To my wonderful family
and friends who remind me that
none of us lives in isolation and that
we must bloom where we are planted.

Maximilian and Carlota

Europe's Last Empire in Mexico

M. M. McAllen

TRINITY UNIVERSITY PRESS

SAN ANTONIO

THE PUBLISHER GRATEFULLY ACKNOWLEDGES THE GENEROUS SUPPORT OF GLORIA GALT, TED AND SHARON LUSHER, AND THE SUMMERLEE FOUNDATION TOWARD THE PUBLICATION OF THIS BOOK.

Published by Trinity University Press
San Antonio, Texas 78212

Jacket design by Rebecca Lown
Book design by BookMatters, Berkeley

Jacket illustrations:

Santiago Rebull, Maximilian von Habsburg, Emperor of Mexico, 1865. Courtesy Castello di Miramare, Trieste, Italy.

Albert Graefle, Carlota Amalia de Saxe Coburg, 1865. Courtesy Museo Nacional de Historia, INAH, Chapultepec, Mexico City, DF.

Coat of Arms of the Second Mexican Empire. Courtesy Museo Nacional de Historia, INAH, Chapultepec, Mexico City, DF.

Frontispiece: Emperor Maximilian and Empress Carlota enter Puebla, 1864

Trinity University Press strives to produce its books using methods and materials in an environmentally sensitive manner. We favor working with manufacturers that practice sustainable management of all natural resources, produce paper using recycled stock, and manage forests with the best possible practices for people, biodiversity, and sustainability. The press is a member of the Green Press Initiative, a nonprofit program dedicated to supporting publishers in their efforts to reduce their impacts on endangered forests, climate change, and forest-dependent communities.

The paper used in this publication meets the minimum requirements of the American National Standard for Information Sciences—Permanence of Paper for Printed Library Materials, ANSI 39.48–1992.

CIP data on file with Library of Congress.

ISBN 978-1-59534-183-9 paper
ISBN 978-1-59534-185-3 ebook

18 17 16 15 14 | 5 4 3 2 1

Contents

Preface   xi

Prologue   I

Introduction. Mexicans, You Have Desired My Presence   3

1. The Right of Kings   20

2. Sooner or Later, War Will Have to Be Declared   38

3. The Red Avenger   53

4. The Siege of Puebla   72

5. Honor of the House of Habsburg   97

6. What Would You Think of Me   114

7. The Future Will Be Splendid   130

8. A Task Worthy of the Damned   147

9. Our Daily Bread   164

10. A Premonitory Symptom   183

11. Every Drop of My Blood Is Mexican   198

12. Like a Lost Soul   210

13. The French Repatriation   225

14. The Empire Is Nothing Without the Emperor   242

15. Beware of the French   254

16. Someone Is Intent on Poisoning Me   275

17. Getting Out of the Toils of the French   294

18. Liberator I Will Be   311

19. War Is War   328

20. The Enemy Is Here   342

21. I Have Cared for You All   358

22. ¡Viva Mexico! ¡Viva el Emperador!   380

    Epilogue   393

    Notes   411

    Selected Bibliography   487

    Acknowledgments   501

    Illustration Credits   505

    Index   511

The Empire is the only way to save Mexico. When one takes charge of the destiny of a nation, it is done at one's own risk, and one never has the right to abandon it.

—Carlota, Princess of Belgium, Empress of Mexico, ca. June 1866

Preface

The violent collapse of the Second Empire of Mexico in 1867 was one of the most spectacular personal tragedies and political failures of the nineteenth century. At the time and over the next one hundred years, the story remained a sensation in Europe and the Americas, though often hidden against the backdrop of the American Civil War. The rise of Mexico's Second Empire succeeded in part because, in the early 1860s, the Civil War so debilitated the United States that it left Mexico, recently emerged from its own War of the Reform under the leadership of new president Benito Juárez, seemingly defenseless. A number of European countries, especially France, continued to stalk territory in the Western Hemisphere, and with the United States otherwise distracted by its own struggle between the North and South, the French recognized an opportunity to prey on Mexico, perceived by them to be feckless but strategic. Europeans believed that it was only a matter of time before the United States annexed additional lands from its southern neighbor, as they had in 1848 and 1853, so they saw a race to grab territory. The path to establishing the Second Empire of Mexico began with an 1861 invasion by the French army under Emperor Napoléon III (Louis Napoléon Bonaparte) using the pretext of reclaiming unpaid bond debt. With a deep-seated desire to defeat U.S. influence in Latin America and to enrich France in the process, Napoléon's experienced and impressive armies were determined to win against a sturdy resistance by Mexico's Republican armies. The French prevailed in pushing President Benito Juárez out of the capital and to the far desert expanses of the north. The war drew out two years longer than Napoléon III anticipated, yet by the end of 1863, the French dominated Mexico City and a large portion of Mexico's population centers. This opened the way for Conservative factions to place a monarch over the established empire of Mexico. Austria's Archduke Ferdinand Maximilian von Habsburg and his wife, Princess Carlota of Belgium, accepted the invitation to take the throne of Mexico, offered by Napoléon III, the Mexican monarchists, and clerics.[1]

This curious story highlights the incongruities that occur when people of numerous cultures, in this case not only from Mexico and Europe but also Asia and Africa, come together under tense circumstances. The liminal qualities of this story—so many foreigners in a foreign land—make for a fascinating glimpse into the nineteenth century, the philosophies of European heads of state, a newly emerging Mexico, and the shake-up of the United States. Maximilian's attempts to anchor an empire in this convulsive climate proved to be a test of Old World methods against a new paradigm in America. During this turbulent time, occupied by armies, officers, and diplomats from abroad, Mexico became a microcosm of erupting European geopolitics, especially in view of Prussia's intent to wage war against Austria and France.[2]

In this book, readers should note that adherents to the Mexican empire are also referred to as Imperialistas and Monarchists. Conservatives and Clerical party members who wanted to maintain a strong central Catholic Church at times encouraged a monarchy or denounced it, depending on Maximilian's actions. Supporters of Juárez are also termed Liberals or Republicans, just as they were in their day. The princess Charlotte was known in Mexico and elsewhere as Carlota—so the history begins and ends with this spelling.

Over the years, the story of the reign of Maximilian and Carlota has been told in myriad ways. Authors have written of this strange and complicated saga as history, but a good many others, inspired by the raw emotion of the epic, fictionalized the story further. A number of plays and songs were written about the Second Empire, as well as a 1939 Warner Brothers motion picture simply entitled *Juárez* (screenplay by John Huston, with Bette Davis, Paul Muni, Brian Aherne, and Claude Rains). Clearly, however, the absurd, complicated, and tragic tale of an Austrian archduke and a Belgian princess on the throne of Mexico produced enough innate drama to stand on its own, without further fictionalization.[3]

Author's note: In 1865, 1 Peso = 1 U.S. Dollar. 1 U.S. Dollar in 1865 = $16.25 in 2010.[4]

Prologue

Bouchout Castle, Meise, Belgium, 1900

Inspired by the spring breezes and emergent blossoms signaling the time for adventure, Carlota, a beautiful, waiflike woman, nearly sixty, princess of Belgium, and, for a brief time, the empress of Mexico, walked gently down the pier on the lake at Bouchout. Wearing a shawl, her cropped gray hair tucked into a chignon and crowned by a straw hat woven with ribbon, her chambermaid steadied her. Carlota placed her slipper on the gunwale of the small wooden rowboat, rocking it in the water. "Today we leave for Mexico," she said, before stepping into the boat for a brief excursion. Rowed about by her attendants, she saw herself gliding over Lake Texcoco escorted by French military officers.[1]

Mexicans, You Have
Desired My Presence

May 28, 1864, two o'clock in the afternoon, Port of Veracruz, Mexico

The captain of the frigate *Novara* advised Maximilian and Carlota to make ready for port at the sultry bay of Veracruz on the Gulf of Mexico. The two emerged from their suites into the swirling, smoky air of the steamship's quarterdeck and strained to see the peak of Mount Orizaba, the highest mountain in Mexico, which stood shrouded in a snowy fog, nearly ninety miles west. The sight of the bastion San Juan de Ulúa, where battalion commanders fired cannon salutes to the sovereigns, encouraged them that their arrival in the new empire of Mexico had been acknowledged. The thirty-one-year-old emperor, Austria's Ferdinand Maximilian von Habsburg, perfectly at home on the *Novara*, Austria's famous flagship, viewed for the first time his new dominion. His wife Carlota, the twenty-three-year-old Princess of Belgium, with her attendants prepared to greet a Mexican receiving committee while the ship's crew dropped anchor, secured the lines, and shut down the loud, droning engines.[1]

The royal couple looked out on Veracruz, an unremarkable town of dwellings and warehouses, yet the main entrepôt of foreign trade and goods going to the heart of Mexico, a site the Americans had bombarded only seventeen years earlier during the Mexican War. Flanking the town stood the fabled and rambling cemetery that had come to be known as the deathbed of nations. The French facetiously called the burial grounds *Le Jardin d'Acclimation*. It represented the ravages of yellow fever, also known as the *vomito prieto*, and the unyielding toll the disease took on newcomers, especially on the thousands of

Port of Veracruz, Mexico, masted steamships at anchor and customs house, ca. 1875

French and Austrian soldiers who had arrived in 1862 and 1863 to fight Benito Juárez's Liberal army and clear the path for Maximilian's new empire. It was a haunting salutation. The Europeans, unlike the natives of Veracruz who had immunity to the disease, arrived highly susceptible.[2]

Buildings around the harbor were garlanded, flowered arches decorated the streets, and the ships at anchor flew celebratory flags of welcome, but only a small gathering of people cheered from rooftops and wharfs, setting off rockets and fireworks. On board, steeping in the humidity, the royals could hear the bugles of a small band.[3] Being celebrities in Europe and accustomed to much pomp and grandeur at their appearances, this small reception seemed anemic and strange, when the country voted to change its government to a monarchy and beckoned them to its new throne. Curiously, Mexico had not orchestrated a grand ceremony to commemorate the historic and monumental occasion of the arrival of their new monarchs. Veracruz appeared mostly vacated, as Maximilian and Carlota witnessed. A large percentage of foreigners comprised the population of 8,000, and most represented Mexican and European shipping companies and financial houses. Many remained opposed to French interference and the new imperial state. Generally, these independent merchants avoided any attempt to organize the business of imports and exports, which might have inhibited the quasi-contraband transactions they thrived upon. As one aide observed, any government that enforced duties remained the traders' enemy.[4]

Maximilian and his administrators had no word from the imperial welcoming committee of Mexican officials who should have been awaiting their arrival, ready to lead them inland through the mountains to the capital of Mexico City. When local imperial prefect Domingo Bureau spied the *Novara* through his telescope, he sent word immediately to Juan Nepomuceno Almonte, lieutenant general of the realm and interim chief commander of the empire, waiting upland at the town of Córdoba, located 3,000 feet above sea level, not wanting to risk exposure to yellow fever. He planned to rush to Veracruz upon the confirmed arrival of the sovereign. Almonte and his wife, with the rest of the committee, immediately started out for Veracruz before the *Novara* anchored, but the journey from Córdoba, over sixty miles west, was slow and rough.[5]

Since the royal party arrived during the time of contagion, French officers and Mexican advisors recommended that Maximilian and Carlota remain on board to reduce the time exposed to infection in Veracruz. According to some, this delay spoiled the emperor and empress's victorious entrance by disappointing onlookers excited to welcome them. However, waiting to disembark, Carlota viewed the Mexican seaport rather cheerfully, writing to her eighty-two-year-old grandmother, Marie-Amélie, the former queen of France, "We are leaving early tomorrow morning for Mexico City and will be en route for a while. I am infinitely pleased with the appearance of Veracruz. It reminds me of Cádiz, but a bit more oriental," recalling her view of the ancient seaport on Spain's western coast.[6]

A short time later, French admiral Auguste Bosse and an aide rowed out to the royal steamer, climbed on deck, and Bosse proceeded to lambaste the captain for mooring in what he considered the most contagious waters at bearings so close to shore. People had died, he said, after only one night in port. Maximilian himself, a former admiral in the Austrian navy, had ordered the ship's captain not to anchor near the French vessels but south of the fort, occupied by Napoléon III's army, to thwart the impression, ironically, that he entered the country under French protection. He wanted his arrival to demonstrate he arrived at the invitation of the people of Mexico, who, he was assured, had voted for a monarchy. Bosse also grumbled on about guerrillas lying in wait along the long and treacherous route to Mexico City. He said that the French military commander-in-chief, Marshal François Achille Bazaine, remained too busy fighting in the field to personally escort the sovereigns from Veracruz. Maximilian tried to view the mix-ups lightly, while others stood aghast.[7]

Maximilian von Habsburg,   Carlota of Belgium, ca. 1864
ca. 1860

Finally, in the evening, Almonte and his wife, Dolores, along with Gen. Mariano Salas and other members of the Imperialist delegation arrived from Córdoba and rowed out in a few small skiffs to the *Novara*. Almonte, a long-time Mexican diplomat having served in France, England, and Spain, had assisted in constructing the conceptual Mexican Imperial government, ruling as chief of the regency until Maximilian's arrival. He and the assembled Monarchists boarded the *Novara*, the deck illuminated by torches and lanterns, and formally welcomed Maximilian surrounded by officers and midshipmen.[8]

The emperor stood tall at six feet in height, a slender man with expressive blue eyes. He had very pale skin, almost pink some said, and silky, blond hair and a short beard that he parted in the middle in Austrian fashion. On this evening, he dressed in a black frock coat, white vest, and white pants, with a black cravat. He greeted the Mexican legation warmly and drew the party into the upper deck salon, where they exchanged welcomes and pleasantries. The imperial prefect of Veracruz, Domingo Bureau, addressed Maximilian as the savior of Mexico, heralding his arrival as a new era under a "benign scepter." At this historic moment, long anticipated by partisans ready for a Mexican monarchy, everyone gathered marveled at Maximilian, their sovereign, thanking God for a return to solid leadership at last.[9]

Maximilian replied, "I view with pleasure the arrival of the day when I can walk the soil of my new and beautiful country, and salute the people who have chosen me," said Maximilian. "May God grant that the goodwill that led me toward you may be advantageous to you; and that all good Mexicans uniting to sustain me, there will be better days for Mexico."[10]

Maximilian then introduced Carlota to the committee. A pretty and tall but delicate-looking woman with dark and flashing eyes, she commanded attention without having to utter a word, accustomed as she was to being understood, the only daughter of the king of Belgium. In conversation, she had the habit of squinting as though trying to focus. She smiled, laughed, and usually conveyed a pleasant demeanor but transmitted the attitude that she was not in the habit of putting up with anyone's trifling.[11]

Joaquín Velásquez de León, the newly appointed secretary of state, made a sincere, welcoming speech to the imperial couple and then addressed Carlota. "The Mexicans, Madam, who expect so much from the good influence of your Majesty in favor of all that is noble and great, of all that bears relation to the elevated sentiments of religion and of country, bless the moment in which your Majesty reached the soil and proclaim in one voice, 'Long Live the Empress.'" In slow but good Spanish, Carlota thanked the delegation, saying how happy she was at arriving in her new country. Afterward, during the reception, Almonte's wife, Dolores, spontaneously embraced Carlota in customary Mexican fashion. The empress recoiled with uncertain awkwardness, unaccustomed to this sort of greeting, against the protocol and formality of the Belgian court.[12]

Maximilian brought with him a sizeable retinue to organize and prepare his court, as he would have arranged it in Europe, where he previously governed. The core group numbered about eighty, including Félix Eloin, his private secretary; Sebastian Scherzenlechner, head of the civil cabinet; Count Félix von Zichy, master of the court; Count Charles de Bombelles, rear-admiral of the Austrian navy, a longtime friend and close advisor; Marquis Giuseppe Corio, his chamberlain; and Jacob von Kuhachevich, the treasurer of the household, along with a number of military and political advisors, both Austrian and native Mexican.[13]

From the *Novara*, Maximilian issued a written statement to the people of Mexico: "Mexicans: You have desired my presence. Your noble nation, by a voluntary majority, has chosen me to watch henceforth over your destinies.

I gladly respond to this call. Painful as it has been for me to bid farewell forever to my own, my native country, I have done so, being convinced that the Almighty has pointed out to me, through you, the mission of devoting all my strength and heart to a people who, tired of war and disastrous contests, sincerely wish for peace and prosperity; to a people who having gloriously obtained their independence, desire to reap the benefit of civilization and true progress."[14]

Soon the French soldiers at Fort San Juan de Ulúa and on shore lit saltpeter torches known as *bengalas*, the blue glow stretching lambently across the water and illuminating the night sky. French sailors, anchored at the nearby Isla de Sacrificios, hung lanterns from their ships' riggings and lines, and the troops fired petards and cannon salutes from the fortress. No one slept that night. Maximilian and Carlota eagerly waited for the moment to disembark and begin the trip to the capital and see their new country.[15]

The next morning, at 4:30, Maximilian, Carlota, and their entourage of ministers and attendants attended mass. Afterward, the sailors rowed them to the breakwater, a mephitic smell rising from the gulf water. The boom of cannon saluted the royals' arrival. A delegation of officials greeted them as they disembarked, welcomed them to Mexico, and presented them with a key to the city on a silver tray. Despite the sincerity of the town council, lady-in-waiting Paula Kollonitz described the reception as "chilling," mostly by the absence of people. After the brief ceremony, Maximilian, Carlota, and their entourage climbed into carriages and traveled through the empty streets under French and Mexican military escort. They passed through a few arches erected to celebrate their arrival. At the perimeter of the town, military officials helped the entourage onto a narrow-gauge train waiting to take them west to the cooler, upper plateaus of Mexico. The unadorned rush seats and rickety condition of the cars unnerved some members of the entourage, accustomed to much grander modes of travel.[16]

The rail line, improved hastily two years earlier by the French military to move their armies out of the pestilent climate of Veracruz, ended only a short way inland. At the small village of Loma Alta, the royal party transferred to carriages, some vehicles in better condition than others, to complete the three-hundred-mile trip. It was difficult finding space, not only for the passengers but also their five hundred pieces of luggage. The large entourage had to divide into several parties, given the impracticality of traveling in one long caravan. Those assigned to set up the royal household went ahead in order to reach Mexico City before the sovereigns. Many rode behind in cramped

Railroad trestle and bridge at La Soledad from Veracruz, ca. 1864

phaetons or mule-drawn covered diligences or simple wagons, and some, like William Heide, the conductor of the royal orchestra from Vienna, rode most of the way with his wife, Kate, on the back of a burro. Although their destination of Córdoba lay not far, the rugged terrain that one diplomat called a "sketch of a road" remained little more than heavily rutted, muddy trails. Maximilian and Carlota rode in elaborate English traveling carriages, solidly built, but for paved roads.[17]

As they approached the Río Chiquihuite on the trail through the mountain pass of Paso del Macho, the climate and vegetation became tropical and dense. Being the rainy season, low clouds and mist hung in the air. The Mexican escorts repeatedly apologized for the condition of the road; however, Maximilian and Carlota assured them they did not mind, having traveled to tropical and rugged places in the past. The lush mountains with their rivers, ravines, and waterfalls astonished the emperor and empress with their beauty.[18]

The royal couple now had their first glimpse of rural Mexico, comprised almost entirely of indigenous peoples living in poverty except for the riches of their gardens, which were bountiful. They had few possessions and lived plainly. The children, only half-clothed, kicked around coconuts playing ball games, while women offered the travelers bananas and mangos.[19]

Members of the entourage worried about the narrow, slick roads and the steep ravines, known as *barrancas*, where guerrillas or highway bandits frequently lurked. Often the guerrillas worked for regional *caudillos*, or for Juárez, against the empire. The drivers kept the carriages steady on the mountain trails. Skilled drivers were paid extra if they went a hundred days without overturning a coach. The imperial military guard comprised of a French column and Mexican troops commanded by Col. Miguel López, a cavalryman known for his fine military record and impeccable protocol, escorted Maximilian's carriage and directed the drivers. Three years later, López would come to play an unexpected role in Maximilian's reign.[20]

Stopping on the twisting route, they ate a hurried supper at the military post of Paso del Macho and resumed their trek to the next town of Córdoba. A storm erupted, and as sheets of water fell over the entourage, a wheel broke on Carlota's carriage, forcing her to change vehicles. The gloom of night brought new worries of possible attacks by guerrillas. Carlota, remembering the warnings of Admiral Bosse at Veracruz, imagined gunmen at every turn but tried to remain calm. "Things looked so odd that I should not have been surprised if Juárez himself had appeared with some hundreds of *guerrilleros*."[21]

As the party approached Córdoba, the local priest sent a number of local people down the road to meet them. The natives carried torches to guide the carriages. They passed through one section known as *Sal si puedes* (get out if you can), named for the deep mire requiring all the energy of the mules. With sixteen reins in one hand and a whip in the other, the drivers whistled, called, and hissed, while a young assistant threw stones at the mule's rumps and flanks, some animals under harness for the first time. Kollonitz thought the drivers picturesque with their short leather jackets, hairy goatskin leggings, and sombreros. When carriages turned over, Carlota later wrote that it required all their "youth and good humor to escape being crippled with stiffness or breaking a rib."[22]

The party arrived at the garrison of Córdoba at two in the morning, exhausted and hungry. Maximilian and Carlota did not complain, although they received many apologies. "We did not feel in the least bit tired," Carlota later remarked. The residents lit torches and lanterns on nearly every building to honor their arrival, a beautiful sight to any traveler. White-clad Indians waved ferns and flowers. French officers in gold-embroidered uniforms wearing ribbons and medals greeted them, and local officials presented the keys to the town and hosted a lavish supper that lasted until nearly daybreak. Maximilian and Carlota retired to a fine home owned by a wealthy *hacendado*, but there were no provisions for the members of the entourage. Some of the women found beds, but the men slept in chairs, in the carriages, or on the pavement. For most of the court staff, the bright lights, fireworks, and all-night celebrations meant another evening with little sleep.[23]

Early on June 2, the royal party resumed its travels over the plateaus, through farm fields of corn, coffee, and fruit trees on the way to Orizaba, a short distance of about fifteen miles. Along the road, the sovereigns saw that people of every little village built arches of welcome over the roads, and most citizens wore a token of their arrival on their hats.[24]

As they reached Orizaba, known for its loyalty to Juárez, thousands of native clansmen came forth from the town to meet them. They surrounded the royal coach to get a look in the carriage at the emperor and his young, beautiful wife. One group wanted to unhitch the mules from Maximilian's carriage and draw it themselves, which he would not allow. For some of the Conservatives, it seemed a little surprising and disappointing that Maximilian bore no royal medals or jewels, and Carlota dressed simply in a brown silk dress, scarf, and hat, unlike the official images of them in full formal attire circulated before their arrival.[25]

At the small fortification of Garita de Escamela at Orizaba, Maximilian addressed the prefect and the crowd assembled: "The love with which our new country greets us profoundly moves us, and we think it a happy sign of an agreeable future." Many of Maximilian's imperial supporters finally met them, including various ministers, ladies-in-waiting, and other attendants, who had waited to greet them there instead of risking a stay in pestilential Veracruz.[26]

After a mass at the cathedral and a hymn of welcome and thanksgiving, or Te Deum, they toured the town looking at the panoramic views and the towering snowcapped cone of Mount Orizaba, the officials explaining its Nahuatl name, Citlaltépetl or Star Mountain. A group from the Naranjal community, an ancient and somewhat isolated region, had descended from their home in the mountains to hold a presentation for the royals and their attendants. Maximilian and Carlota were delighted and fascinated by their ceremonial attire, the men in silver embroidered tunics and short pants, machetes in their belts and heavy gold earrings. The women presented Carlota with a diamond ring said to be from the family of Montezuma, which she placed on her finger, with a promise to remember them always. They toured the nearby villages and heard speeches both in Nahuatl and Spanish. Thrilled with the frenzied greetings, Maximilian then spoke to the natives in Spanish while interpreters repeated the words in the native dialect. The empress presented 300 pesos to the municipal prefect for the local hospital and the poor. Later, during a tour of local convents and factories manufacturing paper and cotton products, they passed a group of unwelcoming but curious Liberals. Maximilian tipped his hat to them and they politely raised theirs in return. Those predisposed not to accept the royal couple could not deny their magnetism and charm.[27]

The next morning, Carlota appeared in her riding habit, or *traje de amazona*, along with a sombrero, since she had chosen to cross the rugged mountains on horseback. For the ascent through the *cumbres*, they left Orizaba with an escort of French and Mexican imperial cavalry and other military numbering over a thousand men. Maximilian and Carlota admired the skill and finery of the Mexican riders accompanying them with their embroidered attire and silver saddles. After stopping at the village of Acultzingo for their first Mexican-style breakfast of tortillas, various sauces of *mole* and chile, along with *pulque* to drink, they continued to wind upward through the Sierra Madre to La Cañada (Morelos Cañada). Here the party learned that guerrillas had been lying in wait for them, but that they had been dispersed.[28]

One carriage bearing the imperial staff took a detour, and the passengers saw the bodies of dead guerrillas killed by the imperial guards. The entourage climbed slowly through the *cordilleras*, and in the early evening the troops lit torches to see the narrow road. Everyone sat silent in their carriages as they bumped up the mountain path, listening for any attackers. Fireflies twinkled in the dense vegetation. Hours passed until they crossed the cumbres and arrived at La Cañada, most of the party exhausted. The next morning as they made their way through Palmar de Bravo, they could see in the distance for the first time the two volcanoes of Popocatépetl and Iztaccihuatl with their snowy peaks of 17,000 feet towering on the western horizon.[29]

On June 5, as they approached the major Catholic center of Puebla de Los Angeles, a cavalcade of riders in full regalia, with silver saddles and bridles embroidered in metallic thread and tassels, rode out of the city to greet them. Many of the men carried their small sons with them on horseback. In the city, women and children in their finest attire cheered in the streets and from balconies. Banners fluttered from buildings and enormous arches decorated the streets. Bells pealed from the city's numerous churches. Their enthusiasm reassured Maximilian, who was greatly moved by the passionate greetings and gladly returned their joy. The people of Puebla, a strong center of Conservatives with a population of 70,000, remained intensely curious about the royal couple, many feeling that Maximilian and Carlota would bring peace and prosperity after a decade of civil war. Priests, who only a year earlier hid from Juárez's Liberals, joyously welcomed the monarchy, expecting a new era.[30]

Everywhere in Puebla, the royal entourage could see the damage the city had incurred from the two intense battles fought in 1862 and 1863 between the French and Liberal forces, resulting in the establishment of the empire and Maximilian's new career. Seeing that atonement was in order from the recent storms of artillery fire, Maximilian pledged his responsibility to restore the buildings in what remained an otherwise beautiful place. Also to demonstrate his magnanimity, he ordered the release of all the prisoners in the jail, even those awaiting death sentences for murder.[31] This sort of clemency he enjoyed immensely.

They were to stay at a lavish home in Puebla, with separate festivities planned for the men and women. Carlota, with her attendants, attended a dinner party at the home of city prefect, Juan E. de Uriarte, but curiously, as she entered the house and was escorted into the dining room, the rest of the guests remained in the drawing room, staring expectantly. After a few awkward moments, someone explained that the empress must invite the guests to join her at the table, which she proceeded to do. During the meal, language difficulties strained conversations, with Carlota's limited Spanish skills and only one woman knowing a little French. At the end of the meal, "we sat looking at each other after supper for a long time before the company gave signs of departing," Paula Kollonitz explained. Carlota seemed unruffled, knowing such tensions could be expected with the arrival of the royal couple.[32]

The next morning, June 7, Carlota marked her twenty-fourth birthday. The day began with a splendid celebration in Puebla with mass at the cathedral conducted by the bishop. Carlota gave 7,000 pesos to repair the local hospital, and Maximilian gave another 1,000 to found a maternity ward. That evening a large dinner at the presidio preceded a grand ball at the Alhóndiga, the old granary refitted as a place for public events. For the occasion, Carlota wore a white silk dress and a crown adorned with red and white roses encrusted with enamel, emeralds, and diamonds, the colors of the Mexican flag. A necklace of large white diamonds completed her stunning outfit. From the street, the royal couple walked over a carpet of flowers to the building's portal. On the way, pyrotechnists ignited a sensational display of fireworks that blazed an image of the castle of Miramar. It seemed the whole town had taken to the streets to celebrate.[33]

As the royal couple entered the building, they could see in the corners of the courtyard pyramids of crystal vases, built to look like the Aztec monuments, emitting various prismatic lights. Maximilian and Carlota seated themselves at two thrones built for the occasion. The guests participated in a quadrille, dancing until dawn, although the sovereigns retired at midnight, their usual habit of leaving well before a celebration's end. The next morning, the royal couple bid town fathers adieu and donated additional funds to repair the almshouse. Carlota thanked them for "a welcome, which on my birthday, makes me feel that I am among my own people, in my own country, surrounded by loving friends."[34]

Moreover, this overland journey to Mexico City revealed to Maximilian, and especially Carlota, the great disparity in wealth and privilege that plagued Mexico. "Everything in this country has got to be begun all over again; one finds nothing but nature, whether in the physical or in the moral order. Their education has to be undertaken down to the smallest details," Carlota wrote Eugénie, empress of France. She seemed bothered by the segregation between the people of European origins and the native peoples.

> Outside the towns, one does not find a single white person. It is like the wave of an enchanter's wand. No sooner does one arrive in a place of importance than one finds prefects with embroidered uniforms and tricolor sashes, almost as in France, except that the embroideries are gold. It forms quite a strange contrast to the rest of the country. . . . Nearby all the Indians can read and write, they are in the highest degree intelligent and, if the clergy instructed as they ought, they would be an enlightened race. . . . The priests do not even teach the catechism in the schools . . . and that is at Puebla, the clerical town par excellence. . . . The ephemeral governments which have succeeded one another for the past forty years have never been more than minorities supplanted by other minorities, for they have never had any root in the Indian population, which is the only one which works and which enables the state to live.[35]

But Carlota knew very little about the man they had come to displace, Benito Juárez, himself from indigenous origins.

Mounted civilians from Puebla accompanied them to Cholula, guiding the royal party to the extraordinary town with its great pyramids. They viewed the church Nuestra Señora de los Remedios, which sat atop the area's largest temple, set against an impressive backdrop of the icy altitudes of the volcanoes. Girls pressed forward through the crowds with flowers. Maximilian and Carlota stayed at a small hotel in San Martín Zoquiapan, six miles north, where they were given a dinner in their honor by Gen. Tomás Mejía, an ultra-Catholic pure-blooded native Otomí, so vital to the Imperialist mission and fiercely loyal to its cause. Maximilian, who had heard a great deal about Mejía's bravery, little knew how much he would come to depend on this general's staunch support.[36]

As they greeted their supporters and came to know more about the military and skeletal governmental provisions made by the regents, they became more confident. "According to all I have seen," remarked Carlota, "a monarchy is feasible in this country and responds to the unanimous needs of the people; nonetheless, however, it remains a gigantic experiment, for we have to struggle against the wilderness, distance, the roads, and the most utter chaos. The level of civilization in this country presents astonishing contrasts."[37]

Early the next morning, as the entourage ascended the hills toward the plateau of Anáhuac, the native name for the valley of Mexico, they forded rivers and struggled through ankle-deep mud when a carriage wheel broke near the pine-shrouded station of Río Frío. After repairs, the small caravan soon descended into the Valley of Mexico. Winding slowly down the steep mountain road, they could see stunning views of the volcanoes and grasslands. In the distance appeared the City of Mexico, beautiful with its church towers and tall trees, surrounded by immense lakes.[38]

On June 11, as they neared Mexico City, Maximilian and Carlota stopped at the Villa de Guadalupe to attend mass at the legendary church of Nuestra Señora de Guadalupe, the site of pilgrimages to honor the Virgin Mary, said to have appeared to the campesino Juan Diego in 1531. At the church, Pelagio Antonio de Labastida y Dávalos, the archbishop of Mexico, along with other clerical hierarchy who had eagerly awaited the couple's arrival, conducted a thanksgiving mass. Recently having returned from forced exile in Europe, the forty-eight-year-old Labastida, with his crooked smile, introduced the royal couple to the presbytery and then invited them to two thrones. After reciting the *Domine Salvum fac Imperatorum* (God Save Our Emperor), the priests gave a tour and Maximilian and Carlota partook water from the sacred well of the church. Maximilian replied to the gathered officials: "I happily receive congratulations, and I salute you with the effusion of one who loves you, and has identified his fate with yours."[39]

When Maximilian and Carlota emerged from the shrine, they saw hundreds of people who had ridden out from Mexico City to welcome them. Attired in their finest black suits and gloves, the men on horseback and women in carriages, all cheered "¡Viva Maximiliano primero!, ¡Viva Napoléon tercero!" The crowd sounded out a salute to them and the newborn empire of Mexico, along

with a few speakers who praised the archduke's plan to rejuvenate the country. A woman representing the assembly's wives read a statement to Carlota,
"with your Majesty and your august husband, who are the objects of public
admiration, and the delight of this vast Empire, commences the dynasty which
takes the name of your new country. It will be able to figure by the side of the
country of Charles V and Mary Teresa, [and] by that of . . . Napoléon III."[40]

From among the crowd, Marshal Achille Bazaine, chief of the French
military, and Marquis Charles F. Montholon, the French minister to Mexico,
looked upon the royal couple. They made their way to the church's domed
chapter house where Maximilian met Bazaine for the first time, the beginning
of their conflicted but mutually respectful relationship.[41]

Carlota related the overwhelming experience of finding their purpose in
Mexico to Eugénie:

> If ever a country [Mexico] was miraculously saved from a condition out
> of which it would never have emerged, it is indeed this one; it knows this
> and understands it, and gives proof of it by its ever-increasing joy and the
> affectionate welcome which it has given us. This is due to the freedom of
> expressing its opinions restored to it by France. . . . There were great shouts
> of "Long live Maximilian the First," "Long live Napoleon the Third," and
> the crowd raised their great sombreros and answered: "May he live long
> (Que Viva)." The sight of the Virgin of Guadalupe touched me greatly . . .
> [as if] a great act of historic reparation [was] . . . rendered to the Indians by
> a descendant of Charles the Fifth on the point of ascending the throne of
> Montezuma.[42]

The next morning, June 12, the one-year anniversary of the French army's
occupation of Mexico City, Maximilian and Carlota entered the capital by rail.
Maximilian wore the formal uniform of an imperial Mexican general with the
ensign of the master of the Royal Order of Guadalupe and gold collar of the
Order of the Golden Fleece. For the occasion, Carlota dressed in a gown of
blue and white silk, a blue scarf, and a hat decorated with fresh flowers. They
boarded carriages and began a long, stately cavalcade through the streets. The
lavish procession, led by the Mexican Imperial Guard under command of Col.
Miguel López, commenced according to protocol dictated by Maximilian. The
elite French and Mexican lancers with their gold and silver burnished arms and
uniforms followed the imperial guard. The Algerian Zouaves in their colorful
uniform of red baggy trousers, cropped jacket, and fez followed, along with
the Chasseurs d'Afrique in riding clothes embellished in galonné. The Italian

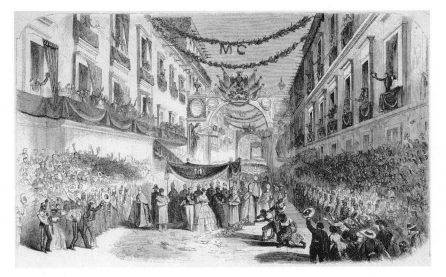

Emperor Maximilian and Empress Carlota enter Mexico City, June 12, 1864

gilded royal coach, with its beveled glass, carved angels and wood scrolls, velvet with gold fringe, and red leather doors embossed with the crest of Imperial Mexico, followed, bearing Maximilian and Carlota, the coachmen driving four white, brilliantly caparisoned horses deliberately and slowly. Behind them rode the heavy-eyed Achille Bazaine at the coach's right door, sword drawn, followed by other French officers in similar fashion, sixty carriages of dignitaries, and various French companies with their officers. The swarming crowds cheered, many waving from balconies and windows rented for a glimpse of the royal couple. The streets, decorated with banners, flags, and hundreds of arches of orange blossoms, ribbons, roses, along with portraits of the royal couple, overflowed with revelers. People in fine clothing, polished carriages, and men in silver embroidered sombreros on horseback whistled and waved at them as they passed. Booming cannon, band music, and church bells added to the celebration.[43]

The people of Mexico City had seen many strident and arrogant leaders come and go, but the day of the arrival of Maximilian and Carlota differed greatly, as even the jaded editor of the partisan French newspaper *L'Estafette* commented, "Today, there was neither clamor, nor boasting, nor a single cry of revenge. All the '*Vivas*' seemed to come from the heart, inspired by a genuine emotion at the sight of these young sovereigns so confident and trusting in their love. And the most touching thing of all was the way in which everyone has made an effort to give them a worthy reception. Even in . . . the outlying districts, far from the center, there was hardly a house that had not made some attempt at decoration—a wreath of leaves, a branch of palm, or a few brightly colored rags. And these humble efforts were as heart-warming as the opulent decorations of the great palaces." The French considered this welcome the consecration of Maximilian's election and that the Republicans, including Juárez, would yield.[44]

The municipal prefect, Miguel María Azcárate, officially welcomed Maximilian and Carlota with gold keys to the city created by a local artist. The royal couple proceeded by carriage to the National Cathedral through the Zócalo, the central plaza, where Archbishop Labastida escorted them inside. Over the cathedral doors, the people of the floating gardens had installed an array of yellow, red, and white flowers that read, "Xochimilco to his Imperial Majesty Maximilian I." The royal couple and the Catholic entourage entered the cathedral quietly amid the glowing candles and decorations bathed in cochineal red and gold. State banners representing Austria, Belgium, France, and Mexico lined the walls. Maximilian and Carlota settled upon throne prepared for the occasion, and the archbishop began the Te Deum and mass accompanied by an orchestra and choir.[45]

Afterward, Maximilian and Carlota followed a carpeted walkway under a canopy to the National Palace. There they received a long stream of diplomats and dignitaries, members of the acting government and military, including Marshal Bazaine. Toward evening, a formal investiture was held in the palace, with Maximilian in formal attire and Carlota in her diamond crown with a mantilla of Brussels lace. She also wore royal heirlooms of the Habsburg and Bourbon families. The entire party viewed the oil lamps of the city, lit very brightly for their arrival. Fireworks boomed through the night air. The people in the plaza continually called to the royal couple, "Let our Emperor come out!" The crowd cheered "¡Viva el Emperador!" and "Vive l'Empereur!" with great clamor, shouting, and sincerity. To Maximilian, it all seemed magnificent in the land where his ancestor Charles V, Holy Roman Emperor, king of Castile and Aragón, ruler of Austrian lands, Flanders, Brabant, and Holland, Burgundy, and Naples, or roughly half of Europe, laid claim to the crown of Montezuma in 1519. Hernando Cortés referred to Charles as "your Majesty to whom the whole world is subject."[46]

The next two weeks of festivities included dramatic performances, operas, fireworks, acrobatics, bullfights, and horsemanship exhibitions including *coleaderos*, offering a competition of Mexican cattle working on the haciendas. Maximilian and Carlota attended most of the events, which gave the people another chance of seeing them take possession of their realm, as they attempted to win their hearts. At the first performance held in their honor at the national theater, Maximilian and Carlota arrived on time only to find the place rather empty, because the other invited guests were accustomed to arriving late, much to the embarrassment of the Mexican ministers. Soon the new sovereigns understood the cultural differences in marking time, and the Mexican ministers and staff did their best to be punctual and adopt European customs. The festivities ended with a gala ball given by Bazaine, with Carlota remaining too shy to dance the quadrille.[47]

The couple spent their first weeks in the crumbling National Palace, little changed or maintained over the last forty years, which remained in disarray. Upon their arrival, attendants of the household hurried about, installing new furnishings, rushing the carpenters who hammered away, painting and cleaning. Despite the expedited effort, the palace remained dusty and disordered. Maximilian spent one night on the billiard table, driven from his quarters by mites and bedbugs, and Carlota slept on a terrace.[48]

In all, it was a tumultuous and adventurous welcome to the capital. After long and arduous negotiations, the voyage across the Atlantic, and the bone-jarring journey from Veracruz, Maximilian and Carlota arrived as foreigners come to lead a troubled land amid improbable circumstances.

The Right of Kings

Ferdinand Maximilian von Habsburg, the son of the Austrian Archduke Franz Karl and Archduchess Sophie, a princess from the royal Bavarian family of Wittelsbach, was born on July 6, 1832, at the summer palace of Schönbrunn, three miles from the heart of Vienna. Maximilian's older brother, Franz Josef, who later became emperor of Austria, was born two years earlier, while younger brother Karl Ludwig arrived the year after Maximilian, and another brother, Ludwig Victor, was born nine years later. Maximilian's baby sister, Maria Anna Karolina, born in 1835, died at the age of four.[1]

Sophie considered Maximilian playful, intelligent, the most tenderhearted of all her children, and a loving son. She described him at the age of three as an energetic, darling, and happy child. "In his long white trousers and loose white shirt, Maxl flutters round me like a great white butterfly," said Sophie, his behavior very different from Franz Josef, who displayed discipline and rigidness even as a boy. When, at the age of seven, Maximilian suffered with his mother in her grief at the death of his sister, he struggled to console her and amend the tragic disruption in their family. To make things right again, the boy saved his money and bought his mother a pet monkey, saying, "I cannot buy you another little girl but at least I can buy you a monkey."[2]

The 500-acre Schönbrunn lands were originally occupied by a hunting lodge and enlarged in the eighteenth century into a magnificent residence of 1,400 rooms. There, Maximilian became a keen reader, thirsty for knowledge of art, science, and great literature taught by some of the greatest minds in the country. One important teacher, the eccentric Heinrich Bombelles, instructed the children to avoid bigotry or piousness because it interfered with true faith. He discouraged the praying or carrying of rosaries, which he considered fetishism and mechanical prayer. His lessons resonated with Maximilian. While Franz Josef became the industrious student, Maximilian, however, often liked to play practical jokes or find ways to challenge his tutors, feeling superior to some of them. He nicknamed his teachers, calling one stuffy French professor "Monsieur Foppabile." But he respected his literature teacher, Charles Gaulis Clairmont, the half-brother of Mary Shelley, who held the chair of English Literature at the Vienna University. His lessons captivated Maximilian's imagination, and he enjoyed English poetry.[3]

Since Maximilian suffered frequent and recurrent illnesses, his mother urged him to be athletic, along with her other sons, to gain strength and resilience. The children played outdoors and learned various equestrian arts. In time, Maximilian became an accomplished horseman with a love for speed and danger. "To walk one's horse is death, to trot is life, a gallop is bliss," said Maximilian. Speed and new technologies fascinated the young student. "If the theories about the air-balloon become a reality, I shall take to flying," he said. However, the young prince immersed himself in a variety of subjects, passionately longing for great adventures around the world.[4]

Maximilian developed impeccable manners and charm but loved play-acting and drama, which made him more popular than the competitive Franz Josef. He became known as the most spirited of the brothers. In family presentations, he captivated his relatives with his theatrical and comic interpretations. Despite the Habsburg characteristic of a long jaw, overbite, and upper lip that somewhat drooped over the lower, which produced the appearance of an almost pouting expression, Maximilian stood out as the handsome, hearty, and much livelier brother, which his mother, Sophie, attributed to her side of the family.[5]

Maximilian's father, Franz Karl, was a weak man, considered not much more capable than his older, epileptic brother, the Emperor Ferdinand. His life was spent languishing in a lackluster court dominated and administered by the powerful Prince Richard Klemens von Metternich. At the time, the Austrian Empire extended from Romania in the east, north to the province of Galicia, in modern-day Poland, to Hungary, the western part of the Ukraine, west to the provinces of Lombardy and Venetia in northern Italy, and south along the Balkan Peninsula on the Adriatic Sea to modern Bosnia and Herzegovina.[6]

As the glories of the old Austrian Empire faded within the vacuum of moldering sovereign leadership, the royal Habsburgs sought to hide the family's internal debility. Powerful grand dame Archduchess Sophie wisely and real-istically assessed the situation and knew the key to preserving the empire lay in promoting her firstborn son as candidate for emperor. At seventeen, Franz Josef, with his particular seriousness and discipline, enrolled in the Austrian army to help crush the Revolution of 1848, repressing turmoil in a number of regions that rejected Habsburg authority. His commanding officer, eighty-two-year-old Field Marshal Joseph Radetzky, a national icon, prevailed in a number of difficult Austrian victories over Italian revolutionaries. When radi-cal mobs attacked Vienna, the uprisings were violently quashed, and the insti-gators, including the women, were shot or whipped, punishments Maximilian abhorred and opposed.[7]

However, this rigid military training helped to shape and further discipline Franz Josef, making him, as the Habsburgs saw it, a worthy disciple trained to carry on the empire's values and vigor. At the end of 1848, Sophie managed to persuade her husband, Franz Karl, to renounce his rights of succession in favor of installing his son as emperor. More importantly, Franz Karl coaxed his brother, the sitting Emperor Ferdinand, Franz Josef's uncle, to abdicate his crown. Franz Josef was invested as emperor in December at the age of eigh-teen. Despite the joy surrounding the revitalization of the Austrian throne, Maximilian resented the lavish attention bestowed on his brother Franz Josef, whom he considered pedantic and a dull doctrinaire. Yet he longed to be an advisor to his brother and sought a role in ruling the empire, but Franz Josef, by then consumed in learning and leadership, refused to consider the idea.[8]

Maximilian's ruling philosophies varied greatly from the draconian policies embraced by his brother and carried out on the empire's own people. He con-demned the hasty execution of radicals, simply because they expressed their desire for something different. He remained independent: an explorer, anthro-pologist, and amateur botanist as well as a devoted, open-minded supplicant of the Catholic Church.[9]

Maximilian embraced honesty, trustworthiness, and honor as his basic tenets, his Habsburg inheritance. He wrote a personal moral guide of twenty-seven pieces of advice to himself, a lexicon of credos, on a small card:

> Let the mind rule the body and maintain it in moderation and morality; Never a false word, not even out of necessity or vanity; Be kind to every-body; Justice in all things whatsoever; Don't answer without reflection, lest one fall into a snare; Nothing offensive, even when it is a sign of wit, for corners tear things; No superstition, for it is the fruit of fear and weakness; Never joke with one's inferiors, never converse with the servants; Take

thought and show delicate consideration for those around one, pay them attentions; When in the right, iron energy in everything; Never scoff at religion or authority; Listen to all, trust few; Never complain, for it is a sign of weakness; Always make a good division of one's time, plenty of regular employment; In judging others' faults, remember one's own; When taking any step think of the consequences; Take it coolly (this he wrote in English); Nothing lasts forever; Keep silence if you can do no better; Two hours' exercise daily.[10]

Through his teens and twenties, he kept journals and wrote copious letters to his family that revealed his longing for adventure, his harsh judgments on other royal courts' poor standards of protocol, along with the thoughts of an impressionable young man, romantic and sensitive. He could be light, humorous, turn ironic phrases, and, like a typical Viennese, he loved music. He generally liked people, often overlooking their political agendas or duplicity, and with his mind open to options, he could easily be persuaded. He could also be impulsive, willful, stubborn, and given to dark moods and malaise. In time, he developed the habit of withdrawing from public until such episodes passed. Despite these tendencies, when he was confronted with decisions, he placed duty above all his personal whims. These juxtapositions in his character created enormous ironies all his life, of which he was well aware but did not explain or attempt to avoid.[11]

When he was nineteen, Maximilian's family sent him on a diplomatic tour of Europe and the Mediterranean to meet various royal cousins and learn about their courts and realms. As Habsburg blood ran through nearly each royal dynastic court in Europe, he easily sought out relatives in nearly every country. This tendency to marry into rather than conquer other sovereign lines resulted in the family maxim: "Let others wage wars, but you, happy Austria, shall marry."[12]

On his mission, his first of many voyages on Austria's flagship, the *Novara*, "the name itself a good omen to every Austrian," he sailed to Italy, Spain, and Portugal. "I was going to realize my much longed-for desire—a voyage at sea. . . . This moment was one of great excitement to me," Maximilian wrote. He observed the way rulers treated their subjects and institutions of these countries. There he observed the government, style of rule, and the institutions of these countries. More importantly, he learned the ways of a seaman, navigating in open waters and maneuvering into ports. He had trained with the Austrian navy for a year, and these travels only helped to fuel his desire to explore the world.[13]

His commanding admiral, Wilhelm von Tegetthoff, observed that young Maximilian was a natural mariner and impressive administrator. In 1854, at the age of twenty-two, Maximilian became the commander-in-chief of the Austrian navy. In this role, he oversaw improvements to the port at Trieste on the northern Istrian coast of the Adriatic Sea and then was assigned to sail the Mediterranean and Aegean seas. As a scholar of Greek and Roman history, he scouted out opportunities to explore the geographic locations he had studied. He visited ports in Albania, Greece, Turkey, Egypt, and Morocco as well as areas of Palestine and modern-day Israel. Maximilian became fascinated with the people he encountered, especially wizened sailors who told their war adventures. An old pirate who had once tortured Turkish soldiers during Greece's war for independence especially influenced his view of sea warfare. He interviewed Albanian natives before sailing on to visit his mother's cousin, King Otto of Greece, a former prince from Bavaria. At Smyrna, he was embarrassed to see naked slave girls in the local market. Arriving in Gibraltar, he dined with the British governor and naval officers, who maintained their territory with a heavy hand, often refusing refugees from nearby Spain. After dinner, the young archduke retreated with the other officers to drink port and smoke, while the women were sent into another room, a tradition he thought appropriate.[14]

Yet in Spain, however, he marveled at the women who were more liberated. While attending a bullfight in Seville, he was awed by their active participation. The young *bellezas* did not faint from the sight of blood but cajoled the matador to kill the bull. Along with his fascination for the stunning girls, he took pride in his Habsburg heritage, learning more about his ancestors Ferdinand I, the Holy Roman Emperor, and Charles V, king of Spain and Christian ruler of Mexico. He came to a fuller understanding of their family motto, *Plus Ultra* (further beyond).[15]

On his tour, while meeting many beautiful women, he began to swoon over a few of them, thinking of them as possible mates. In Lisbon, he fell in love with a cousin, Maria Amalia of Brazil, and planned to marry her. Sadly, soon after his return to Austria, she died from consumption. When he developed an infatuation with the daughter of an Austrian count, she was deemed too low in rank to marry him. According to protocol, Maximilian had to obtain his brother's approval in marriage, and he had to be mindful of any girl's background and royal status.[16] The young naval officer could only focus on his work in the navy and wait.

Meanwhile, in April 1854, in a lavish church ceremony, his twenty-four-year-old brother Franz Josef married the beautiful Princess Elisabeth (Sisi) of Bavaria. Although his mother, Sophie, meant that he should marry the girl's sister, Franz Josef fell deeply in love with the stunningly alluring fifteen-year-old girl, who had a strong and independent personality, and she quickly became devoted to her spouse and her new status as the empress of Austria.[17]

Two years later, the Austrian court sent Maximilian on another diplomatic mission to meet France's Emperor Louis-Napoléon Bonaparte (Napoléon III) and his wife, the Empress Eugénie. This imposing assignment would forever change his life. Louis-Napoléon, a firebrand, was born on April 20, 1808, the son of Louis Bonaparte, King of Holland, who was also the brother of Napoléon I. In 1848, after the abdication of King Louis Philippe and Queen Marie-Amélie of France (the grandparents of Carlota of Belgium, then Mexico), cocksure Louis-Napoléon rose to power with the establishment of the Second Republic. After initially winning the presidency of France, on November 7, 1852, the senate replaced the republic with an empire and reestablished the title of emperor. Louis-Napoléon took the name Napoléon III, in the tradition of his Bonaparte uncle, Napoléon I.[18]

The callow Maximilian considered Napoléon a pretender and a new-comer, or parvenu, as he referred to him in his letters home to his brother, but restrained his personal opinions knowing that Austria must maintain good relations with powerful France. Maximilian thought the French leader more closely resembled a circus master with a riding whip than an emperor with a scepter. From the venue of his young years, Maximilian had little idea how an emperor should comport himself but knew Napoléon's style differed greatly from Franz Josef's. Nonetheless, he admired Eugénie as royal, attractive, polite, terming her "quite a thoroughbred."[19]

During Maximilian's first evening at the summer retreat of Château de Saint Cloud near Paris, Napoléon seemed distracted, uncomfortable, and nervous around the young archduke and his staff. Eugénie did not dine with them, so Maximilian spent a good portion of the evening trying to compensate for the lack of conversation. Maximilian read Napoléon as a leader hostile to the old guard, shy, and defensive; a man with a shuffling gait, standing small and unimposing, twirling his moustache. The next day, however, the two men met in the palace's famous orangery and talked of matters of state, the Crimean War, Russia and its Danubian principalities, and strategies of what Austria could do with regard to Turkey, Albania, and Herzegovina. Napoléon stressed that Austria and France must remain on good terms, despite his belief that the Habsburgs' methods of maintaining their large empire were misguided.[20]

Napoléon III (Louis Napoléon),
emperor of France, ca. 1865

Through the remainder of Maximilian's stay, a series of parties in his honor included bawdy entertainment with the court ladies present, which he thought low class. Napoléon, known for his susceptibility to beautiful girls and his love affairs, blatantly flirted with the women. When Napoléon and Eugénie held a formal ball in Maximilian's honor, he wrote later, "the company was unbelievably mixed, and distinguished by their disgusting dress and tasteless behavior. Adventurers swarmed." He continued, "One can see, moreover, that his suite [entourage] has formerly been that of a president of a republic, it is often hard for them to maintain themselves on a proper level. The behavior of the court ladies toward the empress, too, their shaking hands with her, their hearty friendliness, are a little shocking to our ideas of imperial etiquette."[21]

However, during his visit Maximilian began to see Napoléon's vision. The

French emperor worked exhaustively to redesign Paris with Georges-Eugène Haussmann, in hopes of bringing order, peace, beauty, power, and prestige to the capital in a massive rebuilding scheme, to rival Rome. To modernize the city from its rough, rambling pathways to one of symmetry, avenues were widened and fortified, and parks and public centers built. Maximilian at first viewed this project as pretention but came to appreciate Napoléon's ingenious urban designs, modeled with artistry but also the realities of human need and grand scale. The renovation served as a diminutive microcosm for Napoléon's plan for the world.[22]

By the end of his visit, Maximilian found that he agreed with Napoléon on many issues. When Napoléon brought up the matter of disintegrating peace in Prussia and the German provinces, Maximilian granted that the great powers would face a rearranging of the map in the near future but did not know how this would affect Austria or that Napoléon already had set in motion a number of concepts that would soon materialize. Meanwhile, Napoléon and Maximilian watched an impressive military review of 30,000 French troops, orderly in appearance and well disciplined. The French military machine and Napoléon's vastly expanding empire left an indelible impression on Maximilian. While Franz Josef may have intuited the danger and complications in dealing with France, Maximilian developed an admiration for the emperor's insights, glossing over the complexities existing between the countries. Maximilian concluded that Napoléon was a born empire builder and political genius.[23] Napoléon came to see Maximilian as an advantageous friend to France.

For the next leg of his tour, Napoléon gave Maximilian the use of his yacht to sail to Belgium to visit the court of King Leopold I at Laeken, near Brussels. The first king of Belgium, Leopold was a wizened leader in a flourishing country, highly ambitious, an innovator with superior leadership who personally tended to strategy, and even the smallest details of foreign policy, also tied to nearly all the royal courts of the continent and England through marriage. Earlier, Leopold was offered a proposed throne in Mexico but refused the suggestion, having serious intentions to build an empire in Europe. He was established in the royal house of Saxe-Coburg-Gotha, with the amalgamation of strong and powerful lines of succession. Upon his investiture as the Belgian king in 1831 over a neutral country, he used this nonalignment to passively influence European political movements. In these ways, Leopold artfully maintained Belgium's relevance and even its indispensability. "The very impartiality of [Belgium] drove him to act instead of shutting himself up in that passivity which, after him, became the governing principle of Belgian diplo-

Leopold I, King of Belgium,
Carlota's father

macy," wrote one historian. Being educated in England, he became a devoted friend and guide to his niece, Queen Victoria, and he helped to arrange her marriage to Prince Albert of Saxe-Coburg. With such strong allegiances to Great Britain, Leopold's prestige exceeded many other European sovereigns, and he felt it his duty to avoid all catastrophes between countries, especially England and France.[24]

Maximilian thought Leopold's insights would prove invaluable, but he had more on his agenda than state matters, for Leopold also had a daughter, the Princess Carlota, about whom he had heard great things. While at Laeken, Leopold gave Maximilian long lectures and treatises on political science, which bored the young man endlessly. Leopold liked to tell people that he remained the "Nestor of Monarchs," the aged oracle of heads of state. To his credit, Leopold did possess encyclopedic knowledge on the character of leaders and matters of national security. But at last, Maximilian finally met the sixteen-year-old Carlota and was instantly attracted to the smart, beautiful girl.[25]

Carlota was born on June 7, 1840, at the royal palace at Laeken and christened Marie Charlotte Amélie Augustine Victoire Clémentine Léopoldine by King Leopold and his wife, Queen Louise-Marie. Louise-Marie, the French Princess of Orléans, the child of King Louis Philippe and Queen Marie-Amélie, was thrilled to have a daughter, having previously given birth to three sons: Louis Philippe, who did not survive, Leopold II, and Philippe, Count of Flanders. Queen Louise insisted on naming the baby in honor of Leopold's first wife, Charlotte of Wales, whom he had cherished but who had died in 1817 during childbirth after only a year and a half of marriage. At first shunned by her father, who wanted another son, and adored by her mother, Carlota became Leopold's favorite within a few years. She was a willful child, charming and loving toward her father, winning him over with her curled locks and large brown eyes; she accompanied him to state affairs even when she was very young. Educated by the nuns, who shaped her studies and her strict religious training, they guided Carlota to be a loyal Catholic with a comprehensive worldview. With frequent visits to France and England, Carlota grew quite close to her maternal grandparents, well aware of the pain of their abdication when Napoléon III came to power.[26]

Louise became ill when Carlota was ten, never overcoming the shock of the death of her brother, the prince royal, her sister, Marie, then, in 1848, her father's humiliation and death. Through the fall in 1850, Carlota watched her mother slowly die until she finally succumbed on October 10. Consequently, the grief-stricken Leopold came to spend more time with his children, sending away his well-known mistress. At first, he did not know how to replace the gentle love of their mother; his methods of parenting were rather rigid. Carlota seemed alone and somewhat affection-starved. But frequently at her father's side, the little girl would join him at the podium during public addresses and take his hand. She won his heart. Carlota mirrored the same quiet strength and logic of her mother. As she matured, Leopold came to depend on her resilience. By age thirteen, she had begun to learn the complexities of managing a kingdom and politics. She spoke French, German, Flemish, and English, and had a talent for numbers and finance.[27]

Much advanced in her maturity and astuteness, Carlota grew into one of the beauties of European monarchy. Slender with a small nose and sharp eyes, which seemed to communicate her ever-present thoughts and moods, she kept her thick brown hair in braids encircling her head. Although she could be light-hearted, she preferred the seriousness of matters of state and world politics. Her composure was sometimes mistaken for vanity, but she remained devoted to becoming a useful counselor. Often challenged by her father, she used her keen intelligence to master a subject or solve hypothetical problems. She loved the arts, read great literature, wrote many letters, played the piano, and painted.[28]

During Maximilian's stay at Laeken, the two began spending more time together. Observing Maximilian and Carlota, Leopold saw the attraction and encouraged the match. It became apparent the two young royals were falling in love. At Christmas, Maximilian loaded her with presents, a bracelet and charm containing a lock of his hair, a diamond brooch, a pair of earrings, and a painting of herself. He also shared his diaries of his travels with her. "The archduke is charming in every way and you may imagine how happy I am to have had him here for the past week. Physically I find him more handsome and morally there is nothing further to be desired. He comes to lunch every day and remains until three or four and we talk happily together," she wrote on December 29. Leopold invited Maximilian to return on New Year's Eve 1856, and he issued an announcement of their intent to marry. This news was repeated in the major European capitals.[29]

As was customary, Maximilian's advisors began negotiating the union, the dowry, trousseau, and jewelry. Leopold offered Maximilian little at first, but the Belgian parliament voted to pay $100,000, which Franz Josef matched with an extra $230,000 as a gift. Leopold laughed saying that when he first married, all he received were his wife's debts going back to 1809. After the negotiations, Carlota's dowry of over $1.1 million passed to Austria. Leopold also encouraged Maximilian's older brother, Emperor Franz Josef, to give Maximilian a high position in the Austrian monarchy worthy of his birth and with commensurate pay. Accordingly, with anarchy threatening to erupt across northern Italy, menacing Austrian territories in the region, Franz Josef agreed to award the governorship of Lombardy-Venetia to Maximilian. He expected his brother to quash the unrest and prevent its loss. On April 19, 1857, Maximilian accepted his appointment with his headquarters to be at Monza in Italy's northern province of Lombardy, with full understanding of the people's resentment for Austrian domination and oppressive tactics. Carlota viewed their future position with mixed feelings. Appealing as it was, she said, "It will be a difficult undertaking. It is a mission of good, which we must fulfill. I can feel the thorns already, but I can also foresee the satisfaction to be derived from doing something good." As part of his rule, Maximilian met and had discussions with Pope Pius IX (Pio Nono, as some called him), born Giovanni Maria Mastai, Count of Ferretti, who had remained ambivalent during the unrest in Italy and maintained relations with Austria. The young prince received the pope's benison, or official blessing, as well as a medal knighting him into the Order of Pius, the Holy Father apologizing that the award held no real value, serving only as a token. Touched and humbled, to Maximilian it was a *cosa santa*, a religious relic from his Holiness.[30]

In May, as one last test before the marriage, Leopold arranged a meeting between Maximilian and Queen Victoria, whose assessments he valued. Victoria had in mind another match for Carlota and opposed her marriage to "one of those worthless [Habsburg] archdukes," so it became necessary that she approve of the union and not contradict her previous efforts to find a suitable spouse for Carlota. The beauty and grandeur of the castle of Windsor and Victoria's court overwhelmed Maximilian. He was awestruck by the ancient traditions, the formalities, the ceremony, and the grounds. The queen's cordiality and gentle ways impressed him, and he did his utmost to please her. Victoria's husband, Albert, found Maximilian enlightened, especially his ideas about religious tolerance and his liberal political views. At a luncheon after the royal christening of Victoria's youngest daughter, Beatrice, the queen honored Maximilian by seating him beside her with Prince Frederic Wilhelm of Prussia on her other side. He made clever and intelligent conversation. In light of growing discord between the Prussian territories and Austria, he remarked, "Ich hoff dass es von guter Bedeutung für die Zukunft ist, dass bei dieser Gelegenheit England zwischen Oesterreich und Preussen sitzt" (I hope it is a good omen for the future that on this occasion England sits between Austria and Prussia). His charm won Victoria's wholehearted approval of the match. She wrote Leopold I about Maximilian, "He is charming, so clever, natural, kind and amiable, so *English* in his feelings and likings."[31]

On June 27, 1857, Maximilian and Carlota celebrated their marriage at Laeken in the royal chapel. Carlota wore a gown of white and silver brocade woven in the town of Ghent, and a veil made by the lace makers of Brussels, a gift from the town. Maximilian wore his full dress admiral's uniform, collared by the Order of the Golden Fleece. Over the next few days, Carlota, in a tearful state over leaving her father but happy, said goodbye at her mother's grave and to her lifelong home. During the days after the wedding, Leopold advised them on their future.[32]

A few weeks after their marriage, Maximilian and his new bride traveled briefly to Vienna to meet Maximilian's family, where she was received warmly, then on to Venice, before taking up residence at the royal palace at Monza, ten miles northeast of Milan. Despite Maximilian and Carlota's best efforts to gain popularity and the support of the people, few subjects came to visit their court or attend state visits. Carlota was insulted on at least one trip into Venice. The nationalistic Italians resented domination by the Austrian autocracy, and the two young sovereigns found themselves isolated. Compounding their misery, Maximilian's brother Franz Josef openly distrusted and objected to his brother's efforts to win over the Italians and his liberal attitudes relative

Maximilian and Carlota at the time
of their marriage, ca. 1857

to social unrest. Maximilian held strong feelings about the freedoms of the people, causing such a rupture and personality conflict with Franz Josef that he was not invited to make a report on his work to the ministerial council in Vienna. Despite Maximilian's work to improve the Austrian navy, Franz Josef vetoed appointees or projects that Maximilian proposed, thus adding insult to his brother's endeavors.[33]

By the end of 1858, Maximilian saw rising tension and a potential crisis in Lombardy-Venetia and sent Carlota home to Laeken for safety. It was her first trip home since their wedding. When the Italians raised their flag over the arsenal in Venice declaring revolution against Austria, Maximilian hesitated, while his brother admonished him to use "severity in the event of even the smallest revolt." Maximilian wavered in seizing the offensive against the French fleet anchored at Venice in support, fearing unnecessary damage to the Austrian vessels. The angry and frustrated Franz Josef sent in armed reinforcements and instituted martial law. He subordinated Maximilian to the commanding general of the military, essentially removing him from office without much ceremony, and placed him in charge of a few ships, should open naval battles commence, which never occurred during the ensuing war.[34]

By April 1859, when Austrian demands on the Italian liberals in Piedmont-Sardinia went unmet, war broke out, with Napoléon and the French army assisting the Sardinian cavalry. Napoléon entered the conflict not only to oust the Austrians from Italy, but he needed a campaign to protect his popularity in France. The Austrian commanders moved slowly in northern Italy, without the legendary Field Marshal Radetzky to guide them. After losing two big, bloody conflicts, the Battle of Magenta and the pivotal Battle of Solferino, under the command of Emperor Franz Josef, the Austrians brokered peace negotiations with Napoléon. Under pressure from sparks of revolution in Hungary, Franz Josef ceded Austria's territory of Lombardy to Piedmont but retained Venetia. This had been part of a plan Napoléon had long set in motion, observing the Italians' growing resistance and for which he promised to compensate Austria in due time, while making other deals with Italy and Prussia.[35]

Consequently, Maximilian lost his governorship and, left with no country to rule, was forced to put the Italian conflict in the past and build a new life. Since 1855, Maximilian had begun acquiring small parcels in the rocky outcrops of land near Trieste, on the Adriatic shore across from Venice. He intended to build a castle constructed of white limestone with a magnificent garden, to be designed by the civil engineer Carl Junker and garden architect Wilhelm Knechtel. He and Carlota had planned the house since the time of their engagement as a Moorish pavilion with a winter garden and a chapel. Maximilian named his project Miramar in the tradition of Spanish palaces he admired. He adored the warmth of the Adriatic Sea. Carlota had grown to love the region as well, taking a pilgrimage on her first wedding anniversary to Loreto with supplications to conceive a baby, afterward visiting charming coastal villages and various islands.[36]

Miramar was to be Maximilian's ship of state, although he was a monarch without a state. To be on site during the construction, he designed a small garden house where he and Carlota lived. Planned as a fortress and a breakwater, Maximilian wanted the castle's construction to make the best use of the light summer breezes and to shut out the winter *bora*, the thunderous air masses blasting off the Balkans. Simultaneous to the construction, Carlota planned the grounds complete with olive trees, laurels, myrtles, and statuary, including two sphinxes from Egypt.[37]

Having a large hand in the design himself, Maximilian proceeded to create a home with warm, honey-colored wood and burled paneling, coffered ceilings, and hidden doors leading from one section of the house to another, even between his and Carlota's bedchambers. He could leave a game of billiards and be in his wife's room within seconds. From his study, which was designed as a copy of the admiralty cabin of the *Novara*, Maximilian could look out the windows and see the Austrian fleet, along with merchant boats, and Italian fishermen. Facing the west toward the harbor, in a niche high in the wall below a giant clockface, a stone statue of the image of the Ave Maris Stella, Virgin Mary, the Star of the Sea, raised her arms bidding bon voyage to passing mariners.[38]

Maximilian filled his castle with images and symbols. He displayed the family crests, paintings of his ancestors, his brothers, images reminding him of his childhood and young-adult years. He commissioned scenes from his marriage and investiture as governor of Lombardy-Venetia. Carlota, who was a gifted artist, also provided her work to the home's collection. The couple used light blue damask with an anchor pattern and crest to cover the walls of the salons and private apartments. In the floor of the second-story landing, situated in the ceiling of the front entry, Maximilian designed a fountain with water pouring over a glass lens. The effect of water mixing with natural sunlight emitted sparkling rays of light dashing over the first-floor entryway to the castle, mirroring the shimmering Adriatic.[39]

Chandeliers and lanterns displayed the opposing profiles of Janus, the Roman god of passages, who looked both forward and backward, with a mindful basis in the past. The namesake of January, Janus also represented the sun and the moon, with the benefit of viewing the past and the future simultaneously. He also symbolized new beginnings, and perhaps more importantly to Maximilian, the symbol associated with Rome. An observer could not help but notice Janus's application to Maximilian's life.[40]

Toward the end of 1859, with Austria reeling from its defeats in northern Italy, Maximilian, hoping to avoid the chaos and intrigue, determined to explore Brazil, ruled by his cousin Pedro II. With Carlota, he departed on November 10, 1859, for a three-month tour, much relieved "after a summer replete with anxiety," Maximilian recalled. Although Carlota originally set out with Maximilian intending to go to Brazil, she decided to remain at the island of Madeira, west of Portugal, claiming to be unaccustomed to the roiling and stormy seas. Maximilian sailed on, intent to visit the Amazon and collect and identify plant specimens. According to Maximilian's valet, this was the first step toward Maximilian and Carlota growing apart in their conjugal life. No one knew the cause, for certain, and stories abounded over his possible

Habsburg Archdukes Ludwig Victor, Franz Josef,
Karl Ludwig, and Ferdinand Maximilian, ca. 1863

impotence or disease. Nevertheless, Maximilian seemed content to travel on without Carlota. Venturing through the jungles and visiting various plantations, he learned a great deal about the beauty of the country, the taxonomy of plants, ecosystems, agricultural methods, and mining wealth within Brazil, but at the farms he seemed ambivalent at the agrarian system of landowners and slaves. At one moment, the estate owners seemed adventurous men of action, but their iron rule and the unjust flogging of slaves aggrieved him as morally wrong and sinful. Maximilian also thought the priests too powerful and pretentious in their attempts to teach the natives. He marveled at the richness of forests and worked with botanists to document taxonomic terms for various plants and animals. So impressed with his early travel experiences and Brazil, he wrote a travelogue titled *Recollections of My Life*.[41]

Upon his return to Miramar, Maximilian set out for Vienna with his bride only to find corruption, uneasiness in the royal household, and never-ending stresses. Even Carlota felt palpable tensions in the court, where she found her in-laws most uncongenial. In short, Maximilian and Carlota had no station of duty and little purpose other than building their castle and planning their gardens. They purchased a small island retreat called Lacroma in the Adriatic, in today's Croatia, the retreat of Benedictine monks, where legend had it that Richard the Lionheart shipwrecked and later built a monastery to celebrate his survival. Through those next years, Maximilian traveled to Vienna regularly, while Carlota took up most of her time riding horses, painting, and swimming. However, they both longed for a purpose, a chance to rule, as they had been bred and trained. "I believe the day will come when the archduke will again occupy a prominent position. By this I mean a position where he will govern, for he was made for that and was blessed by Providence with everything necessary to make a people happy," wrote Carlota.[42]

In October 1861, after some talk and rumors, Maximilian was approached with the idea of becoming emperor of Mexico. Offered as partial compensation by Napoléon for Austria's loss of Lombardy, this, he hoped, would improve France's relations with Franz Josef. Maximilian first received a letter of intent from Austria's imperial advisor, Richard Metternich, on behalf of Napoléon, followed by a visit from Johann Bernhard, Count von Rechberg-Rothenlöwen, the Austrian minister of foreign affairs, who traveled to Miramar to discuss the restoration of a monarchy in Mexico, should France mount an expedition. Metternich knew that Emperor Franz Josef was amenable to allowing his brother to assume the empire of Mexico. While Rechberg had advised against it, he nonetheless treated the matter as though it were strictly between Maximilian the candidate and Napoléon III. Although Franz Josef did not trust Napoléon, the opportunity for a fresh distinction in Habsburg prestige, combined with a way to get rid of his brother, proved an irresistible combination. The concept was not new, as royal clans commonly dispatched various family members to govern other countries as it suited them, whether or not they were familiar with the land, language, or culture. The family members viewed it as their duty to lead countries wherever they may be called, and this had worked reasonably well in Europe over the last few centuries. Maximilian, who also waited for such an opportunity, agreed to seriously study the prospect of the Mexican emperorship, an unprecedented challenge in this distant and seemingly exotic land. This led to a roundabout series of negotiations between Napoléon, Franz Josef, and Maximilian and Carlota, advised by Carlota's aspiring and determined father, Leopold, who told her, "The Mexicans are worth more than the Italians." It all worked within Napoléon's scheme for influencing power across Europe.[43]

Despite the enthusiasm of the Mexican Monarchists and their trust in Napoléon's grand scheme, some of Franz Josef's advisors wondered if a trap was not being set for Austria. "Timeo Danaos et dona ferente" (beware of Greeks bearing gifts), said one minister trying to chart Napoléon's scheme, using the Mexican venture as a pawn to rearrange European territories. If Franz Josef objected to Napoléon's manipulations, he could say, "What does this mean, Austria? You have forgotten that I was the one who put one of your archdukes on a rather distant throne. It was fraught with difficulties, I admit, but thanks to my treasury, my fleets, and my influence, I smoothed the way." They wondered to what advantage was a throne in Mexico. While his ministers questioned Napoléon's motives, suspecting his chicanery, Franz Josef did not fully interpret the great movements sweeping Europe in his own time, so in denial were the Habsburgs that circumstances were changing.[44]

This did not bother Maximilian and Carlota, who had ceased to worry about Austria's welfare. They bore in mind sovereign duty, their imaginations blazing, trying to anticipate the vast outlay of political, moral, and financial capital that would become their responsibility in the New World.[45] At the time, they did not seriously question Napoléon's wisdom in occupying a country so far afield, especially under the Habsburg's right of kings, nor the consequences of overturning the determined and devoted president of Mexico, Benito Juárez.

❡ 2 ❡

Sooner or Later,
War Will Have to Be Declared

The curious arrangement of a Mexican empire ruled by an Austrian archduke and Belgian princess did not originate with Napoléon III but stemmed from an idea seeded just after Mexico's independence from Spain in 1821. At the birth of an independent Mexico, a fair number of the elites, political leaders, and a defiant clergy agonized over their loss of power. With the wide disparity of cultures and economic status across the country, they worried Mexico could never sustain a democracy. Moreover, with over 100 native societies distributed over 5,000 villages, each with their own language, customs, and territories, it was difficult to assimilate the people into one national identity, especially against the backdrop of centuries of despotism, which especially set them apart from the powerful ruling classes. Factionalism between political parties and the military led to a succession of fifty-four administrations in the forty years between 1823 and 1863, each regime lasting until the treasury funds to pay the bureaucrats and army were exhausted.[1]

With its vast lands and resources and industrious, inventive people, many recognized Mexico's potential to be a powerhouse that could rival any nation but remained a failed state, unable to withstand the rising power of the United States with its eyes on further territorial expansion. It was perceived that a depressing lack of stable leadership held the country back. "The worst enemies of Mexico are her own [people]," said keen observer Gen. William Tecumseh Sherman.[2]

Three hundred years as a stratified Spanish colony left Mexico and its indigenous people in biting poverty, under a system of regional viceroys. Spanish colonialists ruled by royal mystique and force, subsuming a people who had traditionally lived under various ethnic rulers or *caciques*. In 1810 the cry for independence by Padre Miguel Hidalgo y Costilla and Ignacio Allende y Unzaga, *Grito de Dolores*, inspired Mexican revolt. It would be another ten years until the country achieved independence. Agustín de Iturbide, a brilliant, ambitious, and arrogant *criollo*, proclaimed himself emperor, but public protests resulted in his ouster from office and exile. When he returned to Mexico in 1824, the Mexican people turned on him, and he was executed. But this did not suppress the Conservatives' conviction that only under a monarchy and a structured society could Mexico emerge as a world power based on "the principles of rational order, built upon the nature of man."[3]

When the Mexican Congress instituted sweeping liberal reforms with the Constitution of 1824, it gave the vote to all men, to which the Conservatives strongly objected, arguing that the constitution weakened the country and that the proletariat was not educated or sophisticated enough to rule the country. "Our people, because of their (poor) education, still need to be led by the hand like a child," said controversial President Antonio López de Santa Anna. Despite subsequent constitutions that limited the vote to men with incomes, Conservatives doubted the recalcitrant Republicans had enough discipline to maintain Mexico's independence, especially to fend off any territorial encroachments by the United States.[4]

In 1853, when Santa Anna reluctantly agreed to the Gadsden Purchase, stemming from residual consequences five years earlier with the Treaty of Guadalupe Hidalgo, he permitted the cession of nearly 30,000 square miles of Mexican territory in Arizona and New Mexico to the United States. At the same time, however, Santa Anna determined not to let Mexico fall victim to further aggression from the United States. Feeling that only strong alliances with powerful European nations would help stabilize a strong central government, Santa Anna sent out various proposals to foreign leaders, including France's Emperor Napoléon, to assist in forming an agreement between his country, England, and Spain to protect Mexico. This proposal contained the suggestion that a European sovereign should establish a royal dynasty in Mexico. Although Santa Anna eventually lost support on all sides, the Monarchists continued the campaign for a foreign prince.[5]

Advocating for the old regime, the powerful and ubiquitous hierarchy of the Catholic Church joined in calling for a Mexican monarchy. During the centuries of Spanish rule, the church became the largest landholder in Mexico, and by the mid-nineteenth century, the value of those lands was estimated by Miguel Lerdo de Tejada at three billion pesos. The dead hand of the clergy would not sell properties, depriving the government of revenues from transactions and individuals the right to invest in these lands, which the church rented out to form between eight hundred and nine hundred farms. In many cases, the church failed to fully utilize their properties. There was no religious toleration, and as the church of the whole nation, clerics wielded great influence over the country's 8 million people, only one-sixth descended from European origins. The Constitutions of 1812 and 1824 guaranteed that Catholicism would remain the official national religion and kept the church's power bases centered at Mexico City and Puebla. In regions such as Oaxaca, Catholicism adapted to the traditional cults of the indigenous communities. However, clerics frequently abused their power, and this led to a rising undercurrent of resistance.[6]

After the collapse of Spanish rule, Catholicism remained at the core of Mexican life, although many feared the clergy and clerics who dominated through intimidation. Attempts to stop the unbridled control of the church and make it subordinate to the law gave rise to the Liberals, also known as Republicans. Their democratic values, national identity, and civic virtue offered a serious threat to the power and influence of the clerics, who were determined to protect themselves from state dominance. Simultaneously, this was answered by a strengthening of the Conservative party, not necessarily based on Catholic domination, but which used alliances with the church to further its goals. Conservative leaders recognized that the church tied the country together, while serving as one of the defining characteristics of Mexican nationality, united, reliable, and enduring. To maintain their power, or what they considered the traditional social and political structures of the country, they eventually decided to bring the Second Empire with Emperor Maximilian and Empress Carlota as sovereigns. They molded their objectives in the crucial years between 1855 and 1860, during intense Liberal reforms.[7]

Liberals organized through the 1850s. Many were radical intellectuals, and a cadre derived from Oaxaca and the Pacific coast, arguing for the people's sovereignty and the power of the less fortunate. They put their faith in a strong body of law and in the autonomy of local government, handing rights, independence, and power to the individual states. The debates resulted in proposals for constitutional change, which erupted in factional clashes, often motivated by personal agendas. Moderate Liberals such as Ignacio Comonfort saw themselves not as radicals but called for meaningful changes in federalism without disarming the church. He tried to repair relations. Taking power and

Benito Juárez, ca. 1867

lands from the immovable, and heretofore unquestioned, church hierarchy, he argued, would require careful measures. The church, however, mobilized to stop any erosion of its totalitarianism.[8]

In 1855 and 1856, amid rising conflict, leading to the War of the Reform, Liberals led by Melchor Ocampo, the former anticlerical governor of Michoacán; Benito Juárez, a young lawyer and former governor of Oaxaca; and Miguel and Sebastián Lerdo de Tejada, intellectuals from Veracruz, sought to pass laws that amounted to a departure from the last three hundred years. In the reform, Benito Juárez's reputation would grow legendary as he formed himself into the self-made liberator of the overlooked lower classes—his legacy.[9]

Pablo Benito Juárez, a pure-blooded Zapotec native, was born into humble beginnings on March 21, 1806, to Marcelino Juárez and Brigida García in the mountain village of San Pablo Guelatao in the state of Oaxaca and was dutifully baptized at the church of Santo Tomás Ixtlán, known today as Ixtlán de Juárez. "I had the misfortune not to know my parents . . . Indians of the primitive race of the country, because I was barely three years old when they died and left me and my sisters in the care of our grandparents Pedro Juárez and Justa López, also Indians of the Zapotec nation," the future president later wrote.[10]

A few years later, after the death of his grandparents, his sisters had already married, and the small boy went to live with an uncle, Bernardino Juárez. Although raised as a shepherd, his uncle taught him the rudiments of reading and writing as well as ecclesiastical lessons with the hope that he would one day go into the seminary. When he failed to recite biblical passages correctly, his uncle told Benito to bring him a whip and then punished the boy. At the age of twelve, Juárez left his uncle to seek work in the city of Oaxaca, first staying in the home of Antonio Mazza, for whom his sister worked. It was there he would meet his future wife, Margarita Mazza, the homeowner's daughter. A few weeks later, he found work with a bookbinder named Antonio Salanueva, with whom he bartered his labor in return for sponsorship of an education. He enrolled at the Royal School under Salanueva's patronage in January 1819.[11]

Juárez found the ecclesiastical studies at the Royal School interesting, but the manner in which he was taught offended him. He and the other under-privileged boys were separated from the main body of students and punished for not knowing their lessons. Juárez became discouraged, and for three years he resorted to independent study. At the age of twenty-two, he decided to learn law at the Institute of Sciences and Arts. In the debates over the future of Mexico, the students divided themselves between Conservatives and Liberals, a laboratory of philosophy later reflected during the War of the Reform. At the institute, while waiting tables, Juárez once met the dictator Antonio López de Santa Anna and instantly distrusted him as a fortune seeker. Santa Anna would later remember Juárez as little more than a barefooted boy.[12]

The young scholar, one observer described, was of middle height with a dark-complexioned, round face "made more interesting, by a very large scar across it. He had very black piercing eyes, and gave one the impression of being a man who reflects much and deliberates long and carefully before act-ing. He wore high English collars and a black neck-tie and black broadcloth."[13]

Juárez approached his legal studies seriously. He learned constitutional law and formed radical ideas of how to suppress church power and institute land reform. In Oaxaca, he soon began representing people against the church while working to promote crop rotation with farmers, revive the mining indus-try, and establish a state mint by abrogating a foreign concession. Through methodical work and continuity, he prevailed upon the clergy to provide for the poor and sick, seeking to restore the church to its rightful purpose, which was to minister. More importantly, he entered the realm of politics.[14]

When Ignacio Comonfort, a former colonel and hacendado from Puebla, became president of Mexico in September 1855, the clergy and the Conservatives were uneasy. In December, Juárez, who had been appointed minister of justice, promulgated a law that became, eponymously, the legendary *Ley Juárez*, which limited the church's ecclesiastical courts to rule over its own internal matters but not civil issues. At this time, the true manifestations of the Liberal changes were not yet known, but foreseeing a complete paradigm shift, the bishop of Puebla, Pelagio Antonio de Labastida, protested any changes in church jurisdiction over state matters. Juárez tried to persuade him not to influence his flocks into revolt. Labastida, who would later become archbishop of Mexico, maintained that the resulting public rejection and outrage lay beyond his control, though most knew the clergy encouraged demonstrations. In Puebla, the people mounted a rebellion in December 1855 calling for restoration of the Constitution of 1836 and the absolutism of the church, which required the National Guard to restore peace. To strengthen the Juárez Law, in June 1856 the Liberals instigated the *Ley Lerdo*, named for Miguel Lerdo de Tejada, ordering the immediate divestiture of most church lands and elimination of the special privileges of the clergy, considered by them to have been "only a source of evil." They intended the former church properties to be used to create a middle class of farmers, landowners, and tenants.[15]

The fighting continued through the first part of 1856, while Comonfort struggled to build his presidency in Mexico City. He and the Conservatives remained squarely divided over the position of the church in everyday Mexican life. In response, the two armies clashed in Puebla, and Comonfort quashed the conflict with 15,000 troops. In March he banished Labastida from Mexico, who then fled to Europe, where he found it advantageous to engage in politics and side with other exiled Conservatives in Europe to restore church power. He pled their case at the Vatican over his four-year expatriation.[16]

In Mexico, the Liberals pushed for a complete separation of church and state. They crafted the Constitution of 1857 to decentralize the government, disarm military politicians, and limit the power of the presidency. More importantly, the constitution removed the provision that Catholicism be the exclusive religion of Mexico. Religious toleration remained anathema to the Catholic hierarchy, who rejected the constitution wholesale and excommunicated those who pledged themselves to it, in the tradition of being outside the law. In 1858 Comonfort's regime collapsed, and as chief justice, Juárez assumed power as the constitutional president. In January 1858 Gen. Félix Zuloaga at Mexico City seized control as the candidate selected by the Clerical party. Two rival governments emerged, and violence erupted in what would come to be known as the War of the Reform. Juárez based his presidential capital at Guanajuato, and Zuloaga operated from Mexico City.[17]

At the outset of the War of the Reform, *La Reforma*, militant clergy refused to abandon church properties, hiding in haciendas or in the Dominican and Franciscan monasteries. They collected munitions and funded a Conservative army with gold and silver melted down from the sacristies. The Conservatives also put their faith in the twenty-seven-year-old Gen. Miguel Miramón, a daring, ambitious criollo from Mexico City who had fought in the Mexican War, where he earned the title of "Maccabeus" because his style resembled the ancient biblical soldier and liberator of Jerusalem. The Conservatives also enlisted thirty-seven-year-old Gen. Tomás Mejía, a member of the Otomí culture from Querétaro, a master of the region of the Sierra Gorda and San Luis Potosí through prior military service, known for his high standards in discipline, the uniforms and appearance of his men, the quality of his horses, and devout loyalty to the church party. These men were seen as brilliant military tacticians who would play crucial roles in the subsequent empire.[18]

The fighting swept across the country and lasted longer than anyone anticipated. The Conservatives, who were strong in central and eastern Mexico, were led by Gen. Miramón, a skilled and brutal fighter, while the Liberal military, mostly a cadre of lawyers, came to depend on Gen. Santos Degollado of Guanajuato and Jesús González Ortega from Jalisco. As the conflict wore on, both sides escalated their brutality. At Tacubaya, near Mexico City, Conservative Gen. Leonardo Márquez, known for his ferocity, ordered all his prisoners executed—not only the Liberal officers and troops, mostly in a hospital, but also the doctors caring for the wounded. The clergy and church officials celebrated the victory, while the Liberals condemned the act as barbaric and reminiscent of the Dark Ages.[19]

Although the Conservatives won decisive victories, Liberals including Benito Juárez and Melchor Ocampo displayed enduring patience and determination. In 1859 and 1860 Ocampo and Juárez promulgated the Laws of the Reform that further solidified control over the church, ordering church properties nationalized, monasteries and convents searched, closed, and dispersed, and religious orders suppressed. The war would continue for another year.[20]

Desperation for funds grew on both sides. Juárez needed money for the war and the growing national debt. Accordingly, he sought the United States' assistance and seriously considered formalizing the McLane-Ocampo Treaty, an offer by Robert M. McLane, then U.S. minister to Mexico, of $4 million in return for mining privileges in Sonora as well as the cession of portions of the Isthmus of Tehuantepec and Baja California to the United States, along with rail and telegraph easements. Both the Conservatives and Liberals questioned Juárez's loyalty. The controversial treaty resulted in many Mexicans losing confidence in Ocampo and Juárez, who faced allegations of giving away another large section of Mexican territory, much like Santa Anna. The Americans, some who maintained a morally superior attitude toward Mexico, however, continued to have designs on seizing more Mexican territory, despite its own impending Civil War.[21]

This was with reason. Increasing European interest in Mexico worried the United States, because the Mexican Conservatives invited France and Spain to intercede. To fight the Liberals, Miramón hoped the Europeans would agree to blockade Veracruz, as the Spanish had already engaged in a naval demonstration off Tampico, followed by an Anglo-French demonstration in January, a warning to Juárez not to default on national debt. In June, when Miramón led an attack on Veracruz only to be crushed by a Liberal column twice the size of his, the Liberals burned churches and swept across the central plateau. Forced back to Mexico City and desperate for funds, Miramón broke into the British Legation offices and stole $660,000, a sum Great Britain later charged against Mexico's aggregate debt liability.[22]

Further adding to the debt worries, Miramón contracted with the Swiss banker Jean-Baptiste Jecker in October 1859 to borrow money in the form of bonds for the Conservatives. To facilitate the agreement, he struck a usurious arrangement to borrow 7.5 million pesos against a debt of 15 million pesos, half in cash and half in armaments and munitions. The significance in the Jecker contract lay in the fact that one of its predominant investors was Charles Auguste de Morny, Duc de Morny, the bastard half-brother to Napoléon III and a clever instigator of national movements emerging in France. Two months later, Jecker's banking house was in the hands of creditors who eagerly wanted to reclaim the debt. In March 1860, when Miramón again moved his Conservative army on Veracruz, Juárez succeeded in persuading the U.S. navy to stop Spanish ships sailing from Havana, contracted by Miramón to blockade Veracruz. The United States, motivated by the pending McLane-Ocampo agreement, conferred this benefit on Mexico, although the treaty lost favor soon afterward.[23]

The next month, Miramón declared himself president of Mexico but was defeated by the Liberal armies of Gen. González Ortega in August and December 1860. Leaving Mexico for Havana, Miramón traveled on to Europe where he continued to lobby for the Conservative cause. Juárez claimed Mexico City as president on the first day of 1861.[24]

In April, a few months after Miramón contracted with the Jecker firm for bond funding, France assigned Minister Jean Pierre Isidore Alphonse Dubois de Saligny, a man eager to gain the good graces of Napoléon to manage French interests in Mexico. The French Foreign Ministry, also known by the metonym the Quai d'Orsay, asked him to settle debts and indemnities before the Juárez administration could be officially recognized. A loyal Catholic, Saligny, viewed as a violent, imprudent, quarrelsome man, championed the cause of the church and its restoration of power, arriving with a larger agenda. Labastida, with whom he consulted in Europe before taking his post, convinced him that without their properties, the church had no power to protect itself, and the clergy would be reduced to mere servants. They won Saligny to their cause, who soon began to write about the "social decomposition" of Mexico, intolerable levels of violence toward French subjects, and the country's imminent absorption by the United States.[25]

Within the movement to bring a foreign monarch to Mexico, two other men also stood out most prominently because of their connections and influence with certain courts in Europe: José María Gutiérrez de Estrada and José Manuel Hidalgo y Esnaurrizar, both Mexican-born *criollos* with significant assets in Mexico, who lived as refugees in Europe. After nearly twenty years of watching leaders struggle to make Mexico a republic, only to see them fall time and again against a backdrop of *pronunciamentos* full of condemning rhetoric, followed by coups d'état, they saw their homeland degenerating. They said the Liberal government was tyrannical, oppressive, and governed only by force. These conflicts sucked the lifeblood out of the country. Their profound disillusionment caused them to conclude that Mexico would never be capable of self-rule. As early as 1840, the ultraconservative Gutiérrez de Estrada summed up his frustrations that the "sad experience" of democracy proved that the country could not flourish as a republic and the best solution lay in a church-based constitutional monarchy, which, he claimed, the people were accustomed to as the foundation of the Mexican state. But given Iturbide's failed attempt in 1822, any new sovereign leader should be a foreign prince, thereby unsusceptible to factional infighting.[26]

Gutiérrez de Estrada had spent a great deal of time cultivating relationships as a Mexican diplomat to Vienna and Rome. More comfortable in Europe than in Mexico, he came to acquire a Roman palazzo and married the daughter of an Austrian countess who served in the court of Archduke Ferdinand Maximilian in Italy. Deriving most of his income from henequen plantations in Yucatán, Gutiérrez de Estrada became a great advocate and financial supporter of the pope and the Vatican. So closely was he tied to the Jesuits, he reeked of incense, some said.[27]

Up until the end of Mexico's War of the Reform, Gutiérrez de Estrada scoured the great courts of England and Europe and consulted with authorities in Rome, in a never-ending effort to persuade royals and statesmen alike on the cause of a Mexican monarchy. He wrote long, thirty-page treatises on the subject, arguing that European leaders could not let North America's covetousness go unchecked. It would be only a matter of time, he argued, before the United States would devour the rest of Mexico, and the Europeans would pay dearly for their indifference and inaction.[28]

The second man, José Manuel Hidalgo, was born in Mexico as the son of a Spanish officer and estate owner devoted to Iturbide. He moved to Spain with his family at an early age and worked mostly for his family's Mexican interests. He also came to advocate the return of a Mexican monarchy. In 1858 in Bayonne, France, Hidalgo happened to cross paths with Eugénie de Montijo, Empress of France, his childhood friend. As she descended from her carriage on her way to a bullfight, she noticed the young man respectfully acknowledging her on the street. She recognized him and they reacquainted. As they visited, Eugénie invited him to a seaside excursion at Biarritz. On the trip, Hidalgo explained in detail his mission, the struggles to restore the church in Mexico, and the Monarchists' ideas for a foreign-born Emperor to save the country from itself. Her friendship with Hidalgo, a self-seeking, obsequious, untruthful man, came to be very important.[29]

Neither Gutiérrez de Estrada nor Hidalgo desired to return to Mexico but chose instead to push their Monarchist agendas in European royal circles. While Gutiérrez de Estrada endlessly advocated for church authority, Hidalgo's interest lay mostly in maintaining his father's estates. Both thought themselves Mexican patriots, but men who seemed happiest living away from their homeland.[30]

In Empress Eugénie, Hidalgo found a way to rejuvenate interest in a Mexican monarchy that Gutiérrez de Estrada had worked decades to develop. Eugénie was born María Eugenia Ignacia Guzmán y Montijo in Grenada, Spain, the daughter of Cipriano Guzmán Palafox y Portocarrero, the Count of Teba, and María Manuela Kirkpatrick, descended from an elite Scottish family. Educated in Paris and England, Eugénie maintained close ties with the Spanish court and remained devoted to Spanish causes as well as French. In describing the situation in Mexico, Hidalgo played to her Spanish patrio-

Empress Eugénie de Montijo, Paris, France, ca. 1865

tism and wish to regain control of the country. The church had lost its power under the reforms of the "Godless" Liberals, he argued, and peonage had seized Mexico, ruining all that Spain worked three hundred years to build. The damage to Catholicism and the Spanish descendants there further weakened the country against possible American intrusions, and this compromised European interests in Mexico. To Eugénie, a consummate monarchist, the wisdom of seating a European prince, who was also a Catholic, on a newly created Mexican throne, seemed obvious. France would not only have access to Mexican commerce and forestall American aggression but would also redeem and restore power to the church.[31]

In the creation of a Mexican empire lay an opportunity for Eugénie to assert her political power since she held considerable influence over her husband. She was fascinated by the idea. Hidalgo played not only on her devotion to Spain and Catholicism but also on her disdain for the republic of the United States and its rising power. The regeneration of Mexico and Central America had long been on Napoléon's mind. Eugénie played on this, also as a way to hold his attention, amid the indignity of his various love affairs. Although she knew very little about the United States and Mexico, she had identified a subject that would appeal to her husband's ambition.[32]

After Louis Napoléon formally became Emperor of France as Napoléon III in 1852, he wasted little time in building formidable support to create the most powerful regime in Europe. The French territory of Algeria led to a French protectorate in Tunisia and east to the building of the Suez Canal. Rapid economic expansion and successful victories in the Crimea, China, and Cambodia, where France established regencies and trading centers, further emboldened him to exercise his geopolitical influence. An avid historian who studied the life of Julius Caesar in detail, he later wrote a book, *Histoire de Jules César*, published in 1865, with the preface that "historical accuracy should be no less sacred than religion," because as religion lifted humanity above the interests of the world, history inspired the love of all things beautiful and just. Napoléon III saw himself as a great warrior who would change the world unto his design, namely according to the Napoleonic ideal and utopian philosophies, while expanding upon the ideas of his uncle, Napoléon I, especially in foreign affairs and the guarantees of "Liberty, Equality, and Fraternity." He set out to change the balance of power in Europe and revive the prestige of France. In the case of Mexico, he would fulfill his uncle's dreams, which had become his own, of spreading French superiority in the Western Hemisphere, not necessarily by making war but by putting defeats and humiliations in the past to bring about one peaceful confederation.[33]

His policy for Mexico mirrored his general political policy, which included opposing the ultraconservative papacy and bishops, one of the greatest ambiguities of his reign, since he protected the pope's temporal home in Rome. Further, his long-held great desire to spread French civilization, prosperity, and well-being throughout the world included Latin America and Mexico especially, known for its rich resources but sorely lacking in stability and civilizing influences. Energetic, intelligent, and wily, Napoléon III passionately and, some said, altruistically worked toward his goals, striving for monumental and historic changes. One of his ministers termed Napoléon's plan, "la plus grande pensée du règne (the greatest idea of his reign). Most of all, he determined to be remembered by history.[34]

Even early in their marriage, however, Eugénie had worried about North

American expansion and European interests. She referred to American arrogance and Spain's belief that a U.S. invasion of Cuba was only a matter of time. "Sooner or later, war will have to be declared on the Americans," she said, and Napoléon smiled skeptically. "War, war my love is no longer possible in France; we are, so to speak, hemmed in by material interests and trade, which are all in all," he said. This ideal lasted only a few years. France went to war in the Crimea, and it expanded its interests in Asia.[35]

Napoléon, however, observed other European countries reasserting their authority in the New World, taking advantage of regional unrest. In 1861 Spain restored its control over the Dominican Republic. The reign of Pedro II of Brazil and his wife, Leopoldine, a Habsburg, seemed secure. He pored over maps of Mexico, smoking one cigarette after another, dreaming of a block of control in North America.[36]

By 1858, to align with Napoléon's philosophies, Eugénie was clearly interested in Hidalgo's idea of reviving the Mexican empire. Because Hidalgo had come to be one of her closest courtiers, he spent a great deal of time in her presence and spoke of Mexico often, and she in turn mentioned his ideas to Napoléon. In the fall, while at Compiègne, Napoléon summoned Hidalgo into his office and asked about conditions in Mexico, then in the throes of its War of the Reform. "Very bad, and the country will be lost unless Your Majesty comes to its aid," said Hidalgo. Napoléon wanted to hear more. He motioned Hidalgo to a window seat, offered him some wine, and asked for more information. As Napoléon mulled over diplomatic strategies, he visualized that any assistance from France must be accompanied by similar help from Great Britain, to avoid provoking the United States or the English mining companies. Indeed, Napoléon and Henry John Temple, Lord Palmerston, the prime minister of England, had been in communication, and both agreed that a large army and many millions would be required to subdue Mexico. Britain's minister to Mexico, Charles Lennox Wyke, agreed, saying that Latin America's nations were ripe for monarchies. Napoléon had already set the plan in motion, much to Hidalgo's surprise.[37]

For other reasons, Napoléon had considered the occupation and control of Mexico. France had been facing a silver shortage—the metal had increased in value and was mostly needed for the purchase of cotton for France's cloth industry, worth 700 million francs. But with the onset of the U.S. Civil War, cotton became scarce. When France turned to the less desirable crop grown in India, they demanded payment in silver. When silver supplies became scant, cotton imports fell, and by 1861 unemployment soared. As many as 40 percent of the spinning workers in Normandy were out of work, and export industries like watchmaking and porcelain suffered. To cure the French need for precious metals, especially silver, Mexico's mines, especially in Sonora, seemed a logical solution, further propelling Napoléon to the idea of its occupation, installation of a monarchy, while sending European immigrants to populate the new nation.[38]

Of course, Napoléon and Hidalgo understood that the Americans would allege a violation of the Monroe Doctrine, the unilateral policy to discourage any power grab by European states on the North American continent. This did not bother Napoléon. He scoffed at it and looked forward to testing American power, doubting the Monroe Doctrine could be enforced. With conflict rising in America on the brink of Civil War, and the United States more accurately described as the "dis-United States," Napoléon felt the time was opportune to spread France's influence through the Western Hemisphere. He saw Spain thriving in Cuba and taking territory in the Dominican Republic and islands off the coast of Peru. Aware of the activities of Alejandro Mon, Spain's minister to France, to establish a "strong and durable" government in Mexico, Napoléon was loath to see them claim additional lands. He knew it would take an enormous army and great resources. Nonetheless, France along with Britain assured U.S. president James Buchanan that whatever means they chose to protect their people and assets in Mexico, it would be done without armed interference.[39]

More importantly, they would need a Catholic prince willing to take the throne, and they began to consider possible candidates. Hidalgo mentioned Spain's Juan Carlos de Bourbón, the Count of Montizón. Napoléon paused, turned toward the table, sipped his glass of wine, and said, "We thought of the Duc d'Aumale, but he refuses," referring to Henri d'Orléans, the fifth child of King Louis Philippe and former governor-general of Algeria.[40]

In late 1860, with Mexico's War of the Reform coming to a close and the election of Abraham Lincoln signaling that the United States would slide toward Civil War, Napoléon sensed a unique opportunity to occupy Mexico. The war had caused a 7-million-franc decrease in exports, and since its end, Juárez had encouraged his generals to harass French importers and rob their *conductas,* or wagon trains. He also believed that, given the chance and additional time, the United States would annex another portion of Mexico, as it had in 1848 and again in 1853, just seven years earlier. Many sovereigns in Europe hoped that the South would prevail in the Civil War and remain independent, as an equalizer against an overreaching North, whose leaders they viewed as aggressive in the habit of inciting difficulties and barriers to trade. However, he carefully said many things to rationalize his mission and make it seem even philanthropic, as though France could save Mexico's independence from the United States and preserve the integrity of its lands: "We on the other side of the ocean, shall have restored to the Latin race its power and prestige" in staving off the Americans. Defense of France's national interests in Mexico, financial claims, and creation of an empire for Maximilian aside, "the downfall of Juárez was the only business at hand." Napoléon steeled his determination.[41]

During the next few months, Empress Eugénie and Hidalgo plotted to send an expedition to Mexico and spoke often with Napoléon on the matter. Eugénie prevailed on Prince Richard Klemens von Metternich, the Austrian ambassador to the court of Paris, to find a candidate for emperor. Metternich, who at first opposed the scheme, sensing that in return Napoléon would ask Austria to give up their claim to Venetia, commented that Napoléon's preparation for the Mexican expedition gave him more insight into the emperor's character than years of regular relations.[42] The timing of their scheme did not ripen until 1861, when the plan fit into place. In Mexico, Benito Juárez chose a strategy that so isolated him from the European powers, it changed the course of history for the next six years.

❧ 3 ❧

The Red Avenger

In June 1861 the War Comet, at ten degrees east of Ursa Major and halfway to the North Star, appeared in the northern sky, low and large over the Americas and Europe; its luminous, conical tail sprayed particles of matter through the atmosphere into the biosphere. Its glittering fan seemed to brush the earth and in some places obscured the sun during daylight hours. A number of writers, artists, and observers viewed this Red Avenger, one of several great comets in the nineteenth century, as a portent of unrest, aggression, and a sign of war.[1]

In Mexico, overturning reform measures enacted under the Liberals became the clarion call of Conservatives, clericals, and landed aristocracy, who set their sights on punishing Juárez and the Liberals for disempowering the clergy. They demanded the restoration of church lands and the collection on damages accrued during the War of the Reform. European governments also demanded the immediate payment of loans to Mexico for war financing. While tensions rose, the Liberals fought tenaciously against a return to the old order, no longer wanting to allow the Catholic Church to be the cornerstone of society, viewing the priests' influence as dictatorial, autocratic, and frightening. This conflict led to random violence. In Veracruz, the papal nuncio, Rome's representative to Mexico, was stoned by Liberals. Meanwhile, in Europe, Bishop Labastida, indignant at his ouster from Mexico in 1856, lobbied the Vatican and European courts against the abuses of the new regime, waiting for the opportunity to return to Mexico. His quiet vengeance would prove to be very effective.[2]

When the fifty-four-year-old Benito Juárez entered office on January 1, 1861, he found a host of problems stemming from the War of the Reform. After dismissing his enemies, including papal representatives and the minister from Spain, his new administration immediately faced over $80 million in debts to Great Britain and other European countries, left behind by previous regimes, including that of Miramón. The Swiss banking house operated by Jean-Baptiste Jecker held some of the bond debt, admitted by the Mexican government to total roughly $2.86 million, while the remainder held by Spain totaled $9 million. In addition, the British legation claimed 69 million in silver dollars loaned or stolen from them. International law provided for the payment of government debts, no matter if entered into by previous administrations. With the murder of his Liberal comrade Melchor Ocampo on June 3, political chaos began to stymie Juárez. Opposing Liberals formed a party to elect Jesús González Ortega and put pressure on Juárez to resign. The ongoing unrest, combined with mounting interest, concerned European investors in Mexico who saw no end to the discord, despite Juárez's presidency. Charles Lennox Wyke, who arrived in April 1861 to replace Great Britain's minister to Mexico, Loftus Charles Otway, found Juárez to be powerless in the anarchy, terming him a cypher. "These events," he said, "by proving the miserable improvidence of the present government, have completely discredited President Juárez, and his retirement is now looked upon as an absolute necessity for the good of the commonwealth."[3]

As for the foreign debt, Juárez at first promised to pay as prescribed by treaties and conventions but then failed to remit and made little effort to negotiate with bondholders. Juárez then proclaimed their "nullity" because he did not enter into those debt agreements. As there was no regular system of taxation in Mexico, which left it mostly dependent on customs revenues from trade goods, these debt payments risked bankrupting the Mexican treasury. On July 17, 1861, Juárez called a moratorium on further disbursements, while stating that he hoped to resume payments in two years but gave no firm guarantee. European ministers immediately condemned his act as irresponsible for a progressive and reliant country.[4]

Saligny, the minister to Mexico from France, and Wyke immediately wrote letters of protest. They were furious with Juárez's decision to violate debt obligations and intent to exact justice against Mexico's anarchy. Wyke asked, "Do you think that these lamentable facts . . . inspire us with confidence in a people who thus violate their engagements with us?" The two ministers threatened to terminate all official relations with Mexico if Juárez did not rescind his decree.

Receiving unacceptable responses and general silence, France and England broke off diplomatic relations, although with different motivations. Wyke remained sure that Saligny, whom he termed an "unfortunate man," had a much larger agenda and would impugn England's demands for its legitimate claims to Foreign Minister Édouard Thouvenel if they interfered with France's design, thus jeopardizing their relationship.[5]

When Napoléon learned of Juárez's announcement to suspend payments six weeks later in September 1861, he interpreted the announcement as Mexico's sign of rejection to all foreign governments. He viewed it as a diplomatic provocation, an affront to France and its debt claims, partially deriving from Jecker, associated with his half-brother De Morny. De Morny also served as president of France's Corps Législatif, or congress, and as a key policymaker and cunning crony, he had facilitated Napoléon's numerous expeditions and projects. Additionally, they expressed disappointment at Mexico's inability to conduct itself in a stable manner with respect to its international relations and agreements. Saligny suggested moving on Mexico immediately: "I am more inclined to believe that nothing could prevent a corps of 4,000 to 5,000 European soldiers from marching right to Mexico City without encountering the slightest resistance."[6]

In that year of great transitions, 1861, Napoléon carefully monitored events in North America. One evening while at Biarritz, he had just finished dinner with Empress Eugénie and Hidalgo when the topic of an armed invasion of Mexico was discussed. After supper, Eugénie settled down to her needlework with two of her ladies-in-waiting, while Hidalgo pulled up a little stool alongside her. He said in a low voice, "Your Majesty, I have just received some very interesting letters, events are moving in our direction, and I hope that the idea of intervention and of an empire may become a reality. I would like to tell the Emperor." The Empress rose and, after a moment, escorted Hidalgo into Napoléon's study.[7]

"Tell the Emperor what you just told me," she said. As they entered the room, the emperor held up a letter just arrived from the King of Siam, a curiosity that amused him, his eyes alight with pleasure. He then laid the note on his desk, rose, lit a cigarette, and turned to listen.

"Your Majesty, I had long lost all hope that the ideas I have spoken about with you for the last four years would be achieved, but England, which is as irritated as France and Spain are with the policies of Juárez, is going to send its vessels to our [Mexican] ports. There it is, Your Majesty, the English intervention," for which Napoléon had been waiting. Hidalgo went on to describe the readiness of the Spanish to proceed in association with France, with the idea that together they could have a mighty three-way alliance to cruise into Mexican waters. "The United States are at war; they will not make a move, besides, they would never challenge the three combined powers. . . . I tell Your Majesty that the country will rise up in mass to back the benevolent intervention," said Hidalgo.[8]

Napoléon replied that he had not seen any telegrams yet from his foreign minister, Thouvenel, but "If England and Spain are ready to go and the interests of France demand it, I will go as well, but I will send only a squadron, no landing troops, and if the country says it wants to organize itself, supported by powers of Europe, we will stretch our hand out. Moreover, as you justly say very well, the situation in the United States is very favorable."[9]

Hidalgo thought he was dreaming. "Whatever happens, we owe everything to France alone; please allow me to ask if you have a candidate, because the Mexicans would welcome him coming from your Majesty as if he were our own emperor?"

The emperor turned to his cigarette and said, "I have none."

Hidalgo glanced at Eugénie, "We cannot consider a Spanish prince . . . there was no possible choice there, sad to say."[10]

"In fact," said Eugénie, "there is no possible choice there, and that is unfortunate, because if there were one, he would be the most suitable." She and Hidalgo mentioned a few other candidates, mostly German princes, but they deemed them inappropriate because of their religion and relative unimportance. Hidalgo recalled that, although he had been skeptical, Prince Metternich suggested that an Austrian archduke might accept the crown.[11]

"But which archduke?" asked Eugénie.

"I suppose they were talking about the Archduke Régnier," said Hidalgo.

"Yes," said Eugénie, "for the Archduke Maximilian would not be willing."

"Oh, no. He would not accept," said Hidalgo.

"No, he would not want to," said Napoléon.

Eugénie, who remained standing during the discussion, thought for a few moments. An inspiration came to her and she struck her breast lightly with her fan. "Well. I have a feeling that he will accept."[12]

Napoléon, however, added that the idea must come from the Mexican people themselves, but the project was launched. Eugénie urged Hidalgo to investigate the matter with Maximilian, but of course Mexico must make the ultimate selection. She then called the foreign minister, Alexandre Walewski, onto the terrace and told him of what was happening. Walewski replied, "Mr.

Juan Nepomuceno Almonte,
Imperialista

Hidalgo will recall . . . I always told him that it was not possible, but now the circumstances have changed and I believe it is totally feasible. What can I do for you?"

"Lend me your telegraph a moment," said Hidalgo.[13]

Hidalgo wired Gutiérrez de Estrada, who was acquainted with the Austrian court through his wife, to go to Vienna to sound out the idea with Maximilian and the Habsburgs. With his message, the refugee Mexican Monarchists in Europe began to deploy. Almonte, then in Paris, started to move forward with his plan to overthrow his nemesis, Juárez.[14]

When consulted, Mexican monsignor Labastida, exiled in Rome, greatly supported the plan to place Maximilian on the throne as emperor of Mexico, if it meant a restoration of church power. He admitted, however, that because of the totality of Juárez's reforms in distributing church lands, it would require the greatest "courage, adroitness, strength, patience, and . . . good fortune."[15]

From exile in St. Thomas, former dictator Antonio López de Santa Anna dispatched communications to the Mexican exiles in Paris and to Maximilian to offer his services to the future monarchy. He added that the "immense majority of the nation aspires to reestablish the empire of the Montezumas with your imperial highness at its head, persuaded that this is the only remedy that can cure the grave ills of society, the last anchor of our hope," wrote Santa Anna. The old dictator desperately hoped to find a way to resume some semblance of authority in his former nation and viewed the situation as a possible conduit.[16] For nearly all the campaigners and supporters, the potential of a revived empire carried a unique purpose suited to their motives.

By then, conditions in the United States had degenerated into full-scale warfare. Europeans watched and speculated on a possible outcome in the conflict. Juárez's Mexican envoy to Washington, Matías Romero, hurriedly communicated to American secretary of state William H. Seward that France, England, and Spain were combining to take aggressive action against Mexico. In view of the United States' own domestic chaos, Seward could only make a statement urging the maintenance of a republican form of government. Juárez came to rely heavily on the twenty-four-year-old Romero, a fellow lawyer from Oaxaca, who served as Juárez's tenacious and persuasive chargé d'affaires and key to the Juaristas' knowledge base in Washington. His assertiveness helped remind Lincoln and his cabinet that the plight of the Republican government in Mexico should not be forgotten.[17]

When Napoléon saw that it would be impossible for the United States to get involved in Mexico, he seriously began to plan for a French invasion and called for reconnaissance. Because he considered some of the Mexican exiles a bit fanatical to trust absolutely, he ordered Thouvenel to interview a number of them, including Hidalgo, Gutiérrez de Estrada, and Almonte. Thouvenel with Walewski also made confidential inquiries with the Austrian emperor Franz Josef and his ministers, through Prince Metternich, regarding the candidacy of his brother, Archduke Ferdinand Maximilian. Metternich also pressed the issue with the Austrian hierarchy at Napoléon's request, but seeing that a European alliance and other arrangements had yet to materialize, Emperor Franz Josef waited for the pieces to fall into place. Indeed, Prince Metternich concurred, "What a lot of cannon shots it will take to set up an Emperor in Mexico, and what a lot to maintain him there."[18]

Throughout the fall of 1861, interest and excitement built within the French court for the occupation of a vulnerable Mexico, and many courtiers advocated that France quickly seize the opportunity, anticipating that the United States was too split and internally damaged to assist Juárez. Napoléon contacted British prime minister Lord Palmerston and France's ambassador to England, Count Auguste Flahaut de la Billarderie, explaining France's wish to move on Mexico. He said that although he received many requests to aid Mexico before, he had no reason to until recently. "My conduct was closely tied to that of England, and I thought it would be difficult to agree on the objective they proposed with the cabinet of St. James, that we risked getting entangled with the United States, and that, therefore, it would have to wait. Today, unforeseen events have changed the face of things. The American war has made it impossible for the United States to get involved, and the affronts committed by the Mexican government have given England, Spain, and France legitimate reasons to intervene." He then wrote Leopold I, King of Belgium and Carlota's father, who as a favorite uncle to Queen Victoria and considering Belgium's relationships with Great Britain, could prevail upon her for England's cooperation in a joint expedition to correct the Mexican debt situation. Victoria treated the subject with extreme reserve, the British mining contracts in Mexico having been beneficial to her country, despite that during the anarchy, exports to Mexico had fallen by half.[19]

In Mexico, Wyke reported that bandits and battling partisans attacked British mines at Real del Monte in Hidalgo state, which normally furnished $260,000 a month in silver to England. They feared further harassment, not only on the mines but on their subjects who had been cruelly victimized by "forced loans" of $50,000 and upward by the Liberal army and imprisoned when they did not pay. Meanwhile they extorted these payments in the name of liberty, toleration, and the blessings of a constitutional system, which infuriated Wyke, a shame in "one of the finest and most fertile countries in the world."[20]

Meanwhile, Spain's Queen Isabella II eagerly agreed to participate in the expedition. She lobbied for a Bourbón monarch to occupy the Mexican throne, but no suitable candidate could be agreed upon. Spain's willingness to participate remained important to Napoléon but not so important that he lose control.[21] He distrusted Spain, and England distrusted him.

In October 1861 diplomatic representatives of the three powers convened at London and agreed on the combined expedition to Veracruz. Lord Palmerston, along with his foreign secretary, Lord John Russell, relied on the advice from their minister in Mexico and cautiously committed Great Britain to the expedition, in spite of Queen Victoria's misgivings. The British only wanted to force a repayment agreement with the Juárez regime. Prior demands and naval demonstrations had proved unproductive. Yet fearing what France and Spain might do upon arrival at Veracruz, England insisted on inserting a clause stipulating that the three countries would abstain from claiming any Mexican territory or interfering in any way with the domestic government of

Mexico. The passage, however, which was vaguely worded, remained open to interpretation by France and Spain, hardly giving them pause. "The somewhat loose wording of our present treaty has been a *cheval de bataille* with these knaves," wrote one British minister, George W. Mathew, about how the French dwelled on the liberalities allowed by the London Convention.[22]

On October 31, 1861, after speedy negotiations, the three powers signed the Convention of London and prepared to send their armies to Mexico. They felt assured that Juárez had enough money to pay debt from the sale of nationalized church properties. But they first planned to seize customs duties at the port of Veracruz, estimated at $7 to $8 million per year, until they were satisfied, unless Juárez agreed to some other way to reimburse the debt in a secure, business-like way. The three countries wisely offered the United States a participatory role in the scheme. Of course, neither Seward nor Lincoln could perceive of doing so, although they made America's minister to Mexico, Thomas Corwin, a man opposed to expansionism, available to negotiate Mexican debt repayments to the sovereign states, if necessary. Corwin received orders to carefully monitor the situation and repel any attempts by the Confederate States of America to insinuate themselves with the powers. At the time, it seemed that few in the United States or Mexico realized the gravity of the situation when the flotilla launched in November. Some said it was an amicable mission to demonstrate seriousness over financial responsibility, terming it "a friendly bondholders' war."[23]

The Spanish fleet had the easiest task, with a large portion of their navy already based at Havana, and they reached Veracruz first on December 8, although the three powers had agreed that their fleets would arrive at approximately the same time. Under the direction of the popular and prestigious Gen. Juan Prim, Conde de Ruess, the Spanish landed twenty-six ships with 6,000 troops by December 17 to occupy Fort Ulúa and Veracruz with no resistance. On January 9, 1862, French Admiral Jean Pierre Jurien de la Gravièr glided into the port with fourteen steamships carrying 2,600 troops. The French contingent was composed of nearly 2,000 marines as well as 600 infantrymen, Zouaves, and Foreign Legionnaires, most veterans of campaigns in North Africa. Napoléon had selected some of his best regulars, reassuring Eugénie that he had sent "the red trousers," meaning the army, and "not the blue ones," the marines. The Royal British Navy arrived with 800 marines under command of Admiral Alexander Milne and Commodore Hugh Dunlop, with orders to maintain strict reserve and nonintervention in Mexico's internal affairs.[24]

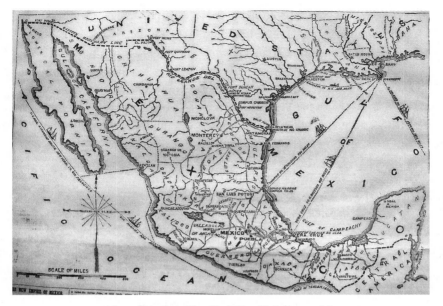

Map of Mexico, *New York Herald*, July 30, 1863

French Admiral Jurien brought with him to Mexico special and covert instructions that upon the rise of the monarchical party, the French officers were to gather a constituent assembly from the provinces of Mexico, men sympathetic to France, and vote to form a monarchy. So confident was Napoléon that his forces would quickly defeat Juárez and the Liberals, they could initiate the canvassing almost immediately. The French emperor expected that the vote could be done without the knowledge of Spain and England, thereby sparing their moral sensibilities.[25]

On January 10, 1862, the three commanders, along with France's Dubois de Saligny and England's Charles Lennox Wyke, the two ministers acting as commissioners, issued a statement to the Mexican people that their expedition resulted from broken treaties. "Three nations who accepted in good faith and acknowledge your independence have the right to expect you to believe them animated by no cowardly intentions, but rather by others more noble, elevated and generous." The three extended a hand of friendship. "Exclusively to you, without intervention of foreigners, belongs the task of constituting yourselves in a permanent and stable manner. . . . Your labor will be the labor of regeneration. . . . The evil is great, the remedy urgent. Now or never can you make your prosperity," read the announcement. The three countries viewed themselves as "anchors" that would lead to a vigorous economic future for the country. Saligny added, "It is only a question of a protective demonstration," offering that their presence could calm the anarchy in Mexico.[26]

Soon after the French arrival at Veracruz, they found the customs house abandoned. Since all import duties were paid in Mexico City due to highway robbers, a procedure they had overlooked in the Convention of London, the naval officers thought at first to collect duties from the area merchants, at least to fund their operations. Seeing no way to collect, officers planned to negotiate with Juárez.[27]

Napoléon instructed Saligny, "Il fallait commencer par le gros bout" (to start with a large demand), so he contrived an ultimatum he knew Juárez would never accept. Saligny compiled and exaggerated damages declared by French merchants and tradesmen suffered during the War of the Reform and other conflicts by roughly rounding the figures upward to 60 million francs, with further petitions to follow. This included the bond debt incurred by Miguel Miramón from Jecker's bank during the war. Wyke and Prim condemned France's exaggerated claims as monstrous and exorbitant, constructed only to provoke the government, which could have never satisfied their demands, and in disgust ended their meeting with Saligny. Both sought a way to assert yet settle their legitimate debts and end their country's role in the expedition as quickly as possible. On the other hand, Saligny completely refused to negotiate with Mexican officials.[28]

Three weeks earlier on January 27, Miguel Miramón sensed an opportunity to return to Mexico, taking advantage of the breach opened by the allied military, and sailed into Veracruz from Europe under an assumed name, with a cadre ready to advocate for the clericals. British commodore Dunlop, unsure where Miramón's motives lay and suspecting him of planning a coup, arrested him on charges connected to his robbery of the $660,000 from the British Legation offices in 1859. Subsequently, the commodore sent him to Havana on a royal cruiser to neutralize him.[29]

When Napoléon received reports on the landing, he read that Spain had sent a superior number of troops. Ever wary of being superseded by the Spanish, who he believed were anxious to reclaim Mexico, Napoléon decided to send reinforcements. In March another 4,500 men under the tall, lean, and deliberate French Brig. Gen. Charles Ferdinand Latrille, the Count of Lorencez, accompanied by Juan N. Almonte, disembarked at Veracruz. These additional troops surged France's numbers to exceed the Spanish garrison. This new military buildup further encouraged the British and Spanish to wind up their

French Imperialist soldiers encamped near Veracruz, ca. 1865. Soldiers included French cavalry, French infantry, Arabs, and Zouaves. Palm thatch was commonly used near Veracruz.

expeditions and go home. Yet Wyke resolved to finish the matter of Britain's debt resolution.[30]

Using the excuse of yellow fever, which traditionally claimed 20 percent of Europeans who remained in the Veracruz port, Napoléon advised the Spanish and British that all troops should quickly move west to the upper plateaus of Orizaba and even beyond. Both the French and Spanish armies carried permission from their home commands to advance inland west from the sea. Queen Victoria had not empowered Commodore Dunlop and his men, however, with the same latitude, sensing that France was preparing to intervene in Mexico. Victoria had little interest staging an invasion, mindful of Britain's relations with the United States.[31]

Before negotiations on the debt issues could commence, however, the Spanish and French officials continued to worry about a possible yellow fever epidemic in Veracruz. None of the commands had bothered to bring overland transportation with them. They had no carts, wagons, or horses, thinking that once they arrived these could be readily obtained. The French expected that the Monarchists would happily provide for their needs, not realizing the Monarchists were mostly elites located far from the remote countryside.

However, on January 25 Juárez promulgated orders that no Mexican citizens could help the foreign invaders, or anyone who threatened Mexico's independence, upon pain of confiscation, and ordered all available carts and horses moved out of the Veracruz area. He promised death to any citizen who aided the interveners materially, politically, or militarily. In the face of such hostility, the French and Spanish were stuck. Prim immediately sent six hundred sick men back to Havana. Jurien issued a statement that unless Juárez allowed them the right to move upland out of the "hot" zone to the temperate plateaus to the west, negotiations could not begin. Juárez responded that he would send representatives to hear their demands and possibly negotiate their claims.[32]

Prim and Wyke observed a growing restlessness in the country with increased outbreaks of anarchy stemming from their foreign occupation. Many people feared Juárez would make a deal with the interventionists and trade Mexican land, as he nearly did with the United States in the McLane-Ocampo Treaty.[33]

After alerting his congress in Mexico City, Juárez dispatched Gen. Manuel Doblado to make initial inquiries with the commanders and commissioners. On February 19 they met at the village of La Soledad and heard the demands of the allies. The final negotiations were planned for April 15 at Orizaba. Prim stipulated that the Spanish troops be allowed to relocate their camps to three healthy locations in the mountains, adding that his country bore no intention to intervene in the independence and domestic affairs of Mexico. France's Jurien also made the same argument. They drew up an agreement, the Convention of La Soledad, which Saligny signed only grudgingly. In making the agreement, however, the allies, who were allowed to make camps outside Veracruz, purchased time, which enabled them to exert pressure on the Mexican government, simply by their presence. For the French, it offered Almonte time to contact other Monarchists, Conservatives, generals, and sympathizers, who had been secretly waiting for his arrival. Juárez perceived that he benefited as well, hoping the pestilential and deadly climate would do its work, decimating the foreigners by disease.[34]

Although Juárez had called for Almonte's arrest if he reentered Mexico, Almonte defiantly continued with his plans to set up an imperial government. He left Veracruz, traveling eighty miles southwest with some of the allied troops, and met a passel of Conservatives at Tehuacán, Puebla. Those present at Tehuacán included Generals Leonardo Márquez, Tomás Mejía, and Félix Zuloaga. Hearing of the rendezvous, Juárez ordered his troops to stop the meeting. When Juarista troops found Gen. Manuel Robles Pezuela en route to the meeting, they lassoed him and shot him in the back as a traitor.[35]

Meanwhile, Napoléon and Eugénie learned with great disappointment that Saligny signed the Convention of La Soledad. Napoléon's minister of foreign affairs, Thouvenel, advised Saligny and Jurien to adhere to the French ultimatum to Juárez's government. They wanted no diversions from their plan. If Juárez did not capitulate, and they knew he would not, Thouvenel authorized a march on Mexico City. Lorencez already had a plan to move inland. Almonte then announced their plan to bring Archduke Maximilian to Mexico as the emperor, with the aid of the French, to pacify and redeem the country. Prim and Wyke then expressed outrage, having already suspected Napoléon's designs. Lord Russell in England guessed some pecuniary motive; "You know [Napoléon] never does a service for nothing," he wrote.[36]

On March 17 Prim tried to warn the French that it would be a mistake to try to overturn the Liberal government to install a monarchy. Unlike in Europe, there existed no deeply rooted hierarchy of aristocrats to support its structure. If they did so, said Prim, "this monarch will have nothing to sustain him, on the day that this support is withdrawn . . . he will fall from the throne erected by Your Majesty," further implying Napoléon did not see the flaws in his plan. This angered Napoléon, who wrote the Spanish government calling for Prim's recall and published the letter in *Le Moniteur* on April 2.[37]

On April 9 the allied commissioners Wyke and Prim lambasted Saligny's decision to move into Mexico's interior. Great Britain and Spain viewed this deliberate action as malicious and "imprudent," and decided to wind up affairs and send their troops home. On April 30 at Puebla, Wyke and Prim met with Doblado and on May 12 signed a treaty with the Mexican government settling their claims. Wyke agreed to accept 13 million pesos for British creditors, with an immediate installment of 2 million and the balance of 11 million pesos to be paid from a loan the Mexican government intended to obtain from the United States. Prim also settled with Doblado on behalf of Spain. Juárez agreed to both pacts without hesitation, and the British and Spanish forces hastily retreated to Veracruz to leave for home.[38]

The French waited to commence any military actions until the troops of England and Spain retired to Veracruz. Then from Córdoba, on April 16, Saligny issued a pronunciamento to the Mexican people announcing France's occupation. As the sole intervener, Gen. Lorencez started an aggressive advance to Orizaba.[39]

Meanwhile, near Trieste, Italy, at Miramar, Maximilian had become infatuated with the idea of becoming Mexico's emperor. As one French minister put it, "The archduke Maximilian is all on fire to be emperor across the seas." Gutiérrez de Estrada's persuasive letters about Mexico's long suffering and its rising moral crisis compelled him to imagine a country under his own tutelage and philosophy, although Maximilian raised important questions about Mexico's desire for a monarchy. Aides in the Austrian court privately expressed their surprise that Maximilian seemed to fully understand the complications involved with leaving Europe for a throne in the Americas. They secretly hoped Mexico would someday become an Austrian province. However, the Austrian government conducted its own investigation that confirmed the unrest in Mexico, witnesses expressing the opinion that oppressive minorities and bands of guerrillas held the country under a paralyzing siege. Mindful of the United States at war, if the Confederate States of America fell, the country would be too distracted to intervene in Mexico. If the Confederates won, they would be useful allies to Mexico. They anticipated that with unrest in Prussia, Germans would immigrate to Mexico, bringing their industriousness and strong work ethic to the country to create order and security.[40]

Maximilian wrote Napoléon to express his gratitude and to begin the process of arranging to go to the New World. "You find me, Sir, deeply imbued with the importance of the mission which you desire to see entrusted to me. . . . The flag which Your Majesty would like to see me unfurl in America has ever been my own, and it will surely be the object of all my efforts to hold it firmly aloft, in case I am called upon to reign." Carlota also wrote to thank Eugénie, "You are so good as to take in the cause of an unhappy country."[41]

Toward the end of December 1862, Maximilian entered into negotiations with his brother, Emperor Franz Josef, over the support he could expect upon taking the Mexican throne. While Maximilian recognized this opportunity as a coup for himself, he reminded Franz Josef it was a great moment for the Habsburg dynasty. But it was important to Maximilian to get certain guarantees tied to his lineage.[42]

Maximilian first addressed the matter of his funding, knowing his brother, who controlled a good part of his life, would be a tough negotiator. Franz Josef's initial offer included 200,000 gulden (about $27,000) for expenses in connection with his candidacy. After he accepted the crown, his appanage, or princely allowance, of 150,000 gulden (about $20,000) per year would reimburse the family for these preparations, along with money loaned him to build Miramar, which would become Austrian state property. To properly supplement his reign in Mexico, it was thought that $25 million could be borrowed through the Rothschild banking house facilitated by Napoléon III. Franz Josef promised to recruit an Austrian voluntary military corps to go with Maximilian with the guarantee that officers would return with the rank they achieved in Mexico. Because Maximilian doubted that Mexican officers would serve under his authority, Franz Josef promised to send ranking generals and veteran artillery units. An escort of European troops, outfitted in a uniform designed for Mexican service, would guard Maximilian and Carlota. Maximilian would eventually build an imperial army made up of Mexicans, serving with the Austrian forces.[43]

Although Maximilian would take leave of his command in the Austrian navy, Franz Josef promised an Austrian warship to transport him across the Atlantic. He also asked his brother to drop the name Maximilian and go by his first name, Ferdinand, leaving the name Maximilian to be used only in the exclusive realm of Austria. This Maximilian absolutely refused.[44]

Austria's Prince Metternich expressed doubts on the success of the Mexican enterprise; there would remain the taint that the enterprise was "the domain of adventure, and that to face it in cold blood a man must have energy and character, and be ready to act at the right moment." Although he was hurt by these criticisms, Maximilian pressed on, eager to move forward and make it work, as though the Mexican empire was an established fact. Both worried about the outcome of the American Civil War and actions the United States might take. Napoléon diffused his qualms by arguing that the outcome of that war remained very much in doubt.[45]

The plan cobbled together by Napoléon's ministers and Maximilian called for a provisional Mexican regency of trusted advisors, consisting of a Mexican bishop and two statesmen to prepare for Maximilian's takeover. Maximilian stipulated which household attendants would serve him in Mexico, and what ladies-in-waiting would accompany Carlota. As Napoléon had hoped, Maximilian placed his trust in Almonte, consulting with him consistently before he left for Mexico. Almonte pledged his loyalty to the future emperor, working to set up a government under this regency in preparation for their arrival. Almonte agreed to perform nearly all the tasks and ideas envisioned by Maximilian, Franz Josef, and Napoléon, even offering to bring in Santa Anna if they wished, because Gutiérrez de Estrada advocated to place him within the new monarchy, although in reality, Almonte and many Mexican Conservatives distrusted the former dictator completely. Fostering his own personal ambitions for his role in imperial Mexico, Almonte facilitated the royal movement, making lavish promises and agreeing to nearly all demands to get the project moving. However, Gutiérrez de Estrada jealously opposed Almonte, campaigning for Santa Anna's return. This political maneuvering and griping became onerous to Napoléon and Eugénie.[46]

Based on these preliminary preparations, Maximilian requested Napoléon to arrange a note of $25 million. Napoléon could not make that promise immediately but mentioned that Almonte should pave the way for the empire. As he dispatched an additional six hundred Zouaves to Mexico, he advised Maximilian to rely on Almonte, "an excellent fellow," to pave the way by giving him full powers and making him the center of his operations to advance his arrival. Maximilian proposed to Austria and France that if they recognized the Confederate States of America, entering into certain commercial and military guarantees with the southerners, he wanted their assurances to defend the independence of Mexico against any attempts at the sale of its territory or allowing Union troops to enter in order to bypass the rebels, which he thought Juárez's Republican government might allow. Recently, the Juárez government had rejected the Confederate States of America, who in turn saw Mexico under Juárez as expendable. Napoléon saw his chance to make an impact. "Never will any achievement have grander results, for the task is to rescue a continent from anarchy and misery, to set an example of good government to the whole of America, and finally, to raise the standard of monarchy, supported upon a wisely directed freedom and a sincere love of progress, against dangerous Utopias and bloody confusion," wrote Napoléon, condemning Juárez's ideas.[47]

When Maximilian learned that England and Spain withdrew from the expedition, he became very concerned with France being the sole supporter of his reign. From the beginning he had made it clear that he must have Great Britain allied with France to support the Mexican Empire, promising to protect its ongoing interests, especially the mines. Maximilian wrote that Napoléon seemed to want "an unlimited extension of French power. . . . In my opinion, the Emperor Napoléon wishes to dominate Mexico without appearing to do so in the eyes of Europe." But after conferring with King Leopold on the matter, who ambitiously thought the prospect in Mexico an excellent idea, he calmed down.[48]

With a recent decline in health, Leopold intently wanted to see his daughter and son-in-law flourish, not only to please them but to see his influence cross the Atlantic. The Belgian king agreed to provide military brigades and guards, not only for general military service but also to protect Carlota. Maximilian also prevailed upon Leopold to intercede with Queen Victoria to support his new post. She had written that if Maximilian succeeded, the undertaking would be one of the greatest and useful of their time. But Victoria, still in mourning for her husband, Albert, who had died nearly a year earlier, would give no more than her kind sentiments. Maximilian never lost hope that England would assist his empire in some way. When Lord John Russell investigated the matter and learned that Austria was not going to provide a large war fleet, he wondered what would motivate Maximilian to give in to Napoléon's folly. He knew that Napoléon could be very persuasive about any project when he wanted to see it flourish. Maximilian began to have his own doubts. From the beginning, their support had been a requisite.[49]

Leopold explained that in Britain, "Guarantees are rather illusory, and they are only obtained from England when it is clearly and obviously to her interest. A good quality of English guarantees is their trustworthiness; hence they are not very lavish with them." He counseled them to move forward and went over every aspect of the mission with Carlota, including government and their personal needs. He advised her they should free themselves from the Austrian traditions and courtiers, "who cost dear and are of no service." He drew up a plan. "Take only a small household, no more than three or four manservants. . . . Above all things, I recommend a good administration and justice, since these two things together are certainly the things to which the Mexicans are least accustomed and which they value most," assuring her that once the country was completely pacified, their government would be accepted by all.[50]

Maximilian also had preliminary counsel with Bishop Labastida, who traveled to Miramar to discuss the role of the pope and the Catholic Church in Mexico. But the conversation remained superficial and light because Labastida would not discuss anything without the pope's sanction. Nevertheless, they concluded that the mission of Maximilian and Carlota would be a holy one, and Labastida conferred his blessings at a mass in Miramar's newly gilded chapel.[51]

Continuing with his plans, Maximilian wrote to Pius asking permission, if necessary to mortgage the remaining church properties in Mexico to raise funding for the war and the expenses of the empire. He knew papal support would win over the Catholic contingency, anticipating they would work in harmony. Unfortunately, in his correspondence Maximilian mentioned reforming the Catholic Church in Mexico and sanctioning its corrupt clergy, prompting concerns with the pontiff, who was aware Labastida remained resolute that all former church properties be restored. The pope, who over his tenure had increasingly asserted a conservative and autonomous church, greatly pleasing ultramontane advocates, passed over Maximilian's mortgage request, writing

Pope Pius IX, ca. 1865

most cordially that he would consider such issues when bishops in Mexico were allowed to go about their business in safety. But the enormously charming Pius invited Maximilian and Carlota to see him when arrangements were complete and they embarked for their new empire.[52]

In the United States, Secretary of State William Seward received word on the potential overthrow of Juárez with France's intent to invest Maximilian with a crown. Previously, the Congress had entertained the idea of loaning money to Juárez to pay Mexico's debts, but the Senate rejected the notion. Over the next years, a number of resolutions designed to punish Napoléon and the French were drafted, but no action could be taken in the midst of the Civil War, one senator remarking, "Have we not war enough already on our hands?" However, Seward issued a statement expressing the dangers involved with the whole scheme and sent it to American ministers in England, France,

Spain, and Mexico. "The setting up of a monarchy in the Republic of Mexico must have grave consequences and would, sooner or later, bring the powers concerned in it into serious conflict with the U.S.," he wrote. Abraham Lincoln saw the successful rise of a foreigner to the throne of Mexico incongruent with the Monroe Doctrine but could do nothing, even though Matías Romero lobbied rigorously.[53]

From his vantage in Washington, Austrian minister Johann Georg Ritter von Hülsemann strenuously disagreed with Maximilian's candidacy. When the Viennese press announced the certainty of the mission and raised doubts, Von Hülsemann, who never thought Napoléon and Maximilian could be serious, objected and emphasized that the prospect of overthrowing Mexico would be impossible.[54]

Napoléon was determined. He prepared for critics to ask him why France wasted so many men and so much money to establish a government in Mexico. Why should they aggress themselves against the United States when they supported French commerce and mercantile goods? They needed America, but he wrote, "It will not be interesting to us if it takes possession of the whole of the Gulf of Mexico, and governs the West Indies and South America, thus controlling the entire produce of the New World. We now see by sad experience how precarious an industry is that which is compelled to seek its raw material in a single market."[55]

In reality, few Europeans had any knowledge of the ruggedness of the Mexican terrain, the vastness of the land, and the staunch resolve of Juárez and the Liberals. Yet in the sierras of Mexico, the French commanders set their compasses toward Puebla de los Ángeles.

❡ 4 ❡

The Siege of Puebla

The withdrawal of England and Spain left the French army alone, according to Napoléon's design. He calculated that Mexico would be in such disarray that overtaking the country, albeit three times the size of France, would be rather seamless. But despite reinforcements that brought troop strength to 7,000 men, only 6,000 French soldiers remained well enough to fight, the remainder laid low by the fatigue of long marches, the hot, humid climate, and disease. Undeterred, on April 26, 1862, Gen. Lorencez, freed up from the moral constraints imposed by England and Spain, wrote that his battalions were "so superior to the Mexican in terms of race, organization, and Moral discipline . . . at the head of . . . 6,000 soldiers, I am now the master of Mexico." Prior victories in China and other far-flung battlefields caused him to think fresh glory in Mexico was assured. He guaranteed the emperor that his command would enter the Mexican capital as early as May 25.[1]

The French commanders hastily planned their advance to the capital, a 310-mile march, not wholly anticipating the resistance that lay before them. After Veracruz and La Soledad, they knew they must cross the rocky climbs of Paso del Macho, the river valleys of the Chiquihuite, Córdoba, Barranca San Miguel, Orizaba, Tecamalucan, Acultzingo, Palmar, Amózoc, and pass Puebla successfully, then move on through San Martín Texmelucan, Río Frío, Peñon Viejo, and into the valley of Mexico. In Paris, Napoléon and Eugénie monitored the situation closely but felt confident in their army's abilities. As "soon as he [Lorencez] crossed the Chiquihuite, he will be master of the country," wrote Eugénie to Carlota. "I have never doubted the success of the enterprise."[2]

Gen. Lorencez next set his sights on reaching the city of Puebla quickly. Located 170 miles west of Veracruz, the leadership passionately supported a monarchy. Because the winding road leading west covered rugged lands, Lorencez left the sick soldiers at Orizaba and started his men toward Puebla. Gen. Leonardo Márquez, the Conservative general known as the Tiger of Tacubaya, for his brutal treatment of prisoners during the War of the Reform, joined Lorencez's French troops with 2,500 of his men. Puebla, an ancient city of 80,000 people and hundreds of religious institutions—churches, convents, and monasteries—was a center of Conservative and Clerical party supporters. It sat nestled in low hills, defended by heavily fortified walls and gates, a series of small forts circling its perimeter. Saligny, who assisted Lorencez with strategy, assured him that Puebla was so much in favor of a monarchy, the people would meet him at the gates with open arms.[3]

Lorencez decided to press forward vigorously. On the high plateaus, his army advanced with speed, but he soon learned that Juárez had dispatched 6,000 troops to Puebla to bring the total defense under Gen. Ignacio Zaragoza Seguín to 12,000 infantry, 200 cavalrymen, and 6 cannon. Zaragoza stationed his men in the citadels of Loreto and Guadalupe on the northeastern outskirts of the city, on the west at San Xavier and Santa Anita, and on the south at El Carmen. The remainder of his troops, he placed in the streets of the city.[4]

On April 27, outside Puebla, knowing he was outmanned, Lorencez planned to start with artillery fire on the northern forts of Loreto and Guadalupe, while surrounding the town. However, when he reviewed the overall situation firsthand, he halted and sent a message to Saligny, who sat in a carriage at the rear with the baggage and supplies. Lorencez asked if there had been any news from Puebla that might influence his approach. Saligny replied that a message had just arrived from Márquez, via a native scout who carried a note disguised as a cigarette, advising them to attack from the east. Saligny thought such maneuvering would be a waste of time but gave him only cursory guidance. "You will make your entrance under a rain of flowers, to the confusion of Zaragoza and his gang." After some debate, Lorencez stood by his original plan to attack the northern forts first but was delayed by heavy deluges.[5]

In the early morning hours of May 5, the French advanced with ten artillery pieces within one and a quarter miles of Fort Guadalupe and at midmorning commenced shelling, inflicting some damage but not as much as they hoped. The artillerymen moved their batteries closer but were forced to aim upward

Porfirio Díaz, Juarista general
in charge of Oaxaca, ca. 1867,
future president of Mexico

from a level below the fortifications, making it difficult to sight in their cannon. Consequently, few of the mortars struck their targets. After the French artillery expended nearly half its ammunition in less than two hours, Lorencez ordered his infantry up the hill to capture Fort Guadalupe. The Liberal batteries fired on the red-garbed Zouaves from Fort Loreto, and they were driven back. By midafternoon the Mexican army's withering musket fire began to take a heavy toll on the French, and the soldiers slipped down the muddy hills when a thunderstorm released another downpour. In the heaviest of the fighting, Zaragoza sent thirty-two-year-old Gen. Porfirio Díaz, a native of Oaxaca, to attack the French infantry. He and his cavalry charged Fort Guadalupe, raising France's death toll.[6]

At four in the afternoon, Lorencez sounded the bugle of retreat. His soldiers marched down to the plain, gathered their knapsacks, and waited for an expected Mexican counterattack, which never materialized. French wagons and ambulances ran the gauntlet dodging final sniping to collect bodies of the dead and wounded. By evening, all survivors were accounted for, except for one company of marines, lost in the dark. The French heard celebrations and songs of victory by the Mexican army, including the "Marseillaise," the well-known French anthem, banned at the time by Napoléon. The French counted 462 men killed and wounded with 8 taken prisoner.[7]

The next morning, the French buried their dead, anticipating another major assault. The Mexicans generals chose, however, not to attack them across the level fields, having much respect for the same French army that had won legendary victories at Sebastopol, in the Crimea, and Solferino, Italy. Two days later, after deciding against a second offensive, Lorencez packed up and the French troops withdrew to Orizaba, all the while blaming the defeat on Saligny. But more importantly, in the minds of the Mexican military, the May 5 victory remained a monumental achievement. In the years that followed, the republic would celebrate the triumph as Cinco de Mayo.[8]

Over the next few weeks, as the French army settled into its camp at Orizaba awaiting orders and reinforcements, various troop units under Gen. Márquez handily defeated Juárez's skirmishers in the countryside against Liberal soldiers. Zaragoza urged Juárez to launch an all-out attack on Orizaba before the French could be reinforced, but Juárez forbade it, saying the only way to beat the invaders was by guerrilla combat. Curiously, he knew the French would never leave until they humiliated him and his government, and his strategy concentrated mostly on defense. Meanwhile, the French troops at Orizaba had to wait longer than they anticipated. In summer 1862 the men, who were anxious to fight, did everything possible to entertain themselves. They drilled, fought off snipers, and struggled against boredom, sometimes producing theatrical performances.[9]

In the face of defeat, Saligny attempted to extract himself from blame and wrote letters damning Lorencez, whom he termed a "fearful person, lazy, sluggish . . . incapable of initiative . . . he never asks for advice and takes offence." Lorencez accused the ignorance of Saligny and Almonte for misleading him regarding Mexican troop strength, calling them "totally inept."[10]

In Paris, Napoléon did not receive news of the French defeat at Puebla until June. The Parisians expressed shock that their seemingly invincible warriors had been routed so easily in Mexico, and there were patriotic calls for *revanche*. When they read between the lines of the censored press reports that the French troops defended four hundred men in the Orizaba hospital, they then learned of the raging yellow fever. Obliged to maintain France's honor, Napoléon determined not to retreat. He wrote to Lorencez to keep up his spirit, "Such are fortunes of war, and occasional reverses sometimes cloud brilliant successes; but do not lose heart; the honor of the country is involved and you will be supported by all the reinforcements you need." To save face with the public, Napoléon's state journalists wrote glowing reports in *Le Temps* and *La Patrie* of victorious battles in the Mexican countryside. Napoléon annealed his resolve, his reputation at stake, with monetary losses to recoup for the Quai d'Orsay.[11]

Soon Admiral Jurien de la Gravièr returned to Paris from Mexico and

Battle of Puebla, May 1862

attempted to explain the defeat at Puebla. They had taken a prudent course, feeling assured that the city would easily surrender, he argued. When they found the place so well fortified with thick walls and numerous defenses, they realized they were understaffed and undersupplied.[12] Disgusted, Napoléon decided to roll up his sleeves and develop a strategy to beat the Juaristas into submission.

On July 3 at Fontainebleau, he met with Gen. Louis Élie Frédérick Forey and appointed him to replace Gen. Lorencez. Napoléon educated Forey on the higher purpose of his mission in Mexico. "If a firm government is established there by the aid of France . . . we shall have extended our benevolent influence to the center of America," he wrote, adding that control of Mexico's raw materials would prove indispensible to France, especially its silver and gold. Napoléon and Forey soon emerged with a plan to augment manpower and matériel in the Mexican project along with certain strategic refinements.[13]

Gen. Forey, tall, with a ruddy complexion and full, bushy moustache, had distinguished himself as a dependable leader in the Crimean and the Italian campaigns and had commanded a large and well-disciplined army under Napoléon for ten years. On July 3 Napoléon wrote a note alerting Lorencez of the change in command, blaming not his leadership but Saligny,

The Siege of Puebla 77

who reportedly had been drinking excessively, although he said nothing about recalling him.[14]

Napoléon paid little attention to criticism from his own people or other European royalty. However, he wanted the approval of France's congress, the Corps Législatif, for additional funds to expand the Mexican intervention to ward off criticism. Because members had the right of address and control of the budget, Napoléon knew he must hone his arguments. He carefully articulated his design for Mexico along with misleading numbers concocted by Minister of Finance Achille Marcus Fould. Amid many reasons, he argued that Mexico could be a lever to control world trade and would prevent the United States from acquiring more Mexican soil. Beyond such geostrategic plans, winning over the Catholic Church and businesses would enlarge France's commercial opportunities. French domination of the Gulf of Mexico, the Antilles, and South America would gain countless sources for commodities and outlets for trade. Simply put, the intervention would reap enormous financial benefits. The Corps Législatif voted unanimously to send more troops, despite protests from the opposition party led by Jules Favre and Adolphe Thiers, who censured the intervention from the outset.[15]

Napoléon also gave clear instructions to Forey to protect religion but not to interfere with the previous sale of church lands by the Liberal government. He mandated that all political decisions made by Almonte and his advisors would be considered temporary until the Mexican population could decide their destiny, convinced they would vote for a monarchy, which, as he viewed it, was really the only choice. He also cautioned Forey to use French resources judiciously, since they wasted a good deal of their munitions at Puebla: "The farther away an expedition is, the more must it be conducted with . . . boldness and caution. A cannon shot in Mexico is a hundred times more precious than in France." He also stated that they should be wary of the United States, to guard against any intrusions, especially from the Union army, believing they sought any opportunity to dominate Mexico.[16]

In September 1862 Gen. Forey and his sea-tossed troops arrived in the bay of Veracruz. As instructed, Forey moved thousands of men, over two hundred guns, horses, and provisions ashore and immediately began planning to march his men west to join Lorencez at Orizaba. Having heard of hazards along the route due to guerrilla snipers and the resulting shortage of food, Forey planned to take only 1,200 men inland.[17]

As for business at hand, it was a whole new slate. Forey assembled the French troops in the plaza of Veracruz and issued proclamations assuring the people that the French arrived only to make war on Juárez, and if his government did not capitulate, France was prepared to send 200,000 men. He prohibited the exportation of gold and silver. Realizing Saligny and Almonte would not work with him, Forey demoted them to subordinate positions and dissolved their staffs. He removed the governor of Veracruz, French-born general Adrian Woll, a mercenary for the Mexican government for the last forty years. He announced he would recognize no political party until the French seized Mexico City. In planning to march to Orizaba and then Puebla, the unhurried Forey deliberated and planned almost too cautiously. Sadly, the wait exposed his battalion to yellow fever.[18]

Simultaneous to Forey's assignment, the French ordered reinforcements between September and November of 28,000 men, many units comprising France's most elite fighters. In early 1863 approximately 20,000 men arrived from Cherbourg and Brest. Another large contingent sailed directly from Algeria. The Mexican expedition proved popular within the army. Far-flung tours of duty and longing for adventure in the New World to get out of the crowded, noisome street of Paris helped to further their careers. The corps was divided into two divisions, one commanded by the fifty-one-year-old Gen. François Achille Bazaine, the son of a mathematician who had briefly served Napoléon I. A man of some heft but not height, Bazaine rose through the ranks of the Foreign Legion, known as a man not sparing in severity. He greatly distinguished himself in Algeria, Morocco, and the Crimea, making sport of the enemy and becoming the youngest man to earn the commission of general in the French army, serving under harsh conditions. Behind his great white moustache and small eyes hid an embroidery of military diagrams, so infinite and detailed, he often failed to take time to illustrate them to anyone.[19]

Napoléon assigned command of the second division to fifty-three-year-old Gen. Félix Charles Douay, also advanced by extensive service with the French infantry in the Crimea and Algeria. He was known for his efficiency and bravery in battle. Before their departure, Napoléon warned the generals against squabbling and to respect the people and calm the minds of the Mexican people, especially regarding the former church lands.[20]

With yellow fever still raging in Veracruz, Bazaine's detail arrived at the end of October, three weeks after Forey. The Gulf of Mexico's waters were running high as a gale pounded the seashore, but in the morning the storm had passed. Capt. Charles Blanchot, who worked on Bazaine's staff, wrote of the desolation and monotony of Veracruz and the leisurely buzzards trolling in the sky.[21]

As Bazaine rowed to shore to assess conditions in the port, he left the landing of the horses to Blanchot. Blanchot discovered that the loading cranes on the *môle*, or stone pier, were crumbling, and they could not maneuver near it, so the men loaded the horses from the ship onto flatboats that served as springboards. Whipping, jeering, and pushing the horses off the scows before they could lame themselves, the horses swam to shore in good order. Meanwhile, Bazaine discovered that Forey had departed for Orizaba, taking only 1,200 men with him, leaving the remainder at Veracruz, against orders. On the way to Orizaba, however, so many of the men had already been exposed to fever that they died or were killed by snipers. Only 50 of the 1,200 men made it there alive. The bodies strewn along the winding road shocked Bazaine and his officers, who could not understand why Forey had not handily dispatched the guerrilla snipers that kept Veracruz blocked. Bazaine quickly deployed his troops to break up the bands of guerrillas and move his men to healthy encampments.[22]

The makeshift hospital, located in a convent, had fallen into a pestilential filth from the countless sick and dying men. Bazaine ordered a thorough cleaning of the rooms and courtyard, scraping of the crusted floors, and care for the rest of the sick and dying. He sent 6,000 men to inland camps via alternate routes to Jalapa.[23]

Bazaine then allowed the remaining troops to disembark, eager to reach shore after having been cramped on their transports for nearly a week. The operation to shuttle them with provisions to Veracruz began quickly; a number of men simply jumped into the water to swim to the môle. By noon it seemed apparent that what they thought was a growing gale was actually a hurricane, and it blew into the port with ferocity. The offloading of the transports ceased in the rising, violent winds. Blanchot watched in the howling storm as a French warship lodged on a craggy shoal. Bazaine ordered whaleboats launched with cables to save the foundering warship. But the boats swamped, and finally the threatened ship sank, flooding the beach with casks, provisions, and drowned sailors. By the end of the second day, thirteen ships, both military and merchant, had sunk. Miraculously, most transports survived and the landing of the men resumed, with more troop ships sailing safely into the port soon afterward.[24]

Meanwhile, Gen. Lorencez retreated east from Orizaba and entered Veracruz in humiliation and disgrace. He saw himself as the second storied and accomplished officer, after Jurien, whipped by Mexico, its environment, and its distance from France.[25]

Another French officer who helped to cut the new path to Jalapa, Pierre Henri Loizillon, wrote about encountering guerrilla fighters in the mountains. Loizillon viewed Juarista efforts as "pitiable," terming them "highway robbers who murder you in a corner and flee like the cowards they are at the first crack of a rifle. There is no glory in fighting such troops." His attitude of superiority summed up the sentiments of a large portion of the French army: he was saddened by the poverty he saw and the way "five or six individuals can terrorize a population of 2,000 or 3,000 souls. The laws are powerless to repress such monstrosities." The guerrillas remained mostly unorganized, formed from the same region and organized in bands named simply for their leader. Some were landholders with a political cause, others simply opportunists. Often these guerrillas, who sometimes called themselves Juaristas, could not be recognized from other regular, hard-working folk who distrusted the French. They often dressed in suits of finely embroidered leather. Many worked as law enforcers, politicians, *rancheros*, businessmen, lawyers, bookkeepers, or even musicians. Confusion about their status remained divided among the French officers; some considered them lawful belligerents, and some considered them nothing more than disorganized resistors. Therefore, if they were not legal combatants, then in the view of the French they were to be treated as criminals upon capture, not prisoners of war.[26]

A few anti-imperial companies stood out by their character. Los Bello for their radical and passionate opposition, making them difficult prisoners; Los Chinacos was a name applied mostly to bands in Michoacán but also used to refer to their bravery; Los Cravioto derived from south and east of Mexico City, and unsuccessfully bargained to switch to the side of the Imperialistas; Los Cristeros patrolled near Zacapu; Los Galeanos were known for their cruelty in Jalisco; and Los Plateados roamed the areas near Morelos.[27]

Loizillon's company camped at Jalapa and was ordered to wait, much to the dissatisfaction of the men who were eager to move on to Orizaba to fight. The mountains were cold, and the local people who resented the occupation kept to themselves, not interacting with the French soldiers. Feeling alienated and homesick for France, he wrote, "For the moment, everyone is bored to death. Not a cat will do us the honor of addressing us. I have even forgotten the Spanish I learned on the crossing." During the long encampment, Loizillon thought they could have organized better, using land near Perote, a wheat-growing center, for food supplies. Instead, the French continued hauling provisions, often rancid biscuits, shipped from Cherbourg, and sent from Veracruz under an escort of five hundred men. Loizillon complained that the men struggled to bring goods over the rugged roads, and "all this to throw away the biscuit which no one can eat. There are times when I think that the stay in the . . . country has . . . destroyed every intelligence. I say no more, because I do not want to sour my character."[28]

Finally, Imperialista Gen. Leonardo Márquez arrived with a column to bolster the French troops at Perote. Upon observing Márquez's ragtag Mexican soldiers assigned to fight alongside them, Loizillon sniffed, "They call this the regular army? When you look at it, you wonder what the word irregular means. This whole scouring of ragged scum is in our pay. . . . They have a way with them, though; they arrived at ten and by noon were all lodged, officers and men."[29]

Bazaine assembled his division and ordered them to push on through the mountains to Perote and assemble on the plateaus, the soldiers much relieved to have a steady commander. One outstanding officer, Col. François Charles du Barail of the 3rd Cavalry Regiment of the Chasseurs d'Afrique, who crossed a shipment of 450 Arabian horses to Mexico, described Bazaine as a man who "sees things from above and views aims from afar, [with a] shrewdness which lies in the moving amid intrigues and making use of them, without seeming to take part in them. His courage was universally recognized and imperturbable, he was absolutely impassive in the thick of danger, and affected the coquetry of indifference, which produced a great effect on all his assistants. . . . [He] wanted everyone to feel at ease at his table." Bazaine reserved his bursts of anger, terrible but brief, for those who failed to execute orders.[30]

As the army moved over the steep and winding passage of the Cumbres de Acultzingo, they cursed the ruggedness and primitive nature of the roads, while marveling at what Lorencez must have gone through simply to get to Puebla. The infinite views, the clear air, and the landscape, spectacular and vivid on many days, however, awed them. By the end of January, as siege materials arrived on transports, the French army meticulously hauled the supplies uphill and readied for another attack on the plains of Puebla, determined to redeem themselves in the eyes of their *citoyens*.[31]

Meanwhile, trying to prop up his defenses, Juárez appealed to U.S. secretary of state Seward through Mexican minister Matías Romero for a loan from the American treasury to buy arms in the United States. While certainly viewing the United States as a protector of republicanism against European interference, Congress hesitated to fund another nation's war. Seward did state to France, however, that America's power had been sufficient protection for Mexico up until 1861 and warned that if they pursued their policy in Mexico,

Marshal François Achille Bazaine, ca. 1866

it would likely result in a "collision between France and the United States." Seward declined active intervention, although the government sold horses and mules to the French and allowed their claims to export tobacco from Virginia. This he allowed, with a stinging rebuke, that while the United States remained "in favor of the commerce of neutrals, it ought to receive such comity as it practiced." Seward emphasized mutual respect between maritime powers.[32]

Through private investors Romero raised enough money and credit to buy over 30,000 guns and 4,000 sabers from an arms dealer in New York. However, Secretary of War Edwin M. Stanton, citing the need to keep all available weapons to fight the Civil War, denied the export license. Illegal blockade running and smuggling served as the only method for receiving guns, for in November 1862 Lincoln issued a decree prohibiting all arms exports from United States for the duration of the war, fearing that munitions shipped to

Mexico or elsewhere would end up in the hands of the Confederates. Pledging customs house funds from the Pacific coast ports still under Republican control, Juárez resorted to getting contraband guns from Matamoros via New York, New Orleans, or Mexico's Pacific ports, San Blas or Guaymas, via San Francisco, although the French attempted to seize these shipments. Soon Confederate officials suggested to the French that they would assist them, if they occupied Matamoros where they could receive shipments of critical war materiel. Also knowing the lucrative port would mean important income to empire, its customs revenues, said to exceed 250,000 pesos in some months and currently going to the Liberals, further motivated the French to occupy Matamoros as part of the conquest.[33]

Forey's unhurried preparation gave Juárez's men time to reinforce the city of Puebla again as well as Mexico City, including earthworks and a plan to flood the enemy by releasing lake water. By December 1862 the Liberal army, with 28,000 regulars and an auxiliary contingent of 5,000 more expected, amassed to defend Puebla. Equipped with twenty cannon and mountain howitzers, they set in for a long siege. Liberal Gen. Jesús González Ortega, the governor of Zacatecas, prepared to defend Puebla, although Juárez longed for the leadership of Ignacio Zaragoza, who had died in the cold and rainy Cumbres earlier in September from typhus. Juárez, who arrived in Puebla to inspect the defenses, was criticized by other officers on his choice of commanders, saying González Ortega's cowardice put the army at risk. Juárez replied, "What are *you* good for yourselves? No one is necessary: ideas are all that matter."[34]

To discourage the French, in locations across the highlands Juárez posted broadsides reprinting a letter from Victor Hugo, the respected and celebrated author as well as bitter enemy of Napoléon, denouncing the Mexican expedition. Reprinted copies of Hugo's *Napoléon le petit,* a pamphlet also condemning the French emperor, were distributed. Juárez also published and posted damning speeches by Hugo's compatriot Jules Favre and other opponents in the French legislature, all weaponized to dispirit the soldiers.[35]

In February 1863, as the French readied for a second attack on Puebla, they had assembled 28,000 men, 600 horses, nearly 6,000 mules, an arsenal of 8 twelve-pounder cannon, a dozen mountain howitzers, and many other arms. Encampments in the peaks near Quecholac, twenty miles southeast of Puebla, were hit by a winter storm. The troops marched through snow, their faces bearded in icicles. The men complained "like the grumblers on the retreat from Moscow," said one of the colonels. The commanders kept strict discipline, Col. du Barail ordering all brass highly polished, horseshoes clean, and equipment in good order, despite the climate.[36]

After dispatching most of his forces to the upper plains to wait, Imperialista Gen. Forey then anticipated difficulties in holding Veracruz and the coast with the onset of the yellow fever season, which would further decimate the legionnaires on duty. He queried his superiors in Paris about the availability of soldiers from Africa, who were more acclimatized to the heat and known to be resistant to tropical diseases. Most were immune to yellow fever. Through authorities in Egypt, then a province of the Ottoman Empire, Napoléon requested 1,500 enslaved Sudanese conscripts as a favor from the government for previous favors to the sultan's viceroy, the Egyptian khedive at Alexandria. On January 1, 1863, a French frigate docked at Alexandria, and 450 Sudanese soldiers serving in Egypt were combined with another 50 pressed into service, against the fervent protests of their families, and sailed to Mexico. One observer noted that Veracruz had become a veritable Babel with the legionnaires from so many countries.[37]

Forey also addressed the subjugation of the lower altitudes of the Huasteca, which the French called the *terres chaudes,* or the hot lands. The region extended over four states: Veracruz, Hidalgo, San Luis Potosí, and north into Tamaulipas. It tended to be a burning, miasmic region, and the European troops, not acclimatized to long marches through such tough semitropical terrain, suffered greatly. The indigenous populations, exploited over the millennium by Europeans, remained remarkably independent there but sparsely scattered in the hot lands. It made excellent territory for the Liberal political fighters and their unorthodox warfare techniques. In the Huasteca, guerrillas could hide from the Imperialistas and reconnoiter to plan further attacks, while cutting off supplies between Veracruz and Puebla. In the name of Juárez, they held up convoys, killed travelers, closed roads, and captured exhausted stragglers from the French army, frequently massacring innocent people. The French army needed a special force for this untamable region.[38]

On February 14, 1863, with the French officers around Orizaba, twenty miles behind the front lines, Minister Saligny threw a celebration and dance at his headquarters. At the fête, Gen. Forey pulled aside Col. Charles Du Pin, who had just arrived from France. The crusty Du Pin, a man of impressive bearing, with a long, white beard and a fondness for cigars, began his service with the French army in Japan as a cartographer, but his reputation as an unconventional and relentless fighter derived from his service in China, where some considered him an "intellectual brawler." When Du Pin was caught shipping rare Chinese art objects to France and selling them to cover gambling losses, Napoléon removed him from his command. When Du Pin recognized the need for volunteers for the Mexican expedition, he sought a chance to regain his rank by offering to serve. So authorized, the forty-eight-year-old veteran warrior set sail for Veracruz.[39]

At the party, Forey said to Du Pin, "Colonel, the *terres chaudes* are overrun by bandits; our convoys are attacked daily . . . communications are too often cut off. I . . . want . . . you to rid us of these brigands and give you command of the counterguerrillas of the hot lands. It involves securing the country and the passage of the army's convoys while I am tied up with the siege of Puebla, which I am about to undertake." Forey gave him full powers as a mercenary; he had only to relentlessly pursue the Liberal "guerrillas" and to get rid of them as he saw fit. Emile de Kératry, who served with Du Pin, said that at the party, the dances went on with the languid notes of a habanera playing in the background. Couples swayed across the dance floor, unaware of the menacing license Forey had just given Du Pin. "Could it be that some of the guerrilla leaders were that evening in the salons of the Minister of France Saligny, disguised as gentlemen, whose smiling faces would grimace later as they swung from the end of a branch?"[40]

On March 16, with Puebla on the horizon, advance columns commanded by Douay and Bazaine began to assemble. The clouds cleared, the weather became sunny and bright, and the imperial troops, numbering 26,000 men, arranged their equipment and provisions.[41] After three days of preparation, on the dry and cool morning of the 19th, the French army in all its splendor and polish fell into formation, called together by the division's drums and trumpets. The cavalry's hoofbeats crunched on the scree and reverberated off the mountain ridges. Occasional artillery fire could be heard from within the city walls signaling the Mexican army's readiness to defend the city. After a brief advance, Forey began his bombardment of Puebla. He deployed his forces to the right and left to swing around the town, and Puebla was surrounded. The initial maneuvers took two days to complete. In the evening, the campfires of the French soldiers dotted the plains, as flares sent up from within the walls of Puebla illuminated the dark sky and countryside. The next day, Forey along with Almonte and the engineers examined the town from all angles but took two long days to decide on a plan.[42]

In all, both sides were well prepared for a full-scale battle, with over 150 artillery pieces. The French brought with them 56 *bouches à feu* (artillery pieces). The Mexican army, with ample time to prepare and provisions, deployed 96

The bombed-out penitentiary at Puebla after the Second Battle of Puebla, May 1863

cannon and positioned 55 other guns along with ammunition, enough for a long siege. After Forey's unhurried and extensive study, he ordered Bazaine to begin with an attack on the penitentiary near the west side of the city, against Bazaine's judgment. Despite his disgust, Bazaine's men set about digging trenches as rapidly as possible.[43]

During those two tense days of inactivity, the Conservatives grew anxious that the French army might lose again. Typical was the comment by Almonte who said, "Forey does not understand anything, he is an ass, literally an ass, and nothing else." Bazaine, whose quick and easy manner reassured his troops, agreed, privately criticizing Forey.[44]

Over the next week, the French made incremental progress as the cannon demolished the face of a convent and gutted a few perimeter structures. But in the late afternoon of March 29, when the French heard the slow chiming of a church bell at five o'clock, the fixed signal, they rose from their trenches and began a long swell up the embankments of the town. They crested the battlements and swarmed into the town against a hail of bullets, many of the Mexican soldiers falling dead or surrendering. Bazaine ordered a halt, quickly realizing that nearly every home and structure in the town had been placed in defensive readiness with munitions. An improved strategy required the soldiers to scour the city block by block and house by house. The French soldiers made camps just at the city's walls, the first night hearing screams of men trapped inside a powder magazine, which some retreating soldiers had tried to destroy in their wake.[45]

Puebla contained 158 blocks of thick stone and plaster, substantial Spanish colonial construction. Mortars damaged the buildings, but the structures as a whole remained standing. Excelling at such urban combat, the Mexican army found the sturdy town indispensable to their resistance. In the bitter cold, the French made little appreciable difference, while the officers agonized over the solidness of the buildings, convinced that the conflict would boil down to raw street fighting.[46]

On April 18, with ammunition and supplies running low, the French officers mulled over their next step. Some wanted to leave and march directly on Mexico City; when word of this leaked out, a riot almost erupted in the French ranks. During the siege, limping troops would return to safe areas every night, sometimes putting up with citizens tormenting them. Across the street from a house where fifty French officers camped in tight quarters, a woman would occasionally come to her window to show off her buttocks to the soldiers. She quit only after someone took a potshot at her. The soldiers could only take so much harassment.[47]

One small unit of forty Zouaves commanded by Lt. Jean Nicolas Galland held off a much larger group of Mexican soldiers for hours. When allowed to surrender, the door opened and the Zouaves emerged jeering because there were only forty of them and they remained bull-necked. "Our Zouaves came out . . . their fezzes pushed back, their pipes clenched between their teeth, their weapons over the right shoulders, the lips black with powder, they went, bugles in the lead, to . . . the parade ground, as calmly as if it were the changing of the guard at the Tuileries," said Paul Laurent, a member of the 3rd Chasseurs d'Afrique. The little post of Zouaves drew the greatest curiosity.[48]

Meanwhile, on the morning of April 30, Mexican guerrillas ambushed a supply convoy from Veracruz, commanded by Capt. Jean Danjou with sixty-four Foreign Legionnaires. As the legionnaires sought refuge at the nearby Hacienda de Camarón and sheltered in a barn, the guerrillas laid siege to the hacienda. Soon their numbers swelled to over 1,000 men. By evening, the legionnaires, comprised of Polish, Spaniards, Italians, and Germans, began to suffer lack of ammunition and water and charged from the barn, their bayonets drawn. Only three survived the deadly attack.[49]

The final push to take Puebla began on May 7. When Forey learned the position of Comonfort's auxiliary force, Bazaine deployed a night attack on his camp on the town's outskirts and caught Comonfort off guard at the village of

Remains of the Convent of Santo Domingo, Puebla, Mexico,
after the Second Battle of Puebla, 1863

San Lorenzo and decisively defeated him, capturing 1,200 prisoners, seizing all their artillery, munitions, and transports. Bazaine attacked from the south, while the remainder of the troops laid siege to the buildings near the penitentiary. The fighting across the town spread vigorously. The Mexican garrison, starving and low on munitions, opted to surrender.[50]

On May 17, 1863, after a sixty-day siege, the French heard a series of blasts at one in the morning that rocked the town. Forey received a note from Gen. González Ortega that he had dispersed his army and destroyed his arsenal. Puebla lay at his disposal. Two days later Puebla was in Imperialista control. Mexican soldiers, starving, ragged, and "crying like animals," went into the French camps searching for food. Quickly, the French officers ordered two depots set up to assist the struggling Mexican soldiers. Men in the Mexican camps, hastily made prisoners, were discovered to be in horrid condition, naked and exposed to the cold.[51]

When the French finally staged their triumphal entry into Puebla, with bugles blaring, drums rolling, and flags fluttering, no one received them. Gen. Forey was surprised. The city was dead. The columns advanced slowly,

Juarista Gen.
Mariano Escobedo,
ca. 1865

picking their way through the rubbled, quiet streets, passing the wrecks of buildings, drawn to the cathedral where they could hear a chorus of priests' chanting a solemn refrain of thanksgiving to honor the end of fighting, their voices reverberating through the ruins of Puebla.[52]

In fact, a good number of people and clergy had fled to nearby Cholula to wait out the siege. Upon learning of the French conquest at Puebla, festivities broke out with the clergy and people in bright regalia dancing and singing for three days. "It was almost a carnival, for everyone wore costumes of the sixteenth or seventeenth century. . . . The clergy directed all this . . . and the Indians prostrated themselves in the dust, beating their breasts. It was touching but a trifle comic. And the music! Clarinets, cornets, trombones, chimes, bass drums, cymbals, whined, brayed . . . thundered waltzes, polkas, schottisches, which the musicians performed from memory and . . . not too badly," reported Col. Charles du Barail, a commander in the 3rd Chasseurs d'Afrique.[53]

In all, the French assumed control of 12,000 men as prisoners—an astounding number—including most of the central command. Leonardo Márquez's battalion absorbed 5,000 infantry into the ranks of the Conservative army, and another 5,000 were sent to work on the railroad under construction near Veracruz. The remainder included 1,500 officers and 25 generals, including Jesús González Ortega, Porfirio Díaz, and Mariano Escobedo. After some deliberation, including a suggestion by Saligny to transport the officers to a penal colony in Cayenne in South America and by Almonte to shoot them all, Forey, citing "laws of honor" and "tradition in the military fraternity," decided it more humane to imprison the officers in France. But over a third of the Republican officers ordered to Veracruz for deportation and imprisonment in France fled their captors en route to Veracruz, including González Ortega, Díaz, and Escobedo, Mexico's most talented military men. The remainder sailed on French war steamers to Brest.[54]

In his battle report, Capt. Pierre Henri Loizillon wondered why the Mexican Republican army had given up, because the French found substantial food stores and munitions hidden in the city's bodegas, which the Mexican army had not used. At first crediting the Mexican's fall to the relentless French attacks, he saw that their mismanagement and starvation made continued defense untenable. The French had suffered a high fatality rate with the loss of nearly 25 percent of their force. In the campaign, Forey lost 47 officers and 283 men killed, with another 1,400 soldiers dead from illness, especially yellow fever.[55]

During the siege, to prevent Juarista reinforcements arriving at Puebla, Col. Du Pin in the *tierra caliente* had assembled an odd assortment of men near Veracruz to scour the countryside. He had adopted the most peculiar costume, "a vast Mexican sombrero and a long white beard with neither a tie nor vest. He wore a colonel's pelisse, either of red or black, white pants with large folds, yellow riding boots with large Mexican spurs, eight or nine prestigious decorations on the chest, a revolver at his side and a tried and tested sword hanging from his saddle." But he was a killer and valuable to the French machine. Partially based on his striking and curious appearance, accompanied by his reputation, this enigma of a fighter terrified many villagers across the Huasteca.[56]

Du Pin's new command revealed an extraordinary array of irregulars. Both cavalry and infantry, the men without uniforms mostly dressed in what could be described as rags. Emile de Kératry wrote:

> It seemed every nation of the world had made an appointment to meet there: French, Greeks, Spanish, Mexicans, North and South Americans, English, Piedmontese, Neapolitans, Dutch, and Swiss rubbed elbows together. Nearly all of these men had left their county to chase after a still-elusive fortune. They included a sailor disillusioned with sea, a slave trader from Havana ruined when typhus wiped out his cargo, a pirate, a gold seeker, the bison hunter from the Great Lakes, and a Louisiana industrialist ruined by the Yankees. This band of adventurers knew nothing of discipline, officers

Charles Du Pin,
ca. 1865, commander
of the counterguerrillas
in Mexico

and soldiers got drunk together in the same tent, and revolver shots often sounded the reveille. As for their dress, if these troops had marched behind the bugles on the boulevards of Paris, one would have thought they were an old gang of vagabonds.[57]

Generally, they arrived fully trained for military service, having served in Africa and China. Because serving as a counterguerrilla abroad spurred soldiers up the ranks, a number of fighters sought to join this corps. Men from noble birth also sought a position in Du Pin's counterguerrillas. The sheer daring and resulting bragging rights at home inspired them to seek missions that seemed exotic or dangerous. "The character of the adventurer is infinitely varied, one is hungry for gold, another thirsting after pleasures, a third driven by the desire to make a name for himself, or who knows?" wrote Kératry.[58]

In Veracruz, supplied with weapons, they convinced the locals, who feared reprisals from the Liberals, to sell them horses. Before they set out for Puebla, however, a man whose pregnant wife was raped by guerrilleros, brutally murdered with the baby cut from her womb, pleaded for intervention. After evaluating his story, they set out to find the murderers and hastily executed them in the early hours of the next day. With this swift action, the Mexican Liberal guerrillas knew that days of formal French warfare had given way to a new and intimate brutality, but they continued to close roads, spy, blow up railroad lines, seize supply convoys, or take prisoners of French soldiers and civilians and kill them.[59]

Du Pin, a swashbuckler and sharpshooter, frequently did things to emphasize his toughness and impress his men, such as impulsively shooting down toucans in midflight. He also demanded strict discipline in the ranks. He could be creatively cruel, a trait Marshal Bazaine highly valued, while remaining fiercely paternal with his men. Du Pin urged his men not to place too much value on their own lives and handpicked the fiercest fighters, largely because of their reputations as hasty executioners. They sowed terror throughout the country. After a court-martial sentenced two peasants to death, a captain of the gendarmerie asked Du Pin, "Is it possible to play with human life that way?"[60]

"Bah!" said Du Pin. "Every Mexican is a guerrilla, or has been one, or will be one. By shooting those in our custody, there is no risk of making a mistake." His flying columns set ambushes for the groups of Liberals who tracked them, then hung or shot all suspects without trial, dispatching them on the pretext of insurrection. Local caudillos made an example of the counterguerrillas when they could. At a place near Rancho Viejo, Du Pin reported, "Five of our soldiers who fell into the hands of the enemy were castrated and died as a result of that horrible operation." Afterward, Du Pin had Rancho Viejo burned. His outrageousness eventually caused scandal for Maximilian and Carlota, who complained to Bazaine that Du Pin must be brought under control, accusing him of wildly escalating the butchery. Carlota called him the "monster of the hot lands."[61]

Convoys carrying goods inland from Veracruz were frequently attacked, and Du Pin and his men searched for the source of the strikes. About six miles off the Veracruz road, in a forest of tall trees, they heard music in the distance, and as the soldiers approached they found the sources of the tunes emanating from a large storehouse. Two hundred men appeared in the clearing as though it were a ballroom, with twenty happy young girls fluttering among the men. When the counterguerrillas were spotted, the men fled, leaving the girls behind. A quick search of the building revealed provisions stolen from various captured convoys including textiles, furnishings, and, curiously, musical instruments. The soldiers gave some of the silks to the girls before they set the place on fire but thought to set aside the trumpets, guitars, and violins. As they bivouacked in the forest clearing, some of the men, who turned out to be virtuosos, played songs and danced to the music from the Latin Quarter of Paris. In the morning the counterguerrillas set off to return to camp, with at least one of the night's trumpeters carrying a beautiful woman on his saddle.[62]

Finally, a combination of new laws requiring passports along the road to La Soledad and a new administrative system at Veracruz for courts-martial and imprisonments began to make demonstrable changes. "The dungeons of San Juan de Ulúa were overflowing with vagabonds and highwaymen, who had been tried by the military courts," said one observer. In mid-April 1863 an immense military convoy carrying ammunition and $4 million in gold for the troops at Puebla made it to its destination, signaling the suppression of vagaries along the road and attacks. By May 1 the counterguerrillas posted a troop of Egyptian soldiers to guard the railroad lines, near La Soledad. Clad in their notable white, billowy, uniforms, these strangers impressed and frightened the native population.[63]

In Mexico City, Benito Juárez witnessed the return of his exhausted and demoralized troops from Puebla and knew they could not be reorganized in time for another heavy defense of the capital. Knowing an overwhelming French juggernaut approached, in order to protect Mexico City, he had to leave. On May 31 he called the congress into session, and after a brief presentation they pledged their confidence. He vowed himself to an eventual Republican victory: "Adversity, citizen deputies, discourages none but contemptible peoples; ours has been ennobled by great feats and we are far from being shorn of the immense obstacles, material and moral, which the country will oppose to unjust invaders. The vote of confidence . . . engages my gratitude to the Assembly of the Nation in the highest degree, though it is impossible for me to engage my honor and duty in defense of our country more than I already have."[64]

Juárez waited until sunset to order the Mexican flag lowered over the National Palace. Facing an unforeseeable future, men held their hats to their breasts as the national anthem was played for the last time. On the balcony of the palace, state ministers handed the flag to Juárez, who pressed it to his lips and cried "¡Viva Mexico!" A crowd standing in the Zócalo responded with cheers, and then it was over. Early in the morning, Juárez abandoned the capital for San Luis Potosí with his cabinet, business files, tax rolls, and financial records, guarded by a small military squadron.[65]

On June 10 Forey, Almonte, Saligny, and the French columns made a triumphant entry into Mexico City, attired in their formal uniforms. The people cheered, trying to make the best of a confusing situation, in a public welcome orchestrated by the commander of the city. The monarchists built triumphal arches with images of Napoléon and Eugénie wreathed in flowers over the main avenues. Forey sent telegrams to France's minister of war that he had occupied Mexico City and that the city had welcomed them enthusiastically. "The soldiers of France were literally crushed under garlands and nosegays of which nothing can give you any idea."[66]

After setting up lodging for the troops, the people saw the town fill with the red trousers of the French army and began adjusting to the new regime. Church officials, eager to reassert their power, reverted to their old schedule of masses and services, ringing the bells at constant intervals to the distraction of the French officials unused to the ubiquity of Catholic ritual. Some felt they were mocked; "All we lacked were tapers in our hands," said one officer. The clergy reinstated the scheduled feast days, and the French consented, even ordering officers to accompany the processions. Labastida distributed wax amulets to the Zouaves in the hospital to protect them from the musket "balls of the sacrilegious enemy." One Zouave put the talisman on and dared someone to shoot at him. Some French officers felt a little humiliated in being ordered to take sacraments to the sick, yet they knew it was important to demonstrate they wanted the reversal of Juárez's reforms, who had wanted "an expulsion of everything that wore a cassock," wrote one observer.[67] They let the people believe it at first.

Many officers felt revulsion at the French pandering to the Church, saying the priests' demands overwhelmed them. The day after their entry into Mexico City was "a monster procession . . . organized for that day and nothing was neglected to give it incomparable effect. The triumphal arches of the day before served for a new parade, which was escorted by three squadrons of cavalry and three regiments of French infantry, and which was hailed by the same enthusiasm, the same flowers, the same acclamations, and the same smiling women. The politicians of the army and the French mission thought we were going too far," said one official.[68]

Within two days of his arrival, Forey began to set up an executive administration. Napoléon had written him, "You must be master in Mexico City without appearing to be." He permitted independent press, within limits, and allowed the French *Monitor Franco Americano*, the *Boletín Oficial*, *El Cronista de México*, and *La Sociedad* to report the news. The general also prohibited the *leva*, or forced conscription of laborers and indigenous poor, into the military ranks. Corruption and wrongful imprisonment were punished. Governmental forced loans from citizens and merchants, or *préstamos forzosos*, were banned. He issued orders to control the venal administration of justice that had been open to bribery and corruption. Armed bands of guerrillas, he announced, would be subject to courts-martial. Most importantly, the incoming government would allow freedom of religion instead of one national faith, an order that caught the Catholic clergy unprepared.[69]

Forey warned his officers to be on their best behavior. He appealed to the owners of the larger houses in the city to take in officers to be billeted in their homes. Many grumbled about this, but it served to integrate the French military into the Mexican society, especially in the elite circles. Although Forey at first closed the Alameda to all civilians because he located the cavalry barracks of the Chasseurs d'Afrique on its perimeter, he soon ordered it reopened, and a military band played there every morning from ten until one in the afternoon.[70]

By June 22 Forey established a triumvirate council to head a temporary government, elected by thirty-five prominent Conservatives, selected by Saligny. The provisional council, known as the Regency, consisted of Almonte, Pelagio Antonio Labastida, the new archbishop of Mexico (who planned to return to Mexico from Europe in September), and Gen. Mariano Salas. They would govern until the arrival of the sovereigns. It was critical that the regents operate efficiently, definitively, and in unison to attain legitimacy and respect. Napoléon expected them to build a stable operating administration and organize the military as an army of Imperialist Mexicans, cultivated and trained by the French officers. Bazaine, with all the diplomacy and tact he could muster, encouraged the regency to work in unison.[71]

After a few months, when Labastida arrived and joined the regency, it became obvious that the three men had severely divergent visions for the Mexican empire. This became a joke to the French military. Capt. Loizillon called Almonte "a reactionary of little value," Labastida "a vigorous man who immediately set foot on the others and directs everything," and Salas "a mummy unearthed for the occasion."[72]

Bazaine, however, doggedly followed Napoléon's plan, and with the assistance of the church assembled 231 citizens, mostly criollo Conservatives, to form what he called the Assembly of Notables. The regency adopted resolutions calling for Mexico to become a nation under a Catholic monarch vested with the title of emperor. The provisional government, as enunciated by the Conservative and Clerical parties, was to take immediate control over the country and its departments with the goal of bringing new leadership to Mexico. The president of the new executive organization, Teodosio Lares, announced the new regime by public proclamation at the National Palace, joined by Forey, the provisional leaders, professors from the university, military officers, and staff. An additional 215 were selected, ostensibly without class distinction, to a National Assembly to select the permanent form of government most suited to Mexico, with implied pressure to bring a monarchy to the country, namely Ferdinand Maximilian.[73]

One French officer compared the assemblymen to larvae plucked off the street. They "are completely free to choose provided it decrees a monarchy," he wrote. It was important to Napoléon to demonstrate to the world that the Mexican citizens voted freely to choose a government for themselves. On July 10 the assembly called for a government ruled by a monarchy, as expected. There was some debate about getting a consensus from beyond the capital, but the rainy season made this almost impossible. "To celebrate this vote, the Mexican army has fired a hundred rounds of cannon in the square, amid the complete indifference of the population," one officer recalled.[74]

In celebration, Forey gave two gala balls at the garrison's ballroom, decorated in campaign flags, trophies, bayonets, and flowers. *Bengalas*, or saltpeter lights, lit the exterior of the gardens, and the officers welcomed spouses or other young Mexican women, some wearing Parisian fashions. Officers called them "wonders of creation" and "alluring and languid." A number of the local women found the French officers fascinating and exciting. Most agreeably, the officers returned their admiration. Sara Yorke Stevenson, a young American woman living in Mexico City, wrote, "They fell gracefully into the Mexican mode of life, and took kindly to the Habanera, the bull-fights, the Paseo, and the style of flirtation preferred by the Mexican women. For this they soon coined a new French word, *noviotage*, hybridized from the Spanish word for *lover*." The semi-platonic arrangement often lasted for a prolonged period in which the man "played the bear" (*hacer el oso*), a somewhat disparaging term for the way the young men made eyes at their chosen one from the street as they walked back and forth for hours in front of her house, or at the Alameda, or followed her carriage on horseback at the Paseo, with the alleged goal of culminating the courtship in a marriage.[75]

The French generals, now at the helm in the capital, saw that an even longer campaign to subdue the country and receive a new monarch lay before them. They settled in, preparing to drive out the Juaristas from the rest of the territories and major cities and to await the arrival of their emperor and empress.

Honor of the House of Habsburg

News of the fall of Puebla reached Napoléon and Eugénie at Fontainebleau, where, greatly relieved, Napoléon admitted that he had "for the last week, simply not lived." Congratulations soon arrived from the European royal heads of state, and the officials and royal administrators in Paris were delighted, as were his ministers. Vendors sold Mexican flags along the Seine. At the Tuileries, the royal chefs experimented with *Bombe Mexicaine*, a layered confection shaped like a dome, with the Mexican national emblem of the eagle perched on a cactus, holding a snake in its beak and talons.[1]

At Miramar on August 8, 1863, Maximilian received a telegram from Napoléon with congratulations that the national assembly in Mexico City had heralded him as the country's new emperor. Napoléon promised that the whole of Mexico would soon fall. While encouraged that his Mexican empire would finally materialize, Maximilian took the charged news with ambivalence, worried about a number of issues, including intervention from American forces. It remained basic to him that England should support his monarchy to legitimize his empire and protect him from possible U.S. reprisals, but to date Queen Victoria had shown only grave reserve, although the prime minister, Lord Palmerston, saw the advantages to trade. The expenses of the campaign and its length remained key. His advisors said that to subjugate the entire country, a great deal more energy, money, manpower, and military force would be required. Moreover, there was much unknown about the harsh arid region of the tierra caliente and in the Huasteca in northeastern Mexico. Maximilian manifested no personal concern about his own welfare; he only needed a mandate and a solid, definite, tangible summons to action, and he was ready to serve.[2]

From Mexico City, at the end of summer 1863, after the Assembly of Notables voted to rebuild the Mexican government as an empire, a Mexican delegation traveled to Miramar to offer the crown to Maximilian. The group arrived on October 2 with high expectations that Maximilian would accept their invitation. The deputation, headed by Gutiérrez de Estrada and Hidalgo, admired the Adriatic setting, which they viewed as a vignette of what it would be like to have the grace, decorum, and power under a monarch controlling their country. Wearing his medal of the Order of Saint Stephen and the royal collar of the Golden Fleece, Maximilian received the deputation, and Gutiérrez de Estrada read a lengthy statement in French about the unhappy conditions in Mexico, the anarchy, and the endlessly changing leadership. He concluded that as a worthy descendent of Charles V, Maximilian was the personification of the primeval heritage under which the aegis of government was legendary, *hoc signo vinces.* He then reported the vote of the Assembly of Notables, with the news that a number of regional leaders representing about 700,000 people, including those from Mexico City, Querétaro, Guerrero, Córdoba, and Toluca, desired a monarch and invited Maximilian to be emperor.[3]

With gratitude, Maximilian accepted the title of Emperor of Mexico but only provisionally. He called for the ratification of his election by the Assembly of Notables, but he also wanted a national vote of the people—a plebiscite—for a constitutional monarchy. Maximilian had been informed that the assembly had no real legal authority, and he knew that he must have support from a solid majority of the general population. Six months should be sufficient time to conduct an election, Maximilian concluded. He demanded the vote be conducted in Mexico City and a majority of states, including Morelia, Querétaro, Jalisco, and Guanajuato, those with populous towns. "A sham vote would produce nothing but a phantom monarchy," he argued. Also, if the majority did not support an empire, he feared reprisals from North America, with the U.S. Congress already alleging a violation of the Monroe Doctrine. When the Mexican legation made the distinction that forty-five towns and villages had declared in favor of a monarchy, Maximilian was heartened and encouraged but noted that they were under French control. He also called for the protection of major cities, cultural sites, and ports for a period of six years by 8,000 to 10,000 French troops. In all, the conference ended on a happy note with Maximilian enthusiastic about assuming the throne that awaited him in Mexico.[4]

Gutiérrez de Estrada and Hidalgo returned to Paris and at a dinner at

José María Gutiérrez de Estrada and Mexican delegation officially
inviting Maximilian to be emperor of Mexico, 1863

Saint Cloud recounted their meeting with Maximilian. Eugénie, who had just
arrived from Spain where she lobbied for support for the Mexican expedition,
explained her modern vision for Mexico, where political enemies would make
peace and function progressively, much like France. Gutiérrez de Estrada
debated that such an ideal would not be possible in Mexico without a very
strong and iron Catholic hand, to which she disagreed, saying the French
would bring humanity without secular control. Hidalgo, as Eugénie's toady,
agreed with her. They all knew, however, that in the eyes of Napoléon it was
important to make the Conservatives' mission appear unified. After dinner
Napoléon asked whether Maximilian had decided about Mexico, and Gutiérrez
de Estrada replied that "in the most categorical and conclusive way," his bags
were packed. Maximilian only waited for the people to declare their will and
merely asked for "assurances, not guarantees," much more feasible than a
meticulous vote.[5]

Throughout this time, Napoléon coached Maximilian for his new role. He
assured him the United States would cooperate. "Once the country is pacified,
both physically and morally, Your Imperial Highness's government will be
recognized by everybody," he wrote. "The United States are well aware that,
since the new regime in Mexico is the work of France, they cannot attack it

without at once making enemies of us." Attempting to manage Maximilian's liberal philosophies, he later added, "Allow me to lay great stress on one point: a country torn by anarchy cannot be regenerated by parliamentary liberty. What is needed in Mexico is a liberal dictatorship . . . a strong power which shall proclaim the great principles of modern civilization, such as equality before the law, civil and religious liberty, an upright administration."[6]

Maximilian conducted his own investigations, however, to understand the true political situation in Mexico. He called on Charles Bourdillon, a former London *Times* correspondent who had recently returned from Mexico. Bourdillon painted a rosy picture of Mexico's liberals, stating that they posed no real threat to the Conservatives. Former British minister to Mexico, Charles Wyke, who distrusted Bourdillon and suspected he was a French agent, was also summoned by Maximilian to give a report. Wyke offered to write his opinion, but the British foreign office prohibited him from meeting with the archduke, fearing French retribution should Maximilian opt out of the Mexican throne. Wyke and the British government well knew that the anarchy and chaos was nearly insurmountable. Austria's Franz Josef, seeing England's lukewarm attitude toward the expedition, wanted only minimal involvement with Mexico. The British refused to jeopardize their interests, not even to warn Maximilian.[7]

Confident that a majority would elect for his appointment, Maximilian began brokering with the French over the finances, seeking a loan of 150 million francs to purchase arms for an army yet to be recruited and the settlement of France's expenses in the expedition. Almost simultaneously Maximilian stepped up negotiations with his brother Franz Josef over Austria's support of the Mexican empire including the thorny issues of family stipends and his succession rights in the Habsburg dynasty. Franz Josef asked him to travel to Schönbrunn to discuss matters in person. While he longed to see the expansion of Habsburg influence in the New World, Franz Josef remained circumspect about Napoléon's motives, refusing to give unlimited support to an endeavor sponsored solely by France. Also, Maximilian and Carlota continued to hope that England would morally and materially support the empire to fully legitimize the enterprise, endorse the dignity of the house of Habsburg, and stave off any intervention from the United States. Maximilian asked Carlota to go to her father in Belgium to inquire again if he could not persuade Queen Victoria. He feared that without England's stalwart support, the nascent Mexican empire would be immediately vulnerable. He wanted guarantees. Many pro-expedition leaders believed, however, that England's participation did not coincide with Napoléon's vision to raise Mexico from its deplorable condition. Any position assumed by Britain would serve its own monetary interests only.[8]

Time ticked on. By the end of 1863 Napoléon had begun to see that France could not indefinitely support the Mexican empire and eagerly waited for Maximilian to make his arrangements and set sail, even without other countries' support. When England's Charles Wyke paid him an unofficial visit in November, Napoléon told him he had been surprised by the Mexican people's attitudes, feeling misled and questioning if they wanted France's guidance. Placing Maximilian on the throne would improve the imperialists' circumstances, he concluded. Politically, he knew he must recall at least a small contingency of the French army soon after their arrival in Mexico. "That is what France wants and what I want," he said. Wyke, nevertheless, pointed out that Maximilian in no way expected an early withdrawal of troops, that this ran counter to France's proposals, and that his power in Mexico would extend no farther that the tips of the French bayonets. Napoléon paused in reflection, and said, no, that the archduke knew that once he established himself on the throne, France's duty to him would come to an end and there was no need to go to "bail for its continuance." Wyke, who had little respect for the Mexican generals, especially Márquez and the Conservative leadership, then proposed that the Mexican regency should dissolve and determine if the country really did want a monarchy. Napoléon again disagreed, "It would be to admit a mistake, and in France I am not allowed to make mistakes."[9]

In Mexico, internecine squabbling between the French generals Forey and Douay against Almonte and Saligny troubled Napoléon. While not partisan to the clerics, Almonte often sided with Bazaine, and Archbishop Labastida went against Gen. Forey. "I confess that I would rather undergo a second siege of Puebla than be placed in a position where I am supposed to be restraining influence on people who do not want to be restrained. General Almonte . . . allows himself to be talked into adopting the most deplorable measures, which I cannot sanction as I do not want the French flag to be associated with actions which are contrary to our policy," said Forey.[10]

Capt. Pierre Loizillon, in his regular reports to Napoléon, insisted that Forey be recalled, complaining about his slow and difficult conquest of Puebla. Forey, Loizillon said, could not even muster enthusiasm to persuade the men to follow him into battle again anywhere in Mexico. Loizillon and the French troops also bore deep contempt for Saligny, whom they termed the "army-killer," largely because of his ill-informed strategic decisions on the battlefield of Puebla, adding that he "deceived the country and the Emperor as to the resistance we would meet in pursuing the course he . . . imposed on us." But Loizillon also resented being attached to Generals Almonte and Márquez, calling them "thieves, immoral, and incompetent."[11]

Napoléon became convinced that he misplaced his trust by appointing Forey and Saligny; particularly bothersome was Forey's inclination to be too lax to control the Conservatives and church party members. In July, after extensive deliberation, Napoléon recalled them. The French soldiers celebrated their summons to France. Forey was shocked and embarrassed, despite Napoléon's decision to simultaneously bestow on him the rank of marshal, one of the highest military distinctions in France. The emperor then awarded Achille Bazaine all of Forey's duties as commander-in-chief of the Mexican campaign. Forey, who had intended to stay on to see Maximilian invested, delayed his departure for at least five weeks, inspiring ridicule and boisterous song. Saligny would not leave either, although he had been ordered to do so three times. He said he needed to settle debts, which Bazaine promptly forbade, and lingered over the next several weeks, eluding authorities, until orders arrived that he was to return to France immediately. After marrying a young woman from an ultra-clerical Mexican family on Christmas Day, he finally set sail for Europe.[12]

Napoléon ordered Bazaine to correct Forey's mistakes and raise more men. He expected an efficient campaign to subjugate the remainder of Mexico. The general announced to the people that his mission was to serve the interim government and asked them to have faith and unite to support a stable regime. He then made his first duty to raise the quality of soldiering in the imperial army, especially those drawn from the Mexican population. The ranks had been filled with forced conscripts, many of them convicts, and he set out with his generals, Leonardo Márquez, Tomás Mejía, and Miguel Miramón, who had returned to Mexico, to improve their enlistment procedures, discipline, and training with an effort to recruit from populations of indigenous natives. "The 175 Indians that are part of these companies seem satisfied to serve under orders of our officers, whom I have instructed to show kindness toward them and look after their well-being," wrote Bazaine. He gave himself six months to tighten operations in the skeletal government, which he thought excessively apathetic and reactionary. During that time, he and his officers would poll the population on the form of government they wanted and announced that they only sought a stable regime to regenerate the country.[13]

As soon as Bazaine assumed command, Labastida intensified his demands to have the church's former properties returned, proposing that courts decide whether or not to punish the purchasers. He also attempted to set in motion a number of mandates given him by the Vatican during his European exile, including restoring religious orders. To do so, he often invoked the authority of Pope Pius IX. Under direction from Paris, Bazaine refused to undo Juárez's reforms over confiscated church lands. The subject remained too raw, and the complications of returning properties, already sold several times over, would have been impossible without causing further insurrection. With his repeated outbursts, Labastida incurred the disdain of the French officers, who saw him as the emblem of the Mexican clergy, unorthodox and ethically compromised, who simply wanted to restore his wealth under various moral justifications. The French quickly came to understand the rationale behind Juárez's reforms. In France, as in other European countries, the clergy did not have unbridled domination, and controls on the Catholic Church had been instituted after intense conflict. Yet Labastida remained outspoken, passionate, and immovable. Gen. du Barail described him as "youthful, fat, with a blooming pink face trimmed by a triple chin . . . the type of the papistical churchman, unctuous, saccharine, and false." People knew him to agree with one position in public but remain stubbornly loyal to ultraconservative ideals when making critical decisions. After a few months Labastida, who wanted nearly absolute control over Mexico, saw a chance to get it and became impossible to please, a torment to Bazaine. "Unfortunately his ideas are those of the Roman clergy," wrote Bazaine, "almost those of the Spanish clergy of the time of Philip IV, with the exception of the Inquisition." Labastida frequently abstained from meetings of the regency or quit, only to rejoin it a few days later.[14]

Bazaine also suffered a storm of resentment against the arrival of a Protestant French chaplain attached to the army "on the virgin soil of Mexico." Bazaine allowed the Protestant service to go on as scheduled despite the archbishop's extreme condemnation.[15]

As a result of these conflicts, clerics fomented bitterness within their own congregations against the French officers. Labastida was so repressive and intolerant that he turned away worshipers who did not conform to strict tradition in dress. When the wife of one of Bazaine's officers arrived at mass wearing the latest in Parisian fashion (meaning a hoop skirt, décolletage, bare arms, and Parisian hat), the officiating priest became offended that she was not wearing the black mantilla customary for most women supplicants. The priest made a rude gesture to her husband, who in reply complained to the priest's superior. When it was decided that the priest was within his right to excuse her from church, Bazaine wrote an angry letter to Labastida asserting that the French were good Catholics, just as reverent as the Mexicans, and French women should be allowed the right to attend mass in the attire of their homeland.[16]

Frustrated, Bazaine also hoped to lay the issues of property ownership to rest by a determined show of force. Supported by a retinue of two hundred Zouaves, he burst into a meeting and demanded the regency issue a decree ratifying the Liberals' nationalization of church lands, guaranteeing rights to those who had purchased them. Almonte and Salas agreed, but when Labastida refused, Bazaine removed him from the regency. He protested that stepping down was inconsistent with his character but decided to boycott anyway.[17]

Labastida intensified his protests against the provisional government's moderate liberalism. He insisted that Napoléon and Maximilian had promised to restore the church from what he called Juárez's "vast swindle." Bazaine, however, whose first goal was to place the monarchy on a stable footing, continued to ask the courts to clear up property rights, titles, and debt, along the lines of Juárez's reforms. The archbishop expressed outrage, condemning Bazaine and the other regents as anti-Catholic, immoral men who sought to deal the pope an appreciable blow. The future emperor of Mexico, Labastida said, would be deprived of valuable economic resources, and the French military had put "many new obstacles in his way," limiting Maximilian's power and latitude, "reducing him to the painful necessity of gnawing on the fleshless bones of a cadaver." However, in conciliation, Bazaine had the idea of punishing the Liberals by confiscating their personal property. He drafted a decree to seize their assets, but it was quickly withdrawn when it was seen as overreaching, likely to cause revolt and panic.[18]

In retribution, when Bazaine took the field in November to supervise troop advances on Guadalajara and San Luis Potosí, Labastida and the Clerical party planned a revolt against the French. The clerics stated their income would be tied to their patronage and service to the emperor, instead of being able to collect tithes or rents as before. Fearing they would be reduced to low wages with few privileges, the priests mobilized. With Labastida calling for public demonstrations, they rallied the indigenous population to hold benign processions carrying flowers and pinwheels. Labastida appointed a synod of seven bishops with the power to deny sacraments or excommunicate any government official who refused to restore their properties. Only upon capitulation would they receive absolution. In support of the church, the Supreme Court, comprised of sympathetic Conservatives, ruled that Bazaine had acted illegally to remove Labastida from the regency. Bazaine, Almonte, and Salas retaliated by dismissing all the justices from the bench.[19]

The Cathedral, Mexico City. Note Aztec calendar affixed to western wall, ca. 1880

On November 18, with Bazaine still out of the city organizing his troops, Labastida called for insurrection against the French, his supporters slipping leaflets under the doors of citizens. He threatened to exclude all who served the regency and closed the cathedral for the spectacular mass held for the French military on Sundays. Labastida slipped out of the archbishop's palace, hiding in different houses to avoid arrest. From the battlefield, Bazaine revoked the archbishop's orders and authorized Baron Gen. Gabriel Niegre, military commander of Mexico City, to simply reopen the cathedral by blowing open the doors with a cannonade if Labastida did not allow his troops to worship. During all the bluster, little actually happened—no one was excommunicated and the military attended mass as usual. But from then on, the French army put limits on Catholic displays and rituals.[20]

"The Archbishop continually repeats to me that we are doing the greatest wrong in not supporting the church, and he repeats interminable homilies, to which I only answer unmoved, 'Monseigneur, I am only a soldier charged with carrying out an order,'" wrote Bazaine. Instead of trying to ameliorate the situation, Bazaine took the hard line with the clerics, which only annealed their resolve to get their way. Although the French offered to support the church with state funds, the priests did not change their minds but temporarily suspended the revolt. Bazaine did not realize then that the priests' support for the new emperor had been severely damaged.[21]

The marshal agonized over the growing tensions as everyone waited for Maximilian's acceptance and arrival. Truly nothing substantial could be completed with the church until they could negotiate with the emperor. The Mexican monarchists agreed. Gutiérrez de Estrada commented that imperial decrees would be worth more than 50,000 troops trying to fight a rebellion promoted by the church.[22]

At this point, the emerging empire moved as fragile clockwork, every gear dependent on the next to make motion. Napoléon refused to fund Maximilian's loan requests until he formally accepted the role as emperor, although bankers from Paris and London had been visiting Mexico to investigate. He also sent French accountant Nicolas Budin to Mexico to take control of government assets, pay creditors, set up commercial trade in raw and manufactured goods, and support the needs of the military. Maximilian remained firm that he needed proof that a majority of the voters supported him. Marshal Bazaine had the mission of securing the plurality Maximilian required while making the country fit enough for him to reign.[23]

In reaction to the clerics' fractious uprisings, Bazaine suggested that France send another 25,000 troops in order to help suppress Clerical party revolts, a difficulty that was not originally envisioned with the Mexican expedition. Bazaine's men, busy in the field, struggled over rugged terrain to fan out across Mexico, but the campaign was slowed by Labastida's insistence on throwing obstacles in his way, the violence requiring determined control. When Napoléon received this news about the archbishop's outrageous behavior, he had Eugénie invite José Manuel Hidalgo to lunch, where Napoléon read Bazaine's letter to him, furious that Hidalgo misled them regarding Labastida's support and facilitation of the new empire. Eugénie ordered Hidalgo to intervene and control the archbishop. At a subsequent large and formal dinner, she had Hidalgo seated to her left and aired the subject again. She upbraided him in front of the guests over Mexico's egregious clergy who tried to stand in the way of a victory for the monarchy. "I admire you, you didn't turn a hair," said a witness to her reprimand.

"No," he said, "but I have hell within me."[24]

Despite the problems with the archbishop, Bazaine, aided by the small but elite 3rd Regiment of Zouaves, the backbone of his command, had launched an intensive push into the Mexican interior provinces to make the land fit for a new reign under Maximilian. It was a campaign of speed, frequently spawning breathtaking violence. The marshal had roughly 40,000 French regulars, Legionnaires, and European troops under his command, at times distributed more thinly than he preferred. Another 13,000 Mexican imperial auxiliaries fought under the direction of Generals Márquez, Miramón, and Mejía. They began with the seizure and occupation of the most populated cities, driving the Republicans north. By January 1864 Gen. Márquez routed one-legged Liberal Gen. José López Uraga near Morelia, taking his cannon, copper ingots, weapons, and ammunition, resulting in Uraga's decision to side with the Imperialistas a few months later, eventually becoming an advisor to the emperor and empress. Uraga's defection further weakened Juárez's forces. Douay and Miramón threw Juarista Gen. Jesús González Ortega out of Zacatecas while Gen. Mejía swept through the chaparral pushing Liberal Gen. Manuel Doblado as far north as San Luis Potosí and Matehuala, hoping to drive Benito Juárez out of the region while opening access to the Texas border. With the assistance of the counterguerrillas, in only ten weeks the French rapidly swept over the vast area of central and western Mexico. At the same time, Gen. Mejía pushed toward the northeastern frontier. Major victories came soon. On November 13, 1863, when the counterguerrillas killed the former Mexican president, Gen. Ignacio Comonfort, in Guanajuato, this setback further demoralized the Liberals.[25]

In six weeks, the "Franco-Mexican flag fluttered on all the plateaus from Morelia to San Luis Potosí . . . from Mexico to Guadalajara," said officer Émile de Kératry. In each town, Bazaine appointed a prefect, established a citadel for a small garrison, and attempted to settle unrest caused by the guerrillas who agitated the people and called for resistance. "If the country is not pacified, it has at least been conquered; the enemy's army, scattered and divided, far from its capital where it can no longer draw on any resources, has taken off into the mountains, where it has advanced toward the north in the poorest states, the most sparsely populated. [The Republic] will collapse with time," wrote Bazaine.[26] However, Bazaine grossly exaggerated his conquest, mostly contained to the interior regions.

One fortunate success in Bazaine's campaign lay in gaining the support of Santiago Vidaurri, the fiercely independent *caudillo* of northern Mexico who controlled Coahuila, Nuevo León, and portions of Tamaulipas. Long recognized for his home rule and personal army, Vidaurri remained loyal to his own trading interests and had informal agreements with American Confederates to facilitate trade in cotton and vital supplies. The "Lord of the North," as

Vidaurri was known, turned against Juárez when the president fled San Luis Potosí, protected by the 6,000 soldiers with Generals Doblado and Miguel Negrete, and arrived in Saltillo in January 1864. Juárez desperately demanded the customs duties of Piedras Negras, estimated at 50,000 pesos per month. Vidaurri refused, protesting that Coahuila and Nuevo León depended on those funds. When Juárez's troops attacked Vidaurri at Monterrey, Vidaurri seized their artillery. After a tense three-day standoff, Juárez summoned Vidaurri to a trial and declared his territory under siege. Vidaurri asserted open revolt and escaped into Texas, where he found refuge with the Confederates. It was a tense period for the Imperialistas, who struggled to hold the northern territory. When Vidaurri returned, he became an Imperialista prepared to help Gen. Mejía solidly control the northeast, key to having Chihuahua pronounce in favor of the empire and holding a grip on the most populated areas of northern Mexico. In the absence of any authority, Republican or Imperialist, Vidaurri's word was law and he controlled the flow of money, despite the diplomatic complexities.[27] Juárez never forgot Vidaurri's betrayal.

By the end of December, Mejía's army, despite being plagued with typhus, occupied San Luis Potosí and the port of Tampico, Tamaulipas. Bazaine quickly ordered restored communications across the region and customs officials to man the port. In the south, Yucatán voluntarily committed to the French. In each of the conquered cities and towns, French officers collected the names, addresses, and signatures of as many citizens possible to record people's votes to elect for an empire. While this polling could not be reckoned as complete canvassing, the French thought it closer than any other vote in the nation's history. "The number of these adhesions is not the result of universal suffrage. But it is nonetheless the expression of the great majority of the liberated states, for the Indian element that inhabits the countryside always follows the Mexican element that lives in the large centers. The Indian masses have never been sincerely consulted by any party and the pretext is simple, they are regarded as creatures without reason. To make them *gente de razón*, one would have to change the whole social organization of the country," Bazaine wrote. Indeed, no president had ever been elected at large, only by blocks of votes or congressional election. This Bonapartist technique typified Napoléon III's methods of masking the wishes of the few behind the petitions of the masses.[28]

It proved effective. Charles Wyke and other British foreign officers watching events in Mexico, however, knew the effort misled the French public and more importantly Maximilian. "The poor archduke will now be told that the majority of the population has declared in his favor, and thus be induced to go out to a country where his presence will only have the effect of prolonging a civil war with all its attendant horrors," wrote Wyke, predicting that soon people would begin to understand the case.[29]

Throughout the winter and into spring 1864, the majority of Juárez's 20,000 battered and defeated fighters, underfunded and undersupplied, either deserted or joined the Imperialistas. The exceptions included the independent and resilient Gen. Porfirio Díaz, who headed to Oaxaca to prepare a defense in the southeast, and Gen. Mariano Escobedo along with González Ortega, who continued to resist the French at Monterrey in Nuevo León. Juárez and his supporting generals were assisted by a number of regional caudillos, like the scrappy Juan Nepomuceno Cortina and American-educated José María Jesús Carvajal, who maintained guerrilla armies sometimes numbering 2,000 men. With town after town, however, proclaiming in favor of the empire, Juárez was forced to move frequently, hiding in the vast deserts of northern Mexico, to thwart the rumor he would set sail from Matamoros and leave the country. Juárez knew he had the moral backing of most of his people as well as the United States but no reliable way to secure material support. In Washington, Matías Romero kept pressure on Secretary of State Seward for aid, with no real results.[30]

Before Juárez left Monterrey, he sent his wife, Margarita, and his immediate family of nine children and grandchildren to the United States where they settled in New York. He then led his ministers and a small militia northwest, arriving in Chihuahua in October 1864. Lonely and isolated, he wrote his family that he lived in "unending torment, knowing nothing of [their] fate." After two months in Chihuahua, Juárez finally heard from his family; his sense of relief tremendous, he focused on regaining his country. The problem lay in his isolation. "Chihuahua is a calaboose where we are in rigorous incommunication; but it will not be long before our bayonets open a way into the interior," Juárez told his family. He was encouraged that so far the French remained less structured, poorly staffed and armed in the northern states, but that did not stop him from lamenting their recent loss at Puebla and seemingly hopeless situation.[31]

With enemies on all sides, his treasury in tatters, and being out of contact with his generals, Juárez could do nothing but simply wait with monklike patience. He continued to have faith in his small corps and the guerrilla fighters who remained sympathetic to his presidency, but conditions began to look insurmountable. In January, to further his misery, he soon heard that his son José, whom he called Pepe, had died of pneumonia in New York. "It is too much that my spirit suffers and I have hardly strength enough to surmount this disaster, which drains me and hardly lets me breathe. My adored son is dead and with him died my fairest hopes. This is horrible, but there is no remedy," he wrote.[32]

The situation and his raw emotion tested his resolve, but he remained unbowed over the following months, determined not to leave Mexico. In March, at a banquet marking his fifty-ninth birthday, he summed up his devotion. "I drink to the independence of the nation, citizens. . . . That we may make it triumph or perish," he said. "To give one's life for Independence is a great good. I repeat that as men we are nothing, that principles are everything."[33]

Indeed, Juárez loyalists refused to abandon him. While Bazaine continued his rapid advances through central Mexico, maintaining a town or region under French subjugation proved a difficult task. When the imperial garrison moved on to the next village, Juaristas reclaimed the territory. To preserve French military progress and avoid undermining his troop's efforts in meaningless victories, Bazaine was forced to establish small garrisons or rural guards in these volatile areas, which took men out of his columns.[34]

Therefore, Bazaine made heavy use of Du Pin and the counterguerrillas, especially in the north where independent caudillos governed vast areas. With light armaments, they could deploy rapidly to areas of unrest. They became so valuable that they were promoted from irregulars to formal units. Bazaine ordered them proper uniforms, a sign of their institutional importance. They received wide-brimmed Mexican straw sombreros, if they did not already wear a turban, red or blue pelisses with black braid and copper buttons, heavy cotton pants, and tall riding boots for the cavalry or shoes and gaiters for the infantry. On Napoléon's advice, Bazaine ordered the Foreign Legion to assist the counterguerrillas and enlist indigenous Mexicans as privates to serve along the Turkish regiments.[35]

By the middle of 1864, soldiers had arrived from twenty-two nations, most European countries, China, Algeria, the Sudan, Egypt, and elsewhere, including Mexico, either by force or volunteerism, and had joined Du Pin and his big-hatted counterguerrillas. They battled to subdue the countryside, with the added duty of preventing the clergy from working against the French army. Near Córdoba, they confronted a parish priest who ran a bar offering *aguardiente* (a sort of brandy) and other spirits, where he robbed intoxicated guerrillas in games of monte. His place attracted so many guerrillas that he was advised to shut down the gambling and work on his own conversion.[36]

Guarding the railroads also taxed the counterguerrillas. Near La Soledad, three carloads of provisions, engineering materials, and railway workers, protected by twenty-two counterguerrillas, were surrounded and attacked by 300 Juaristas. The leader of the counterguerrilla detachment was shot and killed. An old Turk named Soliman, of "Herculean strength and bravery . . . cleared the area around himself by striking terrible blows with the butt of his rifle. In spite of everything, he fell; they all fell, but their bodies were also surrounded by more than one enemy cadaver." Only two *contras* managed to survive, including one cavalryman from Martinique who dragged himself through the brush back to La Soledad.[37]

Leaving the lowlands of Veracruz mostly pacified, Bazaine sent the counterguerrillas to clear the roads in Tamaulipas and to aid Gen. Tomás Mejía and the Fifth Division in the march to occupy the northeastern border. On March 15, 1864, some 550 counterguerrillas and 200 horses boarded the *Eure* and sailed for the port of Tampico, Tamaulipas. Voracious swarms of sharks greeted their arrival as they dropped anchor at the sandbar off the coast.[38]

Mexico's second largest port, Tampico, remained a critically important trading center at the confluence of the Pánuco and Tamesis rivers, two large navigable waterways. Tampico's customs revenues came to $1.2 million annually, making it a highly desirable possession. The port had been under French control since August 1863, but area guerrillas, including the well-known Liberal caudillo José María Jesús Carvajal, strangled trade by terrorizing the countryside. Born in San Antonio de Bexar, Carvajal was educated as a seminarian and saddlemaker in the United States and, after military training, came to dominate swaths of northeastern Mexico. When the counterguerrillas arrived, Du Pin took control of the port, as the navy units set sail for France. Du Pin found Tampico almost completely cut off from the interior. Boats could not bring in fresh food, and the water carriers would not risk bullet fire, leaving the inhabitants to drink brackish water. At the same time, Carvajal and other Liberals blatantly entered the town's café to gloat over the paralysis of the town. Other caudillos, such as Servando Canales or self-proclaimed Tamaulipecan governor Juan N. Cortina, also controlled parts of Tamaulipas and Nuevo León, receiving reinforcements daily.[39]

On April 11 the counterguerrillas blew their bugles in front of the cathedral, calling to arms in preparation for moving against Carvajal. In turn, Carvajal called the Huastecans to war. The counterguerrillas marched south only to be stopped by the swollen, turbid Tamesis River. They drove nearly 200 horses and mules into the water, chasing behind them in canoes laden with equipment, saddles, guns, and ammunition. After following the whinnying, wild swarm, each man chased, caught his animal, saddled up, and rode south to find Carvajal's army.[40]

Carvajal assembled his 1,200-man army, mostly comprised of cattlemen from the area, Texans, and French deserters. As he moved west through central Tamaulipas, he encountered two platoons of Arab counterguerrillas, who with their piercing war cries terrified the local population. The local people believed Arabs ate children. After skirmishing and hand-to-hand combat, Carvajal retreated, leaving the dead and wounded as well as his dagger, engraved "Carvajal. *Libre o morir*," which Du Pin appropriated. In the military storehouses of the town, the counterguerrillas found a number of recently manufactured American rifles and money. Defeated, Carvajal hid in the mountains, as the counterguerrillas reclaimed Tampico, and Du Pin was praised as liberator of the port. La Huasteca lay nearly subjugated by the end of April.[41]

By May 1864 towns with large populations, such as Guadalajara, Querétaro, Guanajuato, and Morelia, fell under Imperialista control. In the battle of Matehuala, the Liberal Gen. Manuel Doblado lost his force of 1,200 men as well as his artillery to the Imperialistas, greatly weakening resistance in northern Mexico. Town after town fell to the Imperialistas. With each defeat, the petitions for a monarchy increased. Soon the long lists of signatures demonstrating the people's vote for a Mexican empire were sent to Paris.[42]

Maximilian's final requirement of the Mexican people had been fulfilled. "Three-quarters of the total territory of Mexico and four-fifths of her whole population have declared for a monarchy. Your arrival is awaited with eagerness and impatience and I hope to hear that Your Majesty will hasten your departure as much as possible so as to start upon the work of regeneration and reorganization which will raise us once more to the position of a great country," Almonte wrote to Maximilian. Indeed, the French looked forward to his coming as well, expecting Maximilian to call for reconciliation with the church and unite the country.[43]

Almonte had exaggerated his claims, however. Although the French army had quickly seized the states of Mexico, Querétaro, Guanajuato, Morelia, parts of Chihuahua, and Tamaulipas—the wealthiest and most populated areas—only about one-seventh of the Mexican territory lay under French control. Bazaine claimed votes of 6.5 million out of a population of roughly 8 to 9 million people, augmenting the numbers by securing referendums from area representatives and then adding the total numbers of the census of the area, as if it were a full, fair, and free poll. "I am convinced that the acts of adhesion represent the opinion of the reasonable people of Mexico and that the archduke can rely on the manifestation without remorse," wrote Bazaine. But from the beginning, truths surrounding the whole Mexican scheme had been incidental or inconvenient to the Monarchists and Napoléon.[44]

¶[6]►

What Would You Think of Me

Seeing the time growing nearer for his acceptance and departure for Mexico, Maximilian stepped up his business negotiations with Franz Josef, who would give only a few concessions of Austrian support to the new empire. To date, he had ordered the *Novara* fitted out for the transatlantic voyage that would take Maximilian, Carlota, and their household to Mexico. He also pledged a corps of Austrian soldiers.[1]

Franz Josef, however, also prepared a provision, aided by his minister, Prince Richard Metternich, that came close to jeopardizing the entire mission. In a meeting, while going over Franz Josef's offers to Maximilian, Austria's minister of foreign affairs, Count Johann Rechberg, mentioned to Maximilian, rather casually, that his brother would grant his blessing to accept the Mexican throne and assist him in setting up his new empire, providing that he relinquish his title and right of succession. This meant giving up his Habsburg titles and rights of legitimacy, especially concerning the children he and Carlota might have in Mexico. Rechberg concluded by saying that Franz Josef wished him well and hoped that Providence would protect him on his dangerous mission. Although Maximilian paused in disbelief and concern, he decided not to raise the issue of his Austrian rights until monetary and military support were in place. The succession issue could be addressed when he saw his brother in person, hoping it would not result in an emotional blowup.[2]

On January 30, 1864, Napoléon made the announcement that France guaranteed to support Maximilian's new empire: the French military would not leave Mexico until the empire was stabilized, and its exit would not jeopardize the regime. France would leave up to 8,000 Foreign Legionnaires for six to eight years. Napoléon also offered Maximilian the most favorable terms to repay France for the expenses associated with the establishment of the empire. Napoléon ordered his minister of finance, Achille Fould, to formalize the paperwork for the loans. A suggestion was also made that Maximilian negotiate the demands of the church and reinstatement of properties with the pope before going to Mexico. Because the details remained vague, Napoléon urged that Maximilian come to Paris to finalize matters.[3]

In preparing to negotiate with Napoléon, Maximilian quietly sent the draft of the French proposal to his father-in-law, King Leopold of Belgium, to review. Foremost was the matter of retaining the French troops in Mexico. Leopold, who believed in a strong defense to protect political interests, warned that if things started to go bad in Mexico, Napoléon would withdraw his troops and he would disown the whole experiment. If he planned to recall his troops, it must be done in gradual phases. "It is you who are acting as the cat's paw for the Emperor Napoléon, and for this very reason, no step ought to be taken without full safeguards as to leaving you the troops. You must at all costs get something done about this officially and in writing, signed by the French ministers . . . and ratified by you and the Emperor," wrote Leopold.[4]

With continuing encouragement from the Conservatives, especially the effusive flattery from Gutiérrez de Estrada and exaggerations from Juan N. Almonte about conditions in Mexico, Maximilian's confidence rose. He abandoned his hope for England's material support when Napoléon hinted vaguely that perhaps a Bourbon in Spain would gladly take the emperorship of Mexico, happy to reclaim former territory.[5]

Feeling enthusiastic, Maximilian announced his pending acceptance to Almonte in Mexico and asked him to prepare to receive him in Veracruz, the date having yet to be decided. Almonte reminded him of the unhealthy atmosphere of Veracruz, with its deadly yellow fever and malaria in the spring and summer. He sketched a plan for the quickest journey from Veracruz to Mexico City through Orizaba and Puebla. Almonte also advised that Santa Anna, the former dictator, had just arrived at the port of Veracruz on February 24 with the intent of seeking a position in the new empire. Fearing the confusion and unrest his presence would cause in the country among his former supporters, Bazaine ordered Santa Anna to leave Mexico. The old warrior returned to his exile in St. Thomas.[6]

At the same time, Maximilian wrote Almonte with instructions, then, strangely feeling he could reconcile with the Republicans, wrote to Benito Juárez, inviting him to serve as prime minister of the new empire and to meet him in Mexico City upon his arrival. It was a great dream of his to unite the political factions. Juárez, who was at the time near Monterrey on the run from the French army, replied diplomatically. Juárez wrote that the intervention had endangered their nationality and that he was "the one called to maintain the integrity, sovereignty, and independence of the nation." He continued:

> You tell me that abandoning the succession to a throne in Europe, forsaking your family, your friends, your fortune, and what is most dear to man, his country, you come with your wife, Doña Carlota, to distant and unknown lands to satisfy the summons spontaneously made by a people that rest their felicity and their future in you. I am amazed, on the one hand, by your generosity, and on the other, my surprise has been great to read in your letter the words "spontaneous summons," for I had already perceived that when the traitors of my country appeared at Miramar . . . to offer you the crown of Mexico with several letters from nine to ten towns of the nation, you saw in all this merely a ridiculous farce. . . . To all this you replied by requiring the will of the nation to be freely manifested through universal suffrage; this was to demand an impossibility but it was the demand of an honorable man. How can I not wonder then, when I see you . . . surround yourself with that condemned part of Mexican society? Frankly, I have suffered a disappointment, I thought you one of those pure beings whom ambition could not corrupt.[7]

He declined the offer to meet in Mexico City. "My occupations do not allow it," he said, adding, "contemporary history records the names of great traitors who have broken their oaths and their promises and failed their own party, and all that is most sacred to a man of honor. . . . It is given to men, sir, to attack the rights of others, to take their property, to attempt the lives of those who defend their liberty . . . but there is one thing which is beyond the reach of perversity, and that is the tremendous verdict of history. History will judge us."[8]

Maximilian would not receive this letter in Europe for some weeks. With the need to finalize matters and say goodbye to relatives across Europe, Maximilian and Carlota set out with their entourage to visit Belgium, France, England, and Austria before sailing to Mexico. At their first stop in Brussels to see Leopold, Carlota radiated excitement about her new station as empress of Mexico and talked at length with her father. But Maximilian's worries over the demands and succession issues pending with Franz Josef had deepened.

Moody and irritable, he sniped at Carlota when she told people that all the arrangements were settled. Mortified by the sheer idea of refusing the crown, Carlota ignored his concerns, reassuring Maximilian that he was "supremely fitted" to be emperor. Despite his ambivalence, he knew she had made up her mind.[9]

By March 5 the young sovereigns arrived in Paris, having determined to exact more concrete promises from Napoléon. Upon their arrival, the French court fêted them with all the honors due a ruling monarch. The officials presented a gala performance at the Tuileries and held a reception at the Austrian embassy. The entire diplomatic corps in Paris attended, with the notable exception of U.S. minister William Lewis Dayton, who was instructed to stay away as a sign of support for Juárez's Republican government. Carlota and Eugénie spent hours together, as the gregarious French empress talked endlessly on a wide variety of subject matters and won Carlota's friendship. As they discussed plans for the Mexican empire, Carlota buried the hostilities she may have borne for Eugénie, the wife of the man who directed the movement that caused Carlota's grandfather, former monarch of France, to abdicate. From her discussions with Eugénie, Carlota grew more confident with her role as empress.[10]

On the business of settling and funding the Mexican empire, military agreements and a financial plan were finalized by Minister Achille Fould and presented in two parts, an official version and a confidential rendering. The plan called for 25,000 French troops to remain in Mexico until a domestic, well-trained army could replace them. Additionally, the Foreign Legion would remain in Mexico for eight years. The convention did not specifically address Maximilian's role vis-à-vis the French military, leaving it under the command of Bazaine. This would later present complications.[11]

Fould devised a tricky financial plan egregiously to the benefit of France and highly burdensome to the Mexican empire. A loan of 270 million francs would be provided to the French expeditionary force through July 1, 1864, after which the Mexican empire would be liable for 1,000 francs annually for each soldier of the French army. But French subjects with war claims sustained during Juárez's War of the Reform must be compensated. Toward this note, 66 million francs would be paid to the French treasury at once, as an installment toward what France had already expended on the Mexican expedition. A commission composed of Mexican, English, and French citizens would monitor repayment. Aside from the military costs and claims, Maximilian figured the expense of setting up a government would be a robust 8 million francs.[12]

In the secret articles, the French emperor promised never to fail the Mexican empire, but in return Emperor Maximilian would abide by all actions of the French commander in chief, Bazaine. More importantly, he extracted the promise that the 38,000 French troops would be withdrawn only gradually, so that Mexico would retain 28,000 men through 1865; 25,000 troops through 1866; and 20,000 through 1867. These measures were vitally important to Maximilian, and he got what he wanted most: financial backing and protection. His persuasiveness surprised the French and the Austrian ministers, who had doubted Maximilian could derive any concrete promises from Napoléon.[13]

A number of people pinned a great deal of excitement and hope on Maximilian's quest. The Confederate commissioner to France, John Slidell, having previously sent an agent to speak with Maximilian at Miramar, felt certain that, once established, the Mexican empire would grant diplomatic recognition to the Confederate States of America. However, after several requests for an audience with Maximilian, through Gutiérrez de Estrada, Slidell soon learned that Maximilian considered it "inexpedient" to make arrangements with the Confederacy. Apparently, the French government advised Maximilian to hold out for official recognition from the U.S. State Department, which in likelihood would occur if the Mexican empire did not mix itself in the business of the Confederacy. Meanwhile, the determined Confederates dispatched another representative, Gen. William Preston of Kentucky, to Mexico to wait for Maximilian's arrival.[14]

On one point, Maximilian would not concede. While in Paris at the request of Napoléon III, Maximilian met with former California senator William McKendree Gwin, who proposed a project in conjunction with the French government to establish a colony and mining projects in the Mexican state of Sonora. A former plantation owner and secessionist, Gwin had fled to Paris during the Civil War, where he persuaded Napoléon that Sonora, thought to possess the richest silver veins in Mexico and fraught with "Indian hostilities," was ripe for development as a French colony. Gwin, who sought to regain his personal wealth lost in the U.S. Civil War, proposed that for the mining rights, the Mexican imperial treasury would receive 6 percent of the gross proceeds of the raw materials, ores, and precious metals, payable in bullion which could be used, in turn, to pay its debt to France. Napoléon proposed that he would support the project in return for all the mineral rights. Maximilian, however, would not discuss it, knowing little about the idea and fearing it would disturb the cohesion of his new empire. Napoléon decided to press the subject with Maximilian again once he was in Mexico.[15]

Before leaving Paris, Maximilian successfully negotiated another loan for 200 million francs from a London-based bank, which he hoped would cover pending British claims against the former regimes of Mexico. He took on more crushing debt mostly to please Great Britain and prove the mission's worthiness. Napoléon and Eugénie wrote notes with praise and thanks. Napoléon lauded his honorable and virtuous courage to regenerate Mexico. "You may be sure that my support will not fail you in the fulfillment of the task you are so courageously undertaking," he wrote. Indeed, Napoléon felt as though he no longer had to shoulder the burden of Mexico alone.[16]

As Maximilian and Carlota bid adieu to Napoléon, Eugénie presented the archduke with a gold medallion of the Virgin Mary. "It will bring you luck," she said. They said warm goodbyes and departed for England. The happy couple arrived fresh and excited from the lavish honors paid them in Paris. As they said farewell to various relatives of Carlota's, including Queen Victoria, many carefully avoided addressing them as "Emperor" and "Empress" of Mexico, as most were not in favor of their new roles. They visited Carlota's exiled grandmother, the former French queen Marie-Amélie, who remained skeptical of their future plans, herself having gone through great ordeals at the hands of Napoléon and the birth of his Second Empire. In an emotional goodbye, she warned Maximilian about being a foreign emperor in a foreign land; she burst into tears and exclaimed, "They will be murdered." The weeks of tension and worry were evident on the faces of Maximilian and Carlota.[17]

After the brief stay in England, Maximilian and Carlota arrived in Vienna on March 19 to finalize business details. Upon their arrival, Maximilian grew serious while Carlota, who usually felt great stress in the company of the Habsburgs, especially when near Empress Sisi, radiated pride and confidence. Carlota would now be her equal. They were received with the highest state honors and given an opulent reception and dinner at the imperial palace of the Hofburg. Carlota wore a diamond and emerald tiara designed for her new rank in Mexico.[18]

The doubts and disbelief of Emperor Franz Josef's ministers remained palpable. They worried over the colossal undertaking by such untested and very young rulers. Six months earlier, during a trip to Ischl, when Maximilian had first presented the idea of Mexico, Maximilian's parents objected to the scheme. His mother, Sophie, attempted to change his mind, worried that he was lured simply by adventure. He reassured her nothing was to be feared. Regardless, the royal family could see all around them that young and adventurous

Austrians considered Maximilian and Carlota's new position very glamorous, and the men could not wait to enlist in the daring Mexican mission, either to improve their rank or see the world.[19]

The next day, Maximilian faced Franz Josef on the issue of resigning his title and succession. Franz Josef, who disdained personal confrontations and preferred leaving such matters to the written word, presented Maximilian with a document called the "Family Pact," hoping to neutralize the ambitions of his brother, should he return to Austria in defeat. It called for the complete renunciation of his Austrian family title and for all his heirs and successors, as long as a male Habsburg of the imperial house still lived, even if he left Mexico. It canceled his annual financial support as well. Franz Josef explained that these demands were not without precedent, and according to Austrian law, he could not take a foreign throne without renouncing his previous title. Maximilian, who expected this would be coming, nevertheless felt deeply wounded and betrayed. He had not plumbed the matter thoroughly and could scarcely contain his anger at being handed a paper and told to sign away his heritage and his fortune. According to Empress Sisi, Maximilian, smoking one cigarette after another, finally exploded with rage and accused his brother of putting him in a helpless position, telling him that he "deliberately misled him by withholding these conditions till now, when he had pledged his word to a population of nine million people, signed the convention and contracted a loan, in all good faith, believing he was free to do so." Franz Josef admitted the timing was poor. "I cannot but be concerned for the future of my wife and the children whom I hope to have in Mexico," said Maximilian. He argued that his brother could not take away what he had inherited from his ancestors. No one could strip him of his divine right.[20]

Maximilian returned to Miramar with Carlota on March 24, seriously contemplating withdrawal from the whole Mexican design. Maximilian protested that Habsburgs had ruled all over the world—no law impeded their succession rights, so why should he be called to forfeit his entitlement? Having refused to sign the pact, he wrote letters to mentors and friends for advice, including Pope Pius IX. He nearly summoned the Mexican legation, at the time in Paris, to announce he would not serve as emperor. Notes in his journal reflected his somber regard for Mexico and that he likely regarded the crown as a temporary term, "As I am about to leave for many years to engage in a dangerous task, for the throne of Mexico is certainly a dangerous one."[21]

Worried that the entire matter would be revealed to his subjects, Franz Josef sent representatives to Miramar to force Maximilian to sign the Family

Pact. Again Maximilian refused, while threatening that he was about to turn down the Mexican throne. In an unlikely move, Franz Josef reported his difficulties to Napoléon and requested he intercede. Napoléon quickly grasped that the whole expensive, dangerous expedition was about to collapse because of terms he thought petty and frivolous. After two and a half years of war to occupy Mexico and 260 million francs ($52 million), he was bound to see his project to completion.[22]

When Eugénie heard about his dithering, she flew into a rage and wrote a harshly worded letter to Maximilian. She warned him of the "appalling scandal" he was about to create for everyone involved for putting "forward a family matter of no importance, compared with the confusion into which you are throwing the whole world. Let us have your last word, for this is a very serious business. Will you please notify your government immediately. Believe me, yours in a most justifiable ill temper, [signed] Eugénie."[23]

Napoléon blamed Franz Josef, Maximilian, and Austria's minister to France, Richard Metternich. Metternich hurried to the Tuileries to reassure Napoléon that they intended no harm to the project, that it was merely family business. In their discussion, Napoléon threatened that the situation could cause regrettable tensions between France and Austria, his project compromised by a private squabble. Napoléon suspected that Maximilian had been aware of these conditions all along but had never addressed them. "The Archduke must have known that beforehand. I must really say that I have no luck with Austria; it looks as though I were being purposely left in the lurch at the last moment," he said.[24]

Napoléon telegrammed Maximilian at Miramar, expressing his disappointment with the family fight, and reminded him of the tremendous outlay of resources expended on his behalf in Mexico. The emperor played upon Maximilian's sense of honor and duty, knowing that mention of certain key values would ring acutely in his mind, because his integrity meant everything. "By the treaty concluded between us and mutually binding," Napoléon wrote. "By the assurances given to Mexico; by the pledges exchanged with the subscribers of the loan, Your Imperial Highness has entered into engagements which you are no longer free to break. What indeed would you think of me if, once Your Imperial Majesty had arrived in Mexico, I were to say that I can no longer fulfill the conditions to which I have set my signature? . . . You are obliged by family interests . . . the honor of the house of Habsburg is at stake."[25]

Maximilian could not bear that his reputation would be shattered. Accordingly, he proposed a counteroffer: to concede to abdication if his annual allowance be continued; moreover, if he voluntarily renounced the throne of Mexico or it was taken from him, Franz Josef would set aside the agreement and reinstate his former rights. While Maximilian dreamed of ruling a country, the notion of abandoning a royal lineage presented an acute obstacle that panicked and crippled him emotionally. This lineage was his identity. The prospect of giving up his Habsburg heritage horrified him.[26]

Franz Josef authorized the emolument of Maximilian's royal allowance at 150,000 gulden or over $20,000 per year. He assured him a volunteer Austrian corps numbering at least 6,000 men and 300 sailors. Then he wrote a kindhearted, personal letter agreeing that if Maximilian's role in Mexico did not go well, a position in the Austrian empire would be promised to him. Yet Maximilian remained wary of signing the documents and desperately wanted to retreat to his island of Lacroma, where he could enjoy his gardens and forget the whole predicament. He sulked around Miramar, realizing what he was leaving behind. Out the castle windows, the sight of sailors busily preparing the *Novara* and the French frigate *Themis* for the voyage to Mexico, both laying at anchor in the bay, made little difference. He wrote a poem of lament, obliquely indicting Carlota's ambition for his troubles.[27]

Carlota understood this dilemma, and Napoléon continued to demand an answer. She herself looked forward to the challenge in Mexico and getting on with the project. As a woman of quick decisions and marked action, she felt she could better negotiate with Franz Josef. So on his behalf, she made a short trip to Vienna to plead Maximilian's case against forced relinquishment. She had gotten her father's advice on the matter: "My beloved child, nothing ought to be given up of the position which is his birthright," but also warned "do not give up the Mexican business, since it will lead to senseless confusion." With her father's words in mind to never release their inheritable rights, she discussed the matter with Franz Josef, but he refused her entire argument. She appealed to Archduchess Sophie to intercede, but she could not persuade her son either. So in the end, Carlota convinced her brother-in-law to travel to Miramar to meet with Maximilian again and come to some kind of an agreement.[28]

On April 9 at 8 a.m., Franz Josef arrived at the family's private royal train station and made his way to Miramar, attended by his two brothers, Archdukes Karl Ludwig and Ludwig Victor. He was accompanied by ministers and chancellors wanting to bid farewell to Maximilian and Carlota, along with representatives from Hungary, Croatia, and Transylvania. Maximilian and Franz

Josef went immediately into the library for their deliberations, which grew heated, smoky, and emotional, as they tried to come to suitable terms. After several hours of debate and stewing, Maximilian signed the Family Pact. When the agreement was announced, the naval orchestra outside the castle played Haydn's *Gott erhalte unser Kaiser*. Following the emotional session, Carlota took Franz Josef's arm and led him into the dining room for a brief lunch. Afterward, Maximilian went with his brothers to the train station. Just before boarding, Franz Josef turned to Maximilian and extended his arms, saying "Max," and kissed him, tears welling his eyes, not knowing if he would ever see him again.[29]

The next day, the Mexican delegation arrived at Miramar from Trieste. The members had lingered in Paris for five months, waiting for his final decision. Again, the committee led by José María Gutiérrez de Estrada and José Manuel Hidalgo arrived to find Maximilian in his formal dress surrounded by his secretaries and Austrian and French diplomats. Carlota, in a pink gown adorned by the Order of Malta and her diadem, stood by his side. With a good portion of the castle still under construction, they moved into Carlota's state apartment, where a parchment roll placed on a small table listed the names of all the Mexican towns that had given their assent to the new monarchy. Observers noted that Carlota smiled and seemed happy, while Maximilian's pale face revealed fatigue and stiffness. He nervously ruffled the papers presented to him.[30]

Speaking in French, Gutiérrez de Estrada lauded the couple and intoned the virtues of his beautiful homeland of Mexico. After his lengthy speech, he proclaimed them emperor and empress of Mexico. Maximilian replied in Spanish, glancing at prepared remarks. He promised to rule as a constitutional monarch and grant the country a liberal constitution. He recited an oath of office and finalized the military convention with France, along with decrees concerning the deployment of the Austrian and Belgian corps. After cheers of "Viva Emperador Maximiliano!," "Viva Emperatriz Carlota!," and a twenty-one-gun salute, they attended mass in Miramar's chapel. The castle guard raised the newly designed imperial standard of the Mexican empire over Miramar, and the *Novara* and *Themis* sounded their artillery in celebration.[31]

Interestingly, the two principal legation members who worked so diligently to bring Maximilian to Mexico decided to stay in Europe. Gutiérrez de Estrada, who had not been back to Mexico in twenty-five years, elected to remain in his palazzo in Rome. Hidalgo, whose family still lived in Mexico, feared that his homeland would be too inclement for him and chose to remain a member of

Napoléon's court in Paris in the company of Eugénie. He did, however, accept the important post of Mexican minister to France, to maintain official relations with Napoléon and the French government.[32]

Among Maximilian's advisors, the question lingered whether he had accepted the throne of Mexico wholly of his own free will or because of Carlota. A number believed Maximilian capitulated to his wife, based on some anecdotes surrounding the ceremony of April 10. The night before, Maximilian let slip, in front of a family member, these words: "For my part, if someone were to tell me that everything was off, I would shut myself up in my room and jump for joy! But Carlota?" That evening after his confirmation ceremony, the radiant empress presided over a grand banquet, while Maximilian took ill with a fever and retired to the Gartenhaus, the two-story cottage where they lived while waiting completion of Miramar. This postponed their departure. He remained secluded there for three days, coming out only to stroll the grounds and admire Miramar, dreading his departure from the calm Adriatic idyll. On April 11, the day the royal couple planned to embark for Mexico, the empress arrived at breakfast with a telegram of congratulations from Napoléon. Maximilian brusquely set his fork down on the table and cried, "I don't want to hear about Mexico now, I tell you."[33]

Carlota and the royal staff entertained an endless procession of visitors, while Maximilian remained sulking and cloistered. She met with various personnel assembling and preparing for the voyage, never mentioning her husband's troubles. She remained busy, calm, and excited, beaming with confidence. After some days of sorting out his troubles and the burdens of his new station in Mexico, Maximilian emerged from his isolation on April 13, seemingly in better spirits and ready to leave. He set about drafting letters and telegrams, replying to Napoléon's wire with congratulations to the newly titled Maximilian I of Mexico, which Carlota tried to give him two days earlier. Maximilian addressed his response to "my brother" Napoléon, as emperors called one another, reporting on the settling of his family matters with Franz Josef and that he would perform his duties with proficiency. Franz Josef and Sisi expressed their hope that God would guide them. His parents, Archduke Franz Karl and Archduchess Sophie, sent a wire from Vienna hoping that God would protect them and bidding them farewell from their native soil, "where alas we may see you no more."[34]

During Maximilian's days of isolation, nearly one hundred porters and longshoremen loaded and ferried trunks, crates, and strongboxes to the anchored *Novara* and *Themis*. They stowed crates of bone china made for the new empire

Maximilian and Carlota depart Miramar at Trieste, Italy,
for Veracruz, April 14, 1864

by Minton, along with crystal, kitchen equipment, furniture, linens, foods, wines, liqueurs, paintings, and art, all chosen for the royal household. A set of Christofle silver flatware, commissioned for their new imperial home with Maximilian's insignia, would arrive later from France on one of the regular transports. Carefully, they also loaded two carriages designed by Milanese artisan Cesare Sala of Carrozzeria Italiana, one lavishly gilded with *putti* and carved scrollwork, the other a more utilitarian town coach, seating four to six, in black with the royal crests. Both were disassembled and ready for shipment. The gilt coach with its complicated harnesses, beveled glass windows, and accoutrements of cast silver and embroidered velvet, would serve as the official ceremonial conveyance in Mexico. In all, to equip the household and ship it to Mexico, they spent nearly 300,000 pesos, with 21,500 spent on wine alone.[35]

On the morning of April 14, the people of the surrounding Italian countryside and villages lined the roads and the Adriatic shore, waiting to send them off. The mayor and chamber of commerce of Trieste arrived on boats sponsored by Austrian Lloyd, a shipping company and insurance consortium, to present an album of views of Trieste and read a proclamation of bon voyage signed by 6,000 citizens. The mayor, councilmen, the royal couple, and the staff were in tears at the end of the presentation, as was Maximilian. By two in the afternoon, it was time to leave. The boilers of the *Novara* erupted into steam. Ribbon-capped sailors from the *Novara* rowed a royal launch decorated with a gold and red canopy, the Mexican imperial crest, flags, and red linens to the castle's jetty, strewn with flowers. Maximilian and Carlota descended the white stone stairs to the jetty and, in a shower of blown petals, steadied themselves into the rowboat, as the Mexican imperial anthem played in the background. As Paula Kollonitz, Carlota's lady-in-waiting, said, it all began with a step.[36]

The *Novara* slowly pulled out of the harbor, escorted by the *Themis*, a few frigates, and celebrating fishermen, sailing down the Croatian coast for some leagues until they were out to sea. Taking in the sea air, Maximilian expressed his joy at being on the ocean again, revived at the prospect of his investiture and new life. Carlota enjoyed his high spirits, as did the rest of the staff and crew. Four days later, they steamed into the Italian harbor of Civitavecchia to a thunder of cannon salutes. From the port, Maximilian and Carlota traveled the thirty-five miles to Rome for an audience with Pope Pius IX. Although they sought his insights and blessings before the thirty-six-day crossing to Veracruz, Maximilian decided to say little regarding the Mexican Clerical party's demands to overturn Juárez's reforms.[37]

At the Eternal City, an array of soldiers, including the Swiss Guard and French troops—Rome being under the current protection of France—staged a formal welcoming ceremony for the young sovereigns. Maximilian and Carlota stayed at the lavish Palazzo Marescotti as the guest of Gutiérrez de Estrada, who arranged an opulent dinner party in their honor. The king of Naples and Pius IX's chief minister, Cardinal Giacomo Antonelli, paid them a visit. The next day in the presence of the pope, Maximilian touched on the need to have a representative, a papal nuncio, come to Mexico to negotiate church issues. The charming Pio Nono gave them holy communion and his blessing. The couple toured the Coliseum by moonlight and the next day visited relatives. After their four-day visit, the royal couple and staff returned to the *Novara* and weighed anchor on April 20.[38]

Arriving at Gibraltar, a grand cannon salute from the British garrison ordered by Queen Victoria greeted the *Novara*, and to Maximilian and Carlota, this meant a great deal, a sign of her best wishes. The Spanish at

Cádiz also fired their artillery in tribute as they rounded the Costa de la Luz. Afterward, the ship turned southwest to the Island of Madeira, where for a few days the Portuguese officials fêted the royal party. With these last expressions of esteem, the young princess Carlota concluded that England, Spain, and Portugal all approved of the mission. "We are in official relations with all the Powers," she wrote happily.[39]

As they cruised the Atlantic, the young sovereigns conferred with their staff, including former valet turned secretary, Austrian Sebastian Scherzenlechner, Belgian Félix Eloin, an engineer, and Mexican minister of state Joaquín Velázquez de León. Mostly they created a set of rules and regulations for the new attendants in Mexico, a court ceremonial, largely drawn from similar royal household protocols in Austria and France. Carlota aided Maximilian in this new guide that came to be entitled *Reglamento para el Servicio y Ceremonial de la Corte*. Meanwhile, Maximilian continued to fume over the Family Pact, feeling that his brother forced him to sign it. He drafted a formal protest and repudiation of the arrangement. Written mostly by Carlota, it was addressed to the various territorial legislative assemblies under the crown of Habsburg-Lorraine, swearing under oath that Maximilian had never heard of Austria's Acts of Renunciation until he had been forced to sign it, after all the commitments for the Mexican empire had been settled. By claiming his brother extorted his signature, Maximilian hoped he would find support in the Austrian parliament. The document later became public knowledge, causing the emperor Franz Josef considerable embarrassment.[40]

The only difficulty on the trip stemmed from the limited amount of coal that could be taken aboard the *Novara*, and without good trade winds, the *Themis* took the steamer under tow to the island of Martinique where they could refuel. During this coal shortage in the Caribbean, Carlota's lady-in-waiting expressed relief at the quiet sailing, without the incessantly droning engines. Much to the staff's amazement, they encountered dolphins, dogfish, and flying fish, which sailors called *blé de la mer*. Then they found jellyfish in the water, which they termed "floating roses." Maximilian ordered the sailors to catch one in a net, and it was brought aboard for inspection, the staff marveling at the "long threads" of rose-color that stung if they touched it. Carlota spent the remainder of the voyage practicing Spanish and planning. Violent weather on the last leg of their trip caused flooding in the cabins of the staff. Carlota's stateroom was unaffected, and she continued to write quixotically about the tropics, the butterflies, and hummingbirds.[41]

In preparation for their arrival at Veracruz, Maximilian's aide, Ángel Iglesias, sent a notice to Almonte via the *Themis*, which arrived first, "to prepare everything that is necessary for their majesties and their retinue, so as not to delay them on their trip to the capital." He attached a precise schedule of the people arriving and a list of events as they should occur. "As you will see in the program, the Majesty wants the people who arrive with him to be divided in two entourages, one to go with the sovereigns and one to go before or after . . . so both entourages can travel [at once]. You know the danger of delays in Veracruz," he wrote.[42] At the time, they did not know that Almonte was not in Veracruz but inland at Córdoba, having made only scant preparation for their landing.

Almonte dissolved the provisional regency to take power as a lieutenant under the emperor. He issued a manifesto to Mexico that inaugurated the policy of the regents, who awaited Maximilian. "A government that owes its existences to the combined action of national interests and of magnanimous and civilizing France, should reflect in its conduct the elements to which it owes its origin," he wrote, blaming the Juárez administration for the poor condition of Mexico, which he recounted in detail. When they founded the regency fourteen months earlier, the government had no employees, important archives had either been dispersed or mutilated, and the public treasury was bankrupt. He wrote that "the resources that were to aliment it [had] entirely dried up, not only by imprudence and incapability but also by the truly criminal system of the failed government that had depopulated the towns and countrysides, annihilated agriculture, killed industry and commerce and destroyed safety, peace, and confidence everywhere." He added, "It would have been impossible to take one step, without the efficient cooperation of men and the politic of intervention," pointing to his temporary government's success in restoring a functioning infrastructure. Then he identified the framework he and the regents expected Maximilian to follow by example: "During its existence, Mexico has seen, as a phenomena, all its public service employees and contracts paid religiously."[43]

A French general, Charles François du Barail, who suffered a rough duty in Mexico with his health forever damaged in Veracruz, chose to retire and leave Mexico in early May 1864. Somewhere on his crossing, as he relaxed looking out at the ocean, he noticed in the distance "two little trails of smoke, ever so light, like that which slips from a cigarette between two inhalations." The captain identified the steamer as the *Novara* transporting Maximilian to Mexico. Du Barail thought to himself,

Poor Maximilian. What are they going to do in that atrocious country which I leave without regret; and those people who have been tearing one another apart for more than forty years . . . in this Mexico without trade or industry; in the Mexico which has been killed by its mining wealth, leaving civil war the only possible branch of human activity. The very defenders of your throne, those Mexicans who have called you, will abandon you, because you cannot go through with their retrograde plans. . . . If you succeed in bringing order out of this chaos . . . you will be the greatest sovereign of modern times. But I very much fear that the task you have undertaken is above human strength. Good luck.[44]

❧ 7 ❧

The Future Will Be Splendid

Chapultepec Palace, Mexico City, June 1864

After only eight days in the hot, dusty, and deteriorated National Palace on the Zócalo in Mexico City, Maximilian and Carlota decided to vacate their plans to live in the city's center. From the first tortuous night on June 12, 1864, in which they suffered from bedbugs and other vermin, the royal couple found the crumbling and noisy administrative building in the main plaza too much like living in a military barracks. The emperor and empress decided to enlarge and refurbish nearby Chapultepec Palace, a Spanish vice-regal home built between 1783 and 1785, approximately four miles west of the city on a high basalt hill overlooking the Valley of Mexico. Their first idea had been to make Chapultepec their summer palace, like Schönbrunn near Vienna, the retreat of the Habsburgs. But it was evident the couple felt more at home outside of the city. For official business and state events, however, they decided to retain quarters in the National Palace.[1]

Chapultepec, known to the Aztecs as Grasshopper Hill, had long been an important site to indigenous peoples and coveted by the Spaniards. It remained a magisterial spectacle. Maximilian deemed it ideally suited for a Habsburg monarch. The magnificent views of the Valley of Mexico, its church domes, and Lakes Texcoco, Xochimilco, and Chalco enchanted the sovereigns, who concluded that they could live nowhere else. The woods remained mystical and enchanted to many of the citizens. The place has a beauty he had "seen

National Palace, Mexico City, Mexico

perhaps only at Sorrento," wrote Maximilian. Cypress trees, or *ahuehuetes*, nearly two hundred feet tall and considered sacred, encircled the plateau, along with an array of vines, flowering plants, and butterflies that created a disarming ecosphere. Summiting its bluffs, visitors could not ignore the stunning, snow-capped summits of the twin volcanoes of Iztaccihuatl and Popocatépetl.[2]

Maximilian happily adopted the old, unfinished castle as his project, and he put his heart into its renovation. With the same fervor with which he created Miramar, he designated enormous amounts of money for the design and restoration of the old palace. He appointed well-known Austrian architect Carl Gangolf Kayser as official court designer to assist with the improvements and brought Julius Hofmann from Miramar to design the interior. In order to renovate as quickly as possible, Maximilian hired over two hundred laborers. He commissioned the Mexican artist Santiago Rebull to decorate the salons and private apartments as well as restore the various murals. To add to the sumptuousness of the royal residence, the couple installed artifacts in the style of Vienna's Hofburg Palace, including huge alabaster vases, French wallpaper, and bronze or gilded candelabras. Crimson silk damask embroidered with the imperial motto *Equidad en la Justicia* (Equity in Justice) milled in Europe covered the walls of one salon. Napoléon also made a gift of tapestries depicting the art of various sports, which they installed in a small parlor. Maximilian's spending on the project somewhat alarmed Carlota, but she did not discourage his enthusiasm.[3]

With Wilhelm Knechtel, his landscape designer from Miramar, he mapped out a circular cobblestone drive that wound up the hill to the summit. Carlota helped redesign the surrounding park and gardens to make them more formal by her standards, while retaining their fascinating native specimens. Maximilian, with his passion for plants and taxonomy, commissioned Dr. Dominik Bilimek, a gentle Moravian priest trained as a botanist and zoologist, to collect, study, and classify the spectacular plant and insect specimens so foreign to Europeans.[4]

At the castle, the staff was instructed on the formal protocols of the household, similar to the procedures employed in Austria, France, and Belgium. The procedures followed the court ceremonial, which Maximilian, Carlota, and their chamberlain finished soon after their arrival. The royal retinue was made familiar with these rules. In some ways, Maximilian viewed the high dress, ribbons, decorations, and pageantry as part of the history of Europe, not Mexico. As much as he loved the fantasy of life without ceremony, he was not ready to go raw and unadorned without these essential elements of royal reign. The manual as written freed him from the unpleasant inculcation of court traditions to staff members unfamiliar with the strict and obscure protocol. In it, Maximilian flouted pomp and ceremony when he could yet imposed strict formalities for the ministers, aides, and military, including seating order for receptions, dinners, and church services, dishes and wines served, the order of outriders and guards, and staffing.[5]

To reward service to the crown, Maximilian and Carlota established three different orders for people who provided beneficial service: the Order of the Mexican Eagle and the Order of Guadalupe, administered by Maximilian, and the Order of San Carlos, for Carlota's dispensation to other ladies. As grand master of the Order of the Mexican Eagle, Maximilian bestowed a medallion of gold and enamel depicting the Mexican eagle holding a serpent in its beak, encircled by the imperial diadem, which hung from a silk blue ribbon. He conferred this honor to a limited number of honorees, including knights, officers, commanders, and grand officers. Decorations went to citizens and foreigners who distinguished themselves in service to the empire. The Order of Guadalupe went to citizens only and was not as exclusive. Carlota awarded two classes of San Carlos, the grand cross and the small cross, to women in her service or who provided extraordinary assistance to the empire. In addition to these, both presented numerous other small awards in the form of enam-

Chapultepec Palace, Mexico City, Mexico

eled rings, pins, and watches with the imperial crest or Maximilian's insignia. Sometimes these sought-after decorations caused anxiety and jealousy among ambitious ministers, envoys, and ladies of the court.[6]

Maximilian maintained a disciplined schedule, often retiring to his quarters in the early evening. At dusk, he often took a stroll on the terraces or roof to think and enjoy the view; "my old treasurer (Kuhachevich) has usually to accompany me, for his sins," wrote Maximilian wryly. He then went to bed by eight or nine in order to rise at four in the morning to begin work during the early sacred hours, following the precept that eight hours of sleep ensured health and a long life and waking early led a wise leader to pray and contemplate in peace. Upon awaking, in his candlelit quarters, dressed in a blue flannel robe and chamois slippers, he looked over papers and correspondence. His secretary slept down the hall, and the emperor usually summoned him with an electric bell, at which time the secretary awoke and dressed quickly. "After tapping lightly at the emperor's door, I would enter, with my portfolio of papers," recalled his secretary, José Luis Blasio, hired when the emperor's previous secretary, the young Austrian Nicholas Poliakowitz, fell from a horse and fractured his arm. Blasio could speak French, while members of Maximilian's staff knew not a word of Spanish. While Blasio read Maximilian his correspondence, valets removed his dressing gown, and standing in his shirt, he washed his face and hands. The valet helped him in his riding clothes and cloak.[7]

"We would finish a little before seven o'clock, I would hasten to don my charro suit, lock my door and proceed to the patio, where grooms were ready with our saddled horses." Maximilian would not let his aide sleep in and miss the ride, no matter the cause; he simply insisted he accompany him. The emperor often rode a gentle horse named Anteburro, whom he named after the South American tapir, an animal that had fascinated him in Brazil. He cantered through the grounds of Chapultepec, to the Alameda, or the adjacent countryside. At 9 a.m. he took an elaborate breakfast with Carlota and a few private secretaries, which involved several courses and wines. After breakfast, Maximilian would ride to the National Palace in his coach with his secretary always seated to his left, and escorted by a small group of mounted guards. The remainder of the day, Maximilian held cabinet meetings, ceremonies, and regular business of state at the National Palace. In his offices and apartments, he kept decanters of water and red and white wine, sweet breads, and biscuits in his apartments. "Whenever Maximilian, who was a heavy smoker, came in without a cigar in his mouth, he took one from a tray. Frequently, he would dip a biscuit in wine and eat it," said Blasio.[8]

Maximilian generally liked to be left to his wiles, uninterrupted, and focused on his own concerns for some hours in the day. "I am not of a particularly happy nature," Maximilian wrote. "Among other defects, I have a feeling of absolute independence, so that even the empress, with her very particular tact, never enters my quarters or disrupts my work without my invitation. She knows my weakness on this point, and because she adapts to it, our harmony has never been troubled." He concluded it was best to communicate with his staff and ministers by memo, following the example of Leopold, his father-in-law, who corresponded with nearly everyone in writing, even with his sons who lived under the same roof. Despite his admiration for such discipline, Maximilian remained too lenient and sensitive to follow that rule, often enforcing policies only to break them later.[9]

Most days Maximilian dressed informally, some said too informally, in a simple frock coat and high-crowned hat, sometimes in Tyrolean style or a small sombrero. In tropical weather, he wore white clothes and a Panama straw hat with a gold cord. He soon adopted Mexican style of dress when riding, much to the amusement of his fellow Austrians. While still in Italy, he became familiar with Mexico's tradition of exquisite dress and gear, had an officer's uniform made, and when he first tried on the embroidered pants and jacket, he felt half-embarrassed, whispering to an aide in German that he looked ridiculous. Later in Mexico, he altered the charro suit and added a gray

Maximilian in charro attire, ca. 1864

sombrero with a white hatband woven with gold. Reportedly, the first time he put on the suit of the *jinete*, to go out riding, he felt so self-conscious that he tried to pass out of the palace doors unnoticed, saying that he felt comfortable only after being seated on his horse. He also appreciated finely embroidered Mexican saddles and accoutrements with silver filigree and detailing. Others came to copy his style.[10]

Carlota's tastes inspired an admiration for all things European, which changed the attitudes of courtiers, the food they ate, the formality of service, and the manner of dress. At court occasions she preferred European standards in dress and etiquette, and this she expected in her guests, but mostly she wore the attire of the Mexican upper classes. "As for our costumes, we dress in Mexican fashion, I go out riding in a sombrero, our meals are in the Mexican style, we have a carriage drawn by mules with quantities of bells, we never use any wraps but serapes. I go to Mass in a mantilla . . . so in all that is external and puerile we conform to all that is most Mexican, to such an extent as to amaze the very Mexicans themselves," Carlota wrote to Eugénie.[11] Although they influenced the spread of European haute customs in Mexico, she and Maximilian wanted to show their commitment by demonstrating adherence to native dress and customs. They wanted to appear Mexican.

Carlota had fourteen ladies-in-waiting, selected from the wives of distinguished gentlemen in the court. They included Dolores Quesada de Almonte; Guadalupe Cervantes de Morán, the Marquesa de Vivanco; and Gertrudis Enriques y Segura, the Condesa del Valle. The ladies' responsibilities included acting as an intermediary to Carlota, accompanying her on walks or carriage rides, to the theater or mass, and court functions. The women reveled in the high social position. Carlota wrote that the *damas* were mostly "honorary, but they take forever when I send them to fetch something." They were expected to be formal with her and not too affectionate. When once the wife of a Mexican general casually offered her a cigarette, she politely informed the woman that her doctor discouraged the practice. In short order, smoking among the women in her elite circles was out of vogue.[12]

Carlota became close with some of her ladies. One attendant, Otilia Jordan de Degollado, the Virginia-born wife of Maximilian's aide and minister to Washington, Mariano Degollado, rode horseback nearly every day with Carlota. While many Mexican women were not trained equestrians, Otilia grew up riding sidesaddle in the American South and could keep pace with Carlota. Afterward they sometimes ate breakfast together, where Carlota attended to matters of state. "I never saw such an industrious woman in my life," said Degollado. "She read a great deal, besides conducting all the correspondence with the crowned heads of Europe."[13]

Maximilian's secretary, Blasio, also worked with her in the executive offices. "She spoke Spanish without the least accent, very slowly, as though she were meditating each of her phrases before uttering it. She was a trifle nearsighted and almost always, when addressing a person, narrowed her eyes as though to see better," he recalled. She usually wore dark colors, her gowns high at the neck with a bit of lace at the wrists or collar, her long, dark hair worn up.[14]

While the sovereigns lived at Chapultepec during its renovation, they authorized a 750,000-peso refurbishment of the National Palace. Small rooms were converted into a large ballroom named the Salon of the Ambassadors. When Maximilian noticed the giant wooden beams in the ceiling were cedar, he ordered them stripped and partially gilded. Carvings in the patios, the chapel, and dining room were restored. Carlota requested from Paris embroidered silks and toile specially depicting the French victories in Mexico. She and Maximilian spent 101,000 pesos on furniture, carpets, and crystal sufficient to reflect "royal dignity." Carlota removed prior decorations and furnishings that she condemned as tasteless, and she was particular about the things she put in the palace. However, when her ladies-in-waiting presented her with a mirrored vanity table, she called it a "jewel" and used it.[15]

Carlota commanded the planning and design of white-tie royal dinners and the occasional ball, which she usually gave on Monday evenings, either at the National Palace or Chapultepec. Known as *Los lunes de la Emperatriz*, the events, which began at eight o'clock, were held for various foreign delegations, military officers, professors, friends, and supporters. Nearly styled in European court traditions, the salons, attended by liveried servants, were decorated according to the occasion with gold candelabras and dinner service in the dining room. At eleven, a formal dinner was served, the menus listed neatly at each place. They spared no expense on the cuisine, prepared by French chefs, and comprised of the finest French and Viennese specialties, including soups, oysters, fish, beef cutlets, vol-au-vent, salmon tartare, quail, and truffles. Numerous wines and cognacs accompanied each course, along with the French champagnes Roederer and Veuve Clicquot. Dessert included asparagus, sorbet, cakes, and puddings. After the meal, the guests were invited to a concert or a dance to the royal orchestra's waltzes. The sovereigns enjoyed listening to the music of Strauss, Verdi, Schubert, and Haydn. They also danced quadrilles, mazurkas, and polkas. During the dancing and drinking, the social and cultural barriers were relaxed. As the champagne flowed, the guests sang "La Marseillaise" and danced the habanera.[16]

Visiting artists performed operatic or orchestral performances, such as Rossini's *Barber of Seville*, Bellini's *Norma*, Verdi's *Un Ballo in Maschera*, Gounod's *Faust Serenade*, Jehin-Prume's *Fantasia*, and Goethe's *Faust*. Private promoters brought comedies, ballets, and burlesque performances, such as *Deux Divorces*, to Mexico City, while the Foreign Legion also produced musicals. The Parisian artists often had a difficult journey from Veracruz but appeared in costume and makeup for private performances at the palace, repeated later for the public at other venues.[17]

At gala events, Maximilian, who was a close observer, noticed nearly everything at social gatherings and commented on almost everything: the ladies' dresses; the young man married to a much older woman, (he could not see how he could wed this mummy of bones and parchment in fine jewelry); the court official with twelve children, whom he termed "patriotic" for adding to the population of the empire; and finally, the women who flashed arduous eyes at him, commenting that they would be formidable lovers. After the entertainment, in his own salon Maximilian handed out gilded cigars and engaged his guests in billiards, while telling scandalous stories about his Mexican ministers, sometimes making crude or bawdy remarks in German, thinking only the most sophisticated guests could understand his dry wit. Losing billiard players would have to crawl under the table, unless Maximilian lost, in which case a servant would do the honor. Maximilian wrote about one dinner, "The diplomatists gorge and swill to such an extent that as a rule after dinner they can only mumble inarticulate sounds." Especially in the first year of their reign, these events displayed all the excesses of the wealthiest courts in Europe, with the bill for one such fiesta totaling 105,000 pesos. With frequent dinners such as these, the royal household went through over seven hundred bottles of wine a month. One frequent guest commented that wines were "said to be a part of His Majesty's machinery of government, and none who had once tasted, ever forgot their flavor or questioned . . . whoever made the selection."[18]

In the eyes of one guest, eighteen-year-old Sara Stevenson, Carlota's fêtes were dull and ceremonious, perhaps too formal for a young, unmarried girl. In the "insufficiently lighted" ballroom, dancing would cease when the emperor and empress toured the crowd before the formal dinner, giving a nod or some superficial comment. Despite the party's atmosphere, she admired Maximilian. She wrote, "Tall, slight and handsome . . . he looked, and was, a gentleman. His dignity was without hauteur." He had a gift of putting people at ease and "possessed far more personal magnetism than the empress," she wrote. Carlota's strong, intelligent face was somewhat hard at times, though "her determined expression impressed one with a feeling that she was the better equipped of the two to cope intelligently with the difficulties of practical life." Stevenson agreed with others: "It is probable that, had she been alone, she might have made a better attempt at solving . . . problems than did Maximilian" as she showed firmness and clear judgments in meetings she conducted. However, Stevenson describes her as "reserved, somewhat lacking in tact and adaptability." She further explained that the empress had a dignity that "at first repelled many who were disposed to feel kindly toward her." Indeed, Carlota at times used great formality or kept a low profile as a defense against awkward situations, her insecurities, and to assure that people took her seriously. Stevenson continued, somewhat presciently, "It is more than likely that under this proud mien, she concealed a suffering spirit, or at least a consciousness of a superiority which had to efface itself."[19]

In the midst of dinner or dancing, thunderous cannon fire sometimes interrupted the festivities as various Republican factions launched forays against imperial troops guarding the city. In response, Maximilian ordered an artillery battery and a squad of soldiers to surround Chapultepec to shield attacks. "My parties end after one o'clock," wrote Carlota in February 1865.

> Next Monday will be the sixth. I dance a few quadrilles, one of which is regularly with General L'Hérillier. I am gradually inviting all the French officers, even the paymasters, who had a great longing to dance. Life here is almost like the Middle Ages, we are . . . contented and calm, and yet there is nothing to prevent a band of guerrillas from falling upon us at any minute. Up here [at Chapultepec] we have cannon and a system of signals for communicating with the city. But that does not prevent us from being always on the lookout. The night before last I got up on hearing cannon-fire; it was a tumultuous celebration in honor of the Virgin of Tacubaya . . . at four in the morning; I suppose it was to allow for the difference of time between here and Jerusalem. All religious festivities take place here at night, amid an explosion of firecrackers, as if the earth were being rent asunder.[20]

When Maximilian took the opportunity to write to his family in Austria, he often boasted about his life in Mexico. He even made gibes at the ways of Europeans and remarked that he was steering Mexico toward a more sophisticated, businesslike approach. Although they had large and sumptuous social occasions, he said, "We very seldom give dinners." He wrote, after a few months living at Chapultepec, "The serious character of the Mexicans, a quality which is much to my liking, demands this, thank God, and leaves me plenty of time for my real work. The so-called entertainments of Europe, such as evening receptions, the gossip of tea parties . . . of hideous memory are quite unknown here, and we shall take good care not to introduce them. The Mexican's only enjoyment is to ride about this beautiful country on his fine horse and go to the theatre frequently."[21]

Maximilian's house staff also included his old friend and aide-de-camp, Charles Bombelles, the son of his former tutor, who managed the royal stables. Bombelles divided the barns into two sections: the European stable held the horses for town and ceremonial use, and the national stables housed the horses and mules trained for overland travel. He also directed twenty-five coachmen and grooms. Maximilian delighted in fine transportation, eventually commissioning thirty-three carriages in his royal fleet, some built by his aide, Feliciano Rodríguez. "You would be much amused to see us in our Mexican equipage, a little, quite open carriage, as light as a feather, the famous Mexican state coachman on the box, with his gigantic white hat, green velvet tunic and full, white linen trousers, with his poncho of three colors round his shoulders . . . driving a team of six cream-colored mules with zebra hoofs, two of them harnessed at the shaft, the four harnessed in a row in front, an outrider on a cream-colored horse with rich silver-mounted Mexican harness; and the whole turnout racing madly along as swift as an arrow," he wrote. On the weekends, he coordinated charro exhibitions and coleaderos at Chapultepec for his ministers and guests, embracing the country's legacy of horsemanship.[22] Life in Mexico City seemed pretty and idyllic, despite serious problems bubbling below the surface.

Both Maximilian and Carlota charmed the Mexican elite, the indigenous tribes, and visiting foreign ministers by learning their customs and their languages. People marveled at how well Maximilian spoke Spanish, albeit cautiously. He spoke ten languages: fluent in German, he could converse in French, Flemish, Italian, Latin, and English as well as Hungarian, Czech, Polish, and Croatian. Carlota preferred to speak German with her husband but was fluent in French, English, Italian, and Spanish. She was a prolific writer and note taker, sending copious amounts of correspondence in her tight, small handwriting using the sharpest nibs, rather as though she wrote with a needle.[23]

From the beginning, it was apparent that Carlota would be a partner to Maximilian in ruling the country. Her first impressions indicated that she knew little about the regime of Benito Juárez but recognized that many more reforms were badly needed: "It is an appalling task, for when a country has spent forty years of its existence in destroying all that it possessed in the way of resources and government, everything cannot be set right in a day. This does not alarm us, I merely state the fact." Carlota knew they must force a paradigm change upon Mexicans from all social and economic levels. She was sure the people had grown tired of pompous and ineffective presidents, although she recognized the people's respect for Juárez. However, they had welcomed a monarch of a plain and simple style, like Maximilian, she reasoned. Because Maximilian was born in Europe, there could be no posturing or infighting among politicians or parties. He intended to lead by example, with honor and fairness. When Carlota and Maximilian spoke, they attempted to communicate to all people, hoping they would support the goals of the empire.[24]

Since one of Maximilian's main precepts included governing coolly, calmly, and firmly, in his first year he attempted to take a firm stance against insubordination, brooking no petty partisanship or interests, reasoning, "The good people must first learn to obey." He drafted various decrees that retained many of the old reforms established by Juárez, while planning to clean up and realign the major institutions in the country. "There are three classes which are the worst thing I have found in the country so far: the judicial functionaries, the army officers, and the greater part of the clergy. None of them know their duties and they live for money alone. The judges are corrupt, the officers have no sense of honor, and clergy are lacking in Christian charity and morality. But all this does not make me lose hope for the future," he wrote.[25]

Maximilian determined to reverse the country's tradition of polarized party affiliations and favoritism. He dismissed the provisional government and formed a council of state on December 4, 1864, retaining only a few conservatives including Teodosio Lares and Joaquín Velázquez de León. He composed the new council of ministers not only of French or Austrians but mostly Mexicans, and a few were former Liberal partisans. He attempted to unify former enemies, to demonstrate a lack of partiality, but moreover to avoid jealousies and indignation within various offices. Rather shocking to the Monarchists, Maximilian appointed Liberal lawyer José Fernando Ramírez, a scholar of anthropology and native dialects, as minister of foreign affairs. As the founder of the Mexican Academy of Sciences and Literature, Ramírez lent a level of erudition and thoughtful insight Maximilian wanted his administration to reflect, opposed to the stringent notions of the reactionary clerics. Therefore, he abruptly raised the suspicions and resentments of the Church party members he excluded. Neither could Maximilian tolerate his ministers' pandering to Napoléon in detriment to Mexico and demoted a few, including Almonte, who had supported France's Sonoran mining scheme. The experienced diplomat managed ceremonies as "High Marshal of the Court" for the first few months. In a country where many people were closely allied to a political party, Maximilian's actions shook up the standard model of the factional rivalries. He wished to publicly distance himself in a spirit of openness. Although he often dined with Ramírez as well as Luis Robles Pezuela, the minister of commerce, and Feliciano Rodríguez, his aide-de-camp, Maximilian kept a closer, private council, comprised mostly of European advisors and military officers, contrary to how he wanted to be perceived.[26]

If any one word could describe Maximilian's doctrine for his empire, despite its limitations, it was "regenerate." He felt, somewhat naïvely, that by extirpating political feuds and finding the virtues within all parties, he could return Mexico to its former glory, grand and splendid as he saw it under the dazzling reign of his Habsburg predecessor Charles V, on whose vast empire the sun never set, despite the fact that his heroic sovereign ancestor never visited the Americas. Maximilian trusted a network of regional advisors and prefects to maintain their respective region's loyalty to the empire. He wrote encouraging letters to his imperial representatives that the reorganization of the country after many years of unrest would take "patience and confidence in God." The empire's official newspaper, *Diario del Imperio,* which carried the court and administrative news, reported his plans.[27]

Maximilian was also very careful to include the indigenous classes of the country, stating they must rise from their "humiliations" and humble existences as the overlooked segment of Mexico's communities and oppressed by the Catholic Church. Groups such as the Nahuas, Otomís, Tarascans, Zapotecs, Mixtecs, Totonacs, and Huastecs, instead of considering themselves part of the Mexican nation, lived in closed worlds with poor-quality farmland and a low standard of living. Maximilian worked to cultivate the goodwill of the native tribes, which he termed the *clases menesterosas* (poverty-stricken classes). He took great labor to understand and speak their languages, such as Nahuatl, and appointed the Nahua academician Faustino Chimalpopoca to his ministry, consulting him not only on the language but also anthropology and the lives of these Aztec descendants. Chimalpopoca, whose name meant "Smoking Shield," had a deep understanding of his brethren. He saw in the liberal-minded Austrian monarch great hope for his long marginalized people. Maximilian developed a plan to provide them with a formal education, grants, and opportunities denied them by the previous administrations. Consequently, Maximilian established a department devoted to the underserved natives and issued a number of decrees relative to their ownership of native territories, also written in Nahuatl. Almost as soon as he arrived, villagers from these ancient communities began petitioning for their ancestral lands, lost through war or property grabs. Maximilian also focused on public instruction for all socioeconomic groups, including the native populations, and mandated that schools provide teaching of the sciences, language, philosophy, and physical education.[28]

Maximilian received an outpouring of enthusiasm from the indigenous people upon his arrival in Mexico, an emotion he returned with zeal and compassion. The French army counted on the natives' support as well and seemed astonished at their acceptance of the occupation. However, these small and relatively isolated communities could do little to provide extra manpower, with the exception that when regional leaders, like Gen. Tomás Mejía, ably organized tribal bands to defend the throne of Mexico, they joined the fight with spirit. Men from communities such as the Yaquis, Opatas, and Pimas fought with such ferocity, their bravery was lauded in the newspaper *L'Estafette*.

Sadly, some of these same groups also suffered massacres in punitive reprisals by the Liberals.[29]

On arriving in Mexico, Maximilian soon realized the country remained quite disorganized and was not as pacified as Napoléon had assured him. Almonte and the regency had done little in the way of forming a government. Maximilian had little knowledge of the overall financial revenues because no imperial officials collected taxes. Maximilian established a central agency called the Imperial Commissioners Office with various departments to administer justice and public service, dismiss corrupt civil servants, collect taxes, and support agriculture and industry.[30]

Maximilian also defined his role as emperor: to govern the military, declare war, maintain the peace, foster commerce between foreign nations, issue laws or decrees, and most important to him, convey amnesty on sentences pronounced in his name. He presided over a ministry composed of nine departments, including the civil list of the Imperial House, comprising the staff and guards; the Ministries of State, Foreign Relations, Development, Government, Treasury, Justice, Public Instruction, and Worship; War; Protection, and eventually Navy. Each minister served on his cabinet. He issued decrees for the management of forests, railroads, courts-martial, roads and canals, a postal service, telegraphs, mining, colonization, statistics, and agriculture.[31]

He demanded that the state's borders be redrawn and a new map created. He also divided the country into eight military departments, each headed by a territorial general, a commissioner, and regional prefects, while a bishop administered the Catholic religious institutions. The *gendarmerie* and *guardia rural* served to police and enforce laws. At the same time, Maximilian also called on the hacendados, large landholders, to defend themselves and property by deputizing them to carry weapons but prohibiting them from giving support to guerrillas. He also mandated that each parish priest report monthly on births, parishioners, deaths, burials, and the sick.[32]

To know more of the country, people, and places, on August 10, 1864, Maximilian set out with a large contingent of soldiers north from Mexico City. He focused on seeing central Mexico, the most pacified area. Dressed in traditional Mexican charro attire, he passed through villages and surveyed the landscape, impassively tending to business but with the intent to show himself to the people and become part of Mexico. He timed the tour to arrive at the town of Dolores to celebrate the national holiday of Independence Day. It was here that Father Miguel Hidalgo y Costilla had given his cry and proclamation for freedom from Spain on September 16, 1810, a major episode in history. The emperor traveled north from the capital through small villages to Querétaro and on to Dolores Hidalgo, 250 miles northwest of Mexico City. Maximilian left Carlota in charge as regent in Mexico City.[33]

The Independence Day celebration blended the role of the church with the state, and Maximilian wanted to associate his reign with the spirit of independence. To embrace such an event seemed only logical. It also reassured the people that he honored the three main national holidays: Independence Day and the feast days of Corpus Cristi and *Nuestra Señora de Guadalupe,* which allowed him to participate in what lay dear to the hearts of his new subjects. To become further part of Mexico's fabric, his own birthday, July 6, was added as a fourth national holiday. The irony of a new emperor, a descendant of Spain's Carlos V, celebrating the anniversary of a movement that extinguished forever Mexico's role as a Spanish colony, perhaps did not occur to Maximilian. To him, the holiday presented the opportunity to exhibit his first major display of statesmanship and devotion to his new *patria.* In his charro outfit, he meant to criticize the pomp of the Spanish viceroys and former president Santa Anna. However, in his simplicity of appearance followed by teams of mules with bells on their harnesses, many people remained indifferent or ridiculed him. One Republican who, despite the church's lavish preparations for the emperor, noted the paradox, saying, "I assure you that never have we seen one of these occasions in which there has been so little enthusiasm. And it could not be otherwise, since the ridiculous and shocking spectacle of seeing a foreign army celebrating the anniversary of independence, it cannot but inspire a profound disgust." He and other Republicans knew that far away, in the northern state of Durango, Juárez, too, celebrated Independence Day with his small retinue.[34]

In Mexico City, left alone for the first time since arriving, Carlota commenced meeting with the cabinet members in Maximilian's absence but experienced frustration, because they constantly challenged her, and she was not sure how to make her wishes understood. After the initial conferences, she wrote Maximilian in her lapidary, succinct manner, "the ministers arrived half an hour late," and some did not attend. A few days later, she wrote again, "You might as well know that your ministers have done nothing of what you told them to do. I am only asked about things which should already have been done." After a few weeks, she overcame her fears and learned how to handily manage the business of state. Attempting to work with the army, she communicated regularly with Bazaine to get news, or she often made suggestions about the placement of certain divisions or commanders, especially in Veracruz, Yucatán, or in the mining regions in the state of Hidalgo where there were violent attacks by the Plateados, bandits known for the rich silver worn on their clothing and weapons. Attentively, she asked questions on strategy, expressing the need to quash unrest. "The most important thing is the pacification of the sierra. As for the Indians who are trying to defend themselves against the Plateados, tell me if you think it is necessary to arm them," Carlota wrote.[35]

Without Maximilian, she decided to experience some things on her own. "Adored treasure and dear love," she wrote, "Today, crowned by fame, I took my first horseback ride. The animal I like most I named 'Chulo' [Dandy] and he walks like he has springs for legs. We rode to . . . Hacienda de la Teja and other shaded trails." However, nights spent alone challenged her the most, and she was not happy being left behind as he went off for adventures. On August 12, she was staying at the National Palace when a torrential rain turned the streets around the National Palace into a quagmire. She remained lonely and restless. "You see, since without you this time has not passed pleasurably, I feel, compared to our interesting life, invalid by your departure and I am mummified in the swamp palace. At night there are such storms, that I cannot climb to the roof," she wrote, referring to their habit of strolling on the rooftop of the National Palace, from which they could view the city, and it was easier than calling the guards to go out to the Zócalo for a walk.[36]

Maximilian arrived at Dolores on the afternoon of September 15, and after dinner at 10:30, an assembly of local officials led Maximilian to Padre Hidalgo's former home, a landmark. According to plan, he stood at a window and addressed a gathering of townsfolk and military officials. Slightly timid about his Spanish skills, his voice quivered a little, but he worked to make himself heard to the hushed crowd. In his speech, he summoned the spirit of unity and deep-rooted pride that existed in 1810: "Mexicans: over half a stormy century has passed since, in this humble house, from the heart of a humble priest, the great word of independence resounded, reverberating like thunder from one ocean to another through the extent of Anáhuac, and before which the slavery and despotism of centuries was destroyed. This word, which shown amid the night like lightning, awoke the whole nation from a long sleep to liberty and emancipation." He concluded by denouncing party hatreds and called on the people to unify and seize their own future in the tradition of their national heroes.[37]

"You cannot imagine how embarrassed I was before a tightly packed, silent mass of people," Maximilian reported to one of his brothers. "It went off well, thank God, and the enthusiasm was indescribable." A local newspaper later reported that at the conclusion, the people, the troops, and local authorities erupted in enthusiastic applause and shouts, which began a celebration that lasted into the morning. "This time, the cheers were for me, not Hidalgo," wrote Maximilian.[38] All this he hoped would spread the word of his earnestness, care, compassion, and magnanimity.

The next morning, the pealing of bells intoned the day's festivities, along with *tronadas* of fireworks. After mass, dressed in the gold-embroidered uniform of a Mexican imperial general, Maximilian conducted a luncheon for seventy honorees from various tribes, towns, and parishes. "Gentlemen, we toast our independence and the memory of its heroes," said Maximilian, raising his glass. He presented the Cross of the Order of Guadalupe to four Mexican veterans and pardoned a convict from Guanajuato. Monarchist party members reciprocated by giving Maximilian the baptismal documents of Hidalgo and fellow revolutionary Ignacio Allende, which he later donated to the national museum. He distributed funds to the poor through his almoner, Monsignor Ignacio Montes de Oca y Obregón.[39]

Meanwhile, in the capital of Mexico City, on the eve of Independence Day, Carlota and Miguel María Azcárate, the political prefect, along with local officials, gathered at the Imperial Theater for an evening of commemorations in tribute to Hidalgo and to the anniversary of the Grito de Dolores. Azcárate read the dramatic call of the 1813 Act of Independence. The next morning, Carlota rode in the gilded royal carriage to mass at the National Cathedral. She presided at a ceremony to lay the foundation for a new monument to the 1810–1821 revolution, distributed imperial medals, and announced the founding of a home for veterans, La Casa de la Independencia. The veterans shed tears as *vivas* rang out. The afternoon continued with concerts, theater productions, bullfights, and a hot-air balloon demonstration, and Carlota attended a performance of *La Traviata* performed by the Italian Lyric Company at the Imperial Theater. "I wore a tri-colored sash over a white dress, and the event went off victoriously," Carlota wrote to Maximilian. Fireworks lit the night sky. As Carlota's first time to play the central role of a monarch in the shimmering capital city, she glowed in the celebration, happy to be part of the country's future.[40]

❡ 8 ❡

A Task Worthy of the Damned

Carlota returned to her work as regent, but not happily. Frustrated, she had been working on the finances of the empire, complaining that few officials had taken care of state funds over the last several years. She longed to be with Maximilian, whom she imagined having high adventure in their new country. "You are not as other mortals. When I hear accounts of your journey, and of all you had to endure, I am so lost in admiration that I see you as an angel rather than as a human being. . . . I am jealous of all the good you do without me, jealous of your very thoughts, those noble, genial and at the same time practical ideas."[1]

Two weeks later, on October 2, 1864, a strong earthquake struck the state of Puebla, and the officials there telegraphed the National Palace of the terrible damage. Carlota wrote to Maximilian to report the incident and tell him of the aftershocks that reached as far as Mexico City. "They were at two in the morning and woke me, everything creaked and the walls made much noise. The house was a like a boat thrown against the rocks and dragged from below as if there were a mine beneath it. Finally, came swells like sighs, each time less and less and then it stopped. I felt a strange movement, like the breast of the earth as though it were breathing with difficulty. We only felt the strongest tremors here. All of nature seems dry and uneasy. The volcanic liquids must be passing with force." After a few more lines about her ordeals with state finances, she signed off, "I embrace you, your loyal Carlota."[2]

From León, Maximilian and his escort traveled southwest to Morelia,

Michoacán, a city known for its Liberal sympathies, but an important commercial center for independent-minded Pacific Coast traders with whom he wanted contact. On this leg of the tour, Maximilian rode horseback through the mountains. He spent twelve to fourteen hours each day in the saddle, crossing rocky mountain trails, rapid rivers, and scummy ponds. Wherever he went, the people flocked to see him, hoping for a glimpse of the new emperor. Then they traveled seventy-five miles southeast to Toluca, where Maximilian planned to meet Carlota, who took an excursion to see the dormant volcano of El Nevado, its crater filled with two cerulean lakes, named for the sun and the moon, amid fields of snow.[3]

On the way to Toluca, Carlota and her escort made camp on the Llano de San Lázaro near the village of Cuajimalpa, a 9,000-foot plain west of Mexico City. Carlota rode horseback up the forested sierra, where she joined Bazaine. She wrote that he sat waiting for them there "with his staff officers dressed in burnouses with flowing headdresses." At Cuajimalpa, the natives greeted her waving colored handkerchiefs from cane poles, and she happily received them. Bazaine's staff pitched two large, white tents in a wide valley of flowers and carpeted the ground with Oriental rugs for Carlota. "A chasseur d'Afrique stood guard, motionless on his horse like a statue on one of the high slopes," she wrote. She could see the tents of Bazaine's staff in the distance, including the marshal's round marquee that he captured in the 1844 Battle of Isly in Morocco. When they arrived, it was time for lunch. "We sat down at the table, the atmosphere was deliciously calm. The soldiers and officers, some lying down and others standing with the bright blue and red of their uniforms, the dazzling white of their neck protectors gave an utterly picturesque effect," Carlota wrote. That afternoon she enjoyed the quiet hum of the camp, the horses drinking at the river, and the panoramic view. In the evening the cooks served a dinner that included fine French foods and wines, followed by fireworks. "Then the tents were latched shut and everyone slept until morning, [until] the music of the Foreign Legion began to play an Austrian tune followed by reveille," she wrote.[4]

The Zouaves and engineering corps made an altar from pine branches and improvised a large cross of greenery. "The army chaplain climbed up on the step of the altar and a sturdy young Zouave in a fez and turban served as his acolyte. It was impossible to look on all of these suntanned faces of a hundred companies from the ends of the earth gathered to attend this open-air mass without being moved," wrote Carlota.[5]

Carlota surrounded by Zouaves and French army officers
near Cuajimalpa, 1865

The next day Marshal Bazaine and several French officers rode along with the empress to meet Maximilian at Toluca. In her joy to see Maximilian, Carlota jumped so hastily from her carriage that the surrounding officers caught a glimpse of her leg, much to their delight. Maximilian heartily greeted Bazaine with congratulations for his accomplishments as a marshal of the army. At the same time, Bazaine gave Maximilian a report of recent victories but added much work lay ahead to entirely suppress the resistance. Maximilian realized the magnitude of the task that awaited them, not only in terms of the necessary military operations but with the organization of the government and the unending complications posed by the church, needling him and demanding the return of their former properties. Maximilian expressed optimism that one European country after another had begun to recognize the Mexican empire, including Prussia. Despite their intention to go to war against the Habsburgs in Austria, Otto von Bismarck sent envoy Baron Anton von Magnus with King Wilhelm's recognition of the Mexican empire. But as much as it was done to associate with the new empire, Prussia also wanted information on the French and Austrian armies in Mexico, with Germans largely viewing the intervention with great distrust.[6]

Many other pressing matters, however, including the establishment of a national bank, departments of government, the budget, and cultural institutions, all needed attention. "The present is gloomy, but the future will be splendid," he told Bazaine. Although Maximilian had contracted malaria during the long journey, he considered the tour a success. On October 30 the royal couple returned to the capital to the cheers of the people.[7]

Once again in Mexico City, Maximilian turned his immediate attention to the empire's relationship with the Catholic Church. He and Carlota held a dim view of the condition of the Mexican clergy in general, previously warned by their advisor in Rome, José María Gutiérrez de Estrada, that the church in Mexico differed greatly from that in Europe. "There is no denying that this country has a character all its own; Gutiérrez was quite right about that . . . except . . . we . . . shall act in such a way as to change it. The masses are excessively stupid and illiberal . . . that explains the stranglehold which the clergy have managed to obtain on them. It does not educate the people, and so they remain as they are and . . . the clergy has a free hand," Carlota wrote Eugénie.[8]

The sovereigns shared the opinion that the clerics were spoiled, overly entitled, corrupt, with little knowledge of their charitable duties, and hardly cared for the people, except for fomenting public reaction and tithing. Maximilian had chosen to uphold Juárez's reforms that nationalized their lands, especially the large ranches and haciendas, a decision that angered the clerical hierarchy. He also allowed for the toleration of other religions, a decision that infuriated Archbishop Labastida. Maximilian would not describe himself as emperor "by the grace of God," or *imperator Dei gratia,* as the Conservatives would have preferred. Instead, the scepters presented him by the Monarchists from Puebla and Pachuca, as well as the Assembly of Notables, were decorated with only secular or royal symbols, flora and fauna. One emblem assimilated Maximilian's attendant duty to both worldly and ecclesiastical things, the unity of Christian spirit with his royal leadership: a crown likening a bishop's miter adorned with eagles and ribboning *ínfulas.*[9] This insignia put forward the leadership and enlightenment Maximilian intended to bring to the Americas.

In order to make peace and progress in the country, the emperor knew that negotiations must begin, and the clergy agreed. Because Labastida remained immovable, Maximilian considered any negotiations futile unless an official representative from the Vatican arrived to set new policy for Mexico's church that squared with the emperor's views. If the clergy were to be reformed, what was necessary was "a good concordat and a nuncio with a good Christian heart and an iron will," Maximilian wrote. "Only thus will the clergy be reorganized, made Catholic (which they are not at present), and acquire the good influence which they have hitherto not possessed." Maximilian wished to moderate the influence and militant activity of the clergy, much as he had seen done in Europe, especially through Leopold in Belgium. However, Leopold urged caution, not to push too harshly, use diplomacy, and the Catholics would be good subjects whose influence would be beneficial. The king wrote Carlota, "One can deal with the Catholic Church, just as well as with the Anglican. . . . Obedience is still the rule in that church and in that lies its strength." However, Carlota reported her current confessor was a Spaniard; she would not "turn to a Mexican" priest.[10]

Many critics saw that Maximilian should have come to an agreement with the pope before he left Europe and signed a concordat on the nationalized properties held in mortmain. If it meant taking losses, promising to prove up titles, and preventing illegal transactions, it would have demonstrated good faith. There was little hope of fruitful discourse so far away in Mexico, with the empire coveting control of those consecrated lands. This deprived the church of its currency, and the church could then split the people from the empire—this especially included the elite Conservatives, Maximilian's power base.[11] The emperor's myopic European and privileged views prevented him from understanding the power and nuances of a dominant Catholic Church within elite Mexican society, blended with indigenous faiths, and the economics of the Romish powerhouse institution touching nearly all aspects of life.

Disregarding the agendas of the Conservatives, Maximilian expressed his views on religion and education very clearly to Manuel Siliceo, the minister of public instruction and religious worship: "Religion is a matter of individual conscience; the less the state gets involved in religious questions, the truer it remains to its mission. We have liberated the church and sciences. To the first I want to guarantee the full enjoyment of her legitimate rights . . . freedom in educating and training her priests." He added that the clergy's important duty was religious instruction, which "regrettably, the clergy of the land until now has not taken any interest [in]." He ordered Siliceo to emphasize religious instruction for children through the parishes. The schools were to be reorganized with open, secular administrations, out of church control.[12]

Maximilian waited on the Vatican to send a nuncio, which Pope Pius IX had promised them during the couple's visit to Rome. On August 25, 1864, when Gutiérrez de Estrada delivered Maximilian's letter to the Vatican asking for the expedited arrival of the papal representative, the pope immediately responded by naming Pietro Francesco Meglia as nuncio to Mexico, and he arrived in mid-November.[13]

The same steamship that transported Meglia also brought others who became key diplomats, including Count Guido von Thun-Hohenstein, an Austrian military officer and diplomatic representative of Franz Josef, from one of the oldest dynasties in the Habsburg monarchy. There was also Sir Peter Campbell-Scarlett, whom Queen Victoria dispatched to Mexico, finally signaling Britain's formal recognition of the Mexican empire, despite her government's heavy misgivings about France's meaningful support and Maximilian's competence. However, Maximilian and Carlota saw these arrivals as wonderful signs.[14]

Maximilian and Carlota had been warned by Eugénie in Paris that Pius selected Monsignor Meglia for his absolute and rigid advocacy, his "iron will," which kept him in strict conformity with conservative church policies, not the iron will Maximilian had hoped for. The Vatican hoped that with Maximilian and Carlota's inexperience, combined with their deep religious devotion, they could be persuaded to overturn the land reforms and the closures of the convents and monasteries. But both sovereigns remained steadfast in their liberality to permit religious toleration and uphold the nationalization of properties. Knowing this, Pius had written a letter to Franz Josef before Maximilian's acceptance, reminding him that freedom of religion and speech in other countries had led to the overthrow of monarchies. By the time Maximilian agreed to the throne, serious religious questions deteriorated to the insoluble, but he still held hope he could come to an understanding of shared power.[15]

Adding to the pressure to give in to the Vatican, Maximilian's own generals, Miguel Miramón and Leonardo Márquez, devout Catholics, complained of Maximilian's intentions to preserve the reform laws, fearing recriminations. They also disagreed with Maximilian's inclusion of moderates and Liberals in his administration. This led the emperor in turn to suspect their motives and listen mostly to his closest advisors, Félix Eloin and Sebastian Scherzenlechner, who with their servile manner and effusive flattery beguiled Maximilian into believing in his own suspicions. When they suggested that Márquez and Miramón worked against the emperor and might be dangerously close to going over to Juárez, Maximilian chose not to confront the generals. But in November, before the arrival of the nuncio, he dispatched Miramón on a special mission to Berlin to study the "Prussian art of war" and the following month sent Márquez to tour Istanbul and then Jerusalem to establish a consulate there and see the holy sites. By sending them on expensive and useless missions, he kept them loyal but removed them from any susceptibility to the malevolent influence of the clerics. Later, Maximilian saw he should have used their support and military talents in Mexico.[16]

The Vatican's nuncio, Pietro Meglia, arrived in Mexico with instructions from the Vatican to be at first very immovable. With a strong preconception that Maximilian had betrayed the church, the Vatican wanted certain large concessions before they could move toward a concordat. Meglia felt, like others, that the reason for bringing a Catholic prince to rule Mexico was to preserve the clerics' stronghold on the country's identity and character but, more importantly, to recover its assets and wealth. The properties, susceptible to land speculators, had already changed hands several times, but this complication seemed irrelevant to the clerics. Sorting through and undoing title transfers and financial agreements would have incited another revolution. Additionally, Maximilian and Bazaine saw these properties as a source of income to fund the war. Around the fragile empire, the disgruntled clergy began circulating pamphlets calling for the restoration of various religious orders. They targeted Maximilian and Carlota mercilessly. Some of these leaflets falsely suggested Carlota's intransigence against the church stemmed from her unhappy marriage to a philandering husband whose sexually transmitted disease caused the royal couple to be unable to have children. These scandalizing attacks were enormously hurtful to both of them.[17]

In mid-December 1864, at his first audience with Maximilian and Carlota, the nuncio Meglia presented a copy of his credentials, a letter from the pope, and a list of demands from the Vatican. These included the annulment of all reform laws enacted under Juárez, a declaration that the Catholic Church remained the exclusive faith of the Mexican empire, latitude for the bishops to exercise their duties without supervision or limitations, restoration of the religious orders, public and private education by the clerics, and removal of all restrictions that made the church dependent on the goodwill of the empire. In response, Maximilian prepared a counterproposal offering to emphasize the Catholic Church's importance as the country's dominant religion, while allowing other faiths to practice. He provided that if the empire renounced its claims on former church-owned properties, the state would support the salaries of the priests. Maximilian went over these points in person with Meglia, asking that they agree, put them in writing, and sign a concordat of unity.[18]

Meglia excused himself to confer with Labastida but only hardened his position. Days later he replied by writing a thunderous denunciation of Maximilian's proposal, that it was in direct opposition to the wishes of the pope, with a warning that his counterproposal constituted a damning insult. Meglia remained unyielding and abusive, saying he had no instructions to negotiate. He threatened that the clerical hierarchy would abandon the sovereigns, and the priests of the country would mobilize to work against them.[19]

Enraged, Maximilian refused to negotiate further and called his council together to discuss the situation. They resolved that if Meglia remained immovable, they would publish a decree reinforcing reform laws made by Juárez, while retaining control of the church.[20]

A week later, Carlota, feeling that she should try to persuade Meglia before Maximilian took any drastic measures, asked to discuss the issues once more, hoping the spirit of Christmas would improve the climate of negotiations. On the 24th, she summoned Meglia and spent two hours presenting her complete argument, which in the end proved to be one-sided. "Nothing has given me a better idea of hell than that conversation, for hell is nothing but an impasse without an issue. To want to convince somebody and to feel that it is time wasted, that one might as well be talking Greek, because he sees things black and you white, is a task worthy of the damned," she later reported to Eugénie.[21]

In the meeting, one of the only comments Meglia uttered to Carlota was to remember it was the church that set up the Mexican empire for Maximilian. Carlota scoffed at this and responded that it was the emperor who established the empire on the day he set foot on Mexican soil. "I made every possible representation to him in every possible tone, serious, playful, grave, and almost prophetic, for the issue seemed to me bound to lead to complications, perhaps even by a break with the Holy See, to the great detriment to religion. Nothing was of any use, he brushed my arguments aside like so much dust, and put nothing in their place but seemed to take pleasure in the nothingness that he created round him and in the universal negation of light," she said. She placed Maximilian's ultimatum before him saying they had done all they could.[22]

As she explained in a letter to Empress Eugénie, Meglia had "a crazed mind, a blindness, an obstinacy with which nothing can compare, and in addition to this he actually ventures to maintain that the country, which is simply steeped in hatred of theocracy, desires that the property of the clergy should be restored." Infuriated, Carlota complained to Bazaine that the only thing to do with Meglia was to throw him out the window. Bazaine could only laugh in response, for the royal couple now came to know his own frustrations with church officials when he first arrived in Mexico.[23]

On Christmas Day, Maximilian called an emergency meeting with Carlota, his ministers of state, foreign affairs, and justice, and summoned Archbishop

Labastida and Teodosio Lares, a vital Clerical party member. Meglia had presented a final summary of his goals, concluding that freedom of worship horrified Mexican Catholics and that priests would never submit to being paid by the state. Although Maximilian considered himself a good and modern Catholic, and a patient and reasonable man, he had difficulty restraining his anger. To the council, he concluded he would ratify Juárez's reform laws, and on December 27, he issued the reconfirmation, while remaining careful not to raise the specter of Juárez by using his name.[24]

On January 7, 1865, to further limit the powers of the church, Maximilian promulgated another decree stating that all papal edicts and arguments would be invalid unless the emperor sanctioned them. In a vitriolic letter, Meglia censured Maximilian. The emperor, however, did not read the condemnation because his aides deemed its language outside diplomatic standards of courtesy. Two weeks later, Maximilian defined religious tolerance by proclamation, allowing all Christian religions the right to practice in Mexico. This was furthered by an order a month later declaring liberty of worship and confirming the alienation of church lands upon the legal review of land transfer contracts.[25]

Predictably, the struggle not only alienated the Clerical party from the new emperor but also unnerved the Monarchists, the upper economic class of Mexican society and his main constituency. When many priests across the country resumed protesting against the empire, Carlota lamented the situation, rightly suspecting Labastida's duplicity, since he stood to gain the most. She knew he stirred much of the discord and even accused Labastida of ghostwriting Meglia's letters to Maximilian. Labastida's "bad Italian I know so well that I can recognize it in every line," she said. "The task of subduing a corrupt clergy is a thankless one." No immediate support could be expected from the Clerical party or the church, and Labastida remained a constant irritation.[26]

Maximilian surmised, "The more I study the Mexican people, the more I am led to the conclusion that we have got to try to make them happy without their help, and perhaps against their will." His rigidity matched the nuncio's, and this further eroded his base of support.[27]

Several weeks later Maximilian dispatched a deputation of representatives to circumvent Meglia and prevail on the hierarchy at the Vatican to conclude a concordat. He directed the deputies to conciliate on certain points, but the pope simply replied that he hoped the emperor would comply with all the demands listed in his letter delivered by Meglia. Thus, the effort to win over the church came to a standstill. Napoléon was not alarmed. He preferred that Maximilian should never have taken up the issue and had relied on

Bazaine's tough methods of handling church affairs. After five months, Meglia slipped out of Mexico to take a post in Guatemala, with no concordat in place, leaving the empire's relationship with the church as fractious as ever.[28]

Maximilian's refusal to capitulate to Meglia and the church resulted in a violent uprising by many priests against the empire. Demonstrations and disorder broke out in areas where before the clericals openly welcomed the sovereigns. However, Maximilian remained strident and refused a request from Archbishop Labastida to go back to Europe in protest. His firmness astonished many observers.[29]

Returning to the matter of finance and the French military, with assistance from King Leopold, Maximilian heavily lobbied Napoléon to send additional funds for the Mexican empire and to aid in setting up a national bank. The European financiers who pledged to fund the institution, however, also demanded control of financial contracts and wanted to have a hand in establishing a French colony in Sonora, an issue on which Maximilian proved immovable. With the Mexican expedition still popular in France, Napoléon agreed to find French financiers to fund a bank and offered a loan of 100 million francs. But he wanted accurate information on conditions in Mexico and total authority of the lending, warning Maximilian that he must demonstrate leadership over the country's productivity and money matters. Maximilian tried to counter any negative news about his regime, remaining buoyant in his letters to Napoléon. To curry favor further, he described the happiness of the Mexican people with the French presence in Mexico and awarded Napoléon the Grand Cross of the Order of the Eagle, along with pearls from the Pacific Coast and a shell crafted as an ashtray "for those nice cigarettes which inspire one so pleasantly to work."[30]

Collaborating with the French army to fully secure the country, however, proved to be tricky, since Maximilian was not in command of the army, contrary to his understanding of his rights stated in the Treaty of Miramar. This made national independence nearly impossible, and instead of uniting their designs, Bazaine and Maximilian, with Carlota and their extremist ministers, began to emphasize different goals while each asserted and contested for power. Maximilian and Carlota began to have confidence in Gen. Félix Douay, who they believed was a more practical leader and honest in his reports to the empire. When it became apparent that the French army's grip on Mexico remained shaky, evidenced by bandit attacks within a mile of Mexico City and whole districts still in play between the Juaristas and Imperialistas, Carlota grew annoyed. Although she said nice things about Bazaine in letters to Paris and remained pleasant to the marshal, she attacked the chief of his clerical staff, Lt. Col. Napoléon Boyer, whom she disdained and wanted removed.[31]

Carlota increasingly took control of the effort to persuade Napoléon to strengthen the military because she knew Maximilian would not, preferring instead to remain diplomatic, to the point of being indecisive and paralyzed. In fall 1864 Napoléon recalled 10,000 French soldiers, an obligatory gesture to his critics, including Fould, while fearful of the arming up of the Prussians and the burden on the treasury. Napoléon placed the responsibility on Bazaine, but Carlota saw through the pantomime. In early 1865, when it was learned that Bazaine, under Napoléon's orders, planned to send the 3rd Regiment of Zouaves back to France without consulting them, Carlota wrote to Napoléon but failed to persuade him to leave the troops or send more sharpshooters from Algeria. She wrote to Bazaine blaming Napoléon, "I moved heaven and earth in order to be able to keep [them], but your sovereign obstructed my efforts," expressing her frustration that each man was worth ten of the regular troops. The timing of this withdrawal greatly alarmed them, and they again questioned Napoléon's logic but could complain little lest they compromise his favor. At the same time it pleased them to see that between December 1864 and January 1865, 400 Belgians troops arrived, along with the first of the Austrian troops, a corps of 7,000 men including Croatian and Polish recruits. Maximilian and Carlota feared any sign of France weakening its commitment to subdue Mexico. Meanwhile the Juaristas kept up their attacks in the countryside. Oaxaca was still not settled, nor the entire border in the north. Parts of Guadalajara and Michoacán were falling back into the hands of the Juaristas.[32]

Maximilian finally ordered the disbanding of what he considered untrustworthy and inferior Mexican troops, retaining only the elite officers, wiping out all of Bazaine's careful work. His intent was reorganization of the ranks with promotions based on merit, discipline, and morality, as they were designed in Europe. As one officer said, "He threw out a mass of individuals, almost all former thieves by profession, who naturally went back to their old trade." The outcasts wasted no time in going over to the Liberals or guerrillas. In disrupting Bazaine's designs, Maximilian, who had little experience in army matters, being a naval officer, helped to add to morale troubles and mass desertions.[33]

Nevertheless, Bazaine pushed on to subjugate areas further north and south and reported new victories across Mexico. He worded his propaganda to sound upbeat, while downplaying the skill of the defeated Juaristas to scatter, regroup, and attack again. Bazaine secretly knew Napoléon watched and waited for the right moment to withdraw his army. The uncertainty of the timing and disagreements caused conflicts within the French ranks, and especially between Bazaine and Gen. Félix Douay, who pushed for troop reinforcements and seemed better aligned with Maximilian's goals. Maximilian, who sensed Bazaine remained loyal only to the French war department and to himself, lobbied, nearly pleaded, Napoléon to replace Bazaine with Gen. Douay. The internecine tensions often became personal and caused the French officers to split into two camps, each trying to undermine the other by sending false reports back to France regarding misappropriations of customs revenues and lack of military funding.[34]

Despite the enormous job of bringing the country under total Imperialist control with an army of only 30,000 men, Bazaine approached the task by planning several systematic campaigns. In June the French navy prepared to occupy the port of Tampico with the objective of landing additional French regiments to secure northern Mexico. Gen. Tomás Mejía was to march northeast from his headquarters at San Luis Potosí to take Ciudad Victoria, the capital of Tamaulipas and then north to capture Matamoros. With Maximilian's changes to the Imperial ranks, however, Mejía suffered a lack of uniforms. He had cloth but no authorization or money to make them; they were assigned to fight but had too few armaments. At Matamoros, Gen. Miramón appealed to arms dealers or military officers for stands of munitions. Their orders were to sweep the Huasteca, spread west to capture the state of Nuevo León, and drive Juárez across the border into New Mexico territory. On September 21 a column of the French army led by Gen. Armand Castagny aided by a large column of Zouaves captured Monterrey. Meanwhile Juárez, his Republican supporters, and a small army headed to the far northern reach of El Paso del Norte on the border of Chihuahua and Texas but did not intend to cross the Rio Grande. Bazaine consulted with a number of military tacticians and diplomats to weigh the prospect of an expedition into the Chihuahuan desert to find Juárez. The British supplied intelligence that the United States planned to send squads of soldiers to chivvy the northern caudillos of Mexico and the outlying Liberals to protect Juárez and organize an offensive. With many towns to pacify in the central plateaus and along both coasts, Bazaine hesitated.[35]

Northeastern Mexico was the birthplace of a number of Republican leaders who wielded great influence, and a few, like the impulsive Juan N. Cortina, often caused chaos with bandit-like guerrilla tactics. To control these caudillos and their loosely allied bands and keep them away from Tampico, Col. Charles Du Pin and the counterguerrillas intensified their swift maneuvers and often

ruthless brutality to clear the trail for Mejía's army. Du Pin's methods of burning villages, hunting down suspects, public torture, and immediate execution
by bullet or noose horrified the public. Du Pin's savage devices even alarmed
the American envoy at Tampico, Franklin Chase, who reported, "The system of Du Pin is to demand from the towns and rancheros sustenance . . . and
if refused or when it is impossible to comply . . . the offenders are severely
flogged and the town or rancho laid in ashes." To further seed terror in the
citizens, Du Pin demanded his Arab soldiers execute all wounded captives
"whose heads are at once severed from their . . . bodies, and sported with as
foot balls while the chief . . . looks with complacency on these savage scenes,"
Chase said.[36]

One French officer thought the counterguerrillas' methods appropriate to
the situation. "One of the sad consequences of guerrilla warfare is that . . .
sometimes inoffensive people whose conduct excites our suspicions are victims
of a situation imposed on us by circumstances," he said, adding that this served
as one of the only ways the French could "impose respect" on a country of
eight million inhabitants with such a small army. However, the French army
attempted to demonstrate restraint by policing, convicting, and executing abusive counterguerrillas as a sign of "impartial" justice.[37]

The counterguerrillas pushed north over the Pánuco River to take the
undefended port of Tampico and, accordingly, all its customs house income.
With the help of Du Pin guarding the rear and 400 sailors of the French navy
at the mouth of the Rio Grande, Gen. Mejía occupied Matamoros with 2,000
French and Austrian troops on September 26, 1864. With Juarista Gen. Juan
N. Cortina waiting with 1,200 men for a moment to attack, Mejía pushed
his army downstream to occupy the port of Bagdad at the mouth of the Rio
Grande. This warehouse boomtown was a valuable possession as the shipping terminal for millions of dollars worth of Confederate cotton and Mexican
trade goods selling to Europe. Clearly Mejía possessed the most lucrative outlet and politically powerful entrepôt on the U.S.–Mexico border. Since 1861,
soon after the start of the Civil War, when Lincoln blockaded the Atlantic
and Gulf ports, American planters shipped their cotton to the Texas border
and crossed it to Matamoros, where it was then sent downriver to Bagdad.
From there as many as 200 ships waited to take cotton by sail to Liverpool,
London, Antwerp, and Bordeaux in return for gold and silver coinage, armaments, or marketable goods. During the course of the Civil War, approximately 320,000 bales of cotton passed through Matamoros to the benefit of the
Mexican customs house. While Maximilian would not formally recognize the

Confederacy, not wanting to damage the chance of establishing relations with Washington, Gen. Mejía and Governor Vidaurri enjoyed excellent relationships with a number of Confederate officials, including James E. Slaughter in South Texas. This opened the flow of goods and supplies both south and north of the border, especially facilitated by Cuban-born José Agustín Quintero, a liaison between merchants and officers. A general calm prevailed for nearly two years.[38]

Carlota received the good news via telegraph while Maximilian still toured the Mexican highlands. She expressed great relief, writing, "Matamoros, which was finally occupied, reports an income of over half a million pesos per month in maritime customs." The French interpreted this territorial gain as the point they seized majority control of Mexico. By the first of 1865, trade flowed easily in Tamaulipas to San Luis Potosí and elsewhere.[39]

In Tampico, Franklin Chase, however, warned of a more sinister threat to U.S. sovereignty. "The French officers . . . invariably speak and act as if the war which they are now engaged in against Mexico is merely an introduction to a war which their Emperor is about to establish against the Northern States," said Chase. But in summer 1863 Union victories at Vicksburg and Gettysburg gave Napoléon indication that a northern victory might emerge. This made him reevaluate his hopes for the success of the southern Confederacy, wondering how long they could support his Mexican intervention. Nonetheless, he ordered his army to keep friendly relations with the rebels.[40]

Soon after Mejía's push to the north, Bazaine began a campaign in Oaxaca to the southeast, against defending Juarista Gen. Porfirio Díaz. Bazaine knew that to reach Oaxaca with his artillery, he must cross impassible mountains, so he set about building an expensive 250-mile road, strong enough to carry a heavy load from Puebla.[41]

The campaign southeast to Oaxaca turned out to be a great exploit. Marching an incremental five miles per road segment completed, Bazaine and his 8,000 troops, including the fierce Chasseurs d'Afrique and his escort of Algerian Spahis, reached the outskirts of Oaxaca in January 1865, only to find that Díaz had entrenched and was ready for a hearty defense. In preparation, Díaz had all the homes on the city's perimeter blown up, so his army could fire without obstructions. On January 11 Bazaine's Imperialistas surrounded the city and began shelling. With an army of only 3,000 soldiers, Díaz and his men diligently defended the capital, dubbing the Chasseurs d'Afrique the *carniceros azules* (the blue butchers). Sorties and hand-to-hand fighting left Díaz debilitated, but he and his men held out for nearly a month. However, when

Movement of siege materials to Oaxaca, Mexico, summer/fall 1864

his troops began to desert and his cavalry joined Bazaine, Díaz, with only 700 soldiers remaining and outnumbered ten to one, rode to Bazaine's headquarters at midnight on February 9 to surrender Oaxaca.[42]

As Díaz's men lay down their arms, Bazaine asked him why he had not given in sooner. Díaz said that Maximilian was not his sovereign. Bazaine then asked why he violated his parole after his defeat and capture at Puebla. Díaz responded that he was never given a parole at Puebla. Apparently, the two men made their peace, and Bazaine invited Díaz to breakfast. The marshal sent word to Maximilian that he had captured Díaz, all his equipment, and his garrison, and inquired what to do with him. Maximilian received the news while dining at Chapultepec, turned to his guests, and convivially asked, "What should I do with this rebel?" After some discussion, one of the women at the table suggested he be shot, "for if you do not he may one day shoot you, they tell me this General Porfirio is a man of great determination."[43]

Díaz and his men were incarcerated at Puebla in Fort Guadalupe under an Austrian guard. But Díaz escaped to rejoin Juárez's resistance. In Paris, Gen. Forey at the Corps Législatif criticized Bazaine, saying that Díaz should have been shot immediately.[44]

French officials also condemned Bazaine's controversial decisions to move slowly and deliberately on Oaxaca, not completely fathoming the impassible terrain. They accused him of wanting to seize glory at government expense. Building a road through the mountains cost an additional 2 million pesos, they said, and was later viewed as a "military promenade." Maximilian congratulated and decorated Bazaine but also pointed out that the campaign "tied up so many of our brave soldiers and forced us to put off so many other necessary operations."[45]

In summer 1864, with Maximilian and Carlota settling into life in Mexico, the Republican Party in the United States renominated Abraham Lincoln. Looking toward Mexico, the party platform reasserted the Monroe Doctrine and specifically denounced any attempt by a European government to overthrow any government on the continent of North America. Although in May the United States had recalled its Mexican minister, Thomas Corwin, in protest, the State Department carefully worded its position so as not to rile Napoléon, risk losing his cooperation, and force his support for the Confederacy. But congressmen wondered, as Corwin suggested, if France was securing a foothold on the doorstep of the United States, a base of operations from which it could attack. France scoffed at these assertions, condemning American "audacity" and interference in European affairs, the Monroe Doctrine in reverse. Maximilian and Carlota agreed, using the existence of the Brazilian empire as a contradiction, and seriously considered prohibiting trade with nations that did not recognize imperial Mexico.[46]

A month before the U.S. presidential election in October 1864, Matías Romero, Juárez's minister to Washington, along with Gen. Manuel Doblado, intensified their appeals to the American government to act, seeing that the Imperialistas were coming close to occupying all of Mexico. But they could only derive a pledge of neutrality from Secretary of State William Seward, who remained cautiously aloof, recognizing France's right to make war on another sovereign power. They traveled south to meet Gen. Ulysses S. Grant on October 24, at City Point on the James River in Virginia, to explain the situation. Grant, who fought in the Mexican War nineteen years earlier, expressed sympathy, but with the Civil War still raging he could do little at the time. He did convey his desire, however, to send some of his "blue men" as volunteers once the Confederacy had been defeated. Grant discussed the situation with Lincoln but knew they must wait. Baron Ferdinand Wydenbruck, the Austrian minister in Washington, commented that when Lincoln discussed U.S. intervention in Mexico, he said, "There will be no more wars while I am president."[47]

The Confederate States of America still eagerly courted Maximilian. Judah P. Benjamin, the CSA's secretary of state, envisioned that by attaining the recognition of the Mexican empire, it would open the way to Austrian acceptance, leading to approval by other European countries. The Confederacy sent James Murray Mason, its envoy to Britain and France, orders to remain in Europe and prepare to visit any other capitals when Maximilian recognized their government. In 1864, shortly after Maximilian's arrival in Mexico, Confederate Gen. William Preston of Kentucky appealed to minister of foreign affairs, José Fernando Ramírez, for an audience with Maximilian; he never heard a response. The Confederates rightly surmised that implications from U.S. secretary of state Seward caused Maximilian to believe that the Union would eventually endorse his empire, which he fervently wished. Seward deftly dangled the indefinite hope of U.S. recognition, which restrained Maximilian from direct and overt relations with the Confederates, who sought a firm alliance. That, however, did not preclude tacitly open trade with the Confederates through northern Mexico or welcoming them as subjects in the empire.[48]

By securing the northern border and Oaxaca, Maximilian concluded that the empire had been pacified. Indeed, the French had most of Mexico under their control by spring 1865, except for the states of Guerrero, Chihuahua, Sonora, and Baja California, home to only 7 percent of Mexico's population. Accordingly, Napoléon felt he could begin to repatriate some of his army to France. But the fight remained far from over. From his tiny, desert outpost in Chihuahua, Juárez continued to send requests for assistance and dispatched a few lobbyists to Washington and New York to raise awareness and funds. He also prevailed on arms dealers to finance and purchase munitions in California and New York for the remainder of his Liberal army.[49]

Juárez's pleas resonated with patriotic freedom fighters in the United States, but because of timing and the tragedies associated with the Civil War, reaction to those calls lay gestating for some months longer. Meanwhile, Maximilian and Carlota forged ahead to build up their empire and regenerate Mexico.

{ 9 }

Our Daily Bread

In January 1865 Maximilian commenced his eighth month as emperor as an enemy of the church hierarchy, an anathema to the United States, and a disappointment to France and Austria. He had pushed away people loyal to him who, for one reason or another, did not agree with him or his changeable concepts. He remained obstinate against any encroachment on his power. Yet there remained little he could do to control Bazaine's military strategies, and it troubled him that sections of the country continued to resist subjugation, including in the states of Sonora, Chihuahua, and Michoacán. Also, huge complications still existed with France's monetary promises.[1]

Yet to Maximilian it remained vital to appear untroubled and in control, especially to his family in Austria. In his letters, he boasted about the joys of living in Mexico and that Carlota had bloomed like a rose, never before so serene and cheerful. He adored his riding horses, especially the highly spirited Orispelo, trained for war, and the soft-gaited Anteburro. In his correspondence, he made a conscious effort to appear industrious and without cares. "My only free moment is from eight to nine in the morning when I generally ride out with Carlota to enjoy the glorious morning air, like everybody here with one of those admirable Mexican saddles in Mexican riding costume, with the broad-brimmed hat, the light jacket, the trousers adorned with their silver buttons and the admirable and picturesque cloak," he wrote. With Carlota, riding on Chulo, he often traveled through Chapultepec and as far as the Alameda. Maximilian felt that he had finally captured the true nature of the country and that his leadership could only strengthen Mexico. Protected by the French, he remained apprehensive of Bazaine's actions and his protean moods but showed him only respect. Soon, he thought, Bazaine would find Maximilian's military policies valid, the entire country would fall under imperial control, and the empire could operate effectively.[2]

Unable to direct the French military, Maximilian focused on other matters. Modernizing Mexico City remained a priority. Maximilian began redesigning the public areas of the city so the capital would resemble the revitalized centers of Europe. Appearances remained a top priority with the Conservatives. He ordered improvements to the city's infrastructure, streets cobbled, new bridges, and gas lighting through the ministry of development. Maximilian designed a plan for a postal system for Mexico, transportation between the interior and the coast, and telegraph lines between major population centers.[3]

Every day Maximilian traveled to the National Palace from the castle, a camber over bridges and canals. "It was on one of these drives to Mexico City that Maximilian conceived the idea, which he carried out, of purchasing land near Chapultepec and constructing a road that would directly connect the castle with the square of Carlos IV," Blasio wrote. Maximilian drew a line from the castle northeast two miles to the statue known as "El Caballito" by Manuel Tolsá with roundabouts or *glorietas* spaced about a third of a mile apart. With his European and Mexican engineers, he planned the wide roadway that emerged as the Paseo de Chapultepec, also known as the Paseo de la Emperatriz, which became the major ceremonial artery through the city. He regularly inspected the work, even going up in the tower of Chapultepec to make more precise surveys. The emperor also planned fountains, statuary, and trees while establishing policies forbidding concerts, funerals, or processions on the avenue, unless authorized.[4]

Maximilian also decided to modernize Mexico's form of exchange, under the encouragement of the French and the Imperialistas who felt that a refigured monetary system would trade more easily in world markets. He redesigned not only the Mexican coinage but moved the system from the Spanish eight-real peso to the more modern decimal system. The new currency used as its base 100 centavos. Coins were minted in denominations of centavos: 1, 5, 10, and 50, with 1 peso equivalent to 100 centavos. They carried Maximilian's profile or that of his and Carlota's, with "Maximiliano Emperador" or "Imperio Mexicano" encircling their faces. Maximilian observed that the imperial twenty-peso gold coin was quickly accepted into the foreign markets, a vote of faith that pleased him greatly.[5]

Placing a strong emphasis on the arts, Maximilian announced the restoration of the portrait gallery of all national rulers. He set out to expand its collection by collecting or commissioning paintings to create a series of the Spanish viceroys and the heroes of Mexican independence. He engaged top Mexican artists such as Rafael Flores, Santiago Rebull, Juan Urruchi, and Petronilo Monroy. He also ordered paintings of himself and Carlota, copied from European originals, along with new bronze busts. Maximilian also contracted for images of the Virgin Mary, various saints, and a series called the "Priestesses of Bacchus" for the corridors of Chapultepec. These he funded with nearly $14,000 from his civil list fund.[6]

France joined him in promoting European arts. Court artist Jean-Adolphe Beauce, a history painter who had recorded French campaigns in Italy and Syria, was assigned to render the sovereigns, the military campaigns, and officers in a series of large oils. The French also shipped thousands of books and hundreds of musical instruments, including twenty-seven pianos, to Mexico in 1864 alone.[7]

With the assistance of Bazaine and the military, Maximilian deployed scientists to study all matters of Mexican plant life, geography and mapmaking, agronomy, history, archaeology, and medical sciences. Bazaine established a prestigious scholarly team of over 150 French, Austrian, and Mexican scientists in biology, zoology, and medicine to work together to familiarize Europe with Mexico, further French business interests, and transform the country into a modern nation. He called for an academy of sciences and a science library to be assembled. Thousands of research and plant specimens were sent to Paris for examination, where Mexican orchids caused a clamor, with botanists longing to propagate them. Bazaine gathered a group of engineers and doctors at the College of Mining to form a scientific commission to study and write papers together. He set up departments to support and regulate the mines, publishing advice and encouraging the use of new mechanized technologies. As Maximilian established an academy of arts and sciences, he contracted with Andrew J. Grayson to publish a series of botanical drawings on the birds of Mexico and other scholars to document the wide variety of flora and fauna of the county. On April 10, the anniversary of his acceptance of the empire, Maximilian distributed awards at the National Palace to accomplished students and researchers in science, geography, and statistics, and to their professors.[8]

Maximilian especially studied and promoted Mexico's indigenous past, either out of passion for the subject or, as some surmised, for underlying political reasons. Nonetheless, he seemed to have a genuine fascination with

Mexico's ancient history and commissioned archaeologists of pre-Columbian artifacts to perform investigations, including a pioneering study at the ancient pyramids of Teotihuacan. He instructed prefects in various districts to protect antiquities "that [give] luster to the history of our country." The Commission Scientifique du Mexique in Paris commissioned French photographer Léon Eugène Méhédin to capture images of artifacts at the new national museum of history, archaeology, and natural history. During his study of Mexico, he focused on the temple site of Xochicalco and made plaster castings of its ornate carvings. He encouraged the sovereigns to restore the pyramid site completely, although the emperor disparaged his work, thinking Méhédin's scientific team would steal archaeological treasures and ship them to France. Carlota and Maximilian also studied the work of American historian William H. Prescott concerning Spanish colonial Mexico and his descriptions of museums. The emperor ordered artifacts from a Tarascan tomb to be placed in the national museum. He also opened exhibits to the public in the National Palace. To further associate himself with Mexico's ancient origins, he minted a medal with his and Carlota's profiles on the front and the Aztec calendar on the obverse. A visitor from Britain noted the emperor was "as much bent on preserving every relic of the past, as the Spaniards [had been in] obliterating them."[9]

It concerned Maximilian that certain national treasures had been spirited out of the country, including to his native Austria, albeit centuries earlier. When Maximilian dispatched Charles Bombelles to Vienna on family business, he persuaded Franz Josef to return to Mexico some of the articles that once belonged to Montezuma, including a feathered shield and field reports sent in 1519 by Hernán Cortés to Charles V in Europe. Maximilian specifically requested an ancient and extraordinary book, known as the *Codex Vindobonensis Mexicanus I*, written in hieroglyphics on doeskin, likely of Aztec origin. The accordion-folded manuscript remained one of the finest examples of written pre-Columbian history. Although Franz Josef declined to let the codex go, he allowed Charles Bombelles to take the feathered shield and Cortés's letters for the Mexican national museum.[10]

Likewise, Carlota contacted their Belgian minister, Giuseppe Corio, to obtain a feather mantle, bow, and quiver said to belong once to Emperor Montezuma, installed at the museum of Porte de Hal in Brussels. In her education regarding all things Mexican before leaving Belgium, she had viewed these items at the museum and in August 1865 asked that they be shipped to Mexico City for the collection of indigenous art and artifacts. She promised to trade the items for an equally significant gift.[11]

Visiting band of Kickapoos, who traveled from northern
Mexico to meet Maximilian about territorial matters.
The Kickapoos had been displaced from western Missouri
amid Civil War conflict. The conference between the
Kickapoos and Maximilian created a major sensation
in the press in a quickly modernizing Mexico, 1865.

Further wanting to create beautiful settings, Maximilian sought to enhance
Chapultepec and the adjoining grounds much as he did at Miramar. He purchased several adjacent pieces of land, mostly haciendas, with the idea of creating a park. This included the historic Molina del Rey and the Hacienda de
la Hormiga. Similar to Miramar, he wanted lavish gardens and riding paths,
a private, quiet oasis for himself and Carlota. Nearby flowed a spring, said
to be where Malinche, the darling of Cortés, bathed, and Maximilian swam
there as well. A half hour before his arrival, imperial valets arrived with fresh
clothes while four guards stood by. His dip would last for fifteen or twenty
minutes, and afterward he returned to Chapultepec, refreshed and happy. On
nice days, the emperor and his secretary Blasio rode through the grounds in
a wickerwork, a light two-wheeled carriage, while Blasio read documents to
Maximilian. They also walked among the ancient cypress trees, the *Taxodium
distichum*, as amateur botanist Maximilian identified them, while dictating letters to Blasio in French.[12]

Kickapoo Indians visiting the court of Maximilian, ca. 1865

On Sundays at Chapultepec, the sovereigns frequently held audiences with people from all social and economic segments—indigenous or criollos, foreigners or Mexican-born. The couple enjoyed greeting their subjects, especially when they arrived in native dress or ceremonial regalia. It served to celebrate the diversity of the people. In January 1865 a band of the Kickapoo tribe visited the imperial government to seek land rights as well as protection against attacks from other hostile tribes and deserting American soldiers raiding in their territory near the Rio Grande. They arrived at Chapultepec in red and blue serapes in ceremonial feathered headdresses, face paint, and beads, their women mostly unadorned. The Kickapoo chieftain wore a Louis XV peace medal awarded to his tribe a century earlier by the French. "Last week we received at the palace a deputation of real, heathen Indians from the northern frontier, regular Fenimore Cooper figures in the true sense of the word. They had dinner here yesterday in Montezuma's cypress grove, on the very place where the Indian emperor used to hold his great banquets," wrote

Maximilian to his brother in Vienna. Three African Americans from Texas accompanied them to translate their petitions into English. Maximilian assured them that the French army would help protect them as subjects of the empire.[13]

By spring 1865, the one-year anniversary of their arrival, Maximilian felt that the empire was coming together and expressed his great pride to friends and family. He wrote his Austrian doctor, Auguste Jilek, that European ideas about Mexico's backwardness were wrong. "They are too proud to admit that we [Mexicans] are a long way ahead in essentials," he said. He liked the openness and progressiveness in the Americas. He remained confident that his liberal policies combined with discipline would bring a new and productive life to the empire.[14]

However, Carlota soon developed a jaundiced view, derived from the lack of promised support from Paris regarding monetary issues, the clergy, the press, and the military. She worried that the finance ministers in France had not completed the additional loans necessary for the government, while Napoléon hinted at withdrawing his troops earlier than guaranteed in the Convention of Miramar. Although the Austrians and the Belgians, including the Cavalry of the Empress, fought industriously for the empire, she knew they were best used for policing in times of peace, "but when the storm comes there is nothing like the red trousers," she wrote, in reference to the French army. The clerics continued to rail against them to give back their lands and engaged the independent press to report their complaints. The royal council suspended two newspapers that published articles questioning Maximilian. Carlota fumed that some in the press represented them as "imbeciles."[15]

In their difficulties, Carlota wondered if the pope had bedeviled them with the *mal de ojo* or "evil eye" during their visit in Rome, which he had joked about in passing. "It is true that since he [Monsignor Pietro Francesco Meglia] set foot in our land we have had nothing but trials and tribulations and we expect just as many in the immediate future," she wrote, referring to the nuncio. With the pressure of trying to unite the country, Maximilian's health presented problems. Since his tour of the central plateaus, he suffered one illness after another: throat infections, influenza, stomach ailments, and dysentery. In all, the progress to take over and organize the country was slow. Carlota spoke out in frustration at the pace with which their policies were implemented, writing "the pyramids of Egypt were not harder to raise than the nothingness [*le Néant*] of Mexico would be to defeat."[16]

On February 3, 1865, through Eugénie, she expressed her desire for industrious French immigrants to Mexico. "It will not be long before France reaps

Algerian Spahis in Paris for travel to Mexico, May 20, 1863

a rich harvest from what she has sown. The traffic between Le Havre and Veracruz was considerable last year and who knows how many French will come and settle here . . . there is nothing to be done with the existing elements," she wrote.[17]

Carlota appealed to Eugénie to prevail on Napoléon to keep large numbers of French soldiers in the country. "I prefer to stick to reality. To civilize this country we must be fully in control, and in order to have room to maneuver, we must be able to make its force felt with large battalions. This is undebatable," she wrote. "I hope the emperor will effect no more reductions before he has heard from General Douay. I think that if we are to do well this year, we shall require an effective force of 40,000 men, including all nationalities. This means that if a few thousand more could come to us from France, by continuing recruiting elsewhere, with the aid of money . . . we might perhaps reach this figure," Carlota wrote. "It seems to me that Monsieur Jules Favre could not but approve of our being assisted in combating the clergy, for it is only the latter which, combined with disorder and Juarista bands, calls for an increase of the troops," she wrote. As Bazaine downplayed the hearty resistance of the Juarista guerrillas who continued to vex the Imperial troops, she reported, "nothing could be less accurate at the present moment," she wrote. "General

L'Hérillier is obliged to dispatch expeditions from Mexico in every direction with the greatest energy, there are so many bands." She suggested they needed more Algerians to sufficiently occupy the country.[18]

By March 1865 funds from the first loan would be depleted, used almost entirely in military operations. The French financiers remained aggressive in collecting customs house receipts to satisfy debt repayment. Fearing the empire would default, French authorities browbeat the local customs house officials to direct the money to France, who in turn often worked to sabotage their fiscal mechanisms. Under political pressure, Napoléon lamented that the slow revenue stream and reimbursement dogged him in the public, with no real resolution in sight, yet more money would be needed to completely defeat the Juaristas. But France's ministry of finance failed to mention that their country's exports to Mexico surged 41 percent over the two years since the occupation to over 57 million francs, or 11.5 million pesos.[19]

In late 1864 Napoléon and his finance minister, Achille Fould, had dispatched Charles Eustache Corta, a deputy of Paris's Corps Législatif (National Assembly) and a genius at economic management, to Mexico City to study and organize the fiscal matters of the Department of Treasury. His aptitude and easy manner quickly won the trust and gratitude of the young emperor and empress, especially Maximilian, who had little interest in monetary policy. The sovereigns, who arrived fully expecting to find the regency had maintained the mines and factories after taking control from Juárez, realized that many businesses had stagnated. Despite occasional attacks, most of the English mining companies continued doing business, however, by hiring their own guards to get silver to Veracruz.[20]

A simple analysis of the untapped natural resources of the nation, the potential wealth of Mexico, astounded Charles Corta. He saw that the mines alone calculated to produce between 57 million and 100 million francs a year, or between 11 million and 20 million pesos. He encouraged Maximilian to extend and renew contracts with additional mining companies and to carry out his plans for colonization. Unlike others, Corta understood the problems of financing the empire and the ever-present military. Bazaine was "the biggest spender in the French army," noted Corta, partially based on his extensive efforts in Oaxaca to capture Gen. Porfirio Díaz. He tutored the young sovereigns and with their approval made vital financial changes. Corta was "as necessary to us as our daily bread," wrote Carlota.[21]

But in early 1865, in the middle of his mission, just as Carlota wanted to entrust permanent management of the finances to Corta, curiously, Napoléon recalled him to the Corps Législatif in Paris. Maximilian and Carlota felt as though Napoléon had betrayed them. Yet Corta did not forget their needs in Mexico.[22]

In a passionate speech to the council in Paris, Corta gave a favorable and adulatory description of Mexico's potential "under the wise and prudent government of the Emperor Maximilian." He said Maximilian's upholding of the liberal laws limiting the powers of the church was largely popular, despite Archbishop Labastida's complaints. "Emperor Maximilian has sanctioned the principle of selling the clergy's assets and decreed that all previous sales that had been made legitimately, in accordance with the eternal principles of law, should be validated. However, wanting to rid the sales of fraud, deception and unfair advantage . . . Maximilian set up a tribunal to review all these sales. Emperor Maximilian's decree caused a certain uproar," Corta said. In response to the sentiments of the Mexican clerics, he added, "the Vicariate [Labastida] retired to his country house, where he wrote to the emperor asking forgiveness for a moment of madness," although it is doubtful that the archbishop made such a lavish apology.[23]

Corta was so persistent and persuasive that new loans were approved in March 1865. He also helped to negotiate the underwriting for a national bank of Mexico. Supported by French and English creditors, the enormous sums raised for Mexico, however, drove the empire dangerously deeper into debt. The loan subscriptions, arranged by the Comptoir National bank of Paris, proved highly popular with investors betting on the lavish natural riches of Mexico. Napoléon wrote that bankers raised a sum amounting to 272 million francs, or 54 million pesos, a stunning figure in world finance. This, however, also provided for deductions for premiums, lotteries, reserves, and commissions. From the bond, Napoléon authorized no more than 34 million pesos for the Mexican empire. In a letter, he cautioned Maximilian to use the funds judiciously, condemning his profligate fiscal habits and resenting the cost of the war, transportation, and maintenance. He also informed him that France would manage the debt repayment with its own officers. "Mexico owes its independence and its present government to France," Napoléon admonished Maximilian, "yet . . . even our just claims are not always treated with consideration. The commission charged with examining the claims of our nationals . . . is working at a desperately slow rate and with an ill will."[24]

While Napoléon was willing to support the empire further in hope of planting it solidly, he did not reveal the whole truth. The French government dumped the whole amount of its loans on the Mexican empire as its complete obligation, despite Maximilian not receiving the total sum borrowed. Just to pay the government, it required more than half of the customs house receipts of 8 percent on imports. Victimized by the duplicity of Napoléon and the French bankers, Maximilian did not yet realize they handed him the entire bill for the expedition plus interest. Although he remained dependent on their goodwill, he insisted the French military make financial cuts as well. Marshal Bazaine had been authorized to loan the emperor up to 2 million francs or 400,000 pesos per month if necessary, which Maximilian appreciated, but it made for an awkward situation.[25] He could hardly bear the thought of appealing to Bazaine for money, a man who could scarcely manage his own spending or agree on how to get the country under control.

By mid-1865 France's deficit for the expedition ran over $60 million, including $2.6 million in nonrecurring expenditures, $500,000 in lost equipment, and $4 million budgeted for transportation and repatriation of the French army. The notes called for repayment using 20 percent of all customs house revenues at all Mexican ports, both Pacific and Atlantic, with Bazaine and a French managerial team to direct the dispensation of funds. Because of revenue losses due to contraband and a reduction in maritime trade, French inspectors replaced Mexican customs officers, although they were not subjects of the empire or hired employees. The French officers increased fines on various infractions to support the military, but they were to be approved by Maximilian, partially as a way to keep good relations with locals. However, the French agents at Veracruz soon alleged that merchants secretly shipped goods into Mexico as though for the royal household, thereby duty-free. They asserted then that Maximilian's personal deliveries were not exempt from searches. While Maximilian allowed that all boxes bearing his name or that of Carlota's be opened and inspected, he asked that other French imports going to the military be subject to the same searches equally. Bazaine then relented, stating that this was impractical because the emperor's containers arrived sealed in zinc, and opening them would cause too much damage. Bazaine amended his order that only shipments for the military be opened and inspected.[26]

Bazaine, who believed himself to be above the law and regulations, however, operated two shops in Mexico City, a grocery and one that sold French goods, lace, dresses, and silk, all imported as arms and ammunition, without duty and transported at the expense of the government. The French military feared him too much to expose his fraud.[27]

As for the financial strain, there was much blame to go around. Maximilian's personal debt increased steadily. The costs of government officials, staff, along with the lavish lifestyle of the imperial household and the military officers, especially that of Marshal Bazaine, thrust the debt upward. Yet the Imperialistas continued to hold opulent balls at Puebla and Mexico City, often trying to include Liberal leaders with the hope of attaining their loyalty.[28]

Simultaneous to these arrangements, however, the sovereigns received the good news that the French army would remain in Mexico. Napoléon strongly warned Maximilian, however, he must accelerate plans to organize his own national army and promoted Charles Loysel, chief of the military bureau, to the rank of lieutenant colonel, to help Maximilian do so. Napoléon knew that Loysel would never serve under Mexican commanders, and promoted him to be of equal rank to Maximilian's advisors. Disputes over seniority remained a sticky problem within the mixed columns of French, Austrian, Belgian, and Mexican troops, who often obeyed only their own commanders. Much of the trouble in organizing an imperial Mexican army stemmed from prejudices of race. In Mexico, sons of Spaniards born in the New World, the criollos, often resented having to serve along side indigenous troops, whom they considered inferior. The European troops in general felt the same.[29]

Now, with new loans and Loysel in place as head of the military cabinet, Maximilian knew they must quickly organize but also realized that Bazaine would not command both his own retreating troops and those of a new force. It was a delicate task, and Maximilian examined the matter with his minister of war, Juan de Dios Peza, and Count Franz von Thun in a conference at Jalapilla. After several meetings, Maximilian wrote Bazaine, "As I share [the] opinion that we must actively pursue the organization of the army as we have not found a French or Mexican general who has wanted to or would have undertaken the responsibility, I have decided to entrust it to General Count Thun."[30]

Gen. Franz von Thun, a bristling military leader, had arrived only four months earlier with 6,000 Habsburg troops, including Austrians, Italians, Croats, and Poles from the Austrian-Hungarian provinces. This stung Bazaine, leaving him full of indignation. In addition to Thun's forces, over the last five months 1,500 Belgian legionnaires under Lt. Col. Baron Alfred van der Smissen had assembled in Mexico, much to Carlota's delight. They were readied for battle and incorporation into fighting units. In spite of Maximilian's support for Thun and Van der Smissen, Bazaine would not allow them to fight alone, unconcerned with cultural frictions, and forced them to serve under French commanders, often alongside Mexican generals. Bazaine could not bring himself to relinquish military control, which furthered the morass. The Belgian Van der Smissen especially resented having to serve alongside Gen. Ramón Méndez in subjugating the Pacific coast at Michoacán. To get an army started under his command, Maximilian ordered Gen. Thun at Puebla to organize an Austro-Belgian brigade that would serve as a prototype. Thun devised a plan to build a force of Mexican volunteers but also vagrants and deserters, to make up a native army. With Alphons von Kodolitsch, Thun seized various communities in the region. By engaging negotiators to listen to the people's needs, such as aid for homes or crops, Thun attempted to build a base of support from which to build loyalty. At Tlapacoyan, a gateway town to the hot lands and Sierra del Norte, which the Austrians attacked but never captured, Thun succeeded in negotiating a long-lasting treaty with the Cuatecomacos led by Juan Francisco Lucas. In turn, Thun encouraged Carlota to support the area hospital. But the people's loyalty eventually eroded as their suspicions ignited against the backdrop of racial abuses laid on them by the Austrians and Belgians.[31] Had Maximilian been less naïve, he would have realized that when he took on so much debt, he could have simultaneously bargained for control of the military, which he had been previously promised, in order to assimilate forces and apply his ideologies.

Nevertheless, Maximilian rationalized that the French military worked in the best interest of the Mexican empire, and indeed every day, slow headway was made in the field of battle, which suited the "character of my people," said Maximilian, struggling to maintain his faith in Bazaine. By March and April 1865 the armies, aided by the brutality of the counterguerrillas, employed strategies that further suppressed the Juaristas. Shortly after the French victory at Puebla, the counterguerrillas received reinforcements. Their pay increased to thirty dollars a month for infantry, as their brand of unfettered warfare became more valuable to the French army.[32]

Within the walls of the palace, Maximilian could not achieve any unity in his executive offices or in his cabinet of advisors. French minister Charles Montholon and José Fernando Ramírez daily disputed over the subject of claims and receivables due French citizens and the French empire. So intense were their disagreements, Montholon was recalled to France. Although this frustrated Carlota, she knew that Ramírez advocated solely for his country out of patriotism, while Montholon represented France.[33]

In Maximilian's executive offices, advisors began infighting and bickering because the emperor relied heavily on the advice of two secretaries, Austrian

Sebastian Scherzenlechner, a pompous former valet, and Belgian Félix Eloin, a civil engineer turned loyal advisor and head of Maximilian's civil cabinet, both of whom disliked the French and liked the Mexicans even less, unfamiliar with the country or its language. King Leopold especially recommended the tall, heavy-set Eloin to Maximilian, for his experience in mining, saying that his ambition would offset his lack of talent. The two arrogant and gossiping men influenced Maximilian to the extent that he often made ill-informed decisions, especially against the church. As obsequious toadies, they kept Maximilian out of touch but entertained, while boasting of their influence with the emperor. Other senior aides, like Count Charles Bombelles, were appalled that Maximilian would rely on the unqualified advice of two men unschooled in matters of state. Maximilian's association with them caused people to speculate on his sexuality. With his gentle manner and enjoyment for design in all fields, such rumors had followed Maximilian since his naval service in Austria. Most could see, however, that Maximilian's greatest difficulty was perceiving when he was being misled and acting impulsively on advice from the fawners and flatterers surrounding him. He made no excuses for them, seemingly unaware of such manipulations.[34]

The rest of the staff especially blamed Scherzenlechner for catalyzing much of Maximilian's conflict with Bazaine and the church. An impolite man of large stature and girth, with a sensitive and overbearing personality, they gave him a nickname derived from the highest and largest pyramid in Cholula called the "Grand Cu." This degenerated into the bovine sobriquet "the Grand Moo." Even Carlota referred to him by that name. It depressed staff members to see the "Grand Moo" twist and maneuver Maximilian. His tactics included trying to persuade the emperor to confer a barony estate and the title of "excellency" upon him. Count Karl von Khevenhüller, a twenty-five-year-old Hungarian prince and colonel in the Austrian corps, remembered Scherzenlechner as "a true upstart, brutal to those below him and creeping up toward those above . . . he looked much like an engorged ox."[35]

Scherzenlechner soon ruined his trust with Maximilian. When he and Eloin began to compete for the emperor's favor, they became bitter enemies. Scherzenlechner claimed the title of "excellency" and demanded to be addressed accordingly but then complained that his pay was too low. Eloin mentioned this to Maximilian, who was then drawn into their quarrel. When the subject of Scherzenlechner's pay and rank came up, Maximilian lost his temper, told him to quit lying, and fired him. The former valet responded by spitefully returning his medals and writing a note to Mexico City's military commander that 7,000 armed Indians were planning to attack. Maximilian considered a court-martial for Scherzenlechner, ordering his aide-de-camp, Gen. Woll, along with Count Bombelles to draw up the papers but instead pardoned him, gave him money to return to Europe, and permission to live on his island of Lacroma.[36]

In March 1865 events in the United States again began to affect Mexico. With the Confederacy near collapse and the possibility of thousands of defeated southerners going into Mexico, the French army took preemptive measures to control chaos at the turbulent Texas-Mexico border. Bazaine warned his armies to expect an influx of Americans. The larger concern, Napoléon realized, was that a northern victory would free Washington to become more active in its opposition to France's occupation of Mexico. He said he did not worry if the United States declared war on France, because the Civil War continued, but he wanted to keep as many French soldiers in the interior of Mexico as feasible, while sending Mexican columns fanning north. He recommended that the country be organized into three large military areas under the command of generals Félix Douay, Armand Castagny, and Franz Thun and dispatched the army in three different directions. Maximilian felt this strategy too scattered to be effective. As one Mexican Conservative in Mexico City said, "As soon as things begin to settle down at Washington, you may look for trouble here." Napoléon prepared for an American storm although he professed otherwise, saying that the United States would never declare war on France. However, Bazaine shored up details, ordering a cleanup of corruption and reorganization of the gendarmerie protecting Mexico City.[37]

With the winding down of war in the United States, Maximilian and Carlota also saw growing uncertainty within the empire. The end of the Civil War meant new problems: they heard reports of men jumping out of the Imperialista ranks to join the Juaristas, rising disrespect in the press, while Juárez and his ministers seeking assistance from the United States increased worries. "Today the fall of Richmond and the uncertainty that prevails with regard to its probable results have put the empire back in the presence of the republic, it is a second crisis from which we will emerge as well as we did from the one involving the clergy's property, but it demands attention. The Liberal party . . . wanted to see what they would get from the Emperor. Now they know that it will not go any further and they are looking elsewhere. The situation is delicate," wrote Carlota.[38]

Maximilian, however, prepared to control any wholesale violence caused by the flood of American émigrés, soldiers unwilling to live under a northern government, wanting to enlist in the imperial ranks, or worse, join Juárez's Liberals. He recognized that a sudden inundation of fleeing Confederates could create mayhem or have a positive influence on the empire in the way of colonization, land sales, and taxation, and he named a commission composed of Europeans and Mexican landowners to plan for new residents.[39]

Carlota, seeing that Americans would make excellent, industrious subjects, was enthusiastic but knew that the empire must enter into favorable relations with the United States soon, lest they use force to stop the exodus. "We must put the situation right with America, since we will draw the southerners, and no doubt we will be forced to allow them, but this should not become a *casus belli*. The South has an army of about 53,000 men and it would be very convenient to have them and keep them as colonists. It would be a laudable enterprise, given the misfortunes these people have withstood. My intuition tells me that we should do something here, that otherwise the opportunity would be lost," she wrote to Maximilian.[40]

In the spirit of openness, Maximilian made provisions for accepting Confederate refugees. In his innocent optimism, he never grasped that he compounded his difficulties with the United States in obtaining diplomatic recognition, a goal close to his heart, and one he never lost. As one observer wrote, "so little did he . . . understand American conditions." France's Édouard Drouyn de L'Huys urged the U.S. State Department to discontinue its recognition of Juárez, "an ex-president flying from village to village is no more the head of a government than a few bands of guerrillas . . . are armies," he wrote.[41]

Maximilian felt sure the end of the American Civil War would finally result in friendly relations with the United States and devised a plan to win over the administration. Using Carlota and newly appointed French minister Alfonse Dano as guides, he drafted a letter to Andrew Johnson, the new president of the United States, expressing condolences regarding Lincoln's assassination with additional information regarding the care of political refugees entering Mexico. In July he dispatched Mariano Degollado to Washington, who attempted to deliver the letter in person. Secretary of State Seward, who remained in office under Johnson, however, refused to acknowledge Degollado, reiterating his policy of neutrality and said to be mortified by rumors that Maximilian planned to cede a wide swath of northern Mexico to France for a colony. Seward had been in regular communication with Napoléon and his ministers, warning them that they should withdraw their army from Mexico, and he likely knew such hearsay about Maximilian's territory cession were not true. France's minister, Charles F. Montholon, reassigned to the United States, repeatedly assured Seward that Napoléon planned to recall his army and evacuate Mexico sometime in the next few months, although he and French foreign minister Drouyn de L'Huys maintained France did not invade but merely responded to the mandate of the Mexican people. "We have not gone across the ocean merely for the purpose of showing our power and inflicting chastisement on the Mexican government," they wrote. However, France wanted to avoid a confrontation with a hostile American nation, whose power would grow rapidly as the business of the nation regained velocity. When American minister John Bigelow in Paris casually asked Drouyn de L'Huys whether the French would evacuate Mexico if the United States agreed to recognition of the Mexican imperial regime, he was told Montholon was authorized to entertain such an agreement, with assurances of an advantageous commercial treaty with the empire. On this point, Napoléon and Montholon misled nearly everyone.[42]

Bazaine did not agree with having an open policy to Confederate immigration, but Maximilian wrote him about his plans to accommodate them and asked for the military's cooperation. Bazaine largely ignored any instruction from Maximilian and ordered Col. Pierre Jeanningros at Monterrey to disarm the Americans and to drive them to the interior as far as possible from the border or to San Luis Potosí or Matehuala. Also, in the absence of funds, the French army had begun using levied fines, without the emperor's approval and much to his displeasure. Bazaine treated these matters as purely military problems, not considering the political aspects of his actions. A letter during that period illustrated the emperor's growing annoyance with Bazaine. "I hope that Dano has already brought you up-to-date on the plan for our diplomatic campaign vis-à-vis our big neighbors, and I flatter myself to think that you will share my views," wrote Maximilian.[43]

In April 1865 Maximilian set out on a new tour of the countryside, this time to the pyramids of Teotihuacan, and then onward to the calm and fertile valleys of Tlaxcala and Orizaba. The trip proved to be instructive and, moreover, inspirational, he reported. "Yesterday we were at Teotihuacan and saw the amazing ruins, pyramids almost as remarkable and colossal as those of Egypt, I climbed the great pyramid of the sun and at the top you have a wonderful view, infinitely extended. This morning I went up again with Ramírez to watch the sunrise, a splendid spectacle. Not in ten years have I enjoyed this same excitement as I did at the pyramid of Cheops in Egypt," wrote Maximilian.[44]

On the tour, Blasio wrote correspondence for Maximilian in a coupé outfitted with a desk. Facing the two seats, a storage compartment held food and wine stocked by the majordomo each morning. One morning on the way to Perote and Jalapa, Maximilian asked Blasio if he noticed how the outdoors sharpened one's appetite. "I'm hungry now," he said, "let us give ourselves a pleasant surprise by eating something quietly." From the locker, he pulled out roasted turkey, cold meat in gelatin, and cheese. He emptied a glass of wine in one draft and offered the bottle to Blasio. After breakfast, they replaced the dishes in the locker and Maximilian looked out at his escort, "Poor fellows, we know how they are envying us, but we can't invite them." He took out a cigar and lit one.[45]

Again Maximilian assigned Carlota to the position of regent in his absence. For all her willful leadership, she heard criticisms of her authoritative decision making. As the only woman working in a circle of men, she tread carefully, trying not to seem like a shrew, but she knew that some joked about her. "It is said that I have influence over Max, that I am responsible for this or that decree. But Max is so far my superior in every way . . . I have never wanted to impose myself. What Max does not choose to tell me, I would never attempt to ask. More so than ever, now that he is a reigning monarch and one has to guard his dignity. I help Max in whichever way I can. I help because Max wants me to help, and because I crave for some useful occupation—not just out of ambition," said Carlota. Maximilian made light of the situation. "The Empress ought to have been the man and I the woman," he joked. "She prefers the drum, I prefer the baton."[46]

Feeling exasperated over what she could not control, Carlota turned instead to what she could influence. She attended to the lower socioeconomic strata of Mexico, and to do so, she reached out to the priests of indigenous origin, despite criticism from church authorities who wanted the sovereigns to tend to the abrogation of reform policies. She disregarded the bishops and prelates, knowing that the needy of the country did not judge their motives. The simple and economical parish priests welcomed their assistance. While Maximilian toured the eastern highlands, she issued a decree forming a council to assist the parishes and the needs of their parishioners. To do so, they went around the elite clerical system, offering the priests direct assistance from the imperial nucleus. In her desire to help the poor of Mexico, Carlota disregarded the chance she might alienate her upper-class supporters. It was important for her and Maximilian to connect with the native populations, and the priests of the villages helped them to meet their congregations, who often welcomed the sovereigns with great enthusiasm. Some critics scoffed that the natives were easy to impress and win over, valuable for the appearance of authority, but with little clout. Despite their efforts, their success with certain native groups varied, and with many communities, the Imperialistas could not reliably confirm their support. This often hinged on the tribal priorities, such as land rights.[47]

It seemed that Maximilian disagreed with the criollos' assessment about native peoples. On April 22, 1865, he wrote to Carlota that he had met a woman who could be a new lady of the court for her, a woman of indigenous background, "with no mixing" of blood, he said, adding she was perfectly educated, spoke French, and was wealthy and single, also known for assisting charities. He noted that that her inclusion at the court would be politically beneficial.[48]

Maximilian endorsed Carlota's efforts to engage the approval of the native Mexicans. He also wanted to right the unfair treatment by the hacendados who paid indigenous farmworkers only a few reales a day, barely sufficient to sustain their families. In a country with over 6,000 haciendas, some so large it would take a person several days to walk across, the hacendados remained powerful lords over their employees and families. These workers purchased goods on credit, usually building debts so high, they lived in virtual slavery. "The more I study Mexico, the more I am convinced that the regeneration of the country must be based on the Indians, who make up the vast majority of the population. It is a duty for me to try to lift up this fascinating and easily governable race from the state of abjection under which large landowners . . . seek to maintain them, and to achieve this goal, I have had a draft decree prepared," Maximilian wrote to Bazaine. He sought to effect a law that employers must pay a living wage to the indigenous worker and outlawed corporal punishment. It also limited the inheritance of debts. However, it caused rancor within his cabinet, one minister saying the native man "is quiet and submissive so long as he is kept under." The hacendados and other landowners would reject Maximilian's disturbance of the old system. When Maximilian did not courageously push the matter, Carlota waited until he was out of town and succeeded in having the decree ratified as law. She wrote Maximilian, "At first they shuddered at the idea, but when it came to voting, there was general enthusiasm, with only one dissenting voice. I really feel today as if I have made history."[49]

A Premonitory Symptom

The height of imperial domination over Mexico occurred in April and May of 1865. Marshal Bazaine commanded 60,000 men, half of them French, claiming three-fourths of the country. France's naval squadrons controlled the waters and ports off both the Gulf and Pacific coasts, while Imperialist armies moved on land to take control of still unsecured portions of Chiapas, Guerrero, Michoacán, Sonora, and Chihuahua. However, while the weakened and demoralized Republicans searched for organized support to rebuild their army, the French expected Juárez to give up soon or join with Maximilian.[1]

Over the last six months, Juárez had become more desperate for U.S. assistance. Early in 1865, when it appeared that nothing or no one could defeat the French army, a rumor surfaced that Lincoln and Seward were preparing to recognize Maximilian's fragile empire. Gen. Manuel Doblado raced to Washington on Juárez's order to authorize Romero to offer the Americans a deal. The secret plan involved selling Baja California and part of Sonora to the United States if they would refuse to accept the empire. Seward reassured the Mexican legation that Maximilian's regime remained counter to the interests of the United States and no offer of Mexican territory need be considered. When the imperial press in Mexico learned of the scheme, they severely criticized Juárez for his idea of giving away more land.[2]

Juárez had led his ministers and small army north, arriving in Chihuahua in October 1864. There, camped near El Paso del Norte in the desert, he faced his darkest days. A corps of only three hundred troops remained in his army, and most of these, with the exception of Porfirio Díaz's small command in Oaxaca, hid along the frontier of northern Mexico. Juárez had lost control of every state capital, and the French held every port, cutting off customs receipts to his near moribund republic. Moreover, he had little contact with the outside world except through Texas or New Mexico. In the isolation of El Paso, he remained in relative hiding in a small house that remained open day and night. It was furnished with bare necessities borrowed from supportive families. Under Napoléon's pressure to send troops back to France, Bazaine did not pursue Juárez to El Paso, remotely situated a thousand miles upstream from the mouth of the Rio Grande, figuring that without forage or masses of people to support him in the bleak wasteland, he would soon lose his army and fold in defeat. Also, rumors abounded that a battalion of Yankee troops headed toward the border to assist Juárez, a clash the French wished to avoid. Meanwhile, Bazaine attempted to negotiate with Juárez's former generals but was unsuccessful.[3]

The few Republican cabinet members and leaders who remained with Juárez bickered, and hampered by financial woes and besieged everywhere, a number of them fled across the Rio Grande into the United States. Over a dozen Mexican generals departed for New York, Texas, Louisiana, or California, some for personal reasons, but a few loyalists clandestinely sought funding. Gen. Mariano Escobedo, a loyal Juarista, moved through the countryside, planning to reconquer Saltillo and other northern towns that had been lost to the French. Escobedo's training as an *arriero*, or teamster and hauling contractor, in northern Mexico made him particularly knowledgeable of the terrain. A tall, slender man with wire glasses, beard, large ears, and steady manner, the thirty-four-year-old Escobedo appeared more like a professor than a warrior, however. Juárez waited patiently, trusting his generals, and that time and tenaciousness would prevail over the French as their funding would dwindle. "Forward and no fear" was his maxim.[4]

Juárez was encouraged that so far the French remained less structured, and poorly staffed and armed in the northern states, but that did not stop him from dissecting and analyzing the Liberals' recent defeats, especially the loss at Puebla. "We lost the action when we had all the advantages for success and all the probabilities on our side, because . . . González Ortega did not engage all his forces but only a small part, which fought heroically, the other, which was the larger part . . . the commanding general let them disband because of neglect or disgust. These facts have not been published nor should be, with the enemy facing us and I inform you of them only so that you may know . . . the causes of our disasters. Ortega is here now, living in retirement in his house," wrote Juárez. González Ortega, as president of the supreme court and rightful successor to Juárez, claimed that soon he would take over as president with the coming expiration of his term. Juárez lived not only on the margins of his country, tenuously holding on to what remained of his government, but with his original tenure expiring, he also had to contend with an ambitious opponent claiming succession to the Republican presidency.[5]

From his sandy hermitage, Juárez continued to issue proclamations while maintaining contact with the Mexican Republican resistance. Through his representatives in Washington, D.C., especially Matías Romero, he appealed for financial and military aid, since they would not accept land. He couched his comments carefully to avoid an outright call for American intervention. Juárez in no way wanted to risk losing more power to the "Northern Colossus," despite the United States' debility after the bloody five-year Civil War. Former Union general Lew Wallace, who would later write the novel *Ben Hur*, wanted to support Juárez, suspecting that fleeing southern rebels would assist the French. Wallace formulated a plan to funnel funds, arms, and ammunition to the desperate Republicans. Meanwhile, Juárez also depended on the Mexican caudillos in the north to attack French encampments, raising the level of danger for the Imperialistas and supply convoys. When some discharged American soldiers joined these freebooting regional companies, Bazaine dispatched battalions into Coahuila and Nuevo León to help the counterguerrillas to fight them.[6]

As anticipated, in the last weeks of the American Civil War, in late spring 1865, 8,000 to 10,000 Confederate soldiers crossed the Rio Grande into Mexico. Some wished to fight for Maximilian as soldiers of fortune, while others took their families with them to resume a southern planters' life. Prominent Confederate generals such as John B. Magruder, James E. Slaughter, and Edmund Kirby Smith, as well as the governors of Louisiana and Texas, went with the soldiers. Just after his flight into Mexico and selling Confederate cotton and artillery to Mejía, Gen. Slaughter opened negotiations with Bazaine, promising to recruit 25,000 ex-Confederates to settle in northern Mexico.[7]

This inevitable development, however pleasing to Maximilian, also brought more complications to the delicate situation of diplomacy and neutrality. While he desperately wanted relations with the U.S. government, he also wished for new subjects. Therefore, while demanding the fleeing Americans give up their arms, he also required their commitment to the imperial government, their promise of no attacks on friendly or neighboring countries, and their agreement to stay away from the border and the Isthmus of Tehuantepec, where

France hoped to develop a railroad or canal bridging the Gulf of Mexico and the Pacific Ocean in the future.[8]

In early summer 1865 in Washington, Grant and Gen. Philip H. Sheridan blamed Seward's "milk and water" policy of neutrality for the French army's near total conquest of the Juaristas. They intensified their criticism of the French occupation as an overt violation of the Monroe Doctrine. Grant said that Maximilian "tried to play the part of the first Napoléon without the ability to sustain the role." In Congress, calls for retribution or war escalated as the United States drafted resolutions asserting its hegemony over the continent. In July, after considerable debate, Grant dispatched representatives to the Rio Grande on an inspection tour to find ways to deliver arms to Juárez. They also devised the idea of having former Union officers immigrate to Mexico as soldier-colonists to fight for Juárez. "It is a determination on the part of the people of the United States . . . that an Empire shall not be established on this continent by the aid of foreign bayonets," wrote Grant. He concluded that a little help now would be better than total war later. He placed Sheridan in command of forts on the lower Rio Grande with over 50,000 troops, a "Corps of Observation," that traveled through Texas with two columns of cavalry led by Maj. Generals Wesley Merritt and George Armstrong Custer. To strengthen his display, Sheridan let rumors fly in San Antonio that an American invasion of Mexico was imminent. Then he rode to Fort Duncan across the border from Piedras Negras, where he opened communication with the Juaristas and spread the word that he only awaited his troops.[9]

To further take matters into his own hands, Grant, with the approval of President Johnson, chose to send Maj. Gen. John M. Schofield into Mexico to organize an army corps and extract the French army with the guidance of Matías Romero. However, Seward skillfully redirected Schofield on a mission to France to wait for the "proper moment" to negotiate the French army's retreat from Mexico. However, that moment never came. Schofield merely enjoyed the glamour and pleasures of the French court and the hospitality of Minister John Bigelow.[10]

Still seeing the thousands of citizens fleeing into Mexico, Grant and Sheridan expressed anxiety at the "slow and pokey methods of the State Department," viewing the French occupation as an excrescence of the recently concluded Civil War. Sheridan wrote, "This . . . is a premonitory symptom of what I have for some time believed—that we can never have a fully restored Union until the French leave Mexico." William Tecumseh Sherman, however, felt differently, preferring to leave Mexico to its fate. "The Mexicans have failed in self-government, and it was a question as to what nation she should fall a prey. That is now solved, and I don't see that we are damaged," he wrote. Nonetheless, Grant, with the permission of President Andrew Johnson, continued the mission to send arms to Juárez.[11]

Accordingly, Bazaine ordered all possible routes into the Valley of Mexico armed and defense structures built, especially in the mountain passes. He wanted the valley's water supply protected. To take "all measures demanded by prudence and honor of the flag," he also ordered stockpiles of supplies and munitions to San Luis Potosí, Durango, and León. Querétaro was heavily supplied and reinforced as an outpost in case superior forces crossed the Rio Grande. He meant for Querétaro to support the entire imperial military for five months, should they be forced to meet the enemy and defend Mexico from this northern position. Additional worries stemmed from a possible American flotilla into Mexican waters and that the French naval presence was not sufficient.[12]

American military officers set up a recruiting station at Fort Brown on the Rio Grande border, enlisting "body guards" and "escorts" for fifty dollars a month to fortify the Liberal forces in Mexico. Many of the men who joined aided Republican Gen. Mariano Escobedo, along with regional caudillos, such as Juan N. Cortina and Servando Canales, who harassed Gen. Tomás Mejía and his imperial army, trying to drive them away from the border. The American military quietly ordered that supplies of gold or silver, muskets, ammunition, cartridges, food, and hospital tents be left at rendezvous points upriver from Brownsville, Texas. These supplies enabled the Juaristas to periodically attack. But Mejía repulsed these assaults and continued to hold Matamoros through the end of 1865. When the French minister at Washington complained to Seward, the U.S. State Department checked Sheridan's efforts temporarily. In relative peace, Mejía made improvements in Matamoros and celebrated his forty-fifth birthday with an elaborate banquet complete with an orchestra that could be heard across the river.[13]

With the promise of expansion by this new influx of settlers, conditions seemed auspicious for Maximilian and the empire, while Bazaine felt positively victorious. Gen. Félix C. Douay, a valued friend and gifted leader, had returned to Mexico, and this both pleased and concerned Bazaine, who knew the man was a logistical expert but with great ambitions. He appointed Douay to the important northern command of San Luis Potosí but not before he placed his worries aside and asked him to sponsor his upcoming wedding.[14]

On June 26, 1865, Bazaine, a fifty-four-year-old and a widower, was to marry the seventeen-year-old Josefa de la Peña y Azcárate, known as Pepita. The niece of Manuel de la Peña y Peña, a former president of the Mexican Republic, the engagement raised some eyebrows among the Liberal loyalists. Carlota described Pepita as pretty, with grace and simplicity and an expressive face. "She speaks French with a pure accent . . . [and] although she is the object of a marshal's attentions . . . has not lost her naturalness. She did not seem to notice either the admiration of which she was the center. . . . To tell the truth there is a very decided attraction, for the marshal has even begun to dance again, and gave us to understand that he had not missed a single Habanera," Carlota wrote. Pepita certainly excited Bazaine, whose first wife, Marie, committed suicide 1863 when she believed her husband in Mexico had learned of her rumored affair in Paris.[15]

When Maximilian, then at Puebla for a grand celebration of Carlota's twenty-fifth birthday, learned of the upcoming nuptials, he reluctantly returned from his tour of the central highlands. He commented on the irony of the old warrior marrying a girl three times his junior, and regarded Bazaine's giddiness as amusing, if not incongruous. "On Monday, the 26th we have, alas, yet another great state entertainment at the palace in Mexico, the wedding between Marshal Bazaine and a charming girl of seventeen, who will do us credit in Europe by her beauty and amiability. In spite of his fifty-four years, the marshal is perfectly infatuated and in love like a ninny (*verliebt wie ein Gimpel*); may this hazardous conjugal happiness agree with him," he wrote his brother Karl Ludwig.[16]

The emperor restrained his anxieties with Bazaine, offering to host the wedding reception at the National Palace. In her exuberance to throw a grand state event, Carlota hurried to finish its restoration. Small salons were opened to create a throne room and ballroom, trimmed with Italian brocade and Venetian chandeliers. Napoléon sent large vases from the porcelain center of Sèvres near Paris. Maximilian brought in his staff from Miramar to design the banquet, equal to the magnitude of one at the Hofburg or Tuileries. The palace guards appeared in clean red and white uniforms and polished helmets. Some citizens sniffed at the expense, but many others were swept up in the splendor and glamour.[17]

The day of the wedding at the National Cathedral, Archbishop Labastida concealed his resentments and displayed a cordial attitude. The carriages of the numerous guests carrying ladies in fine French attire and lace mantillas filled the Zócalo, along with many hawkers selling flowers and goods. The

Wedding of Achille Bazaine and Pepita de la Peña,
June 26, 1865, National Palace, Mexico City

Zouave escorts in their bright and highly festive uniforms dazzled the crowds as the wedding party proceeded to the cathedral.[18]

As hoped, the wedding served to break up some of the tensions that had risen from numerous months of combat and struggle to create a working empire. The relief and simple joy at the occasion lifted the spirits of Maximilian and especially a calm Carlota, who even embraced the bride. At the wedding breakfast, Maximilian toasted Bazaine and Pepita. As a wedding gift, he gave the couple the use of the palace of Buenavista, a nationalized church property. Carlota gave Pepita a set of diamonds.[19]

After the celebrations, Maximilian planned a short respite of quiet work and recuperation from what was attributed to liver pains. In fact, what he truly ailed from was frustrations with his cabinet. The office was in disarray, which Carlota recognized but could do nothing about. "I do not know either what is the matter with the civil cabinet; there are days when letters rain like manna in the desert and others when nothing shows up. It is completely intermittent and not very encouraging for those who arrange the files." Letters would be taken from Maximilian's office without being read and correspondence not handled correctly. She complained that telegrams between the National Palace and

Chapultepec were too slow; "an urgent dispatch takes one hour and until a person receives a reply, one and a half hours. It would be just as well to go over on foot," she wrote.[20]

Unsure how to deal with the disorganization, Maximilian sequestered himself to plan the next steps for his government, knowing that some strong decisions had to be made to build Mexico's economic stability. Carlota concluded he had exhausted himself on his tour and left him alone, as he preferred to shut himself off from the world at times. Evidently, during Maximilian's tour of the highlands, while she remained to work in Mexico City, she found diversion of her own. Charles Loysel had been assigned as her bodyguard and head of her personal staff, which meant they spent hours together, during which Carlota developed an infatuation for him. When duty called her to Puebla, she learned Loysel could not accompany her and when saying goodbye, both had tears in their eyes. "We felt something indefinable in our souls. . . . I spent this whole journey as unhappily as the stones," she wrote him later.[21]

That summer a number of former Confederate officers began to arrive in Mexico City and made inquiries to see Maximilian and offer their services. Imperial officers had allowed the fleeing rebels to pass over the border at various points without objection. Although the adventurers saw a wide array of new possibilities south of the border, U.S. federal officers visualized a number of disastrous scenarios. When the notable Confederate commander of the Trans-Mississippi Department, Gen. Edmund Kirby Smith, headed for a ship to take him to Mexico, Gen. Wallace shared his concerns with Grant: "I cannot do otherwise than suspect that there is a secret arrangement existing between the Mexican Imperialistas and the Texan Confederates contemplating ultimate annexation of Texas."[22] Wallace feared a Mexican invasion of Texas and the southern states almost as much as imperial Mexico worried about a U.S. attempt to intercede and expel the French from Mexico.

Matthew Fontaine Maury, an impecunious former Confederate Navy Department officer who had been stationed in England, arrived in Mexico at approximately the same time "grieved and mortified beyond expression" at the "ignoble end of the Confederacy."[23]

In June 1865 Maury presented Maximilian with a plan to establish a settlement with former rebels to strengthen "the foundations of his dynasty." Maury viewed his plan as an opportunity to bring talented workers to Mexico who would invigorate the country. "Deprived of their homeland, disgusted by [northern] institutions, and loathe to remain there as a conquered race," Maury said the southerners would become good monarchist Mexicans, "under a sky

where the same stars shine . . . on another corner of land of their continent."
Maximilian agreed with Maury, partially influenced by Carlota's well-known
sympathies for the Confederate cause and their material comforts. After a
few weeks Maury had a colonization plan ready, which Maximilian accepted
and formalized in a decree on September 5. But soon Maury found it difficult
to work with certain ministers, especially Eloin, and planned to meet with
Maximilian and Carlota before a dinner at Chapultepec. "It was mail day for
Europe, the emperor had been busy at the palace writing seventeen letters
for the steamer. . . . He went into the sitting room and said, 'Carlota, here's
Mr. Maury.' She came out immediately and commanded me to be seated, the
emperor and the other gentlemen standing," he wrote. After a brief conversation about the plans for immigration, they proceeded to a formal dinner with
four German naval officers. After dinner Maximilian offered cigars to his
guests, along with brandies. The emperor drew up an armchair in the corner,
recent dispatches in his hand. "You have something to say to me?" he asked.
"Yes, sire, I can't manage immigration through the Ministers. I must transact
business with you directly and not through them, nor must they have anything
to do with it," Maury said. The Mexican ministers considered Maury an outsider, bringing in dreaded Americans, whom they did not welcome.[24]

They went over his plan for immigration. As he listened, Maximilian realized Maury's ideas were detailed and asked him to stop for a moment. "I wish
you to continue the conversation with the empress, I have something pressing to do. She will make notes, give me verbal explanations, and have it all
ready for me by four o'clock in the morning, when I will attend to it," Maury
remembered Maximilian saying. Carlota came in from the garden, and Maury
resumed reeling off his scheme for arriving immigrants and appointment of
agents. Maury said Carlota made "notes nearly as fast as I could talk."[25]

From that point on, Maury dealt with Carlota on immigration. Maury's
plan revealed his reasoning for allowing up to 100,000 southerners to bring
slaves with them to Mexico. His intent was to allow former servants to work
on their masters' farms as apprentices, stating that their emancipation had
resulted in their starvation and death, when the public treasury could not offer
support. He surmised that Washington would be glad to see a fair number of
former slaves depart for Mexico. Upon reaching the border, the owners would
free their slaves and have them sign a commitment to work for them for at least
seven years. At the term's end, the boss would give the worker a house as a
tenant, although he would be treated as a minor. "The ability to serve freely
and to not be bought or sold constitutes an essential difference from slavery,"

Maury assured Carlota.[26] This workaround did little to please the antislavery Mexican ministers.

After becoming a naturalized Mexican subject, Maury was given the title of "Imperial Commissioner of Immigration." Following his plan, he placed agents in Virginia, Texas, North Carolina, South Carolina, Missouri, California, Louisiana, and Alabama, forming with Maximilian the "American and Mexican Emigrant Company." Newly naturalized John B. Magruder became the chief of the Mexican land offices, searching for the suitable regions for colonies near Guadalajara, Monterrey, Durango, Mazatlán, Mérida, and Veracruz, where tens of thousands of acres were designated. Maximilian envisioned that colonies would form a strategic line of loyal American settlers who would aid in the defense of the empire, a needed augmentation to his army and a barrier zone for northern Mexico, in case of an intervention by the United States. Additionally, the plan called for the inculcation of modern farming techniques among native populations and deliberate exclusion of certain Confederate corps recruited from "vagabonds."[27]

Maury and his team focused on settlements along the emerging Mexico City railroad, especially tracts made from twelve nationalized haciendas that formerly belonged to the church for a colony west of Veracruz, in the Córdoba region; however, other lands had been reserved near Tampico, at Tuxpan, and in the valley of Acatzingo, or over 500,000 acres. At one site renamed Carlota, Maury marketed the settlement as a haven, and soon Isham Harris, former governor of Tennessee, and Gen. Joseph O. Shelby with fifty members of his former command, the Iron Brigade, settled there. The excitement created by the exodus caused businessmen in the United States, eager for Mexican profits in commercial, rail, and maritime commerce, to call on Congress to approve Maximilian's de facto government.[28]

At Carlota, the government extended credit for 640 acres per family or 320 acres for single men, for a dollar an acre. In less than a year the population jumped to 500 residents. The first settlers were exempt from military duty for five years, and by settling on the land a number of the exiles became Mexican citizens. Town leaders planned a church, cemetery, and schoolhouse. Maury touted the virtues of the land that would grow cotton, corn, wheat, grapes, coffee, sugarcane, and tobacco, depending on the region. Settlers could harvest and sell *cochinilla*, insects used to make red dye. Although many considered bringing slaves, most did not. Settlers either did the labor themselves or hired local workers. The colonists set to making bricks and building houses.[29]

The U.S. State Department and military did their share of complaining that leaders and talented people, albeit former rebels, were fleeing the country instead of aiding the process of Reconstruction. Although word of an amnesty plan offered by President Johnson circulated, the news did not heal the pain and egos of the rebels nor induce them to return. By autumn 1865 an additional 2,000 Confederates had arrived in Mexico.[30]

Meanwhile, other American expatriates felt secure enough in the Mexican imperial government to speculate on gold. In summer 1865 William M. Gwin had arrived in Mexico City to renew his campaign for Sonoran mines in partnership with France. Napoléon remained vitally interested in Mexican silver, and new scientific studies by French surveyors reconfirmed the riches of Sonoran soils. Accordingly, the French emperor encouraged Bazaine to find a way to occupy Sonora, but using only Mexican imperial columns. When a Californian group of filibusters planned to set up a colony claiming President Juárez had granted them land in Sonora, this gave rise to Maximilian's suspicions that the United States might try to annex the territory. He ordered it occupied and pacified by the Imperialistas. Juan N. Almonte had warned Maximilian on the vulnerability of the region. Because ten years earlier Gwin, an expansionist, had helped to orchestrate the Gadsden Purchase of lands in Arizona and New Mexico, Maximilian felt it would not be long until the former senator would be bargaining for the absorption of Sonora as well.[31]

When Gwin realized the emperor remained opposed to French or American involvement in Sonora, he sought a secret meeting with Bazaine, hoping the marshal could persuade Maximilian. Gwin was staying near Mexico City at Casa Amarilla, the Tacubaya home of Col. Andrew Talcott, an American engineer working on the new rail line inland from Veracruz. The marshal agreed to a meeting, after receiving orders from Paris to help Gwin, and planned a surreptitious visit. One afternoon, as the marshal took his usual ride with his aide-de-camp, he dropped in to see the family of Sara Yorke Stevenson, who lived nearby. He invited Stevenson, who spoke French, to come along. "Leaving the horses in our patio with his orderlies, [the marshal joined] us in a walk up the hill, casually dropping in *en passant* at the Casa Amarilla," Stevenson wrote. "The plan had the advantage . . . of providing the marshal, who did not speak English, with suitable interpreters. The interview was a long one. Indeed, there was little to be said on his own side, as the Mexican ministry was absolutely opposed to the project and any change of policy must depend upon a change in the imperial cabinet."[32] Bazaine could only take the renewed proposal to Maximilian, but it was doubtful he would agree. The newlywed marshal seemed unconcerned after the meeting.

"His Excellency, however, seemed in high good humor. As we came out, he merrily challenged us to run downhill, much to the astonishment of the few *léperos* [street people] whom we happened to meet."[33]

In September 1865, although Maximilian never agreed to Gwin's schemes with France, he finally agreed to a few Sonoran settlements, if they pledged to support him. These he viewed as a barrier against aggressions, should they arise, from North American immigrants. He even granted limited use of slave labor there. Mexico had abolished slavery forty years earlier, and more recently, Carlota had attempted to abolish peonage in an August cabinet session. But Maximilian became so eager to attract American immigrants, he made an exception and allowed men and women to be held as property for five to ten years in Sonora. This decision signaled yet another example of how the emperor would create laws that went against what he claimed were his core principles. Juárez and Romero condemned Maximilian's reestablishment of slavery in Mexico. U.S. attorney general James Speed pointed out that only a few years earlier, slaves would have freed themselves simply by treading on Mexican soil.[34]

In Veracruz state, meanwhile, the colony of Carlota never seemed to lose its air of impermanence. After a few months, the majority of the buildings were only half completed. Shabby rooming houses of crumbling adobe and vine-laden ramshackle offices comprised most of the town. Mexican locals in their closely knit communities did not welcome the settlers, who competed for resources and felt exploited, making the situation tense. The immigrants' doubts further increased when Maximilian offered newly arrived colonists an armed guard to escort them to their new homes, though no mention was made about permanent protection.[35]

In summer 1865 Maximilian dispatched Félix Eloin to the Tuileries, with a letter warning Napoléon that additional troop reinforcements were needed to defend against a possible attack by the United States. The mission served the triple purpose of calling for augmentation of the military, having another representative in France, and alleviating tension within his staff. Eloin was intensely loyal but rude, possessive, controlling, and questioned every initiative the emperor tried to launch. The staff accused him of profiting from empire business, and his meddling disrupted or slowed progress. In general, his staff overspent on projects, such as the telegraph lines, but under Eloin's neglect and disfavor, the executive staff often performed hostile acts that ultimately hurt the empire. Eloin was more useful away from Maximilian. When Eloin arrived in Paris, he learned that Napoléon was touring Algiers, so instead he met with the empire's top ministers, accompanied by José Manuel Hidalgo.

Apparently, in his reports to the ministers, including Édouard Drouyn de L'Huys, Achille Fould, and war minister Jacques Louis Randon, he spoke arrogantly and brusquely, outside the normal diplomatic courtesies. Much to Hidalgo's horror, Eloin was maligned in the newspapers as well. Eloin then met with Eugénie, who served as regent in Napoléon's absence. The empress commented again that Maximilian asked for too many guarantees, that he was too nervous, and "too fussy (*trop remuant*)." Clearly annoyed with Eloin, she exhibited pure ennui toward Mexican activities but mentioned she would forward the request to Napoléon. Nothing came of it. Eloin traveled on to Belgium, where he temporarily entered into the service of King Leopold.[36]

Eloin's exit from Mexico coincided with Maximilian's dismissal of his entire Mexican cabinet, which he transformed into a simple administrative secretariat. "The current civil cabinet that, basically, is nothing other than an agglomeration of incapable and lazy men, who, without regulations and without orders, don't really know why they exist," wrote Maximilian. At times, it seemed that he wanted them to act autonomously, because often the emperor did not follow through on his ideas. Maximilian retained only his aide, José Luis Blasio, and appointed his most trusted and amicable confidants to cabinet positions, such as his physician, Friedrich Semelder, as minister of public instruction and Karl Burnouf as chief of finance. Maximilian declined to see members of his military cabinet and walled off their offices from his own. He suppressed rumors and intrigues within his staff, demanding that all requests be in written form. "It can no longer be alleged . . . that the Emperor has said or desired this or that; everything is written or signed," he wrote. Yet he did not like complaints of any sort but often admitted he created the problem himself, and yet again he did not want to deal with the situation. "As regards the personnel of the cabinet and especially the heads, they must know how to accommodate themselves to my character; it is the very least that I can ask them," said Maximilian.[37]

Still, it concerned him that Mexico had yet to fall under complete Imperialist control. Through 1865, Marshal Bazaine worked to subdue all sections of Mexico but had resisted aiding Maximilian to build a transitional and independent Mexican imperial army. He often neglected to report to Maximilian or incorporate the emperor's ideas into the military campaigns. Despite Maximilian's outward appearances of courtesy and friendship toward Bazaine, he harbored grave doubts about the marshal. Maximilian said, "I do not complain of those Frenchmen who serve their emperor but poorly and still conduce to the honor of their flag. I speak of those high functionaries who spend immense sums of money and shed the blood of Mexicans uselessly, who continually

intrigue against me and defeat all my efforts to form a strong national army."
He attributed his toleration of the situation to his deep respect for Napoléon. "I
submit to the gross injustice and humiliations such as I have never experienced
in all my life, because of my love for my new country and of my friendship for
France. I pretend to be deceived because of the future . . . unfortunately, I have
rather too good a memory and I recollect too well the many promises, which
have been made to me and the lies, which have been told to me during the past
fourteen months. Not one of these promises have been redeemed and I repeat
that the military position today is even worse than was the case last year."[38]

Bazaine remained secretive and suspicious of other French officers, including Félix Douay, who had served intermittently in Mexico since 1862. Bazaine
assigned Douay to San Luis Potosí, far from the central administrative sphere
of Mexico City, lessening his influence on Maximilian. But on July 9, before
Douay left for his new post, Maximilian took the opportunity to debrief
Douay, suspecting Napoléon and Bazaine hid the truths about the army and
the mood in Paris. Douay said the exasperated French questioned maintaining
the Mexican project, now in its fourth year, with so little financial return and
territorial splendor. However, he encouraged Maximilian to stand firm, blaming Napoléon for underestimating the scope of the mission and now prodding
Bazaine to return his troops. There were too few men involved in too long a
fight over too much territory.[39]

"You must know that the marshal always opposes all attempts to organize
an army," Maximilian replied. "He has thwarted everything we have wanted
to do. The older Mexican generals have been astonished; they think I do not
want an army. Whereas it is the marshal who will not give me anybody to
organize it," he said. "You know that I first thought of Loysel, whom I made a
brigadier-general. When he returned from the interior, where he had accompanied me upon my tour, the marshal began to treat him like a dog. Later on I
had some trouble in getting him transferred to me as chief of my military cabinet. Thus the marshal has frustrated all my projects." He added that Bazaine's
great faults included laziness, jealousy, and lack of order.[40]

Why not, asked Douay, turn to the Belgian and Austrian regiments? "They
march very well . . . they have taken part in a number of engagements and are
beginning to settle down. As to the Belgians, the great mistake was made of
sending beardless boys, who were disheartened . . . and nobody tried to make
any attempt to raise their morale; in the meantime they were killed like flies,"
said Maximilian.[41]

Maximilian seethed about the cost of the war, causing a shortage of funds for the new army. "In spite of all one's prudence with regard to expenditures, in spite of the cheese-paring which prevails in the Finance Department, there is nothing to be done, for the war alone, the civil war, absorbs everything. You know how punctually we pay all sums as they fall due to France," said Maximilian. Douay reminded the emperor that his duty was to pay his own officials first, despite the loans. Maximilian agreed. "All the more so," he said, "since the ports are our sole sources of revenue. Taxes are as good as nonexistent. Our only real resources are Tampico, Matamoros, Mazatlán, and Veracruz."[42]

Douay also blamed the vastness of the country. "The distances which the troops are made to cover are simply insane. My division has traveled 19,000 miles in seventeen months," said Douay. When the emperor inquired about reinforcements, Douay evasively said that he thought 30,000 men might arrive soon. Maximilian seemed pleased and mentioned that with the new railroad between Veracruz and the Mexican interior nearing completion, things should get easier.[43]

"Good, but we must not rest on our oars," said Douay.[44]

In the last months of 1865, displeasure with the endless war weighed heavily on Carlota. She suspected Bazaine enjoyed a cat-and-mouse game with them, not wanting the battles to be over, while harboring the idea of ruling Mexico himself. He reported brightly to Napoléon but said otherwise to Maximilian and Carlota. In letters to Eugénie, she lamented that Douay, who got along with Maximilian "like two friends, even brothers," was not sent to replace Bazaine but instead sent into the field. She did not comprehend fully that Bazaine was Napoléon's man. The commander's relationship with the sovereigns was immaterial to Napoléon. "Your Majesty appears . . . to desire that General Douay should receive a higher command; he is certainly a very good general, but . . . the marshal is our best soldier . . . his recall would have the disadvantage of making people believe that interest is slackening. I am afraid that the neglect of some formality has given Your Majesty a bad idea of him," wrote Eugénie.[45]

The struggle to remove Bazaine left Carlota demoralized and feeling trapped by the French army. She wore her concerns on her face. "I am growing old. Others may not see it, but I can assure you that my sentiments and feelings are very different from what they appear in public," she wrote to her grandmother, Queen Marie-Amélie in England.[46] Carlota had few friends in Mexico and no family. No children. She had only her riding, her painting, and her charities. This she seemed to lament, simply indicated by her eagerness when she could play a role in ruling Mexico, compensating that the natural order of things had not produced an heir.

Every Drop of My Blood Is Mexican

After eight years of marriage, the public speculated about why no children had been born to the royal couple, each greatly desirous of having a baby, an heir to the Mexican throne. Rumors abounded about Maximilian's impotence, sterility, or that he was homosexual. Others blamed Carlota's frigidity or infertility. Maximilian's valet, Antonio Grill, later spread the rumor to José Luis Blasio that the emperor likely contracted syphilis years earlier from a Viennese prostitute and then infected Carlota. It had also been said that Maximilian contracted venereal disease from a Brazilian woman during his travels. Carlota's doctors speculated that perhaps she had suffered from an unattended uterine disorder. However, some of her correspondence suggested Carlota may have miscarried and the fetus was buried on the island of Lacroma. While the couple considered seeking a specialist in infertility in the United States, they decided against traveling there.[1]

The grief and bad feelings may have been why Maximilian and Carlota slept apart most of the time. Although Carlota demonstrated no signs of preference about these arrangements, it was usually Maximilian who requested the separate sleeping quarters. Blasio noted that on a visit to Puebla in June 1865, Carlota was expected to join the emperor at a private home. When the emperor reviewed the room prepared for their visit, he "manifested his satisfaction at seeing the magnificent double bed, with its canopy of fine lace and silken ribbon, which was waiting for the imperial pair. But as soon as the host was out of the way, His Majesty ordered the servants to find a room at a distance from the bedchamber and set up his traveling cot there. He did this almost angrily," said Blasio. Clearly Maximilian and Carlota cared deeply for one another as evidenced by their daily behavior and in the letters, but their conjugal separation puzzled the staff.[2]

Since one of the emperor's major aims was to establish a dynasty, sometime in 1865, Maximilian seized on the idea of adoption. The opportunity happened almost by serendipity. Since his arrival in Mexico, it had been an irritation to Maximilian that the heirs of Emperor Agustín de Iturbide I, crowned in 1822, continued to live in the country. In 1823 Iturbide was exiled but had returned to Mexico, although warned not to do so. Officials arrested him in July 1824 and he was shot. However, over the intervening forty years, loyalists called for an Iturbide heir to seize his "rightful inheritance" to the Mexican throne. To remove that threat, Maximilian ordered the descendants to leave the country, but they did not immediately comply with his order.[3]

In early 1865 the family proposed Maximilian give them a pension to guarantee their departure, since they had little money to relocate. Iturbide's second son, Ángel, and his American wife, Alice Green, had a darling boy of two-and-a-half years, named Agustín. Once the advisors to Maximilian realized Iturbide had a grandson of a young age, he developed the notion of adopting him as heir to the Mexican throne. This solution would forever associate Maximilian with the Iturbide clan, somewhat similar to Napoléon I's link with the in-laws and children of his sister, Caroline, especially Joachim Murat. This relationship would also countermand any other Iturbides who might lay claim of entitlement. Soon Maximilian proposed to adopt the baby as well as his sixteen-year-old cousin, Salvador, and award their aunt Josefa (also known as Pepa) the title of princess of the empire, if she would remain in Mexico to care for the baby as his nanny.[4]

Although the Iturbides at first rejected the offer with disdain, after some discussion they changed their minds. The idea that their son might someday rule the country dazzled Ángel and Alice, the notion of being the father and mother of an emperor struck them as an immense opportunity. By midsummer the family eagerly awaited completion of the adoption.[5]

José Fernando Ramírez, imperial minister of foreign affairs, drew up the documents termed the "Secret Contract." Maximilian offered 150,000 pesos each to Ángel and Alice and to his siblings, Agustín, Agustín Cosme, Josefa, and Sabina, a nun in Philadelphia. He paid the first 30,000 immediately, as soon as the adoption papers were signed, and the balance was promised in two notes to be drawn in Paris in December and February of 60,000 pesos each.

Agustín de Iturbide y Green,
Prince of Iturbide, ca. 1865

In this way, he made it clear that he wanted the Iturbides to leave not only the country but the continent. As further inducement they would not change their minds, Maximilian promised a lifelong annual stipend to Ángel and Sabina. They all signed the agreement, including the mother, Alice.[6]

A few days later, on September 15, 1865, the family brought baby Agustín to Chapultepec Palace to the emperor and empress. Alice spent a few last hours with her boy, saying goodbye, and then sent his toys and clothing with a motherly note thanking Carlota. Now in their care, Maximilian offered the child and Josefa quarters in the palace as a provisional home, until another could be prepared for Josefa, who apparently made fastidious demands on the staff. But they invited her to become a formal member of the court and to appear at state functions with the child. They covered her necessities and paid a monthly allowance to her and for costs associated with raising little Agustín.[7]

As a new member of the royal court of Mexico, the emperor and empress presented Josefa a crown and earrings of gems, a set of pearls, and other pieces of jewelry. Carlota also inducted her into the royal Order of San Carlos. Perhaps more importantly, the emperor bestowed on her the line of primogeniture. Carlota evidenced some interest in the boys' care, mandating what they ate and when, their daily schedules, bedtimes, and prayers to memorize. After a time, Carlota sent Salvador to the College of Sainte-Barbe in Paris, considered to be one of the finest educational institutions in Europe.[8]

The forthcoming Independence Day celebration added further incentive to Maximilian to complete the adoption. On September 16 the day began with a mass at the Cathedral. In high pomp, Maximilian rode on horseback with court officers, Marshal Bazaine, and his generals, as the palace guard led the procession, with Carlota following in the royal coach. Archbishop Labastida and the cathedral council received the emperor and empress. After a Te Deum in celebration of the monarchs, a palace official read the announcement of the adoption of the grandsons of Agustín Iturbide and the installation of Josefa as a princess of the Second Empire.[9]

Maximilian briefly addressed the festival crowds. "My heart, my soul, my work, and all my faithful endeavors belong to you and to our beloved country. No power on earth shall turn me aside from the accomplishment of my task; henceforth every drop of my blood is Mexican, and if God permits new dangers to menace our beloved country, you shall see me fight side by side with you for your independence and integrity," he said, alluding to a new paradigm in Mexico with the end of the American Civil War and the flood of many new immigrants. Festivities continued throughout the day, culminating in a gala celebration in the theater, much as the year before with the reenactment of "the Grito de Dolores." Additionally, Maximilian ordered a chapel built for the remains of former emperor Agustín Iturbide and decreed that the second battalion of the line be renamed the "Iturbide Battalion" with a new uniform, which he designed.[10]

A week later, as Alice started her journey to leave Mexico, she was struck with grief at having abandoned her baby and stopped in Puebla. From there, she wrote Maximilian pleading for the boy's return: "I appeal to the noble and generous heart of your Majesty. I cannot adjust to this separation from my child, eight days that I have tried have been impossible, and I desire that your Majesty let me take my child until he is five years old, and that is a short time." Bizarrely, she followed with a saccharine letter as though written by the boy asking that he be released to his mother or that she may die without him, which Maximilian read in disgust. She also wrote to Bazaine, asking him to use his influence with Maximilian.[11]

In her alarm, Alice set out for Mexico City. Denied an audience with Maximilian, she appealed instead to Bazaine. The marshal passed Alice's request to Maximilian's office, and she soon received a response through the foreign affairs secretary, Martín Castillo, saying that the contract between the empire and "you and your six siblings was based on your good faith . . . at Chapultepec on the 9th of September. . . . Your Majesty, the Emperor, hopes that you do not bring on the sad necessity of showing to you his good heart can also be severe." Bazaine refused to intercede further.[12]

Alice was determined to regain her son and wrote again. "This prayer is to see my child, and not to be separated from him in his infancy. In my motherly dreams never did I think that my son would one day aspire to the crown, and my delirium to educate him like a good Mexican gave me many ideas to do good for the country . . . and today your Majesty honors my son in the national memory, but should I separate myself from my child when he needs all my solicitude? What guilty conscience could survive this separation?"[13]

On September 29, a palace guard in an imperial coach called at the Mexico City home where Alice was lodging. Informing her that the emperor and empress would see her, she entered the waiting carriage with considerable misgivings but wanting very much to see her son. When the coach did not turn toward the National Palace, she asked, "The court is at Chapultepec, no?" The officers nodded but then sped past the turnoff to Chapultepec and soon they were out of town. When she inquired where they were going, she received only silence. At the outskirts of Mexico City, they encountered a diligence used for overland travel, and it dawned on her that she was being deported. When asked to change vehicles, she descended from the carriage, seated herself on a nearby rock, and refused to budge. The footmen lifted her into the second carriage and she was driven to Puebla, where her husband waited. There they received a telegram from Maximilian saying Agustín was happy and healthy, accompanied by an order to leave the country.[14]

Maximilian realized his conduct would not reflect well on him, especially in the United States. In response, he had his staff draft a report of the situation for Mariano Degollado, his representative in Washington, "for a complete understanding of the patriotic thinking celebrated by our august sovereign." The report described the contract and the departure of the parents for Puebla, Alice's return to Mexico City, and her expulsion. This did not stop the U.S. Congress from passing a resolution to inquire into the matter. A report was also sent to the legations of England and France in Mexico City. Maximilian instructed Félix Eloin, while in Europe, to indirectly leak the secret agreement with the Iturbide family to the newspapers as a defense against any other trouble Alice might cause.[15]

The whole adoption scheme and conduct of Maximilian and his advisors served only as an embarrassment to Carlota. Although the episode publicly highlighted the royal couple's inability to have a child, she remained loyal and accepted the adoption, calling it "a simple act of justice" for them to protect the descendants of a former emperor. At the time, adoptions for societal or economic reasons were not uncommon, even if the child's parents were well and living. The childless couple came to love the child as their own. Yet in the case of Carlota, she seemed to care about her new ward but remained ambivalent. "The child is fresh and rosy, but not too well-behaved at present," she wrote.[16]

As the boy's unhappy parents made their way to Veracruz, they protested to Maximilian that he had no legal warrant to keep the boy. The Iturbides either misunderstood the papers they had signed or as Maximilian saw it, they conspired to betray him, by taking the money and then embarrassing him. The family left Veracruz for New York; en route, Alice received a report that her son was doing well and was cheerful. It would be the last official imperial communication she would receive.[17]

In the United States, Alice appealed to Secretary Seward for intervention, who referred her to American minister John Bigelow in Paris, to request Napoléon's intercession. When she arrived in France, Alice met with Bigelow and afterward with the French minister of foreign affairs, Édouard Drouyn de L'Huys, who apologized but concluded the family was bound by the contract. He said France had no license to interfere in domestic matters in another empire, which seemed an ironic comment considering the damage the French army daily inflicted on the Mexican people. The Iturbide arrangement raised gossip within European social circles.[18]

Juárez and his ministers used the sad and bitter story as a useful gift in their case against Maximilian. When the incident leaked to the press, it was written that Maximilian "kidnapped" an American boy. The U.S. Congress issued a resolution against Maximilian. The incident played into growing disdain in the United States for the Mexican empire. In January 1866 in New York, a large public assembly gathered at the Cooper Institute to discuss the aid of Mexico against France as well as a society called the "Mexican Patriot's Club" and a "Juárez Club" promoting the restoration of the republic. The newspapers printed little positive information on the empire, which Maximilian refuted, while sending representatives to New York seeking entrepreneurs for partnerships in rail and steamship lines. Maximilian contemplated starting an imperial newspaper for an American audience simply to promote good public relations that would lead, he hoped, to an amiable alliance.[19]

What the outside world thought of the Mexican empire mattered greatly to Maximilian. He wrote to a former Austrian aide boasting of his Viennese staff, especially Count Thun. "In spite of all the gossip and tales about robbers, which are disseminated in the European and the Austrian papers by American money, we are very comfortable and contented here and . . . if I could suppose myself back at Miramar again, and the Mexican deputation were to come again, I should not hesitate or impose conditions, but accept with a ready and cheerful 'yes.' Like Guatimozin's [the last Aztec emperor, also known as Cuauhtémoc], mine is no bed of roses, indeed there are many thorns; but . . . I often receive tokens of true gratitude," said Maximilian. "I love strenuous work, but . . . I want to see results. I am under no illusions as to the possibility that the new edifice upon which we are working may collapse if exposed to storms, and that I may perish with it, but nobody can deprive me of the consciousness of having worked devotedly for a sublime idea, and this is better . . . than to molder in inactivity in Europe," he continued. "There is no more pitiable creature than an appanaged [subsidized] prince, leading what is called a carefree life."[20]

In the autumn of 1865, still seeking to have a concordat with the Vatican and to heal the wounds between the sovereigns and the clerics, Maximilian pressured ministers José María Gutiérrez de Estrada and José Manuel Hidalgo to resume talks in Rome. When neither of them felt they could open a dialogue, Maximilian reached out to Father Augustin Fischer, a man of dubious character, who had arrived in Mexico in 1864 and ingratiated himself. A German by birth, Fischer immigrated to Texas in the 1840s, then drifted to the goldfields of California. After training as a Jesuit, he went to work for Durango's bishop but, after committing indiscretions, was dismissed. Charming, persuasive, and intellectual with a gift for flattery and snobbery, he quickly became another officious acolyte of the emperor. Fischer convinced Maximilian that he could sway the pope.[21]

When Fischer suggested he could go to Rome to see papal representatives, Maximilian ordered Fischer to rewrite the proposed concordat to the Vatican. The emperor agreed to soften the guidelines for "liberty of worship" and would allow the clergy to resume public education. He still demanded, however, that ecclesiastical regulations be approved by imperial decree, and the church could not censor books. Fischer set out for Europe accompanied by envoys Joaquín Velázquez de León, Bishop Francisco Ramírez, and Joaquín Degollado, feeling assured that they could mend Mexico's relationship with the clergy.[22] No one knew at the time what a disaster the charlatan Fischer would be for the empire.

In late September 1865 Juárez's Liberals started to reinvigorate. After being misled by a number of American speculators, Matías Romero in Washington and José María Jesús Carvajal in New York made headway in purchasing arms. Carvajal obtained two bond guarantees of $30 million from private investors in New York, thanks in part to Gen. Lew Wallace. With the funding, the Mexican Republicans could at last buy weapons and ammunition from surplus remains held in U.S. munitions factories. But with their credit remaining very uncertain, the bonds sold for little in the way of cash proceeds. A purchasing agent in New York, Herman Sturm, however, convinced American munitions companies to accept the bonds in exchange for guns. Once a few entrepreneurs agreed, other companies consented to sell the agent all sorts of munitions of war and even ships. Wallace purchased guns from manufacturers such as Richard J. Gatling and John D. Mowry. Romero took pleasure that the Liberals used the bonds like dollars. "At a cost of an obligation almost insignificant for Mexico, tremendous material assistance was obtained," wrote Romero.[23]

In the camps of the imperial army in Mexico, morale degenerated as soldiers from the United States joined the Juaristas. Guerrilla attacks on French supply lines proliferated. When captured, the guerrillas took punishment and often seemed unfazed under torture, with whippings by a cat-o'-nine-tails, or even at the prospect of death. The relentless attacks and resistance led to fatigue and tension in the French battalions mixed with Mexicans, Austrians, and Belgians, causing the soldiers of the four nations to come to blows. The lack of communication between headquarters left the European men in remote posts lost and disheartened, not knowing a concrete goal or timeline, and their boredom resulted in complaining and desertions. Many went to the war to make their fortune, but finding a hard fight, disorganization, beer a rare commodity, raw lodging, and woody vegetables, many fled to the United States to settle or asked to go back to Africa to finish their service. A number of the Arabs, angry at the French occupation of their own countries but forced to fight in Mexico, lost all hope. Two men, Bou Medin and Moktar Ben Abdalla, were tried for desertion, as well as other Algerian, Egyptian, and Arab sharpshooters. A number abandoned their units in disgust with their leaders, who, in their own confusion and power struggles, lost the confidence of their men. Some left to join the Mexican ranks, not for better pay but for moral reasons.[24]

In the melee, Charles Du Pin increased brutality in the field. At the little village of Croy near Soto la Marina, when Du Pin learned of a pending ambush, he rode into the town and found the mistress of the local guerrilla chief. When asked where her lover was and what his plans were, he took out his watch and placed it on a table along with a coil of rope. He gave her five minutes to tell him the plot. The terrified woman ran for the door, and the counterguerrillas pulled their pistols. When they placed the rope around her neck, she revealed the whereabouts of her man. With such rash acts and endless reports of brutality, Maximilian finally ordered Col. Du Pin back to France. Not only was he disgusted with his savage methods, but the officers in the regular army had begun to complain, albeit for a different reason. "The attacks against Du Pin came mainly from the regular French army, which witnessed extraordinary rivalries. For many officers, the success of the counterguerrillas could show up their own incompetence," wrote historian Jean-François Lecaillon.[25]

Indeed, horror increased on both sides of the fight. When the mayor of one community advised the French officials of a pending Liberal attack, they shot him. The Liberals mutilated the bodies of captives. Without clear motives, both the Liberals and France's counterguerrillas burned ranches and haciendas, both sides blaming the other. This spread terror throughout regions once loyal to the empire.[26]

Maximilian made the French campaign on Mexico more difficult when, after hard-fought victories against the guerrillas and courts-martial, he often conferred absolution on convicts. He delighted in doing so, thinking it earned him the love of his subjects, but it cost him the respect of the military officers. Bazaine and other generals could not hide their discontent with Maximilian's excessive leniency. French authorities in Paris also urged Maximilian to support the army's extreme severity with the freebooters or he would lose the empire entirely, that they must suppress even the most microscopic of violations that caused morale problems and eroded his position as emperor. The marshal pressured him to stop granting clemency, and finally Maximilian relented.[27]

When Marshal Bazaine received a telegram from Mazatlán that Benito Juárez had abandoned Mexico and fled north over the border into New Mexico territory, the emperor came to believe the Juaristas had no further cause to maintain their fight. Based on this erroneous information, Bazaine and other officers insisted the time had come to finish the war, and they could do so by ruthlessly crushing the Liberals. At Bazaine's urging, Maximilian agreed, but at the same time he blamed Napoléon. "The marshal will have sent you the draconian law I was forced to issue against the guerrillas; the result of this law will be favorable. We would already have rid the country of the scourge long ago, had we not been short of troops," Maximilian wrote Napoléon.[28]

Maximilian signed the infamous "draconian law" on October 3, 1865, known as the "Black Decree," under intense pressure from Bazaine and the military. The seemingly magnanimous, forgiving emperor, consistently averse to injustice and cruelty, in this case ruled that anyone found in armed resistance to the empire or without proper authorization to carry a weapon, whether representing a political cause or not, would be court-martialed and shot within twenty-four hours, without appeal or mercy. Anyone found belonging to an armed band, or who aided, supplied, or protected such groups, would also be condemned to death and executed. The decree promised amnesty to those who lay down their weapons and surrendered.[29] It was the most uncompromising, punitive, and brutal law of his time as emperor.

In the preamble to the decree, Maximilian asserted that the country had degenerated into armed factions claiming to fight to restore Juárez, who now had abandoned his country. "The national government has long been indulgent, and has granted acts of clemency to allow men who have been misguided. . . . From now on, the struggle will be between honorable men of the nation and bands of criminals and brigands. The time of indulgence has passed: the despotism of the bandits, of those who burn villages, who rob and murder peaceful citizens . . . will no longer be tolerated. The government, wielding its power, will hereafter be inflexible in meting out punishment, as required by the laws of civilization, respect for humanity, and the demands of morality," he wrote.[30]

Everyone in the Imperialista ranks, including the French and Austrian commanders, congratulated Maximilian on his "energy" and his "iron hand." They saw this as key to overcoming the frustrations of years of battle and mounting losses in the field. Bazaine followed the enactment of the law with his own orders to the his commanders. "The troops under your orders will take no prisoners," wrote Bazaine. "Every individual, of whatever rank, taken with arms in his hands shall be put to death. In the future, let there be no exchange of prisoners. This is a death-struggle. On both sides it is only a question of killing or being killed."[31]

According to some, Bazaine issued this statement because of a recent and horrific incident on the Veracruz railroad. When running down the line, a mechanic saw the rails had been removed before an approaching curve, so he blew the whistle. As the train slowed to a stop, waiting Juarista guerrillas rushed forth to kill and mutilate the mechanic, an artilleryman, and six French solders. The women on the train were raped. As soon as he got word, the area commander of the counterguerrillas dispatched a unit of forty Egyptians and twenty Mexican soldiers to investigate, and they also fell under attack.[32]

At first, the Black Decree had its intended effect in some areas. The leader of the Liberals in Tamaulipas, including the former Republican governor, came forward to surrender to the counterguerrillas. His fighters also lay down their arms. But most of all, since it pronounced open season on the Mexican Juarista generals, the Imperialist generals took full advantage of it. Gen. Ramón Méndez used the law to avenge personal animosities. He captured Juarista generals José María Arteaga Magallanes and Carlos Salazar Ruíz and hastily executed them. However, overall, the Juaristas experienced a surge in recruits as they planned retribution on the French military and on American immigrants. Minister of Colonization Maury warned Maximilian that the sovereigns' reputations as saviors of the country were quickly eroding. The new law only gave the clergy further reason to denounce Maximilian and stir up anger. In defiance, some parish priests collected arms to give to the Liberals. Often when a local man was executed, the priests lionized him as a martyr.[33]

Morale and day-to-day life in Mexico became harsh and chaotic. The cities and towns saw an influx of begging, and the prisons filled with alleged bandits or those thought to be cooperating with them. The number of widows proliferated, and police could do little to stem the unrest. Newspapers in the United States condemned the Black Decree, but the French army and Imperialistas defended the emperor's act, stating that the international press was ignorant about conditions in Mexico and reiterated the need to be iron-fisted to stop random killings of French citizens. Maximilian, however, seemed to regret the edict, issuing orders to exempt certain Juaristas from death, like Vicente Riva Palacio, if captured.[34]

Maximilian soon learned Juárez had not fled Mexico. He again expressed his wish to unite the country, harboring the illusion that if he could just contact Juárez and the Liberals, whose values he shared, he could win them over and rule in peace. He soon received an ominous message sent indirectly from Juárez, that with the American Civil War over, the United States prepared to aid the Republican cause and Maximilian should leave the country while he still could. "I wish greatly to come to an understanding with Juárez," Maximilian wrote late in 1865. "But before everything, he ought to recognize the determination of the effective majority of the nation which wants calm, peace and prosperity; and it is necessary that he decide to collaborate with his ceaseless energy and his intelligence in the difficult work which I have begun.

If, as I believe, he really has in view the happiness of Mexico . . . no Mexican loves the country and has its advancement at heart so much as I . . . let him come to help me sincerely and loyally and he will be welcomed with open arms like all good Mexicans," he wrote. "I am ready to receive Juárez into my council and among my friends."[35]

Juárez wrote confidently, "With the attitude that the government of the United States . . . Maximilian has now not the slightest probability of cementing his so-called throne. . . . The United States will never permit him to consolidate his power, and his sacrifices and victories will have counted for nothing."[36]

❦[12]❧

Like a Lost Soul

In Chihuahua, Juárez faced political turmoil of his own, despite his isolation. Gen. Jesús González Ortega, who had been threatening a political takeover for some months, although he had left his homeland for the United States, proclaimed himself provisional president of Mexico when Juárez's term of office expired on November 30, 1865. Juárez declared that he would remain as the sitting president, citing that the unique circumstances of the country's occupation extended his term of office and that González Ortega had deserted his post, despite the fact that he left with Juárez's blessing. Through New Orleans, González Ortega arrived at Brazos Santiago, where he was arrested by American authorities and released to Liberal Gen. Mariano Escobedo. The dispute ended when Maximilian, who learned of the debate, invited González Ortega to join his imperial government. González Ortega, at least temporarily, dropped his claim and yielded to Juárez, who wrote, "He did not read the Constitution and found himself in a ridiculous position."[1]

Then tragedy struck Juárez again. In August, his second son, Antonio, died in New York City, causing Juárez immeasurable grief. Shortly before this, Manuel Doblado, who lobbied and raised funds for the Republican cause, also died in New York. Juárez had only a handful of generals and representatives he could trust; the others either joined the Imperialistas or left the country to watch and wait. "Better to be alone than in bad company," Juárez commented.[2]

On the heels of the Black Decree, Jacques Langlais, a new French financial advisor, arrived in Mexico City from Paris with a letter from Napoléon preparing Maximilian for inevitable troop withdrawals. He advised him to immediately begin organizing his own army. "The Mexican army ought not to exceed 25,000 men with the foreign contingents, and ought to cost only 25 million francs. It can be increased only in proportion as the French troops are reduced. The property of the clergy must be made use of. Honesty must be introduced into the administration and then only such persons admitted to your council as are loyal to the French intervention," wrote Napoléon. "I hope that Americans will not trouble the new empire. In any case, Your Majesty's government, on its side, must endeavor to cause us no embarrassment, since France is making such sacrifices."[3]

Presented with yet another auditor, Maximilian accepted Langlais and rolled up his sleeves to work with his new finance team. While he thanked Napoléon for assigning Langlais, whom he found genial and talented, he also attempted to explain complications with money flow and debt. "It is difficult, but not desperate," said Maximilian. "It is only the war that is devouring the resources, the other branches of the administration cost less than in any other country." They tallied the customs receipts and other sources of income, looking for a way to amass a loan payment to French creditors and cobbled together 40 million francs (8 million pesos). But the financiers protested it was not enough. They blamed Maximilian's minister of foreign affairs, José Fernando Ramírez, for not responding to their claims, letting the debt mount. In response, the emperor gave in to their complaints and removed him. Yet Ramírez kept his seat as president of the Council of State and became the director of the Academia de Bellas Artes. Maximilian then worked with the team to reorganize the flow of money to save the country from bankruptcy.[4]

Pressure on Maximilian escalated from his northern neighbors and abroad. When powerful members of the U.S. Congress called for a free and independent Mexico, he knew he must hurry to distance his empire from France. Simultaneously, his Mexican minister to Paris, José Manuel Hidalgo, wrote complaining he had not been paid for his work at the Parisian court, never mentioning that his influence with Napoléon and Eugénie had collapsed. Instead of advocating for the Mexican empire, he only mentioned his personal concerns, stating that his lack of funds caused him to miss marriage opportunities, including to a woman thought to be a Russian spy with ties to the French foreign office.[5]

With these complications, Maximilian set aside a tour of Yucatán planned for November. Over one year earlier, in fall 1864, despite the challenges associated with setting up his rule in Mexico, Maximilian had sent a representative to investigate the possibility of expansion of his empire into Central America. He dispatched Count Olivier Rességuier, a colleague from the Austrian navy, on a secret mission to tour the area. The idea was to construct an alliance between Guatemala, Honduras, El Salvador, and Nicaragua with the goal of eventually unifying the region under Mexico's protection.[6]

Maximilian sent Rességuier with a unit of Austrian officers and his attaché, Maj. Gustav von Boleslawski, to Mérida to learn the political situation under Yucatecan imperial commissioner José Salazar Ilarregui, an astronomer, civil engineer, and mining expert. Salazar had organized the military and the government, and he attempted to pacify the Mayans, who often raided settlements. The Austrians investigated the attacks, collected plants, and recorded climate and topographical data. France was vitally interested in consolidating power in the region and could help extend Maximilian's control to the Isthmus of Panama, where they visualized an interoceanic canal. However, he deemed it critical that Mexico shore up a boundary agreement with the English in control of Belize. Once Yucatán was reinforced and under control, Maximilian planned to make it an anchor from which to ally himself with other Central and South American countries. In preparation for this plan and to build friendships with leaders in the region, Maximilian and Carlota sent a number of significant donations to distribute to the poor and sick through Salazar.[7]

Incomplete pacification of Mexico did not preclude expansion, Maximilian reasoned. In an age of European imperialism, enlarging his dominion seemed natural. It was the sport of kings. After Rességuier's 1864 exploration demonstrated the scheme could work, Maximilian waited for the appropriate time to press for agreements. By summer 1865 Maximilian finally felt that the Central American alliance must progress. But with the financial restructuring of the country, the complexities of building a national armed service, and the Black Decree, departing the capital for a long tour, he feared, would leave the empire vulnerable. Therefore, he asked Carlota to travel to Yucatán on his behalf with instructions to acquaint herself with the people. He proposed Yucatán would become the "center of gravity" for the countries of Central America and concluded, "The Empire [will be] the central power in the new continent, while conceding the dominion of the north to the United States and that of the south to the Brazilian empire."[8]

In her preparations to go to what they believed a raw and untamed region, Maximilian instructed Carlota to "dress simply, which in any case is always more becoming to you." At receptions, the local landowners, village officials, and native deputations should be included, he said, "for the more these people are invited, the more they will be won over, and the more the foreign ambassadors will be impressed." He cautioned her not to be too high-handed, in view of her moods of haughty indignation, adding, "above all, never keep these people waiting." Ambassadors from a number of countries, including Belgium's minister Édouard Blondeel, planned to travel with her, to scout for economic opportunities. As the empress preferred, she took only a small group of advisors, including Félix Eloin, who had recently returned from Belgium to serve as her aide; the one-legged Gen. José López Uraga; José Fernando Ramírez; and Pedro Escudero y Echánove, the current minister of justice. Maximilian also warned her to be wary of the influence of Eloin and Uraga, "who always want to be so aristocratic, which will get you nowhere in Yucatán where the people are very democratic and have no use for pomposity and etiquette."[9]

On November 6 Carlota left Mexico City accompanied by her ladies and entourage, traveling through rain and over mountain passes so rugged and slick she had to go by horseback at times. In the close quarters of travel, the ministers irritated her, however. "The ambassadors are relentless; Uraga says Blondeel sleeps all the time in the coach, and the latter states that Uraga smokes around him too much," Carlota wrote to Maximilian. There was some fun along the way and possibly some shenanigans. Carlota told Maximilian that José Fernando Ramírez knocked at her door while she was undressing. She dressed again, and Ramírez walked in wearing a robe and slippers, happy and wanting to visit.[10]

Taking the train from La Soledad, the party stopped at Paso del Macho, where a committee of ladies wearing the latest in Parisian hats came out to greet her in the damp weather. Several of the ladies accompanied her to Veracruz, where local artisans constructed a ceremonial chariot for her, which she rode in to the port to the people's delight. "Everyone agrees they have never seen such enthusiasm. [Belgian minister Édouard] Blondeel says that my presence is worth more than an army. The cheers are not for me, but because I am your wife," Carlota wrote Maximilian.[11]

It was the first time Carlota visited Veracruz since their arrival over a year earlier. At a couple of dinners, the businessmen impressed her. "The people here are very special . . . all are well dressed and work. They are proud and I think that they care little for the rest of the country," she wrote. After a few days, she gave her impressions of the merchants, whom she had not met upon their entry to Mexico. "They were against us at first, but now they want to show us their respect and gratitude. Everyone here seems to have money and they are all very well dressed," she wrote. "They are not in the least like the Mexicans, much more European in their outlook. There is no dislike of foreigners, and some of the schools, which are very good, are directed by Spaniards. Many of the natives are of the Spanish descent . . . they are very proud and independent. Everyone works, there is no deficit in the municipality, which has just paid 150,000 pesos out of its profits on restoring the local hospital. They are so rich they can afford to give fiestas and receptions like nowhere else." On November 15 there was a dinner with a concert by well-known opera singer Ángela Peralta. "Last night there were fireworks and tri-color paper balloons written with 'Viva el Emperador y la Emperatriz.'" But she slept little, the mosquitos biting heartily. After dropping the nets over her bed, then "about eleven, came a rooster with a hymn and loud cries," she wrote.[12]

A few days later, after a wet norther passed, on November 20 Carlota sailed from Veracruz on a small, shabby Mexican steamer, *Tabasco,* rather than in comfort on the Austrian corvette *Dandolo.* To her, it was a matter of national fidelity. She took no escort of troops or guards. Most of her retinue embarked on the comparatively luxurious *Dandolo,* escorting the sea-bucket carrying the empress. She complained however that she had to pay dearly for her traveling under their flag—the crew was made up of all different nationalities who smoked and chatted noisily all day. They were dirty and ragged and had only one clean shirt they wore at departure and arrival. Two days later Carlota arrived at the port of Sisal. Her rough voyage left her dizzy, tired, and a little beat up. She stayed in her quarters on the ship and ate millet porridge. She wrote her husband that she was like a "sick bird."[13]

Carlota and her party entered Mérida to a 101-gun salute from the town's citadel of San Benito. Church bells rang, and cheering crowds came to meet her in the city known as the *ciudad blanca* ("white city") for its clean, crisp appearance. She was pleased to find an orderly place that she described as beautiful, refined, and unique. Over the next several days, Carlota visited hospitals, factories, shops, and even the prison, where she gave kind words and advice to the convicts. Commissioner Salazar Ilarregui held a ball and quadrille for the empress, and in turn she gave one for the leadership of Mérida, decorating various officials. At the municipal palace, groups demonstrated popular dances of the day, including El Jarabe, El Toro, El Pichito, El Chicix, and El Cardinal. In honor of her visit, Salazar Ilarregui made a public address in which he invited the indigenous and proud Maya to come to Mérida to make peace.[14]

Yucatán, a tropical and unbearably humid region with scrubby vegetation and jungle, remained the center of henequen plantations, which produced sisal fiber from the agave, used for rope, twine, paper pulp, mats, and other floor coverings. Tons were shipped to Europe, much of it as contraband to skirt customs duties. The profit potential was enormous. The land, with its plentiful rains, held great agricultural potential, and the French feared that the British had designs on the area. From the time she arrived, Carlota felt tensions from the merchants and area manufacturers.[15]

To smooth over relations, Carlota met with factory owners of cotton textiles and large henequen plantations at haciendas across the region, including Chimay, Uayalceh, and Mucuyché. She marveled at the indigenous groups and that many were employed in the growing and harvesting of henequen and fiber manufacture. She visited area churches and reported that in contrast to the church attitudes in central Mexico, the priests used moderation and prudence and had honor in teaching students but remained in severe need of support.[16]

After a few days, amid continued salutes and festivities, Carlota and her retinue left for the Mayan ruins of Uxmal. "Half the young men of Mérida accompanied me on horseback," she wrote, "most of whom had never ridden so far." She wore a light traveling cloak, a sombrero held in place by a scarf, and heavy boots to climb the pyramids, all the while taking notes in her precise handwriting and drawing a map of the site for Maximilian. She recorded the ruins' architectural detail and symbols. At the building she termed the "priests' palace," she marveled at the bloody handprints lining the walls. In her letters to her husband, with reports on the humidity and unseasonable temperatures, she also complained about the food, especially a dessert made from the dark fruit pulp of the *zapote prieto* tree that clearly revolted her. She said, "the regional dishes here are all very different from Mexico, and remind me of the black brews of the Spartans." Exhausted from the oppressive weather and her never-ending official duties, she prepared to move on to the last stop on her tour. "We will see how my visit goes in Campeche, and whether it is wise for me to stay there. I am not in the least bit nervous, only one must not tempt Providence too much. It is strange enough for me to be here at all."[17]

Curiously, the Belgian minister Édouard Blondeel noticed on the trip that at times Carlota acted nervous and stressed. She even admitted that in the heat and strain of continuous public appearances, she started to think "sad ideas." On the next segment from Uxmal to the village of Becal, she wrote, "I . . . made part of the trip on horseback to pull myself together a bit, I felt cheerful again and felt a sort of sweet and reverent joy that had more to do with the nearness of God than with the world." Her accompanying physicians noted she appeared upset and unstrung, so much that at times they slipped morphine into her coffee or tea to calm her nerves. This common method for settling the mind likely did her more harm than good.[18]

At the beautiful town of Campeche, the royal entourage was fêted with balls, presentations, and dinners. Before her departure, officials again read proclamations, recited poetry, and released a flock of white doves.[19]

There she received a letter from Maximilian, who remained working in Mexico City. "The further you go, the more I miss you and the more melancholy I feel. I wander like a lost soul through the empty rooms and to add to the depression, the weather is freezing. One needs more furs than in Milan in winter," he said, suffering chills. Maximilian ordered the National Palace staff to light the stoves in his office and adjoining rooms. "They made the temperature as hot as that of a Russian bath," wrote Blasio. "The Emperor reveled in the heat, but we Mexicans almost roasted. . . . If he left the room for a few minutes I would throw open one of the windows to get a breath of fresh air, but on hearing his returning step I would hurry to close it again. Occasionally he would catch me at it and between jest and earnest say, 'What are you thinking of? Don't you see we're freezing?'"

"No, Sir, I see that we are frying."

"These children who have hot blood do not realize that an old man of thirty-[three], like me, is as cold as ice. Close that window, and if you open it again, I'll have a carpenter nail it shut," Maximilian said.[20]

In her absence, Maximilian worked with his ministers and government departments to improve communication and suppress bickering, reminding them he sacrificed his trip to Yucatán for them. He also had ministers negotiating with various bishops and curates regarding the role of Catholicism in Mexico. Attempting to square the logic of the Bishop of Veracruz on a matter, he accused him of violating the church's own disciplines, "directly in opposition of the precepts of the Council of Trent."[21] This no doubt did little to heal simmering contempt emanating from some clergy.

Dealing with the financial headaches of the empire irritated Maximilian. He complained that the French asked him to account for every franc and peso in their audits, and to make deep cuts in what he paid to his servants on the civil list, while Bazaine was allowed to throw parties and live lavishly as a "military expenditure." Much of the strain and misunderstanding between Maximilian and Bazaine stemmed from their tendency to correspond by letter, rather than sit down face-to-face and unite their goals. In some ways, Maximilian wanted to appear detached from the French army, he yet desperately needed them.[22] Despite the conflicts, he struggled to get the marshal to help him.

Preparations for a ball given by Bazaine and the French army.
Note decorations to honor Napoléon III and Eugénie of France, 1865.

In December 1865 Maximilian did his best to appear in command and wrote orders and daily requests to Bazaine to maintain order, but in a remarkably unassertive tone. Since the principal laws defining the rights and duties of the administrative branches were complete, "the moment has come to govern and act. In order to do it successfully, I need loyal, honest, and committed men and I am counting on your assistance to inform me candidly about the officials called upon to enforce these laws," he wrote. He ordered Bazaine to administer the imperial prefects and commissioners of the territorial divisions, writing, "your deep experience in men and things in Mexico . . . makes you necessary for this important work."[23]

As a warrior, there is little indication that Bazaine wanted to administer imperial government districts. He expected to defer all civil authority to Maximilian and his prefects, advising his generals to avoid conflicts of authority. But Maximilian assumed Bazaine would maintain domestic peace, while still subduing the rest of the country. When Bazaine released a battalion of Egyptians at Veracruz to sail to the Sudan to quash an uprising there, Maximilian damned their loss. He had counted on them holding down insurrection along the coast; "their cooperation would have been extremely helpful in the hot lands," Maximilian wrote Bazaine. He worried that this left Veracruz vulnerable to Juarista occupation and demanded to know his plans for the future."[24]

With Carlota in Yucatán, Maximilian felt hemmed in by duties so much that he said he began "to feel as atrophied as a tortoise or an oyster, or what is worse, like one of the former presidents of Mexico who never dared to venture out of the capital," he wrote. To go traveling, he contemplated a tour of the Pacific port of Acapulco, two hundred miles south of the capital, but Bazaine could not allow him to travel through the rebellious state of Guerrero. When he suggested meeting Carlota on her return at the town of Jalapa, Gen. Thun, whose second division covered that region, asked that he reconsider since he had few men to cover the emperor's security detail. So he was left with short excursions, attended by a small military escort on the weekends and his kitchen crew, going where there was no fear of assassination. It seemed worth the risk to overcome his forlornness.[25]

On one of his short tours, Maximilian, with Blasio and a company of hussars, started out at six in the morning for Cuernavaca, a small town fifty miles south of Mexico City, lately made safer to travel with the recent execution of a regional guerrilla and his men. There, Maximilian viewed Hernán Cortés's palace and the town. Recalling his talk with Carlota about his desire for a retreat outside Mexico City on this tour, he walked through a deserted summer house with an immense garden once belonging to French magnate José de la Borda, who had made his fortune surveying and prospecting in the silver mines of Taxco. Built in the mid-1700s, Borda spent over 1 million pesos on the gardens alone. The buildings were abandoned and in disrepair, and the pools were dry. However, the groves of mangos and citrus still existed, overgrown with vines. Maximilian could see the place's potential as a luxurious escape, captivated by its landscape and tranquility. Almost immediately, he put his assistant, Rudolf Günner, administrator of the imperial residences, in charge of the project to possess, renovate, and manage the Borda home and Wilhelm Knechtel to revive the gardens. He also called in architect Carl Gangolf

Kayser, with whom he consulted on nearly every building plan. "In a few days the rooms were hung with tapestries, and the gardens cleared," said Blasio. Maximilian personally augmented planting in the landscape and ordered various trees, including mango, zapote, lemon, lime, peach, and banana.[26]

In the one-story home, the imperial chambers were located in the second patio toward the back of the compound where Maximilian's study, an airy and beautiful space, adjoined the dining room. "Vines and orchids were arranged on the walls. Fish swam in crystal globes and cages were hung containing birds with colored plumage," wrote Blasio. The swimming pool and gardens lay in sight of his office. To friends, Maximilian further described the Borda house as a "simple, secluded quinta . . . a true *buen retiro* full of 100-year-old orange trees and charming rose arbors . . . where one may dream away many a happy minute softly swaying in the hammock after hard work."[27]

Detached from worries about debt and military buildups, as well as his recent stomach ailments, he waxed lyrical to friends and family. "Picture to yourself a broad, level valley, blessed by Heaven, stretching out before you like a golden bowl, surrounded by range upon range of mountains, colored in all the various shades of the rainbow and beyond them the giant volcanoes lifting their snow-covered crests to the deep blue heavens. . . . There are no seasons here, [but] a wealth of tropical vegetation of intoxicating fragrance and luscious fruits—and to crown all, a climate as lovely as an Italian May."[28]

By the first of January 1866 the court officially moved to Cuernavaca for a few months. Col. Feliciano Rodríguez, in charge of the imperial stables along with Charles Bombelles, designed a conveyance for these trips, drawn by twelve white mules fitted with blue harnesses. The coachman, grooms, and footmen wore charro uniforms of leather trimmed with silver and gray sombreros. Maximilian happily traveled through the cambered and switchback mountain passes to Cuernavaca.[29]

Carlota returned from Yucatán on December 20, and even though she was on her return through the cumbres from Veracruz, Maximilian expressed his feelings of desolation, nostalgia, and "dark melancholy" on Christmas day. Upon receiving word that she and her party arrived safely, Maximilian wrote to her saying he had calmed down considerably after worrying about her safety. He was surrounded by his advisors and ministers, and more importantly, he said, little Agustín. He assured Carlota he had been hard at work, only Marshal Bazaine presented the greatest of obstacles.[30] However, it was no secret that he had wonderful times away from the capital.

The people of Cuernavaca had embraced Maximilian. The young men

formed a guard of honor for the emperor called the Cock's Club and persuaded Maximilian to accept its presidency. They wore a uniform of black
trousers, a blue shirt, and gray felt hat with a black plume. They assembled
with a drummer and bugler for Maximilian's public appearances. Additionally,
the city fathers gave Maximilian the use of the Cortés's palace for functions.[31]

In the fresh air of January 1866, Carlota traveled to Cuernavaca for the
first time and loved the beauty and tranquility of La Borda, as laid out by
Maximilian. But sadly on January 6, 1866, the feast day of the Epiphany,
she learned of her father Leopold's death from a heart condition. She and
Maximilian, who had depended on him for moral support and advice, plunged
into despair. "I heard Max sobbing in the room next door and that told me
all," Carlota wrote. "We wept together but we were not alone in our grief.
The whole place shared our sorrow. With the intuitive tact of certain primitive
people, the Indians, in the space of a few hours, had replaced the triumphal
arches by signs of mourning." She derived some comfort from the expressions
of sympathy and affection of her staff.[32]

Maximilian remembered one last word of advice from his father-in-law,
weakening and ill, written on November 12, about their empire in the New
World—and that was to win favor but not pay too much for it. "What counts
in America is success—everything else is mere poetry and a waste of money.
And, now God bless you. I can say no more." Although Carlota's brother Leopold II inherited the Belgian throne, Carlota's true connection to her homeland went with her father, and it left her utterly in shock and bereft of her
mentor. A moral pillar of support for the empire was now gone.[33]

Over the next months into spring, she found Cuernavaca a calming resort.
With her lady-in-waiting, Otilia Jordan de Degollado, Carlota sometimes rode
horseback over the distance of fifty miles from Mexico City, accompanied by
her palatine guard of 150 men. On certain trips, she took time to explore certain
natural wonders, like the grottos of Cacahuamilpa, thirty-five miles southwest
in Guerrero, to see major rock formations in the caves, bringing along Josefa
Iturbide and all the while mulling over economic opportunities for Mexico.
At La Borda house, she and Maximilian swam in the pool and boated in the
lake. She welcomed guests with a relaxed manner, dressed in white crinoline
decorated with black mourning ribbons and fresh flowers at her waist. Their
dinners featured more relaxed and native dining with tamales and local fruit,
albeit prepared by German cooks. She promised people they would not have
tortillas or *tasajo* (dried meat). In the evenings, she played whist with her ladies
and attendants. Manuelita del Barrio, one of her ladies-in-waiting, attempted

to teach her how to play the Habanera on the mandolin. In the gardens, she watched hummingbirds drink from the datura. Her attendants helped her to catch rare butterflies and insects for Dr. Dominik Bilimek, the Moravian priest and botanist assigned to collect insect and plant specimens.[34]

The tall, stout Bilimek, with his gray beard and heavy spectacles, provided Carlota with endless diversion. He spoke little, consumed in study, unless it had to do with natural history or his insects and reptiles, which he referred to as "little creatures of the good God." When he did not know a term in Spanish, he used its Latin equivalent, "making a hash of his laconic remarks. He would start out early in the morning, his favorite hunting ground being one of the nearby sugar plantations. His equipment included an immense yellow umbrella, a cork helmet and a linen duster with capacious pockets. . . . We would see him bobbing about like a gigantic mushroom. He spent his evenings placing in alcohol the vipers and other snakes that represented part of the day's bag. Occasionally he would take off his helmet and display to us centipedes, scorpions, flies, grasshoppers and grubs pinned to the lining," said Blasio, who constantly feared that Bilimek's creatures would escape and slither into his room located next door.[35]

So thrilled was Maximilian with Cuernavaca that he bought a small coffee plantation at Acapantzingo, a mile and half to the southwest where he laid the foundation stones for a home, designed by Julius Hofman from Trieste, Italy, to be an "Indian chalet," called El Olindo. Knechtel supervised the building and grounds design and finished in quick order. Pleased with his new hideaway, he gave a small party for the nearby landowners. The empress was not present, however, he reported to her in superlatives that Olindo "was seductively beautiful and Knechtel had worked wonders with his hard work and good taste. . . . Today I had my first Olindo coffee, which of course, I found excellent." They communicated by letters and ministers traveling between Mexico City and Cuernavaca. The implication was that he longed for a place where he could spend time alone, much like a small house in Austria where he had sometimes stayed as a bachelor. People raised questions about the place eventually known as "Casa de la India Bonita," where it was known he had affairs with the local beauties, amid other speculations about what Maximilian did at El Olindo. Despite what she may have thought, Carlota tried to remain upbeat about the place, praising Maximilian on the walkways and gardens, which she visited in his absence.[36]

Once Blasio, attempting to understand why men with beautiful wives frequently took lovers, asked one of Maximilian's chamberlains about his own affairs. He replied, "Each day you have all sorts of fine food at the imperial table, but now and then don't you enjoy a meal of hot Mexican food, washed down with the white liquor of the country?"[37]

From the beginning of 1866 Maximilian divided his time between Chapultepec and Cuernavaca, only occasionally going to the National Palace, pleasing himself and staying away from frustrations. The court often spent two weeks at Chapultepec, then two at Cuernavaca. At La Borda, Carlota held exquisite dinner parties, the most frequent guests being Prince von Khevenhüller and other bachelor princes in his detail, lavish with wine and bawdy jokes and rumors. At one dinner, Maximilian and the others teased minister Martín Castillo, a recent widower with a jovial manner, who had recently begun seeing a young woman. It was rumored that Maximilian had been with the same woman, and with a knowing and mischievous look, remarked that she *would* make an excellent wife. "It escaped no one's notice that [Maximilian] cast desirous eyes upon various beautiful women about the court, and when discreet mention was made of the topic of [masculine] gallantry, the Empress would smile with a sadness that we all observed," said Blasio. But people also gossiped that Carlota had taken Belgian Col. Van der Smissen as a lover.[38]

After a few months Maximilian and Carlota rarely traveled to Cuernavaca together. Maximilian's secretary later learned that Maximilian had taken a mistress, a seventeen-year-old girl at Cuernavaca. Her name was Concepción Sedano, and although some said she was the daughter of the estate gardener, others said her father held a position in the municipal government. "An innocent, young Indian girl gives me the pleasure of her guileless affection," Maximilian was heard to say. Her maiden name was Leguizano, and she had permission from her father to see Maximilian. When she became pregnant, a hasty marriage for her was arranged with a man named Ignacio Sedano, and the baby son was declared to be fathered by him. Afterward it was rumored Carlota followed Maximilian to Cuernavaca to prevent him from seeing Sedano.[39]

According to his valet, Antonio Grill, Maximilian saw a number of women at the National Palace, Chapultepec, and in Cuernavaca, some of them the sisters of officers in Juárez's army. These women often charmed him at various dinner parties. In a society where taking a mistress was common, according to Grill, there were a number of assignations but no long-term *novias*. There is little doubt that Maximilian adored Carlota, who may have ceased to be a lover but was deeply loved by him. She clearly cared for Maximilian and supported his interests. She collected butterflies and insects for him, trying to enlarge the collection. "I have twenty species of butterflies, large and small and very

Concepción Sedano, ca. 1867

interesting," she said. "The so-called railroad chicharra [locust] squeaks like [the ones] in the forests of Brazil and you will like it."[40]

With the bon vivant Maximilian playing in his own world in Cuernavaca, Carlota often remained busy in the offices in Mexico City, checking his work and trying to keep astride of recent or pending decisions. She frequently called Blasio to her office, where he read documents to her and reported what Maximilian had been preparing. "She would listen attentively, as she paced the floor. Concerning some of the [matters] she would dictate her opinion; in connection with others she would give positive orders and place her initial or signature at the bottom. This would occupy us until ten or eleven o'clock," said Blasio.[41]

Col. Charles Blanchot later wrote that Carlota's distracted husband was beyond her control and she withdrew in discouragement, becoming solemn, severe, and melancholic. She still grieved for her father and seemed uninspired by Maximilian's glowing reports of happy times in Cuernavaca. "While I am delighted by the beauty that reigns in paradise, in the same measure, everything here in the valley is like an ugly plate, dusty, windy, and sad. . . . For the first time I came back to the city along the new street [Paseo de la Emperatriz]. Every day there are more and more pedestrians down in the park, especially of the masculine sex, the only gender that comes out here to walk," she wrote sullenly. In the evening, she sometimes dismissed royal convention and "liked to take an Indian dugout, almost alone, out in the quiet waters of the great lakes of Mexico City under the marvelously starry sky." She felt the expanse of these waters. As a royal wife, she compensated for Maximilian's frivolity and indecisiveness.[42]

On some level, Carlota sensed that Napoléon was about to drastically undermine the Mexican empire and hoped her emperor would begin to face reality.

❦ 13 ❧

The French Repatriation

In early January 1866, in Paris, with the Mexican empire drawing draft upon draft from the French government, Napoléon and Eugénie saw the Mexican intervention had returned little to France. Napoléon gave the impression he was ready to "close his account" with Mexico, expressing as much to American envoy John Bigelow. Eugénie, having recently reread the story of Hernán Cortés and the conquest of Mexico, summoned Gen. Edmond Aimable L'Hérillier, newly returned from his command in Durango and Zacatecas, and asked him why in 1519 so few soldiers were needed to subjugate this country and why so many more were required in 1866. The general, a former commander in the second division of infantry, attempted to demonstrate that things were quite different now, that Cortés engaged the tribal enemies of Montezuma, whereas Maximilian lacked few such internal affiliations. Only a small number in Mexico reliably and permanently adhered to the French, and soldiers often switched loyalties depending on the conditions. To her horror, she began to see that her simplistic reasoning and impassioned advocacy helped lead the French army and Maximilian into a very treacherous adventure.[1]

Napoléon saw his political status in Europe being tested. In France, throughout 1865, disgust with the Mexican venture grew exponentially within the Corps Législatif, among intellectuals, and the press recorded public protests. Prussia's rising power combined with easy territorial victories now threatened Austria and, in many ways, Napoléon's own power base, of which he was acutely protective. Even if the full army was not required to defend

Saddle given to Emperor Franz Josef by Maximilian,
photographed with saddle-maker Josef Kowarz

France, the disbursement of soldiers and sailors through several continents weakened the military presence at home. He wanted to order the French army to return from Mexico but with no specific timetable. Suspecting this, Maximilian argued against it, yet in genial terms, stating that he must allow the French troops to remain. He reminded Napoléon that it was a matter of honor. He did not know, however, that Napoléon had decided that his personal interests mattered more than promises and Mexico.[2]

Amid this climate of uncertainty, Maximilian dispatched his friend and advisor Charles Bombelles to Austria, the land he still referred to as "home," to try once more to conciliate Franz Josef on matters of the Family Pact. He asked Bombelles to see his mother and father to reassure them he and Carlota remained safe and in control of Mexico with no plans to leave. Although he said otherwise, it seemed evident that Maximilian secretly considered abdication and wanted more than ever a secure place for reentry into a life in Europe, not to mention to preserve his Habsburg ties. Bombelles failed to convince Franz

Crossing at Río Frío, en route from Veracruz to Mexico City,
Harper's Weekly, Feb. 9, 1867

Josef that Maximilian would not return to Austria claiming to be emperor of Mexico, and so the Family Pact still stood between them. Nevertheless, Maximilian sent Franz Josef a lavishly crafted parade saddle garnished with silver roses and filigree with intricate embroidery, along with the requisite goat hair chaps and gun bag, made by a staff of artisans in Mexico. The embroidery featured the royal insignias of Mexico with Maximilian's unique monogram.[3]

Meanwhile, it pleased Maximilian that other Europeans loyal to the sovereigns traveled to Mexico to prove their allegiance, a sign of the Mexican empire's legitimacy, he felt. Carlota's brother Leopold II, the new king of Belgium, sent a royal delegation. The commission comprised of members of the Belgian court, including Lt. Baron Frédéric Victor d'Huart, aide-de-camp to her brother Philippe, the Count of Flanders, along with the Count d'Alcantara, an elegant sportsman and playboy, attachés, Belgian Gen. Ferdinand-Louis Foury and Maj. Jean-Antoine Altwies. At the end of the mission, as the officials returned to Veracruz slogging through the rugged elevations of the plateaus, at Río Frío, about forty miles southeast of Mexico City, a group of twenty-five Liberal irregulars attacked the small group and d'Huart was killed. Maximilian immediately summoned a military escort, and he rode to Río Frío himself to bring the baron's body to Mexico City. He telegrammed Carlota "Huart is dead" and escorted the body to Mexico City.

The sovereigns ordered a solemn ceremony for his interment. Carlota blamed Bazaine, quickly adding, however, she did not doubt the intrinsic value of the French army. The incident left Leopold II's respect for the Mexican empire egregiously damaged.[4]

For some months, according to Napoléon's design, Bazaine began consolidating some of his forces in northeastern Mexico, with the exception of leaving Gen. Mejía's troops in control of the mouth of the Rio Grande. When the French evacuated Monterrey, the Juaristas quickly occupied the city. Maximilian agonized that while the Imperialistas still controlled Matamoros's customs revenues, the sudden loss of nearby Monterrey would lead the Juaristas and the U.S. military to think the French were in retreat. "In general, I think we should avoid abandoning these large cities in the north, which . . . have again fallen into the hands of our enemies," Maximilian wrote to Bazaine. "It seems all the more necessary to me to have Monterrey reoccupied by French troops, so that from there they can go to the aid of the brave General Mejía whose position in Matamoros remains difficult." It was really too late. Frustrated, Maximilian could do little to stop him. But he knew the Imperialistas needed to keep the northeast and protect the lucrative Matamoros trade. To maintain a foothold in the north, in desperation, Gen. Mejía resorted to collecting forced loans from Matamoros merchants with the goal of raising $100,000.[5]

Despite all indications that the United States planned to assist with the restoration of Juárez's republican government, Mejía, at this northernmost outpost, wrote that Washington planned to accept the Mexican empire, which Maximilian wanted most. An American commissioner at Matamoros "personally assured me that the government in Washington has decided to recognize the empire soon, but the border situation, depicted in a very negative light by the American generals, will prevent or at least delay it."[6] Based on such rumors, Maximilian believed potential diplomatic relations hinged only on the stability of his empire, not fully comprehending that U.S. disdain stemmed from France's expulsion of an extant republican government.

However, gnawing pressure mounted on the U.S.–Mexico border. Toward the end of 1865, in Tamaulipas the Juarista Gen. Mariano Escobedo had built up a sizeable army, which created havoc for Gen. Tomás Mejía's imperial troops. On the other side of the river, with the consent of American military, including Generals Ulysses S. Grant and Philip Sheridan, Gen. Godfrey Weitzel regularly harassed Mejía's army. Petty sniping, through artillery duels, stolen steamboats, and caustic correspondence erupted on the Rio Grande. Georges-Charles Cloué, chief naval officer of the gulf, anchored near the mouth of the Rio Grande, wrote American officers rebuking them for sustaining the Liberals. He cited France's neutrality in the Civil War and that international laws obliged them to be nonaligned in Mexican affairs. "If we had done the one-hundredth part of what is being done . . . on the banks of the Rio Grande, the American people would have loudly protested, and they would have been right," wrote Cloué. Observers agreed that most of the unlawful activity originated on the American side of the river, but it spawned a general atmosphere of hostility and regular assaults between Imperial and American soldiers. In November, Maximilian dispatched reinforcements on a French barque, writing he meant to demonstrate the strength of the Mexican empire to the "Yankees," adding that they would be won over with both kindness and energy.[7]

On December 30, Liberals, suspected to be aided by American troops, hijacked a convoy of fifteen carts en route south from Matamoros to San Fernando guarded by Imperial troops. When Mejía learned of the attack, he quickly dispatched the counterguerrillas to pursue the marauders. About thirty miles south of town, the red-coated contras ran into the Liberals on a foggy morning, cooking over their breakfast fires; they killed eleven, captured the remainder, and executed them the next morning at Matamoros. This only served to outrage local caudillos, whose ranks included a number of one-time American soldiers.[8]

Using the attack as a motive for revenge, on January 5, 1866, in the dark, cold, and rainy early-morning hours, sixty raiders, many of them African American, fortified by mescal, crossed the river from Texas and sacked the port of Bagdad. The attack, led by former Union general Richard Clay Crawford, who commanded a corps of Liberals in Mexico, targeted merchants' warehouses of goods. The forces overcame Mejía's imperial guards, took three hundred prisoners, and proceeded to plunder and gut the town, killing eleven defenders. After two hours of intense fighting, the Imperial guards surrendered. Merchants' warehouses, stores, residences, and saloons sustained heavy damage. The raiders commandeered rafts to ferry stolen wares across the river to the U.S. side.[9]

American forces under Gen. Weitzel across the river pledged their complete support and sent troops to guard Bagdad. Generals Grant and Sheridan, while urging neutrality, acted otherwise, allowing U.S. soldiers to make mayhem for the Imperialistas. However, Juárez and his generals condemned overt U.S. interference. On January 7 Liberal general Mariano Escobedo, who had been plotting an attack on Mejía for months, had counted on appropriating the items now destroyed. Escobedo at first assumed his own Liberals launched the raid but then admonished Weitzel, accusing him of planning the attack and asked him to surrender the "pirates." Describing the devastation, Escobedo told the American general that the port was the responsibility of the Mexican Liberals and not the U.S. army. American consul Lucius Avery speculated that the raid stemmed from Mejía's requests for hundreds of thousands in forced loans and conscriptions, which caused widespread discontent. However, the attack derived from Crawford's outrage over Mejía's severe measure to secure the area.[10] The shattered commercial activities had the effect of escalating political chaos in northern Mexico, an outcome that Grant and Sheridan desired.

Of the tense situation on the border, Maximilian saw the harsh reality of maintaining the important northern position of Matamoros. "I just learned of the capture and destruction of the important port of Bagdad on the Rio Grande by dissidents. This fateful event, the consequences of which will inevitably be disastrous, besides being an affront to our military, happened as if to persuade the Americans that we cannot overcome our enemies. I am more convinced each day of how right I was to insist in my previous letters on the need to pacify the northern border as soon as possible," he wrote Bazaine. Bazaine agreed and immediately sent Austrian troops, including Col. Alphons von Kodolitsch, two companies of the Red Hussars cavalry, and Ernst Pitner, a young lieutenant colonel who would become an important assistant to Maximilian, to reinforce Mejía at Matamoros, which increased Imperial forces on the lower border to 1,700. The "medley of people from all over the world" at Bagdad and Matamoros greeted them heartily, wanting trade to resume. The Prussian consul, a partner in a large shipping company, gave the Austrian soldiers a sumptuous feast with roasts, pies, German beer, and wine. There was a lot at stake for the Imperial government. Maximilian hoped the attack would fortify the troops' spirit to defend the empire's honor.[11]

As Maximilian read reports that dissident groups were forming near Veracruz and at La Paz in Baja California, he realized how exposed he would be if Napoléon pulled his men out completely. For months, he had lived in denial that the French emperor would break the promises made in the Convention of Miramar and leave him vulnerable. Bazaine had done little to aid the transition to provide a new army. "I tell your Majesty frankly," Maximilian wrote Napoléon, "this situation is a difficult one for me, I add, as a good and true friend, that it is dangerous both for you and for me. For you, in that your glorious reputation suffers by it, for me, since my intentions which are . . . yours too, cannot be carried into effect. Such military and financial proceeding will be the ruin of the great idea of the regeneration of Mexico." He feared that the population's confidence in the empire would crumble. "If the guerrilleros return, everyone who has declared for the empire will be hanged or shot without mercy," said Maximilian.[12]

Much to Maximilian's added horror, the notorious Col. Du Pin returned to Mexico in late January. Several months earlier, Maximilian and Carlota, both appalled by Du Pin's lack of restraint and cruelty in the field, demanded that Bazaine send him back to France. After some resistance, Bazaine transferred him. But in Paris, Du Pin obtained an audience with Napoléon and spoke persuasively for the need of a vigorous offensive against the guerrillas. If allowed to punish the violators "with the utmost severity," his euphemism for a death sentence, he could help finish the work of pacifying the country. This impressive presentation convinced Napoléon to send Du Pin sailing back to Mexico.[13]

Napoléon's decision shocked and angered Maximilian, who wanted to know what had happened to his imperial order. "I had forbidden Du Pin's return, and hope in the future my orders will be carried out. It is the first time that I have been disobeyed since I have been in this country; but I intend to be obeyed and shall take care that I am. Notify the marshal of this from me," Maximilian wrote to Alfonse Dano. Viewing that Du Pin had not changed his methods, he wrote to Bazaine, "I urge you to order Du Pin not to execute or put any individual to death without him first being tried. This warning can only serve to enlighten him and to protect his reputation while covering his liability." The emperor threatened to ruin Du Pin's career, but the French colonel waved it off as nonsense, saying he was merely enforcing the Black Decree of October 3, 1865.[14]

On January 19, 1866, Bazaine informed Maximilian that as soon as reinforcements arrived and were organized, he would undertake a fresh offensive after a brief furlough, although dissidents continued to make mayhem in various districts. "It is my intention to dispatch them in every direction in the Empire at once, and Your Majesty will then see that it is not the military situation in Mexico which ought to cause the greatest anxiety," wrote Bazaine, implying that it was the people who most doubted Maximilian and opposed the empire. Juarista successes were secondary. He cautioned that they must take precautions against a menacing United States and reassured him that the troops would remain in the field and intensify their efforts.[15]

Despite authorizing a renewed campaign across Mexico, Maximilian did not want to think about killing so much as conciliation. Surely there were ways to avoid the death penalty, as authorized by the Black Decree, or to rescind it. He had merely wanted to deport insurrectionists to Yucatán. Bazaine, however, counseled him on remaining tenacious. Maximilian's French secretary, Édouard Pierron, advised Maximilian to let the courts-martial do their work and not to undermine them. The hard line always worked best, said Pierron, adding, "names change and places change, but the human heart remains the same." If they did not resort to harsh measures, the war would drag on infinitely and Mexico would never be pacified. Yet Maximilian still believed the people would admire his leniency, and he pardoned five offenders sentenced to death by courts-martial in Aguascalientes.[16] It became apparent that Maximilian's hard-line measure had no foundation in his heart; he could not be brutal enough to demonstrate the thoroughness of the Black Decree and continued to confer clemency on convicts.

Meanwhile, Napoléon had received impacting news from Washington. On December 4, 1865, in his annual address, President Andrew Johnson denounced France for its ongoing occupation and support of the monarchy in Mexico, which he interpreted as extreme aggression toward the United States. Secretary of State Seward, who had been intensifying his warnings over the last months with the backing of the U.S. Congress, signaled that the United States was serious about intervening. Napoléon received notice from Seward, mincing no words that France must get out of Mexico, threatening trade sanctions in unambiguous terms. He offered no reciprocal tokens and little diplomatic courtesy. Seward's strong line raised the specter of a possible war, with hope this would instill fear in the French ministers, if not Napoléon, to end what they called this "bad business" (*une mauvaise affaire*). Growing more important to Napoléon, however, was that 50,000 troops remained 6,000 miles away in Mexico, which could prove to be serious when the Prussians mobilized on Austrian territories. He also perceived that France's position in Mexico could result in a possible alliance between the United States and Prussia.[17]

Seward's threatening letter offered Napoléon a pretext and justification to expedite the withdrawal of his men. Just as he used the mitigating circumstance of unpaid debt to invade the country in 1861, he had now been given another ostensible reason to get out. With a promise of withdrawal, he could stay the vengeful northern colossus of America.[18]

On January 15, 1866, Napoléon wrote Maximilian a letter amounting to the final solution for France. He wrote:

Sir my Brother,
It is not without regret that I write to Your Majesty, for I am forced to inform you of the decision at which I have been bound to arrive in view of

all the difficulties caused me by the Mexican question. The impossibility of obtaining fresh subsidies from the Corps Législatif for the upkeep of the army in Mexico and Your Majesty's inability to contribute any more to it, forces me to set a final date for the French repatriation. In my eyes, this must be as soon as possible.[19]

Napoléon dispatched a representative, Baron Édouard Saillard, a small, cold-mannered man, reserved and discrete, with orders for Marshal Bazaine on the withdrawal and to fix the schedule for returning the troops to France. Troops would leave, Napoléon wrote Maximilian, "in such a way that it may not happen suddenly (*brusquement*), so that public tranquility and the interests we are set on safeguarding are not imperiled. Moreover, the agreement still holds good that the Foreign Legion shall still remain in Your Majesty's service for a few years."[20]

Napoléon sent a confidential letter to Bazaine with additional orders to help Maximilian organize a full-fledged army and leave some kind of permanence, so that France could feel that all her best efforts had not been wasted. Napoléon gave Bazaine no more than eighteen months to establish a military system and bring home the French army.[21]

So finally it was done. Napoléon had set the systematic and official abandonment of the Mexican empire in motion. He whipsawed Maximilian by leaving him defenseless, refusing to send any more funds, while continuing to charge usurious interest on a debt of funds the Mexican empire never fully received. Maximilian now had nowhere to turn, except to rely on his own skills and, of course, those of his capable wife, Carlota, who was furious.[22]

Maximilian received this news in February while on a retreat to Cuernavaca. It was a withering and humiliating blow, with Maximilian stating, "he had been brought to Mexico with his eyes blindfolded." Having been told nearly two years earlier that a pacified Mexico lay waiting for his leadership, he arrived to find the country only 10 percent under French control. Now the French held him completely responsible for a situation he had not started but was expected to finish against Herculean obstacles and under onerous financial conditions. The French loans' proceeds had been exhausted. Betrayed, Maximilian could scarcely believe that Napoléon's unease with public opinion in France would lead to this betrayal. Maximilian resentfully told the marshal that Napoléon could take all his troops immediately. "We are going to succeed and my counselors and friends can see, I can say it without pride, what energy and tenacity a Habsburg is made of." However, unable to fully except France's abrupt end of its support, he also planned to seek a new treaty of Miramar to define "the positions of the two governments," resolving that "our situation will be greatly strengthened."[23]

Privately, however, Maximilian became frightened and desperate but remained in denial for some weeks. From Cuernavaca, Maximilian emphasized his energy and work in letters to Carlota about ministers and the military reorganization. Telling Carlota not to alert the public and assuring her that Napoléon would not emphasize the issue in France, he set to work developing a new agreement with the French government, hoping to salvage the remains of the Treaty of Miramar, presented to him in 1864. "Working here with more application than in Mexico [City], because, thank God, nobody bothers me all day. I'm almost finished with the points of the new treaty [of Miramar] with France," wrote Maximilian, describing her as "his angel and star of his life." He wanted three more years of support from France and 10,000 more Austrian troops. But he could not focus. On the same day, he also wrote her about Professor Bilimek finding the most beautiful new insect specimens. At the end of April, he recognized her strain and concern and returned to Mexico City to take up his full duties.[24]

On the one hand, he told the French to leave, but on the other, he wanted new guarantees from France in a new treaty. He promised to pay all of Mexico's commitments, knowing this was impossible, but then threatened to back out of those obligations to protest France's abandonment. As for Napoléon's allegations that Maximilian caused Mexico's financial problems, he in turn blamed France's army for excessive expenses. "The French are always like that. Throwing money out the window on one hand, and on the other, screaming that there is no order or thrift in Mexican affairs," wrote Maximilian to Eloin.[25]

But the crisis obviously humbled Maximilian, who questioned his role as emperor. When he wrote about the regeneration of Mexico, he indicated that he did not deserve praise. "A name on the iron plates of history—that is still in the distant future, and the path toward this goal is hard and difficult. I do not lack the will to do good. My whole ambition is that I can help build the great building and if I can only carry a few stones toward that goal, I shall be content knowing that I have not lived in vain."[26]

On the heels of Napoléon's letter, Achille Fould in Paris ordered the French paymaster to close the account of the Mexican government, a sad circumstance since Mexico had to date met almost all its debt obligations. Fould informed their minister of finance in Mexico, Langlais, to suspend army pay, a *coup de jarnac* (an unfair blow) that further crippled Maximilian. Langlais, however, recently completed a list of financial reforms that increased income to fund a new army while reducing costs. He also found funds that had gone unused. Maximilian cut his staff, the civil list, to one-third, and reduced his budget from 1.5 million to 1 million pesos. "In Mexico, the emperor is not a ruler by the grace of God, but a plain and simple head of a purely democratic nation. Therefore, he must think of his duties first. Since he is not of supernatural origin, his path is a practical one and laid out only through the well-being of his fellow citizens," wrote Maximilian. He approved the new budget but also raised taxes and eliminated a number of government expenses. Simultaneously, Langlais informed Maximilian that the European bankers paid themselves from the Mexican underwriting. "I know very well that it is in France that they are stealing Mexico's two loans," Maximilian wrote, adding that the empire had only received a fraction. Langlais had charted the discrepancies but did not know who pocketed Mexico's funds. Maximilian chose to wait to raise this delicate matter, knowing he would need future cooperation from France. Looking the other way could make him a hero.[27]

At first Maximilian attributed Napoléon's harsh decision to withdraw not to his duplicity but rather to Mexico's weak representation at the French court. He had only his military attaché, Charles Loysel, in the conflicted position of also being a French general, to represent him there, along with the ineffective José Manuel Hidalgo. He desperately looked over his staff to find someone to go to Paris and plead the case for leaving the troops according to the Convention of Miramar, signed barely two years earlier. He reached Eloin, then in Belgium, and ordered him to go with letters and papers to make the argument to Napoléon.[28]

Eloin traveled there at once, and upon his arrival in mid-March found a profoundly changed Napoléon. He had aged terribly and appeared nervous, confused, and embarrassed. Maximilian's reply to Napoléon's notice announcing the Mexican withdrawal concerned the aging French emperor, and he grew emotional, saying, "One can see that he is irritated—I do not want him to be so—I understand the impression that reading my letter must have made. But what can be done?" Napoléon blamed Maximilian's inabilities to follow a budget and meet the financial obligations. Few funds could be raised under such a credit risk. It was time to leave Mexico. "I am therefore forced to provoke a solution, but you understand, we shall soon understand each other, the main point is to calm opinion and soften the impression in the United States and in the Chambers [Corps Législatif]," said Napoléon. The timetable for withdrawal would be announced soon. He promised however, that he would allow the soldiers who wished to stay in Mexico to do so. He also pledged to negotiate a loan to provide assistance should an emergency arise, if Maximilian would make certain guarantees.[29]

After the initial business, Napoléon told Eloin to look around and listen to the people in Paris and what they said about Maximilian. The public spoke very poorly of the Mexican expedition. "Since you have been in Europe, you have been able to take account of the state of men's minds: the opinion that Emperor Maximilian lacks energy; he draws up and promulgates decrees, without realizing that they often cannot be executed. It is alleged that, urged by his eagerness to achieve something, he loses himself in Utopian schemes without practicality," he said.[30]

When Eloin started to object, Napoléon artfully glossed over his betrayal of the Mexican empire and placed everything on Maximilian's back. Eloin argued, however, that the situation was more intricate, that Maximilian's decrees reflected his vision for change after forty years of revolution, whether or not they could be carried through. He attributed the financial crisis to first sending Nicolas Budin as financial minister in 1864 and not someone more qualified, like Langlais, who arrived too late. "The army bleeds all the resources. If they are organized, who is guilty? . . . Your Majesty is not unaware that the relations between the emperor and the marshal are very tense and becoming more difficult every day. I have not been sent by my sovereign to discuss this subject, but I believe I am carrying out a duty," said Eloin. "The marshal has never been able to forget that he had preceded the emperor and commanded as master, and recently the return of Du Pin has made his position very difficult."[31]

"I know that your emperor has complained very bitterly to the diplomatic corps," said Napoléon. After the mention of Du Pin, Napoléon reviewed letters Eloin set before him, knitted his brow, returned the letters, and dismissed Eloin with his habitual smile but without a handshake. Just then, Empress Eugénie entered the office dressed for the outdoors. She made a desultory inquiry about the health of Maximilian and Carlota, followed by a comment about the sadness of the passing of King Leopold. She then asked her husband to go for a walk since it was a beautiful, sunny day. She looked at Eloin as though he should leave, and taking the suggestion, he exited the palace.[32]

Over the next few weeks, Eloin with Loysel attempted to see Carlota's brother Leopold II, who was at England's Claremont House in London, to plead for Belgian reinforcements. The new monarch refused, however, to see the Mexican representatives. In Belgium, public opinion on the French intervention and Mexican Empire had fallen precipitously with news of the fatal attack on d'Huart and the legation sent to Mexico City. Leopold II, unlike his father, refused to involve himself in the perils of Maximilian and Carlota.[33]

While Eloin was appealing to the French and Belgian courts, Maximilian called for support from his homeland. In an effort to replace a portion of the evacuating French, he appealed to Austria's foreign minister, Count Alexander von Mensdorff, for more soldiers to maintain the legion. The Austrian court supported the idea, since Vienna hoped to keep the Mexican empire going, if the burden was endurable. In spite of growing Prussian aggression against Austria, on March 15 the ministers in Vienna signed an agreement to provide 4,000 extra Austrian volunteers for 1866, with an additional 2,000 fresh recruits for subsequent years. With this gesture, Franz Josef kept Austria's relations with the Mexican empire active but superficial, mindful of Austria's relationship with the United States. Despite the small number of troops, Maximilian expressed his gratitude. From his minister, Baron Ferdinand von Wydenbruck, he had heard of recent haranguing in the American Congress toward the Habsburg dynasty, asserting that Maximilian was only a mere adventurer.[34]

Soon after, Wydenbruck learned that through Matías Romero's efforts, recruitment for soldiers to fight for Juárez had been established in seven different locations in New York and at least one in Washington. Horrified and fearful for Austria's role in Mexico, Wydenbruck interceded in protest, and received assurances that the recruiting would stop, and a disclaimer was placed in the New York newspapers. But the offices continued to sign up fighters for a republican Mexico.[35]

In order to force the Europeans to leave Mexico entirely, Seward manipulated the complexities in European tensions to stop reinforcements from Austria. In May 1866 the U.S. ambassador to Austria, John L. Motley, received instructions to issue a protest against further recruitment for Mexico. Seward added that if the Austrians did not comply, they could consider themselves in conflict with the United States. Despite pending war in Prussia, Franz Josef planned to the send troops anyway. When Motley then threatened to break off diplomatic relations, they capitulated. No more reinforcements would be sent. In early June, Maximilian learned that Emperor Franz Josef canceled transports of 2,000 Austrian volunteers ready to sail to Mexico from Trieste, blaming Austria's need for troops on a possible defense against Prussia. He did not lie but extracted his country from Seward's scrutiny.[36]

Maximilian had been depending on Austria's continued support. His brother let him down again, and the wounds cut deeper than any of Napoléon's betrayals. In a restrained tone, he lamented the "unpardonable weakness of the European powers toward the United States." Maximilian fully realized the rising tensions between Austria and Prussia, yet he grew bitter at yet another obstacle set in his path by Franz Josef, recalling the Family Pact. "If Austria had been loyal, she would at once have embarked the troops, but such a cowardly and faithless government could not be expected to behave otherwise," he wrote his brother Karl Ludwig.[37] He could not depend on aid from any government, near or far.

In the wake of Europe's crumbling support, Maximilian began to lay blame. He condemned the newspapers across Europe for misrepresenting conditions in Mexico. He worked with Eloin and his representatives in Vienna to try to win over the press, intimating that certain expenditures might have to be made to influence the reporters and editors. He hoped the London *Times* could be persuaded to print good things about him. "There is nothing more important to win in England than the *Times*, cost what it may . . . whoever can rely on this paper can also rely on public opinion in England," he said. Eloin came to an editorial agreement with the *Belgian Independence*, and Maximilian asked him to do the same in Paris and Cologne with papers hostile to Mexico. To persuade the European press to print favorable articles about Mexico, portraying it as less dangerous than perceived, Maximilian planned to establish two press bureaus, one in Paris and another in Vienna.[38]

Recently, Maximilian had assigned Emmanuel Henri Dieudonné Domenech, a Catholic missionary born in Lyons but educated in the United States, as his communications secretary. In press releases, at the suggestion of Charles Loysel, Domenech repeatedly asserted the benevolence of Maximilian, pointedly stating his care superseded that of the French. However, Domenech failed in his role to lift up the reputation of Maximilian in the newspapers. Maximilian wrote to Eloin, "Domenech is nothing but a clown and I have always judged him as such." Domenech later defended himself, saying Maximilian took actions that alienated Mexican authorities at every level.[39]

Maximilian also blamed José Manuel Hidalgo in Paris, who helped create the Mexican empire. Hidalgo had done little to mitigate damage in the press, one of his primary duties. It became evident his main concern lay in currying favor with Eugénie and regaining his social position in the French court. Napoléon's decision to withdraw his army should have put Hidalgo in direct opposition to Napoléon, had he been advocating for Mexico, instead of favoring France. But many times he could not get past the antechamber of Eugénie, much less see Napoléon. "His weakness and lack of ability has done us a lot of harm," wrote Maximilian, who then, in disgust, summoned Hidalgo to Mexico City. Hidalgo had not visited his family for twenty years, so Maximilian invited him to "breathe his native air . . . see the happiness of embracing your good mother." In his place, he dispatched Juan N. Almonte to Paris in April, "the best Mexico can produce," said Maximilian. Almonte arrived in Paris to witness the growing clouds of controversy between Prussia and Austria over the German states, with Napoléon pulled into a protectionist stance. Mexico was now a minor concern. Empress Eugénie wrote Carlota that an outbreak of war would change Europe profoundly. Almonte, nonetheless, began a series of meetings with Napoléon, arguing that he should leave as many soldiers as possible in Mexico.[40]

Hidalgo arrived in Mexico City trembling with fright, a humorous sight to the war-seasoned French and Austrians. A few days into his visit, Maximilian invited him for a ride around the grounds at Chapultepec. Hidalgo appeared "armed to the teeth, and was quite upset because they were to be attended only by one groom. Maximilian laughed at him." The emperor sent an account of Hidalgo's behavior to his press representative in Vienna, saying, "These exhibitions of fright were obviously to be ascribed to the accounts of Mexican conditions in the European press," dismissing the real dangers of his turbulent land.[41]

When Maximilian appointed Hidalgo to the post of counselor of state, in order to ameliorate his demotion, he panicked, realizing his new position meant he must remain in Mexico. If the empire collapsed, he knew this promised his likely execution. In the middle of the night, he fled Mexico City to Veracruz and sailed for Europe. Hidalgo receded into private exile in Paris, watching the fate of the Mexican empire from afar.[42]

Gutiérrez de Estrada, another Mexican monarchist who refused to visit his homeland, continued to harass and question the paralysis of the Mexican empire. Since Maximilian's investiture, he did little more than send long epistles from Rome complaining that the Mexican empire had yet to build an army and had turned its back on the Catholic Church. Maximilian emphatically denied this and curiously defended Bazaine. "I must use a soldierly frankness and say that to this very day, the French marshal has worked day and night . . . by orders and counterorders to render a good and final organization of our brave troops impossible. Never forget, my friend, that French policy has always aimed at keeping Mexico weak in two respects . . . namely, military and financial affairs," he wrote. He also pointed to the lack of education among the Mexican people, a decision made by former narrow-minded politicians.

He prided himself on refusing to play the party machine, but it made his mission difficult, "consequently the anti-patriotic education and clerical exclusivity" kept the people from formal learning. When the immutable Gutiérrez de Estrada stated that Maximilian's lack of faith caused problems with the church, Maximilian protested that the corrupt clergy remained decadent. Maximilian defended himself, citing the feast days the court observed, his diplomatic representatives in Rome and the Holy Land, stating only that he and Carlota dismissed the novenas, the rosary, and the scourge of self-flagellation, practices with which they did not agree. These letters were enormously hurtful to Maximilian, because he also knew that Gutiérrez Estrada shared his correspondence with the pope. Maximilian would not capitulate to placing religious considerations over the priorities of education nor let clergy control the schools, writing to his wife, "Catholicism, as constructed by Gutiérrez, does not exist in Mexico."[43]

Adding to the chaos and setbacks, Jacques Langlais, the primary economic advisor who had achieved new successes in reorganizing Mexico's financial structure, suffered a stroke and died on February 23, 1866. Maximilian felt he lost a true and loyal friend. Suspecting foul play, the French ordered an investigation but found no poisons or other nefarious causes of death. Another French official named A. de Maintenant, Langlais's assistant, moved in to continue the management of over 23 million pesos, the largest line items going to the cost of the war and interest on the French debt. However, with Langlais's death the momentum to implement his previous plans was lost, as Maintenant was only thinking of funneling funds to France.[44]

Maximilian's colonization scheme, which continued to lure away American Confederates, still frustrated U.S. officials. Gen. Phil Sheridan wrote Gen. Grant that more "energetic" actions by the Imperialistas in northern Mexico made him doubt that the French intended to leave Mexico. "The sympathy of the whole South is with Maximilian," he wrote about former Confederates. Edwin Stanton, secretary of war, agreed: "For myself I have never had any faith in Napoléon's promise to withdraw." In March 1866 Gen. William T. Sherman refused to allow two former Confederate ships to embark for Veracruz. The ships sailed anyway. In his inability to stop them, Sherman fumed, saying he wanted to "break up [Matthew Fontaine Maury's] nest of Confederates which was agitating the public mind of the South and preventing the people there from quietly submitting to subjugation." In some ways, newly arriving Confederates caused additional chaos for the imperial government. Many became guns for hire. When they did not find a position with the French army or Foreign Legion, some of them joined the various guerrilla groups against the empire. Maury also lamented the slow progress of the colonization, saying he got little support from the "absentee" emperor, Maximilian spending more time chasing butterflies in Cuernavaca than attending to business. As a possible indication of the looming demise for the Confederate colonies in Mexico, Maury sailed for England, and although he intended to return, never did. The emperor officially discontinued his office in April 1866.[45]

❧ 14 ❧

The Empire Is Nothing
Without the Emperor

Marshal Bazaine and his French generals had now set a schedule for troop consolidation and transports to Europe. Knowing that Maximilian and Carlota had been lobbying for his removal, Bazaine kept his plan of withdrawal confidential. The army would depart in three sections, one in November 1866, the next in March 1867, and the final in December 1867. Bazaine announced he would sail with the first transport, leaving Gen. Douay to complete the process. "As regards military conditions, the land was as much pacified as it ever had been," Bazaine stated, which was a gross inaccuracy. Juarista forces grew in strength every day, and mayhem broke out in villages and towns across the country. In May, as the Imperialistas' northern division barely held on, Juaristas reorganized in the western and southern sections of the country. Maximilian struggled to contain his considerable anxiety. "Although everyone believed that an open rupture was imminent, in appearance Maximilian's dealings with the marshal were cordial. Bazaine's first son had just been born. Their Majesties were godparents and the child was baptized in the imperial chapel," said José Luis Blasio.[1]

Soon after Bazaine scheduled the withdrawals, he finally set to planning the domestic imperial army and submitted a plan to Maximilian. Bazaine combined units of French and Mexican soldiers, along with Austrians and Belgians to form nine battalions of 400 men each, which Maximilian called the Cazadores, a term similar to chasseurs in the French army. He wanted them to be like the Jäger, the light Austrian infantry known for their survival skills and stealth. He saw the need to appoint a minister of war who was European, spoke Spanish, was familiar with Mexico, and came from the ranks of the French army. Each battalion would contain twenty French officers and over 100 French soldiers from those who requested this transfer. From each officer Bazaine obtained a four-year commitment to serve Mexico, emphasizing they would have a positive effect in earning the dedication of the Mexican soldiers. Although the marshal was not authorized to pay the Austrian and Belgian soldiers, he found a loophole that if the corps could be combined with the French Foreign Legion, under a French officer, then France could cover the wages. Maximilian agreed but wanted the force to number at least 15,000 men and to allow the Austrian and Belgian troops to function under their own country's regulations and methods.[2]

Bazaine, torn between masters, moved slowly. Because Maximilian knew that the marshal's primary duty was to Napoléon, he realized he must hold him to the task. With great enthusiasm that the process of building his army was underway, the emperor said despite France's prior efforts "to muddle our affairs," he was determined to have an intact fighting force if it required going *contre vent et marée* ("against wind and tide") and set forth to pacify the country at last. He blamed "inertia on the part of the marshal" and France's fear of the United States. Nevertheless, he reminded Bazaine that Napoléon authorized him to assist building a national army composed of mixed and volunteer corps. Maximilian sent him his own revised plan, which included the establishment of garrisons in northern Mexico and the perimeters of Mexico City, and dispatched his political prefects to send reports from their respective territories. Maximilian asked Bazaine to attend a weekly planning session at which Maximilian presided, reminding him that Napoléon said he would "give every assistance in the organization of a stable army and to 'make haste.'"[3]

The marshal felt this an impossible task. Few funds were available, because the treasury had lost the customs income from Tampico and Mazatlán, and Matamoros was cut off from Monterrey, but he refined the procedures for organizing a corps nonetheless. "As for the Mexican army," he wrote, "the enclosed chart will show your Majesty that its effectives have a certain importance but it needs to be moralized, to attach itself to the cause it serves and that is not the work of one year. Its units must be fed by all races and classes of Mexican society . . . but it is to be feared that sons of good families will still fight shy of the ranks." Soldiers from the native classes would not gladly serve foreigners, he added. Bazaine could not allow the Mexican generals to operate under their own methods, scoffing at their lack of military discipline.[4]

Bazaine, who would hardly take direction from Maximilian, rarely showed up at military council meetings. Maximilian thought of complaining to Napoléon but decided to focus on organizing and drilling the troops over the summer. He planned his own campaign to pacify the country quickly and finally, dismissing Bazaine's strategies, which he said employed "useless fantasies." Maximilian even received disparaging remarks from his brother Franz Josef in Vienna that he had never organized an army, being only a naval commander. Accordingly, Maximilian sent him the schedule for the deployment of his new army. "I send you herewith a scheme for the reorganization of my army, that you may convince yourself that your former admiral has, since his sojourn in free America [Mexico], acquired the capacity to introduce a good organization into a completely disordered military system," he wrote with scorn on May 28.[5]

Maximilian continued to prevail on Bazaine to work with him, and when the marshal finally gave in, the new army slowly coalesced. Contradictory orders and money shortages caused unbelievable stress. The emperor cut ministerial costs from 51 million pesos to 10 million, which aggrieved him greatly, relying on the French despite his dislike for them. Although five new customs collectors were tasked to raise cash, the Mexican empire continued to borrow from French war funds. Bazaine's challenges ran from the ridiculous to the insuperable, knowing that recruitment and training could not happen in a year. Nevertheless, Maximilian urged Bazaine to keep to the job; sensing his resentment, he tried to cajole and reassure the marshal that the mission depended on his guidance. "To promptly complete the organization of the army, what we need most of all is unity of action. The ideas you sent to the council . . . are very sound and full of common sense. You are already the commander-in-chief of the army and the sole director of all military movements, that is to say, a better judge than anyone else of what needs to be done and the one in a position to carry it out. Therefore, I hereby invest you with the absolute authority to organize the Franco-Mexican battalions and to reorganize the national army," wrote Maximilian on June 3, 1866. Following orders and his own agenda, Bazaine saw that provoking Maximilian to abdicate and leave with the French army would save the reputation of the military, so it was to his benefit not to organize a national Mexican army.[6]

Amid the recruiting for the Cazadores, a satirical skit entitled "Messieurs les Voyageurs pour Mexico, en Voiture" was produced by a visiting Frenchman, Alexandre Philippe Régnier, Duc de Massa, which hurt and angered Maximilian. The play, featuring a young Belgian officer, an American girl from Paris, an orchestra leader, and other female roles, skewered Maximilian's financial decrees, his dependence on the French, and his efforts to train a new army. Maximilian had recently compared his new land force to the elite Zouaves, which the producer found wryly humorous. Many found the sarcasm and wit intensely funny. The satire also mocked the French who promised to back Mexico in all endeavors, Régnier not knowing that by July 30, 1866, Napoléon would have reversed every promise made to the Mexican empire. In addition, satirical newspapers in northern Mexico lambasted and railed against the empire and against Santiago Vidaurri, the Imperialistas, and all their collaborators. These publications, with their constant rumors, prodding, and jabs, further emboldened the regional Liberals to organize. There were many others: *La Orquesta, La Cuchara, La Sombra,* as well as poems, *corridos,* and parodies, complete with double entendres.[7]

Seeking refuge from these attacks in Cuernavaca, however, brought little comfort to the sovereigns, especially Carlota who worried excessively about their situation while considering possible solutions to their predicament. Grounds supervisor and botanist Wilhelm Knechtel observed Carlota, "beautiful and slender, yet healthy," taking long, vigorous walks through the gardens and along the adjacent porticos. Often, with her hands clasped behind her, she held the corner of her monogrammed linen handkerchief in her mouth, chewing on it pensively. In this manner, she gnawed holes in the corners, making a shred of her hankies.[8]

In Mexico City, under pressure to maintain appearances, on June 4 Maximilian and Carlota entertained 700 people at a *tertulia.* Carlota celebrated the feast day of Corpus Christi with a lavish procession, and later with Maximilian gave a general inspection of the charitable and educational institutions of the city, in which they noted growth and improvement. A week later they gave another ball for 2,000 guests at Chapultepec, including the entire diplomatic corps. In her first public appearances since returning from Yucatán, Carlota wore her jewels, partly to check the rumor that she sent her finery to England for safekeeping. Amid the evacuation of the French troops and Imperialista defeats in sections of the country, gossip abounded that Carlota would soon leave Mexico.[9]

During this time, Maximilian began to drink too much sherry and champagne to dull his anxiety over the seemingly insurmountable task of raising one army while another left the country. His stomach illnesses returned. With lagging momentum, maintaining confidence seemed overwhelming. To distract himself, he supervised the building of a new national theater and expanded the archaeology museum by moving all artifacts to the College of Mining. He also managed the final tree plantings and amenities along the Paseo de la Emperatriz.[10]

But truly believing that Bazaine would not act in his best interest, Maximilian reached out for more manpower and stable leaders to build and maintain the national army. He seized on the idea to place experienced French officers in key military positions by establishing an office of Mexican affairs. Controversially, he appointed Gen. Auguste Adolphe Osmont as minister of war and Intendant Jean Nicolas Friant as minister of finance. It appeared to be a rather desperate measure by Maximilian, condemned by outside observers. Previously, Osmont served as the French army's chief of staff and Friant as chief of administration. Maximilian could transition with two highly experienced officers without solely depending on Bazaine, who on August 4 had no choice but to accept, although he termed the arrangement "provisional," since regulations prohibited officers from assuming rank in a foreign army. The two men immediately set to work, and Maximilian felt quite satisfied by the new appointments.[11]

Soon the Imperialistas at Mexico City received news of a disaster on the Rio Grande. On June 7 a massive caravan conveying $3 million in merchandise composed of 200 wagons pulled by 2,000 mules had departed Matamoros toward Monterrey. A combined Imperialist force of 290 Austrians (including Lt. Col. Ernst Pitner), 1,110 Mexicans, counterguerrillas, rural guards, *zapadores* (sappers), and artillery protected the convoy. Following a road without dependable sources of water in the stifling summer of Tamaulipas, soldiers began collapsing from heatstroke and dehydration. Some men resorted to eating the fruit of the prickly pear cactus and quickly developed diarrhea. The water barrels empty, the cavalry troops drank wine, which worsened their dehydration.[12]

Anxious to reach water at the Río San Juan at Camargo, the train had to cross deep arroyos, dodging snipers' bullets, and paused at a plateau called Santa Gertrudis. Warned of an imminent attack by an advance guard of Liberals, at dawn the Austrians rode out to find its location. Charging from out of the *monte* (brushland), Gen. Mariano Escobedo's Liberals, armed with American guns, attacked. They blunted the Imperialista flank and began fighting hand to hand. Taking advantage of his men's ability to fight in hot, arid conditions, Escobedo's force rapidly reduced the Imperialistas by half, as "the men in their ranks fell down dead in droves." Taking cover under the wagons, the remaining contingent of 350 Austrians surrendered. Escobedo seized the

Austrian officers and troops, French Foreign Legion, and French naval officers
and sailors upon retreat from Matamoros, Mexico, 1866

merchandise, 1,000 muskets, the artillery, ammunition, and even the musical
instruments belonging to the Imperial orchestra.[13]

The Imperialista defeat at Santa Gertrudis severely rattled the Fifth
Division under Gen. Mejía and his 600 troops remaining at Matamoros. In
all, he lost over half of his garrison. He immediately withdrew his remaining
soldiers from the port of Bagdad after a flurry of desertions into Texas. Facing
certain defeat, Mejía negotiated an agreement with Juarista Gen. Carvajal,
newly arrived from New York, to transition authority. On June 24, 1866,
Mejía's army marched out of Matamoros in silence. For the most part, specta-
tors in Matamoros remained solemn, except for a few who shouted, "Death to
the Emperor." Across the Rio Grande, U.S. army officers at Fort Brown also
watched the withdrawal of Mejía's army.[14]

At Bagdad, Mejía and his Army of the North hurriedly loaded several
steamships to avoid capture, including the French man-of-war, *Adonis*. Then
tragedy struck again, as one transport sank near Tampico; only sixty-one soldiers survived. Docking at Veracruz, Mejía and his army, along with Du Pin
and the counterguerrillas, marched inland to San Luis Potosí. Much to Liberal
general Mariano Escobedo's mortification, Gen. Carvajal had allowed one of
the emperor's best generals to slip away to fight the Juaristas again.[15]

With Mejía's withdrawal from northeastern Mexico, revenue from the

lucrative trade at Matamoros returned to Liberal control. His abandonment of Matamoros made a big impression in France and Austria as well as
in Mexico City. "I was surprised and painfully affected by the news of the
almost complete destruction of Mejía's division. On one hand I was pinning
part of my hopes for the future on these brave troops, and on the other, the
opening of communications between Matamoros and Monterrey, necessary
to shore up our finances," wrote Maximilian to Bazaine, closing, "but I have
confidence . . . in your long experience and ask that you send me the plan for
the campaign to redress the misfortune." The French still controlled Veracruz
and Mazatlán but lost domination over the other gulf and Pacific ports. When
American arms dealers showed up demanding that the empire buy arms from
them or they would be delivered to the Juaristas, Maximilian became furious. On July 9, attempting to quash trade that might benefit the Juaristas,
Maximilian declared all ports in Mexico closed to foreign commerce at the risk
of confiscation of shipments.[16]

The retreat from the northeast proved to be a major turning point.
Maximilian recognized a return to the open partisan fighting in Mexico:
"We now see the struggle with the empire from both unfortunate extremes
which have always ruined our homeland." In Tamaulipas, Nuevo León, and
Coahuila, the northern caudillos and Liberal generals began to assemble and
organize to move south. In order to apply diplomatic pressure on the empire,
five weeks later President Andrew Johnson declared Maximilian's closure of
the ports held by the Juaristas an act of belligerency, in violation of neutrality
laws and treaties between the United States and Mexico. Johnson then dispatched an American warship, the *Tacony*, previously used by the Union army
to block Confederate ports during the Civil War, to sail to various Mexican
seaports as a demonstration of disfavor. The quasi-blockade effort crippled
businesses. Against the United States, Maximilian wrote, "Neutrality has
never been respected except from our side and only too much by France. This
has proven once again the president's proclamation on the subject of the blockade of Matamoros and Tampico and the permanence of American war vessels
in these ports."[17]

At the same time, in Washington, the U.S. State Department intensified
its demands. Seward criticized the schedule of the French withdrawal and
demanded that Napoléon shorten the timeline for departure. The Congress
approved resolutions condemning the French but voted against a proposal to
send $50 million to Juárez. The irritability reflected in Congress was mirrored
in the executive and military branches and followed closely by the press.[18] When

the U.S. State Department received reassurance that the French withdrawal would be expedited, Seward was pleased to see Napoléon capitulate, despite the variety of reasons that contributed to his decision. In self-congratulation, Seward wrote Lewis D. Campbell, U.S. minister to Mexico, "A friendly and explicit arrangement exists between this Government and the Emperor of France . . . he will withdraw his expeditionary military forces from Mexico."[19]

Seeing developments that might lead to the restoration of the Liberals, Santa Anna, at the time staying in New York, declared his support for Juárez, contemplating a possible reentry into Mexican politics. While the Juaristas repudiated him, Gutiérrez Estrada also attempted to discredit him with the Liberal Mexicans by printing his early letters supporting a monarchy. Santa Anna attempted to explain his devotion to the Republicans by publishing a manifesto on June 5, 1866, explaining that numerous supporters called for his intervention and that his goal was to fight for independence and to die in his mother country. Maximilian viewed his manifesto as enormously helpful to flush out the Juaristas' plans and the factionalism that began to form within their cadres. More importantly, he exhibited confidence, hosting dinners and writing to Carlota that the people warmly greeted him and prayed for her.[20]

Meanwhile, Americans on both coasts began to mobilize against the Imperialistas. In San Francisco, California, Juarista Gen. Plácido Vega sold leases to American companies for rights to salt and other deposits in Mexican mines and then purchased over $600,000 in munitions, including rifles, Colt pistols, and percussion caps. He shipped them into Mexico by bribing the commissioner at the port of Mazatlán. When the port manager of San Francisco found out about the illegal shipments, he stopped a subsequent cargo of 20,000 rifles and 18 cannon. Col. George Mason Green and his brother, former California legislator Alfred A. Green, serving as agents for Juarista Gen. Gaspar Sánchez Ochoa, used their influence to persuade San Francisco's bankers to sell $10 million in bonds. Sánchez Ochoa purchased uniforms, horses, sabers, Henry repeating rifles, and ammunition. Also, from San Francisco, the Greens helped recruit the Legion of Honor, a group of freedom fighters financed by Sam Brannan, a capitalist, leader of the Mormon church, and friend of Juárez. The men, disguised as miners, traveled to Juárez's camp in Chihuahua, where the lancers gave them lessons in Mexican-style warfare. The Legion of Honor soon assisted in subsequent Juarista victories.[21]

Meanwhile, Gen. Wallace traveled to New York City to supervise the loading of secret shipments of arms and equipment for Mexico, enough to equip 7,000 soldiers. Wallace took great pains to avoid public attention, knowing that only a few members of Congress recently learned the War Department planned to arm the Mexican Juarista Republicans. Wallace worried about a reversal in the attitude of the War Department should the public learn of the mission. "All I fear is that something may have transpired since leaving New York to alter the policy of the government toward us. Sheridan, in that case, would be uglier than any Frenchman," wrote Wallace. Arriving at Brownsville, the general began unloading his shipments and moving them into the Mexican interior. As many as 30,000 muskets arrived from the Baton Rouge arsenal alone. Wallace also intended to meet with Juárez to propose several business ventures on behalf of private American investors, including a telegraph concession in Mexico, should the republican government be restored.[22]

In Mexico City toward the end of May, Maximilian heard from Father Augustin Fischer and Joaquín Velázquez de León in Rome that they had made superficial progress toward reaching a concordat with the Vatican. Fischer worked to curry diplomatic favor but only succeeded in annoying the prelates. Maximilian realized the damage Meglia, the nuncio, had done within the Vatican's Roman Curate, who clung to their power and punished governments. "They have honey in their mouth and ice in their heart," wrote Maximilian. He seemed philosophical about their hypocrisy, however, vowing to get on with his plans to rid Catholic influences in education, recognize civil marriage, restrict mass in secondary schools, and take the rosary out of the professional schools. His civil code allowed not only for divorce but mandated parents to educate their children. He felt Mexico must be more liberal-minded about the church, like France and Austria. "Las manzanas deben [estar] maduras para caer [de] la altura del árbol" (Apples must be ripe in order to fall from the height of the tree), he wrote Velázquez de León, sure they would get a concordat in time.[23]

Meanwhile, Almonte reported from Paris that Napoléon and his ministers rejected any idea of leaving the remainder of the French troops in Mexico. At the same time, Napoléon tightened conditions for the repayment of debt related to the Mexican intervention. He dangled the possibility of more loans and funds to set up a national bank but demanded 50 percent of the receipts from the customs houses in an amended Convention of Miramar drafted on July 30. If Maximilian would accept those terms, Napoléon agreed to allow the Foreign Legion to remain for another three years and Bazaine to advance 100,000 pesos per month to fund the military. Maximilian, of course, could not fathom any contract with France that deprived Mexico of three-quarters of its revenues. The imperial government was already paying England 24 percent of its income for debt repayment. Napoléon's severity surprised Maximilian, who should never have sent the soft-spoken Almonte to bargain for him, realizing now that France's only interest in Mexico lay in extracting whatever funds possible before their disengagement.[24]

Léonce Détroyat, the undersecretary of the navy and a French officer who served as an advisor to Maximilian and had been ordered back to France by the marshal, wrote to him with ominous advice before his departure. "The fate of the Empire is at stake at this moment. The veil has been drawn aside. Napoléon's policy, which has been equivocal for some time past, is now clear for all eyes to see. It will end in Your Majesty's fall. The Convention of Miramar can no longer be appealed to, the friendship of a brother sovereign can no longer be believed in." The French departure placed Maximilian's life at serious risk, and he strongly believed that Bazaine's motives lay against the emperor's interests.[25]

Maximilian should plan to abdicate, wrote Détroyat, advising him to issue a proclamation to the Mexican citizens. It should state that when he came to Mexico he thought he had come to save them from anarchy but took on an insurmountable task, blindly trusting the emperor of France who vowed to support him and never abandon him. Instead, Napoléon had changed his mind and the rules. Without the major support he was promised, he could not complete his task as emperor and should return to Austria. He encouraged him to unmask Napoléon and expose the truth to the world.[26]

Détroyat's words moved Maximilian deeply. He admired his bravery since France could have easily shot him for treason by expressing such notions. Maximilian thought Détroyat was right; he must divorce himself from the man who ostensibly gave him an empire, which turned out to be a Pandora's box. Exposing Napoléon's betrayals would mean vindicating all those naysayers who had spoken against the project even before he left Miramar. It seemed he had little left to lose.[27]

Abdication was the only option, Maximilian realized; he readied his head around the notion and rehearsed how he might go about it. There was only one person who might stand in his way—his love, his partner, his conscience. Who knew what Carlota might say? So he proposed the idea to her.[28]

Carlota heard him out. She thought about it carefully but could not transcend her previous experiences with the stigma of abdication. Although she sympathized with her husband's difficulties and logic, she disagreed wholeheartedly with the idea of abandoning the Mexican throne. She could only think of her grandfather Louis Philippe, who under pressure from Napoléon

III relinquished the throne of France, his exile leading to his premature death. This was much on her mind, having recently learned of the March 24 death of her grandmother, Marie-Amélie, former queen consort of Louis Philippe.[29]

Now the same irascible character had betrayed her husband. Carlota had learned from her father, Leopold, that by tackling problems head-on, recovery from mistakes could often make a ruler wiser and stronger, but if handled improperly, those mistakes could destroy him. She saw that Maximilian acted impulsively upon the latest advice. Because he lacked decisiveness and was too dependent on advisors, he would not be strong-minded unless the mission was clear. She elected to give Maximilian her own history lesson:

> Charles the X [the King of France who relinquished the throne in 1830] and my grandfather [Louis-Philippe] ruined themselves by abdicating. This must not be repeated. The first made it impossible for his descendants to ascend the throne and broke the fleurs-de-lis in the sack of the archbishop's palace. [My grandfather], after a prosperous reign of eighteen years, condemned his family to a long exile and his government appeared in the eyes of his contemporaries to be a government of rhetoricians.[30]
>
> Abdicating means handing down a sentence on yourself, and writing yourself a certificate of incompetence, and this is acceptable for old men and the weak in spirit. It is not the thing for a thirty-four-year-old prince, full of life with his future before him. Sovereignty is the most sacred possession there is in the world, one does not abandon the throne like one leaves an assembly surrounded by a police force. . . . When one takes charge of the destiny of a nation, it is done at one's own risk, at one's own danger, and one never has the right to abandon it. I do not know of a case where abdication was not negligence or cowardice . . . it is an excuse and an expiation, it could be nothing else. A man can still abdicate when he has fallen into the hands of the enemy in order to deprive the acts he is forced to carry out.[31]

Carlota quoted Louis the Great of the fourteenth century: "'Kings must never give up in the face of defeat.'" She continued: "Very well, then, I say the emperors do not give up. As long as there is an emperor here, there will be an empire, even if it is no more than six feet of earth. The Empire is nothing without the Emperor. The fact that he has no money is not an excuse, it will be obtained with credit, but credit is obtained by success, and success is won by struggle."[32]

Carlota used a well-crafted argument. "The Empire is the only way to save Mexico. Everything must be done to save it, because we swore our commitment and nothing can release us from our oath. . . . The Empire must be

The Imperial Habsburgs of Austria
Back row: Emperor Franz Josef, Ferdinand Maximilian,
Carlota of Belgium, Ludwig Victor, Karl Ludwig.
Front row: Empress Elisabeth, Rudolf, Gisela,
Archduchess Sophie, and Archduke Franz Karl.

Édouard Drouyn de L'Huys, French minister of foreign affairs, ca. 1865

Achille Fould, minister of finance, France, ca. 1865

Gen. Miguel Miramón,
former president of Mexico

Gen. Leonardo Márquez, ca. 1865.
Sent abroad to Istanbul, then
Jerusalem, Márquez returned to
assist Maximilian with the defense of
Querétaro, only to desert him later.

Imperialista Gen. Tomás Mejía, 1865,
executed with Maximilian at
Querétaro, 1867

Imperialista Gen. Ramón Méndez,
executed after the fall of Querétaro,
June 1867

Charles Lennox Wyke,
British envoy to Mexico

Jean Pierre Isidore Alphonse Dubois
de Saligny, ca. 1865, French minister
to Mexico, 1861–63. On May 5, 1862,
at the first assault of Puebla, he cost
many lives in the French defeat, with
the mistaken belief that the citizens
would meet the French army "under
a rain of flowers." This overconfidence
resulted in Mexico's celebrated victory
over the French.

Juan Prim, Conde de Reuss,
Spanish fleet commander, ca. 1865

José Manuel Hidalgo y Esnaurrizar,
Imperialista in Paris, ca. 1865

Belgian Félix Eloin,
Imperial aide, ca. 1865

Admiral Jean-Pierre Jurien
de la Gravière, ca. 1865

Minister José Salazar Ilarregui, imperial
representative from Yucatán, member
of imperial ministry, ca. 1865

Santiago Vidaurri, regional
caudillo and Republican general,
ca. 1865, served as the last minister
of the treasury for the empire.

Matías Romero, Mexican minister
to United States for Benito Juárez and
the Republican government

Count and Gen. Franz von Thun, commander of the Austrian battalions, ca. 1865

Charles Bombelles, Maximilian's friend, head of palatine guards and stables

Dolores Quesada de Almonte,
lady of the court and wife
of Juan Nepomuceno
Almonte, ca. 1865

Manuela del Barrio,
lady of the court, ca. 1865

Pelagio Antonio de Labastida y
Dávalos, archbishop of Mexico,
ca. 1867

Pietro F. Meglia, papal nuncio
to the court of Maximilian

José Luis Blasio, secretary
to Maximilian and Carlota,
ca. 1865

A *cochero*, one of Maximilian's
drivers, 1865

Maximilian in riding attire. Note the
slouchy and highly embroidered chaps.
He poses with head groom Feliciano
Rodríguez in jaguar chaps, ca. 1865

French officer, Mexico City, ca. 1864

Father Augustin Fischer, ca. 1866, aide and confidant of Maximilian, largely credited with the emperor's decision not to abdicate

Mariano Degollado, imperial envoy to Washington, D.C.; and Otilia Jordan de Degollado, riding companion of Carlota

Josefina de Iturbide, aunt of the Prince Iturbide adopted
by Maximilian and Carlota, 1865

William H. Seward,
U.S. Secretary of State,
ca. 1865

Matthew Fontaine Maury,
former Confederate officer,
who fled to Mexico to become
minister of colonization for
the empire of Mexico, ca. 1865

Prince Félix zu Salm-Salm and his wife, Princess Agnes

French Gen. Félix Charles Douay

Gen. François Castelnau

Mariano Riva Palacio,
Maximilian's lawyer,
1867

Frederic Hall,
American lawyer for
Maximilian, 1867

Imperialistas imprisoned after the fall of Querétaro.
Front row: I. L. Casanova; Manuel García de Aguirre, minister of justice;
Gen. C. Moret; Gen. M. M. Escobar; José Fernando Ramírez, president of
council of ministers; Félix zu Salm-Salm; his dog, Jimmy.
Second row: Mariano Monterde; V. Herrera y Lozada; Reyes; Severo del
Castillo, imperial general; Gen. Pedro Valdés; Redonet; Gen. Calvo.
Back row: Díaz; Tomás Prieto; Adame; Othon, ca. 1867.

preserved, it must remain standing, and defended, if necessary against any attack," she said. Regarding Détroyat's idea of abdication, she said he had no comprehension of the situation:

> The words 'too late' cannot be used here, but rather 'too early.' . . . What is at issue is loyalty, love of country, and honor. You do not abandon your post before the enemy. Why would you abandon a crown? Kings in the middle ages at least waited until their states were about to be snatched away before handing themselves over. Abdication was not invented until sovereigns forgot how to jump on a horse in times of danger. . . . My grandfather wanted to avoid bloodshed and was directly responsible for the blood spilled in France. . . . The civil war no longer exists [in Mexico] because there is no longer any pretext for it, Juárez's reign has passed.[33]

Carlota's pitch seemed clear and logical. She felt sure Napoléon would never truly sever himself from the Mexican expedition, and nor should they. She encouraged Maximilian to buck up, concluding,

> There is just one step from pathetic to ridiculous. We were to start out as champions of civilization, as the liberators and regenerators; and then to withdraw on the plea that there is nothing to civilize, nothing to liberate, nothing to regenerate, all this under an intimate agreement with France, which has always passed for the country of intellectual power, you will admit that for both sides this would be the greatest absurdity committed under the sun. . . . Even if it is permitted to play with single individuals, one does not play with nations, for God avenges this.[34]

Beware of the French

To save the empire, Carlota determined to cross the highlands, descend through the tierra caliente, sail the Atlantic, and travel to Paris to see Napoléon in person. She felt that if she could simply meet with Napoléon and Eugénie, she could make them understand Maximilian's position and persuade them to support the Mexican empire a while longer. In preparation, she set to work with Maximilian to draw up arguments and a proposal. Since funding remained critical with the budget in deficit, they agreed to ask for an immediate subsidy of 500,000 pesos, the amount the French treasury had recently suspended. They also wanted a promise that the Mexican army of 20,000 mixed troops would receive pay through the end of 1867 and monthly financing of 500,000 pesos to support the government. They demanded a reassignment of the commanding generals, with Marshal Bazaine recalled to France or Algeria, and that the French army be removed en masse only after the complete organization a new national army. Maximilian asked Carlota to learn the raw truth from Napoléon.[1]

To underwrite Carlota's voyage, Maximilian withdrew 30,000 pesos from a fund set aside for repairs after inundations, floods being a frequent occurrence in a Mexico City surrounded by lakes and marshes. This remained one of the last viable accounts in the imperial treasury. For the journey, she planned to take the most traveled and helpful courtiers: Martín Castillo, the minister of foreign affairs; the Count del Valle Juan Antonio Suárez Peredo, her grand chamberlain; Felipe Neri del Barrio, chamberlain, and his wife, Manuelita, her

lady-in-waiting; Charles Bombelles, chief of the palace guards; Carlota's doctors Friedrich Semelder and Karl Bouslaveck; Léonce Détroyat to serve on the
steamship; Jacob von Kuhachevich, the imperial archivist and personal treasurer, and his wife, who was the lady of her chamber. The Von Kuhachevichs
had been with them from the beginning and dreaded leaving Maximilian to his
own devices. It was likely they were sent away because the wife was a known
busybody and gossip. She revealed Maximilian's love interests at Cuernavaca
to a number of people and wrote about Maximilian being "blind" and a "pup-
pet" over a weak government, and that "this entire business is a lie and won't
last long . . . but no one has the courage to tell the truth."[2]

At first Carlota's mission was planned in secret. In cipher, Count General
Thun, the governor-general of Puebla, received a missive from Charles
Bombelles asking him to reserve twelve cabins on the next mail packet leaving Veracruz for Saint Nazaire on the French coast. The bookings were to
be made in the names of soldiers in the hospital, ostensibly being discharged
home. Outside of their immediate aides, others were told that Carlota was taking another tour of Yucatán and the imperial authorities there were instructed
to prepare for her visit. Bazaine, however, robbed the mission of any secrecy
when he had the *Moniteur* print an article on July 7, "the empress leaves tomorrow for Europe," seeking the resolution of various Mexican and international
concerns.[3]

On July 6, 1866, the cathedral held a celebration and Te Deum in honor
of Maximilian's thirty-fourth birthday. Although he was unable to attend as
the result of a raging fever, Carlota attended the service without him. Rumors
of Carlota's imminent departure had swept the capital, and curious onlookers
commented that she seemed very serious and remained on her knees in prayer
longer than usual. Adding to the somber tone, Maximilian had just received
a telegram, which took three weeks to arrive, announcing the June 15 com-
mencement of the Austro-Prussian War. He knew this spelled much stress for
Napoléon and hoped the battles would be over by the time Carlota arrived in
Paris.[4]

Maximilian and Carlota spent their last evening together reviewing the
documents prepared for Napoléon, along with account sheets compiled by
their secretary, Pierron, for the French finance ministers. Carlota rehearsed
her presentation to Napoléon. They reserved the threat of resignation as an
ultimatum, not aware that Napoléon really no longer cared as long as he could
extricate himself from Mexico without a loss in credibility.[5]

At four in the morning on July 9, Carlota said goodbye to her ladies-in-waiting. "I will be back in three months," she said. One of the ladies, Concepción de Pacheco, was in tears and asked if she could embrace Carlota because she might never see her again. As she clasped the empress, all the ladies began to cry, and Carlota had trouble containing her emotions. She entered her carriage, and her entourage left Mexico City headed for the mountain passes escorted by wagons bearing trunks, her valuable possessions, a kitchen wagon, and a detachment of cavalry and the *Emperatriz* regiment of Belgian and Mexican soldiers, commanded by Miguel López. Although he was still ailing, Maximilian rode with Carlota about twenty miles east as far as the town of Ayotla. The sun began to rise over the snow-white summit of Popocatepetl, bathing the landscape in soft orange and purple hues. When they finally said goodbye, both broke into tears. So weakened by fever and sadness, Maximilian had to be helped to his transport for the return to Mexico City. Carlota wrote to him from the crossing at Río Frío, saying that seeing him break down made her "so miserable that [she] became half-unconscious and wept quite openly in front of the muleteers." She remained determined that the French were not going to cause their downfall, however, and pulled herself together. "Beware of the French. Even the nicest of them . . . is supposed to have said that I will never come back. Do not listen. It would break my heart, wherever I should be, if I ever heard that you had been talked into giving up the throne for which we have sacrificed so much and which can still have such a glorious future. There are many here who are loyal and who would never betray you," she wrote.[6]

Baron Karl Malortie, acting as Gen. Thun's aide-de-camp, escorted the twenty-six-year-old empress and wrote that her courage inspired the young officers. He described their ride one evening:

> There was something ghostly, uncanny, in this procession of horsemen and vehicles cantering and panting through the deep sand road, wedged in by monumental hedges of aloes . . . the gigantic cactus throwing mysterious shadows. Preceded by a troop of our Polish lancers, cocked carbines on hips, and lances planted firmly in the stirrups, Her Majesty advanced alone, a truly glorious vision, a Juno-like appearance on her splendid thoroughbred charger, lit up by the silvery rays of a full moon. A white dust-mantle over her gray well-fitting habit, and a large sombrero with long floating veil contributed to the empress the appearance of an elf-like fairy queen.

Gen. Thun and Charles Bombelles frequently rode beside her, conversing in German and making light social talk or outlining strategic plans, concealing themselves well from the Spanish and French speakers in their midst.[7]

After riding about thirty-five miles southeast, they arrived at a large hacienda at Río Prieto where they were to spend the night. A lavish dinner had been prepared, and they were late. Malortie recalled that Carlota "jumped out of the saddle ere any one of us could hurry to her assistance, and leaning on Count Thun's arm, stiff after two days on horseback, mounted the half-dozen steps leading into the house." The empress hurried through the hall in her riding clothes, where the guests waited for her. She whispered to her hostess, "I shall not be ten minutes, the time to jump into my tub, and put on a tea gown. Do tell the ladies."[8]

She arrived a short time later, looking radiant and composed, keeping up appearances. She quickly greeted the guests, making her rounds with a word or a smile, not wishing to betray the urgency and seriousness of her mission. The dining gallery looked out onto a garden where an Austrian string ensemble played traditional Tyrolean music, including the Ländler. "The dinner was, like all official functions, somewhat stiff, the Empress endeavoring in vain to make people feel at home," said Malortie.[9]

Departing Puebla, the journey through the highlands and over the cumbres was hindered by rain and stormy conditions. With a strong escort of Chasseurs d'Afrique, they passed through the treacherous hills, while watching for guerrilla snipers. Near Córdoba, the swirling, yawing clouds of a *norte* dumped torrential sheets of rain. Carriages began to get stuck or overturn. When a wheel on Carlota's carriage broke, she prepared to ride horseback but was advised against it. Instead, she took shelter at a small roadside inn where noisy and drunk travelers reveled in the next room. Her armed bodyguard did not announce the identity of Carlota or ladies to anyone. Some of the rowdy men were singing songs including *Mama Carlota*. "*Adiós, Mama Carlota, Adiós, mi tierno amor, Se fueran los Franceses, Se va el Emperador*," they sang. ("Farewell Mama Carlota, Farewell my tender love, When the French go, the Emperor goes too.")[10]

In this awkward scene, the ladies-in-waiting looked away and the French guards did not move, reluctant to get into a row. Carlota, however, viewed the singers as secret enemies plotting to do her or her husband harm. She got up to go, wanting to mount her horse and ride on. Fortunately, another carriage arrived from Córdoba, and she left with the guarded carriages.[11]

On Friday, July 13, after crossing the Paso del Macho, Carlota rode into Veracruz, met not by crowds but by the ubiquitous vultures that preyed on carrion along the coast. Her quiet mission drew almost no one's notice. The mercantile workers who gathered at the wharf removed their hats when she passed, and Carlota noticed their uncertain looks. In this sad climate, she felt they speculated on her state, why she was leaving. When Carlota saw that the flag of France flew from the mast of the steamer *Empress Eugénie* instead of the Mexican royal standard, she could not allow the people to think she too was abandoning the country. The small launch waiting to convey her to the steamship bore no insignias either. Annoyed, she blamed the city council, whom she thought idiotic, for not conveying a spirit of patriotism that should have been timed with her arrival. To leave with dignity, she refused to embark until the crew flew the Mexican imperial emblem. After some embarrassment and a flurry of activity, the commander of the French gulf squadron, Georges-Charles Cloué, and the French crew hoisted the appropriate colors. Carlota calmed and thanked Commandant Cloué for his cooperation. There was also some confusion on the bookings, for the Compagnie Transatlantique had been told only scant detail. The company bumped a number of the French passengers to make room for the royal retinue. Carlota remained in her cabin with a raging headache for most of the first leg of the voyage to Havana and ordered mattresses to pad her cabin from the noise of the churning engines.[12]

In Mexico City, with Carlota's mission troubling his mind, Maximilian wrote to his brother Karl Ludwig about the pain of letting his wife go to Europe. "Carlota's voyage is the heaviest sacrifice I have yet made to my new country. It is all the harder since she has to travel through the deadly yellow fever zone during the worst season. But duty demands this sacrifice and, God willing, it will not be in vain." He said that although it was "extremely difficult and deeply sad," the weakness and fear of European governments toward the United States obliged him to know if they could rely on anyone and hear it firsthand.[13]

Marking the two-year anniversary of his arrival in Mexico, Maximilian turned to his projects to improve the county's infrastructure and beauty. He ordered expansion of railroad and telegraph lines to the Pacific coast while completing short lines in the Valley of Mexico. In Mexico City, he continued work to renovate the Plaza de Armas; clean up the market square; construct a hydraulic system to pump water to the city's monuments and public fountains; repair the dilapidated bull ring; and wire electric street amenities, including a system of clocks. All would be paid, he envisioned, with a new city property tax, similar to Paris and Vienna. Also, Maximilian passed time by examining schools, awarding scholarship prizes, having formal military dinners, and traveling on small excursions out of the city, sometimes going out on his boat in Lake Texcoco, on warm days that he said reminded him of the Adriatic.[14]

After steady reinforcement from the United States, by the end of summer 1866 the Juaristas regained Tabasco, Chiapas, Guerrero, Sonora, Baja

California, Chihuahua, Tamaulipas, and the Isthmus of Tehuantepec. More importantly, French had evacuated the ports of Mazatlán and Guaymas on the Pacific coast and Matamoros in the Gulf of Mexico, further depriving the Imperial government of needed cash. The only ports the empire still held were Veracruz, San Blas in Nayarit, and Manzanilla in Jalisco. Despite offensives by the Juaristas throughout the country, Marshal Bazaine continued building the new army while consolidating his French troops and complaining a great deal. The process was tricky. If he disbanded some of the regiments before consolidating them into the new mixed units, many would attempt to desert or mutiny, especially the Belgians. When discontent led to a riot, more than thirty Belgian officers demanded to return to Europe, citing the end of their enlistment. This only encouraged the Juaristas. Bazaine disbanded the Belgian units, dismissed the recalcitrant officers, and assigned the rest to Mexican imperial units. Bazaine hurried the process because his troop transports were arriving in September to evacuate the French army, an irony not lost on some observers because of his previous passivity in aiding Maximilian to form his own army.[15]

In addition to Maximilian's doubts about Bazaine's strategy, not all the military commanders agreed with the marshal's plan for consolidation, which they viewed as haphazard. When ordered to complete the organization of the Austrian troops and move them from Puebla seventy miles north to Tulancingo, Gen. Thun refused, and on August 23 announced his plan to leave Mexico. Thun felt he had received little support, protesting endlessly throughout his assignment to assist in building the imperial national army. After expending so much shoe leather to subdue the country, many soldiers felt demoralized. Furthermore, they had not been paid, and food and provisions were scarce. Thun wanted to stay nearby the quickest exit route from the country.[16]

This rising panic affected French civilians and other foreigners loyal to the crown, and a number of residents determined it was time to abandon Mexico, including a number of European ministers. "The poor French . . . have been forced to leave everything, wealth and interests of all kinds, to save their lives," said Capt. Pierre Loizillon. "It is a complete fiasco, and very sad because of all the personal misfortunes. French and Mexicans alike curse the French intervention. Everything that is happening is so appalling that I cannot believe we left Mexico in such a shameful way. Sooner or later, the emperor is going to have to go; so I hope some sort of accord will be reached with whoever the president might be," he wrote.[17]

Through the spring and summer of 1866, with support eroding, Maximilian knew he could not depend on the Conservatives and Clerical party with his current policies. Yet his open-minded, liberal ideals had done nothing to cement support with the Republicans. "A grand and influential class of the country disgracefully abstains from supporting my efforts, the concluding proof that the country wants peace building," he wrote. Gutiérrez de Estrada wrote from Europe to say that Maximilian's only salvation would be to give over to the Clerical party, those who brought him to Mexico in the first place, and he finally agreed, even though they could not provide him with the men and armaments he needed. He had no choice. He called upon Teodosio Lares, the former president of the Assembly of Notables and a devoted Catholic, a man he did not like or agree with, to rejoin the cabinet but retained the moderate José María Lacunza as prime minister. Minister José Salazar Ilarregui, Gen. Auguste Adolphe Osmont, and Gen. Jean Nicolas Friant, who was a personal friend of Archbishop Labastida, remained on the cabinet. Bitterly hostile against Bazaine and the French army, Lares's appointment publicly signaled Maximilian's reversal from his progressive albeit irresolute ideals. He ordered the arrest of twenty-four outspoken opponents of the empire, whom he labeled as traitors, although most had done little more than complain about the French. Maximilian ordered them expelled to Yucatán, writing, "Since the deportation was carried out and openly announced in the *Journal*, the mood improved significantly up in the capital." As the time for the military's departure neared, the more anti-French and stringent Maximilian became.[18]

In August 1866 Bazaine issued his final orders to recall his soldiers from previous strongholds. Most left scornfully. Gen. Félix Douay started south from northern Mexico in shame and anger. Tampico was evacuated and the Liberals in support of González Ortega moved in almost immediately to set up a gallows in the main plaza where they hanged the Imperialista prefect of the region and seized the customs funds. Juarista Gen. Mariano Escobedo lauded the French army's withdrawal from the northernmost provinces, calling it a definitive victory. French citizens living across northern Mexico were massacred in a number of settlements, as well as Mexicans who cooperated with the French or served the empire in some way. Hearing of such violence and the loss of so much territory rent Maximilian's heart, and he wrote of his sadness over every drop of blood spilled. He urged Bazaine not to remove military protection from the towns without providing for the contingency of attacks on Imperialistas remaining in each place. Maximilian reminded him that his throne would be left with the residue of his actions after his departure. "For just as the marshal is responsible for the honor of France, so am I for that of Mexico," Maximilian said.[19]

General anarchy spread. Men deserted their colors, garrisons were captured by Liberals, only to be recaptured by Imperialistas. When regional leaders organized bands of guerrillas, they attacked civilians and military alike along the roads. Maximilian prepared to proclaim martial law, but Bazaine said there were not enough soldiers to enforce it, which would cause embarrassment and more damage. Bazaine mendaciously assured Maximilian that when the Juaristas tired, the Mexican imperial army would be able to reclaim those places, including the previous northern strongholds.[20]

All Maximilian could do was to organize his own army. Distressed, he cut the pay of the civil list again, discreetly sold carriages, horses, harnesses, and equipment, and halted his expenditures and gifts to send more revenue to the troops. At the same time, bad news arrived from Vienna. On July 3, 1866, the Austrians had suffered a humiliating defeat by the Prussian army at the Battle of Sadowa, sixty-five miles northeast of Prague, with a shocking and staggering loss of life. The battle engaged just under 500,000 troops, 250,000 Prussians against nearly the same number of Austrians, the largest number ever assembled in a European conflict. Reportedly Franz Josef had returned to Vienna to a silenced crowd of disillusioned onlookers. Some exclaimed, "Long Live Maximilian," since a number of Viennese proposed a regime change and the recall of Maximilian to succeed the throne. While Napoléon attempted to remain neutral, others saw that his power and influence in European affairs had begun to slip. With his well-organized military machine, Prussian chancellor Otto von Bismarck now held daunting control. Maximilian knew that the prospect of returning to Europe, even if he dared, would be very difficult. Austria was under martial law, had abolished civil liberties, and was cracking down on dissidents perceived to be collaborating with Bismarck. Such a return would be compounded by the unresolved Family Pact, still standing between him and his family.[21]

During her four-week Atlantic crossing to Europe, Carlota mostly stayed in her humid cabin, fighting seasickness, giving rise to a rumor among her ladies that she was pregnant. She took walks and stood for a long while at the ship's railing, looking out at the ocean, worrying, and nervously shredding her lace handkerchiefs. She slept very little.[22]

On August 8, 1866, Carlota arrived at the French port of Saint Nazaire to learn that the Austrian defeat at Sadowa four weeks earlier had greatly disturbed the balance of power in Europe. She disembarked to find only the Almontes to greet her, Dolores Almonte carrying a small bouquet of sad-looking roses. Although the town officials of Saint Nazaire knew of her pending arrival, few preparations had been made. At the last moment, they scrambled to form a welcoming committee and, unable to locate a Mexican flag, used a Peruvian one instead. Carlota thanked the dignitaries, sent a few telegrams—including one to Napoléon—and retired to the hotel. The next day she boarded the train for Paris, via Nantes, in the company of her retinue.[23]

Although Carlota heard that Napoléon was suffering from a bout with bladder stones and was recuperating at the palace of Saint Cloud, she nonetheless remained intent to meet with him. Undaunted, she knew that France remained in good shape despite European turmoil, and she sent a purposeful message to the emperor announcing her arrival. Her telegram hit like a bombshell. She hoped her visit would trouble him as much as his January letter announcing the early withdrawal of the French troops had devastated her and Maximilian. Napoléon replied, "I have just returned from Vichy, and I am forced to stay in bed, so that I am not in a position to come and see Your Majesty. If, as I suppose, Your Majesty is going first to Belgium, this will give me time to recover." She did not intend to go to Belgium, in view of her brother Leopold II's refusal to send additional support to the Mexican empire, and told Napoléon so in response to his message. She sent notice of her arrival to Maximilian's mother, the Archduchess Sophie but had no wish to go to Vienna. Franz Josef's capitulation to the United States had illuminated his regard for their empire.[24]

Carlota rejected Napoléon's suggestion that they postpone their meeting, no matter the excuse. Scheduled to arrive in Paris the next day, she telegraphed that she fully expected to see him. She also alerted the Mexican delegation of her pending arrival, but as the train pulled into the Montparnasse station, hardly anyone awaited her arrival. The Mexican deputation had gone to the Gare d'Orléans terminal instead. Only Gutiérrez de Estrada and the adopted Mexican prince, Salvador Iturbide, knew exactly where she would be arriving. French officials who had just learned of her arrival also had gone to the wrong rail depot. She was close to tears. When Almonte failed to book transportation, she took Gutiérrez de Estrada's carriage to the hotel, leaving her entourage to search for cabs or landaus. Carlota checked into suites on the first floor of the Grand Hôtel. Fatigued and apprehensive, she locked herself into her suite to cry. She knew the salvation of the Mexican empire lay in her best arguments—a great deal of pressure for a young princess. That evening, one lady-in-waiting commented that the exhausted Carlota looked "like a walking ghost." When news of Carlota's arrival was received, the alarmed Eugénie sent Napoléon's representatives, making their apologies, and asking when Carlota could receive Eugénie and how long she would be staying.[25]

The next morning Carlota's servants and chambermaids found her sitting on a sofa, not having slept during the night. Unstrung, she worried about her meeting with the emperor and if she could persuade him to change his mind. She visualized having to beg for their hold on the empire he promised them. Yet the whole day passed without any word from Napoléon or Eugénie.[26]

Upon Carlota's arrival, Alice Green Iturbide, then living in Paris because of her exile by Maximilian, contacted the court for an audience with the empress regarding her son, Agustín, prince of Mexico, then with his aunt Josefa in Mexico. A meeting was arranged at the hotel. Carlota knew issues still lingered over the adoption payments, but Alice only wanted her child returned. When she arrived, the empress who was seated on a sofa did not rise and did not ask Alice to sit down. So Alice seated herself on the same sofa.[27]

"You are much changed since I saw you last," Carlota said. Alice replied that ten months of suffering had taken a toll on her appearance, adding that Carlota looked quite different, too. Carlota looked away. After a few moments, Alice asked her about Agustín and again requested that she might be able to have custody of him.[28]

"I have done you great honor in giving you this interview. You should not make me regret it. I wished simply to tell you that your child is well, and improving every day in person and intelligence," said Carlota. Alice felt her grief rising within her as Carlota spoke, which the empress could plainly see. "I am treating your child with the greatest kindness; I am supporting him with my own money," said Carlota. "If we give you back your child, you should return the money the Emperor paid to your family." Alice said if Carlota insisted, they would return the funds—she would do anything.[29]

A month earlier, the Iturbides sent letters complaining they had not received their funding as promised, and Maximilian immediately ordered his secretary to forward each heir 3,000 pesos, but they regarded the contract as void. Alice told Carlota that she had consulted a lawyer to review the adoption documents, and the lawyer had concluded that they had not legally given up possession of their son. Alice also complained of the way in which the emperor and his palace guard deceived her when they cruelly expelled her from Mexico City.[30]

"The Emperor did right. You should not have come back to Mexico, and you did wrong after coming there to address yourself to Marshal Bazaine instead of the Emperor," said Carlota.

"I did not know, at the time, of the misunderstanding, which I have since learned, exist[ing] between the Emperor and the Marshal," said Alice.[31]

"There is no misunderstanding, but it was not an affair for the Marshal. You have always acted badly toward us. You stood aloof from us when we first came to Mexico, and now you show no gratitude to the Emperor for having made your son and nephew princes."

"My husband and brothers are the sons of a legitimate Emperor, and if they have not borne their title of princes, it is because they have not cared to," said Alice.

"What advantage can your son be to me? The Emperor and I are both young; we may have children of our own," Carlota said.

"I earnestly hope so, if that will restore me mine," said Alice.

Finally Carlota softened a bit. "For how long are you willing to give him up to us?"

"Not an hour longer than I am compelled to," said Alice.

Carlota promised to write Maximilian on the matter, and she advised Alice to do the same. "I have done so many times and received no reply," said Alice, worried that Maximilian might be preparing to abdicate, and if he brought the baby to Europe, she would have less power to have her son returned.

"Write again, and write politely," said Carlota.[32]

At the palace of Saint Cloud, Napoléon remained greatly preoccupied by the decisive Austrian defeat at the hands of the Prussians, because it was unlike him to hesitate over a major conflagration affecting his border. In bad health, he made a number of efforts not to enter another war. Moreover, France remained debilitated with 30,000 troops still tramping through the deserts and highlands of Mexico. When Eugénie had asked why France had not intervened in the Austro-Prussian conflict, Napoléon in turn asked her who was at fault that all his best generals and men were still on the other side of the Atlantic. He squarely blamed her for the complications. As one historian said, "Lack of synthesis was always the Emperor's greatest problem. Not only did the Empress not contribute to its solution, she was herself a major cause of his problems." Despite everything, Eugénie tormented herself over her role in the Mexican expedition, and she was troubled about the fate of Maximilian and Carlota.[33]

On August 11 Eugénie determined to pay Carlota a visit the next day at the Grand Hôtel. In preparation, all that morning Carlota worked with her Mexican ladies-in-waiting to perfect their etiquette, sharpening their manners to make "a good impression of the elegance and good breeding of the Court of Mexico." She knew some members of the French court snobbishly condemned the lack of sophistication of Carlota's attendants and felt it crucial that her court reflect the standards of the European courts. That same day, to prepare to meet the French sovereigns, Carlota also met several ministers, diplomats, bankers, and military brass, all with connections in some way to the Mexican empire. To them and Napoléon's aide-de-camp, she spared no criticism of the military's strategy of repatriating their French troops, which violated all the promises made to them.[34]

The next day at two in the afternoon, Eugénie arrived at the hotel, accompanied by her lady-in-waiting, Madame Bouvet Carette. Clothed in a light muslin dress and flowered bonnet, Eugénie appeared sunny and elegant, looking much younger in her forty years than Carlota, who wore black, still in mourning for her grandmother, Queen Marie-Amélie. Tense and strained, Carlota carried herself upright. Eugénie rushed to kiss and embrace her, but Carlota only halfheartedly returned her affection.[35]

The scene was rather awkward. When Eugénie broke into light conversation, Carlota interrupted her. In simple language, Carlota told the French empress she needed her help for Mexico and her people. Without the support of the French military, the empire would founder and the Liberals would exact retribution on all those who had supported their reign. Maximilian had met his obligations, and he ruled according to principles similar to those of France. He had done all that Napoléon asked. If France could reinforce them a while longer, said Carlota, the United States would have no choice but to recognize the Mexican empire and accept its permanence. Eugénie became emotional and nervous and tried to steer the conversation toward lighter topics, like the charming dinners she heard Carlota conducted at the National Palace, how the ladies in Mexico developed a fancy for French couture, and how people in Paris had come to love the song "La Paloma."[36]

Carlota stared at her with disbelief. Eugénie had glossed over her very real descriptions of the national crisis in Mexico. Carlota interrupted her to ask when she might return the visit, and the empress looked a little stunned but said the day after tomorrow, if she wished. "And what about the Emperor, will I see him then?" asked Carlota. Eugénie hesitated a moment. "Alas, that will be impossible. The Emperor is far from well and is still confined to this bed." Carlota knew, however, that Napoléon soon planned to travel to Camp

Châlons in Champagne-Ardenne, and her window of time to see him would soon close.[37]

She said that she would see him soon at the palace of Saint Cloud, leaving Eugénie with no response. "If the Emperor refuses to see me, I shall force my way in," said Carlota with a smile. Although she was startled by the curt, light remark, Eugénie had little doubt that Carlota might do so. She returned to Saint Cloud feeling sad and guilty about the young empress, who had quickly aged in a short time.[38]

On August 13 Carlota wrote a note reconfirming her intent to see Napoléon as soon as possible. She asked if she could come to Saint Cloud at 2:30 in the afternoon of the next day. "I have a few documents to bring in support of what I said the other day, so that the Emperor may acquaint himself with the situation by tangible proofs," Carlota wrote. She also asked to see the financial minister, Achille Marcus Fould, and minister of war, Marshal Jacques Louis Randon. "I will bring Monsieur Castillo, who knows the finances of Mexico by heart, in order to present him to the Emperor," she wrote.[39]

The next day Napoléon's first chamberlain arrived at the hotel and asked to see Carlota. On behalf of Napoléon and Eugénie, he invited her to lunch at the palace of Saint Cloud. Not wanting to leap at an invitation of a mere lunch, having been slighted already, Carlota declined but said that if it was convenient, she could be at Saint Cloud by three in the afternoon. She wanted a business meeting. "I don't think I ever saw anything more dignified, more queenly, than Her Majesty's reception and dismissal of the Emperor's envoy, and by the nervous movement in the Count's eyes, I could see that he understood the mute lesson," said Manuelita del Barrio.[40]

At twenty minutes past two, Carlota boarded a landau with her ladies-in-waiting, followed by another coach carrying her attendants. Carlota wore a black dress and a mantilla over a new white hat, purchased for her by her ladies the day before. As she emerged from her hotel, a crowd of onlookers cheered. There had been much speculation in the press about Carlota's visit and her pending arguments to Napoléon, and the public was intrigued. But she was absorbed in her mission, her eyes were red, and she looked exhausted after a sleepless night rehearsing her presentation. In the carriage, she fidgeted and fingered the lace of her mantilla. Her attendants tried to soothe her nervousness. As they approached Saint Cloud, Carlota took a deep breath and consolidated her thoughts on what she termed the plan of "conversion." On arrival, she appeared composed and confident, despite the circumstances.[41]

The honor guard of chasseurs, uniformed in fur bearskin shakos, lined the entryway at Saint Cloud, and the members of the imperial household stood at attention. Amid drum rolls, Carlota acknowledged the French flag. Ten-year-old Prince Napoléon Eugène, the son of Napoléon and Eugénie, wearing a fine charro uniform sent to him by Carlota, bounded down the stairs to help the empress. He took her by the hand and led her up the stairway to his mother, who waited, smiling calmly. Carlota nodded in acknowledgment. Eugénie walked with Carlota into the palace followed by Dolores Almonte and Manuelita del Barrio, whom a courtier sniffed at as "two plain little women with neither the elegance nor grace" of the ladies of the French court.[42]

With Eugénie, she glided through a number of staterooms to the emperor's reception salon, and they disappeared into the private chambers. After a few moments, Napoléon emerged from his private suite so that Carlota could present her staff to him. Twisting his waxed mustache, Napoléon greeted her retinue, moving around the room in his "peculiar, swinging, waddling way of his own," with a forced smile against his obvious pain from his bladder stones. After the royals retreated to talk, the ladies settled onto sofas and chairs in the outer chamber, and the men withdrew into the aide-de-camp's room to smoke while the staff served refreshments.[43]

In Napoléon's office Carlota calmly began her presentation. "Sire, I have come to save a cause which is your own." She recited the history from the beginning with the promises made to Maximilian by the French empire, including command of the expeditionary corps, the inadequate funding of the army, and the shortfalls in maritime customs revenue. She then began her arguments why the French army should stay to support the empire, that the work of occupation was not finished. She presented chronological maps, showing Juarista movements and the ports they now controlled, against the third of Mexico still held by the French, depriving the empire valuable customs revenues. She carefully explained Bazaine's clumsy strategies, pointing out that one town had changed hands between the Liberals and Imperialistas no less than fourteen times. She stated that the Mexican empire launched without an adequate financial foundation or resources, and now the French took no responsibility. Napoléon and Eugénie sat silent, impressed with her presentation.[44]

Later, she wrote to Maximilian, "I did everything that was humanly possible; I immediately gave the emperor an ultimatum." Carlota had pleaded, begged, and tried to shame Napoléon into recalling Bazaine, whom she said undermined their administration. She argued for the continuation of monthly salaries for the Mexican imperial army and an agreement to leave the French expeditionary force in Mexico until the country was entirely pacified. "How is it possible that your Majesty, the master of a nation of 30 million souls, holding its supremacy in Europe, with immense resources and the most extensive credit in the world with victorious armies always at the ready, can do nothing for the empire of Mexico, where France has great interests to protect?" asked Carlota. Her fevered presentation had lasted nearly two hours.[45]

At one point, Carlota's attendants suggested to Napoléon's staff that the empress enjoyed a refreshment in the midafternoon, and Eugénie's lady, Madame Carette, ordered a decanter of orangeade sent into the meeting. When a servant entered with the tray, Eugénie poured a glass and offered it to Carlota, who in midsentence did not want to be distracted and initially refused. When Eugénie offered again, Carlota took the orangeade and drank some. She later mentioned to her attendants that Napoléon and Eugénie were trying to poison her in the middle of the meeting. This offhand remark was an exaggeration, likely due to her irritation at being interrupted. Nonetheless, the Mexican entourage made much gossip over the comment.[46]

During Carlota's presentation, however, Napoléon listened while great emotion arose within him. He dabbed at tears streaming down his cheeks, made a few comments, and stared with glassy eyes. Carlota had the impression that he had already forgotten all about Mexico. The signs of age evident in both Napoléon and Eugénie revealed the weight of their tensions over the last three years. Carlota wrote, "They have become old, both of them are childlike; often they both cry. I do not know whether this makes matters any better." Napoléon promised her that she could meet with his ministers of war and finance to make the same case for the desperate situation in Mexico. He blamed his ministers for the problems, but she suspected he was making excuses. She thanked the emperor and because her coachmen had been told to be back in two hours and were off walking on the grounds, she paced up and down the corridors waiting. When she finally entered the carriage, she began to weep.[47]

"I know more about China than these people here know about Mexico," Carlota wrote to Maximilian, "where they have assumed one of the greatest enterprises in which the French flag as ever been engaged. . . . The Empress has lost much of her youth and energy since the last time I saw her and in the midst of all their grandeur, [they] can no longer withstand any sort of pressure, real or imagined," she concluded. "The throne of France quickly ages those who sit upon it and yet history has taught us as Fortune does, their warrior nation smiles only on the young."[48]

The next morning the ministers arrived, including Foreign Affairs Minister

Édouard Drouyn de L'Huys along with Marshal Jacques Randon and Achille Fould. She made impassioned arguments to each of them in turn, requesting the French army to remain and at least half a million pesos per month from the treasury for their support. They remained evasive but polite, and Fould agreed to meet again in a few days. The Austrian ambassador to France, Richard Metternich, warned Carlota not to place her heart in Napoléon's hands. The jaded French ministers had advised their emperor to get out of Mexico with haste.[49]

A few days later, Napoléon met with Carlota again at Saint Cloud, in what she called a "working visit." This time, instead of persuasion, she tried coercion. She brought Martín Castillo with the financial data and the written promises and contracts that set up imperial Mexico. Napoléon, sitting irritably at his desk, was in no mood to hear about Mexican finances and almost lost his temper. But Carlota, with controlled vitriol, presented the French emperor with his own letter written to Maximilian on March 28, 1864, when he thought the archduke was about to refuse the throne of Mexico. "What would you think of me if, when Your Royal Highness was once in Mexico, I were suddenly to say to you that I cannot fulfill the conditions to which I have set my signature?" Napoléon had written. It was a withering argument that he could not reconcile. The emperor sat wiping his eyes, wanting no more questions. Carlota commented later that he shed even more tears than in the previous meeting.[50]

With Napoléon visibly agitated, Eugénie intervened and convinced Carlota to end the session. She informed Carlota that the ministers waited for her in the next room. Carlota stormed out of the meeting to speak to Ministers Randon and Fould in Eugénie's quarters. Eugénie tucked herself into a sofa in the next room to eavesdrop on their conversation. Carlota began by saying she suspected the French ministers of self-dealing and swindling at Maximilian's expense. She started by demanding an explanation of why the French government had cut Maximilian's annual budget of 34 million francs by demanding half of all the customs revenues, a sum under which no government could function. Expenses of the Mexican military ran in excess of 64 million francs alone, she said. With two loans totaling 516 million francs, the imperial Mexican government received only 126 million to cover the 150 million francs in war costs. Yet Mexico's government remained responsible for the entire debt. She railed against Jecker and other bankers who she believed appropriated the balance of the funds. "Who are the persons whose pockets are filled with gold at Mexico's expense?" she asked, clearly enraged that their cupidity knew no limit. "If those in Paris had conspired to bring about the ruin of the empire, they could not have acted otherwise."[51]

Marshal Randon sat in nervous shock with nothing to say. Totally disarmed, Fould told her the details with more candor than she anticipated. He said the first loan had been undersubscribed and the second was offered at a discount of 63 percent to offset the high credit risk of the Mexican government. The bankers deducted 17 million francs in commissions, 20 million was forfeited back to the bankers, and 800,000 went for bribes to keep the press quiet. It had all been a dazzling international scheme. Fould blamed Maximilian's inexperience and incompetence along with wide-scale corruption in Mexico. The ministers alleged that the expedition nearly ruined France but would not admit the effort only cost 300 million francs. Incredibly, sometime over the last few years, the Jecker debt had been liquidated and eliminated, at Napoléon's request, for his half brother the Duc de Morny. All the costs of sending and sustaining the French military in Mexico had been put on the backs of French taxpayers, yet Mexico continued to pay on the notes. She asked for an extension of the $500,000 once promised to the Mexican treasury. At the conclusion of his explanation, Fould congratulated Carlota on her forensic accounting and financial proficiency and begged to be excused before she could argue further. She objected to the French government's duplicity, but Fould would not stay any longer to receive an embarrassing dressing-down in the emperor's chambers. He concluded by saying the Mexicans were "dishonest, distrustful, and ungrateful," and there were only so many sacrifices France could make for such an unworthy people.[52]

Eugénie sank into the sofa, sobbing into a handkerchief. Carlota was too disgusted to hear more. In a final word with Napoléon in his quarters, she again presented her argument to him. The emperor firmly but softly refused her demands. "Then we shall abdicate," she said.

"Abdicate," said Napoléon, tired and ravaged.[53]

"It is all slime from beginning to end," Carlota wrote later to Maximilian. She felt some moral victory at refusing to give in. "Here every word is a lie, but you must not believe that I begged these people. I told them just what I thought and I stripped them of their masks, but with no lack of courtesy. Certainly nothing so painful has happened to them in their lives." She disparaged Napoléon. "He is an amiable Mephistopheles [the evil spirit], he even kissed my hand when I took leave today, but it is all play acting." She urged Maximilian to send Bazaine out of Mexico by force. "That they want you to abdicate I can see very clearly here, but I think you should wait as long as possible," she wrote Maximilian, with the notion that Napoléon was in decline and would be thrown out soon, therefore it would be Mexico's turn to be the great empire. "The old world is nauseating and depressing. He [the Devil] is so near. I feel his presence every time blood is spilled or in each movement of national unity. He spreads his propaganda in every country and laughs at the victims who fall. . . . On the other side of the ocean we can defy him. You cannot exist in the same part of the world as him, he would burn you to ashes." Feeling somewhat ennobled by her cause, in closing she wrote to Maximilian, "Your faithful one for life."[54]

The French cabinet council met the next day. Outraged at Carlota's condemnation of the French government, many felt justified with cutting off Mexico. Her explanation of the Mexican finances, the shortage of native Mexicans in the military corps, and growing strength of the Juarista guerrillas only proved that further expenditure would be a waste, they said, especially in a country where the people had so little initiative. The ministers never regarded her mission as serious and important. Accordingly, the cabinet council voted against reviewing her proposals, and the evacuation of the French forces should commence immediately. Instructions were sent to Bazaine confirming their decision.[55]

After their vote, the ministers handed their verdict to Almonte to give to Carlota, but she refused to accept any last word from anyone other than Napoléon himself. By then, Napoléon had left Paris for Châlons, and she decided to give herself another week in Paris to see if she could not turn the tide in some way. She brainstormed ideas on alternative approaches and slept very little while she made notes and met with advisors. "I cannot change their will but I shall attack all evasions and groundless lies," Carlota wrote. She met with bankers and economists, all the time worrying that she had let Maximilian down tremendously. Carlota did make small victories. She coaxed the bankers into agreeing to make outstanding bonds nonconvertible to prevent them from calling immediately for gold or silver or increasing their debt, and made arrangements for further concessions from French financiers. While in Paris, she received news from Maximilian of fresh victories over the Liberals, news that invigorated those who still supported the Mexican empire.[56]

She refused offers of gala dinners and flowers and fruit sent by Eugénie from the imperial gardens. She wished that her brothers could have come to her aid.[57]

Maximilian, who knew nothing of Carlota's progress in Paris, decided to commemorate the great technological advancement of the trans-Atlantic telegraph cable, just completed by a French firm, a development that he had been impatiently waiting. At last, communications from Mexico to Europe could be sent within a matter of days through New York, instead of four to six weeks by steamer. On August 15, he sent a cable to Napoléon, "I avail myself of the greatest scientific triumph of the age to send Your Majesty my most sincere congratulations." Optimism lived on in Maximilian's dreams. Hoping to propose profit incentives to entice the French military to remain, he offered a concession in southern Mexico across the Isthmus of Tehuantepec for a canal and a railway. He wrote Napoléon offering land rights there, some 6 million acres, to French colonists.[58]

Ten days later Bazaine returned to Mexico City with a large segment of his army. He cursed the Juaristas and damned the citizens from the areas they left. "The people have no sympathy at all for the new order of things, and the country does not offer enough resources to maintain a garrison sufficient to keep order and assure security," he wrote to Maximilian. The situation across the country looked desperate with the Juaristas, aided by American filibusters, closing in on Mexico City. The French still held a large part of the central plateaus, but the brutality of the war escalated. When the Juaristas captured any French or Imperialist troops, they executed their victims with the same effectiveness as the Black Decree had dictated against them. Conditions began to verge on the chaotic.[59]

At the same time, Father Augustin Fischer returned from Europe having done little to reach an accord with the Vatican. He left the pope with a promise to convene the Mexican bishops and report his progress to Rome. Maximilian rewarded him with a seat on the cabinet, a suite at Chapultepec, and the position of librarian of the court. Maximilian wrote Carlota with the news that he had transformed his whole cabinet into a body of Conservatives and Clerical party members. He chose large landowners and a group with "sensibly conservative ideas without in any way sacrificing political and religious freedoms." The Mexican bishops were meeting with his ministers to find reconciliation and draft a new concordat, allowing for the return of properties to the church not already sold. These, however, would not be exempt from tax, Maximilian saying they could not accuse him of "having dubious ideas on religious questions." He suggested she next go to Rome to see Pope Pius IX to tell him this. Then she should ask the pontiff to intercede with Napoléon.[60]

On August 20 Napoléon, who had returned to Paris, reluctantly agreed to visit Carlota again at the Grand Hôtel. He had hoped she had already left. "The look of anguish on her face" continued to haunt him, said Napoléon.

Carlota had continued to study the empire's financial options and proposed that Napoléon call together the Corps Législatif to ask for an 18-million peso loan; should that prove impossible, he should then turn to the French people for support. She was sure that it could work. "The prosperity of Mexico means the prosperity of France," Carlota asserted. Napoléon tried to interrupt her argument, but she refused to stop talking while pacing up and down the room. He finally took the floor and told her bluntly that the Legislative Assembly and the French people could bear no more. She flushed with grief at the finality of being told no. Pungently she said, "Your Majesty is as much concerned in this affair as we are, so it would be better if you did not indulge in any illusions either." With a seething look, Napoléon rose from his chair, bowed to her, turned, and left.[61]

"To me he is the Devil in person, and at our last interview yesterday he had an expression that would make one's hair stand on end, he was hideous, and this was the manifestation of his soul, the rest is merely a façade," Carlota wrote.[62]

The next day Napoléon wrote a letter to Maximilian memorializing the meeting and regretting his inability to capitulate. "We had great pleasure in receiving the Empress Carlota," he wrote, "yet it was very painful for me to be unable to accede to her requests. We are in fact approaching a decisive moment for Mexico, and it is necessary for Your Majesty to come to a heroic resolution; the time for half-measures has gone by. . . . It his henceforward impossible for me to give Mexico another *écu* or another soldier."[63]

By the state-of-the-art telegraph, Carlota sent a short but penetrating message: "Todo es inútil." All was useless.[64]

Her servants began to pack her belongings, and the royal party prepared for an overland trip to Miramar. The day before she left Paris, Carlota wrote one last letter to Maximilian. She began referring to Napoléon as "The Devil," and clearly vented her frustration, dejection, and sadness. "My darling, early tomorrow morning I leave here for Miramar via Milan. This proves to you that I am leaving empty-handed. . . . I have the satisfaction of having refuted all their arguments, brought all their false pretexts to naught, and thus given you a moral triumph, but He [Napoléon] curtly refuses, and no power can aid us, for he has Hell on his side and I do not," she wrote. She asserted that Napoléon only pretended to be weak and cowardly, using the alibis of the French legislature and the pressure coming from the United States to evacuate Mexico, in order to mask a deeply wicked intent. "Seeing the Devil so close could make atheists believe in God," she wrote.[65]

She recalled the Albrecht Dürer woodcut prints of the Apocalypse from her childhood palace in Belgium and felt assured that the old governments of Europe were crumbling, nearing the end-time, and the continent was full of the "Devil." He could be smelled in the bloodshed on the battlefields of Europe and signaled that the close of Napoléon's empire was near: "Le règne touche à sa fin." She concluded that they must stay in Mexico at all costs, partially to vindicate themselves. About Napoléon, she said, "From beginning to end, he never loved you because he does not love and is incapable of loving; he has mesmerized you like a serpent, his tears were as false as his words, all his deeds are deceptions. You must escape his claws as soon as possible. Since his last 'no' he has delighted in your ruin." Feeling justified, she concluded, "To Him, my journey was the most violent blow He has received for a long time." She believed that once the rest of Europe learned Napoléon left them stranded, money and credit would flow from everywhere.[66]

At Miramar, Carlota could recuperate and think of ways to save Maximilian and the remains of their battered empire.

❦ 16 ❧

Someone Is Intent
on Poisoning Me

On August 23, 1866, Carlota left Paris for the castle of Miramar. Much had occurred in Europe over the past two years, and she knew she would receive no sympathy in Austria, where Franz Josef still staggered from his humiliation in the Austro-Prussian War. Carlota's brothers showed little interest in her return to Europe either, not involving themselves with Mexico. Neither Napoléon nor any of his council members offered continued assistance to Maximilian. She felt alone in her quest but determined.[1]

As she traveled in her private car, the train made its way through the Alps to Turin and Milan in northern Italy, where people waved and cheered at each stop. With these spontaneous expressions of welcome, she felt great relief at having left France. At Milan, after an official ceremony in the town and a mass, she stayed at the beautiful Villa d'Este at Lake Como once owned by her father. Moved by its calm, she recalled previous visits when Maximilian served as governor of the territory of Lombardy. "In this land so full of memories of happiness and enjoyment, of the best years of our life, I never cease thinking of you and send you these lines apart from my Paris letter. Everything here breathes of you, *your* Lake of Como, of which you were so fond, before my eyes in all its blue calm, all is the same, only you are over there, far, far away, and nearly ten years have passed," she wrote Maximilian.[2]

After a few days of rest, Carlota pushed on to Miramar by rail. Maximilian wrote with his instructions that she must visit with Pope Pius IX to exact an agreement. First, however, she intended to check on the castle and grounds, as

Maximilian had never ceased sending orders from Mexico to the architects for its building and garden design. But she had in her mind to keep up the pressure on the French court through the pope, who would certainly come to their aid with a concordat and possibly convince Napoléon to maintain his support. To her surprise, however, the next leg of her journey proved to be most fascinating, as the Italians lay waiting with welcomes and surprises.[3]

At Desenzano, located on Lake Garda about sixty-five miles east of Milan, a column of Gen. Giuseppe Garibaldi's red-shirted volunteers met her at the station with a Mexican imperial flag flying beside the Italian standard. It became clear to her that they regarded her as Carlota of Mexico, not the sister-in-law to Austria's oppressive Franz Josef. They presented her with an embroidered imperial banner made by women of Bari, a town in southern Italy. Curiously, the Italians, known to be sympathizers with the Prussians hoping to be rid of Habsburg occupation, celebrated her former leadership. In view that Franz Josef had turned his back on Maximilian and Carlota, she was particularly touched by their emotional greetings. It was as if they treated her like part of the newly emerging Italy.[4]

The officers escorted her to Verona and on to Padua, about one hundred miles west of Miramar, where she stopped at the train station. So much had changed for the better, and the people seemed natural and readily accepting of her. The enigmatic Italian king, Victor Emmanuel, also related to the Habsburg clan, traveled north from the town of Rovigo to meet her. The short, squat, and unusual-looking man, with his bushy moustache and awkward, shy, but intelligent manner, sat in the rail station beside her, as other senators and officials came in to offer their greetings.[5]

While she visited with Victor Emmanuel at the Padua station, she saw another old friend, an Italian statesman standing by, wanting to welcome her. She greeted him, praising Italy's stability and happiness. He smiled, looking at the king, while joking, "Oh, it is very disorganized." She later concluded "Italy is becoming a great power," feeling vindicated about their former liberal leadership in Lombardy seven years earlier, and added that Victor Emmanuel was "one of the best rulers in Europe because he loves his people." Had they been allowed to rule as they wished, perhaps things would have been different.[6]

After a stormy voyage from Venice east to the harbor of Trieste, Carlota arrived to the cheers of the Austrian naval crews anchored at the port. Despite Austria's recent territorial losses, the imperial naval fleet remained at Trieste, and Admiral Tegetthoff, Maximilian's old commander, greeted her warmly. Arriving at Miramar, she was relieved to be in familiar surroundings. Her royal entourage expressed their amazement at the small fortress, the blue Adriatic splashing against the stark white foundations of the warm and inviting home. "Everyone is astonished by the accomplishments of the absent prince," Carlota wrote to Maximilian. "The Mexicans are all enraptured with Miramar, and that I too appreciate it to the fullest for the first time." While in Mexico, Maximilian continued to work with architects to finish Miramar, adding a museum and artworks, and he was eager to know the progress.[7]

She walked through the rooms, reacquainting herself with their contents. She found her own paintings hung on the walls of burled wood. Other artworks commissioned but not completed before their departure for Mexico had been delivered, and to her amazement, the castle as planned had taken shape without them. In the ceiling to the entry hall to the castle, a little fountain on the second floor, designed to have water splash over a lens of glass and resemble the motion of the sea, worked as designed by Maximilian. She admired the table on which Maximilian had signed the Convention of Miramar, promising to become emperor of Mexico. It was a gift from the pope. She fingered the surfaces of the furniture and other objects, as if to memorize these details before her voyage back to Mexico. Her new empire seemed impossibly distant in this small, intimate nest of their own creation. The Mexican imperial crest had been suspended in the dining room from the molding of its honeycombed ceiling, which surprised her. Curiously, it was garlanded with a wreath of thorns. Her personal physician and friend, Dr. Auguste Jilek, who had strongly opposed Maximilian's role in the Mexican empire, arrived to meet her and revealed that he had put the thorns on the royal ensign as a joke.[8]

After Carlota checked on the gardens to see how their plantings fared over the last two years, she wrote Maximilian that the palms, weeping willows, pines, and cedars had grown large, as had the ivy trellising their garden house. It seemed odd, even to the members of her retinue, that Maximilian was not there. In the ocean, south of the castle toward Trieste, they could see the Austrian fleet approaching. Wilhelm von Tegetthoff, the admiral, had ordered a pass in review in squadron battle formation in honor of the empress's visit.[9]

Tegetthoff named Austria's new flagship after Maximilian, the *Erzherzog Ferdinand Max*, which touched Maximilian deeply, who later wrote, "I can hardly control my grief that I was not [aboard] the flagship that bears my name, among my splendid officers and my beloved . . . Istrian sailors." He telegrammed his former commander with congratulations. Carlota said, "It is the navy's last salute, for it is leaving Trieste, and perhaps disappearing from history. It cast the first ray upon your coming power, upon your dearly bought independence, it saved the coast which was so dear to you, now it too will leave Austria and your brother to their fate. Its mission is accomplished. So is yours. The honor of the house of Habsburg crossed the Atlantic with the name of one of their last victories, the *Novara*." She assured him that, as the power of Austria was fading, his was rising. "The motto of your forefathers was *Plus Ultra* [further beyond]. Charles the Fifth showed the way. You have followed him. Do not regret it. God was with him."[10]

Meanwhile in Mexico, Maximilian reported that he moved most of his staff and closest advisors to Chapultepec. "For me this is a good arrangement, we've gathered at the Alcazar like a great warship," he wrote Carlota. "There are many at the table and at night we play billiards. . . . I need a few distractions, for your absence makes me fall into deep melancholy."[11]

Rumors abounded that Maximilian's own Mexican advisors plotted against him. Baron Magnus believed that in Tacubaya, Gen. José López Uraga along with José Fernando Ramírez and other confidants prepared for an uprising in the valley of Mexico.[12]

With Father Fischer, Maximilian continued to draft a new concordat for the Vatican. He alleged that the pope, by not allowing certain leniency, decidedly placed all the hatreds toward the church on the Mexican empire, and for this they suffered their difficulties with the bishops. Speciously, Fischer continued to exude cheerfulness and said everything would work itself out, but Maximilian had his doubts, going against what he termed the "fanatics," the ultramontanes. "What I can do honestly on my part, I will do, but I do not give one step against my conscience vis-à-vis God, and if they count on concessions they are very wrong," he wrote. He expressed his love for Carlota, writing at three in the morning from Chapultepec, preparing to leave for Cuernavaca within two hours. "[There is] the most beautiful moonlight, a sky without clouds and the snows on those gigantic volcanoes bathed in the light of the moon. We now have a climate so magnificent and beautiful, as I have not seen in the two and a half years," he wrote, reassuring her that the finances were starting to be organized, Teodosio Lares had brought new vigor to the Justice Department, and his new army, under the direction of Auguste Osmont, would be ready by the first of October to start a new campaign to regain positions abandoned by the French army, against his advice to Marshal Bazaine. He added that he recently had dinner with Bazaine and his wife, and the marshal seemed contrite, scolding Napoléon's government for its military directives. Additionally, Tomás Mejía and Santiago Vidaurri prepared to lead the operations with the freshly organized army as planned by Osmont.[13]

However, Maximilian received security and military reports from the field, and the news was not good. On July 26 the French under Gen. Pierre Joseph Jeanningros abandoned Monterrey, and on August 7 they deserted Tampico. Subsequently, as Maximilian reported to Carlota, Tampico had fallen to the Liberals, resulting in the murder of the political prefect. He asked her to relate this news to the Parisian ministers, a further condemnation of Bazaine's lack of care in his strategies and his wasting of francs and resources. As the French army rapidly withdrew from one town after another, the Juaristas moved in and were attempting to approach Veracruz and Jalapa. The partisan newspapers made light of these accounts, reporting that the counterguerrillas would soon repacify the Huasteca. Despite all the bad dispatches, Maximilian signed the agreement to give over half the customs duties to the French government. He viewed this as a new alliance treaty with Napoléon that "give[s] the most positive guaranties . . . on the customs duties. . . . In this way, nothing on my side will have been done that can cancel out the signed commitment that France entered into with Mexico," wrote Maximilian. He did not know, as Carlota did from her meetings in Paris, that much of the grossly inflated debt claims had been already liquidated.[14]

The officers in the French army waited to learn of Napoléon's reply to Carlota's efforts. Loizillon said, "In spite of what the newspapers say, I am convinced that the Empress Carlota was turned down flat by our emperor. General Uraga came by today on his way to board the French ocean liner, supposedly to go fetch the empress. On the other hand, they assert that the poor woman is not coming back and that Maximilian is packing his bags. What a mess." He suspected that the rushed and disorderly evacuation was designed to force Maximilian to panic and leave as well.[15]

However, a number of the Austrian and Belgian troops rallied to Maximilian's aid when others were resigning or deserting. In the fight against the Juaristas, Alfons von Kodolitsch assumed command of the Austrian infantry and cavalry regiments. Twenty-five-year-old Count Karl Khevenhüller, in Mexico City, volunteered to raise, train, and provision a regiment of Red Hussars with his own funds.[16]

Félix Eloin wrote from Brussels to reassure Maximilian that people still thought him a wise and capable leader but warned him to act as though failure was a possibility. He should raise money in Mexico to continue, but not leave with the army. "The French government wishes that an abdication should precede the return of the army . . . nevertheless, I have a firm belief that the abandonment of the cause before the return of the French army would be interpreted as an act of weakness," he wrote. However, Eloin mistakenly sent the letter, marked "Confidential," through the Mexican consul in New York, assuming it would be delivered to the imperial Mexican consul. Instead, the letter went to the Republican consul representing Juárez, who opened and read the letter, and disseminated the notion that Maximilian's resignation was imminent.[17]

On September 9, however, Carlota wrote Maximilian examining the positives, somewhat deludedly, in that she viewed the withdrawal of French troops as an opportunity for the empire to prove itself and stand firm. "I consider the abandonment of direct support [by France] to be very fortunate, so fortunate it may compensate for the lack of material help and money. France is still Mexico's ally." She concluded the French commercial interests and the citizens would still participate in Mexico, because they wanted only successes and wanted to align themselves with the growing power of the American continents. Because Austria was collapsing and with European powers unstable, the result would be an influx of immigrants to Mexico. The power base would shift to the Americas. "I also know from a reliable source that the United States will recognize you as soon as they know that you are the independent sovereign of Mexico, because nothing in the Monroe Doctrine objects to empires," she wrote. The Liberal party would rally around him; if not, it would cease to exist. "Juárez was not the champion of the national cause until you arrived, since then you have represented the independence and autonomy of all the Mexicans, because you alone join the three colors that make up the people," meaning white (the clergy, like a Catholic prince), green (the Conservatives), and red (the Liberals). Maximilian had the flag—he had the empire. She advised him to fight to keep his power as the rightfully elected emperor and to use the Chinacos (the Liberals) to form a new militia.[18]

Four days later she wrote to say that the Europeans were growing even more anxious about the rising power of the United States: "Things appear here in a strange fashion. They are talking about American ships as if they were going to destroy everything."[19] Her sustaining optimism aside, she also harbored resentment and fear under the extreme pressure. Carlota and Maximilian, now on different continents, could not muster a rational view of their situation.

Miramar began to fill with ministers and staff readying for her next mission, to see Pope Pius IX. On September 14 José Luis Blasio arrived at Trieste from Mexico with papers from Maximilian and further instruction. She had been waiting on documents, which he delivered to the empress's staff. Carlota called for him half an hour later. "She was in deep mourning. Her face already showed her intense sufferings, there was a slight melancholy smile on her lips," Blasio said. They remained standing.

"Why are you so late? Since you arrived at Saint Nazaire we have lived here in the greatest impatience," she said.[20]

"Señora, I stopped only two days in Paris with a night in Vienna. . . . As soon as I reached Saint Nazaire I obeyed the emperor's instructions and transmitted to the Minister [Almonte] in Paris the cipher message, which he must have sent to Your Majesty. As this was the most important part of my mission, I believed that I had complied with it faithfully. Excepting for two days and a half, I have spent all my time on railroads in order to get here immediately and place myself at Your Majesty's orders," said Blasio.

Carlota responded, "Probably you are unaware that the cipher telegram sent by Señor Almonte is full of mistakes and incomprehensible." Blasio replied that he did not know this, but he had the original with him. She said, "Give it to me so that Señor von Kuhachevich can translate it immediately. Are you sure that no one has touched the emperor's letters that you brought on your crossing or on your way through France?"[21]

"Señora, those letters have not been separated from me an instant, either on the boat, in hotels, or on trains. They have been constantly in a small portfolio inside another which was locked, and the key was always in my pocket," said Blasio.

"I do not doubt you . . . but you come from America, you . . . suspect no one. That would not happen if you knew the intrigues of the European courts. I am always fearful of Napoléon, who is our mortal enemy," Carlota said, dismissing Blasio for the evening. When Kuhachevich deciphered the letters with directions for her negotiations with the pope, she calmed. Carlota agreed that a favorable solution with the Vatican had to be found.[22]

On September 18 Carlota started out for Rome. She and her entourage traveled by train overland through the Tyrolean region because of cholera epidemics around the Adriatic. As she pushed on, a seed of dread began to grow in her mind against what traps Napoléon might have set for her. She feared she would be poisoned and also warned Blasio, Bouslaveck, and her staff to watch for spies as they set out in advance to prepare accommodations and transportation for her.[23]

As Carlota grew more nervous on her way to see the pope, she seriously considered giving up the mission. Her staff telegraphed Blasio, who was ahead of them, that she was returning to Miramar. Blasio with Bouslaveck retraced their route to find out what had happened, but at Mantua they found a second telegram telling them that the empress had changed her mind and they were to go on. While her train clattered west, the official welcomes became increasingly spectacular.[24]

However, as they neared Rome, Carlota began to fidget and tremble nervously. She complained of discomfort and heart palpitations, no doubt caused by extensive stress over many weeks. They arrived in the Eternal City on September 25 at eleven in the evening in a torrential rain. She emerged from her private car to find the station decorated and an immense crowd waiting, including a delegation of cardinals, members of the foreign diplomatic corps, and Roman aristocrats. She was dressed in black, which made her look even more pallid and exhausted. After the formalities, she was quickly led to the royal carriage provided by the Vatican. The pope had dispatched his Guardia Nobile and French gendarmerie to escort the empress, along with a cavalry column of cuirassiers in their gleaming breastplates. By torchlight, the security escort drove her with haste to the hotel. They arrived at the Albergo di Roma on the Via del Corso.[25]

The next morning, sunshine broke over Rome to reveal a glistening and beautiful city. Having heard of her arrival, Roman citizens seemed fascinated with the empress. Throngs of people crowded around the hotel, hoping to glimpse Carlota, the fame of the Americas. They appeared to be transfixed at the stylish uniforms of her drivers and male servants resplendent in their charro uniforms. Adding to the excitement, the cuirassiers and French army changed guard duty every few hours in the front of the hotel, complete with ceremonial music. Carlota determined to tour the city with Manuelita del Barrio. They boarded a carriage to view the churches, piazzas, and the hilltop parks. Blasio, who could not stand being shut up in the hotel, procured a horse and saddle and went out to explore Rome. On his ride, he found Carlota and Del Barrio in their carriage and as he passed them, he raised his cap in salute and saw the empress smile and say something to Del Barrio. Later, he learned Carlota said, "These Mexicans can't keep away from a horse. See how quickly Blasio obtained one to show himself off."[26]

At the Albergo, Carlota began to receive visitors in the early afternoon. Various ministers arrived, as did Cardinal Giacomo Antonelli, in a lavishly styled carriage. The tall dignitary, dressed in a red robe with a mantle flowing over his shoulders, strode with his attendants to the hotel entrance, all the while giving them orders in his deep and resonant voice. He passed through the gathered crowd, making gestures of blessings as he approached, and ducked through the door.[27]

Carlota knew that Pius had sent Antonelli, the Vatican's minister of foreign affairs, to debrief her, so the Holy Father would not have to deal with the Mexico matter directly at first. Their conversation, in private, lasted for nearly an hour. It was later revealed that most of the discussion centered on why the concordat had not been concluded, including the mention of Maximilian's liberal ideals and Carlota's feelings that the clergy of Mexico needed reform. In their conversation, Carlota expressed her hope that the pope would intercede with Napoléon and convince him to continue his support, although she knew he would not anger the French emperor and risk his abandonment of Rome. Antonelli remained evasive.[28]

At the end of their meeting, Carlota suspected the pope's answer to reaching consensus on the concordat would be "non possumus" (we cannot) as in other attempts through the archbishop and nuncio. She felt uneasy about launching an argument with the Holy Father, knowing Pius IX had become one of the most reactionary and intolerant popes in recent history. For the remainder of the day, she received a number of nobles, diplomats, clergy, and friends. She also had a brief meeting with the Holy See's commissioners to discuss the proposed concordat. Others observed that Carlota seemed somewhat anxious but for the most part gracious and dignified as usual.[29]

On September 27, after another sleepless night, she arrived at eleven in the morning at the gates of the Vatican in a ceremonial coach, escorted by columns of guards, cuirassiers, and liveries. Her retinue followed in other carriages. A large crowd cheered the arrival of the empress and royal entourage. With the highest honors, the Swiss guards in silver helmets and brilliant uniforms lined the passage to the throne room, each holding a halberd at attention. As she moved down the marbled and frescoed rooms, Carlota could see Pius waiting for her, flanked by other church officials.[30]

The pontiff, dressed in a white wool cassock and mantle, sat in his large red and gilded chair. As she grew nearer, he rose to greet her, smiling charmingly. Kneeling to kiss his slipper, he stopped her and instead offered his papal ring. He motioned to a small chair on his right and invited her to sit. Her ladies-in-waiting and attendants, one after another, kneeled before the pontiff and kissed his shoe. The seventy-four-year-old vicar smiled, said a few affable words of welcome, and then blessed the group. He then indicated they may leave the room so that he and Carlota could speak in private.[31]

As Carlota's retinue left to tour the art galleries, chapels, and gardens of the Vatican, she turned to the pope and handed him a draft of a new concordat. After an hour and a half of discussion, their talks concluded, and a group of cardinals conducted Carlota to her carriage. Her staff entered their coaches, waiting for news about the results of her meeting. By her demeanor, it seemed clear that there was little the pope could do to reach an accord with Mexico, too extreme was their impasse. At the hotel, the empress with a rueful expression bowed slightly and said only, "You may retire" to the staff.[32]

Carlota remained distant the next day, although she held a formal dinner for the Mexican legation to Europe. During supper, she remained dour and tired, making clipped remarks, so that no one really spoke for fear of an angry rebuke. When dessert of coffee and sherbet arrived, she refused to take any until the others had been served and then ordered away the coffee when she saw the silver pot had a dent. She looked around at the guests at the table, her eyes moving in rapid saccades across their faces. "It is obvious that someone is intent on poisoning me."[33]

The next day she refused to eat the foods prepared for her. In her room, she would eat only oranges that she inspected and peeled for herself and nuts that she examined and cracked. When she learned Velázquez de León was ill, she summoned him from his sick bed to ask if he had been poisoned. He pretended to be well, in order to avoid encouraging further her anxiety and fears. The whole staff lived in dread, since the pope planned a visit to her the next day. They suspected that her self-imposed asceticism derived from her feelings of failure.[34]

On September 29, when the pope arrived at the hotel to see Carlota, accompanied by his prelates and guard, she seemed perfectly normal. The guards and band had returned to the front door of the hotel, and a flurry of onlookers waited to see the pope's coming and going. The pontiff had brought along Cardinal Antonelli with him as support. Carlota spoke with the pontiff for a long while, and before leaving, he again blessed the imperial staff and held mass in Carlota's honor. At the end of their conversation, he said to Carlota, "The weather is very beautiful, a symbol that the conversation we had was peaceful and lovely."[35] Carlota maintained her poise and grace.

Over the next days, Carlota's paranoia and frustration grew incrementally. Those who suffered Carlota's wrath, however, were her most devoted attendants. Her chamberlain, Count del Valle, had to decipher her strange orders and countermanded a number of illogical commands. Jacob von Kuhachevich and his wife, long in service to both Carlota and Maximilian, took her scolding when they made the slightest suggestions. When Dr. Bouslaveck put a sedative in her coffee, as one of her doctors had done with morphine in Mexico, she caught him at it and dismissed him, thinking he was giving her a toxin instead of a palliative. The doctor refused to leave her service, however. Carlota wanted no strangers in her presence, as her nervousness reached horrifying dimensions. Finally, the despairing staff telegraphed Charles Bombelles and Auguste Jilek at Miramar to come to Rome to assist, thinking the empress would capitulate to her longtime attendants and rally. The two started out from Trieste immediately.[36]

At about eight o'clock on the morning of September 30, having had nothing to drink the night before, Carlota called for Manuelita del Barrio and asked her to summon a carriage. She emerged from her suite wearing a black dress, a cloak of black velvet, and a bonnet with black silk ribbons. She appeared gaunt, hollow-eyed, and flushed because she had a slight fever. She had the driver stop at the Trevi Fountain where she drank long and heavily from the flowing water with her cupped hands. "Here at least, it will not be poisoned. I was so thirsty," she told Del Barrio. Carlota feared that if she consumed water at the hotel, it would be toxic. She then directed the driver to the Vatican, where she demanded to see the pope, although Del Barrio told her she was not dressed for a papal audience, wearing a bonnet and not a mantilla. "You forget, Manuelita, that emperors and empresses rule etiquette and etiquette does not rule them," said Carlota. After some hesitation by the Vatican staff, Carlota was allowed to enter the pope's apartments. Pleased, she dismissed the coachman and told him not to return.[37]

It was just after morning mass, and the pontiff was taking a cup of hot chocolate and his breakfast. Carlota entered as he was eating, and upon seeing him, tears came to her eyes. She knelt before him and asked the pope to protect her, that her staff wanted to assassinate her, ordered to do so by Napoléon. Pius reached out to calm her, as though she was a panicked child, speaking to her gently, but she would not rise until he promised refuge. He said it was all a mistake, no one wanted to kill her, and that her Mexican staff remained very loyal. She repeated over and again that no one could make her leave the Vatican. Napoléon's spies crawled all over Rome. Her entire staff was in his pay. If they could not provide her with a place to stay, she would seek shelter in the corridors and sleep there.[38]

When the pope suggested she have something to eat, she eyed his cup of chocolate and dipped three fingers in it, putting them in her mouth to taste the cocoa. "I'm starving. Everything they give me is poisonous," she said. The pope repressed his shock and called for another cup of chocolate and something for Carlota to eat. She protested and wondered if she might not be able to share his cup, in case a new service was tainted. Becoming flustered with her irrational behavior, the pope nonetheless treated her kindly and gave her his cup. She quieted and spoke rationally and measured, discussing the conditions in Mexico and all the political melees. However, a few times in their conversation, she stopped him to ask what he considered the most effective antidote to poison. "The rosary and prayer," he said with some annoyance. Overall, he could not believe the change he saw in the beautiful, dignified woman, now a cloying wreck one minute, negative and bitter the next, while struggling to contain herself and be understood. It was a heartrending scene.[39]

Trying to distract her thoughts, Pius continued asking about Mexico. Rising to her full height, Carlota launched a long explanation and tirade on the empire, interspersed by moments of silence. After a couple of hours, the pontiff told Cardinal Antonelli to summon two doctors, who should, he wrote in a confidential note, appear in the guise of chamberlains less Carlota become hysterical. Simultaneously, the pope ordered Antonelli to contact Velázquez de León to vacate the hotel with the majority of the empress's staff, since she suspected them of plotting to kill her. That way Carlota would return to the Albergo di Roma without hesitation, the royal staff moved to other lodgings and out of her sight. They planned to tell Carlota that the suspected assassins had been dispersed before they could harm her.[40]

Antonelli immediately took the situation under his control, comprehending the plight of the pope and seeing his dilemma. After a quick meeting with Carlota's staff, including Castillo and Velázquez de León, he decided to telegraph her brothers: Leopold II, the King of Belgium, and Philippe, the Count of Flanders, relating the situation and asking one of them to come to her relief, that she suffered some sort of mental upset. They also decided that Dr. Bouslaveck should return to Mexico to inform Maximilian of the details of her behavior and malady.[41]

After the pope diverted Carlota's attention with a tour of the Vatican's art treasures, she stopped to admire an ancient illuminated manuscript, a book of holy doctrine written on gilded pages interleaved with fine artwork. This was enough distraction to allow the pontiff to slip out of the chambers undetected by the empress. Carlota spent the rest of the day in the Vatican gardens with her lady-in-waiting Del Barrio, the empress still stooping at various fountains to drink and quench her thirst. At midday, she showed no signs of departing, so Cardinal Antonelli invited them to lunch, where the empress behaved in a normal mien. Although she insisted on sharing her plate of food with Del Barrio, this remained the only exception to her otherwise normal mood.[42]

In the afternoon, according to plan, Velázquez de León arrived at the

Vatican to tell Carlota that all the suspected assassins in her entourage had been arrested and removed from the hotel. Relieved, she agreed to return with him to the Alburgo, along with one of the papal chamberlains, who was actually a doctor, to the vacated lodgings. But before she left, she asked the pope if she could take a goblet with her from the Vatican, not trusting the glassware at the hotel. "Of course," he said. On the way to the hotel, she again stopped at the Trevi fountain to drink. Then she walked around the equestrian statue of Marcus Aurelius in the Piazza del Campidoglio and bought and drank a glass of lemonade from a street vendor, wanting to put off her return to the hotel.[43]

When Carlota walked into her room, however, she saw that the interior keys had been removed from the keyholes, a decision made by Edouard Radonetz, the caretaker of Miramar, who was in Rome to manage her stay at the Auberge. Though designed for her safety, she interpreted this as a clear sign that she was about to be locked in for the night or killed. Crying hysterically in despair, she claimed that the assassins laid a trap for her. Carlota rushed out of her suite and insisted on returning to the Vatican. Velázquez de León and the doctor finally agreed, not knowing what to do next.[44]

At ten o'clock at night, the weeping, disheveled empress climbed up the steps to the Vatican and asked for admittance to the pope's apartments. Monsignor Edoardo Borromeo, along with Antonelli, objected, saying that in 1,800 years, this situation had never arisen in papal history. Whether or not this was true, Carlota pleaded so adamantly that Pius was aroused from sleep and consulted. It seemed Pius, a known epileptic who ably controlled his seizures, sympathized with Carlota's mental strain. Although exhausted by the day's stresses from the addled empress, the pontiff allowed her to enter and ordered his attendants to convert his Vatican library into a sleeping quarters for the night, rubbing his face saying, "Nothing is spared me in this life—now a woman has to go mad in the Vatican." The chambermasters brought two bronze bedsteads with coverlets of linen and lace, gold candelabras, a dressing and washing table, and other provisions to the library to create a lavish and comfortable repose for Carlota and Del Barrio, with the stipulation that Carlota move to the hotel the next day. She then sent a carriage to retrieve her personal articles. Once settled, an attending physician, in the guise of a chamberlain, prepared a cup of hot milk with a bit of sedative added to encourage sleep. Carlota soon rested comfortably, like a baby at the end of a long day of tantrums. Del Barrio sat up the entire night worrying that the empress might awaken.[45]

The next morning Carlota awoke overjoyed at having spent a night in safety. She dressed at once and wanted to take mass with the pope in his private chapel but was refused by the Vatican staff, who suggested she might attend mass at the Basilica of St. Peter in the royal pew. She said, "How can I go to St. Peter's, a place of public worship? I should be a dead woman before the service was over, there would be one of those scoundrels behind every pillar." Carlota refused to leave the Vatican apartments, again expressing her fear of being assassinated, saying she would sit quietly and be no bother. She also declined food, unless she ate in the company of the pope. However, Pius would not spend another nerve-shattering day with Carlota.[46]

Knowing she must return to the hotel as she promised, she felt death was near and sat down to write a note to Maximilian. "1 October 1866, My darling, I am taking leave of you. God is calling me to him. Thank you for the happiness you have always given me. May God bless you and grant you eternal joy. Your devoted wife, Carlota." She then wrote to the pope asking for his benediction and communion, since she would be dead soon. She scribbled out a last will asking for his benediction and testament leaving all her jewelry to her brother Leopold II, followed by a note to the pope and Kuhachevich's wife telling them that she would like to be buried in the Basilica next to St. Peter and did not want to be autopsied or displayed after death. She thought she had been poisoned and was ready to die.[47]

When a papal carriage arrived to take her to the hotel, she again refused to leave the Vatican. The news of her erratic behavior leaked out, and rumors flew around the city. Pius returned from his morning ride to find that the empress had not left, and he tiptoed quickly about the corridors to avoid her. The situation became desperate, so Cardinal Antonelli resorted to a ruse to get her out of the Vatican. He informed the Mother Superior of a nearby convent that Empress Carlota would like to tour the St. Vincent de Paul orphanage, so the abbess issued an invitation expressing how much the children would like to meet her. Carlota agreed. She visited the building and the nuns introduced her to the children, which she enjoyed, kindly speaking with them. Carlota offered the Mother Superior a generous donation for their support. When they toured the kitchen, however, Carlota, overtaken by hunger, showed great interest in a stew boiling on the stove. The sisters offered a bite of the ragout, but the utensil handed her by the kitchen staff was oily and Carlota refused, saying that the residue on it was poison. Determined to eat, she said, "I felt so hungry, and they can't have poisoned this morsel" and then reached into the boiling pot to snatch a piece of meat. Feeling the scalding pain on her hand, she shrieked in pain. The nuns rushed to treat her burns, but the famished empress fainted.[48]

At 1:30 in the afternoon, the papal staff helped the disoriented empress into a carriage to the hotel, but in the moving coach she recovered consciousness and demanded to return to the Vatican, calling out for help. "Murder, stop the carriage," she shouted. No one could calm her. At the hotel, two muscular men of the Guardia Nobile from the Vatican forced her, struggling, into the hotel as she screamed at them. Catching sight of other guests staring at her, however, she composed herself, and with the assistance of Manuelita del Barrio and her maid, Mathilde Doblinger, she walked up the stairs to her apartment.[49]

Carlota dismissed Del Barrio and locked herself in with only Doblinger to attend to her. She brooded and paced, and soon she asked Doblinger to summon Mrs. von Kuhachevich. Once she arrived, Carlota turned to her and said, "I never would have believed that a person like you, whom I have known for so many years and loaded with favors and to whom I have given my love and confidence, would sell herself to Napoléon's agents so they might poison me." The woman gasped and began to sob. She bowed to the empress and then threw herself at Carlota's feet. "Get out, Madam, and say to your accomplices that I have discovered their plots and that I know who the traitors are," Carlota said. "Tell the Count del Valle, your husband, and Dr. Bouslaveck to flee, if they do not want to be arrested at once. You too, I never want to hear your name."[50]

The woman left Carlota's quarters weeping, sure that the empress had lost all logic and reason. Carlota then demanded a carriage and emerged from her suite clutching a crystal pitcher. She entered the carriage with Manuelita, and the Pontifical Dragoons followed as an escort. One lieutenant, Count Emich Linange, rode astride his horse near her carriage as they rounded from the Piazza della Pilotta to the Trevi Fountain, and was amazed to see the empress drink from the fountain jets and fill her pitcher. Returning to the hotel with most of the attendants gone or in hiding, Mathilde Doblinger arrived at Carlota's suite with two live chickens and a basket of eggs. Attendants delivered an iron stove and charcoal. Carlota had ordered a kitchen set up in her suite, so that she could control what she ate. She drank only from the glass she had taken from the pope's private quarters. Carlota refused to eat fruit, bread, or anything she did not know the origins of, saying everything was poisoned. Mathilde had to kill, clean, and cook the chicken in the makeshift kitchen and taste it before the empress would eat. She also brought in a cat to eat her food first.[51] She even ordered the commander of the papal guard at the hotel to go buy roasted chestnuts in their shells. "I'm hungry, and my wishes are orders," she said. When the commander arrived with the chestnuts, she devoured them immediately.[52]

The days that followed served to be a trial of nerves and patience for the few staff members whom Carlota allowed to approach her. She feared she would be attacked in her sleep and refused to change her clothes or go to bed. She paced the floor most nights talking to herself softly, agreeing to sit down only for a little while. Some days she refused to have her hair groomed, fearful that the comb had poison in the teeth. Except for Mathilde, who was on call full-time, Carlota only occasionally summoned other attendants to her suites. After a few days under intense strain in cramped quarters, Mathilde began to suffer exhaustion and only with great effort convinced Carlota to accept the auxiliary services of another housekeeper, so she could get some rest.[53]

On October 5 Carlota received a packet of documents from the Vatican, including the draft of the new concordat she had presented and left with the pope to examine. Pius wrote asking her calmly to accept the papers, to keep the drinking glass she had taken from his quarters, and that he would pray every day for her peace of mind. His last words read, "I bless you with all my heart."[54]

The next day, Carlota asked Manuelita del Barrio to call José Luis Blasio to her suite, if he was still in Rome. Blasio had remained quietly in the background, ready to help when he was needed. He found her dressed in black, as though in mourning, with her hair perfectly coiffed. Despite her mental disarray, her appearance seemed normal. The day before, Bombelles and Jilek arrived in Rome, and reportedly Carlota spent several lucid hours in conversation with Bombelles regarding her Belgian inheritance, almost perfectly like normal, although Jilek was not convinced. He saw the strain on her face.[55]

At the meeting, she asked Blasio if he could help her to write a number of letters. It was the first time the secretary had been in her quarters for a week. "Everything seemed peaceful in the room, and occasionally I would steal a glance at the Empress's face, upon which a few days of emotion and suffering had wrought so many changes," he said. Her sunken cheeks flushed from agitation, and her eyes roamed vaguely and absently around the room. There were plenty of signs of her troubled mind. In the room stood "a table on which was the charcoal stove used by Mathilde Doblinger in cooking the empress's meals. Some hens were tied to the legs of the gilded table and on it were eggs and the pitcher of water which Carlota procured for herself," said Blasio.[56]

Blasio turned to her and said he was in her service. She motioned to a small table with paper, pen, and ink. "You have seen much in Rome and want to go to other European cities and you may, but first I want you to write some decrees for me to sign. Sit down," she said. She began to unreel the names of staff members she wanted dismissed, based on what she believed to be an organized, widespread, and covert conspiracy to poison her. She termed them all traitors who had betrayed her and Maximilian. The first note addressed to her grand chamberlain, Juan Antonio Suárez Peredo, the Count del Valle de Orizaba, accusing him of scheming an attempt on her life. The order continued, "We have thought well to deprive him of all of his titles, charges, and honors and to command him to leave the court without returning to it for any reason, and to communicate to His Majesty, the Emperor Maximilian, this disposition which I have signed . . . for the information of our officer in charge of the Civil List and Minister of the Imperial Household." She ordered him to leave for Mexico at once.[57]

This was only the beginning. The flurry of dismissals included her most loyal and intimate courtesans along with a demand they return their orders and decorations: the chamberlain Felipe Neri del Barrio, Manuelita's husband; Dr. Bouslaveck, personal physician; the Von Kuhachevichs; and sadly, Martín Castillo, one of the most loyal and caring ministers of the imperial household. She dictated, "In the name of the emperor, I have to demand the return of the decoration of the Order of Guadalupe," she wrote, or named the other honors they had bestowed on them. Blasio wanted to question her decision to terminate her most devoted attendants, especially that of Martín Castillo. Blasio could do nothing but obey. "My God, how she had changed, in so short a time as a result of her hardship and emotions," wrote Blasio. Finally, and perhaps most tragically, Carlota sacked Manuelita del Barrio, the woman she had most trusted and relied upon for her support and, of late, her sanity.[58]

After Blasio wrote the last words, he arose and bowed to Carlota. She said he may travel wherever he desired. Carlota next ordered Castillo to come in and sign the decrees, including the very order that dismissed him. Blasio lied and told her that it was likely that Minister Castillo had left Rome already, having been dismissed earlier by Her Majesty. "Never mind," she said, "Look for him until you find him and have him come as soon as possible." Blasio, with tears welling in his eyes, asked if he might kiss her hand. She agreed, and he knelt before her, pressing her hand to his lips, and quickly said goodbye.[59]

Blasio emerged from Carlota's quarters to a phalanx of ministers anxious for some news, hopefully positive. Blasio told Castillo of his dismissal and her order to hunt for him so that he might sign the decrees, including the one ordering his own sacking. It was suggested that Castillo report to Carlota, refuse to sign the decrees, and destroy them in the process. After much deliberation, however, they decided to do nothing, hoping that her brother, Philippe, the Count of Flanders, would arrive soon. On October 7 Philippe came to his sister's aid, to the relief of the shattered staff. Del Valle, del Barrio, and Castillo, who spoke French, related the events leading to her break with reality. Philippe immediately went to Carlota at the hotel, and she embraced him with all the vigor of greeting her greatest hero. They spent the day together, and in preparation to leave Rome, Carlota ordered a silver votive offering to the Virgin Mary for "having been freed from mortal danger on 28 September 1866" and had it displayed in the Church of San Carlo al Corso, for her namesake. Meanwhile, her brother sent telegrams to various banking institutions and businesses advising them not to act on any documents that were not countersigned by Edouard Radonetz, the prefect of Miramar.[60]

Carlota engaged Philippe in a long and intense talk, her thoughts more organized than in the past days. Her brother, whose partial deafness caused him to be a man of few words, said little and let his sister rattle on about whatever subject she wanted. She warned him not to touch any of the food at the hotel, that it was all poisoned. That evening he sent the maids away, saying he would look after his sister, assuming she would sleep. She didn't. Carlota stayed awake all night, talking about Maximilian, Mexico, its great wealth, the rebuilding of the capital, and Napoléon's jealousy. The next morning, arm in arm, the two left in a carriage for the rail station to board a train for Miramar. Quietly, the count thanked the staff warmly, saying he would send word to Martín Castillo about Carlota's mental status and to expect his telegram in Paris. It was decided that Velázquez de León would be the only Mexican attendant to see her off at the train station. "Where are my ministers and where are my servants?" she asked. One of Philippe's Belgian staff made a cursory reply, and she seemed satisfied. After saying goodbye to the Belgian minister and the papal representatives, Carlota and Philippe set off for Miramar.[61]

Felipe del Barrio telegraphed Maximilian with the news of Carlota's illness, hoping he would not first learn of the empress's mental state from other sources. The cable stated, "Her Majesty, the Empress Carlota, on October 4, was attacked by a very serious cerebral congestion. The august princess has been conducted to Miramar," the cable read.[62]

While in Europe, away from Mexico and her husband, starved for rest and paranoid about being poisoned, something snapped and Carlota could restrain her emotions no longer. The fear poured out of her. Much had changed in three months. Carlota, once flush with enthusiasm, armed with her logical and forthright arguments, her prestige and glamour, had transformed into a fragile, shattered, and fearful child. Her mind twisted kind gestures into attacks, and she rejected any stranger as evil. On her behalf, Drs. Auguste Jilek and Karl Bouslaveck searched for a psychiatric professional knowledgeable of emerging techniques in the field of mental illness. Tragically, Carlota could not go back to Maximilian, the man who most needed her, who would be left alone to sort out his fate.[63]

❦[17]❧

Getting Out of
the Toils of the French

By late September 1866 Maximilian had learned little of Carlota's negotiations with Napoléon or the pope, but he waited intently. In her absence, Maximilian had been suffering periodically from a number of ailments deriving from respiratory difficulties and liver problems but also dysentery and malaria. Without Carlota, he was not only sick but depressed.[1]

Finally on October 1, he received the troubling telegram from Carlota telling him "all was useless" and Napoléon's letter stating that France would not spend another "écu" on the war in Mexico. Napoléon intimated, however, that he would allow the French troops to stay in Mexico if Maximilian did not abdicate and could repay France's investment in the imperial adventure. Of course, by then Carlota had told him that Maximilian might resign. Napoléon instructed Maximilian how to run the country after the French withdrawal, including hints on how best to leave, if that was his intent, and how to issue a manifesto to the Mexican people. Napoléon suggested that while the French army was still present, Maximilian should convene a national assembly to decide what form of government the Mexican public wanted. The French emperor courteously closed the letter with the warning that "we ought not to indulge in illusions," writing the same words Carlota had used with him in Paris. Maximilian sensed that Napoléon cruelly twisted Carlota's logic to taunt him from his catbird seat in Paris.[2]

Maximilian understood Carlota's hysterical denunciations of Napoléon in her letters and her fury at the ministers' remarks on Maximilian's lack of strength. They knew it was Napoléon himself who had set the military, financial, and political barriers from the beginning, making their rule impossible. Maximilian seethed that France had recently deemed Osmont's and Friant's duties incompatible with the building of a Mexican imperial army. Everyone else seemed to see Napoléon's treachery; even in the Mexican battlefields, the regular officers of the French army realized Napoléon betrayed the Mexican empire. They read his duplicity from across the Atlantic.[3]

Therefore, he searched for new commanders to streamline the treasury and halt the retrograde progress of subjugating the country. He also wrote his ministers in Rome, urging them to ignore dissension with the ultramontanes, meanwhile calling for his own meeting of Mexican bishops to thoroughly examine the proposed concordat. He hoped the bishops would reconcile their philosophies with his and this, in turn, would influence the Vatican. Although time ran hopelessly short against the Liberals, he still manifested an aura of optimism.[4]

It was during Carlota's absence, when Maximilian felt most alone, that he made frequent trips to see his lover. Many gossiped that the woman, Concepción Sedano, had given birth to a baby boy on August 30 in Cuernavaca. Lt. Col. Antonin Vieil, the Marquis d'Espeuilles of the Mexican hussars, said that despite the pressures of his office, "do not believe that Emperor Maximilian was that upset by it, because his concern was to make constant trips to Cuernavaca to visit a young Mexican girl who had just given birth to his son, who delighted him. . . . He is very proud to have thus confirmed his ability to father a child, a point that was strongly contested." This may have been true, but while she was away, Maximilian wrote the most affectionate letters to Carlota.[5]

Maximilian eagerly anticipated her return and planned to meet her in port about October 25. He ordered an aide at Veracruz, Nicolas Poliakowitz, to prepare lodgings for them and that Bazaine provide an escort, emphasizing her safety. His plan was to meet her at Veracruz, then stay indefinitely at Orizaba to allow the congress to vote whether they should continue the monarchy. "If the nation proclaims in favor of the Empire, we shall be returning to the capital, stronger and more powerful than before and prepared to devote the rest of our lives to the service of our country. If the nation desires another form of government, then we shall retire with dignity, conscious of having done our duty," he told Carlota.[6]

Then on October 18, through two telegrams received at the National Palace, Maximilian learned of Carlota's mental collapse in Rome. The first, sent from Martín Castillo, calmly explained that the empress had been put under the care of Dr. Karl Bouslaveck. The second came from Bombelles, which confirmed Carlota's safe arrival at Miramar and that she was in the care of Dr. Josef G. Riedel. Stefan Herzfeld, a young Austrian naval officer and a close counselor to the emperor, deciphered the encrypted letters and thought he had made a mistake. At first he told Maximilian the letters could not be untangled, reluctant to reveal their content. "I am sure that it must be something terrible. You had better inform me because I am prepared for the worst," said Maximilian.[7]

After reading them, Maximilian, with tears in his eyes, asked Samuel Basch, his physician, "Do you know Dr. Riedel in Vienna?"

"He is the director of the insane asylum," said Basch.[8]

Josef Gottfried von Riedel, a seasoned sixty-three-year-old Austrian doctor and a pioneer in mental illness, had worked to bring humanity to the treatment of patients through various remedies including exercise and art education. Dr. Jilek had called him to Miramar. "The professor has not yet given up hope of a cure," Bombelles added, although Riedel wrote that Carlota suffered from "obsession with persecution." Maximilian went pale and worked to contain his self-presence. The *Diario del Imperio* soon reported her ailment as meningitis, while others speculated she had a delayed reaction to poisonous *toloache*, the datura plant.[9]

Basch, who shared these intense moments with Maximilian, said, "The Empress had fallen victim to Mexico. There hardly was any prospect of holding on in Mexico without the support of French bayonets," knowing that should Maximilian return to Europe, even the possibility of scorn and embarrassment for his failed monarchy no longer mattered. As Basch accompanied Maximilian on an evening walk on the roof of the National Palace, they discussed abdication and the emperor asked, "Will anybody believe that I am going to Europe because of the illness of the empress?" Basch replied, "Your Majesty certainly has sufficient reasons for leaving Mexico. Europe will acknowledge that you are no longer obligated to remain here, now that France has prematurely canceled its treaties." But Maximilian also turned to his small cadre of advisors, including Herzfeld and Father Augustin Fischer. Basch and others remained deeply suspicious of Fischer's motives, calling him an evil genius, yet others distrusted the motives of Herzfeld because of prior monetary transactions for the empire.[10]

At Miramar the staff and physicians watched Carlota carefully. At times she tried to escape the grounds by simply walking out, without a hat or coat in the rain or high winds, saying she must help Maximilian. Some days she expected Maximilian to come for lunch; other days, she thought she was about to be poisoned by Napoléon. She gladly welcomed her servants and old friends, like Bombelles, but when a small orchestra was brought into the conservatory for her saint's day celebration, November 4, she began to tremble, fearing the musicians were there to do her harm. She thought workmen on the grounds were spies come for a "fresh slaughter." Carlota avoided taking well water, recalling that Maximilian had once thought someone tried to poison his drink at Orizaba, so she drank watered-down wine. She would not eat soup, or liquids in general, unless the doctors tasted it first. She painted for four to five hours a day, played music, read, and walked in the garden.[11]

She often spoke of Maximilian, the financial straits of imperial Mexico, the war scenes with the Juaristas. She imagined Maximilian as a "magus," a leader of a secret society, joined with others around the world in setting the actual course of history. "Everything is made, nothing has become, every incident, as minor as it may be, is the result of providence and calculation by these great men and their countless tools. Everything is surrounded by Masonry," she remarked, saying that Maximilian was Freemason as well as certain staff members in the Vatican. She was sure Maximilian would return to Europe to take over the rule of all countries. The doctors merely hoped for his return to help soothe her and make basic decisions.[12]

Dr. Jilek gave a detailed report to the royal staff at the Hofburg in Vienna, who advised him that he must not allow any tragedy to overtake her. Returning to Miramar with Dr. Riedel, along with the staff at Miramar, it was decided the best place for Carlota to stay and be cared for was the two-story garden cottage near the castle, where she lived before leaving for Mexico. They nailed the windows shut to prevent her escape, and Carlota violently rejected the notion of staying there. Not fathoming being penned up, she ran away, refusing to stay and attacking her doctors. Her alarming behavior confounded them because she was an empress. Protocol dictated that they must treat her gently and could not give her orders. When the doctors confronted her in unison, she felt convinced she was about to be killed. In her upset, Carlota fainted, and she was carried to the garden house, where she lived for several months, attended by two nuns and her maids.[13]

Three months earlier, while Carlota made her way to Europe, the United States had been applying additional pressure to France to comply with its promise to evacuate Mexico. Secretary of State William Seward informed France's minister Montholon that when Maximilian appointed Auguste Osmont and Jean-François Friant, the two French military officers organizing the Mexican military, this further compromised U.S. diplomatic relations, close to the breaking point. In reality, the two officers had been tremendously effective in building up a reliable fighting force for the empire, the Cazadores.

Despite the obstacles, Osmont and Friant honed an army of 40,000 men by the end of September.[14]

In deference to Seward and the United States, Napoléon tried to trivialize France's role in the Mexican empire, and intimated that perhaps the United States could assume the restoration of law in Mexico after France's departure. Marshal Bazaine admitted nothing but put the crisis squarely on the shoulders of President Andrew Johnson. "The moral influence of the United States has destroyed the empire, and thus the obligation rests upon the United States to keep Mexico from anarchy and protect the thousands of foreigners residing there," he argued. In the American Congress debate centered on a plan to intervene militarily to expel the French and Maximilian. Many of those who entertained the thought were veterans of the Mexican War twenty years earlier and were not hesitant to make bold threats. The French legation lobbied intensively for the United States to prevent anarchy after the army's withdrawal. The U.S. State Department, however, declined to appear antagonistic, holding back to allow freedom of action. This relaxation displayed a sense of an ethical victory while heightening France's discomfort.[15]

Maximilian saw Napoléon capitulating under political and military pressure, especially reacting to Austria's crushing defeat at Sadowa against the Prussians. On September 20 the emperor wrote Charles Bombelles at Miramar, "I refuse to believe that [his] illness and the Prussian needle gun have so far crushed the Emperor Napoléon that he is tottering helpless towards an abyss. He will recover his accustomed fortitude, and the cool judgment of the Empress [Carlota] . . . will succeed in reviving his sick mind." Although they closely monitored telegraph communications for news of the Prussian War, they received conflicting messages on France's military positions, indicating confusion within the war department.[16]

The revenues of the empire steadily shrank. Édouard Pierron, who served as paymaster for the military, could barely scrape together enough money to pay the cavalry, municipal guard, the engineers, and the new Cazadores regiment. He warned Maximilian that pay for his servants and members of the civil list would have to come from his private funds, since there was so little money remaining in the treasury. Under this stress, Maximilian made even more irregular decisions. Pierron complained of Maximilian's haphazard management of the country and the treasury. "He faults his differences with me, but in the same way, issues orders without logic, without method . . . it is impossible for me to continue my work in an area that is under the chairmanship of your Excellency the Emperor," Pierron wrote. Maximilian complicated matters, trying to sail a ship in stormy seas while taking in bilgewater.[17]

In September 1866 Capt. Pierre Loizillon wrote from Puebla that the vigorous consolidation of troops while trying to maintain order and defense proved difficult and demoralizing. Marshal Bazaine issued orders, only to countermand them, or left officers with incomplete instructions. "I have never worked so much in Mexico. Here I am alone with a single French officer; the Austrian officers I have at my disposal can't write French, and are no good to me other than to translate the German documents I receive. I feel like I'm in the middle of the Tower of Babel: telegrams of all kinds come in, in French, Spanish, German, and Hungarian, dealing with civil and military administration, with the organization of the Austrian and Mexican troops, with the courts, finances, and to top it all off, all the troop movements to try to deal with the enemy that is closing in on us from all sides. In addition, I am at work from six in the morning until I don't know what time in the evening or night. In addition, if I had the satisfaction of doing something well, it wouldn't matter . . . I feel like I have worked, as they say, for the King of Prussia [doing useless tasks]," said Loizillon. He complained that he got no solid direction from the commanders. "One minute we get the order to march one way, then suddenly we're stopped. . . . Currently everyone is *floating* in the higher realms, without any fixed direction."[18]

With chaos and violence rising in Mexico and the French troops preparing to leave, Napoléon dispatched his aide-de-camp, Brig. Gen. François de Castelnau, to assist in France's peaceful and complete disengagement. Castelnau arrived at Veracruz on the *Emperatriz Eugenia* in the first week of October 1866 with orders that placed him over Bazaine in authority. This only served to confuse the army officers further. Castelnau, who knew little about Mexico, was told to try to encourage Maximilian to abdicate, while expediting the troop repatriation to France. If Maximilian left Mexico, Napoléon quietly reasoned, the United States would have no cause to intervene, saving France embarrassment. This was too sensitive to discuss publicly, for if word got out, public imagination would be inflamed, and people in their sympathy for Maximilian and Carlota would blame Napoléon and Eugénie for the debacle. Although Maximilian considered abdication on his own, he refused to discuss it with any French officials, his disdain for them growing everyday. He vowed to stay detached from Bazaine and Castelnau.[19]

Pierron, who remained in the confusing position of working for the French but acting as Maximilian's military secretary, met Castelnau at Veracruz. On the trip back to Mexico City, Pierron debriefed Castelnau thoroughly. He described Maximilian as a loyal and honorable commander but someone who could not rule with a firm hand. The chief of their military escort, the notorious Col. Charles Du Pin, who owed his position in Mexico to Castelnau, gave the commander his view as a counterguerrilla who had fought many months and miles across tough terrain. In his battle-scarred, swaggering style, Du Pin said Maximilian was "a superficial weakling, swayed by every adventurer who comes his way and good for nothing but botanizing."[20] While he understood Maximilian to be inept, this in no way gave Castelnau a true picture of the situation. Many influential elites, the military, and the clergy still supported Maximilian, ready to safeguard the throne and his honor.

Lt. Col. Alfred van der Smissen, a baron and loyal commander of the empress's Belgian corps, who had been senior commander of Michoacán, urged Maximilian to take to the field with his men to defend his empire, a notion the emperor considered seriously. Van der Smissen, whose Belgian troops hated the French and threatened mutiny, came up with a simple plan to win back the northeastern region of Mexico. He advised driving back the encroachments of Juarista general Escobedo, who was aided by American filibusters. He said it would require only one division, led by the emperor, to halt his advance, and such a victory would electrify the Mexican people. Van der Smissen suggested the division be composed of a Mexican brigade under Colonel Miguel López, who he characterized as brave and reliable, along with two battalions of the French Foreign Legion, Mejía as chief of the general staff, and himself in command of the Austro-Belgian brigade. "I would beg Your Majesty to allow me to lead the main attack against the enemy and I pledge my word as a man of honor that we shall gain a brilliant victory and take at least 3,000 prisoners. A shout of triumph will arise from the whole empire, and thousands will rally around the throne," Van der Smissen said.[21]

Within days, however, Van der Smissen, against the orders of Bazaine, led his troops into a battle in a heavily Juarista-fortified area near Tula, some fifteen miles southeast of Mexico City. Some of his men, both Mexican and Belgian, defected during the bloody, hard-fought battle, which went against the Imperialistas. Van der Smissen had three horses shot from under him but survived the vigorous attack. In all, eleven Imperialista officers were killed.[22]

At the same time, the domestic imperial Mexican army faced numerous obstacles. Maximilian's repurposed French officers assigned in his new army fought to find purchase but failed when France undermined the scheme. When

Friant prepared to pay the Cazadores from French funds, Bazaine objected because his position as Mexico's finance minister conflicted with his role as paymaster. Friant, who learned this through secretary Édouard Pierron and suspected that he worked with Bazaine to get Maximilian to abdicate, angrily asked, "What do they want? Do they want to overthrow Maximilian? If so, why don't you say so at once?" Friant and Osmont continued to sympathize with the emperor, against the French army.[23]

Maximilian hoped that his new national army would be ready by October 1, 1866. He informed Bazaine he would also assume control of the French Foreign Legion, as promised to him in the Convention of Miramar. Bazaine, busily managing the evacuation of the west coast, evaded the emperor, mainly because he was not sure the convention even remained in effect. According to Bazaine, it had been void since July, but Maximilian pressed on to enforce it. When the troops evacuated northern Mexico, Maximilian reminded Bazaine that he had enough funds to pay troops to fight the Liberals. Not doing so, he said, "would be the means of giving to the [Juarista] rebellion a fictitious importance, to which, up to the present time, it has never attained."[24]

Bazaine informed Maximilian that the evacuation would proceed nonetheless, that he would be staying with his troops until the last column had boarded the last transport, and extended limited support by giving military advice. A few weeks earlier, Napoléon had objected to Osmont and Friant's role in ministerial positions while simultaneously holding French commissions. He sent orders to Bazaine to halt work in organizing the Cazadores, effectively gutting the planned October unveiling of the new and independent army. Maximilian's special requests to keep them on task were denied. The sudden withdrawal of the two officers left the newly emerging Mexican command in confusion, with orders incomplete and communications cut off. Under these worsening circumstances, Maximilian, again feeling victimized, eagerly awaited the French departure. He was convinced that Napoléon, a weak, sick man, had completely lost his mind. However, resigned to push on, he appointed Gen. Ramón Tavera as new minister of war. Friant's tightening of budgetary procedures endured, however, so much so that in August, when Maximilian wanted to organize troops in San Luis Potosí, he had to request the funds. Friant granted him $15,000.[25]

The Independence Day celebrations on September 16 included the usual festivities in Mexico City, masses, fireworks, and the Grito de Dolores. During the week of celebration Maximilian toured Mexico City in an open carriage, decorated supporters, and made a speech to the public stating emphatically,

"In moments of danger, a real Habsburg does not abandon his post." Despite the departure of the French, he pledged to remain at the helm, his personal dignity not allowing him to cower from duty. The emperor was convinced he would have the support of the indigenous population, as his ministers told him, and they would rally to his support. They would rise up, away from the subjection of landowners and away from centuries of abuse. He was optimistic with new ideas of how to secure the empire and defend the people against all enemies. But at that time, he did not know about Carlota's health.[26]

On October 18, when he received the shocking news of Carlota's mental collapse, this only compounded the multitude of insurmountable problems: the financial situation, France's withdrawal, and the rapidly growing strength of the Liberals. Since Carlota's departure, much of his resolve had melted away. He bent to every prevailing notion of his advisors. Maximilian also received word of a massive Imperialista defeat at La Carbonera in Oaxaca. The routed volunteer corps had been captured. These defeats demoralized Maximilian and the army corps even further. There were rumors of a pending attack on Chapultepec, for which the Austrian engineers prepared and loaded cannon. Knowing he could not face life in Mexico without his wife and under the mounting defeats, Maximilian quietly announced his abdication to his closest staff members and planned to take the next ship to Europe.[27] In this way, Maximilian wanted to mend his nets. Then he could leave with a clear conscience.

He determined to go immediately to Orizaba during the preparations. Most people only knew Carlota was sick with a "cerebral fever" and did not know yet of her mental breakdown. He used the excuse of his health. When Bazaine wrote a letter of concern about Carlota, Maximilian thanked him and his wife, Pepita. "The terrible blow caused by the late news, which has so grievously wounded my heart, and the bad state of my health caused by the intermittent fever . . . have necessitated (under express order of my physician), a temporary sojourn to a softer climate." His last hours at Chapultepec were spent in urgency and lament.[28]

Early on the morning of October 20, Maximilian and his staff left for Orizaba, leaving the capital by a circuitous route, not wanting to panic the city. He took only the most anodyne advisors including Augustin Fischer, Samuel Basch, Pedro Ormachea, Dominic Bilimek, and others. In the process of fleeing to Orizaba, Maximilian agonized over his next steps. At their first stop en route to Orizaba, at the Hacienda Socyapán, he seriously contemplated his abdication. Risking schadenfreude from the French, he nonetheless wrote

Bazaine that he wished to relieve himself of his responsibilities. He asked the marshal to suspend all courts-martial on political offenses resulting from the Black Decree of October 3, 1865, along with resulting persecutions, lamenting he had ever enacted it. He also asked that the military tribunals no longer handle political offenses. He implored the marshal to keep the news from the public and preserved the accompanying documents of abdication under lock and key until he notified him via telegraph with his final decision.

While dodging known guerrilla hideaways along the route, one night they encountered Gen. Castelnau and his staff on their way to Mexico City, but Maximilian refused to meet with the general. While passing the night at Acultzingo, the six white mules that drew the royal carriage were stolen. Respect and order began to collapse. While the newspaper *Diario del Imperio* reported that the emperor was going to Orizaba to convalesce, Maximilian could not overcome the rampant gossip that he was leaving the country. This information spread quickly to Puebla.[29]

The day before he left Mexico City, Maximilian wrote to Alice Green Iturbide telling her that he could no longer protect her child and was willing to place Agustín with anyone she desired. A few days later, determined not to be forgotten, Josefa Iturbide, the tutor and nanny of Prince Agustín, worried that she would be left behind to face the fallout. "Friends and enemies are persuaded that your Majesty abandons forever the territory of the Empire," she wrote Maximilian.

> I solely have not given rise to such suspicions. I identified with the fate of your Majesty by my affection for the title your Majesty gave me, like my nephew, and count in the number of family that will not leave you abandoned. If against my knowledge, your Majesty had decided to leave the territory of Mexico, I venture to beseech you to bring us in your company to get out of the country to the United States, taking in my company the innocent child that your Majesty sought worthy to put in my care with the love of a true mother. I also must ask your Majesty to send orders to give me certain funds, because I have none.[30]

After fleeing from Mexico, Princess Josefa Iturbide moved to Paris with her butler. Her relatives said she spent lavishly and wore her imperial diamonds on a regular basis.[31]

After the controversy with the Iturbides and with the news of Carlota's illness, Maximilian said he wanted no more scandal or pain. Alice received word from the archbishop's office that the baby would go with his uncle and a clerical representative by a steamer to Havana. She immediately sailed for Cuba, where the mother and child were finally reunited.[32]

Maximilian also drafted confidential letters granting the estate of Olindo at Cuernavaca to Feliciano Rodríguez, his aide-de-camp. The imperial stables were left to Col. Pedro Ormachea and Gen. José López Uraga, despite their indefinite plans to stay in Mexico.[33]

Rumors of Maximilian's possible exit from the country resulted in a flurry of letters from Conservatives during his hiatus in Orizaba begging him to stay in Mexico, fearing for their safety should he leave. Beginning on October 18, people who learned of Carlota's mental illness also flooded the emperor with letters. On October 19 Maximilian's council of ministers resigned in panic, but after consulting with Bazaine, they all agreed to stay in office. Many with the government and the church expressed their sympathies and concern, hoping that Maximilian would not abandon them. "I send my profound sentiments. I remain asking God, our savior, to free us from a major disgrace, that would be extremely emotional for all Mexicans," wrote Labastida. In all, Maximilian received over one hundred messages from various ministers, clergy, wealthy Conservatives, and prominent women at Mexico City, Puebla, and as far away as Havana, Cuba. Teodosio Lares, president of the regency that brought Maximilian to Mexico, conveyed his sadness. "These are fateful consequences for the whole nation that adopted Carlota as a mother, who has duly sacrificed generously, exposing her precious life," wrote Lares. Her ladies-in-waiting also wrote as well as a group of women from Puebla who held a series of masses for the empress, urging him to stay in Mexico. But groups of prominent leaders from Mexico City and Puebla could not immediately convince him.[34]

Maximilian sought counsel with his ministers including Samuel Basch, Augustin Fischer, and Stephan Herzfeld. Fischer had his own agenda, which mainly had to do with sympathies for the Conservatives and Clerical party. However, Fischer, also looking out for his personal well-being, kept his motives well concealed. Maximilian had not understood Fischer's failure to negotiate a concordat in Rome and did not suspect that the man was power-less and a fraud. In Blasio's absence while traveling with Carlota, Fischer had become Maximilian's secretary. From that point on, he knew all the business of the empire and how to influence Maximilian with his effusive flattery, san-guine optimism, and toadying lightheartedness. Fischer argued to Maximilian to let the French army go in peace, suggesting the small corps of Austrians and Belgians could take over. Moreover, he counseled that a national congress should decide Mexico's future and negotiate an end to the fighting. His ministers Teodosio Lares and José María Lacunza, who managed the country's finances, could prevail. He urged Maximilian not to abdicate.[35]

On the other hand, Herzfeld keenly viewed the situation more seriously and clearly, and advised the emperor to leave Mexico immediately. Conditions had become untenable, volatile, and too dangerous for him to survive. With the decampment of the French, he would be left with insufficient forces to survive the growing Liberal resistance, and Mexico's empire would fall into oblivion.[36]

Maximilian agreed with Herzfeld and covertly expedited his plan to abdicate. He ordered his household managers to pack his possessions at Chapultepec, the National Palace, and Cuernavaca. He gave Gen. Paolino Lamadrid the task of surreptitiously transporting his goods to Veracruz, where quartermaster Nicolas Poliakowitz would secure them. The steamships *Dandolo* and *Elizabeth* had been assigned to take Maximilian, and the captains awaited his orders. The items for shipment to Europe were packed in twenty-three large crates, including boxes prepared by Professor Bilimek containing over six hundred specimens of butterflies, beetles, and plants. Poliakowitz inventoried and separated his personal items from goods that would be placed at Miramar, Lacroma, or in museums. This included, "table linen, oil paintings and . . . private property such as clothing, personal linen, portraits and keepsakes of their majesties, including books, writings, and photographs." Herzfeld rented a villa in Havana and transferred funds to Europe. Maximilian rushed his aides, writing that he could not review Poliakowitz's inventory until they reached port at St. Thomas. This was an important historic moment, he said, and also ordered Poliakowitz to write an official record of the preparations. He cautioned the captain of the *Dandolo* to maintain enough coal to make it nonstop to St. Thomas.[37]

The citizens of Orizaba received Maximilian with considerable fanfare, orchestrated by Father Fischer. The padre reminded Maximilian that he left many matters unresolved: the Austrian and Belgian corps were still in the field fighting for him, as were his loyal Mexican regiments. The emperor's flight would be unbecoming of such a resolute soldier and talented leader, he said. Maximilian thought carefully about this. When he saw the outpouring of patriotic sentiment, he felt humbled and duty-bound. It flattered his vanity and motivated him to renew his passion for serving Mexico and her people. Greeted by fond well-wishers in the streets, Maximilian was overcome. Letters of goodbye he had planned to write were postponed. He avoided appearing with French officers, to stem any suspicion about his loyalties. He reduced the size of his personal guard to appear courageous and closer to his subjects.[38]

Staying at the home of Bernabé Bringas in Orizaba, Maximilian's health began to improve, and each day additional Conservatives sought meetings with him. Teodosio Lares arrived to remind him of his pledges, that his leaving would bring dishonor and great misfortune to the nation. He reminded him of his words of only six weeks earlier, that a Habsburg did not desert his post. "What would the world say, what would history say?" asked Lares.[39]

Still with plans to abdicate, at Orizaba he contemplated how best to do it. Maximilian began discussions, asking many for advice on whether to stay or go. Basch advised him to ease up and think carefully, as much for his health as his well-being. Fischer kept referring to Maximilian's departure and abdication as a "flight," meant to seem derogatory, an abrogation of duty, and a challenge. Basch recognized Fischer's careful manipulations of Maximilian. "Any postponement, any delay benefited him. Every day the emperor remained in Orizaba was a victory. By all kinds of little maneuvers, he painstakingly dodged every open yes or no." He would delay or neglect to pass on orders relating to Maximilian's departure preparations. He never courageously spoke the truth, while playing adroitly on Maximilian's proud but vacillating nature, growing bolder in his scheming and twisting, keeping the emperor unsteady and confused. If Maximilian asked him, "Should I abdicate?" Fischer often sighed in agreement. When asked if he should leave without abdicating, the father shrugged his head and nodded. When Fischer suggested that Maximilian should resign, sharply adding "in favor of Napoléon," impugning his scruples, Maximilian replied, "This idea is Machiavellian. It would be better if I went away without abdicating."[40]

Stefan Herzfeld, at Veracruz en route to New York, wrote Maximilian urging him to leave soon and warned Fischer to protect him. Maximilian never saw Herzfeld's letter, for Fischer never delivered it. Pierron, still in Mexico City, advised Maximilian to put a new regency of moderate Mexicans in place, for once he left, he feared that civil war would erupt. However, Bazaine attempted to leave the Mexican government with a transition plan that would block Maximilian's efforts and force him to retire. Without approval from the emperor, he tried to arrange negotiations with various Juarista generals for a peaceful takeover of Mexico. None of Juárez's generals would meet with him, however, except for Gen. Vicente Riva Palacio, but little resulted from their discussion.[41]

Despite pleas for him to remain in Mexico, Maximilian still prepared to set sail, and fixed the date of departure from Veracruz for November 8. He began to the see the fallout from his rumored abdication as Imperialist troops deserted. Across Mexico, moreover, the remaining Imperialist divisions continued to suffer stunning defeats. In Oaxaca, Gen. Porfirio Díaz decimated a regiment of Imperialistas. When Bazaine dispatched a column of 800 Austrian and Mexican troops to aid the survivors, Díaz's troops anticipated their movements and set upon them. A good number of the royal Mexican troops fell out of the ranks, and the Austrians who survived were demoralized, ready to leave Mexico forever.[42]

Maximilian also read conflicting and inaccurate reports from the military in the field. He was at a loss to know how to act. He finally received Eloin's letter sent from Brussels in September, the one delivered by accident to the Republican Mexican consul in New York, and he read the words carefully. "I firmly believe that abandoning the party before the French army has returned would be interpreted as an act of weakness, and as the emperor holds his office by a popular vote, it is to the Mexican people, free of the pressure of foreign intervention, that it must make a new appeal . . . for the material and financial support essential to survive," wrote Eloin. This gave Maximilian pause. Eloin had written this letter just after consulting with Carlota in September at Miramar, before her mental collapse. By the tone of the message, it seemed as though she had spoken these exact words to Eloin, her signal to Maximilian. "Perhaps I shall return to Europe soon," he said, mulling over his thoughts.[43]

Maximilian had sought advice from British diplomat Sir Peter Campbell-Scarlett, with whom he shared Napoléon's letter advising him about abdication. The minister stopped in to see Maximilian at Orizaba. One of the first things he said was that his precipitous exit from Mexico City certainly gave rise to suspicions that Maximilian was about to flee the country. However, he agreed with Napoléon's advice, that Maximilian should convene a Mexican congress and test the people to see if they supported a monarchy. It would be the only course commensurate with his power and prestige. "It is by no means sure as yet whether . . . the Mexican people will not decide to maintain the empire, if its organization proceeds hand in hand with the cessation of French intervention," wrote Campbell-Scarlett later. No one wanted the French there anymore, but that did not mean they rejected imperial rule. "It is quite certain that after the departure of the French, a strong party would prefer to rally around the imperial flag, so as to save Mexico from being rent asunder by a civil war."[44]

Maximilian's troubles made an impression on Campbell-Scarlett, especially his comment, "If the empress dies, I shall not have the courage or desire to remain in Mexico. I came here more on her account than on my own and I have no ambition to continue alone after her death, and especially . . . as I have no children." At the end, however, Campbell-Scarlett, who was unaware of Fischer's shadiness, agreed with the priest when he suggested Maximilian should return to Mexico City and let the people decide.[45]

While mulling over Campbell-Scarlett's advice, Maximilian continued with his plan to step down, writing farewell letters to his ministers in Mexico City and to his mother informing her of his return, preparing to leave for Veracruz. Then on November 7, 1866, he received a telegram from Pierron in Mexico City with news from the Austrian ministry responding to his last inquiries to resolve the Family Pact with Franz Josef. They stated that if Maximilian arrived in Austria claiming a right of succession as an emperor, he was forbidden to return. If he chose to return as an archduke, no one would prevent his repatriation, and the Austrians would find a suitable position for him. This shocked Maximilian. His old fears and angers surfaced as he remembered past conflicts with his brother. Even though Maximilian harbored a plan to return to Austria, even inquiring about the purchase of the Castle of Artstetten to be nearer to Vienna, the prospect of returning as a prodigal son, to live a tainted life in Europe after losing a throne in the Americas, had little appeal for him. After Maximilian requested a copy of the communication, Baron Alfred Lago, the Austrian minister, denied such a letter had been drafted; he had not seen it but vowed to investigate the matter. Maximilian did not doubt Pierron's report, knowing that with the French army's withdrawal, the Austrians believed he might be contemplating a return and claim to a title. As Maximilian's anxieties compounded with memories of the conflicts with Franz Josef, the concept of staying to fight for his adopted country seemed far more fitting than returning to a crumbling Habsburg empire.[46]

Fischer made much of this news to argue against abdication. On November 10, during his vacillations and anxiety, Maximilian ordered Fischer to cable Poliakowitz at Veracruz to postpone the departure for three or four days. Fischer did so and effusively thanked Poliakowitz for the inventory of the emperor's personal and household goods loaded on the *Dandolo*.[47]

That same day, Generals Miguel Miramón and Leonardo Márquez arrived at Veracruz, having returned from their frivolous assignments in Europe and the Middle East, and they immediately went to Orizaba to see Maximilian. As a former president of Mexico, Miramón, who returned without Maximilian's permission, urged him not to leave and pledged his total loyalty. Márquez vowed the same. They assured him they could pacify the country without the support of France. They supported Fischer's argument, knowing that

Maximilian bristled when others said he could not survive without the French. They preyed on Maximilian's self-esteem, arguing that Napoléon only wanted his abdication to rationalize his mistakes. However, despite being moved by their support, Maximilian continued issuing orders related to his departure, making plans for transportation for the remainder of the Austrian and Belgian corps.[48]

Then Maximilian received two more letters that had great impact. From Europe, Gutiérrez de Estrada urgently reminded him that as a Habsburg he could not walk away from his commitment to Mexico. "What general would leave his position of command in the hour of battle for any private reason of whatsoever nature?" Gutiérrez de Estrada ended by saying that a glorious victory was imminent, but if the empire collapsed around him, he would know that he had done everything possible to save it.[49]

Lastly, his mother, Archduchess Sophie, sent a letter through the Austrian ministry telling him not to compromise his honor. She said that abdication under the present circumstances would mean his reception in Austria and Europe would be a disaster. "Better to be buried under ruins in Mexico than to give in to the French," she was rumored to have written. She advised him to exhibit noblesse oblige and honor, to deal with the political struggle, despite the dangers. The message reinforced what Maximilian had been taught from the cradle. With these last letters, Maximilian made a monumental change in plans, to stay and fight for the Mexican empire.[50]

This news prompted Miramón and Márquez to reconfirm their loyalty, and Maximilian gave them full authorization to augment Imperialist troops and organize the army. The Conservatives pledged 4 million pesos to support the empire. Maximilian could pay his army, raise additional troops, and prevail. His hope was to reconcile with Juárez and convene a national congress to determine the will of the nation. Then in all probability, Maximilian would leave Mexico to tend to his wife. He wrote this in another letter to Juárez, which went unanswered. The war must continue. However, he wanted a vote by his councilors to reinforce this decision.[51]

On November 18 Maximilian gathered his ministers and the Council of State in Orizaba to decide on his abdication and how best to form the government. Of the twenty-three men invited (all Conservatives except for three who had no party affiliation), eighteen arrived on November 24 led by Teodosio Lares. Maximilian stayed away from the deliberations but sent a letter to the assembly outlining his reasons for abdication and conditions under which he would stay, which he listed as "(1) Getting out of the toils of the French;

(2) Arrangement with America; (3) Raising of money; (4) Organize the army; (5) No more bloodshed; (6) Official suspension of the law of [Black Decree] October 3; (7) Courts-martial for nonpolitical bandits only." He promised that he would act according to whatever the council decided. If he stayed, however, he expected financial and military support from a congress.[52]

The next day Maximilian left them at the estate of Casa Bringas, sequestered to decide. "Deseo de salir, llamado de los consejos," he said. As he waited, Maximilian decided to issue a *pronunciamento* regarding the assembly's vote. The power entrusted to him should be decided freely. "This congress will determine whether the empire is to continue into the future and if so will help to form the laws vital to strengthening the public institutions of the country," he wrote. As in other times of doubt, Maximilian disowned any conviction, refusing to decide his destiny. Suspecting the outcome of the council's deliberations meant he would remain in Mexico, he ordered a few boxes of his possessions unloaded from the *Dandolo* and brought to him at Orizaba. Then he went out bug collecting in the meadows with Bilimek.[53]

Over the next few days of discussion and debate over finances, the military, and resources, Maximilian left them with papers to review, particularly a promise from Bazaine to return all munitions to Mexico should the emperor return to the capital to hold his position there. After much debate and consideration of raising funds, the members voted. With the committee heavily represented by the Conservative party, the results of the election seemed assured. Two Liberal members voted for immediate departure, eleven voted for abdication (but only after Maximilian facilitated a peaceful transition of government), and ten voted to preserve the empire at all costs. "We ask Your Majesty not to abdicate and to gain new strength to tirelessly continue to fight for our fatherland, for which we offer weak, but loyal, support," they wrote. They asked him not to leave without securing independence from the Liberals. With the council's endorsement, Maximilian's aides, generals, and staff reinvigorated and committed to organize the military to win back the country, each having his own agenda. Fischer later vowed to get right to work on drafting a new concordat with the Vatican. The night of the vote, Fischer and the ministers celebrated with champagne and a fine dinner in Orizaba, which, knowing the sort of work that lay ahead, Maximilian resented. "I find this very tactless of the ministers," he said.[54]

Maximilian wrote to Carlota that he hoped he would see her again in the spring, expressing his longing for her.[55] However, despite the wretched circumstances, Maximilian recommitted to duty and command as the chosen sovereign, without France as a crutch.

Liberator I Will Be

On December 1 the *Diario del Imperio* reported the glowing news that Maximilian "has decided to retain power and to return to the capital soon. This noble and patriotic decision by the sovereign, who made his final decision yesterday, has left an impression of ineffable joy in Orizaba, where it was celebrated with the pealing of bells, firecrackers, music, and all kinds of joyous demonstrations." Maximilian said he was "deeply moved by the evidences of love and loyalty" and would again renew the "work of regeneration." Multitudes cheered at the front of the palace.[1]

Maximilian wrote Pierron, however, that he had hoped that the assembly would vote for his abdication but was honored when they asked him to stay. Pierron reassured the emperor but warned of their eagerness. Not once did the council members caution him on the difficulties of fulfilling these initiatives. He quoted Roman philosopher Lucretius: "It is pleasant, when the sea runs high, to view from land the distress of another; not that anyone's afflictions are in themselves a source of delight, but to realize you are free from those troubles is a joy indeed."[2]

Too late to convince Maximilian to abdicate, Austrian colonel Von Kodolitsch, who vowed to stay with the emperor, also warned him that Castelnau brought new orders from the minister of war, Randon, in Paris to disband the French Foreign Legion. He knew that Maximilian never saw that development emerging because he was personally planning their reorganization, according to agreements with Napoléon. Randon viewed the Convention of Miramar as a dead letter and encouraged Castelnau to have Maximilian return from Mexico with the French. However, by this time the emperor was so distracted from reality by his conniving advisors, he only cared that the French left for good. His mind made up, he appeared emboldened, resolved not to part with his crown in fear.[3]

On December 3 Teodosio Lares and the other Conservative ministers alerted Bazaine, Castelnau, and French minister Dano in Mexico City that the emperor would not be abdicating. They could only be dismayed. With Maximilian preparing to return to the capital, Bazaine hastened his plans to leave. Under severe pressure from Castelnau and the bureau of military expenditures to control costs, he discharged the French from the newly organized Cazadores to return to their former units and begin marching toward Veracruz, partially dissolving Maximilian's new army. In order to wring as much cash from Mexico and deprive the emperor of badly needed funds, Castelnau also invoked the stipulations of the newly signed customs contract and began to call for France's full share of the duties. Lares instead demanded restitution to the empire of Veracruz's customs revenues for October. Maintenant, the inspector general of finance, denied their claim, along with Bazaine and Castelnau. When Lares and the imperial ministers insisted that the French turn over munitions, artillery, and supplies to the imperial government before their departure, Bazaine had most of the guns spiked and munitions destroyed, leaving only a portion of their stores for the defense of the capital. Instead of leaving a surplus of horses, they were put down. Bazaine intended that these simple acts of sabotage would force Maximilian to leave the country with the French.[4]

Many of the Austrians and Belgians released from the ranks refused to abandon Maximilian, promising to support him with their own regiments. This demonstration of brotherly support gave the emperor hope. They had a few conditions, including that they would no longer serve in mixed units, many refusing to serve under Mexican commanders fearing that their true loyalties lay with Juárez. In all, 173 officers and some 650 men pledged to remain with the emperor. Austrian minister Alfred de Lago scoffed, saying they ought to return to Austria; by staying in Mexico, he said, they would only earn "drinking money." They were too few in number to make a difference in battle, but it was a place to start rebuilding. Maximilian knew he would have to take an active role in raising troops, possibly through the *leva*, or forced conscription. He would be entering Mexico City amid the flurry of French rushing to get out but was heartened by the news that members of the imperial Mexican units vowed to support him.[5]

On November 29, anticipating that Maximilian prepared to leave Mexico for Europe, Americans Gen. William T. Sherman and Lewis D. Campbell, having been assured of Maximilian's abdication, arrived at Veracruz on the frigate *Susquehanna*, to assist in reinstating the government of Juárez. With orders from President Andrew Johnson and Gen. U. S. Grant, Sherman and Campbell planned to establish contact with Juárez and offer support, if desired, providing assistance with land or naval forces.[6]

"Everything about Veracruz indicated the purpose of the French to withdraw and also that the Emperor Maximilian would precede them, for the Austrian frigate *Dandolo* was in port, and an Austrian bark, on which were received . . . as many as 1,100 packages of private furniture to be transferred to Miramar," wrote Sherman. By messenger, Admiral Cloué assured them if they waited eight days, Maximilian would be gone.[7]

They elected to anchor offshore at Isla Verde, not daring to disembark due to a blasting norther, which compounded the dangers in the small port full of French men-of-war and transports. Sherman's aide, the seasick Joseph Audenried, wrote they must be patient and "like Micawber, wait for something to turn up." After celebrating an American-style Thanksgiving dinner on board, the French soon arrived and informed Sherman that Maximilian remained at Orizaba.[8]

Then they received the emperor's proclamation stating he would stay and "shed the last drop of his blood in defense of his dear country." Sherman wrote, "The most substantial people of Mexico, having lost all faith in the stability of the native government, had committed themselves to what they considered the more stable government of Maximilian, and Maximilian, a man of honor, concluded at the last moment he could not abandon them."[9]

The consuls had made a major blunder in their reports assuming Maximilian would soon leave. Bazaine invited Sherman to confer with him in Mexico City, but Sherman declined in view that the United States had not recognized the empire. With thoughts on his own mind, Maximilian sent a representative to invite Sherman and Campbell to Orizaba, but the agent arrived too late. On December 2, after a brief tour of the town and not gleaning any more information, Sherman and his staff sailed north for Tampico, escorted by a gunboat. Learning that the port was in possession of the Liberals, Sherman and Campbell went to the American consulate to see Consul Franklin Chase. Failing to reach Juárez in Chihuahua, they left word with his minister of foreign affairs, Sebastián Lerdo de Tejada, of their desire to make contact. They cast off for Brazos Santiago at the mouth of the Rio Grande, having heard that

Juárez would soon arrive at Matamoros. The general had double purpose to try to halt further Confederate immigration to Mexico and wanted to meet U.S. officers at Fort Brown, across the river from Matamoros.[10]

On December 7 Sherman learned from Gen. Sheridan at Brownsville that Liberal general Mariano Escobedo, commander of the Army of the North, now controlled Matamoros, which Audenried called a "wretched place." Sherman and Audenried took the ferry across the Rio Grande to meet Gen. Escobedo, and with an escort of "banditti-looking cavalry who were mounted on mustangs" and a salute of "prolonged tooting" from a band, they found Escobedo, who served them wine. Through an interpreter, in the interview with Escobedo, they were informed that Juárez was traveling toward Monterrey, and they should appeal to Sebastián Lerdo de Tejada to allow Campbell to meet him. Stranded for a few days when a storm broke their vessel from its mooring, Sherman and Audenried planned general frontier protection with Sheridan. When they finally steamed toward New Orleans, Campbell left for Monterrey, never found any authorities, and left frustrated. Sherman wrote his brother that Juárez was as far away, "up in Chihuahua for no possible purpose other than to be where the devil himself cannot get at him. I have not the remotest idea of riding on mule back a thousand miles in Mexico to find its chief magistrate."[11]

American officials clamped down the U.S. recruiting offices for the Mexican colonies. Seward repeated his demand that Napoléon's troops fully abandon Mexico, receiving assurances from the Tuileries that they were in the process of withdrawing. Napoléon's tone, however, remained defiant:

> We were obliged to have recourse to redress legitimate wrongs, and we endeavored to again raise up an ancient empire. . . . The idea which guided the expedition to Mexico was a grand one; to regenerate a people; to implant among them ideas of order and progress. . . . Such was my desire . . . but on the day that the extent of our sacrifices appeared . . . to be beyond the interest which called to us from the other side of the Atlantic, I spontaneously decided upon the recall of our army. He refused to admit that any diplomatic pressure from the United States caused France's retreat.[12]

As Gen. Phil Sheridan kept up aggressive efforts to aid the Juarista fighters along the Rio Grande, many of the former Confederates who remained in Mexico fell victim to the fighting Liberals. In November 1866 Gen. Jo Shelby, who ran a transport company, had been ambushed by Juaristas on his way with a delivery to one of the French garrisons. When French reinforcements arrived to defend the outpost, the Juaristas quickly dispersed. After that last battle, more of the French encampments closed, Shelby finally lost his customers, and his colony became history. A French financier, Baron Enrique Sauvage, promised Shelby another start at the port of Tuxpan on the coast north of Veracruz with a large supply of imperial arms. Shelby purchased two schooners, and soon he and his 200 Confederate and Mexican colonists were shipping fruit from Tuxpan to New Orleans. A displaced band of the indigenous Toluca regularly attacked the Tuxpan colony, and Shelby defended his community in hand-to-hand fighting. Finally, in February 1866 a swarm of 2,000 guerrillas and natives assailed the settlement. Advance warnings enabled Shelby to evacuate most of the settlers, but those in the outlying areas were massacred. After retreating ninety miles up the coast to Tampico, his boats were scuttled, and his crews murdered and tossed into the sea. Defeated, Shelby returned to the United States, as did many American colonists.[13]

On December 10, 1866, as Maximilian and his ministers strategized to save their government, the French battalion of the First Regiment of Zouaves left Puebla, escorting the sick and wounded eastward to Veracruz to meet ships bound for France, expected in mid-January. They hauled artillery accompanied by a number of the counterguerrillas, who took advantage of the protection of an armed convoy to return to their posts in the hot lands. The arrogant Lt. Col. Gaston Alexandre de Galliffet, a veteran of the Crimean wars and survivor of a severe abdominal wound at Puebla, replaced Col. Du Pin as commander of the counterguerrillas. As the fighting continued through sections of the Huasteca and the state of Veracruz, Bazaine consolidated various regiments ordered to march toward the port, which was hastily under repair to handle the large-scale embarkation. Many of the men, still displaying their Gallic joie de vivre, were reluctant to leave. The soldiers could not help but recall their first thrill at going to Mexico, the memories of hard-fought sieges, seeing their comrades fall in battle, and their many triumphs, all of which haunted them. They had marched over many thousands of miles to far-flung corners of the country, overcoming fatigue, hunger, thirst, Juarista guerrillas, and impassible deserts. "All of us, even the most humble, had the honor of giving our best," wrote Count Jules de Saint Sauveur, who served with the counterguerrillas.[14]

Reaching the village of Palmar, approximately forty miles east of Puebla, the battalion and the counterguerrillas encountered squadrons of Austrian hussars and Mexican gendarmerie in a cloud of dust billowing toward them. It was a guard of cavalrymen escorting the emperor on his return from Orizaba to Mexico City after his decision not to abdicate.[15]

At the little town, Maximilian's worn and mud-splattered carriage stopped, and the emperor descended to greet 1,000 natives who had come from nearby villages to greet him. Count Saint Sauveur, who witnessed the scene, said, "The Prince, who by nature tended toward the most noble inspirations, appeared deeply touched by the tumultuous demonstrations that welcomed him; the naïveté of the population was just what it took to move him." The people, some down on their knees before him, called him "Liberator." The public admiration was a balm to his soul. Despite his fatigue and grief, his spirits lifted and he said, "Liberator I will be." Saint Sauveur wrote, "He felt his courage grow in the face of struggle. So it is with some kinds of people: weak in prosperity, strong in the face of danger." Standing pale from illness and the ordeals of the last months, the emperor looked about the crowds of the poor indigenous people and with compassionate resignation said, "Had I known in Miramar what I know now, I would have come anyway—I would have come for them."[16]

After spending two weeks in Puebla, where he was toasted by Conservative party members and devoted military, Maximilian set out for the capital. The Austrians and Mexicans now served as his anchors. At Río Frío, Gen. Leonardo Márquez joined the growing entourage with 1,000 men. While en route to Mexico City, he met Lt. Col. Van der Smissen and the Belgian corps marching in retreat toward Veracruz, preparing to return to Europe. Despite Van der Smissen's devoted service, Maximilian met him coldly, speaking to him in Spanish, having vowed no longer to converse in French, symbolic of his dismissal of all Europeans who chose to desert the Mexican empire.[17]

Maximilian issued a report to the diplomatic corps condemning the fact that, for political reasons, Napoléon had removed the troops before the date set by the Treaty of Miramar. He alleged that France had entered into negotiations with the Americans to suppress the Mexican empire, but he intended to maintain his country. The circular also included a veiled description of Bazaine's attempts to mislead him. The U.S. consul to Mexico, Marcus Otterbourg, also believed to be in sympathy with Maximilian, knew that Bazaine had been in negotiation with various Liberals, he surmised, intent to arrange a position for himself by taking advantage of the politics of his powerful in-laws. Castelnau had guessed that Marshal Bazaine played games with the ministry so forbade him to attend their meetings because he could not control what he might say. They suspected that the marshal contemplated delaying the evacuation, which would only confuse the situation.[18]

On December 20 Castelnau with Alfonse Dano met with Maximilian at

Puebla and found him gracious and open to discourse on the subject of abdication. Maximilian said that he would call a national congress, seek an armistice, and give the Mexican people a chance to express their choice for a government, as encouraged by Napoléon. He acknowledged he could not keep the crown forever but wanted to renounce it honorably and to benefit the country. Castelnau said he was one year too late. On December 22, at their next meeting, Castelnau again raised the subject, terming abdication a noble action, but Maximilian objected, saying a soldier did not leave his post until relieved of duty. To the discomfort of Castelnau, Maximilian produced a telegram from Bazaine, sent the day before, urging him to keep his crown. "You do not seem accustomed to the methods of the Maréchal," said Maximilian on Bazaine's duplicity. Castelnau returned to Mexico City in frustration, trying to unravel Bazaine's purposes. He launched an investigation and nearly called for the marshal's removal.[19]

In the end, the intrigues of Castelnau and other officers against Bazaine likely resulted from their frustrations that Maximilian would not abdicate. Bazaine's ambitious wife, Pepita, who in Carlota's absence from Mexico became the leading social hostess in the city, likely attempted to persuade the marshal to stay and prolong the empire. Detractors agreed that Bazaine gained more position and influence in Mexico than he would have achieved in France. Pepita visualized a great career for her husband in Mexico, some said. However, more than anyone, Bazaine saw the limitations of his army and the enemies he had cultivated within the ultra-Conservatives. There could be no chance of his survival. Yet if he returned to France with Maximilian in possession of Mexico's crown, his reputation would remain intact. His mission to place a monarch over a restored empire in Mexico would be accomplished. Therefore, it would not have been implausible that Bazaine had encouraged Maximilian to stay.[20]

On January 6, 1867, the Feast of the Epiphany, with church bells ringing and fireworks booming, Maximilian made his official return to Mexico City. The Austrians and Márquez's Mexican corps escorted him through the streets, but the people did not come out to see him as they had done before. Many in his own party seemed terrified. In the explosive climate, Maximilian refused to go back to Chapultepec, with most of his furniture and possessions already packed up and shipped or hidden. Moreover, he refused to be attacked there and see it occupied. Instead, he decided to stay at the Hacienda de la Teja, only a few hundred yards from Chapultepec, owned by Luis Francisco Somera, a Mexican Imperial sympathizer.[21]

Marshal Bazaine, his wife, Pepita, infant son,
and other family, Mexico City, ca. 1866

At the Hacienda de la Teja, Teodosio Lares, president of the Imperial
Council along with the rest of the ministers and generals, filed in to pay their
respects to Maximilian, relieved to find that they would not be left alone to
face the retribution of the advancing Liberal troops. "They were jubilant,
they were too corrupt to understand what a sacrifice their victim was making. They did not think to hide their joy," said one loyal officer. A few staff
members, who had switched sides from the Liberals to support Maximilian,
chose to leave the country to avoid capture and bid Maximilian goodbye at La
Teja. Meanwhile, Lares took more authority as head of the Imperial Council
and used the opportunity to harass Bazaine for leaving their army incomplete
and untrained.[22]

With the exiting of the French, both the Conservative ministers and the military saw their opportunity to take control at last and, sadly, used Maximilian. Lares and the ministers worked to get the imperial finances in order and promised to raise at least 2 million pesos to pay the soldiers. The emperor's account for the imperial house had nearly run dry. He needed money to pay the civil list, councilors, some military, and ministers: Karl Burnouf, his personal assistant and councilor of finance; aide-de-camp Gustav Boleslawski, who managed the library and effects; Oliver Rességuier, his Austrian minister for expansion and planning; and his private account, thought to be for the maintenance of his mistress in Cuernavaca.[23]

Maximilian met with Generals Miramón, Márquez, and Mejía, who reported for duty at the hacienda. They organized the military regiments: the Austrian hussars under Count Karl Khevenhüller; the infantry under Lt. Col. Baron Freiherr von Hammerstein; and the Austrian gendarmerie under Count Edmund Graf Wickenburg. Miramón, Márquez, and Mejía organized their Mexican soldiers into new units and began drilling. Meanwhile, Maximilian, partially kept in isolation by Father Fischer controlling access to him, left the generals to their own methods, and they began to show their rogue tendencies, which at first the emperor did not realize. To raise additional troops, Márquez caused major controversy when he authorized a tax on the citizens and set out to induce 8,000 men into his ranks by using the *leva* or forced conscription in the name of the emperor. When Maximilian received complaints of Márquez's heavy-handedness, he did not take them seriously.[24]

Under this uncertain and gloomy situation, Maximilian summoned Bazaine to the hacienda. The emperor took Bazaine by the arm and led him toward the garden. It was a congenial meeting in which they began with a discussion of Carlota's health. They spoke of Miramón's campaign and Castelnau's mission. Maximilian then asked him what he thought about the future of the monarchy since the Foreign Legion's recall. With this frank question, Bazaine tried to make him understand the futility of staying in Mexico. "From the moment that the United States boldly pronounced their veto against the imperial system, your throne was nothing but a bubble, even if your majesty had obtained the help of 100,000 Frenchmen," said Bazaine. Maximilian replied that he no longer had any illusions, he knew he had been deceived by the Conservatives but would not surrender his authority to any faction, only to the nation, consistent with how he had received it. After their conversation, however, Father Fischer and Maximilian's council controlled who he saw and interrupted all communication with the French officers. Lares wrote a fierce letter accusing Bazaine of collaborating with Juárez and deliberately hindering the pacification of the country, acting against the empire's interests. Because of the severity of the language, Bazaine replied he would have no further communications with Lares or the council. He added, however, he would be at the emperor's service until the final hour of his stay in Mexico. It would be the last time Bazaine saw the emperor. Although Fischer and Lares restricted Bazaine's access to Maximilian, the emperor took one last opportunity to thank and decorate certain officers of the expeditionary force before their departure. Napoléon had cabled Gen. Castelnau on January 10 not to force Maximilian's abdication but to get under steam by March, as planned.[25]

Conservatives buoyed Maximilian's spirits by lavishing him with encouragement, urging him to organize a national congress. He had doubts. At the Hacienda de la Teja, he called together another junta of thirty-three advisors to review again the feasibility of an empire, whether to decide to fight or vacate the country. His ministers of the departments of war and finance submitted a plan complete with dubious financials and estimates of projected income.[26]

On January 12 Austrian minister Baron Lago tried to persuade Lares of the hopelessness of Maximilian remaining in Mexico. He called into question the number of available troops and financial resources. He felt certain that the garrisons of the major cities were not strong enough, and the likelihood of an American intervention seemed assured. He advised damage control and Maximilian's abdication. At the National Palace, Lares issued a long speech to the confidential junta with the ministers and members of the state council and Bazaine, Fischer, and Gen. Márquez in attendance. He used the word "honor" repeatedly. Maximilian did not attend but in a letter pledged his resolve to support the welfare of the country. Bazaine argued against Maximilian's continued rule, stating that it would be no use to recapture territories lost to the Republicans, survival of the empire was impossible, the imperial troops had no chance after the withdrawal of the French, and Maximilian should leave immediately. Certain of the ministers argued against Bazaine, calling him arrogant. Gen. Márquez argued for war, saying the recent losses of Imperialista strongholds were due to rumors of Maximilian's abdication. If he stayed, these could be easily reestablished. Twenty-six, including Father Fischer, voted to continue the fight for the empire, with seven for abdication and the church abstaining.[27]

By January 13, 1867, Tomás Murphy, minister of war, reported that three corps comprised of 29,663 men, 10 artillery batteries, and 6,691 horses were consolidated under the emperor. He informed Maximilian that Juárez relied only on bandits who could easily be overcome. Maximilian was inspired by the outpouring of spirit and support and announced he would command the military directly. Despite developing another fever, he was resolved. Amid the challenges, it did no service to him that he continued to receive conflicting reports on Carlota, some saying she had recovered, others reporting that her condition remained unchanged.[28]

On February 1 Juarista forces were estimated at 34,500 men. Márquez reported that the Imperialistas had lost Zacatecas, Guadalajara, and San Luis Potosí, but Maximilian thought they could be recaptured in due time. The generals felt that the road between Veracruz and Mexico City should be made safe, to secure communications to the coast. They also recommended prohibiting American troops from entering the country upon the departure of the French to prevent further chaos. Mexico City stood practically undefended— only its walls and artillery protected the city, along with a full arsenal. The marshal ordered *chevaux de frise* placed at the embankments adjacent to the gates and had the keys to the citadel and warehouses turned over to the imperial commanders.[29]

Bazaine then issued a statement to the Mexican people in the French newspaper *Ere Nouvelle* and on broadsides posted in the city to announce their final departure and deny any ill intent, saying France never sought to impose a government contrary to their wishes. "All of our efforts were intended to establish internal peace," he wrote. Bazaine, headquartered at the Hotel Iturbide, soon had 26,000 men ready to leave Mexico. He also invited people who wished to leave Mexico to do so under his protection. Many of the Belgians and a good number of the Austrians joined in the French evacuation. Bazaine resolved a few last details, such as provisions for French prisoners, which he worked out with Liberal Gen. Vicente Riva Palacio. He also expected Maximilian's administration to pay an outstanding billeting fee for feeding the troops. When Maximilian refused, the French threatened to take the empire's best bronze cannon as payment.[30]

In the dark, early-morning hours of February 5, Marshal Bazaine led the last columns of French troops out of Mexico City, a little over three years after they had first arrived. Maximilian made no formal adieu or thanks and refused an audience requested by Bazaine. The editor of the *Ere Nouvelle de Mexico* wrote that at ten o'clock in the morning, the French flag ceased to wave over Buenavista, Bazaine's mansion given to him by Maximilian. The house stood bare and empty, Bazaine having sold all the furnishings. An escort carried a very pregnant Pepita Bazaine on a litter, in tears over leaving her mother and family. The columns of soldiers passed through the city with drums beating and standards waving, while the citizens lined the streets, calm and silent.

Some interpreted this as an eloquent and severe expression of their dashed hopes and disappointment with the disaster Bazaine left behind.[31]

As the French military marched out of Mexico City, Maximilian stood in his office in the National Palace looking out from beyond partially closed curtains. With some of his staff members by his side, he peered out the window through the lifted corner of the curtain, so that he could not be seen. "At last, I'm free," he said turning to his secretary of the treasury, Rafael de Mangino and other attendants.[32]

Although the empire felt the vacuum of the French evacuation immediately, Maximilian tried to appear nonchalant. "Faith has been reborn in the future, and the greatest activity and patriotism reign. The [people of the] Capital behaved with a dignified coolness upon the exit of the last troops of our ex-allies, for not even a child paid attention to them, since on this day they celebrate the feast of San Felipe de Jesús . . . no one bothered to go out to see the French retreat in their sad and humiliated position," wrote Maximilian. He appointed Gen. Leonardo Márquez as governor of the capital to keep order and repel the Liberals. Known for his severity, the people called him "Leopardo." When he assumed duty, Márquez issued a public announcement, "You know me, so I don't think I need to tell you anything. . . . I have taken all precautions to ensure your safety, I have sufficient armed forces. . . . I hope that no troubled mind will be mad enough to try disturbing the peace, so that I do not have to enforce the law." He followed this with a city lockdown procedure signaled by alarm bells, and the people knew they must obey, go home, and enclose themselves in their houses.[33]

Maximilian fumed that Archbishop Labastida, after all his boorishness and resistance, left with Bazaine in the evacuation. To his minister Salazar Ilarregui, Maximilian wrote, "Unfortunately, the only person who abdicated his Mexican dignity, forgot his high position, and accompanied the troops, as if their chaplain, was the Archbishop, who fleeing from his house, not only failed to say goodbye to his sovereign and to his friends but did not even advise his vicars, parish, or chancellors." Labastida scribbled a brief note resigning his position, left the city, and abandoned the emperor he worked to bring to Mexico. The bishop of Tulancingo and other clergy accompanied him, fearing the reprisals should the Liberals prevail. Looking only superficially, Maximilian remarked that the people did not seem too upset. "The same afternoon that the French left Mexico, I walked the back streets of the city and found everywhere a tranquil population, happy, and friendly," he wrote.[34]

Simultaneous to the French exit, the emperor received a letter from his mother describing their traditional Christmas in Vienna. In it, Archduchess Sophie confirmed that Franz Josef influenced the assembly's resolution not to accept Maximilian back to Austria, presuming he expected lavish privileges if he returned. She praised Maximilian's attention to duty over personal impulse. "In spite of your natural desire to hasten to Carlota, you have stayed in Mexico, for you have thus avoided the appearance of having been got rid of by intrigue (to which you would in any case never have lent yourself) since it is your great love, sympathy, and gratitude . . . I can only rejoice in it, and hope profoundly that the wealthy people in the country will make your remaining there [in Mexico] possible," she wrote. She added that the Viennese newspapers reported on Campbell and Sherman's visit—but they encountered no great support for Juárez, only hostile Liberal factions. Sophie praised him for his perseverance. "Your poor Carlota wrote me such a pretty, loving, quite rational letter, in which she expressed great joy, as she also seems to have done about the Christmas presents from Papa and me," wrote Sophie. This killed him inside, since he had written to Carlota on December 25, "Christmas without you provokes unspeakable sentimentality."[35]

"I am bound to want you to stay in Mexico as long as this is possible, and can be done with honor," wrote Sophie. "Farewell dear Max, we all embrace you from our hearts and send you best wishes for your happiness in the New Year." All of Maximilian's exaggerations over the last three years about the wonderful conditions of his new empire played against him. His family did not dream of the obstacles and dangers in Mexico, as Carlota's father, Leopold, would have in an instant. But he was gone. Maximilian's brother Karl Ludwig wrote, "You have done quite right to let yourself be persuaded to stay in the country, in spite of the grievous sorrows which have come upon you."[36]

Maximilian could only turn to his work in the dangerous, dusty, and precarious campaign to revive and save the empire. The emperor and his generals evaluated the Juarista forces, the territory held or lost, and devised a military strategy. Maximilian's generals still maintained crucial points outside of Mexico City. Generals Méndez and Mejía held San Luis Potosí and the areas near Querétaro, about 100 miles northwest of Mexico City, and Aguascalientes, 220 miles beyond. Gen. Márquez held Toluca, 60 miles to the southwest.[37]

During the last month Juárez left Chihuahua with a portion of his revitalized army, moving incrementally south to secure a headquarters in Zacatecas in mid-January 1867. At the government palace, he arrived to fanfare, fireworks, and a gala dinner, where the citizens presented him with a lavishly crafted walking cane, some said the counterpart to a royal scepter. Meanwhile, Gen. Mariano Escobedo, who controlled most of northern Mexico, followed Juárez with military coverage. Gen. Ramón Corona was in control at Mazatlán, and more importantly, its lucrative customs house. Gen. Nicolas Regules, with Riva Palacio, held parts of central Mexico. Gen. Porfirio Díaz continued to hold the south and southeast at Oaxaca. The Juaristas crept closer to Mexico City in hopes of surrounding the emperor and the Imperialistas.[38]

Not waiting for Maximilian's approval, Gen. Miramón reacted impulsively to Juárez's move south and launched a surprise attack on Zacatecas, eager to lay siege to the headquarters before the Liberals gained any more momentum. Advancing over the 350 miles north through vigorous forced marches, while adding troops along the way, Miramón led his 4,000-man army to confront Juárez and his army on January 27. At the last minute, the Liberals learned of Miramón's advance. Juárez considered fleeing but determined to stand with the people of the city. He did not want to discourage his supporters by running from a challenge in the Republicans' first attempts to regain control of the country. "In short, my view was that if the city was to be lost, this disaster should not be the result of the retreat of the government, but [for] its cause," Juárez later wrote.[39]

Nevertheless, Miramón's unexpected early-morning attack stunned Juárez and his seasoned military, who had too few men and reinforcements. As Miramón's cavalry penetrated the city, Juárez scrambled to evacuate. The Americans in the Legion of Honor sprang forward to defend and slow Miramón's columns, which gave Juárez a few more minutes. "Then I mounted a horse, and Señores [Sebastián] Lerdo [de Tejada], [José María] Iglesias, and [Manuel E.] Goytía accompanied me," Juárez said. While he first thought of riding north, he learned that the roads were blocked, and set out for Jerez de García, 27 miles southwest. "Miramón with most of his force took it for about three leagues [approximately eight miles], but as often as he tried to destroy our force, he was repulsed, until he was obliged to give up the attempt and return to Zacatecas," wrote Juárez. He later added, "If we had delayed a quarter of an hour more in leaving the palace, we should have given a happy moment to Miramón, but we escaped because the hour had not arrived."[40]

In Zacatecas, a column of Gen. Miguel Miramón's imperial troops, led by his brother Joaquín, ransacked Juárez's quarters. Juárez's housekeeper, Salomé, had hidden his personal effects in a nearby house, but the Imperialistas found and destroyed most of his goods and murdered a young servant boy. They overlooked only his cigar case and the cane the townspeople had presented to him. Miramón's men also destroyed the government palace. Three days later, when Miramón evacuated Zacatecas, Escobedo's Republican forces gave chase.[41]

On February 1 the Juaristas caught up with Miramón's exhausted columns at Hacienda San Jacinto. They killed or captured 3,000 soldiers, including 101 Europeans, mostly French, a war chest of 25,000 pesos, and 22 cannon. One of those captured was Joaquín Miramón. On February 6, when Maximilian learned of the Zacatecas attack, he wrote to Miguel Miramón instructing him that when Juárez and his ministers were captured, courts-martial should try them, but not to act upon the sentences without his approval. The Juaristas intercepted this note and became enraged that their arrests seemed assured and Maximilian would decide their fate.[42]

Juárez considered many of the captured French soldiers vagabonds and filibusters waging unofficial warfare on Mexico, disloyal to their own army, having refused to go back to France. He ordered no mercy on them, hoping to set a bloody example and cause mass defections within the Imperialist ranks. After a hasty series of courts-martial, Gen. Escobedo had all 101 men executed by firing squads. One evening by candlelight, Miramón's brother Joaquín, whose feet had been badly damaged in the attack, was perched onto a chair and shot. The remainder of the Imperialistas under Gen. Miramón struggled to get to the Imperialista-controlled Querétaro.[43]

On the heels of Miramón's defeat, a column of Juaristas attacked Gen. Méndez's garrison at Toluca, thirty-five miles southwest of Mexico City, and his army sustained heavy losses. Things looked even bleaker when Maximilian learned that Gen. Mejía at San Luis Potosí was ailing from typhus. Maximilian finally began to realize so little had been accomplished to stabilize the empire that any hope of its continued existence had begun to dim. He turned on Father Fischer for having been no help in securing the concordat with Rome, merely swilling the imperial wine at dinners. Moreover, the only money the empire could get came through surreptitious sources, the treasury exhausted. Maximilian prevailed on Teodosio Lares and the council for a plan, admitting, "the empire has neither moral nor material strength; men and money flee it, and opinion condemns it on all sides. On the other hand the Republican forces, which have been so unjustly characterized as disorganized, demoralized and motivated only by the desire to pillage, prove by their acts that they are a unified army." He left the future in the hands of the ministers completely and pitifully: "I have made a solemn promise to Mexico never to be the occasion for prolonging the bloodshed. The honor of my name and the immense responsibility that weighs on my conscience, before God and history, require that I no longer put off a great decision that will end so much suffering. Therefore, I hope you will be kind enough to tell me . . . what measure you recommend to resolve the current crisis." It was agreed that they could only salvage their interests and perhaps approach Juárez to ask for a truce and amnesty, hoping for a small chance of success.[44]

Amid the rising violence with no sign of peace imminent, Maximilian's council urged him to leave the capital to spare Mexico City the calamities of war and to go to the heavily reinforced city of Querétaro, where he could count on his supporters. They said that "only the complete extermination of the adversaries can ensure victory." Lares outlined a political and military plan that bordered on fantasy, desperate to continue the imperial fiction, and its hyperbole captured Maximilian's imagination. The scheme appealed to his sense of military leadership, a soldier's life on the battlefield, ending in the possibility of being the Conservatives' political arbitrator with Juárez.[45]

During this time, supposedly at Maximilian's orders but more likely Bazaine's, a representative approached Gen. Porfirio Díaz, who had been obliging in prisoner exchanges, for a peaceful transition in government. Maximilian offered that in return for surrendering Puebla and Mexico City, he would leave the country. "I had to make a real effort to respond seriously that, as general-in-chief of the army corps . . . I can have no relations with the archduke," said Díaz. He later wrote, "Was it for this that I spent part of 1865 in jail?"[46]

Meanwhile, the Austrian commanders, with whom he felt such kinship, promised to convey him safely out of the city, but Maximilian did not view Khevenhüller's or Hammerstein's commands as ready for battle. The Conservative advisors convinced Maximilian that he should take only the most experienced Mexican elite regiments to Querétaro. Gen. Márquez agreed because he felt the Austrians would not obey Mexican commanders. The Conservatives wanted the loyal European troops to spare and protect the capital, despite the Austrians' protests, who had only stayed in Mexico to defend their brother, the emperor. Maximilian ruefully approved the strategy, surmising that if the possibility of truce existed, it may better emerge between the Liberal and Conservative Mexican commanders instead of foreign. He did insist, however, on leaving Gen. Tomás O'Horán Escudero, a former Liberal leader turned Imperialist, as political prefect of Mexico City, since he did not trust Lares would work in the empire's best interest. He also appointed Gen.

Ramón Tavera to command the garrison. He wanted to defend his empire his own way.[47]

On February 12 Maximilian through his minister of justice, Manuel García de Aguirre, wrote a letter to Juárez with a peace proposal. The emperor had not given up hope of finding an honorable way out, desiring to avoid further fighting and bloodshed. His greatest wish was to unite with the former president, recognizing that their two visions for the country remarkably mirrored each other. His plan included calling together a new congress and holding public elections to decide if the country wanted a monarchy or a republic. He also proposed a general amnesty for all political offenses. He asked Juárez to appoint three commissioners to arrive in Mexico City to work with the Conservative party. Juárez never replied. Because they fought for a national cause, he had the upper hand, and he determined to let the generals settle the matter with bayonets and cannon, knowing they had time and manpower on their side. He suspected Maximilian did not have the funds to sustain a long engagement.[48]

On February 13, 1867, as Marshal Bazaine neared Orizaba on his way to Veracruz, he learned of Miramón's savage defeat at Zacatecas. He could see that Maximilian was falling victim now to the Conservatives' agenda, just as his commanders in Paris predicted. Thinking Juárez's severe punishment of the captured Imperialistas may have changed Maximilian's mind about abdication, he dispatched a note to Mexico City, via French minister Alfonse Dano, who was not leaving, to encourage the emperor once more to go with him back to Europe. Bazaine said he would wait one week for him at Orizaba.[49]

But at that moment Maximilian, in his familiar gray topcoat and white hat, astride his steady horse, Anteburro, had left Mexico City for Querétaro. Gen. Leonardo Márquez, Col. Miguel López, and a force of 2,000 cavalrymen of the Empress and Municipal Guards accompanied him, hauling eighteen cannon. The emperor of Mexico had decided to lead his army to the center of the fray.[50]

❦ 19 ❧

War Is War

With faith in his four generals, Tomás Mejía, Miguel Miramón, Leonardo Márquez, and Ramón Méndez, Maximilian believed the Imperialist army could hold a position of strength at Querétaro and quickly prevail. Although he had not built enough troops to replace the retreating French, he assumed that the talent and courage of those that remained would prevail against the Juaristas once the two armies met en masse. His troops possessed quality arms and sufficient munitions, and his ministers had raised additional funds to support the army. Yet notwithstanding his optimism, Maximilian could field only 21,700 soldiers after the losses in Miramón's and Méndez's units. They estimated they would face a Republican army of nearly 60,000 fighters. The Imperialistas felt secure because they still held Mexico City, Puebla, Veracruz, and Querétaro, although most of the country had reverted to Juarista control.[1]

Aside from his ministers' advice to spare Mexico City the ravages of a siege, Maximilian chose to make a stand in Querétaro for a number of reasons. Bazaine had previously designed, equipped, and stocked the town as a frontline bulwark against an army encroaching from the north. Those reinforcements remained in place. Also, by organizing a defense, he could stop Miramón from launching any other spontaneous attacks on the Juaristas. He expected the campaign to last only a few days, which his ministers and generals reassured him as they joined forces. Maximilian and his generals held out hope of negotiating with Juárez, but in a city occupied by the Conservatives. Since Querétaro remained a stronghold of loyal supporters, Maximilian knew he could count on the citizens for essential funds and supplies. The clergy in the city, the monasteries, and the nuns in their ministering convents held Maximilian in high regard. Indeed, Juárez complained, "All the people of Querétaro are hostile to us."[2]

Before his departure from the capital, Maximilian thought carefully about whom he should take with him to Querétaro. José Luis Blasio had returned to Mexico at the first of the year after his assignment with Carlota in Rome and, despite the dangers, offered to assist Maximilian on this expedition. "You shall be my cashier and have charge of my expenses," said Maximilian, cautioning him on the dangers of the mission. That evening, he ordered Blasio to receive funds from Carlos Sánchez Navarro, his grand chamberlain and one of the largest landholders in Mexico. Maximilian had directed Sánchez Navarro to sell quantities of the royal silver, furniture, carriages, horses, and other possessions to his friends to raise cash for the imperial army. "You may get ready to leave day after tomorrow, but say nothing about it," said Maximilian to Blasio.[3]

The emperor allowed only the most essential officers and assistants to accompany him to Querétaro. His cabinet remained in Mexico City, including José María Lacunza, president of the ministry, Tomás Murphy, minister of war, Teodosio Lares, minister of justice, and Santiago Vidaurri, minister of the treasury. His generals offered protection, but Maximilian chose his friend Col. Miguel López to command his personal escort. López had earned the emperor's trust over the previous three years and had been awarded the cross of the Legion of Honor for military service. His personal relationship to Maximilian was so close, the emperor served as godfather to his child. López worked well with the French and Austrians and was a regular guest at their home in Cuernavaca, where he played the Habanera on the guitar or organized tertulias. Maximilian also selected his physician, Samuel Basch, his cook, José Tüdös, and his valet, Antonio Grill, two aides-de-camp, servants, and grooms.[4]

After setting off for Querétaro, the royal escort encountered a band of Juaristas twelve miles northwest of the capital, and the soldiers sprang to action. Maximilian rode to the head of the column with his pistol drawn as the Juaristas fired rounds of rifle fire into the Imperialista lines. "Maximilian was not only serene during the skirmish, but took part in it, and after several hours of fighting, the enemy retreated," wrote Blasio, who remained by the emperor's side during the fusillade. About four miles up the trail, as they approached the village of Cuautitlán, they were upset to see the guerrillas had strung up one of the dead Imperialist soldiers, feet first, and hacked his body with a machete.

When one of the women camp followers discovered a suspected guerilla hiding in a ditch, submerged in water up to his neck, the soldiers pulled him out, interrogated him, and Márquez ordered him to be shot. Maximilian intervened and ordered the prisoner to be incorporated into one of his cavalry regiments.[5]

At dinner at Cuautitlán, a lighthearted Maximilian talked and laughed with the men while reviewing the day's victory. Soon the emperor saw that Gen. Santiago Vidaurri had arrived from Mexico City, escorted by the Austrian hussars. The hussars had gone against Maximilian's orders by serving as Vidaurri's bodyguards in order to join the emperor. The Austrian officers seemed delighted with their cunning rationale, to bring Vidaurri to Querétaro, on whom Maximilian was depending. Known for his unbending independence and control of northern states of Nuevo León and Coahuila, the tall and vigorous Vidaurri sustained his own army and brought these keen fighters along to support the Imperialistas at Querétaro.[6]

The next day before the army resumed the march toward Querétaro, Maximilian reviewed the troops. As he saluted the columns, the emperor was startled to find a newcomer in the ranks whom he had asked to stay in Mexico City. Prince Félix zu Salm-Salm, a Prussian officer, stood at the head of Vidaurri's guard, smiling with his shining buttons and waxed mustache. "Zounds, Salm, how did you come here?" asked Maximilian.

"Your Majesty would not take me with you, as I would not remain idle . . . I requested General Vidaurri to take me with him," said Salm-Salm.

"You know the reasons why I refused your request, [yet] I am very glad to see you," said the emperor. With Austria's recent defeat at the hands of the Prussians in Europe, Maximilian thought it best to reject service from Prussians rather than mix them with Austrian soldiers. When Prince Salm-Salm requested a post in Maximilian's staff, he was refused. Only because Maximilian liked the Prussian minister to Mexico, Baron Anton von Magnus, was Salm-Salm given a chance to serve the empire. His loyalty and energy won Maximilian over.[7]

Salm-Salm had served in the U.S. Civil War and after its termination went to Mexico seeking further adventure, where he joined a Belgian unit under the irascible Col. Alfred van der Smissen. He had brought his plucky wife, Agnes, with him. The twenty-two-year-old daughter of an American general, she was an energetic woman of strong character who would not be left behind. Upon their arrival on the upper plains of Mexico with Van der Smissen, Agnes and her husband were forced to outrun a pursuing Juarista force under Gen. Carvajal. As Agnes galloped with the Belgian forces, her terrier Jimmy balanced on the pommel of her saddle. Agnes complemented her hotheaded husband, who enjoyed combat, dueling, and sword fighting. Saying that he was "just like a cocked pistol always ready to go off," she calmed him down.[8]

While Agnes remained in Mexico City, Félix accompanied Vidaurri to Maximilian's camp at Cuautitlán. Taking to their saddles again for Querétaro, Maximilian invited Salm-Salm to ride with him. In German, Maximilian freely discussed news and information with Salm-Salm in a way he could not with his Mexican generals. Feeling he was surrounded by good company, along the route Maximilian rode with the troops almost jubilantly, riding ahead to speak to commanders or survey the distance, then slowing to return to his column of guards. He gibed his secretary Blasio for not being a better rider, "saying that secretaries were men of the pen and not of the sword," after he traded in his mule for a more spirited horse. After Blasio fell off that mount, Maximilian ordered him back on the mule. "He laughed and said . . . that on this beast it would be possible for him to dictate notes to me, which in fact he did," said Blasio.[9]

The next day Márquez received word of a planned ambush by Juaristas at a place called Arroyo Zarco, about sixty miles from Mexico City. As they advanced, they found the Juaristas lining the hills on one side of the road. When fighting erupted, Maximilian was hustled into a wagon with his staff for protection. At one point in the confusion of the fight, Maximilian left this cover and took refuge near a stand of trees, which soon became the target of Juarista musket fire. Vidaurri encouraged the emperor to take shelter behind a rocky hill. "What do you want me to do, run away the first chance I get?" asked Maximilian. "It is all right for me to expose myself a little," he said, as bullets flew around them.[10]

After the skirmish, the column arrived at San Juan del Río, thirty miles southeast of Querétaro, after a hard march. Here Maximilian issued a proclamation declaring himself the head of the army, reminding them of his determination to fight for the two sacred principles of the empire: independence and peace. He appointed Márquez chief of staff and divided the military into three corps to be commanded by Miramón, Márquez, and the "intrepid General Mejía," who had been forced back to Querétaro from San Luis Potosí because of his health and diminished army. Vidaurri would also help to organize the troops and deploy them once they arrived in Querétaro. "We trust in God, who protects and will protect Mexico, and we shall fight under the sacred invocation: ¡Viva Independencia!" declared Maximilian.[11]

On the morning of February 19, 1867, Maximilian and the army arrived just outside Querétaro at a panoramic place called Cuesta China. They surveyed the city of 40,000 inhabitants, the peaks and valleys cut by the Río Querétaro that made the town particularly problematic, defensible from some vantages but containing certain heights where batteries could be set up and barrages launched. The solidly constructed buildings and houses of stone and plaster crossed rectilinearly, built with roofs well suited for defense. It was, said one observer, a "regular mousetrap," a town almost impossible to reduce to ashes. The commanders could see the convent of La Cruz in the center of the town and beyond it, by about a mile to the west, the rocky and cactus-studded Cerro de las Campanas (Hill of the Bells). On the north side of the city lay a higher elevation called Cerro San Gregorio. From this, another rise called Cerro San Pablo ran north. East of the town rose the Cerro la Cantera, which swept south to the Río Blanco. In the valley, the emperor and troops could see the town's aqueduct and fields of maize, orange trees, and other sources of food supplies to feed their army.[12]

Maximilian determined to set up his headquarters in a building called the Casino in the town center. Before entering Querétaro, the emperor and troops took a moment to tidy their appearance, arranging the little equipment they had, and addressing the condition of their uniforms. Maximilian removed his gray topcoat and white hat and put on his Mexican general's uniform, then tied on the ornamental cordon and medal of the Mexican Eagle. He exchanged Anteburro for the spirited Orispelo, and set out for the southwestern gate of the town. "We descended from the mountain and reached the entrance of the city at 11:30, where we were met by Generals Miramón, age thirty-six, almost exactly Maximilian's age, and the seasoned Mejía, age forty-six," said Blasio. Mejía had just returned to Querétaro after launching attacks to intercept Juarista general Carvajal, who planned to lay siege immediately. Mejía seized a quantity of his artillery, wagon trains, arms, and took prisoners.[13]

The people of Querétaro welcomed Maximilian with excitement, waving from the streets and balconies, which heartened and encouraged the emperor that he had their loyalty. He and his generals rode to the Casino building, where the town prefect and military officers waited to greet them. As Maximilian approached on Orispelo, however, the horse stumbled, considered since the Middle Ages to be a bad omen, but no one seemed to notice except Salm-Salm. From there, the emperor went to the cathedral for a Te Deum and mass, then retired for the night. Later, at a reception at the Casino headquarters, Miramón, looking pale but still bristling after his recent defeats resulting from his attack on Zacatecas, delivered a speech. Afterward at dinner, the

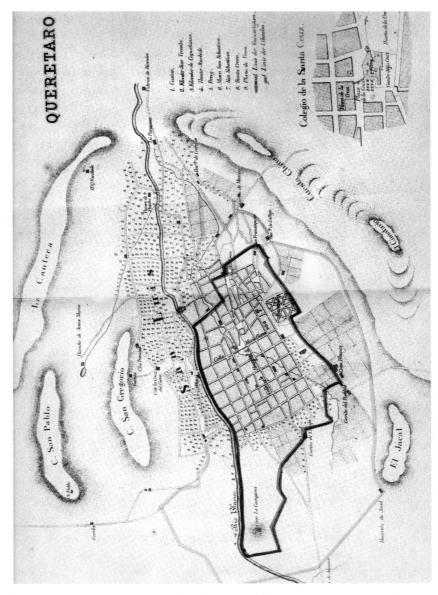

Querétaro, ca. 1865

cunning Márquez toasted Miramón's youthful inexperience, which annoyed Miramón who had a long-standing grudge against him.[14] This was only the beginning of the generals' personality clashes.

Three days later Gen. Ramón Méndez, plump and regal in his red hussar jacket, decorated with the French Legion of Honor and medals, arrived at Querétaro from Michoacán followed by his army comprised of four infantry battalions and two regiments of cavalry. These elite fighters numbering 4,000, some of the best imperial Mexican troops, faithful and hardened, reflected the energy of their commander. Méndez was not afraid to act swiftly and severely. His well-equipped units, including two munitions batteries, brought the imperial army to 9,000 soldiers with thirty-nine pieces of artillery. As the soldiers began organizing, Maximilian inspected his army, distributed medals, and said a few inspiring words about the battle that lay ahead. He seemed optimistic, and at a splendid dinner that night he presided with a positive look of conviction.[15]

At Querétaro, Maximilian appointed a regency council of Teodosio Lares, José María Lacunza, and Leonardo Márquez to replace him if he was killed in battle. With power as regents, they could summon a national congress to reconstitute the government.[16]

Over the next few days, Maximilian gave each general his own particular and autonomous assignment: Márquez served as head of staff; Miramón commanded the infantry; Mejía, the cavalry; and Méndez, the reserves. Col. López would serve as the lead subordinate officer. On February 24 the emperor convened a council of war to finalize strategies and contingencies. Miramón, known to prefer surprise sorties, thought a rapid, vigorous attack would be best. Márquez believed this was too reckless and would leave Querétaro defended by inexperienced troops, while others said the Juaristas should be allowed to concentrate before the assault.[17]

The days passed quietly over the first weeks. Maximilian rose at five, dictated letters, reviewed documents, and frequently surveyed the city on foot. "Maximilian, in civilian clothes, would stop to watch passing soldiers, mingle with the people or, as he was always smoking, ask a light from a passerby or offer one to some gentleman. Other days he would ride in Charro costume or in a plain blue uniform," Blasio wrote. After breakfast, he met with his generals and others for the rest of the day. At dinner, there were always guests. After a round of billiards, *boliche*, or whist, he retired at nine. During this quiet period, plays in the theater were adapted for the officers, which Salm-Salm assessed as "pretty bad," but the taverns were full.[18]

As the Imperialist troops waited, Maximilian sought solutions to their growing financial predicament. Of the 50,000 pesos Maximilian started out with in cash specie from Mexico City, he quickly dispensed 40,000 to pay troops. When additional funds did not arrive from Mexico City, the emperor declared a forced loan on the merchants of Querétaro.[19]

On February 21 Juárez and his aides arrived to make a headquarters at San Luis Potosí, 100 miles north of Querétaro. Almost immediately, he began to send instructions to Gen. Mariano Escobedo in the field as he advanced on Querétaro with 16,000 troops. Generals Corona and Regules with another 10,000 Liberals approached from the west. From scouting reports, Miramón learned of the Juarista movements and, eager to seize the moment along with the limelight, wanted to ride out to confront their columns before the two armies united. Márquez disagreed, however, saying they needed to consolidate their own troops, lay in wait, then "annihilate the enemy at a single blow."[20]

At the port of Veracruz, in the first few days of March, Bazaine's final units of French troops prepared to depart on the last transports to France. Civilian refugees, fearing the consequences if the empire fell, crowded into the port seeking passage to Europe, creating chaos. Cases of yellow fever soared. The saloons filled with thirsty soldiers seeking whiskey. Col. Du Pin raided the customs house. Guerrillas set fire to the bridge leading to the port. In his haste, Bazaine "had whole loads of powder thrown into the water, gun carriages shattered, and cannons blown up. Grenades were buried in the earth to keep them hidden. . . . Nearly all the war materiel on hand . . . was destroyed," said one observer. "The marshal of France did not hesitate to commit acts of crudest irresponsibility and dirtiest avarice." Many Imperialistas condemned these acts, feeling the munitions should have been left, since they had been purchased with the Mexican debt and would be needed to defend the empire. But Bazaine feared that the huge stores of imperial arms and artillery would fall into the hands of the Liberals or be used by fanatical Conservatives against the French who remained in Mexico. Yet others believed that Bazaine meant them to be found by the Liberals. General panic prevailed.[21]

A number of French officers waiting to leave blamed Bazaine for the failure of the Mexican expedition. After all the suffering, the casualties, and five years' worth of blood and hard-won victories, nothing remained. Morale was at its lowest and the men grumbled endlessly, leading Bazaine to convene a meeting at which he produced Napoléon's orders, arguing that he was not at fault. He had heard nothing from Maximilian. After finally agreeing to leave 50,000 pounds of powder, a quantity of arms, and 35,000 rounds of ammunition for the imperial authorities in Veracruz, Bazaine was the last man to board the *Souvereign* and set sail for France on March 16 with Admiral Cloué at the helm.[22]

In Querétaro, on March 6, the two Liberal armies converged on the outskirts of the city, and the first columns stationed themselves around its perimeter. The Liberal troops arrived in various conditions of readiness, some with uniforms and bayonets, while others were dressed only in white linen pants and shirts, shod in sandals, and bearing old muskets. There were not enough guns for all, and there were no reserves. Some camps had scant supplies and a small cache of ammunition. Therefore, the Imperialistas, although outnumbered, felt they had a good chance of defense by breaking through their lines.[23]

Maximilian, ready to go on the offensive, agreed that they should wait, in order to retain secure, defensible positions. However, he decided to do some reconnaissance of his own and make a statement. At four o'clock the next morning, the emperor and his staff galloped out of the city to the foot of the Cerro de las Campanas. Dawn began to break and fog stood thickly on the hillsides as they rode up to the heights. The rising sun caused the haze to dissipate, and the emperor and his staff could see their own troops in the town. Beyond them, toward the horizon, Blasio said they could see "another extensive line of soldiers, whose bayonets gleamed in the rising sun. These were the Republican troops. Behind the emperor, we galloped along our entire line to the sound of bugles and enthusiastic cries of *¡Viva el Emperador!*" The Imperialistas' spirits soared. Miramón again wanted to ride out to meet the Liberal lines, but Maximilian and the other generals held him back.[24]

The emperor moved his headquarters to a campsite on the Cerro de las Campanas. He slept on his camp bed near the fire, while his generals rested on blankets nearby. Early the next morning, the Imperialist troops began to dig trenches and construct thick embankments built of earth and large bricks. Maximilian studied the dangers and possible places to breach the walls. Residents from the town guided by Maximilian helped push cannon into place. When Blasio arrived with paperwork and correspondence, Maximilian said, "Come to my office." He led Blasio over the scree, down the north side of the hill along a narrow path. "What do you think of this office?" asked Maximilian, motioning to a recess in the rock hidden by bushes and scrub. They entered, and Blasio could see it was a shelter with a natural stone bench covered with turf. "Don't you think we can work here, without being bothered? I, Dr. Basch and Severo [his servant] are the only ones who know about this place, which I found yesterday."[25]

Blasio went over the paperwork with Maximilian, while keeping watch over the Juaristas in the distance. At midmorning the servant Severo entered the den with a breakfast of cold turkey and beef, eggs, cheese, bread and a bottle of wine. He spread a tablecloth over the grassy bench. "Our breakfast isn't very abundant or fine, but war is war. The open air will sharpen our appetites and make up for the quantity and quality of the food," said Maximilian. After a brief nap on a plaid blanket, he resumed dictating letters, smoked his cigar, and watched the enemy camps assemble. As he readied for the large-scale combat, he felt his moral fortitude and courage rising. He could make up for his missed opportunities in Europe to prove to his brother and to the world he was a warrior, unafraid and, above all, dedicated to his people.[26]

During the second week of March 1867, small groups of Imperialista cavalry frequently rode out of Querétaro's walls to challenge and insult the Liberals. In these forays, each side sniped at one another, and men were lost from both armies. Some sorties were particularly damaging to the Liberals. During one sally, an Imperialist colonel and his men brought back two hundred steers appropriated from the Liberals. The Juaristas in turn succeeded in capturing a few Imperialist messengers, however, and hung them upside down from a tree and smashed their skulls. On March 11 Miramón conducted another raid, bringing in more cattle, one hundred goats, and a good supply of corn. Unfortunately, the same day the Liberals destroyed part of the aqueduct, which Salm-Salm called a "magnificent monument" from the time of the Spanish conquest that supplied the town with water. "We could see the cascade formed by the escaping water which fell from the damaged arches and flooded the plains," said Blasio. Fortunately, the river, and plenty of wells and cisterns within the city, remained to provide water.[27]

When the commanding officer of Maximilian's elite fighting Cazadores was wounded, they were left without a commander. Therefore, Maximilian offered the command to Salm-Salm, who eagerly accepted the position of colonel. "The Cazadores consisted of nearly 700 men, of whom the greater part were French; but there were also Germans, Hungarians, and about 150 Mexicans. It was a wild corps of the bravest soldiers that could be found," Salm-Salm wrote about his new detachment, which were placed within the lines of Gen. Severo del Castillo's troops and given four twelve-pounder cannon.[28]

The Imperialist generals continued to watch and bicker over strategies, while waiting for the Liberals to attack. Maximilian remained at his camp on the Cerro de las Campanas, watching the Juaristas by day and the flickering light of their campfires by night. Mejía and Miramón finally hauled some tents to the camp and set them up for the emperor and staff. Blasio, who moved to the *cerro* as well, since Maximilian thought he might need him on short notice, complained of a rampant flea infestation. On March 13, after observing the Liberals reorganizing into battle positions, Maximilian and the generals decided that the convent of La Cruz would become their fortified citadel. Established on the east side of the town in the sixteenth century, it was constructed of solid stone. Cannon shot bounced off the walls and roof. The emperor and generals moved into the building as the Liberals prepared to attack.[29]

Maximilian chose for his quarters one of the cells in the cloister that opened onto a corridor. In the two-chambered room, the emperor placed his camp bed, a washstand, and clothes rack on one side, and used the other as his office. Nearby, Blasio set up a makeshift quarters where he stored tins of preserves, provisions, and wines for the emperor's table as well as the royal decorations, crosses, and medals. Also flanking Maximilian's room lodged Dr. Basch, Salm-Salm, military aides, and servants. Through the night, the emperor could hear the call of "*¡Alerta!*" from the sentinels when they detected suspicious movements. He and his men got little rest.[30]

Early the next day, on March 14 at 5:30 in the morning, Escobedo's artillery units began shelling Querétaro. As mortars from three sides exploded overhead, shrapnel rained down on the convent. Maximilian and his generals sprang into action under a hail of grenades. The emperor mounted his horse and rode to the front lines, as the men shouted *vivas*. The Liberals trained their artillery fire on Maximilian, but their aim was poor. Salm-Salm deployed the Cazadores and was amazed at their skill. "The wild fellows were always fighting among themselves . . . but as soon as they were led against the enemy, they were like one man, and everyone tried to outdo his comrades in daring deeds. Even the very buglers, boys between fourteen and sixteen, stole sometimes outside the lines, armed with a gun and box full of cartridges, to hunt the 'Chinacos' (Liberals) on their own hook," he wrote.[31]

Maximilian interrogated a number of captured prisoners, one of whom was an American soldier. "Why do you fight against us?" Gen. Méndez pulled the hat off the young man, who had not removed it out of respect for the emperor. "Because I am a Republican," said the prisoner. "If you really are a Republican, you should never side with Juárez, but Ortega," said Maximilian, smiling at the prisoner. He dismissed him.[32]

In all, the Cazadores killed three hundred men and captured a valuable Parrott gun, a fine cannon manufactured in the United States. As they hauled the gun to the convent of La Cruz, Salm-Salm ran into a correspondent for the *New York Herald*. The man, H. C. Clark, had been ordered out of Querétaro by Márquez, who suspected he was an American working with the Liberals. When he saw Salm-Salm, Clark nearly pulled the colonel off his horse trying to get his attention. While asking him to intercede, he said that he was English, and wanted to remain to report on the siege. Maximilian agreed to allow Clark to stay, providing he had no communication with the Liberals and reported truthfully. Under these conditions, Clark sent reports out of the city. Later, he was nearly killed by a cannon ball that came through the window of his lodgings.[33]

By three that afternoon, the intensity of the fighting began to slow as Escobedo's exhausted army fell back, but the bombardment of the convent continued until nine o'clock in the evening. Despite their full vigor, the Liberals lost thousands of dead and wounded and much of their munitions. They suffered 750 captured, and yet only succeeded in taking the hill of San Gregorio. Not only did they suffer from a lack of ammunition, they needed reinforcement, slowing their attack temporarily.[34]

As the Imperialist battalions returned to camp, many of the men felt great joy after a successful day's battle. Salm-Salm recalled that when a Capuchin friar approached a group of his men at rest, he had "the image of the Holy Virgin hanging by a rope around his neck. The Mexicans amongst my troops, whose hands were not cleansed yet from the blood they had spilt, rushed up to the priest with exultation, crossing themselves, and devoutly kissed the image."[35]

The next day, March 15, Maximilian called several of his officers and men into formation in the patio of the convent, around the captured Parrott gun. Thanking them he said, "You have all behaved so bravely that I cannot make any distinction. We therefore resolved to decorate the whole battalion." Then he proceeded to hand out the Cross of the Mexican Eagle. To the Cazadores who had captured the cannon, he awarded the gold and silver medal for bravery and gave them a twenty-peso gold piece embossed with his image. One of Salm-Salm's more ferocious killers became emotional when given a gold medal, and was "so beside himself with pleasure that he gave me, before the whole front, the Mexican *abraço*, beating with his hand my back and shedding torrents of tears," said Salm-Salm. As Maximilian spoke of coming attacks and preparations, the Liberals on the Cuesta China, southeast of town, began a new artillery barrage. Maximilian remained at his place, unfazed, as the shells began to drop and continued to ask for staff reports from the generals. Over the many weeks of the siege, people remarked that while under active bombardment, Maximilian often displayed a nonchalant attitude by strolling into the courtyard or the street, or asking for a light for his cigar, much to their fascination. He often rode outside the lines with great composure. However, when the soldiers began shouting "¡Viva el Emperador!" the Republicans used the cheering to take aim at the emperor, launching projectiles in rapid succession. The generals then began prohibiting the *vivas*.[36]

However, his army also began suffering shortages of food. The emperor learned that Porfirio Díaz recently set out north from Oaxaca targeting the city of Puebla and its garrison of 2,500 men, then under the command of Imperialist Gen. Manuel Noriega. If Puebla fell to Díaz, there would be little chance of receiving any supplies. No communications from Veracruz would go through, and they would be cut off from funds from the customs house. The sudden confluence of all these factors called for immediate and vigorous measures by the generals at Querétaro.[37]

This gave Gen. Leonardo Márquez, who had grown increasingly unhappy serving as chief of staff and bickered constantly with Miramón, an idea to leave. Because they had heard nothing from Mexico City, the telegraph lines having been cut, Márquez told Maximilian that his ministers and aides in Mexico City were too frightened to send support to him in the field. He offered to ride through the lines and get needed funds, reinforcements, and supplies from Mexico City and return. Having convinced the other generals of his sincerity and abilities, they devised a plan to get Márquez out of the city walls. Maximilian excluded himself from this planning session to allow the generals freedom to make their own decisions, squarely handing his fate to them. It was decided that Márquez would gather additional troops, provisions, and 1,000 horses at Mexico City and reenter Querétaro through an attack on the Liberal lines. The plan was kept secret, known only to the emperor and close advisors.[38]

The scheming and ambitious Márquez asked the emperor about what to do when he arrived with little authority in Mexico City, although he held the important title of regent. Maximilian conferred the title of "Lieutenant of the Empire" on Márquez with unrestricted authority and orders to dismiss all ineffectual ministers, the "old women" he termed them, who failed to support the army, and to replace them. Meanwhile, Maximilian sent word to Mexico City asking for additional money. He had expected proceeds from the sale of his private property, much of it in the hands of Augustin Fischer and palace official Karl Schaffer, and was disappointed that Sánchez Navarro's men had not arrived with those funds.[39]

Maximilian again ordered a turnover in his advisory council. He wrote letters of instruction for Márquez to deliver to Schaffer, Fischer, Sánchez Navarro, and Eloin, who by then had returned to Mexico. He ordered them to dissolve the ministry, relieving Lares, and that Santiago Vidaurri was appointed minister president, in view that the situation had become purely military. Others appointed included Tomás Murphy, minister of foreign affairs; José María Iribarren, minister of government and ecclesiastical affairs; Gen. Nicolás de la Portilla, minister of war; and Carlos Sanchez Navarro, minister of the imperial household. He asked them to aid Márquez in protecting Mexico City and the government archives and send funds, ordering his unsold private property to be placed with the English or Austrian diplomatic corps for shipment, in case Mexico City fell. Assuming Márquez would bring the bulk of the Imperialista soldiers with him back to Querétaro, Maximilian warned Eloin that Mexico City would not be safe after the army's departure. He advised Eloin to come to Querétaro, "to join us, where you will be at complete liberty to share the dangers of the arduous war that we have undertaken and that we hope leads to a good outcome," or he could return to Europe, closing, "I have not forgotten you." He also demanded that Günner, Fischer, and Schaffer come to Querétaro, telling Fischer specifically to bring him a letter copybook containing orders, a better telescope, a better map, all remaining medals and decorations from the strongbox in his private quarters, some good books, and Bordeaux wine.[40]

Early on the morning of March 22 Márquez rode out of Querétaro, promising to return in two weeks. "God be with you," Maximilian told him, promising they would remain in good spirits while they awaited his return. Maximilian rode to the Cerro de las Campanas to watch as Márquez approached the Liberal lines. To distract the Juaristas and allow Márquez and his 1,000-man cavalry to escape Querétaro, Gen. Miramón and 2,000 soldiers launched an attack on the other side of the town. In his surprise sortie, Miramón forced the Liberals out of their camps. The column of fleeing Juaristas left behind a good number of arms and provisions. Miramón returned with twenty carts full of arms, ammunition, and supplies, along with sixty head of cattle and hundreds of goats and sheep.[41]

They all hoped for Márquez's speedy return with much needed reinforcements.

❦[20]❧

The Enemy Is Here

Márquez and his cavalry arrived in Mexico City five days later. Almost as soon as he entered its walls, he made his authority known. With oppressive bearing, Márquez began to raise troops using the *leva*, or mandatory conscription, and forced loans as high as 10,000 pesos from merchants and foreign citizens. When they refused to pay, they were arrested. Soldiers sent into their homes to await payment refused to let the residents eat or drink, a mother was forbidden to breastfeed her child, a Spaniard was tied to a bench. Agnes Salm-Salm, waiting at Mexico City, who was anxious for news about her husband, visited Márquez and wisely deduced what was happening. Márquez took martial control and "behaved and spoke as if the emperor was only his pupil and he himself the most important person in all Mexico," Agnes wrote.[1]

In Querétaro, the generals worried aloud about Márquez's motives for leaving, while also insisting to Maximilian that he placed too much trust in Father Fischer, a dishonest man who was known to travel with women and had fathered a number of children. But Maximilian waived off these revelations, saying that he found Fischer amusing and all would be well. But his advisors knew Fischer would not to come to his aid on the battleground.[2]

Meanwhile, outside the walls of Querétaro, furious at the escape of Márquez, Escobedo redoubled artillery barrages sending skyward as many as four hundred projectiles an hour. Most of them flew over their heads and lodged in the sandy terrain. Blasio watched the shells fall, saying, the "next day we had plenty of them, for we paid boys twenty-five centavos a piece for every shell they salvaged which could be used."[3]

On March 24, from a position near the city gates, the Liberals once again opened heavy artillery fire on the city. Mejía hesitated to move his men against the Juaristas, but seeing that Miramón set his column in motion, he charged, crying, "This is the way a man dies." In short order his men drove the Juaristas back and captured 400 prisoners, including a good number of officers. They also seized a campaign flag. But over the next few days the Liberals ceaselessly pounded the Imperialistas.[4]

News of the conflagration at Querétaro reached Europe and the United States. Emperor Franz Josef demanded news from Ferdinand Wydenbruck, his minister in Washington. "The Emperor of Austria, my gracious sovereign, has been informed that his brother is surrounded in Querétaro by the Liberals. The fate of the prisoners after the battle of Zacatecas makes the emperor anxious for his brother's safety, should he fall into the hands of the Liberals," Wydenbruck wrote American secretary of state Seward. He asked Seward to use his influence with Juárez to intervene on behalf of Maximilian. Anticipating Maximilian's defeat and probable incarceration, Wydenbruck added, the American government "seems to have a right to demand from Juárez to respect prisoners of war, as it is in great measure to the moral support of the American government that the Liberal party in Mexico owes its present successes."[5]

In early April, learning that the Imperialistas struggled to hold Querétaro and mindful of the severity with which Juárez treated the captives from the Zacatecas attack, Seward ordered Lewis D. Campbell, the American minister to Mexico, at the time in New Orleans, to go to Mexico and communicate to Juárez. "You will communicate to President Juárez . . . the desires of this government, that, in case of his capture, the Prince and his supporters may receive the humane treatment accorded by civilized nations to prisoners of war," wrote Seward. However, Campbell did not want to venture into a field of battle and delayed the trip indefinitely.[6]

However, even Juárez's representative, Matías Romero, had expressed concern about the potential of a wholesale slaughter of all who participated in the empire. Campbell sent Seward's sentiments and wrote a few anemic letters from New Orleans to Juárez and Sebastián Lerdo de Tejada that the United States sympathized with the restoration of Mexico, but outright executions of prisoners of war would be a stain on all republics. He sent these by way of an

American sergeant, instead of an official high-ranking envoy. Campbell had no intention of going to Mexico, and when Seward pressed him, he turned in his resignation, pleading illness.[7]

Juárez's staff, their patriotic sensibilities wounded by heavy-handed advice from the United States, replied to Seward, "The constant practice of the Government of the Republic has always been to respect the life, and treat with the greatest consideration the prisoners taken of the French forces, while, by the greater part of them, and even by the order of the chiefs, prisoners which they took from the republican forces were frequently assassinated." They planned to consider only "what the principles of justice demand."[8]

At the end of April, Bazaine and his military units arrived in France, but no official ceremony greeted him nor any of the pageantry normally associated with the return of a prestigious marshal. Napoléon issued a low-key announcement to accompany the French army's return but little else. He and his subjects prepared to forget the entire Mexican affair. As Bazaine became an easy scapegoat for Napoléon to offset pressure on himself and Eugénie, he stood by obediently and patiently, settling his wife, Pepita, and baby into Parisian life, awaiting the arrival of a second child. Many felt convinced he had done a disservice to Maximilian by leaving him without support and thereby damaging France's image. Gen. Douay wrote, "The Mexican affair will be a veritable catastrophe. The government will do well to leave it, if possible in the shadows and in silence. Marshal Bazaine may escape . . . the punishment which he deserves for his culpable intrigues, but he will not escape the infamy to which he is vowed by all decent people."[9]

In Mexico, throughout the siege of Querétaro, Juárez communicated with Escobedo at least three times a week. Juárez gave much thought to the fate of prisoners, instructing both Escobedo and Díaz not to shoot the ordinary solders, "but this should not apply to the leading figures and commanding officers." They would be subject to the law of January 25, 1862, requiring all armed opponents of the Republican government to be executed. He hardened his position toward Maximilian, whom he termed "a wretched, rash, intruding fool" who had the opportunity to leave with the French but decided to stay and spur further civil war. Those commanders responsible for the bloodletting, therefore, could not upon capture "be considered mere prisoners of war, since such responsibilities are defined by the law of nations and the laws of the Republic," wrote Juárez. It is evident that Juárez intended to ignore growing international pressure to release Maximilian and began to construct the legal framework to convict him and his generals, even before the cannon fire quieted in Querétaro.[10]

In the midst of battle Maximilian began walking for exercise in the afternoons, saying he needed to keep up his health. Around the convent of La Cruz, a number of sidewalks crisscrossed the Alameda, and the emperor walked vigorously there and back. Often he dictated new orders and sometimes trivial details to Blasio, including his plan for a new court ceremonial, a protocol guide for the imperial court. Blasio had little doubt that the enemy could see him from their field glasses and were drawing a bead on his route, because as soon as he began his daily walk, artillery fire would resume. Whooshing mortars and cannonballs flew well over Maximilian's head, slamming into the walls of nearby buildings, already riddled with holes from previous shelling, followed by the cracking of shrapnel. Even though the generals pleaded with him not to take his diurnal walk, they could not control him—instead of trying to support his health, it seemed like he wished to give the Liberals a perfect opportunity to kill him. Salm-Salm sensed Maximilian's darkening mood and became convinced he wanted to advance his own death to put an end to the siege. When Gen. Miramón pointed out the unnecessary risk he presented to the public as well as the virtue of dying on the battlefield versus performing calisthenics, Maximilian stopped the daily ritual.[11]

Within the city walls, the more pressing need was for food, namely meat and corn. The situation was so bad that soldiers turned to killing their horses and mules. Sometimes, the most unexpected sources turned up as victuals. "One day while we were at dinner an orderly came from Miramón, bringing a fine [meat] pie. It was delicious, and we were enjoying it, when the general appeared and asked us how we liked it. We all answered that it was excellent and he remarked, 'When you want another one, there are still plenty of cats at my place, so you will never lack pies such as the one you are eating,'" Blasio wrote. Maximilian, in on the joke, knew what had happened and laughed, not having eaten the meat, only the crust.[12]

To boost morale, on March 30 Maximilian again decided to award those who defended and won a fair number of confrontations. Under a canopy strung across the plaza of La Cruz decorated with pennants and flowers, with the martial band playing patriotic tunes and a cannon salute, Maximilian briefly spoke and bestowed these medals with more solemnity than any others before. During the ceremony Gen. Miramón stepped forward from the line and approached Maximilian with a copper decoration usually given to privates for bravery, saying that the emperor deserved the medal more than any soldier. The men admired his willingness to fight beside them, Miramón said, and that he had exposed himself every day in the most intense battles. The emperor, despite his many other decorations, had never worn a medal for bravery and was greatly humbled by the honor. Miramón affixed the medal to his lapel and the two embraced. The assembled officers and troops applauded and cheered wildly. "The Emperor wore the medal constantly," said Blasio.[13]

The next day, March 31, the Republicans surrounding the town celebrated Benito Juárez's recent birthday with intensified bombardment of Querétaro. During the blitz, Maximilian's topographer, Johann Fürstenwärther, presented Maximilian with fresh maps of the area with a plan to regain territory. Miramón looked at the map and gave some vague advice, which Maximilian thought too simplistic, but said little. Later, when the cartographer asked if Miramón could read map markings and elevations, Maximilian smiled and said, "this is not one of the strong suits of my generals." The next day, Maximilian sent Miramón to take back the Cerro de San Gregorio, seized some weeks earlier. Miramón led his men forward but was thrown back and routed with heavy losses. After the battle the Liberals ruthlessly shot Miramón's wounded men, not allowing their army to collect them for treatment. They then sent the bodies floating down the river, which contaminated the city's most important source of water and demoralized the troops as they saw the bloated and mutilated bodies of their comrades in the water.[14]

Meanwhile, in Mexico City, Gen. Leonardo Márquez learned that Gen. Díaz prepared to attack Puebla, occupied by the Imperialistas under Gen. Noriega. Knowing Puebla's strategic importance, Márquez reasoned that he could go with the Austrian hussars and his cavalry to Puebla, intercept Díaz's columns and defeat them, instead of returning immediately to Querétaro, as promised. Any resulting captives, he thought, he then could use as reinforcements, planning then to return with them to Querétaro. In violation of Maximilian's orders, Márquez started for Puebla with his cavalry and new recruits.[15]

Learning that Márquez had left Mexico City to intercept him, on April 2 Díaz expedited his mission and hastily laid siege to Puebla. His army quickly captured the city's forts and broke through Noriega's imperial defenses. Noriega, thinking all was hopeless and not knowing that Márquez was on his way, surrendered Puebla on April 4. After allowing the soldiers to join his ranks, Díaz ordered the execution of Noriega and his seventy-four officers, saying that even though they had not lived like men, they could die like men.

After the hard-fought battles over Puebla in 1862 and 1863, Díaz's quick victory appeared extraordinary but solely attributable to Noriega's hasty surrender. Díaz could not resist bragging, however, that he had captured Puebla in one day, which the "best soldiers in the world," the French, could not do without a prolonged fight.[16]

After taking Puebla, Díaz pursued Márquez and his army back to Mexico City, and near there on April 8, the two armies clashed. Many of Márquez's Mexican troops panicked and deserted or joined Díaz's army. Márquez lost most of his guns. The artillerymen cut their horses from their harnesses, mounted them, and fled. The Austrian regiment of four hundred hussars, led by Col. Kodolitsch, remained to fight and successfully brought the remaining Mexican troops back to Mexico City. Kodolitsch's swift and bold action was lauded, but it was a futile act of bravery.[17]

Falling back, Márquez then prepared to defend Mexico City with his remaining imperial Mexican troops and Austrian detachments. Within days, Díaz's army was reinforced by Republican soldiers across Mexico with artillery from Puebla. Díaz equipped canoes with little mountain guns and formed mobile defense lines across the lakes surrounding Mexico City. The Imperialistas attempted to cut through the formations, but Díaz drove them back into the city walls. When Díaz ordered the storming of Chapultepec, the Legion of Honor with their accurate Henry repeating rifles assisted in picking off imperial artillerymen at the defenses of the castle. After his victory, Díaz set up headquarters at Chapultepec while his men sought to loot the palace, a scene that Maximilian had dreaded. Under orders from Díaz, much of the alcazar's possessions were left intact. Soon after his occupation of Mexico City, Father Fischer, tasked to defend Chapultepec, attempted to negotiate with Díaz for Maximilian's release. Díaz replied, "You plead for the life of Maximilian, but who is there to plead for your life?" Defeated, Fischer said his life did not matter.[18]

Márquez, with the aid of the Austrian troops, remained in Mexico City for the next seventy days. Life ground to a halt. The people became prisoners in Mexico City, as Díaz and his 28,000 troops held them under siege, refusing to attack. Márquez sequestered men who came in from Querétaro so that the Austrian troops would not hear any bad news about Maximilian, for if the emperor surrendered, the European troops would lay down their arms. Márquez lied that Maximilian was returning to Mexico City to save them, but outside observers knew he could not sustain the standoff much longer. Food shortages caused misery and panic as vendors would not cross Díaz's lines.[19]

Otilia Jordan de Degollado, Carlota's former riding companion, engaged a group of expatriate American soldiers to go with her to Querétaro with the assistance of Gen. Tomás O'Horán. She planned to use unemployed former soldiers to seize Maximilian and take him to Tampico to sail for Europe. When she asked Father Fischer to send a secret message through the lines to Maximilian, however, the plot was discovered, and Díaz imprisoned the American soldiers. Fortunately, Degollado was spared incarceration, although she was warned by her co-conspirators, "your sex would not have prevented your arrest. The Liberals have been arresting women upon the slightest pretexts."[20]

With the evacuation of the French and the resulting fight to hold the empire, all business throughout central Mexico halted for months. The railroads did not run, commerce stalled, and people were paralyzed. "All other business is pretty much annihilated owing to the condition in which the French intervention has placed the whole country, everything is dull and gloomy but there will be a favourable change soon," said mining engineer John C. C. Hill, looking forward to the return of Juárez.[21]

In Querétaro, Maximilian, his generals, staff, and 7,000 soldiers waited for Márquez. He was supposed to return by April 5, but the day came and went with no news. From that day forward the Imperialistas constantly scanned the landscape to spot his return. Messages arrived every day for the Imperialistas via priests, who passed the Liberal lines without a search, or native messengers who carried notes in their cigarettes, so word could have reached them. Stories circulated that the general had been captured, but Maximilian sensed something more sinister. And yet every time he mentioned his suspicions, he stopped himself and said, "No, no, it is impossible." The generals argued about going out to find Márquez. Maximilian considered sending Mejía or Salm-Salm, but he needed them to defend the city.[22]

Miramón and Méndez insisted someone must go to Mexico City. On April 11 Miramón with the Chasseurs and Méndez's second battalion tried to breach enemy lines and get control of the main road. Against a withering firestorm of bullets causing heavily casualties, they fought furiously for an hour before turning back. During the bitter fight, Lt. Ernst Pitner, who replaced Salm-Salm as commander of the Cazadores, was hit in the head by a musket ball. He fell right before Salm-Salm, who wrote that Pitner's blood spattered his boots, "but though stunned for a time, he was not fatally wounded." Maximilian continued to send couriers with notes to Márquez, but the messengers were seized, killed, and strung up on a pole with a sign pinned to their chests reading "The Emperor's Messenger." Salm-Salm grew so angry and frustrated that he gathered a column of his cavalry and tried to run the gauntlet through the lines. At every point he was repulsed. The terrain was so full of trenches and the defense so strong, he abandoned his efforts after two hours, taking the wounded with him.[23]

The Imperialistas became more resourceful as food, provisions, and munitions ran dangerously low. The nuns baked Maximilian a loaf of wheat bread every morning, using flour that remained to make consecration hosts for mass. He shared this daily gift with his staff members. Having run out of beef, mutton, and goat, the men began to rely almost solely on mule and horse meat, beans, and tortillas. For munitions, Gen. Manuel Ramírez de Arellano fashioned a powder works and crucible in the convent of Carmen. Here they made paper cartridges. From lead taken off the roof of the theater, they cast cannonballs and molded bullets.[24]

Day after day Maximilian visited the men in the trenches, asking them if they were well, and more importantly, knowing their commanding officers at times stole their pay, asked if they received their salary. "This care had a very good effect, and was so new and flattering to the soldiers, that they loved the emperor for it, especially as he shared with them all dangers and privations," said Col. Salm-Salm. The colonel, on duty one night in a foxhole, fell asleep as the firing slowed toward dawn but suddenly sprang awake to see Maximilian standing near him, without any bodyguard, holding up his small field glass and scanning the landscape. He looked down at Salm-Salm, who was still rubbing his eyes, and smiled. It frustrated Salm-Salm that Maximilian would not keep from harm's way.[25]

On April 22, upon the interrogation of two newly captured prisoners, the Imperialistas learned that Puebla had fallen to Díaz. They also related that the Liberals occupied part of Mexico City. At first, Maximilian said nothing and withdrew to think. The same day, a flag of truce went up from the Liberal lines and an emissary arrived to suggest negotiation, saying the emperor could leave Mexico in freedom if he surrendered the city and his army. Gen. Miramón complicated any possible negotiations by making demands on the Liberals regarding the safe retreat of the rest of the imperial officers. When Gen. Escobedo replied he was not authorized to discuss these issues, Maximilian declined to negotiate, since the proposed terms only involved his welfare and not that of his men. Reinforcements continued to join the Liberal lines, increasing their troop strength to approximately 40,000 men, against Maximilian's 7,000-strong force that eroded steadily.[26]

Over the next week the news of Márquez's defeat leaked out among the soldiers. "Dianas," or the ringing of bells in celebration, could be heard through the Liberal camps. Desertions accelerated and the imperial troops began losing as many as fifty men a day. Maximilian fought to keep his spirits up, continuing to plan a break through the enemy lines. However, his health turned for the worse. With the bad food and water, he suffered from stomach ailments and dysentery.[27]

His generals had not given up hope. Miramón prepared to launch a series of sorties commencing on April 27 with the intent of opening a breach for Maximilian to escape. According to the plan, at a certain hour the town's church bells would ring, like they did when signaling a warning, and the generals would circulate a false report that Márquez was about to attack from the rear. Then, the Imperialistas would rush the Liberal lines. Descending from the heights of El Cimatario, Miramón's offensive proved brilliant, and the Imperialistas drove the Juaristas back within an hour, many of the Liberals deserting their positions. Escobedo called for the seasoned Juaristas under Díaz's command for reinforcement and more ammunition, but these arrived too late. The Imperialistas captured twenty-one artillery pieces, took many prisoners, and seized several flags. Maximilian galloped out to admire Miramón's work. Early that morning, Maximilian's valets packed his belongings and his escorts saddled their horses, ready to flee at the appropriate moment. However, in their celebration and self-congratulation, the Imperialistas became hungry for further victory.[28]

Miramón launched additional attacks on May 1 and 2, but after initial gains they could not overcome the Juaristas. A number of Maximilian's most devoted officers of the Cazadores, who had served him loyally over the three years, were killed in the fighting. One had a shot to the head "which laid bare his brains but he lived through the afternoon," said Salm-Salm. Another fellow, a handsome, blond officer named Joaquín Rodríguez, engaged to be married soon, worried that his end was near and expressed his feelings to Blasio, who attempted to calm him. However, in a few hours soldiers led his body back into camp, draped across his saddle. As the openings in the line began to close, Méndez and the other generals urged Maximilian to escape while he could, but he would not leave without the officers. As proof, he demanded that his refusal be documented, so that history would not brand him a coward, but honorable. He squandered the chance to escape.[29]

The generals did not stop their efforts to protect the emperor or hold out hope for an exit, however. Maximilian seemed to long for a mortar or bullet to take him, to die a hero's death, carelessly exposing himself while walking freely along the front lines or standing on rooftops in full exposure to artillery fire. Where men had died, he lingered, troubled and restless, even though Salm-Salm and others tried to get him to seek shelter. He believed that the fate of the city depended on his leadership, not his cowardice. Nothing mattered materially, his health in tatters, and Mexico a losing proposition. He was tired.[30]

On May 5 the Liberals celebrated Cinco de Mayo, their 1862 victory over the French, mostly to taunt the Imperialistas. After the brief hurrahs, they commenced shelling the town anew. In the convent where he camped, Salm-Salm observed: "Lying on my field bed, a cannonball passing down through an adjoining hall and knocking down a pillar, struck the opposite side of the wall." He said, "Fortunately the wall held."[31]

Incrementally, the Liberals cut the Imperialistas off from their water sources. It was only a matter of time until cholera broke out. Maximilian and his generals were down to 5,000 men, little food, and no forage for the horses. Salm-Salm bought some old straw beds to chop up for his animals. The generals agreed that they must break out of the city with the whole garrison and push northeast into the Sierra Gorda, Mejía's home country, to the coastal regions. The time and date for escape would be the late evening of May 14. Their secret plan would be announced only a few hours before deployment. Mejía's units, numbering about 3,000 men, planned to distract the Liberals on one side of the city with gunfire. Everything was set for the surge, the men and muskets in place, when Mejía asked Maximilian for one more day to prepare. The emperor had no choice but to grant the postponement until the next night.[32]

Salm-Salm, infuriated by Mejía and this delay, confronted Maximilian. "Your Majesty, I must confess that I am little satisfied with this delay. . . . I should think 1,200 muskets and four guns were perfectly sufficient for masking our attack with noise."

"Well, one day, more or less, will be no matter. Take care that the hussars and the bodyguards remain saddled," said Maximilian.

Salm-Salm went to his quarters in a foul mood but summoned his valet to bring a bottle of champagne, which he finished with another officer. He slept in his clothes with his saber beside him and his pistol under his pillow. About 4:30 in the morning, voices jolted him awake and he heard Col. Miguel López shout, "Quick, save the emperor. The enemy is in La Cruz." Salm-Salm jumped off his cot and put on his gun belt. In a few moments, Maximilian's

Col. Miguel López,
Imperialista officer and
bodyguard to Maximilian,
who later betrayed
Maximilian to the
Republican army, ca. 1865

steward, Grill, entered the room saying that Maximilian had summoned him. Dr. Samuel Basch entered the hallway with Salm-Salm and asked what the commotion was. Rushing down the hallway and checking their gear, Salm-Salm said they were under siege and to alert the hussars to be ready to mount their horses and escort the emperor.[33]

Blasio also awoke in the tumult, hearing that the Liberals had surrounded La Cruz. When someone yelled, "Hurry and wake the emperor," he leaped from bed, half dressed, and lit a candle. Blasio said:

> Then I saw that the man who was speaking to me was López's second-in-command, Lt. Col. Antonio Jablonski. I ran immediately to Maximilian's cell. As I passed along the corridor I could see that the soldiers wore the uniform gray with very tall shakos of the *Supremos Poderes* (Supreme Powers, a Liberal regiment). . . . They were on guard at the doors of the cells. . . . The emperor was sleeping quietly. I told Severo to arouse him, which he did, but he still questioned the truth of what I said and began to dress very slowly. Then Jablonski came and implored him to hasten.

When Dr. Basch arrived, Maximilian was dressed. Basch asked why he was called. "It is nothing," said Maximilian, "the enemy has got into the gardens. Get your pistol and follow me."[34]

When Salm-Salm reached Maximilian's quarters, the emperor turned to him and said, "We are betrayed. Go down and let the Hussars and bodyguard march out. We will go instead to the cerro. . . . I shall follow you directly."[35]

Salm-Salm hurried out to the plaza, but curiously he found none of the regimental guards at their posts. There was no one. Finally locating the confused commander of the hussars, he ordered his unit to report to the convent plaza. The colonel then noticed that the gun batteries were somewhat dismantled, and seven or eight soldiers dressed in the gray uniform of the Liberal officers crept in and out through a breach in the wall.[36]

Salm-Salm hurried back to the convent and met Maximilian just as he was descending the stairs. The emperor dressed in his general's uniform with his white felt sombrero rimmed with gold. He wore a thick coat as well as his sword buckled at his waist and carried a revolver in each hand. He appeared pale and ill but calm. Salm-Salm reached out to the emperor as he tottered down the steps. Carrying Maximilian's pistols as they entered the courtyard, he remarked softly, "The enemy is here." One of the Liberal soldiers, among the column filing into the plaza told them to halt. *"Atrás,"* he shouted. "Involuntarily I raised one of the emperor's revolvers, but he [Maximilian] made a gesture with his hand and I dropped it," said Salm-Salm. Imperialist Col. Miguel López, who had been standing among the Liberals speaking in low conversation, came forward saying these men were *paisanos*, fellow countrymen, and to let them pass. The soldiers parted and Maximilian, Salm-Salm, Blasio, and two military attendants stepped past the guard.[37]

"You see, it never does any harm to do good. It is true, you find amongst twenty people nineteen ungrateful; but still, now and then, one grateful. I have just now had an instance of it. The officer who let us pass has a sister who was frequently with the empress, and who has done much good to her. Do good, Salm-Salm, whenever you have an opportunity," Maximilian said.[38] They had an opportunity to flee, a chance they did not fully realize.

As Maximilian made his way through the courtyard, the rest of his staff were arrested, disarmed, and robbed by the Supremos Poderes. "I now declare you my prisoner," one said to Samuel Basch. "I am aware of that," he replied to the soldier, who continued to rummage through the doctor's pockets.[39]

Salm-Salm and the others still wondered what López was doing among the Liberal officers. They guessed the colonel had found a means of escape for Maximilian by going to the Liberal camp and offering to betray the imperial army while leaving a small window of time to allow the emperor to escape. Maximilian believed the same. Certain stealth communications had passed from the Liberal camp to the Imperialistas. Knowing they were suffering food shortages and illness, Liberal generals including José Rincón y Gallardo approached Gen. Miramón, who knew him well, to negotiate surrender, but he would hear nothing of it. In April Liberal general Silverio Ramírez wrote Gen. Mejía pleading with him to persuade the Imperialistas to lay aside their arms, to begin the healing from the fratricidal war that only irritated the open wounds of the country, adding that Maximilian did not want a government for Mexicans. Mejía would not consider turning against Maximilian. López, however, conceived that he could work out a solution on behalf of the emperor to free him and acquire a pardon for the Imperialistas. He met with Gen. Escobedo, who reportedly declined, saying he was not authorized to negotiate such an arrangement but only accept surrender. López acted on his own with the subordinate Liberal officers, which none of the superiors appreciated. Several days earlier, López, who had a history of insubordination, mentioned his ideas to fellow soldiers, which likely involved bribing certain officials.[40]

The day before, on May 14, when Blasio received the proceeds from the last of the Imperialistas' forced loans imposed "on the luckless citizens of Querétaro," the amount totaled about 5,000 pesos. Maximilian ordered the money apportioned among the cavalry of the municipal guard, who prepared to secretly escort him out of the city. The silver coinage went to pay the servants. López, on his way to a meeting with Maximilian at about 10:30 that night, stopped by Blasio's room to angrily demand part of the funds, in gold, not knowing that the money had already been distributed. Blasio reluctantly gave him 100 silver pesos, and López left to meet Maximilian.[41]

In Maximilian's quarters, López discussed plans for the next day's maneuvers. The emperor presented the colonel with a medal of merit for recent distinctions in battle and told López that in the event the escape sortie failed, to do him the blessing of putting a bullet in his head. López told Maximilian not to worry, everything would go well, and if not, surely the Liberals would be open to negotiation. Afterward, Maximilian went to bed but awoke with a fit of colic at 2:30 a.m. Dr. Basch attended to him with opium pills to calm his stomach pain, and the emperor slept solidly until he was roused two hours later.[42]

When López left Maximilian's quarters at about midnight, he slipped through the Liberals' lines to the camp of Gen. Escobedo, which apparently he had done the previous night as well, saying that he was an intermediary between the two camps. The colonel thought he had arrived at a solution to end the siege. He proposed surrendering the Imperialistas, if Maximilian would be allowed to go free. Escobedo demanded an unconditional surrender, however, and access to the convent of La Cruz, but would only guarantee López's personal liberty. While he could not obtain any promises, in some way López became convinced that Maximilian would be allowed to quietly sneak out of Querétaro before the Liberal army seized the entire city.[43]

During the early morning hours, with López's cooperation, a squad of Liberal soldiers led by Col. José Rincón y Gallardo followed López to La Cruz convent where they occupied the building in complete silence. Following López's commands, the gendarmerie, the emperor's battalion, and the Querétaro volunteers surrendered their arms before they were fully aware of the situation. The Liberals seized control of the artillery in the plaza, readied to be used in the sortie the following evening, as well as the church, supply room, and hospital. No one fired shots or cried out in alarm. The buildings fell to the Juaristas in a strange calm. When every Imperialist guard was rendered harmless, López gave the signal by running into Salm-Salm's room and shouting that the Liberals had infiltrated the convent.[44]

The sun began to rise over the eastern hills of the city on the morning of May 15. As Maximilian, Salm-Salm, Blasio, and his stunned aides walked out of the convent, they learned the hussars were still making preparations, and they went to the Plaza de Independencia to wait. Maximilian's attendants urged him to mount one of their horses and ride away to the Cerro de las Campanas, but he refused to leave and summoned Miramón and Mejía to meet him at the hill instead. At that moment, López rode up and said the emperor should go to the nearby house of Carlos Rubio, a prominent banker and textile manufacturer, to take cover from the Liberal generals who would likely be looking for him. "I do not hide myself," said Maximilian. Nonplussed by the emperor's defiance, López left promptly, but then Maximilian noticed that the colonel had brought with him the royal groom, who stood on the street with his warhorse, Orispelo, waiting for him.[45]

The hussars still had not arrived, but they saw a battalion of Liberals fast on their horses approaching, with López in their company. Salm-Salm implored Maximilian to mount his horse and ride away. "If you gentlemen walk, I will walk also," he said. Surprisingly, when the columns of Liberals saw the emperor striding down the street, they slowed their pace and followed him to the base of the Cerro de las Campanas, still held by a fortified Imperialista camp with a few officers, one hundred infantrymen, and four cannon.[46]

As they climbed, it became apparent that one of Maximilian's military attendants, the aging Gen. Severo del Castillo, had trouble with the steep slope. "The emperor took one of his arms within his and I the other, and thus we dragged him between us up the cerro, which was occupied only by one battalion. It was not bright daylight and a most beautiful morning. Suddenly we heard the bells from the Cruz [the convent] give the agreed signal that the vile treason had been successful," later wrote Salm-Salm. The Liberal battalions answered with *dianas* answering the bells' announcement. The rest of the Imperialista troops had fled or surrendered their arms to the Liberals. Miramón, who was hit in the cheek by a bullet that morning as he rushed to Maximilian's aid, remained at the home of a doctor who tended to his wound. Mejía arrived on the heels of Maximilian, with hussars and additional horses, including Anteburro, and they continued to climb to the top of the hill. At the same time, Liberal batteries on the surrounding rises opened fire on the emperor and his entourage, as Juarista cavalry surrounded the foothills.[47]

At that point "on the Cerro de las Campanas was a truly poignant moment," wrote Albert Hans, an artillery lieutenant. "There was a sort of square fortification, a redoubt, atop the hill, full of officers and soldiers of every rank and unit, who had taken refuge there like the victim of a shipwreck on a raft. Each moment, newcomers arrived who were forced to abandon their horses and . . . come through the doorways [of the fortification]," wrote Hans. The Liberals trained all their guns and grenades to the middle of the redoubt. Maximilian asked Mejía if there was still a chance of breaking through the lines. "Sire, it is impossible to get through; but if Your Majesty orders it we will try; as for me I am ready to die," said Mejía. "Ojalá" (if God wills it), said Maximilian. The emperor asked him twice more, and both times he responded negatively, that there was no hope. "Let us hope for a lucky bullet," said Maximilian.[48]

Although Maximilian had been given an opportunity to escape, as he ascended the Cerro de las Campanas and learned the wounded Miramón could not reach them, he saw that leaving together would be impossible. The emperor gave Blasio his field glass to protect and instructed him to burn his letters and papers, which the secretary carried. Blasio ducked into a nearby tent, found a candle, and destroyed the documents and letters. Maximilian contemplated one last time how to escape, but Mejía said there was nothing left to do but lay down their arms. Accordingly, Maximilian sent a notice of surrender with a messenger carrying a white flag to Gen. Escobedo. After a number of tense minutes, the shelling stopped. Liberals began to climb toward the emperor and Mejía. Maximilian leaned on his saber and calmly waited for the group of soldiers led by Gen. Ramón Corona and Gen. Miguel María Echegaray to arrive. Echegaray stepped up to the emperor and said, "Your Majesty is my prisoner." He asked Maximilian to mount Anteburro, and they rode down the hill to meet Gen. Escobedo.[49]

Escobedo invited Maximilian into a hastily erected tent. The two men faced each other in silence for a long, tense moment. After years of struggle against the empire, Escobedo remained stunned that the fight had ended and his enemy stood before him. Because Escobedo said little, Maximilian explained that his surrender meant he was no longer the emperor. In a strong, steady voice, he explained that he had abdicated earlier in March, leaving the papers with José María Lacunza in Mexico City, stating his intention of going back to Europe. He added that he had a copy of this document with him in his quarters. "If a victim must fall, let it be me alone," said Maximilian, but added he wished nothing more than to leave Mexico peacefully by the nearest port. He asked Escobedo to spare his staff and his aides, for they had been loyal and valiant.[50]

The war-weary Escobedo replied that the news of his surrender and his requests would be related to Juárez, and until the president made some sort of decision, the emperor and his staff were his prisoners. "If that is so, I hope you do nothing outrageous and treat me with the considerations due a prisoner of war," said Maximilian. Offering his weapon to Escobedo, he said, "I surrender to you my sword, owing to an infamous treason, without which tomorrow's sun would have seen yours in my hands." Escobedo, after a moment of disbelief and some embarrassment, handed it off to an assistant. At Maximilian's request, the officers escorted Maximilian through the back streets of Querétaro to the convent of La Cruz, where he was detained in his old quarters. Before leaving, Maximilian asked for food for his staff.[51]

On May 15 Juárez sent notes to his supporters and family. "*¡Viva la patria!* Querétaro has fallen by force of arms this morning at eight o'clock. Maximilian, Mejía, Castillo, and Miramón are prisoners." This note was telegraphed ten days later to Washington, D.C., and from there the news was broadcast to Europe.[52]

I Have Cared for You All

In Querétaro's convent of La Cruz grew a legendary shrub that produced thorns in the shape of a cross. It multiplied its cruciform spines discreetly in the abbey's courtyard but represented a grace-filled miracle to many who staged pilgrimages to the holy site. Occupying the cloisters as a fighter, Maximilian possibly overlooked the plant during the chaos of battle. As an avid botanist it is more likely, however, that in quiet moments he noted its rarity and the significance of its fundamental existence while trying to tease out its taxonomy, *Gleditsia triacanthos*, indeed a curious and rare specimen.[1]

In all, the siege of Querétaro lasted seventy-one days. Juárez's forces captured the whole garrison including 15 generals, 357 officers, and above all, the emperor. At Escobedo's orders, Gen. Vicente Riva Palacio, a man whom both the Liberals and Imperialistas respected, calmly escorted Maximilian, who was mounted on his own horse, back to the convent of La Cruz. Riva Palacio's troops treated the captives like gentlemen and shared their breakfast with the captured officers, a relief to the starving men who either had no food or had been made to pay exorbitant prices to opportunists for the few scraps they could buy. Of this, the open and guileless Maximilian commented about his captors, "They are better than I had imagined. Moreover, I am proud that I have educated them by my methods during the siege. They see the results of my clemency toward our prisoners."[2]

As they passed through the streets, the shocked, glassy-eyed Imperialistas began to realize López's betrayal that ended the fight. "In the midst of this tumult, we . . . spotted López in front of his former quarters. The scoundrel was on foot, still in full [imperial] uniform, his elbow resting on the saddle of his magnificent horse, looking out with apparent impassivity over this scene which was his doing," Albert Hans wrote.[3]

Maximilian had wanted to avoid the jeers of the Juarista soldiers who celebrated with pulque and other spirits singing the dreadful lyrics of "Mama Carlota," but he could not avoid them. One of the Liberal officers, who appeared to be an irregular, appropriated the emperor's steed, Orispelo, but as he led the horse away another man demanded the animal, seized the reins, and shot and killed the man, taking the mount away, possibly to be sold. Blasio, who walked back through Querétaro with Maximilian's fine Russian gold-embossed spyglass slung around his neck, encountered an American soldier serving in the Liberal army. The American put his pistol to Blasio's chest, and demanded the telescope. Blasio could do nothing more than give it up.[4]

When Maximilian arrived at the convent of La Cruz, he dismounted Anteburro and handed over the reins to Riva Palacio, giving him his last and favorite horse in return for considering his privacy and circumstances amid the chaos in Querétaro. If losing his last warhorse caused him great emotional pain, he did not show it. As Maximilian and the other captives entered their quarters at the convent, they found their rooms ransacked and their possessions stolen. Looters tore Maximilian's mattress to shreds looking for cash. They took Maximilian's silver grooming set with brushes and razor and his washbasin, along with canned goods and wine, leaving only a few broken bottles. His strong box with decorations and medals was smashed and emptied. A few hours later Maximilian's personal items were discovered in López's room. Two suitcases of clothing and personal effects were returned to the emperor. Maximilian, however, managed to save his medications. He showed a small box of opium pills to Samuel Basch, who had prescribed them. "You see, you must never lose your head," said Maximilian.[5]

When word circulated that the Liberals had stripped Maximilian of his possessions, and despite hard feelings over the forced loans he levied during the battle, the townsfolk came forward with tenderly crafted gifts. The women, who heard he was bereft of undergarments or "interior linen," sent him a number of articles of clothing. "I have never had so much underlinen in my life," he said, laughing with his attendants.[6]

Aside from the revelers in the Liberal ranks and those who resented the Imperialista occupation, there was considerable grief over the possible fate of the fallen emperor. Women walked about in mourning, in their black dresses and mantillas. Many cooked fine meals and delivered them to the convent for Maximilian and his officers. Daily, the emperor received gifts of fruit and vegetables. Foreign merchants slipped him cash for food and essentials or hoped he could bribe his way to safety. Many people remained anxious about their own futures but seemed just as worried about Maximilian's. His princely bearing and selflessness during battle brought together not only a brotherhood of fighters but also the genial emotions of many in Querétaro.[7]

In all, the Republican victory turned out to be larger than Juárez had imagined due to López's betrayal of the emperor, a stroke of fortune he and his generals never anticipated, especially in view of their struggles against dwindling ammunition and desertions. A number of Juarista officers came to visit the emperor, including Gen. Rincón y Gallardo and his brother Pedro. They told Maximilian of how López had led them to the convent and, curiously, spoke of him as a coward and a traitor. "Men like him serve when they are needed, but afterward one kicks him out the door," said one officer.[8]

Soon Mariano Escobedo visited Maximilian and his officers. Since he considered them prisoners of war according to international standards, he said they would be treated with all courtesies. He asked Maximilian if he wished to be joined by his staff and he asked for Samuel Basch, Félix Salm-Salm, and Pedro Ormachea, who were allowed to lodge near his room. He tried to remain positive and naïvely said to his friends, "I am happy that everything has happened without more bloodshed. I have done what I intended to do. I have cared for you all." Later that evening, allowed to see his generals, Maximilian said he expected the Juaristas to rush them to the firing squad. "I am ready for anything. I am finished," said Maximilian.

"I too am ready," said Mejía. "Your Majesty knows that I have never been afraid to die."[9]

On April 23 Escobedo received instructions from Juárez's headquarters at San Luis Potosí regarding the treatment of prisoners. While Juárez agreed with Escobedo that ordinary soldiers should not be executed, he did not feel the same when leading figures or commanders were apprehended. "Special circumstances" and the full force of the law would bear upon their cases.[10]

Escobedo's officers issued calls for all Imperialistas to give themselves up in twenty-four hours or they would be shot when found. They began a search for Gen. Méndez, who had hidden himself, but they had no luck in finding him. Over six hundred Imperialista captives were forced into the nave of the church at La Cruz convent. In addition to the devastation of being penned up, most were offered no food by the Juárez troops, although citizens brought what they could. Men with a little money bought meals, but the remainder starved. Many became convinced they were destined for a mass burial. The church where the Liberals put the captives had also served as the repository for the Imperialistas' gunpowder. The night after their capture, one of the Liberal guards, smoking on duty, accidentally dropped his cigarette, which ignited the powder and quickly spread to boxes of cartridges nearby. A huge explosion could be heard throughout the town. In the church a number of men were killed or wounded as men pushed toward the door. Thinking the prisoners had staged an uprising, another of the Liberal guards rolled a mountain howitzer up to the door, ready to open fire on the prisoners. Fortunately, an officer told him to hold fire. After three days the Liberals started distributing food. As Albert Hans said, "It was about time."[11]

Blasio worked to keep up protocol in La Cruz, which Maximilian admired but also joked about, as there remained so few who appreciated such formalities. Friends and family were kept away for the first few days. This infuriated Salm-Salm, who conspired to make an escape, earning the title of "the lion in the cage." In La Cruz, over those first few days of captivity Maximilian felt a general relief that the fighting had ended. All those who scrutinized his every move saw that he needed rest, the fatigue of battle and his stomach ailments making him very weak. Worse, curious Juarista officers came by Maximilian's quarters to observe him, to get a glimpse of the renowned emperor, whom they now called "archduke."[12]

After two days, with Maximilian's health declining, Dr. Basch contacted the head doctor of the Liberal army, Ignacio Rivadeneira, for assistance. They both thought La Cruz too unhealthy and appealed to Gen. Escobedo, who responded by ordering the emperor and his staff to the Convent of the Teresitas. Maximilian boarded a carriage while his staff walked behind. On the way Blasio spotted López on the street in a general's uniform and sombrero, holding Maximilian's gold-embroidered kepi in his hands. The hat had disappeared from the emperor's room after his capture, and it now became clear who took it. The men snarled about López's betrayal. Salm-Salm recalled to Maximilian that a week before his capture, López had entered his quarters to whisper something to him while Salm-Salm sat writing at a nearby desk. When López approached, Maximilian's King Charles spaniel, Baby, normally a docile animal, leaped up barking and bit López on the leg. He felt they should have regarded this as an omen.[13]

As they approached the convent, the staff ran ahead to form a receiving line at the door of the building, uncovering their heads in respect. "No other monarch can boast of having a court like this," Maximilian said, as he passed into the convent's cloisters. This abbey, however, turned out to be dirtier and more foul smelling than La Cruz.[14]

A month earlier, in late April 1867, while the Battle of Querétaro remained in full engagement, Agnes Salm-Salm had been supplying food and support to the Imperialista prisoners in Mexico City while going to Díaz and attempting to negotiate abdication and a release for Maximilian. As she moved between Tacubaya where she lodged and Mexico City, she approached each camp by turn under a hail of bullets suspended only after her waiving a white cloth. After some weeks Díaz, annoyed by her constant interference and suspecting that she was trying to bribe his subordinates, gave her permission to leave for Querétaro with his blessings. When he would not guarantee her a military escort for safe passage to Querétaro, she purchased an old, bright-yellow fiacre and harness but had no horses to pull it. She found and imposed on the English superintendent of the railroad to give her mules and a driver. A business-man heading north from the capital with his bodyguard provided protection for Agnes, along with her maid and her dog, Jimmy. "I had my little seven-shooter revolver and only three 'ounces' in my pocket," she said. On the way, they encountered an executed man hanging from a tree, a sight Agnes could not remove from her memory.[15]

On April 30, when she pulled up to Escobedo's headquarters at Querétaro, in the midst of combat and flying bullets, she created a sensation. This beauti-ful woman, with her dog and small entourage, had traveled in the odd little carriage over one hundred miles through dangerous territory to find her hus-band in a war zone. "General Escobedo received me at once in a very small and most miserable tent, propped up with sticks, furnished merely with a table made of raw boards and some wooden chests as a seat. The general wore a uniform similar to that of Porfirio Díaz only with rather more lace and brass buttons," said Agnes Salm-Salm. When she demanded to see her husband, whom she thought had been wounded, Escobedo replied that he had not been wounded but only President Juárez could permit her to see him, and he was in San Luis Potosí. Therefore, after a night in a fine hacienda, the next morn-ing, with a letter from Escobedo and a military escort, she traveled another hundred miles north, over three days, to find Juárez.[16]

When she met Juárez in the municipal palace, he was nothing like the ogre she expected. Instead, she found a gentle and seemingly wise man. "The President gave me his hand, led me to the sofa on which Jimmy had already established himself and said he would listen to what I had to say," she wrote.

After hearing her request, however, he refused to allow her to return to the scene of active war. So she remained in San Luis Potosí, where she could hear the "freshest news." When word came that Querétaro had fallen to the Liberals, she rushed to Querétaro on May 19.[17]

After the battle, many Liberal officers with a fair-minded view of their victory, like Riva Palacio and, to a certain extent, Escobedo, wanted a blanket amnesty or even clemency for the Imperialistas. Many had political aspirations and knew they needed support from all Mexicans and that their actions would be scrutinized in the future. Other Juaristas, however, called for blood. On May 18, when the Liberals found Gen. Méndez hiding in the home of a supporter, they dragged him to the Convent of the Teresitas and decided to put him before a firing squad. Before his execution, the Liberals allowed Méndez to say goodbye to Maximilian and the other generals. Mejía, with tears in his eyes, tried to comfort him. Maximilian said, with some emotion, "Méndez, you are only the vanguard. We shall soon follow you on the same road." After a farewell to his family, the Juarista guard led Méndez to the Alameda between rows of soldiers. Méndez refused to be blindfolded and kneeled. As the firing squad prepared to shoot him in the back as a traitor, he turned around and faced the enemy fusillade.[18]

That same day Escobedo with a retinue of Liberal generals and colonels came to the convent to see Maximilian, which caused a great stir and anxiety among the prisoners. They worried that Escobedo, having just executed Méndez, prepared to issue the same pronouncement on Maximilian and the rest of them. After an hour's visit Escobedo and his men left, having made only a courtesy call on Maximilian.[19]

Hours later Agnes Salm-Salm met Maximilian for the first time. "I found him in a miserable bare room in bed, looking very sick and pale. He received me with the utmost kindness, kissed my hand, and pressed it to his and told me how glad he was that I had come," she wrote. When Maximilian asked Agnes about Gen. Leonardo Márquez's actions in Mexico City, she reported that he "assumed rights and an air of command which could not be allowed to any [imperial] subject. He distributed decorations and titles as if he had been emperor himself." Maximilian grew disgusted and upset when he heard this.[20]

She also reported that Juárez and his advisors, Sebastián Lerdo de Tejada and Manuel Aspiroz, were unlikely to grant clemency to the Imperialistas. This compounded Maximilian's worries. Juárez meant to rely almost solely on the law he declared on January 25, 1862, in reaction to the invasion of the French, English, and Spanish, stating that all enemies of the nation, if captured with arms or any Mexican citizens who aided them, would be subject to the death penalty. It mattered little if the accused was a poor beggar or a charming Austrian prince.[21]

Agnes then helped to arrange for Maximilian to make a return visit to Escobedo. With the Salm-Salms, Maximilian rode in an open carriage to his headquarters, the Hacienda de la Hércules. The general, in the middle of a little victory party with his family, appeared somewhat embarrassed when Maximilian arrived.[22]

In their conversation, Maximilian offered a written proposal to surrender what remained of his army at Mexico City and Veracruz to prevent further bloodshed. With a total abdication, he requested that he be allowed to leave for Europe, taking with him all his staff and the Austrian army. In return, he promised never to return to Mexico or interfere in its politics and would persuade his former advocates to be loyal to the new government. Escobedo listened and spoke thoughtfully, their meeting lasting over an hour. Maximilian came away with the impression that Escobedo supported the idea and that Juárez might as well. Escobedo expected final orders regarding the prisoners any day.[23]

Meanwhile, Agnes, who feared for the health of Maximilian in the unsanitary convent of Teresitas, prevailed upon Escobedo to move the emperor's quarters and that of his staff to a cleaner and quieter place. She had obtained fresh linen for the men and was anxious to render their living situations more comfortable. Escobedo assigned them to a beautiful home in the town and ordered it furnished. However, another general, Refugio González, charged with guarding the prisoners, objected and reproached Escobedo, asking him if he wanted to treat the prisoner like a prince in direct violation of Juárez's instructions. González refused to guard him in these lavish lodgings. Somewhat alarmed, Escobedo rescinded the order and told González to find another place for them.[24]

Because the telegraph wires were cut between central Mexico and Veracruz, news of the fall of Querétaro took several days to travel abroad. Soon, however, the press in the United States and around the world reported Maximilian's capture. Royals throughout Europe began appealing to U.S. president Andrew Johnson and secretary of state William Seward for intervention to save Maximilian. There were few officials to bargain with in Mexico, the Europeans having only tenuous or no diplomatic relations with Juárez. The Habsburg family anxiously hoped for Maximilian's release. Being Austrian, Minister Wydenbruck and Emperor Franz Josef correctly assumed they had no sway with Juárez, but they placed their hope in intervention from the United States. Seward sent an appeal with defense arguments cobbled together from a statement from Maximilian, written several months earlier, leaving all business of government in the hands of his ministers, renouncing his power, along with petitions from the Austrian ministers.[25]

Nevertheless, by Juárez's accounting, the United States seemed rather indifferent, although Seward quickly appointed Edward L. Plumb as chargé d'affaires to intervene. Plumb reported that while Juárez might be inclined to grant wishes of clemency, "the army demands the execution of the leaders, and in case of refusal, boldly threaten revolt." While appreciative of the United States for supporting his government, Juárez could not honor their requests.[26]

Persistent pleadings by the European elite to let Maximilian free served only to anneal Juárez's determination to make a decisive statement. He resolved to push for the birth of the Mexican nation as he and others envisioned before the intervention. Maximilian's release would do little to reconcile party differences in the country, established long before the emperor's arrival. The European royals, who viewed the world with a sense of entitlement, could not comprehend that their ardent promises and implicit threats only reminded Juárez of Mexico's long struggles against European domination.[27]

On May 22, the day after their meeting with Escobedo, Gen. González ordered that Maximilian and his staff be moved to the convent of the Capuchin nuns, overall a cleaner, more open, well-lit place, but only a little less wretched than the Teresitas convent, where they suffered horrible conditions. After enduring a morning cramped together and insulted by the Mexican soldiers who taunted them, Maximilian and his staff were escorted by the guards to the convent. Shockingly, González intended that they spend their first night in the damp and dark burial crypts used by the nuns of the convent. When Maximilian was shown where he would sleep, he said, "Certainly that cannot be my room, why this is a vault of the dead. Indeed this is a bad omen." No doubt this reminded Maximilian of the Capuchin crypts in Vienna where the royal Habsburgs interred their forebears. When Dr. Samuel Basch arrived to attend to Maximilian, he asked Félix Salm-Salm where he could be found.[28]

"He is in a crypt," said Salm-Salm.

Basch gave him a horrified look.

"Calm yourself, he is alive, but he really is in a crypt. I will show you to him."

The two opened the door to the stagnant and cold underchamber where the deceased nuns lay. In the far corner, they spotted Maximilian reclining on a makeshift bed. On a little table, a candle provided the only light for him, and he was reading *The History of Italy* by Cesare Cantù. Seeing Basch, Maximilian arose and said, "They have not had time yet to prepare a room, and so temporarily they have had to give me a bed among the dead."[29]

"They have outdone themselves with this brutality, confining a prisoner who expects to die in a crypt," Basch wrote later. For the night, the doctor and other staff slept on the hard floor among the graves. "After the hours of uneasiness I have undergone this afternoon, the dead will leave me alone," wrote Basch.[30]

The next morning Maximilian and the others were given rooms upstairs where they could look out onto a courtyard filled with plants and orange trees. Again, citizens brought them food, clothing, linens, and money. Over the next few days, as they awaited Juárez's decision on their fate, Dr. Basch insisted that Maximilian walk for exercise despite his chronic stomach problems. As he strolled in the courtyard with his staff, shadowed by his guard, Col. Miguel Palacios, whom he called "the hyena" for his squinting eyes, he allowed his imagination to wander. Aloud he told Blasio and Salm-Salm of what he would do when he returned to Europe. "You shall go with me, first to London. We'll stay there a year, have my papers brought from Miramar and write a history of my reign. Then we shall go to Naples and rent a house in one of the beautiful suburbs which surround the city with a view of the landscape and the sea. On my yacht *Ondina* with Basch, old Bilimek, and four servants we'll make little voyages to the Greek archipelago, to Athens, to the coast of Turkey," he said. He said he would send Blasio back to Mexico, if the political climate had calmed, or he would find him a place in a European legation.[31]

Maximilian continued to improve gradually in the Capuchin convent. His guards allowed his meals to be prepared by his cook, Tüdös, who served him soup, hash, chicken, tea, coffee, and red wine. Basch reported that his appetite improved and he looked better in general.[32]

During another of his turns about the convent one afternoon, he and Salm-Salm strolled in a yard outside the chapel. "I saw lying on the ground a thorn crown, which had fallen from the head of a wooden image of Christ, which had been used by the soldiers as firewood," said Salm-Salm, who picked it up. "The emperor took it from my hand and said, 'Let me have it, it suits well with my position.'" He ordered his valet, Grill, to hang it in his new room, which he did. He later told Dr. Basch, who commented on the crown on his wall, "I have a claim to this, they will not dispute it with me. When I leave here, I shall take it back to Europe as a souvenir."[33]

López, the traitor, had been rewarded 7,000 pesos in gold by the Juaristas for his service to the Republic and was released from Querétaro. Without shame, he stopped in to visit Maximilian at the Capuchin convent, asking to see the emperor in his room. The emperor refused to see him, rife with contempt that his former friend would betray him. López had come to be despised by both the Juaristas and Imperialistas alike, and even his wife soon left him, asking, "What have you done to our compadre?"[34]

When Juárez learned of López's duplicity, he decided not to order the emperor summarily shot and to allow some semblance of due process. But he refused to listen to Maximilian's proposals that he be released to return to Europe. The president determined that Maximilian and his generals would be tried by court-martial for violating the law of January 25, 1862, the only legal basis that existed for prosecution. He made few provisions to allow Maximilian or his generals a legal defense. Ironically, the 1857 Constitution, which Juárez helped foster, banned the death penalty for offenses. Not only would Maximilian pay for the French intervention and his four-year expulsion from office, Juárez articulated his fate. "After all we have suffered by the foreign nations, and what we just suffered from France, our susceptibilities cannot allow the appearance on the horizon of another country, not even the shadow of any dependence," he said. "Our constant benevolence towards other nations throughout the period of our independence should have earned their good will, but has merited rather their contempt. This benevolence, perhaps because of the weakness of our previous governments, in their view reflects a lack of energy and dignity, little spirit, poor stamina, poor vitality. We have now proven this is not so." They planned to commence a trial within a few days.[35]

Maximilian wrote Prussian minister Baron Anton von Magnus in Mexico City, asking for assistance and to hire the best legal minds for his defense. Over the years, the amiable Magnus had managed to maintain good relations with both Maximilian and Juárez. The emperor wanted to hire lawyers who had political influence with the Liberals and might help sway their decisions. Depressingly, the only word he heard from the Austrian minister Baron Alfred Lago and the Belgian chargé d'affaires Frederic Hooricks was that they planned to arrive soon to help him settle affairs and witness his will. But Magnus telegrammed immediately to ask Juárez for a trial delay in order to prepare a defense.[36]

Simultaneously, Agnes Salm-Salm panicked when she learned of the swift rush to trial. If Juárez would not give Maximilian the same rights due a prisoner of war, then he should be allowed full rights in a civilian court proceeding. When the Prussian vice-consul Johannes H. Bahnsen, who became an intermediary between Juárez and the prisoners, told Agnes nothing could be done, she objected, saying someone must go to San Luis Potosí and plead for a delay. "Nobody will go. Ask for time? It is quite useless. You do not know Juárez, I know him well," said Bahnsen. That challenge was enough for Agnes. Although it was after midnight, she informed her husband, still imprisoned at the convent of the Capuchins, that she was going back to San Luis Potosí to plead with Juárez for additional time. They awoke Maximilian, who wrote a quick letter to Juárez asking for two weeks. He handed her the letter with tears in his eyes and much appreciation. Thinking a letter of permission would expedite the mission, she sought out Escobedo at his headquarters, although it was almost one in the morning. "The general was just returning . . . from some place of amusement and I found him fortunately in good humor. He gave me not only a letter to Juárez, but also granted my request for an order to take the mules of [a] diligence," she wrote.[37]

She traveled with two bickering drivers through the night and all the next day, suffering delays with a broken carriage part, to arrive at Juárez's headquarters. When Juárez saw her the next day, she presented her argument and the letter from Maximilian. "I declared that it was barbarous to shoot a prisoner without having given him even time for his defense and to treat him as a traitor who had come in the honest belief that he had been elected and called by the Mexican people," said Agnes. A few more days would not matter, and if Juárez refused, people in the civilized world would say that he and the Mexican government had acted in a "hasty, cruel manner." She asked Juárez not to decide until five o'clock in the afternoon. If he decided against it, she would accept his decision, but with a heavy and sad heart.[38]

At five o'clock she returned to meet Juárez's secretary. He emerged from his office with a document granting the delay. "I was so overjoyed that I nearly hugged that worthy gentleman. I wished to see Mr. Juárez in order that I might thank him, but he was out," said Agnes. On her return trip, through a torrential downpour, she was accompanied by an associate of Bahnsen's, who drove as fast as possible to Querétaro. Against the gloom, they lit torches, but rain doused them. They stuck in the deep mud, which required everyone to get out, and Agnes and her maid picked their way over the rocky terrain on foot. "I had to walk for some leagues, which was indeed no joke on such a night and in such weather. I had, moreover, only one pair of thin boots, which were soon cut by the sharp stones," she said. The next morning they arrived at the Capuchin convent. "I was worn with fatigue, my boots torn to pieces, and my feet sore, my hair in disorder, and my face and hands unwashed. I must indeed have looked like a scarecrow, but I was very happy and a little proud too," said Agnes.[39]

The enigmatic princess, who had become a favorite with American reporters, later wrote that when a young soldier saw her returning to the convent he yelled in joy, "La Señora!" Félix Salm-Salm, who was in Maximilian's quarters, ran to embrace his sunburned and disheveled wife. With the good news from San Luis, they returned to Maximilian's room, with Jimmy leading the way, who jumped onto the emperor's bed. "They have granted the delay. Oh, your Majesty, I am so glad." she said. The emperor took her hand and kissed it. "May God bless you, Madam. You have been too kind to one who is afraid he can never serve you."[40]

The date for the trial was set for June 12, 1867, on the stage of the Teatro Iturbide, also known as the Teatro de la República. Juárez ordered that all communications between Maximilian and his generals, along with anyone other than his legal counsel or doctor, cease. The emperor was moved to another room away from his generals. As the date of the trial neared, Maximilian attempted, on his own behalf, to meet with Juárez to plead his case in person. Juárez refused. Meeting the persuasive gentleman captive would make it infinitely more difficult to pronounce a death sentence if the court-martial ruled against him.[41]

Meanwhile, Félix Salm-Salm felt that a reasonable chance of escape existed prior to Maximilian's trial. He trusted a number of the townspeople and Liberal officers who would be willing to spirit Maximilian and his generals out of city, allowing him go north and into the wild, blue mountains of the Sierra Gorda. They could make their way to the coast and be retrieved by two Austrian frigates, still cruising the gulf, the captains awaiting news of the emperor, as well as the Austrian corps.[42]

Prince Salm-Salm set the date of escape for Sunday, June 2. He and Agnes had bribed officials and guards with 3,000 gold pesos. At first, Maximilian would not consider "running away," but Salm-Salm persuaded him to prepare. Over the course of a week, Salm-Salm and Maximilian spoke in code and in German, sprinkling in a few words in Spanish here and there, to satisfy the guards who insisted that their conversations must be understood. The emperor made a list of provisions he would need, including black thread, beeswax, and spectacles to make a disguise, along with two serapes, two revolvers, and a sword. To the list, he added bread, red wine, and chocolate. "The Emperor would not cut off his beautiful beard, but tie it around his neck and put on spectacles. He said he would look so ridiculous without a beard if he should be retaken," said Salm-Salm. Maximilian laughed about an Imperialist general who cut off his big moustache to disguise himself, but afterward not even his best friends recognized him. Maximilian planned where he would rendezvous with his staff and other details, including how to get fast horses and obtaining a guide through the Sierra Gorda, using darkened lanterns. As the date for departure grew nearer, however, he began to have doubts, worried that the plan was too disorganized and would fail, meaning further suffering for everyone. Also, Maximilian would not leave without Miramón, who was still recovering from his facial injury and whose wife, Concepción, had just arrived with their new baby. He protested that his lawyers and Baron Magnus were on their way and could not leave. Salm-Salm despaired.[43]

On June 5 Baron Magnus arrived in Querétaro with Frederic Hooricks and two of the five lawyers hired to represent him: Mariano Riva Palacio, the father of the Liberal general Vicente Riva Palacio, and Rafael Martínez de la Torre. Two days earlier Frederic Hall, an American lawyer from California who represented American business interests in Mexico City, along with two other advocates from Querétaro, Jesús M. Vásquez and Eulalio Ortega, also arrived at the convent to prepare Maximilian's defense. Magnus came to see Maximilian, picking his way over the wives and children of the ragged guards who hung about the corridors of the convent. Magnus wrote that he was incensed at having to answer to each sentinel, especially those who smoked, spit, and talked loudly and disrespectfully. He was pleased to see that Maximilian's cell looked clean with fresh linen. His tiny room, four by six feet, had a large window that opened to the outer walk and courtyard. Maximilian hung a serape over it for privacy. Beside his bronze bed, he had a table and chairs with his luxuries of four silver candlesticks, an ivory crucifix, and his books, meticulously kept arranged in a certain way that revealed his interests in history, religion, and philosophy. His few servants freely came and went. Magnus marveled that Maximilian seemed to be businesslike, even good-humored, although resigned to the bad situation. When Magnus commented on his composure, Maximilian said, "When one has no longer the power to give orders, one has perforce to accept them. I am not the first sovereign to have been taken prisoner. My grandfather the Emperor Franz was also for a time prisoner, and I consider I have a duty towards my fellow monarchs and to history in general, to show that I am worthy of my breeding." Magnus felt great sympathy for him. Maximilian later added, "I know that Juárez wants to see my blood. I always thought the Republicans were inspired by high ide-

Iturbide Theater, Querétaro, site of the trial
of Maximilian and Generals Mejía and Miramón, 1867

als. I thought highly of them. But now I recognize they are bloodthirsty and even worse than some of my own supporters, which unfortunately is not an understatement."[44]

Maximilian continued, "If I had to choose again, I would act in the same way. I prefer my current luck to the embarrassment of being forced by the French to leave the country." He confessed his hatred for the French and said that if he were able to go back to Europe amid the rising tensions between the Germans and France, he would "ask your king permission to participate in the war against the French." He concluded, "I cannot hope for anything from this disgraceful court-martial or Juárez. I have only the escape, and everything is prepared."[45]

From Querétaro, Magnus traveled on to San Luis Potosí to give Juárez a message from the king of Prussia, Wilhelm I, guaranteeing that if he released Maximilian, he would never interfere in Mexican affairs again. During their discussion, Juárez told Magnus that the Mexican people demanded "the blood of the two traitor generals and of the foreign usurper who after the departure of the French had merely prolonged the civil war." Magnus, who suspected that the court-martial and defense was all for show, anticipated its outcome.[46]

Meanwhile, Frederic Hall spent several days interviewing Maximilian for trial and assisting Vásquez and Ortega. Hall realized the complication of the prosecution's argument holding him accountable for crimes against the people of Mexico. "The Treaty of Miramar placed your Majesty in an exceedingly difficult position; while it gave the French commander full control over the military actions and movement of the French troops, as well as over any body of mixed French and Mexican forces, it made the sovereign head responsible for their acts," Hall told Maximilian.[47]

"Yes, I know it, and I am almost ashamed of it, but I submitted to it, thinking it would be the best for the country," said Maximilian. After Hall's first two visits, he asked Maximilian permission to speak in English or French, in order to express the spirit of the law more specifically. Inviting him to speak in English, Maximilian seemed to comprehend well but hesitated over a word, occasionally saying it in French, and Hall would supply the English translation. "Since my practice with you, I speak better English," said Maximilian. "I do not speak as well as I did fifteen years ago; when I was in the Navy, I was in the habit of meeting officers who spoke it."[48]

Hall brought him Henry Wheaton's *History of the Law of Nations in Europe and America* translated into Spanish, so that he might further understand his rights under international law as set by moral standards between "civilized" nations. "Is it a good translation?" asked Maximilian. He noted that an American wrote it. "The Americans are a great people for improvements. And besides they are great lovers of justice. They pay much respect to the laws, that I admire them. And if God should spare my life, I intend to visit the United States," said Maximilian.[49]

Maximilian looked through the book along with various Mexican constitutional laws that favored his case. Hall left behind a copy of the accusations Juárez and his lawyers leveled at Maximilian. He studied papers, marked Wheaton's book in red pencil, and interpreted the unconstitutionality of certain charges brought against him. Hall and the other lawyers agreed with Maximilian, but Juárez chose to act against the constitution. They knew this prosecution would be about passion, not the law. Maximilian said the accusations were written so poorly, "I had to put my hand over my mouth to keep from laughing," he said.[50]

The emperor was allowed to speak to his generals, the embargo of communication lifted. Between long conferences with the lawyers, Maximilian played dominoes with Mejía, Miramón, Salm-Salm, and Basch. On one of his visits Hall was about to enter Maximilian's room but hesitated when he saw them in a tournament. Maximilian motioned Hall to join them. "This is a stupid game, it's like children's play," said Maximilian, thinking it seemed foolish for men of great military talent to be shuffling dominoes. But it was better than sitting idle.[51]

A few days later Escobedo learned of Salm-Salm's plan of escape and ordered that he and a few imperial officers, including Lt. Ernst Pitner, be separated from Maximilian and returned to Convent de las Teresitas as punishment. Maximilian said, "We have only the women to thank for that," blaming Concepción Miramón, the general's wife, for sharing the plot with too many people and trying to bribe a guard. Salm-Salm and Pitner were furious and upset when they realized they might not see the emperor again. In Maximilian's wing of the convent, Escobedo ordered the candles and lamps lit all night, the sentinels replaced and doubled in number.[52]

The prosecuting attorney, or *fiscal*, examined Maximilian in his cell in the convent. Maximilian had prepared for the meeting and vowed, as his attorneys advised, to refuse to answer any questions. The fiscal began by reading the thirteen charges against Maximilian, including his attempt to destroy the constitutional democracy, the usurpation of the sovereignty of a free country in violation of the law of January 25, 1862, effecting the law of October 3, 1865, known as the Black Decree, and the authorization of atrocities and murders of vast numbers of people. Maximilian said little in his defense, except that the citizens who wished for a monarchy had called him to Mexico. Beyond answering his name, his parents' names, where he was born, and his life experiences, he would not say much more. "The prosecutor did not get a word from me related to the indictment," said Maximilian.[53]

Maximilian's lawyers prepared a defense stating that Maximilian had been properly elected by a majority of the people according to their desire for a monarchy, well before his arrival in Mexico. He had been recognized by the nations of Europe and desired a high tribunal of competent authority. They sent this request to the members of the diplomatic corps, in order that they may bring pressure to bear on Juárez.[54]

On June 10 subordinates of the Imperialist army, the colonels and generals, were summarily sentenced to seven years and ten years in prison, respectively. The trial of Maximilian, Mejía, and Miramón was next. Feeling tired and ill, Maximilian went to bed at five in the afternoon that day, not much earlier than his routine. He asked Basch how he thought things would end for him. Basch replied that the whole trial was a game to demonstrate the mercy and fair play of the Liberals, which would eventually result in his freedom. "No, I do not believe that, they will simply shoot us. It is a mathematical problem you can calculate on your fingers. Colonels are sentenced to seven years in prison, generals ten. The only higher penalty under Mexican law is death."[55]

The trial opened in the Teatro Iturbide on June 12. The six judges, prosecutors, defendants, and defense lawyers sat on the stage. A restricted number of the general public, including family and some press, sat in the auditorium. The prosecutor selected the presiding judges from a cadre of young, subordinate officers serving under Escobedo: Rafael Platón Sánchez as president along with Vicente Rodríguez, Emilio Logero, Ignacio Jurado, Juan Rueda y Auza, José Verástegui, and Lucas Villagran. "God forgive me," said Maximilian, "but I believe they have sought out for the court-martial only those with the best uniforms, so that externally at least everything has a decorous appearance." Seeing the farce of the proceedings, Maximilian refused to attend, seeking a pretext. Basch issued a medical order to excuse him because of acute dysentery but truly assessed that the emperor was too ill to attend.[56]

During the trial Agnes Salm-Salm could not bear to see Maximilian wait out an unjust trial with no one to advocate for him behind the scenes. Again she determined that the guards must be bribed to allow him to escape. Now she played on her own personal charms without the assistance of her husband. Escobedo likely knew of her activities but turned a blind eye, thinking that if his captive escaped so too would all the controversy over a possible execution, for which his record would always be branded. Knowing that Maximilian had little cash left in hand, Agnes learned from one of the guards that bribes would be accepted in the form of a check or debit bills, if signed by the emperor. Maximilian approved of the scheme and bills were written for 6,000 pesos to be drawn against his account in Vienna.[57]

Maximilian, who had not been able to count on the Austrian chargé d'affaires Lago for much, prevailed on him nevertheless to cosign the voucher. Lago, a hostile, nervous sort of man who feared reprisals from the Austrian government, at first refused. Maximilian persuaded Lago to sign the checks anyway. But after a short while Lago panicked and, "forgetting all his diplomatic dignity, jumped about the room like a rabbit pursued by Jimmy, tore his hair, and cried, 'We cannot sign them. If we do we will be hanged.'" Almost immediately he cut his name out of the checks with a pair of scissors. The next day Maximilian wrote out two more promissory notes, this time for 100,000 pesos each, payable upon his release.[58]

With these notes, Agnes Salm-Salm planned to approach "the hyena," Col. Palacios, about taking the money and letting Maximilian go free. Although the small paper was not actual cash, it amounted to more money than he had ever seen. After her nightly visit to the convent to see her husband, she asked Palacios to walk her to the private home nearby where she was staying and where, curiously, Maximilian's captor Gen. Echegaray was also lodged. That day she had spent time with Maximilian. In a somewhat melancholy mood himself, he had given her his signet ring, saying that if Palacios accepted the bribe he was to return it to Maximilian afterward as a sign of his silent cooperation.[59]

Palacios agreed to walk her to her house. On the way he explained that he had risen through the ranks to superintend military executions. Agnes knew he could barely read or write, had a young wife and child, and hoped for a better future. She saw her angle of attack—she would prevail upon him to take the check to support his family. She wrote, "I invited him to the parlor. He followed and I began to speak of the emperor in order to ascertain . . . whether I had any chance of success. He said that he had been a great enemy of the emperor, but after having been so long about him and having witnessed how good and nobly he behaved in his misfortune," he felt differently. He agreed, saying he had looked many times into the emperor's blue eyes that did not flinch, and he knew that Maximilian was honest. She held up the emperor's ring and said that if he agreed, he should take it to the emperor as an indication that his escape would not be impeded.[60]

After Palacios pledged secrecy, Agnes offered him the check, explaining it would be redeemed in gold, paid by the imperial family in Austria. He mulled it over for a moment and said he felt sympathy for Maximilian but could not make a decision in five minutes. He took the check from her and looked at it with curiosity, never having seen one before. "A bag full of gold would have been more persuasive," said Agnes later. When he handed her back the paper, she said, "Well then . . . you are not well disposed. Think about it and remember your word of honor and your oath. You know that without you nothing can be done and to betray me would serve no purpose whatever."[61]

Palacios left the house but went immediately to tell Escobedo of her proposal. "Before the next morning, a guard was placed at my house," said Agnes.

The superintendent of the patrol, Refúgio González, met her at the door and said, with a large grin, that Escobedo wished to see her immediately. She went to his headquarters, and when Escobedo arrived, "he looked black as a thunderstorm."

"In a polite but sarcastic tone he observed 'that the air here in Querétaro did not seem to agree with me, that it was indeed very bad.'" She assured him she felt fine, but he said a carriage waited to transport her to San Luis Potosí.

"I told him I had no desire whatever to go there, but I thanked him for his kindness. . . . His anger overmastered him. He said he found it so extremely wrong in me . . . after he had shown me so much kindness and treated me so well, [that I] tried to bribe his officers and to bring him into an embarrassing situation."[62]

"I have done nothing, General, of which I need be ashamed and what you yourself would not have done I my position," she argued.

"We will not argue that point, madam; but I wish you to leave Querétaro," said Escobedo.[63]

She was indignant that the guards followed her through the house as she packed her belongings. One officer tried to grab her arm to escort her. "As quick as lightning, I drew from under my dress my little revolver, and pointing at the breast of the terrified captain, I cried, 'Captain, touch me with one finger and you are a dead man,'" she said. She hastily gathered her things and, with Jimmy and her servant, jumped into a waiting carriage for the long trip to San Luis Potosí. On her way out of town she saw Generals Mejía and Miramón being escorted to their court-martial by fifty riflemen. Mejía looked drawn and weak from illness while Miramón appeared defiant and almost giddy.[64]

On June 13, on the stage of the Teatro Iturbide, Mejía and Miramón sat on a bench and listened to the charges levied against them and Maximilian in absentia, the emperor substituted for by a vacant stool. The trial captivated the people. "You could have heard the wings of a fly," said one observer, because they thought the emperor was almost sacred and the "majority of the public was in favor of the Empire, and therefore believed . . . they should not touch a hair." Mejía was tried first, followed by Miramón. Both were led, one after the other, to a stool on the stage. The prosecution accused the two of a series of charges including treason and executing prisoners without due process. Mejía argued that he had regularly shown clemency for his captives, even refusing to execute Escobedo, when once before he captured him and then set him free. Miramón reminded the panel that until recently he had been in Europe and had returned to pick up the sword of the imperial government only when the

French began leaving Mexico. He also described a number of instances when he had refused to execute prisoners.[65]

After Miramón's session ended, the government pressed thirteen charges against Maximilian in his absence, especially the Black Decree of October 3, 1865, that caused the deaths of hundreds of innocent people. Prosecutors stated that in civilized nations, prisoners of war should not be executed; however, the war conducted by France, supported by Maximilian, was illegal, barbaric, and deprived the people of international law and individual guarantees. They argued that Juárez's law of January 25, 1862, applied. These foreigners took up arms to destroy the country's independence. Defending attorney Eulalio Ortega unreeled the story of Maximilian's path to Mexico, how he had been the tool of the French and, in fact, arrived only after a vote representing the will of the people calling for an empire in Mexico. Ortega, Vásquez, and Riva Palacio asserted that the January 25 law did not apply to the facts of the case and was therefore irregular and unconstitutional. The defense attorneys reminded the judges that Maximilian upheld Juárez's reform laws, that he had refused the French any lands and mines in Sonora, and generally opposed many of the demands of the French military. As for the Black Decree, that order was made only after the emperor had been told Juárez had abandoned Mexico. Despite the decree, he consistently granted clemency to the accused.[66]

Ortega attempted to define the difference between matters governed by international law and matters that required the application of constitutional law, two different systems. He argued that Maximilian came into power as the result of civil unrest and the people's choice of a different system. "When civil war rages among a people, it is ended by the same means as international wars: by an agreement—once the parties become tired of destruction and end their fighting. . . . One party succeeds ultimately in becoming ruler over the other." He closed his arguments with a final thought: "If you condemn the archduke to death I am not worried about a coalition in Europe or the threatening attitude the United States may assume against the republic. But I fear the universal reproach that will fall upon our country, as an anathema more than even the sentence of death, but because of the nullity of the proceedings of this court."[67]

On the first night of the trial, Miramón returned to the convent. Upon seeing his wife, he pressed her hand to his lips while in the presence of Maximilian. Seeing that the emperor had noticed their exchange of affection and was weeping quietly, Miramón apologized, knowing that Maximilian was certain to be missing Carlota terribly. "I am only weeping because you do not deserve to endure these sufferings on my account, when otherwise you could be so happy," Maximilian said. Miramón took his wife's hand again and said, "I am here because I would not listen to this woman's advice." Maximilian replied, "Do not feel remorse. I am here because I did listen to my wife." They both smiled despite their despair.[68]

Maximilian had been in the process of writing letters of farewell to his family in Austria. He also wrote to Carlota: "If God grant that you should recover your health and are able to read these lines, you will understand the cruelty of the fate which has been dealing me its blows without respite since your departure for Europe." He said that all his hope was broken. "Death is to me a happy release. I shall fall proudly as a soldier, like a king defeated but not dishonored. If your sufferings are too severe, and God calls you to come and join me soon, I shall bless the hand of God which has been heavy upon us. Adieu, Charlotte," he wrote.[69]

The next day Maximilian heard that Carlota had died, based on hearsay told to the spouse of Mejía. The generals knew that Carlota's illness weighed heavily on Maximilian and that it tormented him that he had not returned to Europe upon hearing she had suffered a mental breakdown. Word of Carlota's death devastated him beyond imagination. "One less string that binds me to life," he said to Basch. The proud and now broken emperor wrote to the Austrian consul Baron Lago lodging nearby. "I have just heard that my poor wife is released from her sufferings. The news, however heartbreaking, is at the same time an unspeakable consolation to me. I have now only one wish on earth, that my body should be laid beside that of my wife. With this mission I entrust you, my dear Baron."[70]

Midmorning on June 16, the fourteen-hour trial ended in a verdict of guilt for Maximilian and the generals. As most suspected, the decision was predetermined, and the defense's arguments amounted to wasted words and pantomime. The court-martial found all three men guilty of treason. Three voted for a sentence of banishment, three voted for execution. However, the tie-breaking soldier represented Juárez's wishes, and the panel announced the death penalty. The judge read the sentence of execution by firing squad to be conducted on the Cerro de las Campanas at three o'clock that afternoon. Escobedo left the city for a nearby hacienda, unable to be present for the executions.[71]

In a daze, Miramón and Mejía returned to the convent and conveyed the news to Maximilian. As the generals spent time with their wives and children, he wrote final letters to relatives and friends, thanking them for their kind words and attempts at intervention. Maximilian, who over the last weeks had seemed ambivalent about his fate, was transcendently calm. "It is strange that from my earliest youth I have always had the feeling I would not die a natural death, and for a long time I have known that I would never leave this country alive," he wrote Baron Magnus. Father Manuel Soria, Canon of the Cathedral of Querétaro, set up an altar and said mass followed by the rite of extreme unction in preparation for death. They could hear the entire Republican garrison march to the Cerro de las Campanas for the execution.[72]

He wrote his last thoughts to his parents, his brothers, Count Charles Bombelles, Professor Dominik Bilimek, the Conservatives who brought him to Mexico, including José María Gutiérrez de Estrada, and others. In the shortness of time, many of the letters were dictated to Dr. Basch, who remembered Maximilian looking like a "living dead man." He divided his possessions among his friends. He made his last wishes known, asking that he not be shot in the head, "For it is not seemly for an emperor to writhe on the ground in his death agony." The condemned took their last mass with confession and communion. The only sign of Maximilian's nervousness was his constant touching of his beard.[73]

In Querétaro, Maximilian and the two generals spent their final hours in prayer. Maximilian read the *Imitation of Christ* by Thomas à Kempis. He also drew up instructions for his embalming, according to his family's royal traditions, since such postmortem preservation was rarely performed in Mexico and certainly not to standards for Habsburg royals. Liberals stipulated that an appointed state doctor perform the work but would allow Basch to supervise. Maximilian asked Carlos Rubio, the banker in whose home Maximilian refused to hide on the day he was captured, to pay for his embalming, "being completely devoid of money." He also asked that his body be shipped to Europe, promising that his family would reimburse the expense. After these communications, Maximilian told Basch, "I can tell you that dying is much easier than I had imagined. I am completely ready."[74]

All that remained was for Maximilian, Mejía, and Miramón to be led to the firing squad. The minutes passed very slowly, like lead. They looked out at the orange grove in the patio of the convent, hoping to see any sign, any word. The hour of three o'clock arrived with the chiming of the church bells, and then it passed. All seemed deafeningly calm now. It was a cruel, cold, prolonged torture. This gave rise to the hope that maybe a pardon had been granted.[75]

Everyone prayed for Juárez's leniency.

❦[22]❧

¡Viva Mexico!
¡Viva el Emperador!

Finally, late in the day, Col. Palacios arrived smiling with a dispatch from San Luis Potosí announcing a deferral of the execution for three days. Maximilian and the generals, as well as Escobedo, interpreted this hesitation as a sign that Juárez was reconsidering their sentences. All felt guarded relief and hope. Baron Anton von Magnus, while at San Luis Potosí, had asked for the postponement under the pretext of wanting to be able to travel to Querétaro to be with the sovereign in his last moments. He had begged Juárez in the name of humanity to let the three men live. In his request he relayed messages from Queen Isabella II of Spain, Queen Victoria of England, Leopold II of Belgium, and many other influential sovereigns in Europe who wanted to see Maximilian released. William Seward forwarded similar requests received in his office.[1]

Additionally, Magnus hoped Juárez would take time to reflect on the severity of the punishment. He wished the president would realize the setback this would be for the future of the republic. Afterward, world powers would not consider Mexico a country that abided by the same rules of war, prisoners, and diplomatic courtesy as more civilized nation-states. Magnus thought Juárez might reconsider if he remembered his position as a leader and tempered his vindictive desire, the overzealous military, and passions of his advisors. Surely Juárez would want to demonstrate that he was a levelheaded man averse to hastily rushing the former emperor before a firing squad. Despite these efforts, Maximilian had become resigned to his fate. "Come what may, I no longer belong to this world," he said. He did, however, express his anger and frustration at the torture of the last hours. He felt that Juárez was mulling over the pleas of assistance from monarchs of European states and the United States. They all offered him and his country a better chance if he released Maximilian, and the archduke knew it.[2]

Although they sent numerous telegrams, upon learning of Juárez's order to postpone the execution, Maximilian's lawyers rode day and night to reach San Luis Potosí in the early morning hours of June 15. They met with Juárez's counselor, Sebastián Lerdo de Tejada, who seemed sanguine and relaxed but refused a pardon, saying that the Mexican army would never tolerate Maximilian's freedom after six years of bloody war. If they did not punish him, how could they execute his subordinates Mejía and Miramón?[3]

Agnes Salm-Salm, who had also recently arrived in San Luis Potosí, heard the news of the verdict and sped to the municipal palace. She pushed her way into Juárez's office to get some reassurance on the fate of her husband and hopefully, somehow, still save Maximilian. Juárez promised that her husband would be freed. However, nothing could be done about Maximilian's pending execution. The princess viewed the three-day delay as "an act not only of sickly weakness, but of cruelty, for it could not but inspire the poor emperor with delusive hopes." She was equally angry with Magnus, who hurried back to Querétaro, but with an embalmer for the emperor. "He was walking about like a man who had lost half a dozen of his five senses," she said of Magnus.[4]

Agnes sent a telegram to President Andrew Johnson in the United States, urging him to send another, more strongly worded protest to Juárez. Overestimating her influence, she informed Juárez that he would be hearing soon from the president. He responded that no further delay could be granted, and indeed, he regretted allowing the first deferral.[5]

Under pressure from numerous individuals and the press, Johnson ordered Secretary of State Seward to contact Juárez personally by cable asking for clemency for Maximilian, feeling sure he would grant it. Accordingly, Seward did so immediately. He also forwarded telegrams from the governments of England and France on June 15. All was futile. The telegrams did not bear enough political weight with Juárez to make a difference. In the United States, it seems that few took the possibility of Maximilian's execution seriously. Seward either did not fully comprehend Maximilian's fate or did not care as much as was implied publicly. At a dinner party, on June 17 in Washington, he remarked to Austrian minister Wydenbruck that Maximilian's "life is quite safe as yours and mine."[6]

The night before the execution, Agnes Salm-Salm in San Luis Potosí tried once again to persuade Juárez to release Maximilian. He received her at once. "He looked pale and suffering himself. With trembling lips I pleaded for the life of the emperor," she recalled. Juárez said he could not grant her wish, that the execution would happen in the morning as planned. Plunging into despair, Agnes knelt before him, weeping, and grasped his knees, further imploring him. Juárez tried to raise her to her feet, but she would not let go until he conceded to a reprieve. "I saw the president was moved, he . . . had tears in [his] eyes but answered me with a low sad voice, 'I am grieved, madam, to see you thus on your knees before me, but if all the kings and queens of Europe were in your place I could not spare that life. It is not I who take it, it is the people and the law, and if I should not do its will the people would take it and mine also.'"[7]

She pleaded that he might take her life instead. He raised her hands so she would stand and repeated that her husband's life was spared and that was all he could do. She thanked him and left. In the antechamber of his office she saw a crowd of ladies from San Luis Potosí waiting to see Juárez. They, too, came to plead for the lives of Maximilian, Mejía, and Miramón. When Miramón's wife, Concepción, appealed to Juárez and asked why they could not be pardoned, his reply was the same. "I can do nothing," he said. He also refused appeals by other dignitaries who happened to remain in Mexico.[8]

To outside observers, Juárez seemed cold and aloof. Nevertheless, he felt a deep conviction that the world needed to see one swift, final answer to interference in Mexico. "The impatient are going to the devil because they want everything to be over at once, the great criminals will go unpunished, and the future peace of the nation will not be guaranteed, but the government, without heeding them, continues to make haste slowly and with the firm determination to do what best befits the country, and without being influenced in its decisions by personal vengeance, misguided compassion, or any foreign threat. We have fought for the independence and autonomy of Mexico, and it must be a reality," wrote Juárez to his family.[9] Maximilian had been in Mexico little more than three years and three weeks.

Now only a miracle could save Maximilian. His ministers thought of trying to bribe Juárez. But the president remained immovable and, from all outside appearances, dispassionate. This was his moment to stand firm after five years of powerlessness. Maximilian's life represented his chance to demonstrate to Europe and the United States that no continued usurpation of Mexico's republican integrity or its territory would be tolerated. He did not have the luxury of flexibility. "The law and the sentence are unstoppable, because they are required for the public good. This also accommodates for the economy of blood, and his will be the greatest pleasure of my life," said Juárez. But when Seward prevailed on him to release former Imperialistas also sentenced to capital punishment or death, including Félix Eloin and Prince Félix Salm-Salm, he commuted their sentences to a few years' imprisonment and then, under further pressure, granted amnesty, wishing to demonstrate his magnanimity.[10]

On June 17 Maximilian learned that Carlota was alive and, greatly relieved, he penned a note to Edouard Radonetz, the prefect of Miramar Castle, expressing gratitude and asking him to remain at Carlota's side and be devoted to her as long as she lived at Trieste. Maximilian remained composed and dignified, which made the process more difficult for every observer to witness, Liberal or Imperialist. He remained concerned for others' welfare but worried for his soul, he wrote to Pope Pius IX. "As I leave for the gallows, for a death I do not deserve, my heart is touched with the total affection for the Holy Church. I address your Holiness, with full honesty and satisfaction, to forgive, as a good father, the faults that may have been against you, Vicar of Jesus Christ, and your fatherly heart." If possible, he asked for a mass in his name.[11]

The generals wrote farewell letters to their spouses and families. Both had newborn babies, rendering it especially difficult. For that, Maximilian felt much empathy. He dictated one last telegram to Juárez, asking him to stay the generals' executions: "On the point of suffering death in consequence of having wished to prove whether new political institutions could succeed in putting an end to the bloody civil war which has devastated this unfortunate country for so many years, I will gladly yield up my life, if its sacrifice can contribute to the peace and prosperity of my adopted country. . . . I implore you in the most solemn manner . . . that my blood may be the last to be spilt." Juárez denied his request.[12]

Maximilian's former generals wrote letters conveying their loyalty and admiration for the man who had fought by their sides in the last stand at Querétaro. "We the defeated generals, your admirers and friends, are also in the path to the place of execution, and should implacable fate be unfortunate to us all, then sire, in heaven we will unite around Your Majesty," they said. Gen. Escobedo made one final visit to the convent of the Capuchins to make peace with Mejía, who had once spared his own execution. He greeted the general and, with emotion, offered to try with all his power to release him and let the Otomí leader leave for his ancient homeland in the territory of the Sierra Gorda. Escobedo seemed ready to let Mejía walk out unguarded. Mejía replied that he could only accept a pardon if Maximilian and Miramón were also allowed their freedom. When Escobedo said this possibility lay beyond his power, Mejía said, "Good, then let me be shot with His Majesty." Escobedo also visited Maximilian in his cell to say farewell. The emperor gave him a small portrait of himself and asked him to do his best for Mexico.[13]

On June 19 Maximilian awoke well before dawn, at three. He dressed in traditional civilian Austrian clothing, with black pants of a wide waistband secured with embossed buttons, a black vest with horn buttons, a white blouse, and his black frock coat. He carried his white hat. Padre Manuel Soria, a priest who had come all week to conduct services and comfort the emperor and generals, appeared at Maximilian's cell to give him and the generals one final mass. The archduke received communion on bent knees, which moved the priest to tears. Other witnesses wept, but immediately they found Maximilian comforting them, telling them they must yield to God's all-knowing mandates. He removed his wedding ring. This, with a rosary and scapular given to him by the priest, he asked Basch to take to his mother. He took the little medal of the Virgin Mary given to him by France's Empress Eugénie and pressed it into Basch's hands, asking that he send it to his cousin, the empress of Brazil.[14]

He stepped toward Mejía and Miramón. "Are you ready, gentlemen? I am already prepared." They embraced each other soundly. "Soon we shall meet again in the other world." Miramón, who had been resigned to his fate since the day before, seemed calm but asked if they were going up to heaven or down to hell. "Without a doubt, up, and very soon, the guns are already being prepared," said Maximilian. As he stood, Mejía staggered a bit, weakened by his ongoing bout with typhus. Just before 6:30 a.m., Maximilian descended the staircase of the convent into the open air. The beautiful morning emerged clear, cool, and cloudless. "What a glorious day!" said Maximilian. "I have always wanted to die on just such a day."[15]

Escobedo's troops took Maximilian with Miramón and Mejía, in a dusty caravan of hacks, to the Cerro de las Campanas, the site of his surrender thirty-five days earlier. Each vehicle carried the condemned and his father confessor. A large detachment of cavalry and infantry escorted the three carriages. There was a profound silence among the ranks and in the city, which remained largely shuttered. Mejía's wife, Agustina Castro, crying and carrying their new baby, ran after the coach. Maximilian's Hungarian cook, Tüdös, and his valet, Grill, followed in another carriage. The rest of his staff was forbidden to attend the execution. The European ministers could not bear to look upon the scene, except for Magnus who hid among the crowd of soldiers to watch. Gen. Escobedo did not attend.[16]

Coach that delivered Maximilian to his execution, ca. 1867

When they arrived at the Cerro de las Campanas, Maximilian's carriage stopped, and he exited brushing the dust off his jacket, grasping a crucifix in his hand. Tüdös followed behind Maximilian along with Father Soria. The two generals walked behind him to the firing line. Soria and Tüdös stumbled to help Mejía, who struggled to walk over the scree, barely lucid. Three thousand soldiers waited at the cerro, ordered to witness the execution. The emperor, who looked somewhat pale, held his head high. "He already seemed to belong to another world. Beside him trotted his little Hungarian cook like a faithful dog hanging on his last words," said Magnus. Maximilian turned to Tüdös, who had lived in denial that his master would be put to death. "Now do you believe that they are going to shoot me?" he asked. "To die is not so difficult as you think." He wiped his brow with his handkerchief and handed it to Tüdös along with his sombrero, and asked him, in Hungarian, to take them to his mother, the archduchess. He kissed the crucifix and returned it to the padre.[17]

Maximilian, Mejía, and Miramón positioned themselves, bareheaded, before a low thick wall of adobe brick. Miramón stood at his left, Mejía at his right. They looked down at the city of Querétaro below, the site of their battles, as they had done while camping atop the hill. The verdict of the trial and order of execution was read aloud, with a threat that whoever tried to stop the proceedings would be shot summarily. The emperor, with a transcendent calmness, looked around the crowd of Mexican soldiers and recognized almost no one. As they took their places before the firing squad, Maximilian embraced Mejía and Miramón, saying, "In a few moments we will meet in the

When the Mexican military would not allow François Aubert to photograph
the execution of Maximilian and his two generals, he took out a sketch pad and
quickly made a rendering on the spot. Although re-created photo images were
made later, this is the most accurate depiction of the execution as it
occurred on the Cerro de Campanas on June 19, 1867.

other world." Then he turned to Miramón and said, "General, a brave man
must be honored by his monarch even in the face of death. Allow me to give
you the place of honor." He stepped back and traded places to allow Miramón
to take the center position. He turned to Mejía and said, "General, what is not
rewarded on earth will surely be in heaven." Mejía whispered only a few words
to his compatriots.[18]

Seeing the fifteen-man firing squad from the first battalion of Nuevo León
get into formation only five paces from them, Maximilian held up his hand
and said a few words to the confused and reluctant squad commander. "You
are a soldier, you must obey," he said. Maximilian stepped forward and gave a
gold coin to each one, saying, "Muchachos, aim well, aim right here," pointing to his chest, saying they should not hit him in the face, so that his mother
could look upon him. He then returned to his place before the executioners but
appeared as though he had more to say. He beat his chest with both hands to
assure, again, that his torso should be the target.[19]

Maximilian straightened his posture and said in Spanish, "Mexicans. Men
of my class and origins are appointed by God to be the happiness of people or
their martyrs. Called by some of you, I came for the good of the country, I did
not come for ambition, but animated by the best wishes for the future of my

adoptive country, for the brave who died before in glorious sacrifice. Mexican people, I hope that my blood will be the last to be spilled and I pray that it regenerates this unhappy country. ¡Viva Mexico, Viva la Independencia!" He then crossed his hands on his chest for a moment, raising his eyes to the heavens.[20]

Miramón and Mejía prepared to die. Miramón took a scrap of paper from his pocket and read "soldiers of Mexico and my countrymen, I find myself here sentenced to die as a traitor. When my life does not belong to me, when in a few brief moments, I will be no more, I proclaim before you and the whole world that I have never been a traitor to my country. I have fought for her . . . I have children, but they can never blame their father for this infamous calumny that I am today charged with," and then he shouted, "¡Viva Mexico, Viva el Emperador!" After Mejía repeated the *viva* in a muted, drained voice, clutching a rosary, the three embraced again and solemnly faced the death squad preparing its aim. Maximilian, with a peaceful expression, turned his face left and right, looking around at the soldiers and people. Magnus reported that only about fifty civilians attended.[21]

Upon the order to fire, the commander lowered his saber and six bullets ripped into Maximilian's body. He uttered a final word, "hombre," staggered, and fell to the ground, dead. Four musket balls imprinted the sign of the cross. Three of the chest wounds felled him, penetrating the heart and lungs, through the body. The others went through the abdomen. His death throes lasted only a few moments. Miramón and Mejía also fell dead. Miramón died almost instantly, but Mejía suffered a prolonged agony. Magnus noted the time by his pocket watch: 6:40. Because the shots were fired from a short distance, the garments of the three men ignited, smoldering. Two Mexican physicians doused the bodies with water.[22]

The *Boletín Republicano* reported dispassionately that at seven in the morning on June 19, 1867, "Archduke Ferdinand Maximilian of Austria ceased to exist." The Querétaro *Sombra de Arteaga*, however, printed the death notice on red paper. The editors could not express sadness or joy without offending Maximilian's supporters or his executioners, who remained bitterly divided. Sebastián Lerdo de Tejada announced the executions in a low-key statement, telling the Mexican ministers that it was necessary under the circumstances.[23]

In Washington, D.C., the next day, June 20, Secretary of State Seward received a notice from Franz Josef through Austrian minister Wydenbruck. "Request Mr. Seward to let Juárez know, and if possible, Prince Maximilian, that the Emperor of Austria is ready to reestablish Maximilian in all his rights

Firing squad that executed Maximilian, Gen. Miguel Miramón,
and Gen. Tomás Mejía, June 19, 1867

of succession as Archduke of Austria after his release and his renunciation of all his projects to Mexico." Immediately, Seward forwarded this request to Matías Romero to transmit to Juárez.[24] At last, Franz Josef opened the door to welcome his brother's return, dropping the restrictions of the Family Pact. All had been forgiven, a day too late.

Two other appeals reached Juárez after the executions, arriving after the fact. The liberal writer and opponent of Napoléon, Victor Hugo, wired on June 20 from his exile in the Channel Islands, saying that to free Maximilian would be an act of heroism. "This will be your victory, Juárez. The first in overcoming usurpation is superb. The second, in forgiving the usurper, will be sublime." One of Italy's most famous military and political figures, Giuseppe Garibaldi, sent a letter of intercession from Italy on July 5. Both men begged Juárez to show the world his moral superiority and spare Maximilian's life, despite the effusion of blood. The two opposed the French intervention and the Mexican empire but appealed in the name of humanity.[25]

Over the next two weeks, newspapers in the United States and Europe reported the execution. Most members of the U.S. Congress seemed relieved that the French occupation and the Mexican empire had ended, no matter how tragically. They quickly congratulated themselves that Juárez had begun to rebuild the republic. However, Maximilian's death horrified most Europeans, who blamed Napoléon. Austrian ambassador Prince Richard Metternich wrote that Napoléon's motivations were inconceivable. As a "prestidigitateur de premier ordre," he saw that the French emperor unwisely transferred all his hopes to the Habsburg prince, who against insuperable odds remained unable to garner sincere and deep support from the richly varied societies of Mexico but remained loyal to his new empire and to France. A number of royals lamented that they had not more vigorously urged for intervention. After the fact, many lauded him as their beloved martyr. Maximilian's worst crime was "accepting the treacherous gift of empire, but his misfortune was greater than his fault." He tried to fulfill his obligations and live up to the standards exhibited by those forebears he admired. "The fame of my ancestors will not degenerate in me," he said, according to one observer.[26]

Later, Alfonse Dano said that the second greatest obstacle to the last Mexican empire, next to the objections of the United States, was Maximilian. "The Austrian reasoned well and acted entirely to the contrary," wrote Dano. Although he said he thrived in the air of the New World, he could not free himself entirely from the decadent ways of Europe or the protocol of the Habsburgs. To please others, he hemmed in his own sense of adventure and altruism, unable to let common sense outweigh conventions he thought he should impose on the country.[27] He said he wanted to teach the people to obey, but he really wanted to lead and inspire.

In the end, critics also blamed Maximilian for deliberately clashing with the Conservatives and Catholic Church in order to demonstrate his progressiveness to his European countrymen. While he could have made some guarantees to the church on their former properties, he also could have used the nationalized lands to fund his empire. His free thinking, poor strategies, and vacillations caused him to insult the Conservatives by placing Liberals on his cabinet, who had no real desire for an empire, although they admired the emperor, a highly charming, warm, and likeable man. He thought he was making himself popular by choosing advisors freely and willfully. When Maximilian could have struck an agreement with the Vatican while still in Europe, he did not. Then he arrived in Mexico, and because he was unable to translate his openness to the intransigent Pius IX across the ocean, the open disagreement amounted to a stillborn empire in the view of the omnipresent Catholic Church. His disdain for detail or conflict of any sort within his cabinet and his tendency to defer or deny problems led him to blame others or turn to frivolous pursuits. With the French still waging war, Maximilian could not stabilize the empire's operations or funding, so he built railroads, telegraph lines, and redesigned Mexico City. While genuinely good at the heart of things, he never truly mas-

Concepción Miramón in mourning after the execution of her husband, Miguel Miramón, ca. 1867. Disgraced after her husband's death and with a pension from Eugénie, she lived in the United States and educated her children there.

tered Mexico. Napoléon III's underestimation of the size and ruggedness of Mexico and the resilience of the Republicans also contributed to the failure of the empire. It required twice the troops to completely conquer the country. The Imperialistas could have maintained an army under their own methods, but the French, Austrian, and Belgian commanders remained too arrogant, stubborn, and anticlerical to work with the Mexican officers. On the other hand, the Mexican generals were not allowed to develop one consolidated plan. Benito Juárez's convictions paired with the moral and material backing of the United States brought about the dénouement of the French "Grand Design" to regenerate the country.[28] These things combined simply crumbled Mexico's Second Empire both from within and without.

Maximilian and Carlota, the naïve victims of Napoléonic greed, their own desires, and Mexican pride, changed Mexico forever during their short reign. Rulers by paper rights, their chimeric empire, set on a loose foundation in a time of international conflict, foundered but left Mexico with a more solid sense of patriotism, unachievable in the forty years prior. Mexico took the opportunity to telegraph to Europe that they would reject any other incursions. Many, though, reflected on what Mexico may have become if Maximilian and Carlota had succeeded. Moreover, the human factor persisted. Although the sovereigns failed to charm all Mexicans, this last empire of Mexico united the people, ignited imaginations and passions, and impacted future governments. No matter how the world considered Maximilian's reign or ambition, his life ended tragically as the victim of two nations: France and Mexico. It was a dazzling, unforgettable episode that said more about the people of the nation and its place in geopolitics than its rulers.

Epilogue

After the execution, two surgeons verified the death of Maximilian, along with Mejía and Miramón, and ordered their bodies wrapped in coarse linen. The remains of the two generals were placed in crude boxes and released to their family members, but Maximilian's remains were conveyed to the church of the Capuchins for embalming under the supervision of Dr. Samuel Basch. Doctors covered Maximilian's body with a sheet and placed it in a coffin ordered by Escobedo, then transported it back to the town. Salm-Salm thought the doctors handled Maximilian's remains disgracefully, his boots visible, the cloth too short. The doctor Ignacio Rivadeneira, who was little familiar with the procedure of embalming, brought in Vicente Licea, a doctor more versed on the method. Despite this, Basch, whom Maximilian desired to perform the procedure, thought they mismanaged the task, taking eight days to prepare the body. Salm-Salm said they took their work very lightly, smoking while cutting into Maximilian's body and making crude comments about washing their hands in the emperor's blood, as some of the guards looked on laughing. They placed his heart, liver, and lungs in an ossuary, according to Habsburg burial customs. "Those ought to be given to the dogs," joked one guard, as the body parts were removed. One onlooker, a young diplomat named Ernst Schmit von Tavera, was shocked to see Maximilian's body blindfolded and suspended by ropes to aid in the desiccation. Dr. Licea made a death mask of Maximilian's face and an inventory of the clothing, which he gave to Dr. Basch, who then

Maximilian after his embalming,
ca. July 1867

delivered the bullet-riddled garments to the secretary of the Austrian embassy with orders to ship them to Vienna.[1]

After the body's preparation, Baron Magnus immediately asked Gen. Escobedo to release the archduke's remains. Escobedo replied that he could not under orders from Juárez but would make the request and have the answer in a few days. More insistently, Magnus traveled to San Luis Potosí to demand the body from Lerdo de Tejada. He learned that Baron Lago had made the same request, but the body could only be released to family of the archduke or some other duly authorized person. Magnus produced a letter written by Maximilian authorizing Magnus's mandate to receive the corpse. Lerdo promised to take up the matter with Juárez. Magnus assumed that antirepublican demonstrations would erupt should the body be transported to Veracruz. Lago and Magnus promised no pomp and no cortege in association with removing the remains. On June 30 Magnus's requests were rejected. The diplomats speculated that Juárez wished to use the remains as a bargaining chip for official recognition by European powers.[2]

The embalmers placed the body in a zinc liner, then in a wooden coffin, which they positioned across two benches in the convent. They covered the

Maximilian in casket in Querétaro

box with a black pall garnished with inexpensive gold lace. The lid had three windows through which Maximilian's body could be viewed, the middle pane embossed with an "M" in gold. Sadly, observers could see that his mouth and eyes remained partially open. Dr. Licea had ordered blue glass eyes, but the ones used seemed terribly unnatural. He was dressed in a navy blue coat and pants, and his heavy cavalry boots. Soiled gray gloves covered his hands. It was thought that the embalmers had removed part of his beard and reportedly sold locks of his hair. In two small compartments at the foot of the coffin, the doctors placed the containers with Maximilian's organs. The doctors treated the body with charcoal and a chloride of lime, but much to their alarm the skin began to darken quickly.[3]

On July 7, 1867, Juárez on his triumphant return to Mexico City stopped at Querétaro to view Maximilian's body. He observed his former nemesis in repose, the first time he had ever seen him in person.[4]

Juárez received a note from Secretary Seward in the United States telling him that the swift execution of Maximilian "would not raise the character of . . . Mexico in the esteem of civilized peoples." Unmoved, Juárez replied, "The government which has given numerous proof of its humanitarian principles and its sentiments of generosity, is also obliged to bear in mind, according to the circumstances of cases, what is required by the principles of justice and its duty to the Mexican people." He seemed to have a clear conscience on the matter, having tested the laws of the former republic's written constitution.[5]

Juárez dismissed the matter, saying, "Maximilian of Habsburg knew our country only by geography. To this foreigner we owe neither blessings nor evils."[6]

Taken from the church of the Capuchins, Maximilian's corpse was stored by Octaviano Muñoz Ledo, the former imperial minister of foreign relations, in the second story of his house in Querétaro. A soldier stood guard at the door of the darkened room. The body remained in the home for some time.[7]

The last of the Imperialistas did not fall until two weeks after Maximilian's death. Upon learning of Maximilian's execution, Leonardo Márquez and Santiago Vidaurri went into hiding. Porfirio Díaz, with troop reinforcements, set out to arrest or kill them and the remaining imperial commanders. He offered a 10,000-peso reward, and his men searched house to house throughout Mexico City. On July 8 at midnight, Díaz's soldiers found Vidaurri hiding in the home of an American citizen. His hands tied with a lasso, Vidaurri was thrown into a coach and taken to the military barracks. The next morning he was taken to the cemetery of Santo Domingo at Tacubaya, where he was forced to kneel and was shot in the back of the head. A newspaper reported Vidaurri "was conducted with a band to play the march of the crabs" at his execution, an insult underscoring his retreat.[8]

The wily Gen. Leonardo Márquez withdrew funds from the national treasury and escaped by being carried in a coffin and hiding in an empty grave for two days. He then disguised himself as a fruit vendor and went on foot to Veracruz and finally to Havana, where he lived unrecognized working as a pawnbroker. He moved back to Mexico City, where some said he received a pension from Porfirio Díaz, who was elected president in 1876. Márquez spent much of his time writing justifications for abandoning Maximilian at Querétaro. In 1913 he died at the age of ninety-three while visiting Havana.[9]

On July 15 Juárez entered Mexico City in triumph to rebuild his republic. Although fans cheered for his return along the route, some gauged his reception as lukewarm. Juárez's decision to extend his presidency without a new election left many Mexicans feeling uneasy about his restoration to power and what future lay in store for the county. He quickly set out to rebuild public trust by convening a Liberal congress and reorganizing the government.[10]

The news of Maximilian's death reached the Tuileries in Paris on June 30, via the Austrian minister in Washington, just as the city was celebrating the

Russian and Prussian ball, Universal Exposition, Paris, June 1867

Universal Exposition, Napoléon's enormous orchestration intended to promote the newly rebuilt capital. With this spectacle, Napoléon also hoped to wipe out the memories of his failed Mexican venture as well as other debacles. The festivities far exceeded anything beheld before in Europe. The pageantry, the glittering galas, masked balls, operas, ballets, and street performances were billed as the greatest fête of the century in a newly rebuilt city. With over 50,000 exhibits, the 1867 showcase contained twice that of the prior Parisian 1855 exposition. The United States sent hundreds of inventions and their creators, including sewing machines, power looms, cotton gins, automatic reaping scythes, and telegraph line techniques. European inventors also displayed their new creations: Alfred Nobel presented a new explosive called dynamite; Belgian Adolphe Sax, a musical invention called *le saxophone;* and Alfred Krupp, a new fifty-ton cannon capable of firing 1,000-pound shells. Overall, 11 million people attended the exhibition.[11]

As other countries from around the world built pavilions celebrating their cultures, Carlota saw that Mexico must be part of it. She had sent artifacts and art from Mexico, including wax replicas of the country's fruits, a charro outfit and saddle, a fine carriage, items made from tortoiseshell or tropical woods, models of various ancient ruins, silk and wool serapes, hammocks of henequen, maguey plants and a figure depicting how pulque was made, indigo, Yucatecan cigarettes, coffee, marble busts of herself and Maximilian sculpted by Mexican artist Felipe Sojo, coinage, and an almanac of the court.[12]

The sensation attracted royalty and celebrities from around the world, including Russia, Bavaria, Portugal, Egypt, and Turkey. Otto von Bismarck, Prussia's minister-president, tall and rotund, impressive in his white uniform, who had most recently defeated the Austrians, strolled the grounds. He had only started his mission to conglomerate the various German-speaking princedoms into a super-state to rival France, for which he had purchased Napoléon's neutrality by promising land along the Rhine but then mocked him by showing no signs to hand it over.[13] Therefore, certain international tensions wove through the spectacle.

On the evening that the telegram with the news of Maximilian's execution arrived, sponsors of the exposition were to be awarded for their corporate participation. Napoléon and Eugénie, along with Abdul Aziz, Sultan of Turkey, and Albert Edward, Prince of Wales, prepared to attend the ceremony. As Eugénie dressed for the event, she read the news of Maximilian's death first. Shocked, she blanched and ran to Napoléon's quarters, nearly fainting. She told him the news, and they discussed postponing the event but then thought perhaps the notice could be wrong, it was so outrageous.[14]

Since the public remained unaware of the tragedy at Querétaro, they decided to go forward with the medal presenting. Eugénie could only think of Maximilian, knowing not only that France was responsible for his fate but that she had had a hand in selecting him as emperor. After the award program she returned to the Tuileries where she collapsed and had to be carried to her bedchamber. From then on, her self-confidence failed her, compounded by other diplomatic disasters of their reign, squabbling in the ministry over her authority, and public criticism of her influence on affairs of state.[15]

The next day, *L'Indépendence Belge* newspaper carried the shocking news from Mexico quoting dispatches from the Austrian ambassador in Washington. As another newspaper suggested, Juárez had lobbed a bomb on France. Maximilian's death became the only topic of conversation in Paris. The announcement served to revive bad memories—the high loss of life, millions of francs expended, investors without returns, and now Maximilian's execution. Most remaining events at the Universal Exhibition were canceled, and the visiting sovereigns went home. Napoléon's enemies used the calamity to lay further criticism on the emperor, which quickly reached consensus among the public. They accused Napoléon of the crime of abandoning Maximilian

The Mexican cartoonist for *La Orquesta* interpreted Maximilian's execution
as a bomb lobbed by Benito Juárez and Mariano Escobedo at Napoléon III
and his activities in Europe, particularly the Universal Exposition, July 1867.

and squarely blamed him for his death. Also, they alleged he made France look
foolish across the world. "He will never recover from this curse, this outrage
will overwhelm him with the contempt of France," said one of Napoléon's
political enemies.[16]

Austrian minister Richard von Metternich, who learned the news and
left the award ceremony before it was finished, wrote of the "thunderbolt"
Maximilian's news had on the exhibition. He witnessed the stunned silence
of the people and the tears of Napoléon and Eugénie during at least one final
event. "It can hardly be imagined what a deep impression the news from Mexico
has produced here," he said. Artists in Paris saw possibilities in Maximilian's
tragic end. "Shakespeare could not have imagined a more shocking fifth act,"
wrote one art critic. Édouard Manet painted his own version of the execution.[17]

Emperor Franz Josef promptly canceled a planned trip to Paris to meet with
Napoléon, which would have been his first since the loss of Lombardy eight
years earlier. Austria alienated itself from France, and any hope of allying with
Napoléon to contain Otto von Bismarck and German unification temporarily
died. Napoléon wrote Franz Josef a letter of sympathy. "The appalling news
which we have just received has plunged us into deepest grief. I at once deplore
and admire the energy displayed by the emperor in insisting upon fighting
single-handed against a party which has only triumphed by treachery, and I
am inconsolable at having with the best intentions, contributed toward such a

The effects of Maximilian shipped back to Trieste, October 1867

lamentable result. Will Your Majesty accept the expression of my sincerest and deepest regret?" wrote Napoléon. Many recognized that Napoléon's days as a dynamic European powerbroker were fading fast.[18]

Maximilian's mother, Sophie, grieved inconsolably. The shocked citizens of Vienna and Trieste mourned and held ceremonies and masses. Franz Josef cautiously replied to Napoléon that the Habsburgs remained horrified and bereft, not understanding how the Mexican Republicans could have behaved so barbarically. He hoped, however, that the news of Maximilian's death would not forever damage relations between the two countries. Sophie, however, never forgave Napoléon for Maximilian's death.[19]

Franz Josef sent Admiral Wilhelm von Tegetthoff with the flagship *Novara* to Veracruz to collect Maximilian's body and any Austrians who might be fleeing Mexico. When Admiral Tegetthoff arrived on August 25, minister Baron Magnus and Dr. Basch were told that Maximilian's body could not be released "for serious reasons." This made no sense to the Austrians, since Magnus and Lago had been asking for possession of the remains since the execution day. The Mexican foreign minister explained that because a family member or a document from the empire of Austria had not formally petitioned for possession of the body, according to Mexican decorum, it could not be released.

Maximilian's remains aboard the *Novara* in the port of Trieste, 1868

Knowing this was meant only to harass them, the Austrians scrambled to get approval from the Habsburgs authorizing Tegetthoff to return Maximilian's remains. After many delays, by the end of October, Juárez finally consented to allow the body to return to Austria, if Franz Josef would officially recognize the republic of Mexico.[20]

It seemed that weeks earlier, when Juárez had ordered the body moved to Mexico City from Querétaro and stored at the San Andrés Hospital, officials realized his body was decomposing fast and soon Maximilian's face would be unrecognizable. In order to delay the decomposition, they had cloth bandages removed from the corpse and bathed the body in arsenic. It was an embarrassment for government officials. They transferred the remains and the zinc coffin liner into a fine outer box made of carved and highly polished Grenadilla wood.[21]

Meanwhile, the Austrian frigate *Elizabeth*, which had been waiting at Veracruz since Maximilian's pending decision to abdicate in October 1866, was loaded with fifty trunks of personal goods and records. The clothes he wore at the time of his execution, including his familiar white sombrero ornamented with a cord of twisted gold thread and rosettes of silver, one of the emperor's favorite hats, were carefully packed and stowed.[22]

On November 9 the Mexican officials released Maximilian's body to Mag-

Funeral of Maximilian, Saint Mary of the Angels Church,
Vienna, Austria, 1868

nus and Tegetthoff. Three days later Austrian officials and Dr. Basch supervised the removal of Maximilian's body from the San Andrés Hospital and took it to Veracruz. The sailors loaded the coffin, draped in red, white, and Austria's war insignia, onto the *Novara* and embarked for Trieste with the barren remains. After five months the Habsburgs felt relief that Maximilian, their adventurer, had come home to rest among them. It was not lost on anyone that the very vessel which had carried the young sovereigns to their new throne in Mexico only three years earlier, the *Novara*, bore Maximilian's body back across the Atlantic.[23]

The frigate arrived at Trieste on January 16, 1868, to an artillery salute and considerable pomp and pageantry. People lined the shore or waited in boats in the harbor. Although it was a Thursday, the area stores closed, and funeral knells rang out from the domed churches. Civil and military authorities met Admiral Tegetthoff at the wharf to facilitate the landing. The Austrian royal family, represented by Maximilian's brothers Karl Ludwig and Ludwig Victor, arrived on a light shallop, decorated with two crowns and a couched lion, to help convey the coffin ashore. Before leaving Mexico, the sailors had placed Maximilian's zinc enclosure in a copper coffin. The Imperial family placed wreaths on the casket reading "To the Valiant Hero," "To

Maximilian's casket in the Kapuzinergruft, Vienna, Austria, 1868.
The ribbons read "Brother," "Hero," and "Christian."

the Beloved Brother," "To the Good Christian." Maximilian's medals of the Mexican empire were placed on black velvet cushions. Eight marines with drawn swords formed an honor guard around the coffin as it was conveyed to a funeral coach. The bishop of Trieste gave a benediction and blessing, and the staff of Miramar with the royal family and military conveyed Maximilian's remains to the rail station in the city. The casket was placed in a specially prepared car and the train pulled away toward Vienna, where his body was delivered to the Hofburg Palace and placed in a royal sarcophagus. According to one historian, when Archduchess Sophie saw her son's body, she said, "That is not my son," so badly had it decomposed.[24]

On January 20, 1868, after a mass and royal ceremony at the Church of Saint Mary of the Angels at the monastery of the Capuchin friars, Maximilian's family laid him to rest in the imperial crypt, the Kapuzinergruft. His suffering mother, Sophie, followed her son's remains into the tomb. Blasio noted that all of Maximilian's Austrian and Belgian attendants, including Bombelles, Khevenhüller, Eloin, Basch, Pitner, and others filled the church and surrounded the casket. Few of Maximilian's ministers from Mexico who had received gold, medals, and great distinction, now living in Europe, attended the funeral.[25]

Carlota still struggled with reality and could not attend her husband's funeral. She lived at the Gartenhaus for over a year after her collapse. Fears of poisoning still haunted her, and her brother attributed this to Jilek's prior treatment of her with morphine, which made her more suspicious. Jilek, ever dutiful, tended to her faithfully. The doctor ate with her, took walks in the gardens with her, and played cards or board games. She was watched constantly by her doctors, maids, and ministering nuns. Jacob von Kuhachevich, Carlota's aide at Miramar, not knowing yet of Maximilian's death, wrote to him on June 28 to say that his brother, Franz Josef, would soon visit Carlota and from him she would learn of his defeat in Mexico. He reported that Carlota refused to be seen in public and was fearful of strangers. He worried what reaction Franz Josef's appearance would produce. She was cut off from the world and read no newspapers, as her doctors and attendants thought it best that she not learn news from Mexico. She received letters only from her family and scolded them for keeping her in isolation.[26]

Meanwhile, Carlota's obsessions spread. She worried incessantly about her failure to bear children with Maximilian, and the doctors therefore recorded her menstrual periods. Rumors persisted that Carlota had relations with Lt. Col. Van der Smissen in Mexico and became pregnant with his child, and Maximilian sent her to Europe. This proved to be nothing more than groundless gossip. According to doctors' records, there was no pregnancy, and she apparently remained unaware of this rumor. Carlota took her regular menstruation to be a happy sign that she was taking less poison. "During meals, she stole glances of herself in a small mirror to look for signs of poisoning from the food she had just ingested: flushed cheeks or green and brown traces at the neck," said one doctor. From then on, she tried to manage her sleep, eating, and daily routine in an effort to avoid any toxins. Dr. Jilek observed her grandiose ideas of herself and her excessive pride and recorded how she constantly boasted of her royal status and her superiority and referred to Maximilian as "Sovereign of the Universe." "She does not want to be scolded or reprimanded, to have her ideas criticized or contested," wrote Jilek. Most of the time she was left to do what she loved most. She resumed her piano playing and painting landscapes on canvas or fans. Her paintings were vivid, and many thought she was particularly gifted.[27]

Carlota's panic and paranoia began in Mexico, as related in a report by her doctor Friedrich Semelder that was sent to Dr. Jilek, along with other files on her health sent on board the *Empress Eugénie* when she sailed to Europe. Nearly a century later, after her letters and these doctor's descriptions of her behavior had been analyzed, psychiatrists concluded that she suffered from a mild form of bipolar disorder, with her fear of poisoning and her paranoia likely developing in adolescence. Psychiatrists also indicated that she suffered from monomania, an inflated sense of self, obsessiveness about certain goals, and feelings of excessive superiority. Under the conditions of her bipolar disorder, she had delusions of grandeur mixed with episodes of despondency or frustration.[28]

In spring 1867 her brother King Leopold II, realizing that the isolation of her stay in the Gartenhaus at Miramar was not making her any better, requested that Carlota come to Brussels to live with him at Laeken. She arrived on July 31, and according to her brother she was nothing but "skin and bones." Leopold's wife, Queen Marie Henriette, became her constant companion, concerned for her health and well-being. Carlota accompanied them to their summer home at the castle of Tervuren, in the province of Brabant. Almost immediately she shed her fear of being poisoned and went on carriage rides and walks, and for a time she forgot her fear of strangers. Carlota still demanded the keys to her room and refused to be locked in. Upon her arrival, anxious at being alone, she asked Marie Henriette to sleep in the same room with her, but she refused. At first Carlota slept in a chair, but over the next few days she calmed enough to sleep in her new bed. After many days, she seemed rational and calm. She read, painted, and played the piano.[29]

More importantly, Leopold II heard that the Austrian government restored Carlota's citizenship, but he chose to keep her close by in Belgium, suspecting that Franz Josef coveted her inheritance. However, the Austrians continued her payments as a legitimate royal. Leopold II managed her money, worried that the Austrian ministers would use the funds to pay Maximilian's outstanding debts. He also filed legal papers to have her restored to her status as a member of the Belgian kingdom.[30]

As fall approached, the family moved to the palace at Laeken, for Tervuren was not well heated. During this time Carlota vacillated between acting irrational and perfectly normal. The queen arranged her apartment on the second floor of the palace at Laeken, where she hoped Carlota would be comfortable. Here, she loved her piles of jewelry, lace, shawls, capes, fans, and parasols, sometimes regressing into the behavior of a small child. Some days she had her hair styled like a ten-year-old, and other days she came to breakfast elaborately dressed as though for a ceremony. She refused to go to mass on Sundays and stayed in bed. At times she would not eat. During visits by relatives, however, she impressed them with the breadth of her mind and her depth of understanding on certain subjects. Her memory remained sharp, unless clouded by one of her nervous relapses.[31]

With the return and interment of Maximilian's body, her family felt Carlota could no longer be shielded from the truth. In January 1868 the Belgian royal family had one of their ministers tell her of Maximilian's execution and the eventual transportation of his remains to Vienna. The family began a novena, the traditional nine days of prayer for a departed loved one. Marie Henriette said, "I took communion this morning with our beloved child who cried with joy. The novenas ended, we told her everything. She cried for a long time in my arms, and her first words were, 'Oh, if only I could make my peace with Heaven and make my confession.'" She asked the queen to pray with her through the night, so she stayed for a while, and by the morning she had calmly accepted the news and resumed her regular activities. She was allowed to read notes from Austrian officers who sent her mementos and stories of their return to Austria with Maximilian's remains. "I find a sad satisfaction in the tributes and general admiration that surrounds his memory, but which make me cry again with each proof I find in such beautiful articles. What really moved me was to see that from Trieste to the Church of Capuchins, the naval officers and sailors never left, and that on his native soil at least, he was buried in his victory." Her writing skills were left unimpaired by her mental illness.[32]

After the funeral the Belgian legation presented José Luis Blasio with a photograph of a painting portraying Maximilian on a stormy sea, which Carlota signed to him and asked for his prayers. This intensified his wish to see Carlota and he traveled to Laeken, where he requested an audience. When denied by her doctors, he stood at the palace gate where he saw Carlota, dressed in mourning, walking with two attendants under the trees lining the park. "She was strolling along slowly, dressed and groomed with extreme elegance and care. Her gentle and kind face was profoundly sad. Her large eyes, so black and beautiful, appeared even larger and more beautiful under their purple lids. But they stared vacantly, as though questioning her destiny," he wrote. As the three ladies neared, Blasio almost called out to her, but they turned and went another direction. Blasio left the next day.[33]

At Laeken, Carlota's moods became erratic and unpredictably outrageous. She described her brother as "mean" and her sister-in-law as "treacherous." She denounced her retinue of attendants who "made her life unbearable." She hated her physicians who, she said, prevented her from "acts of violence on objects, which they remove by force . . . or of the keys, which they take even from [her] closed fingers." As Carlota became incoherent, Leopold and

Marie Henriette decided to move her back to the summer home of Tervuren Castle and ordered amenities to make it more comfortable year round. The royal couple had two young daughters, Louise and Stéphanie, who remained impressionable. It seemed that Carlota had developed the habit of "undignified conduct," often undressing and whipping herself masochistically with a riding crop, like the scourge she had seen used in Mexican Catholic penance rituals. This became more frequent, and when Marie Henriette confronted her in one of her lucid moments, Carlota said she could not help herself. Therefore in 1869 she moved into Tervuren, where doctors monitored her daily care. They shunned experimental treatments, including mercury and calomel, only administering magnesium and potassium supplements. But this did not control her outbreaks of rage, and Marie Henriette authorized shutting her in her bathroom for her own protection. She eventually outfitted one room with padded walls to keep Carlota from hurting herself during her fits.[34]

In 1869 Carlota wrote a cryptic letter to Belgian officer Charles Loysel, with whom she had been infatuated in Mexico. "The marriage that I made left me as I was, I never refused to give Emperor Maximilian children. My marriage was consecrated in appearance, the emperor made me believe it, but it was not, not because of me because I always obeyed him, but because it is impossible, or I would not have remained what I am," she wrote, in an obscure reference to Maximilian's possible impotence that left her a virgin, which was often a topic of rumor. However, it was likely that her earlier miscarriage was the cause of her infertility. In Belgium she became obsessive about sex and lost all sense of modesty. The doctors feared she tried to seduce her guards and that at least one of them may have taken advantage of her. She sent letters of a sexual nature to Gen. Douay, that she was "nine months pregnant by the redemption of the devil, nine months by the Church, and now I am pregnant by the army" and would give birth soon. But she did not.[35]

She also wrote letters in Charles Loysel's name, seemingly to work out their disaster. It was her only outlet. "Quill of the world, I am because I only write," she said.[36]

In 1879, when the castle of Tervuren burned nearly to the ground, the royal family moved Carlota back to Laeken for a month. Her health improved remarkably; she strolled the grounds and wanted to see people socially. She spent time with her nieces, especially enjoying Clementine, Leopold II's daughter, and playing in the gardens. However, her brother soon purchased the castle of Bouchout, a few miles away, and moved Carlota there. Her ladies-in-waiting reported that she loved to go on boat rides around the castle's lakes.

Every spring, as she stepped into the little rowboat, she said she was ready to go to Mexico. She never forgot her days there, or the tragic death of Maximilian, although at times she wrote that he was not dead but living in London. She lived quietly, following a routine of playing the piano, reading, sewing, or taking walks. However, she was prone to episodes of violence when frustrated. She tore her hair, scratched her skin, or ripped her clothing and would sometimes slap whoever happened to be dining with her. Once, while playing the piano, she tore up a music score but finished the piece from memory.[37]

In 1914, during World War I when the Germans invaded Belgium, the royal family retreated to De Panne on the northern coast of Belgium. Carlota remained ensconced at Bouchout. The Germans battled all around the grounds and the wounded lay everywhere in the vicinity, but they did not enter the castle, possibly because the majordomo flew the Austrian flag over Bouchout. Carlota discovered the existence of airplanes, as German bombers dropped their payloads on the lands surrounding Bouchout; fortunately, they did not target the castle. During one battle she sought protection in the basement, afterward wisely commenting on how the war would end: "It will be a final catastrophe, sir, and one that will not come all at once, but little by little."[38]

After the war Carlota became a tourist curiosity, even among her own relatives; certain royalty showed up unexpectedly to see the enigmatic former empress. After a prolonged bout with pneumonia, on January 16, 1927, at the age of eighty-six, Carlota passed away quietly with no known heirs. A witness at her death described her last days. She ordered the door leading to the drawing room closed so that she could no longer see Maximilian's portrait. "It's as the Archduke would have wanted it," she said. Then, after a small dinner, she collapsed onto her bed. The death rales started soon afterward, but not until she uttered her final words: "It is all for naught. We shall not succeed." After two days she finally succumbed at seven in the morning. A private funeral was held at the chapel at Bouchout during a heavy blizzard, but afterward crowds braved the snowstorm to follow her body through the forest where she was laid to rest in a public ceremony at Laeken. Bouchout Castle was locked, and her faithful personnel thanked, most wondering where to go, many having been devoted to Carlota for nearly six decades. Leopold II and his ministers invested the bulk of her fortune in establishing a colony in the Congo.[39]

The Mexican people twice reelected Benito Juárez president of Mexico. During the next five years, he faced peasant revolts, the embarrassment and threat of separatism in Oaxaca, and constant challenges to his authority. Additionally, Juárez took great measures to ensure that Maximilian and the

Second Empire would not be remembered favorably. Official accounts condemning and discrediting Maximilian and Carlota were published for a time after Juárez's return to office. When imperial loyalists began to meet at the chapel of the San Andrés Hospital, where Maximilian's body lay in storage after his second embalming, Juárez made certain the building was condemned and destroyed, laying a road over the site. Additionally, he made sure the Mexican people never forgot their victory over the French at Puebla on May 5, 1862. Despite the French victory in taking Puebla one year later, Mexico continued to commemorate Cinco de Mayo.[40] Admiration for Juárez grew exponentially after he reclaimed office, despite his enemies.

In the early morning of July 18, 1872, Juárez suffered a heart attack. After summoning a doctor, he took to his bed, and within a few hours his heart convulsed again. The doctor poured boiling water on his chest to revive him, which worked, and he remained in his bed. Incredibly, that evening, when a visitor arrived seeking political advice, he rose from his bed to meet with him. After the meeting, Juárez returned to his bed and died near midnight, with only his houseboy as a witness.[41]

In Europe, Napoléon paid for the crushing Mexican defeat. A combination of factors, including Napoléon's unpreparedness to appease public opinion and reluctance to bargain with Prussia, despite reassurances from Marshal Jacques Louis Randon, the minister of war, proved to be the beginning of the end of the Second Empire in France. A series of calamitous French losses culminated in a Prussian victory on the battlefield of Sedan in September 1870, a huge conflict personally led by Napoléon although he was outmanned, unprepared, and in severe pain from bladder stones. The defeat set the stage for his departure and exile from France. He died three years later, on January 9, 1873, in England after a series of operations to break up the stones that had tormented him for years, compounded by kidney disease.[42] Napoléon's chief financier of the Mexican debt, the scheming Jean-Baptiste Jecker, was shot in an ordered execution during the Paris Commune in 1871.[43]

Despite the extraordinary and artificial means by which Napoléon III created an opportunity for Maximilian to take the throne of Mexico and the utter failing of the endeavor, many across the world remain fascinated by the theatrical drama associated with the last empire of Mexico. The Mexican people acknowledge how Maximilian's regime came to influence the *Porfiriato*, or the tenure of Porfirio Díaz. Díaz became the longest-termed president in Mexico's history, serving for over thirty years, until the Mexican Revolution of 1910. During his grandiloquent tenure, he maintained rooms with possessions from

Maximilian's reign, including the silver, furnishings, pianos, artwork, even preserving the coaches, the lavish ceremonial vehicle and the utilitarian one. He held "audiences" in the manner of the Second Empire, in the same rooms of the National Palace, and people often commented on his elaborate state dinners for which he used Maximilian and Carlota's crystal, silver, and china.[44]

Even with all the lives lost, the bloodshed, disgust, and withered hopes, the short reign of Maximilian remains an important part of Mexican history. The Austrians refer to the expedition as a disaster but remain fascinated that the Habsburgs would venture so far afield in the name of their forebear Charles V to spread the ideals of their royal leadership. They blame Franz Josef and his minister Metternich for Maximilian's tragedy. For the French, it represents a major turning point caused by the fantasies, chauvinism, and ethnocentricity of Napoléon III, leading to his ultimate downfall. In the United States, the story is largely forgotten. For partisans of Juárez, it represents their victory over a common enemy, bloodthirsty Europe and all enemies of republican values.[45]

As Carlota said, the Mexican empire was a gigantic experiment. However, Maximilian and Carlota brought an opulent court to Mexico, pouring millions of pesos into their new investment. Napoléon convinced Maximilian that Mexico was his "pearl of the New World."[46] Perhaps the play would have played on had the money not run out.

What Maximilian and Carlota did not anticipate was that the Mexican nation no longer remained open to discourse about its future or to interference by foreign countries, and vowed not to blindly accept an outsider, even a Habsburg, to run their country. A modern Mexico had arrived with the *Reforma* that began in 1855, and seismic shifts in the nation were set into motion. The Liberals wanted to avoid the least whiff of monarchy or outside control. The glamorous couple arrived to interrupt this time, full of optimism and hope for a second Mexican empire, not knowing it would be its last nor that everything they symbolized would be rejected. One sovereign paid with his life and the other with her sanity, but they remain an indelible part of the soul of Mexico, considered by many among the most colorful figures in Mexico's rich historical pageant.

Notes

The book's epigraph is drawn from Hélène de Reinach Foussemagne, *Charlotte de Belgique, Impératrice du Mexique* (Paris: Pon-Nourrit, 1925), 278–79.

Preface

1. Shirley Black, *Napoléon III and Mexican Silver* (Silverton, CO: Ferrell, 2000), 73; Percy Martin, *Maximilian in Mexico* (New York: Charles Scribner's Sons, 1914), 4–6.

2. Anton von Magnus, Konrad Ratz, eds., *El Ocaso del Imperio de Maximiliano Visto por un Diplomático Prusiano, Los Informes de Anton von Magnus a Otto von Bismarck* (Mexico, D.F.: Siglo Veintiuno, 2011), 10.

3. Alan Palmer, *Twilight of the Habsburgs* (New York: Atlantic Monthly Press, 1994), 160–161, 165–169, 173–176.

4. Conversions by Dr. John J. McCusker, Trinity University, San Antonio, Texas, Aug. 24, 2009.

Prologue

1. Dominique Paoli, Memorandum of Carlota at Castle Bouchout, March 4, 2010, notes in possession of the author; Joan Haslip, *Crown of Mexico* (New York: Holt, Rinehart, and Winston, 1971), 505 (quotation); Hélène de Reinach Foussemagne, *Charlotte de Belgique, Impératrice du Mexique* (Paris: Pon-Nourrit et Cie.), 378.

Introduction. Mexicans, You Have Desired My Presence

1. Paula Kollonitz, *The Court of Mexico*, trans. J. E. Ollivant (London: Saunders, Otley, and Co., 1867), 81–83; Hall, *Mexico and Maximilian*, 105–106; Joseph Audenried to Mary Colket Audenried, Dec. 4, 1866, Joseph C. Audenried Letters, 1865–1866, Nau Civil War Collection, Houston, Texas. The *Novara* was named for an 1849 Austrian victory against the Italians. Haslip, *Crown of Mexico*, 412.

2. James Robb Church, ed., *The Military Surgeon*, (Washington, D.C.: Association of Military Surgeons of the United States, 1920), vol. 47, 442; Kollonitz, *Court of Mexico*, 82–84.

3. Kollonitz, *Court of Mexico*, 85–86; Hall, *Mexico and Maximilian*, 105–106; Egon Corti, *Maximilian and Charlotte of Mexico*, trans. Catherine A. Phillips (New York: Alfred A. Knopf, 1929), 417 (hereafter cited as Corti, *Maximilian*); María de la Fère, *Recollections*, 1907, Maximilian, Emperor of Mexico papers, M108, Special Collections, University of Arizona, Tucson, Arizona (hereafter cited as Maximilian Papers, UASC).

4. Kollonitz, *Court of Mexico*, 85–86; Hall, *Mexico and Maximilian*, 105–106; Corti, *Maximilian*, 417; Carlota to Maximilian, Nov. 16, 1865, in Konrad Ratz, *Correspondencia inédita entre Maximiliano y Carlota* (Mexico City: Fondo de Cultura Económica, 2003), 233.

5. Kollonitz, *Court of Mexico*, 83, 85.

6. Jean-François Lecaillon, *Napoléon III et le Mexique* (Paris: Éditions L'Harmattan, 1994), 103; Kollonitz, *Court of Mexico*, 83, 85; Haslip, *Crown of Mexico*, 243 (quotation).

7. Kollonitz, *Court of Mexico*, 84–85; *New York Times*, June 25, 1891.

8. Kollonitz, *Court of Mexico*, 85–86; Hall, *Mexico and Maximilian*, 109.

9. Hall, *Mexico and Maximilian*, 109, 110 (quotation), 111; H. Montgomery Hyde, *Mexican Empire: The History of Maximilian and Carlota of Mexico* (London: Macmillan, 1946), 8; Kollonitz, *Court of Mexico*, 85–86.

10. Hall, *Mexico and Maximilian*, 109–111; *New York Times*, June 15, 1864.

11. Hall, *Mexico and Maximilian*, 111, José Luis Blasio, *Maximilian, Emperor of Mexico: Memoirs of his Private Secretary*, ed. Robert H. Murray (New Haven, CT: Yale University Press, 1934), 24 (hereafter cited as Blasio, *Maximilian*).

12. Hall, *Mexico and Maximilian*, 110 (quotation) 111; Haslip, *Crown of Mexico*, 223–224.

13. Reinach Foussemagne, *Charlotte de Belgique*, 174–176; Ángel Iglesias to Juan N. Almonte, May 25, 1864, Karton 9, Kaiser Maximilian's papers, Haus-, Hof-, und Staatsarchiv, Österreichisches Staatsarchiv, Vienna, Austria (hereafter cited as Maximilian Papers, OS).

14. Hall, *Mexico and Maximilian*, 107–108 (quotation); *New York Times*, June 15, 1864.

15. Kollonitz, *Court of Mexico*, 86–87.

16. Kollonitz, *Court of Mexico*, 88; *New York Times*, June 15, 1864.

17. Known also as La Soledad de Doblado. Kollonitz, *Court of Mexico*, 89–90; *New York Times*, June 15, 1864; Hall, *Mexico and Maximilian*, 113 (quotation); *St. Louis Globe Democrat*, Jan. 22, 1928, Karton 58, Maximilian Papers, OS.

18. Kollonitz, *Court of Mexico*, 89–91; Hall, *Mexico and Maximilian*, 113; Arnold Blumberg, "The Diplomacy of the Mexican Empire, 1863–1867," in *Transactions of the American Philosophical Society* 61 (Nov. 1971), 30.

19. Haslip, *Crown of Mexico*, 245.

20. Corti, *Maximilian*, 418–419.

21. Kollonitz, *Court of Mexico*, 93–96; Hall, *Mexico and Maximilian*, 114; Haslip, *Crown of Mexico*, 246 (quotation).

22. Kollonitz, *Court of Mexico*, 93–96; Corti, *Maximilian*, 419 (quotation).

23. Kollonitz, *Court of Mexico*, 96–97; Hall, *Mexico and Maximilian*, 114–115; Haslip, *Crown of Mexico*, 247 (quotation).

24. Hall, *Mexico and Maximilian*, 115; Kollonitz, *Court of Mexico*, 98; Corti, *Maximilian*, 420.

25. Kollonitz, *Court of Mexico*, 98–99; Hall, *Mexico and Maximilian*, 115; Haslip, *Crown of Mexico*, 247–248.

26. J. Bernardo Aburto, *De Miramar a Mexico: Viaje del Emperador Maximiliano y de la Emperatriz Carlota, Desde su Palacio de Miramar cerca de Trieste hasta la Capital del Imperio Mexicano* (Orizaba, Mexico: Imprenta de J. Bernardo Aburto, 1864), 104; Kollonitz, *Court of Mexico*, 98–99; Hall, *Mexico and Maximilian*, 115 (quotation); Haslip, *Crown of Mexico*, 248.

27. Kollonitz, *Court of Mexico*, 98; Hall, *Mexico and Maximilian*, 116–121; Haslip, *Crown of Mexico*, 248; Susan Deans Smith, *Bureaucrats, Planters and Workers* (Austin: University of Texas Press, 1992), 114–115 ; Hall, *Mexico and Maximilian*, 120–121; *New York Times*, July 2, 1864.

28. Hall, *Mexico and Maximilian*, 122; Haslip, *Crown of Mexico*, 248; Jeffrey Pilcher, *¡Que Vivan los Tamales!* (Albuquerque: University of New Mexico Press, 1998), 70; *New York Times*, July 2, 1864.

29. Hall, *Mexico and Maximilian*, 122; Kollonitz, *Court of Mexico*, 99–102; W. Harris Chynoweth, *The Fall of Maximilian* (London: self-published, 1872), 6–7.

30. Corti, Maximilian, 419–420; Kollonitz, *Court of Mexico*, 105–106; Hall, *Mexico and Maximilian*, 122; Haslip, *Crown of Mexico*, 249.

31. Kollonitz, *Court of Mexico*, 106; Hall, *Mexico and Maximilian*, 122–124, 140; Martin, *Maximilian in Mexico*, 168.

32. Kollonitz, *Court of Mexico*, 108–110; Aburto, *De Miramar a Mexico*, 143.

33. Hall, *Mexico and Maximilian*, 124–125; Haslip, *Crown of Mexico*, 249; De la Fère, *Recollections*, Maximilian Papers, UASC; José de J. Nuñez y Domínguez, "Los Cumpleaños de la Emperatriz," *Divulgación Histórica* 2 (June 15, 1941), 395.

34. Hall, *Mexico and Maximilian*, 124–125; Joseph M. Nance, "Adrian Woll," in Ron Tyler et al., eds., *The New Handbook of Texas* (Austin: Texas State Historical Association, 1996), 6: 1035–1036; Haslip, *Crown of Mexico*, 249 (quotation).

35. Haslip, *Crown of Mexico*, 249–250; Carlota to Eugénie, June 18, 1864, in Corti, *Maximilian*, 838 (quotation).

36. The Otomí are indigenous to the central highlands of Mexico. Kollonitz, *Court of Mexico*, 115–120; Hall, *Mexico and Maximilian*, 124–125; Corti, *Maximilian*, 420.

37. Corti, *Maximilian*, 836.

38. Kollonitz, *Court of Mexico*, 121–124; Haslip, *Crown of Mexico*, 250.

39. Hall, *Mexico and Maximilian*, 125, 126–127 (quotation); De la Fère, *Recollections*, Maximilian Papers, UASC.

40. Hall, *Mexico and Maximilian*, 126–127, 128 (quotation); Corti, *Maximilian*, 421.

41. Philip Guedalla, *The Two Marshals, Bazaine–Pétain* (New York: Reynal & Hitchcock, 1943), 98–99.

42. She refers to Maximilian, descendant of Charles the Fifth. Carlota to Eugénie, June 18, 1864, in Corti, *Maximilian*, 835.

43. Konrad Ratz, *Maximilian und Juárez, Querétaro-Chronik* (Graz, Austria: Akademische Druck-u, 1998), 2: 89 n.1; Corti, Maximilian and Charlotte, 421; Hall, *Mexico and Maximilian*, 129–131; Haslip, *Crown of Mexico*, 252; Sara Yorke Stevenson, *Maximilian in Mexico* (New York: Century Company, 1899), 128; De la Fère, *Recollections*, Maximilian Papers, UASC; Blasio, *Maximilian*, 4. A Zouave was a distinctive type of infantry officer in the French army, deriving from service in French North Africa in the nineteenth and twentieth centuries, famous for their colorful dress and courage. For further information, see Charles Wellington Furlong, "Turcos and the Legion: The Spahis, the Zouaves, the Tirailleurs, and the Foreign Legion," in *The World's Work Second War Manual: The Conduct of the War* (New York: Doubleday, Page & Co., 1914), 35–37.

44. Achille Bazaine to Jacques Randon, June 1, 1864, Achille François Bazaine Papers, Genaro García Collection, Benson Latin American Collection, University of Texas at Austin, Austin, Texas (hereafter cited as BLAC); Haslip, *Crown of Mexico*, 251 (quotation).

45. Hall, *Mexico and Maximilian*, 130–132.

46. Corti, *Maximilian*, 836 (quotations); Hall, *Mexico and Maximilian*, 132; Haslip, *Crown of Mexico*, 251–252; Bertita Harding, *Phantom Crown* (Mexico City: Ediciones Tolteca, 1960), 169; Hugh Thomas, *The Golden Empire: Spain, Charles V, and the Creation of America* (New York: Random House, 2011), 35 (quotation); James D. Tracy, *Impresario of War: Campaign Strategy, International Finance, and Domestic Politics* (Cambridge: Cambridge University Press, 2002), 22. To properly celebrate Maximilian's arrival, the city council spent over 54,000 pesos on the decorations, triumphal arches, and fireworks. Gómez Tepexicuapan, "El Paseo de la Reforma, 1864–1910,"

in *Historia del Paseo de la Reforma,* ed. Wendy Coss y León (Mexico City: Instituto Nacional de Bellas Artes, 1994), 29–31.

47. Kristine Ibsen, *Maximilian, Mexico, and the Invention of Empire* (Nashville: Vanderbilt University Press, 2010), 12–13; Haslip, *Crown of Mexico,* 258–260.

48. Haslip, *Crown of Mexico,* 253; Dominique Paoli, *L'Impératrice Charlotte: Le Soleil Noir de la Mélancholie* (Paris: Éditions Perrin, 2008), 112.

Chapter 1. The Right of Kings

1. Corti, *Maximilian,* 41–42; Haslip, *Crown of Mexico,* 7, 11.

2. Haslip, *Crown of Mexico,* 11 (quotations), 14; Alan Palmer, *Twilight of the Habsburgs,* 3–4.

3. Haslip *Crown of Mexico,* 14–15 (quotation); Corti, *Maximilian,* 41–42.

4. Corti, *Maximilian,* 41, 42 (quotation).

5. Haslip, *Crown of Mexico,* 15–16.

6. Jasper Ridley, *Maximilian and Juárez* (New York: Ticknor & Fields, 1992), 44; Nancy Nichols Barker, *Distaff Diplomacy: The Empress Eugénie and the Foreign Policy of the Second Empire* (Austin: University of Texas Press, 1967), 106 (see map).

7. Haslip, *Crown of Mexico,* 8–9; Ridley, *Maximilian and Juárez,* 46–47; Corti, *Maximilian,* 42.

8. Ridley, *Maximilian and Juárez,* 46–47; Palmer, *Twilight of the Habsburgs,* 45–47.

9. Ridley, *Maximilian and Juárez,* 46–47.

10. Corti, *Maximilian,* 44.

11. Maximilian, *Recollections,* 2: 98–100; Corti, *Maximilian,* 42–44.

12. "Kriege, sollen andere führen! Das glückliche Österreich heiratet!" In Latin: "Bella gerunt alii, tu felix Austria nube. Nam quae Mars aliis, dat tibi diva Venus!" Courtesy Ralf Weber von Froisberg, memo, September 2, 2008.

13. Maximilian von Habsburg, *Recollections of My Life* (London: Richard Bentley, 1868), 1: 2 (quotations), 57–59, 157–159, 220, 291; 2: 2, 16, 48, 89; Corti, *Maximilian,* 46. The *Novara* was named for the Austrian victory over Italian nationalists in 1849. Palmer, *Twilight of the Habsburgs,* 51.

14. Ridley, *Maximilian and Juárez,* 50–51; Martin, *Maximilian in Mexico,* 27.

15. Maximilian, *Recollections of My Life,* 1: 201, 256–257; Ridley, *Maximilian and Juárez,* 15, 48, 50–51; Corti, *Maximilian,* 46–47.

16. Ridley, *Maximilian and Juárez,* 49; Haslip, *Crown of Mexico,* 52–54; Palmer, *Twilight of the Habsburgs,* 76–77.

17. Haslip, *Crown of Mexico,* 60–61.

18. Martin, *Maximilian in Mexico,* 44–45; Jonathan Steinberg, *Bismarck: A Life* (New York: Oxford University Press, 2011), 121; Ridley, *Maximilian and Juárez,* 51–52.

19. David Baguley, *Napoléon III and His Regime: An Extravaganza* (Baton Rouge:

Louisiana State University Press, 2000), 8–9, 17, 91–93; Ridley, *Maximilian and Juárez*, 51–52 (quotation).

20. Corti, *Maximilian*, 48–49.

21. Ridley, *Maximilian and Juárez*, 51–52.

22. Michael Carmona, *Haussmann: His Life and Times, and the Making of Modern Paris*, trans. Patrick Camiller (Chicago: Ivan R. Dee, 2002), 9–11, 227–232, 343, 386, 409; Alfred Jackson Hanna and Kathryn Abbey Hanna, *Napoleon III and Mexico: American Triumph over Monarchy* (Chapel Hill: University of North Carolina Press, 1971), 9.

23. Corti, *Maximilian*, 51–52, 57–58.

24. Louis de Lichtervelde, *Léopold First: The Founder of Modern Belgium*, trans. Thomas H. Reed (New York: Century, 1930), 138, 267–268, 269 (quotation); Corti, *Maximilian*, 60–61; Ridley, *Maximilian and Juárez*, 52; Haslip, *Crown of Mexico*, 167.

25. Ridley, *Maximilian and Juárez*, 52; Corti, *Maximilian*, 62, 64.

26. Lichtervelde, *Léopold First*, 155; Reinach Foussemagne, *Charlotte de Belgique*, 9–10; Paoli, *Charlotte*, 13–14; Ridley, *Maximilian and Juárez*, 53–54.

27. Lichtervelde, *Léopold First*, 157; Reinach Foussemagne, *Charlotte de Belgique*, 9–10; Paoli, *Charlotte*, 13; Haslip, *Crown of Mexico*, 75–78, 83.

28. Corti, *Maximilian and Charlotte*, 65.

29. Hyde, *Mexican Empire*, 67 (quotation); Corti, *Maximilian and Charlotte*, 67, 70–71, 73.

30. McCusker, memo on historic valuations of money, August 24, 2009, notes in possession of the author. Konrad Ratz, *Tras las Huellas de un Desconocido, Nuevos Datos y Aspectos de Maximiliano de Habsburgo,* prologue by Patricia Galeana de Valadés (Mexico City: Conaculta, INAH, 2008), 38–39; Ratz, *Correspondencia Inédita*, 356; Hyde, *Mexican Empire*, 67 (quotation), 69, 74; Corti, *Maximilian*, 67, 70–71, 73, 81; John Julius Norwich, *Absolute Monarchs: A History of the Papacy* (New York: Random House, 2011), 395, 410.

31. Corti, *Maximilian*, 72–73; Haslip, *Crown of Mexico*, 97 (first quotation); Hyde, *Mexican Empire*, 75 (second and third quotations).

32. Haslip, *Crown of Mexico*, 100–101.

33. Hyde, *Mexican Empire*, 7–77, 80–83; Corti, *Maximilian*, 80–83, 86–87.

34. Haslip, *Crown of Mexico*, 100–105; Ridley, *Maximilian and Juárez*, 56 (quotation).

35. The enormous loss of life and bloodshed caused Swiss observer Henri Dunant to found the Red Cross. Steinberg, *Bismarck*, 152–153; William E. Echard, *Napoléon III and the Concert of Europe* (Baton Rouge: Louisiana State University Press, 1983), 152–153; Ridley, *Maximilian and Juárez*, 56; Norwich, *Absolute Monarchs*, 396, 403–404, 409.

36. Hyde, *Mexican Empire*, 67; Haslip, *Crown of Mexico*, 113; Rosella Fabiani and Lorenza Fonda to M. M. McAllen, interview, June 8, 2009, Miramar Castle, Trieste, Italy; Ratz, *Tras las Huellas*, 124–125.

37. Maximilian, *Recollections*, 2: 281; Corti, *Maximilian*, 88; Haslip, *Crown of Mexico*, 120–121; Interview by author with Rosella Fabiani and Lorenza Fonda, June 8, 2009, Miramar Castle, Trieste, Italy.

38. Research at Castello di Miramare. Lorenza Fonda to M. M. McAllen, June 8, 2009, Miramare, Trieste, Italy. Notes in possession of the author. André Castelot, *Maximilien et Charlotte du Mexique: La Tragédie de L'Ambition* (Paris: Librairie Académique Perrin, 1977), 115–116; Martin, *Maximilian in Mexico*, 32.

39. Rossella Fabiani, *Il Museo Storico del Castello di Miramare* (Vincenza: Terra Firma, 2005), 11–12.

40. Interview with Rosella Fabiani, June 8, 2009, Miramar Castle, Trieste, Italy.

41. Maximilian, *Recollections of My Life*, 2: 281 (quotation); 3: 152–153, 281, 315, 328, 357–359, 403; Ridley, *Maximilian and Juárez*, 56–57.

42. Ridley, *Maximilian and Juárez*, 57 (quotation); Corti, *Maximilian*, 90–92; "Lacroma," *The Rosary Magazine* 7 (New York: Rosary Publication Co., July–December 1895), 571; Nancy Nichols Barker, "France, Austria, and the Mexican Venture, 1861–1864," *French Historical Studies* 3 (Fall 1963), 226.

43. Blumberg, "Diplomacy of the Mexican Empire," 9; Echard, *Napoléon III*, 154, 172–173; Barker, "France, Austria, and the Mexican Venture," 225, 226 (quotation); Haslip, *Crown of Mexico*, 159–161.

44. Mülinen reasoned that Napoléon should send a Murat prince to Mexico instead. Count Rudolf Mülinen to Metternich, Oct. 15, 1861 (quotations), ad no. 11, Haus, Hof, und Staatsarchiv, MD, LOC; *New York Times*, Dec. 14, 1924.

45. New York Times, Dec. 14, 1924.

Chapter 2. Sooner or Later, War Will Have to Be Declared

1. Luis González y González, "Liberals and the Land," in Gilbert Michael Joseph and Timothy J. Henderson, eds., *The Mexico Reader: History, Culture, Politics* (Durham, N.C.: Duke University Press, 2002), 243, 245; *Mexican Times* (Mexico City), September 3, 1866; Ralph Roeder, *Juárez and His Mexico* (New York: Viking, 1947), 1: 41, 76–77; Haslip, *Crown of Mexico*, 142. Some blamed the factionalism on Joel Poinsett, the first United States minister to Mexico. *The Extraordinary* (Mexico), May 25, 1861, Records of Confederate States of America, Department of State, reel 5, Manuscript Division, Library of Congress, Washington, D.C. (hereafter cited as MD, LOC).

2. William T. Sherman to John Sherman, Dec. 3, 1866, in *The Sherman Letters*, 283 (quotation); Guedalla, *Two Marshals*, 77.

3. A *criollo* is a Creole or Spaniard born in the New World. *Mexican Times* (Mexico City), September 3, 1866; Roeder, *Juárez*, 41, 76–77; Erika Pani, "Dreaming of a Mexican Empire: The Political Projects of the 'Imperialistas,'" *Hispanic American Historical Review* 82 (Feb. 2002), 13 (quotation).

4. Will Fowler, *Santa Anna of Mexico* (Lincoln: University of Nebraska Press, 2007), 214–216 (quotation), 217, 248.

5. In many ways, Santa Anna wanted to be that sovereign. In his dictatorship of 1853 to 1855, he became Su Alteza Serenísima (His Serene Highness). José Manuel Hidalgo to Your Majesties [Maximilian and Carlota], April 19, 1865, Haus-, Hof-, und Staatsarchiv, no. 46, Karton 19, MD, LOC; Fowler, *Santa Anna of Mexico*, 301, 304–305, 317.

6. Luis González y González, "Liberals and the Land," in Joseph and Henderson, *Mexico Reader*, 243; Fowler, *Santa Anna of Mexico*, 117; *New York Times*, Aug. 18, 1859; Brian Hamnett, *Juárez* (London: Longman Group, 1994), 87–88; Lord John Emerich Edward Dalberg Acton, *Historical Essays and Studies*, ed. John Neville Figgis (London: Macmillan, 1907), 145; Emile de Kératry, *The Rise and Fall of the Emperor Maximilian*, trans. G. H. Venables (London: Sampson Low, son and Marston, 1868), 9.

7. Hamnett, *Juárez*, 15, 58–62, 65, 88–90, 97; Roeder, *Juárez*, 59, 142; Fowler, *Santa Anna of Mexico*, 220–221

8. Krauze, *Mexico*, 168; Hamnett, *Juárez*, 12, 14, 25, 56–57, 60–61, 65; Brian Hamnett, "Mexican Conservatives, Clericals, and Soldiers: The 'Traitor' Tomás Mejía through Reform and Empire, 1855–1867," *Bulletin of Latin American Research* 20, no. 2 (2001), 190.

9. Matías Romero, "The Situation of Mexico, Speech Delivered by Señor Romero," (n.p.: Wm. C. Bryant, 1864), 5, Andrew Johnson Papers, MD, LOC; Roeder, *Juárez*, 94–96; Ibsen, *Maximilian*, 111.

10. Benito Juárez, *Apuntes para mis hijos* (Mexico City: Universidad Nacional Autónoma de México, 2003), 9 (quotation); Roeder, *Juárez*, 5–6.

11. Juárez, *Apuntes*, 9, 13.

12. Roeder, *Juárez*, 9, 46, 50.

13. Roeder, *Juárez*, 5–8, 46–55; Agnes Salm-Salm, *Ten Years of My Life* (New York: R. Worthington, 1877), 188 (quotation).

14. Hamnett, *Juárez*, xii (quotation); Roeder, *Juárez*, 5–8, 46–55, 79–80. Bad behavior on the part of clerics also motivated Melchor Ocampo, governor of Michoacán. When a poor widow could not pay for her husband's burial, and the body began to decompose, the local curate commented that the woman could salt and eat the remains. Ocampo paid the interment fee, but he made the case a public mission to reform the church.

15. Romero, "The Situation of Mexico," 6, Andrew Johnson Papers (quotation); Hamnett, *Juárez* 58–62, 97; John F. Schwaller, *The History of the Catholic Church in Latin America: From Conquest to Revolution and Beyond* (New York: New York University Press, 2011), 146.

16. Hamnett, *Juárez*, 97–98; Roeder, *Juárez*, 274.

17. Romero, "The Situation of Mexico," 5–6, Andrew Johnson Papers; Hamnett,

Juárez 12, 14, 25, 56–57, 60–61, 65, 72, 74, 82–84, 102; Roeder, *Juárez*, 59; Ridley, *Maximilian and Juárez*, 28–29; Krauze, *Mexico*, 169.

18. Ratz, *Maximilian und Juárez*, 2: 50; Haslip, *Crown of Mexico*, 148; Hamnett, *Juárez*, 82, 276; Hamnett, "Mexican Conservatives," 188; Krauze, *Mexico*, 156.

19. *New York Semi-Weekly Times*, July 12, 1867; Hamnett, *Juárez*, 103, 199; Krauze, *Mexico*, 169.

20. Roeder, *Juárez*, 205; Krauze, *Mexico*, 169–170; Carl H. Bock, *Prelude to Tragedy: The Negotiation and Breakdown of the Tripartite Convention of London, October 31, 1861* (Philadelphia: University of Pennsylvania Press, 1966), 95; Schwaller, *History of the Catholic Church*, 148.

21. Charles L. Wyke to Russell, Aug. 29, 1861, Lord John Russell Papers, PRO 30/22/74, National Archives of the United Kingdom, Surrey, England (hereafter cited as NAUK); Hamnett, *Juárez*, 150–152; Black, *Napoleon III and Mexican Silver*, 65–66; Roeder, *Juárez*, 209–213; 229, 237, 241.

22. Hamnett, *Juárez* 151; Haslip, *Crown of Mexico*, 149.

23. This international event became known as the Antón Lizardo Incident and cost great political capital to some congressmen in Washington. Hamnett, *Juárez*, 148–152, 168, 276; Hanna and Hanna, *Napoleon III*, 36; Bock, *Prelude to Tragedy*, 444. Schedule of Jecker debt taken from Mexican Embassy in Paris, France, as found in papers of Nancy Nichols Barker, Dolph Briscoe Center for American History, University of Texas at Austin (hereafter cited as Barker Papers and CAH).

24. Roeder, *Juárez*, 259, 263–265; Hamnett, *Juárez*, 168–169.

25. Barker, "The French in Mexico," 21, unpublished manuscript, Barker Papers, CAH; Roeder, *Juárez*, 274–277; Wyke to Russell, Oct. 29, 1861, Russell Papers, PRO 30/22/74, NAUK.

26. Fowler, *Santa Anna of Mexico*, 202–203; José María Gutiérrez Estrada, *Carta dirigida al Exmo. Sr. Presidente de la República*, 35 (quotation); Pani, "Dreaming of a Mexican Empire," 17–18; Romero, "The Situation of Mexico," 8, Andrew Johnson Papers.

27. José Manuel Hidalgo to Your Majesties [Maximilian and Carlota], April 19, 1865, Haus-, Hof-, und Staatsarchiv, no. 46, Karton 19, MD, LOC; Haslip, *Crown of Mexico*, 142–145.

28. J. M. Gutiérrez de Estrada, *Cartas Dirigidas al Excimo Sr. Presidente de la República* (Mexico City: Impresa por I. Cumplido, 1840), 9, 35; Haslip, *Crown of Mexico*, 143–145.

29. José Manuel Hidalgo to Your Majesties [Maximilian and Carlota], April 19, 1865, Haus-, Hof-, und Staatsarchiv, no. 46, Karton 19, MD, LOC; Romero, "The Situation of Mexico," 11, Andrew Johnson Papers; Haslip, *Crown of Mexico*, 145–146; Barker, *Distaff Diplomacy*, 87–88; Castelot, *Maximilien*, 138.

30. Haslip, *Crown of Mexico*, 143–145; Robert Ryal Miller, "Arms across the Border," *Transactions of the American Philosophical Society* 63 (Dec. 1973), 5.

31. Barker, *Distaff Diplomacy*, 4–8, 87; Corti, *Maximilian*, 74–76; Baguley, *Napoléon III*, 177–178; Hanna and Hanna, *Napoleon III*, 191 (quotation).

32. Corti, *Maximilian*, 75–77; Baguley, *Napoléon III*, 178; Bock, *Prelude to Tragedy*, 99, 482; Barker, *Distaff Diplomacy*, 87; José Manuel Hidalgo to Your Majesties [Maximilian and Carlota], April 19, 1865, Haus-, Hof-, und Staatsarchiv, no. 46, Karton 19, MD, LOC; Martin, *Maximilian in Mexico*, 46–47.

33. This duty included the well-being of three million Arabs. Alain Plessis, *The Rise and Fall of the Second Empire, 1852–1871* (Cambridge: Cambridge University Press, 1989), 149–150; Napoléon III, *Histoire de Jules César* (New York: D. Appleton, 1865), 5 (quotation); Baguley, *Napoléon III*, 77–79, 170–172; Guedalla, *Two Marshals*, 79; Echard, *Napoléon III*, 151, 174, 208; Hanna and Hanna, *Napoleon III*, 81; Steinberg, *Bismarck*, 121–122; Ridley, *Napoleon III and Eugénie*, 498; Roger L. Williams, *The Mortal Napoleon III* (Princeton, NJ: Princeton University Press, 1971), 107.

34. Plessis, *The Rise and Fall of the Second Empire*, 149–150; Guedalla, *Two Marshals*, 79 (quotation); Hanna and Hanna, *Napoleon III*, 80. "The greatest idea of his reign" referred to Napoleon's great plan of alliances in Europe and a block of countries in North America under French domination. Guedalla, *Second Empire*, 79.

35. Corti, *Maximilian*, 77.

36. Hamnett, *Juárez*, 168; Haslip, *Crown of Mexico*, 129; Guedalla, *Two Marshals*, 79.

37. José Manuel Hidalgo to Your Majesties [Maximilian and Carlota], April 19, 1865, Haus-, Hof-, und Staatsarchiv, no. 46, Karton 19, MD, LOC (quotation); Corti, *Maximilian*, 78–80; Bock, *Prelude to Tragedy*, 449.

38. Black, *Napoleon III and Mexican Silver*, 23–26, 34–35; Hanna and Hanna, *Napoleon III*, 303.

39. Valori-Rustichelli, *L'Expédition du Mexique*, 17; Miller, "Arms across the Border," 5 (first quotation); *New York Semi-Weekly Times*, July 12, 1867 (second quotation); Russell to Mathew, Nov. 1, 1860, Russell Papers, PRO 30/22/95 C511085, NAUK.

40. José Manuel Hidalgo to Your Majesties [Maximilian and Carlota], April 19, 1865, Haus-, Hof-, und Staatsarchiv, no. 46, Karton 19, MD, LOC (quotation); Corti, *Maximilian*, 79.

41. Barker, "The French in Mexico," 20, unpublished manuscript, Barker Papers, CAH; Kératry, *Rise and Fall of the Emperor Maximilian*, 14–15 (quotations); Romero, "The Situation of Mexico," 10, Andrew Johnson Papers; Corti, *Maximilian*, 95; Philip Guedalla, *The Second Empire: Bonapartism, the Prince, the President, the Emperor* (New York: G. P. Putnam's Sons, 1922), 319; José Manuel Hidalgo to Your Majesties [Maximilian and Carlota], April 19, 1865, Haus-, Hof-, und Staatsarchiv, no. 46, Karton 19, MD, LOC; Mathew to Russell, Dec. 31, 1860, Russell Papers, PRO 30/22/74 C511085, NAUK.

42. Ridley, *Napoleon III and Eugénie*, 506; Corti, *Maximilian*, 96–97.

Chapter 3. The Red Avenger

1. New York Times, July 4, 8, 1861.

2. Roeder, *Juárez*, 273–274.

3. Hamnett, *Juárez*, 127; Corti, *Maximilian*, 98–99; *New York Semi-Weekly Times*, July 12. 1867; Mexico's debt totaled $82,315,446. Miller, "Arms across the Border," 6; Charles Wyke to Lord John Russell, *The Present Condition of Mexico: Message from the President of the United States*, 37th Congress, 2nd Sess., House Ex. Doc. 100, 270, 271 (quotation); George W. Mathew to Russell, May 21, 1861; Wyke to Russell, May 27, 1861, Russell Papers, PRO 30/22/74, C511085, NAUK. Pesos and US dollars were equivalent at that time. This amount equaled about $1.3 billion in 2008 dollars. Historical international currency equivalents by McCusker, Aug. 24, 2009, memo in possession of the author.

4. Bock, *Prelude to Tragedy*, 98 (quotation); Ridley, *Maximilian and Juárez*, 81; Miller, "Arms across the Border," 6; Lord Acton, *Historical Essays*, 147.

5. Alphonse Dubois de Saligny to Manuel de Zamacona, July 24, 25, 1861, 80, 86; Wyke to Manuel de Zamacona, July 25, 1861, 87, 89 (quotation), *Correspondence Relative to the Present Condition of Mexico Communicated to the House of Representatives by the Department of State, 1862*; de la Fère, *Recollections*, Maximilian Papers, UASC; Lord Acton, *Historical Essays*, 148; Michele Cunningham, *Mexico and the Foreign Policy of Napoléon III* (Hampshire, England: Palgrave, 2001), 34–35; Bock, *Prelude to Tragedy*, 445. Wyke said Saligny would term them "le perfide Albion." Wyke to Russell, Dec. 31, 1861, March 3, 1862, Russell Papers, PRO 30/22/74, NAUK.

6. Default on debt felt especially acute given France's dependency on silver, which spilled over into other countries' currencies and economies, who were dependent on silver through France. Black, *Napoleon III and Mexican Silver*, 30–33; Bock, *Prelude to Tragedy*, 482–483; Cunningham, *Mexico*, 81–82; Stevenson, *Maximilian in Mexico*, 18–22; Barker, "The French in Mexico," 21 (quotation), unpublished manuscript, Barker Papers, CAH.

7. José Manuel Hidalgo to Your Majesties [Maximilian and Carlota], April 19, 1865, no. 46, Haus-, Hof-, und Staatsarchiv, Karton 19, MD, LOC (quotation). Although Hidalgo tended to exaggerate his role in setting up the whole of the Mexico empire, "from the whole condition of affairs and taking other sources into account . . . things passed very much as Hidalgo described," said Corti. Corti, *Maximilian*, 99–100, 104 n.6; Castelot, *Maximilien*, 138.

8. José Manuel Hidalgo to Your Majesties [Maximilian and Carlota], April 19, 1865, no. 46, Haus, Hof, und Staatsarchiv, Karton 19, MD, LOC.

9. Hidalgo to Your Majesties, April 19, 1865.

10. Hidalgo to Your Majesties, April 19, 1865.

11. Hidalgo to Your Majesties, April 19, 1865; José María Gutiérrez de Estrada to

Richard Metternich, July 1861, no day, no. 9 c/II, Haus-, Hof-, und Staatsarchiv, MD, LOC.

12. José Manuel Hidalgo to Your Majesties [Maximilian and Carlota], April 19, 1865, no. 46, Haus-, Hof-, und Staatsarchiv, Karton 19, MD, LOC; Count Alexandre Walewski to Richard Metternich, July 16, 1861, Hausarchiv, Archiv Kaiser Maximilian von Mexiko, Karton 1, no. 1–100, MD, LOC (quotation); Castelot, *Maximilien*, 140–141.

13. José Manuel Hidalgo to Your Majesties [Maximilian and Carlota], April 19, 1865, no. 46, Alexandre Walewski to Richard Metternich, July 16, 1861, no. 9, Haus-, Hof-, und Staatsarchiv, Karton 19, MD, LOC.

14. José Manuel Hidalgo to Your Majesties [Maximilian and Carlota], April 19, 1865, no. 46, Haus-, Hof-, und Staatsarchiv, Karton 19, MD, LOC; Castelot, *Maximilien*, 141; Report by Count Rudolf Mülinen, Sept. 27, 1861, no. 5, Haus-, Hof-, und Staatsarchiv, MD, LOC.

15. Corti, *Maximilian*, 123.

16. Antonio López de Santa Anna to Maximilian, Dec. 22, 1863 (quotation), Haus-, Hof-, und Staatsarchiv, MD, LOC; Fowler, *Santa Anna*, 321, 322.

17. Corti, *Maximilian*, 95–96; Seward to Thomas Corwin, April 6, 1861, 8; William Seward to Thomas Corwin, Dec. 6, 1861, 36; Matías Romero to William H. Seward, Sept. 30, 1861, 101–103, *Correspondence Relative to the Present Condition of Mexico, 1862*; Thomas D. Schoonover, *Mexican Lobby: Matías Romero in Washington, 1861–1867* (Lexington: University of Kentucky Press, 1986), xi.

18. Napoléon III to Count Auguste de Flahault, Oct. 1861; José María Gutiérrez de Estrada to Richard Metternich, Oct. 1861, Kaiser Maximilian's papers, Haus-, Hof-, und Staatsarchiv, Karton 1, MD, LOC; Corti, *Maximilian*, 103–106, 122 (quotation), 123; Richard Metternich to Roger, no last name, Sept. 25, 1861, Haus-, Hof-, und Staatsarchiv, MD, LOC.

19. Napoléon III to Count Auguste de Flahault, Oct. 1861 (quotation), no. 15, Haus-, Hof-, und Staatsarchiv, MD, LOC; Cunningham, *Mexico*, 53–54; Corti, *Maximilian*, 94, 109–112. British exports fell from £887,862 in 1856 to £441,831 in 1858. Edward E. Dunbar, *The Mexican Papers, The Mexican Question, the Great American Question* (New York: J. A. H. Hasbrouck, 1860), 170–171.

20. Wyke to Russell, July 29, 1861, Russell Papers, PRO 30/22/74 C511085, NAUK.

21. Barker, *Distaff Diplomacy*, 88, 191; Cunningham, *Mexico*, 45, 65–66, 69; Corti, *Maximilian*, 129–130.

22. Barker, "The French in Mexico," 20, unpublished manuscript, Barker Papers, CAH; Cunningham, *Mexico*, 49, 58; Corti, *Maximilian*, 113–114; Mathew to Russell, Dec. 30, 1860, Russell Papers, PRO 30/22/74 C511085, NAUK.

23. Bock, *Prelude to Tragedy*, 446–447, 456; Cunningham, 32, 36, 48–49; Haslip, *Crown of Mexico*, 165, 169–170; Ridley, *Maximilian and Juárez*, 73–74; British For-

eign Office, *British and Foreign State Papers, 1862–1863* (London: William Ridgway, 1868), 53: 390–391, 423; William Seward to Thomas Corwin, April 6, 1861, 8; William Seward to Thomas Corwin, Dec. 6, 1861, 36; Feb. 15, 1862, *Correspondence Relative to the Present Condition of Mexico*, 1862, 48; Harding, *Phantom Crown*, 92 (quotation); Gerardo Gurza Lavalle, *Una Vecindad Efímera: Los Estados Confederados de América y su Política Exterior Hacia México, 1861–1865* (Mexico City: Instituto Mora, 2001), 44.

24. British Foreign Office, *British and Foreign State Papers 1862–1863*, 53: 423; Corti, *Maximilian*, 126 (quotations); Haslip, *Crown of Mexico*, 165, 169–170; Hanna and Hanna, *Napoleon III*, 38–40.

25. Cunningham, *Mexico*, 60–63; 71–72; Hanna and Hanna, *Napoleon III and Mexico*, 42–46; Corti, *Maximilian*, 129.

26. Statement of Charles Lennox Wyke, Hugh Dunlop, E. Jurien de la Gravièr, Saligny, El Conde de Ruess, Jan. 10, 1862, *Correspondence Relative to the Present Condition of Mexico*, 177 (quotations); Martin, *Maximilian in Mexico*, 53.

27. Bock, *Prelude to Tragedy*, 311–312.

28. For decades French merchants, drawn to Mexico by its legendary riches, suffered tumultuous relationships with Mexican leaders, and they often expected France to set things right. Alfonse de Saligny to J. M. Arroyo, Claim on behalf of Mesón de Santa Julia, Sept. 3, 1863, Claim by Pierre Maurel, Sept. 9, 1863, Exp. 4, fo. 3, GD3000, Relaciones Exteriores, Archivo General de la Nación, Mexico City, Mexico (hereafter cited as AGN); Wyke to Russell, May 11, 1862, Russell Papers, PRO 30/22/74 C511085, NAUK; Barker, "The French in Mexico," 3–6, 11, unpublished paper, Barker Papers, CAH; Bock, *Prelude to Tragedy*, 94, 447, 480 (quotation).

29. Bock, *Prelude to Tragedy*, 313–314, 450; Corti, *Maximilian*, 134–136; Stevenson, *Maximilian in Mexico*, 31.

30. Cunningham, *Mexico*, 63, 66, 69.

31. Corti, *Maximilian*, 129; Martin, *Maximilian in Mexico*, 74–75.

32. This 1862 law was later used against Maximilian. Bock, *Prelude to Tragedy*, 310, 316; Cunningham, *Mexico*, 63, 66; Jack A. Dabbs, *The French Army in Mexico, 1861–1867* (The Hague: Mouton, 1963), 19–20.

33. Roeder, *Juárez*, 300; Stevenson, *Maximilian in Mexico*, 31; Hamnett, *Juárez*, 151–152.

34. Dabbs, *The French Army*, 21–23; Stevenson, *Maximilian in Mexico*, 36; *New York Times*, March 18, 1862.

35. Corti, *Maximilian*, 166–167; Ridley, *Maximilian and Juárez*, 88.

36. The *Illustrated London News*, April 5, 1862; Corti, *Maximilian*, 163–164, 167 (quotation); Cunningham, *Mexico*, 73; Bock, *Prelude to Tragedy*, 321; Ridley, *Maximilian and Juárez*, 90.

37. Ridley, *Maximilian and Juárez*, 89–90.

38. Wyke to Russell, May 12, 1862, Russell Papers, PRO 30/22/74 C511085, NAUK; Bock, *Prelude to Tragedy*, 321; Ridley, *Maximilian and Juárez*, 91–92.

39. Martin, *Maximilian in Mexico*, 89–90, 441–442.

40. José María Gutiérrez de Estrada to Maximilian, Oct. 4, 1861, no. 12, Oct. 14, 1861, no. 17, Richard Metternich to Roger Aldenburg, Oct. 6, 1861, Maximilian to José María Gutiérrez de Estrada, Nov. 12, 1861, Haus-, Hof-, und Staatsarchiv, MD, LOC; Auguste t'Kint de Roodenbeck to Maximilian, Dec. 28, 1863, Karton 5, Maximilian Papers, OS; Barker, "Maximilian's House of Cards," 7 (quotation), unpublished manuscript, Barker Papers, CAH.

41. Barker, "Maximilian's House of Cards," 8, unpublished manuscript, Barker Papers, CAH.

42. Hyde, *Mexican Empire*, 116–118.

43. Hyde, *Mexican Empire*, 116–118; Haslip, *Crown of Mexico*, 176; Barker, "France, Austria, and the Mexican Venture," 242. A gulden equaled about $.13 or 1.80 thaler in 1861. A U.S. dollar equaled about four thaler. John J. McCusker, memorandum on historical currency evaluations, Aug. 24, 2009, notes in possession of the author.

44. Corti, *Maximilian*, 140–141; Ridley, *Maximilian and Juárez*, 78.

45. Corti, *Maximilian*, 171–173, 172 (quotation).

46. Ridley, *Maximilian and Juárez*, 78–79; Corti, *Maximilian*, 141, 145–151.

47. Corti, *Maximilian*, 142–143, 144 (quotations); Hanna and Hanna, *Napoleon III*, 53.

48. Blumberg, "Diplomacy of the Mexican Empire," 9; Carlota, "Observations," in Luis Weckmann, *Carlota de Bélgica: Correspondencia y Escritos Sobre México en los Archivos Europeos, 1861–1868* (Mexico City: Editorial Porrúa, 1989), 155–156; Kératry, *Rise and Fall of the Emperor Maximilian*, 9; Ridley, *Maximilian and Juárez*, 79 (quotation).

49. Blumberg, "Diplomacy of the Mexican Empire," 9; Queen Victoria, *The Letters of Queen Victoria: A Selection from Her Majesty's Correspondence and Journal between the Years 1862–1878*, ed. George Earle Buckle (New York: Longmans, Green & Co., 1926), 1: 110; Hyde, *Mexican Empire*, 121–122; Kératry, *Rise and Fall of the Emperor Maximilian*, 9; Carlota, "Observations," in Weckmann, *Carlota*, 155–156.

50. Hyde, *Mexican Empire*, 121–122 (first and third quotations); Lichtervelde, *Léopold First*, 151 (second quotation).

51. Ridley, *Maximilian and Juárez*, 78–79; Interview with Lorenza Fonda, Castello di Miramare, June 9, 2009, notes in possession of the author.

52. Marvin R. O'Connell, "Ultramontanism and Dupanloup: The Compromise of 1865," *Church History: Studies in Christianity and Culture* 53, no. 2 (1984), 200–203; Ridley, *Maximilian and Juárez*, 76; Corti, *Maximilian*, 160–161.

53. William L. Shaw, "McDougall of California," *California Historical Society Quarterly* 43 (June 1964), 123–124 (first quotation); Herr von Geralt to Count Berstoff, March 5, 1862, as cited in Corti, *Maximilian*, 157 (second quotation).

54. Corti, *Maximilian*, 153–154.

55. Martin, *Maximilian in Mexico*, 170.

Chapter 4. The Siege of Puebla

1. Haslip, *Crown of Mexico*, 179; Cunningham, *Mexico*, 114, 115 (quotation); Kératry, *Rise and Fall of the Emperor Maximilian*, 20.

2. Ratz, *Maximilian und Juárez*, 2: 111; Kératry, *Rise and Fall of the Emperor Maximilian*, 7; Corti, *Maximilian*, 175 (quotation). Eugénie wrote this letter June 7, 1862, not yet knowing of the May 5 defeat.

3. Ridley, *Maximilian and Juárez*, 96–97; Corti, *Maximilian*, 176.

4. Ridley, *Maximilian and Juárez*, 98; Martin, *Maximilian in Mexico*, 109.

5. Ridley, *Maximilian and Juárez*, 98; Roeder, *Juárez*, 444 (quotation); Martin, *Maximilian in Mexico*, 109; Cunningham, *Mexico*, 120.

6. Díaz first trained as a priest, then followed Benito Juárez's example to study law. The outbreak of the Mexican War provided him with his first experiences in battle, diplomacy, and management, which carried him through what would prove to be an extensive and powerful career. Ridley, *Maximilian and Juárez*, 99; Roeder, *Juárez*, 445; Krauze, *Mexico*, 207–208.

7. "La Marseillaise" was a liberal song that condemned invading armies. It is now the French national anthem. Ridley, *Maximilian and Juárez*, 99; Roeder, *Juárez*, 445–446.

8. Ridley, *Maximilian and Juárez*, 99–100; Corti, *Maximilian*, 177; Martin, *Maximilian in Mexico*, 110.

9. Ridley, *Maximilian and Juárez*, 102–104; Martin, *Maximilian in Mexico*, 111–112; Corti, *Maximilian*, 179–180.

10. Cunningham, *Mexico*, 120–121 (quotations); Kératry, *Rise and Fall of the Emperor Maximilian*, 21.

11. Barker, "Monarchy in Mexico," 18, manuscript (later published in *Journal of Modern History*), 18, Barker Papers, CAH; Ridley, *Maximilian and Juárez*, 102–103; Roeder, *Juárez*, 453 (quotation); Hamnett, *Juárez*, 171; Bock, *Prelude to Tragedy*, 452; Ridley, *Napoleon III and Eugénie*, 510.

12. Corti, *Maximilian*, 179.

13. Roeder, *Juárez*, 454; Miller, "Arms across the Border," 6 (quotation); Charles Rieken to J. P. Benjamin, June 16, 1863, CSA Papers, Dept. of State, MD, LOC.

14. Ridley, *Maximilian and Juárez*, 103; Corti, 178; Roeder, 454; Cunningham, *Mexico*, 123.

15. Roeder, *Juárez*, 436, 456–459; Ridley, *Maximilian and Juárez*, 103; Cunningham, *Mexico*, 117–118; Plessis, *The Rise and Fall of the Second Empire*, 151; Lecaillon, *Napoléon III et le Mexique*, 187–189.

16. Cunningham, *Mexico*, 124–126; Roeder, *Juárez*, 456–458 (quotation).

17. Charles Rieken, "Vessels of War off Sacrificios, Veracruz," Sept. 30, 1862, Reel 6, Confederate States of America Papers, Department of State (hereafter cited as CSA

Papers, Dept. of State), MD, LOC; Martin, *Maximilian in Mexico*, 114–116; Corti, *Maximilian*, 190–192.

18. Charles Rieken to J. P. Benjamin, Sept. 30, 1862, June 16, 1863, Reel 7, CSA Papers, Dept. of State, MD, LOC; Martin, *Maximilian in Mexico*, 116; Cunningham, *Mexico*, 134–135; 146–148. Woll would eventually serve in Maximilian's court. "Datos biográficos," 1864, in Weckmann, *Carlota*, 228.

19. Guedalla, *Two Marshals*, 4, 8–9, 11, 73, 82; Corti, *Maximilian*, 180; Ridley, *Napoleon III and Eugénie*, 511.

20. Corti, *Maximilian*, 180; Roeder, *Juárez*, 466.

21. Roeder, *Juárez*, 468.

22. Roeder, *Juárez*, 469; Joseph Audenried to Mary Colket Audenried, Dec. 4, 1866, Nau Collection. An estimated 2,000 French soldiers had died by August 1862. Wyke to Russell, Aug. 28, 1862, Russell Papers, PRO 30/22/74, NAUK.

23. Roeder, *Juárez*, 469.

24. Roeder, *Juárez*, 469–471.

25. Roeder, *Juárez*, 472.

26. Pierre Henri Loizillon, *Lettres sur l'Expédition du Mexique, Publiées par sa Sœur, 1862–1867* (Paris: Librairie Militaire de L. Baudoin et Cie, 1890), 8 (first quotation); Roeder, *Juárez*, 473–474, 475 (second quotation); Emile de Kératry, *La Contre-Guérrilla Française au Mexique, Souvenirs des Terres Chaudes* (Paris: Librairie Internationale, 1868), 15–20, 23–24; Dabbs, *The French Army in Mexico*, 34 n.12, 268.

27. Dabbs, *The French Army in Mexico*, 268–270.

28. Roeder, *Juárez*, 474–475; Loizillon, *Lettres*, 11, 14 (quotations); Wyke to Russell, June 28, 1862, Russell Papers, PRO 30/22/74, NAUK.

29. Roeder, *Juárez*, 475, 478 (quotation).

30. Roeder, *Juárez*, 480 (quotation); Kératry, *La Contre-Guérrilla*, 53.

31. Roeder, *Juárez*, 481.

32. The 2,260 hogsheads of tobacco (over two million pounds) had been purchased by the powerful Rothschild's banking house through Richmond before Lincoln blockaded American ports. John Slidell to Robert Mercer Taliaferro Hunter, Feb. 19, 1863, Reel 3, CSA Papers, Dept. of State, MD, LOC; Miller, "Arms across the Border," 12; Frederick W. Seward, *Seward at Washington as Senator and Secretary of State, a Memoir* (New York: Derby and Miller, 1891), 190, 191 (quotations).

33. Romero in *Responsabilidades Contraídas por el Gobierno Nacional de Mexico en los Estados Unidos, en Virtud de los contratos celebrados por sus agentes* (Mexico: Imprenta del Gobierno, 1867), 8–9; Ridley, *Maximilian and Juárez*, 118–119; Miller, "Arms across the Border," 11; Hanna and Hanna, *Napoleon III*, 54; A. Supervièle to Adrian Woll, Nov. 9. 1863, Karton 5, Maximilian Papers, OS; *L'Estafette*, Aug. 29, 1864; Tuffly Ellis, "Maritime Commerce on the Far Western Gulf, 1861–1865," *Southwestern Historical Quarterly* 77 (Oct. 1973), 210–211. The customs house traditionally collected a half-

cent in gold per pound. For additional information, see also M. M. McAllen, *I Would Rather Sleep in Texas* (Austin: Texas State Historical Association, 2003), 275–276.

34. Randon, in Jacques Louis César Alexandre, *Mémoires du Maréchal Randon* (Paris: Typographie Lahure, 1877) 2: 75; Hamnett, *Juárez*, 138; Corti, *Maximilian*, 193; Roeder, *Juárez*, 483, 488, 489 (quotation) 489, 490; Ridley, *Maximilian and Juárez*, 104; Wyke to Russell, Sept. 27, 1862, Russell Papers, PRO 30/22/74, NAUK.

35. Corti, *Maximilian*, 193–194.

36. Randon, *Mémoires*, 75; Roeder, *Juárez*, 493 (quotation), 495.

37. James F. Elton, *With the French in Mexico* (London: Chapman and Hall, 1867), 11; *Blumberg*, "Diplomacy of the Mexican Empire," 60–61; Ridley, *Maximilian and Juárez*, 116–117.

38. Kératry, *La Contre-Guérrilla*, 9, 114–115; Achille Bazaine to Napoléon III, Nov. 18, 1863, Bazaine Papers, García Collection, BLAC.

39. Du Pin formerly went by the name of Dupin, but petitioned the court in Gallic, France, to let him spell his name "Du Pin" to appear more aristocratic. Gérard Mignard, Memo, Feb. 18, 2009, notes in possession of author; Gérard Mignard, *Charles-Louis Du Pin, Un intellectuel baroudeur né à Lasgraïsses* (Self-published, 1997), 4, 12–14; Kératry, *La Contre-Guérrilla*, 10.

40. Kératry, *La Contre-Guérrilla*, 10–11.

41. Roeder, *Juárez*, 493, 495; Ridley, *Maximilian and Juárez*, 121.

42. Roeder, *Juárez*, 495–496.

43. Roeder, *Juárez*, 497.

44. Roeder, *Juárez*, 497; Corti, *Maximilian*, 209, 210 (quotation).

45. Roeder, *Juárez*, 498–499.

46. Kératry, *La Contre-Guérrilla*, 312; Roeder, *Juárez*, 499 (quotation).

47. Roeder, *Juárez*, 504; Corti, *Maximilian*, 210.

48. Laurent, *La Guerre du Mexique*, 58–59.

49. Ridley, *Maximilian and Juárez*, 129.

50. Roeder, *Juárez*, 507–508; Corti, *Maximilian*, 210–211.

51. Roeder, *Juárez*, 501 (quotation), 508.

52. Roeder, *Juárez*, 508–509; Loizillon, *Lettres*, 78.

53. Roeder, *Juárez*, 509.

54. Loizillon, *Lettres*, 77; Corti, *Maximilian*, 210–211; Roeder, *Juárez*, 508 (quotations), 510; Edward Lee Plumb to Allan McLane, March 11, 1865, Edward Plumb Papers; Charles Rieken to J. P. Benjamin, June 16, 1863, CSA Papers, Dept. of State, MD, LOC.

55. Martin, *Maximilian in Mexico*, 127; Roeder, *Juárez*, 509.

56. Mignard, *Charles-Louis Du Pin*, 16–17 (quotation); Kératry, *La Contre-Guérrilla*, 11–12.

57. Kératry, *La Contre-Guérrilla*, 1–14.

58. Kératry, *La Contre-Guérrilla*, 54, 56–57 (quotation); Memo of Dr. Girard Mignard, La Roque sur Cèze, Sept. 1, 2009, in possession of the author.

59. Kératry, *La Contre-Guérrilla*, 15–20, 23–24, 39–41.

60. Mignard, *Charles-Louis Du Pin*, 18.

61. Mignard, *Charles-Louis Du Pin*, 18 (first quotation); Ridley, *Napoleon III and Eugénie*, 512; Jean-Yves Puyo, "The French Military Confront Mexico's Geography," *Journal of Latin American Geography* 9 (2010), 142 (second quotation).

62. Kératry, *La Contre-Guérrilla*, 68–70.

63. Kératry, *La Contre-Guérrilla*, 66–67.

64. Roeder, *Juárez*, 511, 512 (quotation).

65. Carlota to Napoléon, Aug. 11, 1866, in Weckmann, *Carlota*, 177; Roeder, *Juárez*, 511 (quotation), 512.

66. Roeder, *Juárez*, 512 (quotation); de la Fère, *Recollections*, Maximilian Papers, UASC.

67. George H. White to Russell, Oct. 25, 1863, Russell Papers, PRO 30/22/74 C511085, NAUK (second quotation); Stevenson, *Maximilian in Mexico*, 93; Roeder, *Juárez*, 519–520; 521 (first quotation); 522 (third quotation).

68. Roeder, *Juárez*, 520.

69. *New York Times*, July 16, 1863; Roeder, *Juárez*, 521–522, 555; Corti, *Maximilian*, 222; Hanna and Hanna, *Napoleon III*, 89 (quotation).

70. Ridley, *Maximilian and Juárez*, 134–136.

71. Labastida returned on Sept. 17, 1863. *Documentos Relativos a la Asamblea General de Notables que dió por Resultado la Adopción del Sistema Monárquico en México* (Mexico: Imprenta Literaria, 1864), 10–11; Roeder, *Juárez*, 539–540.

72. *New York Times*, July 16, 1863; Roeder, *Juárez*, 523 (quotations); Loizillon, *Lettres*, 98–99.

73. *La Sociedad* (Mexico City), July 18, 1863; de la Fère, *Recollections*, Maximilian Papers, UASC, México; *Documentos Relativos a la Asamblea General de Notables que dió por Resultado la Adopción del Sistema Monárquico en México* (Mexico City: Imprenta Literaria, 1864), 8–9; Francisco de Miranda; Ignacio Aguilar y Marocho, Antonio Suárez Peredo, Conde del Valle, et al., Ratification of vote by Assembly of Notables, July 26, 1863, Karton 9, Maximilian Papers, OS.

74. Roeder, *Juárez*, 522 (first quotation), 524 (second quotation); *New York Times*, July 16, 1863; Ridley, *Maximilian and Juárez*, 136.

75. French and other European officers also brought the game of cricket to Mexico and played in the fields near Chapultepec. François Aubert, "Court of Mexico Playing Cricket," ca. 1865, Getty Research Institute, Special Collections and Visual Resources (photo); Roeder, *Juárez*, 524; Stevenson, *Maximilian in Mexico*, 96 (quotations). See also June Edith Hahner, *Women through Women's Eyes: Latin American Women in Nineteenth-Century Travel Accounts* (Lanham, MD: Rowman & Littlefield, 1998), 148–149.

Chapter 5. Honor of the House of Habsburg

1. Corti, *Maximilian*, 212 (quotation); Haslip, *Crown of Mexico*, 203.

2. Queen Victoria, *The Letters of Queen Victoria*, 1: 104; Corti, *Maximilian*, 212–213; Haslip, *Crown of Mexico*, 191; Carlota, "Observations," in Weckmann, *Carlota*, 155.

3. "In this sign (Christ), you will prevail." Teodosio Lares, Antonio Morán, Juan Rodriguez de San Miguel, announcement of preliminary vote, Nov. 23, 1863, Karton 5; Report of Regions Pledged to Empire, Nov. 1863 (quotation), Karton 9, Maximilian Papers, OS; Roeder, *Juárez*, 559; Corti, *Maximilian*, 261–262; de la Fère, *Recollections*, Maximilian Papers, UASC.

4. Statement of Regions Pledged to Empire, Nov. 1863, Karton 9, Maximilian Papers, OS; Maximilian to Juan N. Almonte, Nov. 4, 1863, Fondo XXIII, no. 19, Centro de Estudios de Historia de México Condumex, Mexico City, Mexico (hereafter cited as Archivo Condumex); Martín de las Torres, *El Archiduque Maximiliano de Austria en Méjico* (Madrid: Librería de D. A. San Martín), 238–239; Roeder, *Juárez*, 560; Corti, 225 (quotation), 226, 305; Carlota, "Observations," in Weckmann, *Carlota*, 157.

5. Corti, *Maximilian*, 278–279.

6. Ridley, *Napoleon III and Eugénie*, 515.

7. Wyke to Russell, Sept. 7, 29, 1863, Russell Papers, PRO 30/22/74 C5110685; Russell to Wyke, Sept. 11, 1863, PRO 30/22/95 C511085, NAUK; Hyde, *Mexican Empire*, 119.

8. Corti, *Maximilian*, 228–230, 261–262, 263–264, 304; John De Havilland, *Le Mexique sous la Maison de Habsbourg* (Vienna: C. Gerold, 1863), 25; Hanna and Hanna, *Napoleon III and Mexico*, 113.

9. Hanna and Hanna, *Napoleon III and Mexico*, 113–114; Wyke to Russell, June 29, 1861, Russell Papers, PRO 30/22/74 C511085, NAUK.

10. Blumberg, "Diplomacy of the Mexican Empire," 47; Haslip, *Crown of Mexico*, 194 (quotation).

11. Roeder, *Juárez*, 532 (second quotation), 533–534, 535 (first quotation); 539–540.

12. Roeder, *Juárez*, 530–531, 534–535; Dabbs, *French Army*, 63; Stevenson, *Maximilian*, 106–107; Randon, *Mémoires du Maréchal Randon*, 2: 85.

13. Achille Bazaine to Napoléon III, Nov. 19, 1863, 30 (quotation); Achille Bazaine to the Mexican people, Nov. 22, 1863, Bazaine Papers, García Collection, BLAC; John Walsham to Russell, Oct. 10, 25, 1863, Russell Papers, PRO 30/22/74 C511085, NAUK; Roeder, *Juárez*, 555–556; Dabbs, *French Army*, 63, 65, 69–70, 78.

14. Hamnett, "Mexican Conservatives," 189; Roeder, *Juárez*, 541; Labastida to Gutiérrez de Estrada, Nov. 21, 1863, K5, OS; Achille Bazaine to Minister of War (Jacques Randon), Nov. 17, 1863 (quotations), Bazaine papers, García Collection, BLAC; Dabbs, *French Army*, 77–80; Ridley, *Maximilian and Juárez*, 134.

15. George H. White to Russell, Oct. 25, 1863, Russell Papers, PRO 30/22/74 C511085, NAUK.

16. Ridley, *Maximilian and Juárez*, 146; Dabbs, *French Army*, 225.

17. Achille Bazaine to Napoléon III, Nov. 19, 1863, Bazaine Papers, García Collection, BLAC; Ridley, *Maximilian and Juárez*, 146; Blumberg, "Diplomacy of the Mexican Empire," 47.

18. Antonio Labastida to J. M. Gutiérrez de Estrada, Nov. 21, 1863 (first quotation); Antonio Labastida to J. N. Almonte, Mariano Salas, Nov. 10, 1863 (second quotation), Karton 5, Maximilian Papers, OS; Antonio Labastida to Achille Bazaine, Nov. 17, 1863; Antonio Labastida to José Ignacio Pavón, Nov. 21, 1863; Achille Bazaine to Napoléon III, Nov. 30, 1863, Bazaine papers, García Collection, BLAC; Dabbs, *French Army*, 82–83; Kératry, *Rise and Fall of the Emperor Maximilian*, 33.

19. Hanna and Hanna, *Napoleon III*, 106; Roeder, *Juárez*, 552–553; Ridley, *Maximilian and Juárez*, 146.

20. This includes the Eastertide tradition of burning Judas in effigy. Guedalla, *Two Marshals*, 97–98; Roeder, *Juárez*, 553–554; Ridley, *Maximilian and Juárez*, 146–147; Corti, *Maximilian*, 273; W. Preston to J. P. Benjamin, June 30, 1864, Reel 7, CSA Records, Dept. of State, MD, LOC.

21. Antonio Labastida to José M. Gutiérrez de Estrada, Nov. 21, 1863, Karton 5, Maximilian Papers, OS; Roeder, *Juárez*, 553–554; Ridley, *Maximilian and Juárez*, 146–147; Dabbs, *French Army*, 81 (quotation), 94–95.

22. Achille Bazaine to Napoléon III, Nov. 30, 1863, Bazaine papers, García Collection, BLAC; Corti, *Maximilian*, 275–277.

23. The brothers Armand and Michel Heine were some of the bankers. Achille Bazaine to Napoléon III, Nov. 19, 1863, Achille Bazaine to Nicolas Budin, Nov. 20, Dec. 25, 1863, Bazaine Papers, García Collection, BLAC; Corti, *Maximilian*, 306, 308; Stevenson, *Maximilian*, 105–106; Guedalla, *Two Marshals*, 95.

24. Achille Bazaine to Napoléon III, Nov. 10, 1863, Achille Bazaine to Nicolas Budin, Nov. 20, 1863, Bazaine Papers, García Collection, BLAC; Dabbs, *French Army*, 65; Corti, *Maximilian*, 291, 292 (quotations); Dabbs, *French Army*, 87.

25. Kératry, *La Contre-Guérrilla*, 102; Corti, *Maximilian*, 292–293, 309–310; Guedalla, *Two Marshals*, 90–91, 95–96; Carlota to Maximilian, March 19, 1866, in Ratz, *Correspondencia Inédita*, 272; Carlota to Marie Amélie, July 24, 1864, in Weckmann, *Carlota*, 270.

26. Kératry, *Rise and Fall of the Emperor Maximilian*, 35 (first quotation); Achille Bazaine to Jacques Randon, Nov. 17, 1863, Achille Bazaine to Napoléon III, Nov. 30, 1863, Achille Bazaine to Juan N. Almonte, Dec. 29, 1863, Achille Bazaine to Jacques Randon, Jan. 5, 1864 (second quotation), June 1, 1864, Achille Bazaine to Napoléon III, Dec. 12, 1863, Achille Bazaine to Jacques Randon, Jan. 5, 1964, Bazaine papers, García Collection, BLAC; *L'Estafette*, July 6, 1864.

27. These governors were Ignacio Pesqueira in Sonora and Luis Terrazas in Chihuahua. Ronnie Tyler, *Santiago Vidaurri and the Southern Confederacy* (Austin: Texas State Historical Association, 1973), 11 (quotation), 13–14, 136–137; Achille Bazaine,

circular to the officers, June 3, 1864, Bazaine papers, García Collection, BLAC; Gurza Lavalle, *Una Vecindad Efímera*, 10–11, 73–74; Roeder, *Juárez*, 549; William G. Hale to J. B. Magruder, Jan. 24, 1864, Confederate Papers Relating to Citizens, RG 109, National Archives and Records Administration, Washington, D.C. (hereafter cited as NARA); Col. Edouard Alphonse, Baron de Amyard, to Bazaine, March 17, 1864, in Achille Bazaine, *La Intervención Francesa en México según el Archivo del Mariscal Bazaine*, 2nd ed. (Mexico City: Editorial Porrúa, 1973), 1119.

28. Achille Bazaine to Juan N. Almonte, Dec. 29, 1863; Achille Bazaine to Napoléon III, Dec. 12, 1863, Jan. 5, 1864, Bazaine Papers, García Collection, BLAC; Roeder, *Juárez*, 544 (quotation); Col. Edouard Alphonse, Baron de Amyard to Bazaine, March 17, 1864, in Bazaine, *Intervención Francesa*, 1119.

29. Wyke to Russell, Jan. 30, 1864, Russell Papers, PRO 30/22/74, C511085, NAUK.

30. Achille Bazaine to Jacques Randon, Nov. 17, 1863, Bazaine Papers, García Collection, BLAC; Corti, *Maximilian*, 293, 310; *L'Estafette*, Aug. 14, 1864; *Revista de los Últimos Sucesos en México*, Feb. 26, 1864, found in Karton 25, Maximilian Papers, OS; Romero tried to convince Seward that the Clerical party of Mexico was strikingly similar to the "slave party" in the U.S. Romero, "Situation of Mexico," 11, Andrew Johnson Papers.

31. Roeder, *Juárez*, 578 (quotation); Charles Allen Smart, *Viva Juárez: The Founder of Modern Mexico* (Philadelphia: J. B. Lippincott, 1963), 326.

32. Smart, *Viva Juárez*, 330–331; Roeder, *Juárez*, 578 (quotation).

33. Smart, *Viva Juárez*, 330–331, 333; Roeder, *Juárez*, 578, 580 (quotations).

34. Achille Bazaine to Napoléon III, Nov. 30, 1863; Achille Bazaine to Juan N. Almonte, Dec. 25, 1863, Bazaine papers, García Collection, BLAC; *L'Estafette*, March 25, 1865; Scarlett to Russell, Feb. 12, 1865, Russell Papers, PRO 30/22/74 C511085, NAUK.

35. Napoléon III to Achille Bazaine, Dec. 10, 1863, Bazaine Papers, García Collection, BLAC; Kératry, *La Contre-Guérrilla*, 78–79; Guedalla, *Two Marshals*, 94; Elton, *With the French in Mexico*, 78.

36. Kératry, *La Contre-Guérrilla*, 91–93, 120.

37. Kératry, *La Contre-Guérrilla*, 105–106.

38. Kératry, *La Contre-Guérrilla*, 102–106.

39. Hubert Howe Bancroft, "José María Jesús Carvajal," in Tyler et al., *The New Handbook of Texas*, 1: 971; Chance, *José María Jesús Carvajal*, 6–9; 80–82; Kératry, *La Contre-Guérrilla Française au Mexique*, 104–109, 110–112.

40. Kératry, *La Contre-Guérrilla*, 112–113, 117–119.

41. Kératry, *La Contre-Guérrilla*, 130 (quotation), 131–135, 141–142; *Pájaro Verde*, May 23, 1864.

42. Haslip, *Crown of Mexico*, 205–206; Achille Bazaine to Jacques Randon, May 28, 1864, Bazaine Papers, García Collection, BLAC.

43. Haslip, *Crown of Mexico*, 205, 206 (quotation).
44. Roeder, *Juárez*, 543, 544 (quotation).

Chapter 6. What Would You Think of Me

1. Corti, *Maximilian*, 312.
2. Roeder, *Juárez*, 564; Corti, *Maximilian*, 320–321.
3. The British firms of Glyn, Mills & Co., F. de Lizardi & Co., and Barings Brothers, as well as Crédit Mobilier of France funded much of the loan. F. de Lizardi & Co., *Mexican Debenture*, April 1, 1842; Philip Ziegler, *The Sixth Great Power: A History of One of the Greatest of All Banking Families, The House of Barings, 1762–1929* (New York: Alfred A. Knopf, 1998), 229–230; Corti, *Maximilian*, 315–316.
4. Lichtervelde, *Léopold First*, 273–274; Corti, *Maximilian*, 316 (quotation).
5. Haslip, *Crown of Mexico*, 207.
6. Fowler, *Santa Anna of Mexico*, 320–321, 323–326; Hanna and Hanna, *Napoleon III*, 109.
7. Roeder, *Juárez*, 566 (quotation); Magnus, *El Ocaso*, 18.
8. Roeder, *Juárez*, 566.
9. Haslip, *Crown of Mexico*, 209–210.
10. Ridley, *Maximilian and Juárez*, 158–159; Hyde, *Mexican Empire*, 127; Haslip, *Crown of Mexico*, 204, 210, 213.
11. Ridley, *Maximilian and Juárez*, 158–159.
12. Corti, *Maximilian*, 325–326. This would be equivalent to approximately $26 million in 2009 dollars. John J. McCusker, evaluation of historical currencies, Aug. 24, 2009, unpublished memo in possession of the author.
13. Hyde, *Mexican Empire*, 128; Corti, *Maximilian*, 326.
14. Blumberg, *Diplomacy of the Mexican Empire*, 17.
15. Napoléon pressed Almonte and the provisional government to give him unworked mining concessions in Sonora before Maximilian's arrival, but nothing came of it. Napoléon III to Achille Bazaine, Jan. 5, 1864, Bazaine Papers, García Collection, BLAC; William M. Gwin to Maximilian, Jan. 5, 1864, Karton 25, Maximilian Papers, OS (quotation); Stevenson, *Maximilian in Mexico*, 174–176; Black, *Napoleon III and Mexican Silver*, 61, 86; Ana Rosa Suárez Argüello, *Un Duque Norteamericano para Sonora* (Mexico City: Consejo Nacional para la Cultura y las Artes, Dirección General de Publicaciones, 1990), 71, 122–123.
16. Richard J. Salvucci, *Politics, Markets, and Mexico's "London Debt," 1823–1887* (Cambridge: Cambridge University Press, 2009), 245–246; Corti, *Maximilian*, 328, 331 (quotation).
17. Reinach Foussemagne, *Charlotte*, 139; Hyde, *Mexican Empire*, 128–129 (quotations); Corti, *Maximilian*, 328, 332.
18. Haslip, *Crown of Mexico*, 215.

19. Ernst Pitner, *Maximilian's Lieutenant: A Personal History of the Mexican Campaign, 1864–1867,* trans. Gordon Etherington-Smith (Albuquerque: University of New Mexico Press, 1993), 168; Corti, *Maximilian,* 279, 329.

20. Hyde, *Mexican Empire,* 129–130; Haslip, *Crown of Mexico,* 217 (first quotation); Roeder, *Juárez,* 564 (second quotation); Corti, *Maximilian,* 334–335; Barker, "France, Austria, and the Mexican Venture," 239.

21. Ridley, *Maximilian and Juárez,* 159; Haslip, *Crown of Mexico,* 208, 209 (quotation).

22. Haslip, *Crown of Mexico,* 210, 219.

23. Eugénie to Maximilian, March 27, 1864, in Barker, *Distaff Diplomacy,* 127 (quotations); Corti, *Maximilian,* 338–339.

24. Interview with Christiana von Habsburg, June 4, 2009, notes in possession of the author; Hyde, *Mexican Empire,* 129 (quotation), 130.

25. Napoléon III to Maximilian, March 28, 1864, in Hyde, *Mexican Empire,* 130 (quotation); and Corti, *Maximilian,* 399–400.

26. Hyde, *Mexican Empire,* 130–131; Corti, *Maximilian* 345, 352, 399–400.

27. Corti, *Maximilian,* 345–347; Haslip, *Crown of Mexico,* 224. A U.S. dollar was equivalent to 7.35 gulden in 1865. John J. McCusker, historical currency values, Aug. 24, 2009, memo in possession of the author.

28. Corti, *Maximilian,* 348–350.

29. Hyde, *Mexican Empire,* 132; Haslip, *Crown of Mexico,* 226 (quotation).

30. Roeder, *Juárez,* 560; Corti, *Maximilian,* 353; Hyde, *Mexican Empire,* 133–134.

31. Hyde, *Mexican Empire,* 133–134; Corti, *Maximilian,* 353–355, 354 (quotations).

32. Hyde, *Mexican Empire,* 134.

33. Reinach Foussemagne, *Charlotte de Belgique,* 165 (quotations); Napoléon III to Maximilian, April 4, 1864, Karton 25, Maximilian Papers, OS.

34. Archduchess Sophie to Maximilian, April 4, 1864 (quotation), Franz Josef to Maximilian, April 10, 1864, Karton 9, Maximilian to Napoléon III, April 13, 1864, Karton 25, Maximilian Papers, OS; Hyde, *Mexican Empire,* 134.

35. Description is taken from the royal carriages at Chapultepec, as well as accoutrement in the archives, Ámparo Gómez Tepexicuapan to M. M. McAllen, interview, Chapultepec, Mexico City, D.F., Oct. 16, 2009, notes in possession of the author; Mario Doeberl to M. M. McAllen, interview regarding royal carriages, June 4, 2009, Wagonberg, Schönbrunn, Vienna, Austria; Robert H. Duncan, "Political Legitimation and Maximilian's Second Empire in Mexico, 1864–1867," *Mexican Studies* 12 (Winter 1996), 42; Kollonitz, *The Court of Mexico,* 222. In contemporary dollars, equipping the new palace would have been nearly $5 million, $350,000 on wine alone. Dollars were equivalent to pesos in 1864. John J. McCusker, monetary evaluations in the U.S. and Europe, August 24, 2009, memo in possession of the author.

36. Haslip, *Crown of Mexico,* 231–232; Kollonitz, *Court of Mexico,* 6.

37. Emmanuel Domenech, *Juarez et Maximilien* (Paris: Librairie Internationale,

1868), 3: 180; *L'Estafette*, March 21, 1865; Haslip, *Crown of Mexico*, 232; Hyde, *Mexican Empire*, 137–138.

38. Domenech, *Juarez et Maximilien*, 3: 180; Hyde, *Mexican Empire*, 137–138; Norwich, *Absolute Monarchs*, 400–402.

39. Haslip, *Crown of Mexico*, 237 (quotation); Kollonitz, *Court of Mexico*, 49–50; Hyde, *Mexican Empire*, 139.

40. Haslip, *Crown of Mexico*, 237, 239–240; Hyde, *Mexican Empire*, 141; Kollonitz, *Court of Mexico*, 57; Hubert Howe Bancroft, *History of the Pacific States of North America* (San Francisco: The History Company, 1888), 9: 138; Ferdinand Maximilian von Habsburg, *Reglamento para el Servicio y Ceremonial de Mi Corte* (Mexico City: Self-published, April 10, 1865), Enrique E. Guerra collection, Linn, Texas.

41. Kollonitz, *Court of Mexico*, 51–56, 62–63 (quotations), 79–80.

42. Ángel Iglesias to Juan N. Almonte, May 25, 1864, Karton 9, Maximilian Papers, OS.

43. Domenech, *Juarez et Maximilien*, 3: 183.

44. Roeder, *Juárez*, 567.

Chapter 7. The Future Will Be Splendid

1. Hyde, *Mexican Empire*, 148–149; Duncan, "Political Legitimation," 46, 48.

2. Corti, *Maximilian*, 428–429, 431 (quotation). Before the arrival of the Spanish, various indigenous royals, including Montezuma, used the famous hill for defense. Ruben M. Campos, *Chapultepec: Su Leyenda y Su Historia* (Mexico: Talleres Gráficos de la Nación, 1922), 7, 15, 24–26.

3. Campos, *Chapultepec*, 25; Duncan, "Political Legitimation," 48; Corti, *Maximilian*, 428–429, 460; Nanda Leonardini, *Santiago Rebull* (Mexico City: Círculo de Arte, 1999), 18.

4. Ratz, *Tras las Huellas*, 126; Campos, *Chapultepec*, 25–26. Maximilian later appointed Bilimek as the conservator of the natural history museum of the National Museum and oversaw specimens, books, and reference materials at the National Library. Proclamation, May 2, 1866, GD 137, Despachos, vol. 1, fs. 220, GD125; Instrucción Pública y Bellas Artes; caja 21, exp. 30, fs. 1–18, AGN; Martín Castillo to Carl Gangolf Kayser, Feb. 11, 1866, Agustín Fischer to Poliakowitz, Oct. 27, 1866, Karton 16, Maximilian Papers, OS. Interviews with Lorenza Fonda, Castillo Miramare, Italy, June 9, 2009; and Ámparo Gómez Tepexicuapan, Castillo de Chapultepec, Oct. 16, 2009.

5. Ferdinand Maximilian von Habsburg, *Reglamento para el Servicio y Ceremonial de Mi Corte*, April 10, 1865; Kollonitz, *Court of Mexico*, 220.

6. The order of San Carlos, named in honor of San Carlos de Borromeo, Carlota's patron saint, was meant to be an exclusive sorority, but resulting jealousies caused Carlota to be more liberal in granting it. Martin, *Maximilian in Mexico*, 171–172; Bla-

sio, *Maximilian*, 13; Carlota to José Fernando Ramírez, n.d., in Weckmann, *Carlota*, 305–306.

7. Maximilian, *Recollections of My Life*, 3: 406–408; Corti, *Maximilian and Carlota*, 464 (first quotation); Blasio, *Maximilian*, 5, 7–8, 10, 12–14, 31 (second quotation).

8. Ridley, *Maximilian and Juárez*, 167; Blasio, *Maximilian*, 7–8, 12–14, 23 (second quotation), 31 (first quotation).

9. Reinach Foussemagne, *Charlotte de Belgique*, 250 (quotation); Domenech, *Juarez et Maximilien*, 216–217.

10. Hall, *Mexico and Maximilian*, 160–161; Corti, *Maximilian*, 431; Kollonitz, *The Court of Mexico*, 221; Ibsen, *Maximilian*, 12–15; Albert Hans, *Querétaro: Souvenirs d'un Officier de l'Empereur Maximilien* (Paris: E. Dentu, 1869), 289; Octavio Chávez, *Charrería: Arte y Tradición* (Mexico City: Fomento Banamex, 2008), 110.

11. Carlota, "A Letter from Mexico," in Joseph and Henderson, eds., *Mexico Reader*, 267.

12. Paul Louis Marie Laurent, *La Guerre du Mexique de 1862 à 1866: Journal de Marche du 3r. Chasseurs d'Afrique* (Paris: E. de Soye Imprimeur, 1867), 165; Haslip, *Crown of Mexico*, 258; Corti, *Maximilian*, 430–432; "Duties of the Ladies of the Palace," undated, Karton 16, Maximilian Papers, OS; Carlota to Condesa Grunne, March 14, 1865, in Weckmann, *Carlota*, 300 (quotation).

13. Mrs. Alec Tweedie, *Mexico as I Saw It* (London: Hurst and Blackett, 1901), 272 (quotation); Materials relative to Otilia Jordan de Degollado, ca. 1885, Enrique Guerra Collection, Linn, Texas.

14. Blasio, *Maximilian*, 24.

15. Duncan, "Political Legitimation," 46 (first quotation). Carlota did try to economize on some things, refusing to be abused by merchants. She wanted to pay no more than 1 franc, 27 centimes, per meter for toile. Carlota to the Councilor of State, Fabric Order, Feb. 21, 1865, Karton 9, Maximilian Papers, OS; Carlota to Dolores Quesada de Almonte, June 17, 1864 (second quotation), Maximilian Papers, UASC; Blasio, *Maximilian*, 22–23.

16. Blasio, *Maximilian*, 37–38; Corti, *Maximilian*, 465, 472; Martin, *Maximilian in Mexico*, 174–177. Weckmann, *Carlota*, 228. The china came from Vierzon or Paris from the firm of A. Hache & Pepin Lehali. Their fine china came from Minton porcelain through Goode & Company, also purveyors to the court in England. Ámparo Gómez Tepexicuapan to M. M. McAllen, interview and tour of collection at Chapultepec Castle, October 17, 2009. Notes in possession of the author.

17. Maximilian and Carlota enjoyed Verdi's work, especially "Los Lombardos," in honor of Leopold I. They ordered Meyerbeers's "Mon Fils" and Donizetti's "Brindisi de Lucrezia." They often played at the Teatro Iturbide or other venues. *L'Ere Nouvelle*, Oct. 15, 1864; *Mexican Times*, Oct. 21, 1865; Martin, *Maximilian in Mexico*, 174–177.

18. Hyde, *Mexican Empire*, 167 (first quotation); Duncan, "Political Legitimation," 42 (second quotation); Blasio, *Maximilian*, 38–39; *L'Estafette*, July 2, Aug. 14, 1864.

The gala expense of $105,000 would be roughly equivalent to $1,700,000 in contemporary dollars. John J. McCusker, monetary evaluations in the U.S. and Europe, August 24, 2009, memo in possession of the author.

19. Stevenson, *Maximilian*, 223–224.

20. Corti, *Maximilian*, 472; Carlota, "A Letter from Mexico," in Joseph and Henderson, eds., *Mexico Reader*, 268 (quotation).

21. Corti, *Maximilian*, 431 (quotation), 432.

22. Invitation to Coleadero, July 29, 1865, Karton 16, Maximilian Papers, OS; Corti, *Maximilian*, 432 (quotation); Weckmann, *Carlota*, 228.

23. Martin, *Maximilian in Mexico*, 28, 100; Blasio, *Maximilian*, 24; Ridley, *Maximilian and Juárez*, 169.

24. Corti, *Maximilian*, 422 (quotation), 423; Magnus, *El Ocaso*, 19.

25. Maximilian, Nov. 1864 (no day), Drafts of decrees regarding guerrilla and partisan fighting, Karton 14, Maximilian Papers, OS; Corti, *Maximilian*, 425 (quotation), 438.

26. Lecaillon, *Napoléon III et le Mexique*, 104; Blumberg, "Diplomacy of the Mexican Empire," 27; Corti, *Maximilian*, 426–427; Barker, "Mexican Monarchists," 9, unpublished papers, Barker Papers, CAH; Robles Pezuela's title of Minister of Fomento, roughly translated to minister of "development" or "commerce," Blasio, *Maximilian*, 8.

27. Hall, *Mexico and Maximilian*, 116; Thomas, *Golden Empire*, 514; Maximilian to José Salazar Ilarregui, Oct. 4, 1864, José Salazar Ilarregui Collection, Hispanic Society of America, New York, NY; Maximilian to Bazaine, Sept. 20, 1865, Bazaine Papers (first quotation); *Diario del Imperio*, March 10, 1865 (second quotation).

28. Faustino Chimalpopoca to Maximilian, Nov. 6, 1866, Maximilian Papers, OS; Maximilian to Édouard Pierron, June 10, 1866, Karton 40, Maximilian Papers, OS; Florencia Mallon, *Peasant and Nation* (Berkeley: University of California Press, 1995), 137, 172; Luis González y González, "Liberals and the Land," in Joseph and Henderson, eds., *Mexico Reader*, 243.

29. Lecaillon, *Napoléon III et le Mexique*, 194–197.

30. A. Supervièle to Adrian Woll, Nov. 9. 1863, Karton 5, Maximilian Papers, OS; Johann Lubienski, *Der Maximilianeische Staat, Mexiko 1861–1867*, Verfassung, Verwaltung und Ideengeschichte (Wien: Böhlau Verlag, 1988), 86–88; *Diario del Imperio* (Mexico City), May 5, 1865; June 7, 1866; *Mexican Times*, Oct. 28, 1865.

31. Maximilian, Provisional Organization Decree of the Mexican Empire, 1864, Karton 9; Maximilian, Fomentos, Jan. 18, 1865, Karton 14, Maximilian Papers, OS.

32. Lubienski, *Der Maximilianeische Staat*, 88–89; Maximilian, Proc. no. 6, Nov. 7, 1864, Proc. no. 7, Nov. 3, 1864, Karton 9, Maximilian Papers, OS; Orozco y Berra Manuel, *Carta General del Imperio Mexicano*, 1864, courtesy Lusher Collection.

33. They used a heavily armed escort because the French courts-martials under Forey during the prior two years left many hostile feelings in the region. *L'Estafette*,

Sept. 17, 1864; Robert H. Duncan, "Embracing a Suitable Past: Independence Celebrations under Mexico's Second Empire, 1864–1866," *Journal of Latin American Studies* 30 (May 1998), 249, 259–262; Ibsen, *Maximilian*, 4, 14; Corti, *Maximilian*, 434.

34. Said by Antonio Riba y Echeverría. Duncan, "Embracing a Suitable Past," 260, 262–263, 266 (quotation). The local pulque vendors used bells on their harnesses, giving rise to people ridiculing Maximilian as the "pulquero." Magnus, *El Ocaso,* 65–66.

35. Carlota to Maximilian on Aug. 11, 1864, in Ratz, *Correspondencia Inédita*, 114 (first quotation); Haslip, *Crown of Mexico*, 280; Carlota to Achille Bazaine, Sept. 13, 1864, Bazaine collection, HC 378/388, HSA (second and third quotation); Kératry, *La Contre-Guérrilla*, 170 n.2; Carlota to Salazar Ilarregui, in Weckmann, *Carlota*, 162–163.

36. Carlota to Maximilian, Aug. 11, 13, 1864, in Ratz, *Correspondencia Inédita*, 114–116 (quotations); Konrad Ratz, memorandum, Feb. 9, 2010. Notes in possession of the author; Samuel Basch, *Memories of Mexico: A History of the Last Ten Months of the Empire* (San Antonio, TX: Trinity University Press, 1973), 24.

37. Duncan, "Embracing a Suitable Past," 262–264.

38. Corti, *Maximilian*, 432, 434 (first quotation); Duncan, "Embracing a Suitable Past," 257–258, 260, 262, 263 (second quotation), 266.

39. Duncan, "Embracing a Suitable Past," 261–264, 265 (quotation), 268; Maximilian to J. N. Almonte, Sept. 18, 1864, legajo XXIII, no. 30, Archivo Condumex.

40. Carlota to Maximilian, September 1865 (no day), (quotation), Charlotte and Maximilian Collection, Woodson Research Center, Fondren Library, Rice University (hereafter cited as WRC); Duncan, "Embracing a Suitable Past," 261–262; *L'Estafette*, Sept. 17, 1864.

Chapter 8. A Task Worthy of the Damned

1. Carlota to Maximilian, Sept. 4 (quotation), Oct. 3, 1864, in Ratz, *Correspondencia Inédita*, 128; Haslip, *Crown of Mexico*, 280.

2. Carlota to Maximilian, Oct. 3, 1864, in Ratz, *Correspondencia Inédita*, 151.

3. *Tri-Weekly Telegraph*, Dec. 8, 1864; Carlota of Belgium, *The Llano de San Lázaro and the Camp of Cuajimalpa* (Mexico City: privately published, 1865); Maximilian Papers, Hispanic Society of America, 1–3; Haslip, *Crown of Mexico*, 275.

4. Carlota of Belgium, *Llano de San Lázaro*, 1–3 (quotations); Guedalla, *Two Marshals*, 103.

5. Carlota of Belgium, *Llano de San Lázaro*, 2–3.

6. Corti, *Maximilian*, 446 (quotation); Ridley, *Maximilian and Juárez*, 173.

7. Basch, *Memories*, 16; Corti, *Maximilian*, 436, 442,; Ridley, *Maximilian and Juárez*, 172–173; *L'Ere Nouvelle*, Oct. 15, 1864; Blumberg, "Diplomacy of the Mexican Empire," 36–37; Magnus, *El Ocaso*, 8–10, 76.

8. Carlota, "A Letter from Mexico," in Joseph and Henderson, eds., *Mexico Reader*, 268–269 (quotation). Worried that her freely expressed ideas would become public,

Carlota asked Hidalgo to prevail on Eugénie to destroy her letters. "I wouldn't want a lot of what I say about the Mexicans to be passed on unnecessarily to posterity." Carlota to José Manuel Hidalgo, Nov. 23, 1864, Charlotte and Maximilian Papers, WRC.

9. Maximilian derived his ideas of "enlightened absolutism" or more liberal Catholic policies from the Habsburg Josef II, the Holy Roman Emperor from 1765 to 1790. Memorandum on Josephism; on holy and royal insignia, Konrad Ratz, Jan. 25, 2011, Sept. 26, 2012, in possession of the author. Memorandum to M. M. McAllen on royal scepters and collars in the Schatzkammer, Vienna, Austria, Thomas Kuster, November 5, 2009, in possession of the author; Corti, *Maximilian*, 433; images of crown and scepters of Maximilian and Carlota, Schatzkammer, Hofburg, Vienna, Austria, May 31, 2009, in possession of the author.

10. Corti, *Maximilian*, 433, 438 (first quotation); Lichtervelde, *Léopold First*, 207 (second quotation); Carlota to Condesa Grunne, March 14, 1865, in Weckmann, *Carlota*, 300.

11. Domenech, *Juarez et Maximilien*, 3: 181.

12. Basch, *Memories*, 19–20.

13. *L'Ere Nouvelle*, Oct. 15, 1864; Ridley, *Maximilian and Juárez*, 179; Corti, *Maximilian*, 433, 438.

14. Walsham to Russell, July 9, 1864, Russell Papers, PRO 30/22/74, C511085, NAUK; Steinberg, *Bismarck*, 117; Haslip, *Crown of Mexico*, 284–285.

15. Ratz, *Tras las Huellas*, 76; Barker, *Distaff Diplomacy*, 132; Martin, *Maximilian*, 258–259; Blumberg, "Diplomacy of the Mexican Empire," 48; Corti, *Maximilian*, 438 (quotation).

16. Ratz, *Correspondencia Inédita*, 162 (quotation); Domenech, *Juarez et Maximilien*, 197; Haslip, *Crown of Mexico*, 290.

17. Lecaillon, *Napoléon III et le Mexique*, 190; Barker, *Distaff Diplomacy*, 132; Martin, *Maximilian*, 183, 259; Patricia Galeana de Valadés, *Las relaciones Iglesia-Estado durante El Segundo Imperio*, 104, 131–132.

18. Galeana de Valadés, *Las relaciones Iglesia-Estado durante El Segundo Imperio* (Mexico: Universidad Nacional Autónoma de México, 1991), 107, 131–132; Corti, *Maximilian*, 451–452; *L'Estafette*, March 21, 1865.

19. Ámparo Gómez Tepexicuapan, Chapultepec, July 21, 2009, notes in author's possession; Galeana de Valadés, *Las relaciones Iglesia-Estado durante El Segundo Imperio*, 132; Corti, *Maximilian*, 452; *L'Estafette*, March 21, 1865.

20. Martin, *Maximilian*, 259; Carlota to Condesa Grunne, March 14, 1865, in Weckmann, *Carlota*, 299.

21. Carlota to Eugénie, Dec. 27, 1864, in Corti, *Maximilian*, 864 (quotation); Roeder, *Juárez*, 586.

22. Carlota to Eugénie, Dec. 27, 1864, in Corti, *Maximilian*, 864.

23. Ridley, *Maximilian and Juárez*, 180; Carlota to Eugénie, Dec. 27, 1864, in Corti, *Maximilian*, 863–864 (quotation).

24. Carlota to Eugénie, Dec. 27, 1864, in Corti, *Maximilian*, 865.

25. Maximilian, draft of decree of tolerance of worship, Jan. 26, 1865, Karton 9, Maximilian Papers, OS; Ratz, *Tras las Huellas*, 76; Campbell-Scarlett to Russell, Feb. 23, 1865, Russell Papers, PRO 30/22/74, C511085, NAUK.

26. Roeder, *Juárez*, 588 (quotation).

27. Corti, *Maximilian*, 460.

28. Martin, *Maximilian*, 261–262; Roeder, *Juárez*, 587.

29. Martin, *Maximilian*, 262.

30. Edward L. Plumb to Matías Romero, March 25, 1865, Plumb Papers; Corti, *Maximilian*, 425, 448, 462 (quotation).

31. Carlota, "Observations," July 29, 1865, in Weckmann, *Carlota*, 187; Lecaillon, *Napoléon III et le Mexique*, 110; Corti, *Maximilian*, 457–459.

32. Carlota to Bazaine, March 29, 1865, Bazaine papers, HSA (quotation); Dabbs, *French Army*, 97, 112, 126; Ridley, *Maximilian and Juárez*, 196; Wyke to Russell, Sept. 26, 1864, Russell Papers, PRO 30/22/74, C511085, NAUK.

33. Lecaillon, *Napoléon III et le Mexique*, 105–106.

34. Dabbs, *The French Army*, 96–97, 99, 104–105; Stevenson, *Maximilian*, 194–197; Hyde, *Mexican Empire*, 160.

35. Leonard Pierce to William H. Seward, June 6, 1863, Dispatches from U.S. Consuls at Matamoros, Roll 4, NARA; Achille Bazaine to Juan N. Almonte, Dec. 29, 1863; Achille Bazaine to Maximilian, June 5, 1864; Achille Bazaine to Napoléon III, Nov. 30, 1863, Dec. 12, 1863, Bazaine papers, García Collection, BLAC; Tomás Mejía to Adrian Woll, July 28, 1864, in Domenech, *Juarez et Maximilien*, 197–199; Campbell-Scarlett to Russell, Feb. 23, 1865, Campbell-Scarlett to Russell, Feb. 23, 1865, Russell Papers, PRO 30/22/74, C511085, NAUK.

36. Franklin Chase to William H. Seward, May 14, 1864 (quotations), Reel 83, William H. Seward Papers, Microfilm, Lamont Library, Harvard University, Cambridge, Mass. (hereafter cited as LLHU); Roeder, *Juárez*, 607–608.

37. A military tribunal convicted Mohamed-Ben-Ouden, an Algerian counterguerrilla who murdered innocent Indians. *L'Estafette*, Aug. 29, 1864; Roeder, *Juárez*, 607 (quotation).

38. Leonard Pierce to William H. Seward, Sept. 1, 1864, Dispatches from U.S. Consuls at Matamoros, 1826–1906, Roll 4, NARA; Dabbs, *The French Army*, 113; Amberson, *I Would Rather Sleep in Texas*, 189, 275; Carl Coke Rister, *Border Command: General Phil Sheridan in the West* (Norman: University of Oklahoma Press, 1944), 14; Gurza Lavalle, *Una Vecindad Efímera*, 73, 138.

39. Carlota to Maximilian, Oct. 6, 1864, in Ratz, *Correspondencia Inédita*, 153–154 (quotation); Tomás Mejía, Reclamaciones Americanas, Aug. 29, 1865, Relaciones Exteriores, Siglo XIX, GD 3000, AGN.

40. Franklin Chase to William H. Seward, May 14, 1864 (quotations), Reel 83, William H. Seward Papers, Microfilm, LLHU; Hamnett, *Juárez*, 171.

41. Ridley, *Maximilian and Juárez*, 182.

42. Elton, *With the French in Mexico*, 34; Ridley, *Maximilian and Juárez*, 183; Kératry, *La Contre-Guérrilla*, 79.

43. Ridley, *Maximilian and Juárez*, 183–184; De la Fère, *Recollections* (quotations), Maximilian Papers, UASC; Carlota to Leopold I, Feb. 14, 1865, in Weckmann, *Carlota*, 244.

44. Ridley, *Maximilian and Juárez*, 183–184.

45. Maximilian to Bazaine, Feb. 14, 1865 (quotations), Bazaine collection, HC 378/388, HSA; Ridley, *Maximilian and Juárez*, 184.

46. *L'Estafette*, March 22, 1865; Corti, *Maximilian*, 421, 426; Amberson, *I Would Rather Sleep in Texas*, 248; Stevenson, 147; *Mexican Times*, Dec. 16, 1865, Carlota, "Observations," in Weckmann, *Carlota*, 155.

47. Doblado died in New York City on June 19, 1865, while still working to get U.S. intervention for Juárez. Death announcement, June 21, 1865, *Message of the President of the United States of March 20, 1866 Relating to the Condition of Affairs in Mexico*, H. Exec. Doc. no. 73, 39th Congress, 1st Sess., 1866, 134; Ridley, *Maximilian and Juárez*, 201, 202 (quotation); Schoonover, *Mexican Lobby*, 50–51; Blumberg, *Diplomacy of the Mexican Empire*, 76.

48. R. T. Ford to Imperial Minister of Foreign Affairs, Oct. 11, 1864, Nov. 9, 1864, Reel 7, CSA Records, Sec. of State, MD, LOC; Blumberg, "Diplomacy of the Mexican Empire," 16–19; Gurza Lavalle, *Una Vecindad Efímera*, 12.

49. Ridley, *Maximilian and Juárez*, 203.

Chapter 9. *Our Daily Bread*

1. Revue Militaire de la Quinzaine, Sept. 11, 1865, Karton 25, Maximilian Papers, OS.

2. Maximilian to Louise von Sturmfeder, Feb. 25, 1865, Maximilian Papers, UASC; Corti, *Maximilian*, 463.

3. *Diario del Imperio* (Mexico City), May 4, 5, 1865; Gómez Tepexicuapan, *El Paseo de la Reforma*, 29–33; Dabbs, *French Army*, 254.

4. Today the avenue is called Paseo de la Reforma. Duncan, "Political Legitimation," 50; Gómez Tepexicuapan, *El Paseo de la Reforma*, 34–36; Blasio, *Maximilian*, 31 (quotation).

5. Juan N. Almonte, "Despacho de Hacienda y Crédito Público," related to newly reapportioned currency, April 8, 1864, Charlotte and Maximilian Collection, 1846–1927, WRC; Duncan, "Political Legitimation," 45–46, Oscar Muñoz Almada, "El Paseo de la Emperatriz," in *Mexico en el Tiempo: Revista de Historia y Conservación*, 1996; Benjamin Betts, *Mexican Imperial Coinage* (n.p.: Organization of International Numismatists, 1899), 34–38.

6. Inventory of Commissioned Art of the Emperor, May 11, 1865, Karton 16, Maxi-

milian Papers, OS. Many of these artists were alumni of the Pelegrin Clavé school. Ida Rodríguez Prampolini, *La Crítica de Arte en México en el Siglo XIX, Estudios y Documentos* (Mexico City: Universidad Nacional Autónoma de México, 1997), 114; Corti, *Maximilian*, 512.

7. Achille Bazaine to Jacques Randon, Nov. 30, 1863, Bazaine Papers, García Collection, BLAC; Dabbs, *The French Army in Mexico*, 244.

8. Maximilian to "Primo" Pedro of Brazil, May 18, 1866, Karton 40, *Revue Militaire de la Quinzaine*, Dec. 18, 1865, Karton 25, Maximilian Papers, OS; Maximilian to Félix Eloin, April 9, 1866, Charlotte and Maximilian Collection, WRC; *Mexican Times*, Feb. 10, 1866; Juliette M. Hood, "*Andrew J. Grayson: The Audubon of the Pacific*," *The Auk* 50, no. 4 (Oct. 1833), 398–399; Dabbs, *The French Army in Mexico*, 240; *Diario del Imperio* (Mexico City), May 4, 5, 1865; Paul Edison, "Conquest Unrequited: French Expeditionary Science in Mexico, 1864–1867," *French Historical Studies* 26 (2003), 460, 466, 468, 491; Corti, *Maximilian*, 512.

9. Military Review of the Fortnight, Dec. 18, 1865, Karton 25, Maximilian Papers, OS; Duncan, "Political Legitimation," 52–53 (second quotation); Coin with profile of Maximilian with Aztec calendar on obverse, ca. 1865, collection of author; Carlota to Maximilian, May 4, 1866, June 21, 1866, in Ratz, *Correspondencia Inédita*, 280–281, 292; León Méhédin to Carlota, March 17, 1866, in Weckmann, *Carlota*, 97–98; Edison, "Conquest Unrequited," 480–482, 483 (first quotation). See also Peter E. Palmquist and Thomas R. Kailbourn, *Pioneer Photographers from the Mississippi to the Continental Divide* (Stanford, CA: Stanford University Press, 2005), 433–434.

10. The shield had been in the Royal Collection of Armors in Brussels but was brought to Laxenburg, near Vienna, during the Napoléonic Wars. While the shield remains in the National History Museum of Mexico at Chapultepec, at the end of Maximilian's reign, the field notes of Cortés went back to Vienna. Gerard van Bussel to M. M. McAllen, Oct. 6 and 7, 2009, May 2, 2011; Curator of Nord und Mittelamerika, Museum für Völkerkunde, memos with information on feathered shield and other goods from Mexico in Museum für Völkerkunde, notes in possession of the author. Bussel indicated the hieroglyphics appeared to be of Aztec origin. Also, Corti, *Maximilian*, 591. Interview about shield, depictions in art, and Cortés's field reports, Ámparo Gómez Tepexicuapan, Oct. 15, 2009, interview, notes in possession of the author.

11. Carlota to Corio, Aug. 8, 1865, in Weckmann, *Carlota*, 151–152.

12. *Diario del Imperio* (Mexico City), May 3, 1865; Martín Castillo to Maximilian, Aug. 14, 1865, Karton 9, Maximilian Papers, OS. Castillo wrote regarding the purchase of rancho "La Hormiga" from Dr. Martínez del Río for 25,000 pesos and boundary issues with Molina del Rey, on the boundary with Chapultepec. He pointed out that the properties were within the view of the castle. Blasio, *Maximilian*, 33–35; Samuel Basch, *Recollections of Mexico: The Last Ten Months of Maximilian's Empire*, ed. and trans. Frank Ullman (Wilmington, DE: Scholarly Resources, 2006), 107. Although

Basch mentions the cypress or *ahuehuete*, as *Taxodium distichum*, the correct name is *Taxodium mucronatum*, but the distinction had only recently been made in 1853, and it is likely Basch did not know this new label. Tom Wendt to M. M. McAllen, Apr. 5, 2010, memorandum.

13.   Wilhelm Knechtel, *Las Memorias del Jardinero del Maximiliano,* ed. Ámparo Gómez Tepexicuapan (n.p.: Jean-Gérard Sidaner, 2011), 110; Maximilian to Karl Ludwig, Feb. 24, 1865, as quoted in Corti, *Maximilian,* 464–465 (quotation); Esther Acevedo, Fausto Ramírez, and Jamie Soler Frost, eds., *La Fabricación del Estado, 1864–1910* (Mexico City: Patronato del Museo Nacional de Arte, Instituto Nacional de Bellas Artes, 2003), 48; Philip Sheridan to J. A. Rawlins, July 22, 1866, Records of the Headquarters of the Army, entry 35, RG 108, NARA; Felipe A. and Dolores L. Latorre, *The Mexican Kickapoo Indians* (Mineola, NY: Dover Publications, 1991), 5, 20; Ratz, *Tras las Huellas,* 127.

14.   Maximilian to Auguste Jilek, Feb. 10, 1865, Maximilian collection, Series 2, Maximilian Papers, UASC; Corti, *Maximilian,* 468.

15.   Carlota to Eugénie, Jan. 26, 1865, as quoted in Corti, *Maximilian,* 874 (quotation), 469; Enlistment Certificate, "Rejimento de Caballería de la Emperatriz," Sept. 5, 1865, MMMA collection.

16.   Carlota to Eugénie, Jan. 26, 1865, in Weckmann, *Carlota,* 121 (first quotation), 122 (second quotation); Carlota to Félix Eloin, no day, 1865, Charlotte and Maximilian Papers, WRC; Roeder, *Juárez,* 588.

17.   Carlota, "A Letter from Mexico," in Joseph and Henderson, eds., *Mexico Reader,* 266–267

18.   Carlota to Eugénie, Jan. 26, 1865, in Weckmann, *Carlota,* 122 (quotations).

19.   Notes on annual exports, 1827–1864, Barker Papers, CAH; Haslip, *Crown of Mexico,* 298.

20.   Charles Eustache Corta, *Mexique: Discourse de M. Corta, Députe au Corps Législatif et de S. Exe. M. Rouher* (Paris: Typographie E. Pankoucke, 1865), 22, 39; Roeder, *Juárez,* 592–593.

21.   Corta, *Mexique: Discours de M. Corta,* 12 (first quotation); *New York Herald,* July 30, 1863; Haslip, *Crown of Mexico,* 282 (second quotation).

22.   Carlota to Napoléon, Aug. 11, 1866, in Weckmann, *Carlota,* 177; Corta, *Mexique: Discours de M. Corta,* 12.

23.   Corta, *Mexique: Discours de M. Corta,* 12.

24.   Charles de Germiny and José Manuel Hidalgo, Comisión de Hacienda de México en Paris, "Obligación de 500 Francos, Imperio de México," Bond certificate and coupons, April 14, 1865; Lecaillon, *Napoléon III et le Mexique,* 189; Martin, *Maximilian in Mexico,* 194–195; Roeder, *Juárez,* 592–593; *Papers Relating to Foreign Affairs, Accompanying the Annual Message of the President,* 39th Congress, 2nd Sess., part 3, 286–288; Corti, *Maximilian,* 489–490 (quotation); *Diario del Imperio,* Sept. 16, 1865. This note would amount to approximately $880 million in 2009 dollars. McCusker,

monetary evaluations in the U.S. and Europe, August 24, 2009, chart and memo in possession of the author.

25. Maritime customs for 1865 totaled 17 million pesos. Dabbs, *The French Army*, 126; Carlota Memorandum, July 1866, in Weckmann, *Carlota*, 182–183; Corti, *Maximilian*, 489–491.

26. Lecaillon, *Napoléon III et le Mexique*, 190; Sub-Secretary of Treasury and House of Jecker to Maximilian, April 8, 1865, Series I, Maximilian Papers, UASC; Corti, *Maximilian*, 489–490; Dabbs, *The French Army*, 114, 140.

27. Salm-Salm, *Ten Years*, 158.

28. *L'Estafette*, June 25, 1865; Ridley, *Maximilian and Juárez*, 173; Roeder, *Juárez*, 592.

29. Corti, *Maximilian*, 484; Maximilian to Bazaine, May 5, 1865, Bazaine Collection, HC 378/388, HSA; Roeder, *Juárez*, 555.

30. Orders to Van der Smissen, Aug. 10, 1865, no. 4, Corps Expéditionnaire, Correspondance Confidentielle 13/7 au 29/9/1865, Service Historique de la Défense, Vincennes, France (hereafter cited as SHD); Martin, *Maximilian in Mexico*, 98; Ridley, *Maximilian and Juárez*, 196; Corti, *Maximilian*, 487, 492–493; Ratz, *Tras las Huellas*, 114–115; Mallon, *Peasant and Nation*, 54–57; Blasio, *Maximilian*, 11; Magnus, *El Ocaso*, 151n.

31. Maximilian to Bazaine, May 5, 1865, Bazaine Collection, HC 378/388, HSA (quotation); Corti, *Maximilian*, 491–492.

32. Mignard, *Charles-Louis Du Pin*, 16–17; Corti, *Maximilian*, 499 (quotation).

33. Carlota, "Observaciones," in Weckmann, *Carlota*, 188–189.

34. Domenech, *Juarez et Maximilien*, 202–203; Haslip, *Crown of Mexico*, 289 (quotations), 294; Blasio, *Maximilian*, 5; *New York Times*, Dec. 14, 1924.

35. Brigitte Hamann, *Con Maximiliano en México: El Diario del príncipe Carl Khevenhüller, 1864–1867* (Mexico: Fondo de Cultura Económica, 1994), 126 (quotation); Hyde, *Mexican Empire*, 166; Carlota to Maximilian, May 23, 1865, in Ratz, *Correspondencia Inédita*, 205; Corti, *Maximilian*, 416, 473–475; Domenech, *Juarez et Maximilien*, 203.

36. Corti, *Maximilian*, 476–477.

37. Napoléon III to Achille Bazaine, March 1, 1865, Charlotte and Maximilian Papers, WRC; De la Fère, *Recollections* (quotation), Maximilian Papers, UASC; Miller, "Arms across the Border," 44; Joseph Smith to Lew Wallace, May 18, 1865, Lew Wallace papers, microfilm roll F645, IHS; Amberson, *I Would Rather Sleep in Texas*, 250–256; Orders to Charles Loysel, Aug. 12, 1865, no. 5, Corps Expéditionnaire: Correspondance Confidentielle 13/7 au 29/9/1865, SHD; Carlota to Napoléon, Aug. 11, 1866, 178, Napoléon III to Bazaine, 246, in Weckmann, *Carlota*.

38. Carlota to Félix Eloin, April 26, 1865, Charlotte and Maximilian Collection, WRC.

39. Stevenson, *Maximilian in Mexico*, 169–170.

40. Carlota to Maximilian, Sept. 25, 1865, in Ratz, *Correspondencia Inédita*, 207 (quotation); Edward L. Plumb to Matías Romero, March 25, 1865, Plumb Papers; unnamed to William H. Seward, Dec. 3, 1864, "The Condition of Affairs in Mexico," H. Exec. Doc. 73, 39th Congress, 1st Sess., 1866, 514–515.

41. Stevenson, *Maximilian in Mexico*, 179 (first quotation); Ridley, *Napoleon III and Eugénie*, 521 (second quotation).

42. William Seward to the Marquis de Montholon, Feb. 12, 1866, "Evacuation of Mexico by the French," H. Exec. Doc. 93, 39th Congress, 1st Sess., 27–28, 32 (quotation); Corti, *Maximilian*, 504–505; Blumberg, "Diplomacy of the Mexican Empire," 77, 83. Carlota also sent her sympathies to Mary Todd Lincoln. Weckmann, *Carlota*, 137–138.

43. Maximilian to Bazaine, June 22, 1865, Bazaine Collection, HC 378/388, HSA (quotation); Dabbs, *The French Army in Mexico*, 138–140.

44. Maximilian to Carlota, April 22, 1865, in Ratz, *Correspondencia Inédita*, 167.

45. Blasio, *Maximilian*, 14–15.

46. *Diario del Imperio* (Mexico City), May 1, 1865; Martin, *Maximilian*, 184; Haslip, *Crown of Mexico*, 329–330 (first quotation); Tweedie, *Mexico as I Saw It*, 272 (second quotation); Ratz, *Tras las Huellas*, 115.

47. Dabbs, *French Army*, 111; Maximilian to Leopold I, May 12, 1865, as quoted in Corti, *Maximilian*, 502; Orders to Charles Loysel, Aug. 14, 1865, no. 6, Corps Expéditionnaire: Correspondance Confidentielle 13/7 au 29/9/1865, SHD; Lecaillon, *Napoléon III et le Mexique*, 194; Mallon, *Peasant and Nation*, 51–52.

48. Maximilian to Carlota, April 22, 1865, in Ratz, *Correspondencia Inédita*, 167.

49. Maximilian to Bazaine, Sept. 20, 1865 (first quotation), Bazaine Collection HC 378/388, HSA; Haslip, *Crown of Mexico*, 323–324 (second and third quotations); Lecaillon, *Napoléon III et le Mexique*, 108; Luis González y González, "Liberals and the Land," in Joseph and Henderson, eds., *Mexico Reader*, 243.

Chapter 10. A Premonitory Symptom

1. Achille Bazaine to Jacque Randon, June 1, 1864, Bazaine Papers, García Collection, BLAC; Miller, "Arms across the Border," 7, 44; Dabbs, *The French Army*, 99.

2. Roeder, *Juárez*, 596–597.

3. Scarlett to Russell, Feb. 23, 1865, Russell Papers, PRO 30/22/74 C511085, NAUK; Roeder, *Juárez*, 596–597; Achille Bazaine to Jacques Randon, June 1, 1864, Bazaine Papers, García Collection, BLAC.

4. Joseph Audenried to Mary Colket Audenried, Dec. 15, 1866, Nau Collection; Roeder, *Juárez*, 599; Miller, "Arms across the Border," 7; Corti, *Maximilian*, 785.

5. Blumberg, "Diplomacy of the Mexican Empire," 84; Roeder, 577, 578 (quotations); Smart, *Viva Juárez*, 326.

6. Roeder, *Juárez*, 599; Lew Wallace to U. S. Grant, April 18, 1865; Lew Wallace to José María Jesús Carvajal, May 5, 1865, Microfilm roll F645, Lew Wallace Papers, IHS.

7. Amberson, *I Would Rather Sleep in Texas*, 268; Charles Thoumas, *Les Français au Mexique: Récits de Guerre, 1862–1867* (Paris: Bloud et Barral, 1891), 401; Maximilian to Bazaine, June 22, 1865, Bazaine Collection, HC 378/388, HSA; "Reclamaciones Americanas," Aug. 29, 1865, exp. 44, caja 92, GD 3000, Relaciones Exteriores, AGN.

8. Blumberg, "Diplomacy of the Mexican Empire," 78; Plessis, *The Rise and Fall of the Second Empire*, 150.

9. Rister, *Border Command*, 16 (first quotation); Miller, "Arms across the Border," 14–15; John M. Schofield, *Secret Mission to Paris Regarding the French Empire in Mexico, 1865–1866* (Reprint of *Century Quarterly*, 1897. Laurel, MD: Preservation Reprint #8210, Wordmax Books, n.d.), 1, 2 (second quotation), 3; Andrew Johnson, *Message of the President*, H. Exec. Doc. 73, 39th Congress, 1st Sess., 434–435; 437–438; 460–461; 495–496; *Message of the President of the United States, Resolution Regarding Mexican Affairs*, H. Exec. Doc. 20, 39th Congress, 1st Sess., 1866, 11; Philip Sheridan, *Personal Memoirs of P. H. Sheridan* (New York: Charles L. Webster, 1888), 2: 211, 215; *New York Herald*, Aug. 19, 1866; John Bigelow to William H. Seward, in John Bigelow, *Retrospections of an Active Life* (New York: Baker and Taylor, 1909), 3: 279–281.

10. Blumberg, *Diplomacy of the Mexican Empire*, 82 (quotation); John M. Schofield, *Secret Mission to Paris*, 1, 11–12.

11. Sheridan, *Memoirs*, II, 217 (first quotation); P. H. Sheridan to U. S. Grant, November 26, 1865, *The War of the Rebellion* (cited hereafter as OR), Ser. 1, vol. 48, pt. 2, p. 1258 (second quotation); W. T. Sheridan to H. Halleck, Sept. 17, 1863, in William T. Sherman, *Memoirs of William Tecumseh Sherman* (New York: Library of America, 1990), 366–367 (third quotation); U. S. Grant to W. T. Sheridan, Oct. 22, 1865, Records of the Headquarters of the Army, 1864–1865, RG 108, NARA.

12. The engineers for Querétaro came from a special reserve unit sent from Courcy, France. Achille Bazaine to Engineering, Aug. 19, 1865, no. 8, Achille Bazaine to Intendant, Aug. 19, 1865, no. 9 (quotation), Achille Bazaine to Engineering, Sept. 20, 1865, no. 12, Corps Expéditionnaire: Correspondance Confidentielle 13/7 au 29/9/1865, SHD; Carlota to Eugénie, no date, in Weckmann, *Carlota*, 255.

13. Ernst Pitner, *Maximilian's Lieutenant*, 102–103; Sheridan, *Personal Memoirs*, 2: 216–217; Rister, *Border Command*, 15; Magnus, *El Ocaso*, 104.

14. Roeder, *Juárez*, 556; Miller, "Arms across the Border," 7.

15. Carlota to Eugénie, March 28, 1865, in Corti, *Maximilian*, 506–507 (quotation); Hyde, *Mexican Empire*, 162 n.2; Ridley, *Maximilian and Juárez*, 153; Guedalla, *Two Marshals*, 93.

16. Hamann, *Con Maximiliano*, 137; Maximilian to Karl Ludwig, June 20, 1865, in Corti, *Maximilian*, 507 (quotation). The translation is "in love like a bullfinch" or loopy like a ninny. Ralf Weber von Froisberg, translation, Sept. 4, 2009. Notes in possession of the author.

17. Stevenson, *Maximilian*, 179–180; Haslip, *Crown of Mexico*, 319–320; Hyde, *Mexican Empire*, 162.

18. Haslip, *Crown of Mexico*, 320; Hyde, *Mexican Empire*, 163.

19. The military also subsidized the house. Gen. Maussion to Gen. Willette, July 27, 1867, Bazaine papers, García Collection, BLAC; Stevenson, *Maximilian in Mexico*, 179–180; Blasio, *Maximilian*, 29.

20. Domenech, *Juarez et Maximilien*, 219 (quotation); Corti, *Maximilian*, 508.

21. Paoli, *Charlotte*, 118–119 (quotation); Corti, *Maximilian*, 508.

22. Amberson, *I Would Rather Sleep in Texas*, 259–260; Jerry Thompson, *Cortina: Defending the Mexican Name in Texas* (College Station: Texas A&M University Press, 2007), 149–150; unnamed to William H. Seward, Dec. 3, 1864, H. Exec. Doc. no. 73, 39th Congress, 1st Sess., 1866, 515; Lew Wallace to Ulysses S. Grant, May 16, 1865, Lew Wallace papers, Microfilm F645, IHS (quotation); William H. Seward to the Marquis de Montholon, June 12, 1865; Marquis de Montholon to William H. Seward, July 6, 1865, House Exec. Doc. 73, Part 2, 39th Congress, 1st Sess., 331–333.

23. Ferdinand Maximilian, Immigration Proclamation, Sept. 5, 1865; Matthew Fontaine Maury to "my dear sir," May 19, 1865, Matthew Fontaine Maury Papers, transcription, Preston Library, Virginia Military Institute, Lexington, Virginia.

24. *Mexican Times*, Sept. 16, 1865; Thomas Corwin to unknown (possibly William H. Seward), Oct. 28, 1865 (first quotation); "Dispatches from U.S. Ministers to Mexico, 1823–1906," Roll 31, National Archives, College Park, MD (hereafter cited as NACP); Carlota, "Conversation with Mr. Maury," in Weckmann, *Carlota*, 173 (second quotation); Frances Leigh Williams, *Matthew Fontaine Maury: Scientist of the Sea* (New Brunswick, NJ: Rutgers University Press, 1963), 431–432 (third and fourth quotations); Domenech, *Juarez et Maximilien*, 203.

25. Carl Coke Rister, "Carlota, a Confederate Colony in Mexico," *The Journal of Southern History* 11 (Feb. 1945), 39–40; Ridley, *Maximilian and Juárez*, 216; Williams, *Matthew Fontaine Maury*, 431 (quotation), 433–434.

26. Carlota, "Conversation with Mr. Maury," in Weckmann, *Carlota*, 172.

27. Andrew F. Rolle, *The Lost Cause: The Confederate Exodus to Mexico* (Norman: University of Oklahoma Press, 1965), 37; Rister, "Carlota," 39–40, 42. In Durango, over 60,000 acres became known as Llano Grande y el Jaral, touted as having water and located near pine forests for building material. *Diario del Imperio* (Mexico City), June 14, 1866. Carlota noted that the army of Gen. James E. Slaughter at Brownsville was not a desirable corps because they were "vagabonds." Carlota, "Conversation with Mr. Maury," in Weckmann, *Carlota*, 173.

28. Rister, "Carlota," 39–40, 42; Daniel O'Flaherty, *General Jo Shelby* (Chapel Hill: University of North Carolina Press, 2000), 295; *Diario del Imperio* (Mexico City), May 1, 1865; Thomas Corwin to unknown, possibly William H. Seward, Oct. 28, 1865, "Dispatches from U.S. Ministers to Mexico, 1823–1906," Roll 31, NACP; *Mexican Times*, Sept. 16, Oct. 14, Dec. 23, 1865.

29. Rister, "Carlota," 41–44; O'Flaherty, *General Jo Shelby*, 296; Rolle, *The Lost Cause*, 92; Ridley, *Maximilian and Juárez*, 216; Stevenson, *Maximilian in Mexico*, 170, 173–174.

30. Anderson, *Gen. Jo Shelby's March*, 170–171; William C. Davis, *An Honorable Defeat: The Last Days of the Confederate Government* (New York: Harcourt, 2001), 348; Rolle, *The Lost Cause*, 80 n.2.

31. This transaction was also known as the Treaty of La Mesilla. Black, *Napoleon III and Mexican Silver*, 79–81; Suárez Argüello, *Un Duque Norteamericano*, 104–105; Stevenson, *Maximilian in Mexico*, 174–179; Napoléon III to Bazaine, in Weckmann, *Carlota*, 246. For more on Napoléon's interest in Sonoran and Sinaloan mines, see Andrew Watkins Terrell, *From Texas to Mexico and the Court of Maximilian, 1865* (Dallas: The Book Club of Texas, 1933), 43.

32. Stevenson, *Maximilian in Mexico*, 176–178.

33. Stevenson, *Maximilian in Mexico*, 177 (quotation); Black, *Napoleon III and Mexican Silver*, 91–93, 101. Frustrated by Maximilian's obstinacy, Gwin left Mexico in January 1865.

34. William Corwin to William H. Seward, Sept. 10, 1865, in Condition of Affairs in Mexico, 39th Congress, 1st Sess., Exec. Doc. 73, 1865, 473–474; Blumberg, "Diplomacy of the Mexican Empire," 79; Ridley, *Maximilian and Juárez*, 216; Félix Eloin to José Manuel Hidalgo, Oct. 29, 1865, Charlotte and Maximilian Collection, WRC; Suárez Argüello, *Un Duque Norteamericano*, 117–118.

35. Rister, "Carlota," 45, 48–49; Rolle, *The Lost Cause*, 93–94.

36. José Manuel Hidalgo to Maximilian in Weckmann, *Carlota*, 152–153; Blasio, *Maximilian*, 58; Corti, *Maximilian*, 501, 515 (quotation); Domenech, *Juarez et Maximilien*, 203–204.

37. Domenech, *Juarez et Maximilien*, 213–214, 215 (first quotation), 216 (third quotation), 217; Hyde, *Mexican Empire*, 165 (second quotation); Blasio, *Maximilian*, 58. Friedrich Semelder, a Viennese doctor, was an expert on the treatment of the ear, nose, and throat. He invented a process of rhinoscopy and laryngoscopy in 1862. *The Lancet* (London), 1 (March 10, 1866).

38. Martin, *Maximilian*, 210–211 (quotations); Bazaine to Napoléon III, Dec. 12, 1863, Bazaine papers, García Collection, BLAC.

39. Corti, *Maximilian*, 520–521.

40. Corti, *Maximilian*, 520–521 (quotation); Weckmann, *Carlota*, 206.

41. Corti, *Maximilian*, 519.

42. Corti, *Maximilian*, 521–523.

43. Corti, *Maximilian*, 521–523.

44. Corti, *Maximilian*, 521–523.

45. Military return, December 1865, Karton 25, Maximilian Papers, OS; Corti, *Maximilian*, 523–524. Letter dated July 15, 1865. Corti, *Maximilian*, 524 (first quota-

tion), 525 (second quotation); Carlota to Félix Eloin, Feb. 9, 1865, Charlotte and Maximilian collection, WRC.

46. Haslip, *Crown of Mexico*, 328.

Chapter 11. Every Drop of My Blood Is Mexican

1. Weckmann, *Carlota de Bélgica*, 229; Hyde, *Mexican Empire*, 155; Ridley, *Maximilian and Juárez*, 57; Paoli, *Charlotte*, 243.

2. Blasio, *Maximilian*, 15–17.

3. John Bigelow, "The Heir-Presumptive to the Imperial Crown of Mexico," *Harper's New Monthly Magazine*, April 1883, 735–736, 739.

4. Before deciding on Maximilian, one of the Murat princes was considered as a candidate for the Mexican emperorship. Rudolf Mülinen to Richard von Metternich, October 15, 1861, Hausarchiv, Karton I, MD, LOC; Bigelow, "Heir-Presumptive," 739; C. M. Mayo to M. M. McAllen, memorandum, Oct. 18, 2012, notes in possession of the author.

5. Bigelow, "Heir-Presumptive," 739; Alice Green Iturbide to Carlota, Aug. 12, 1865, Karton 16, Maximilian Papers, OS.

6. Andrew Johnson, *Papers Relating to Foreign Affairs, Accompanying the Annual Message of the President*, 39th Congress, 2nd Sess. (Washington: Government Printing Office, 1867), 3: 145; Secret Contract, Maximilian and Ángel Iturbide, Sept. 9, 1865, Maximilian Papers, OS. Maximilian offered nearly $2,500,000 each in contemporary dollars. Based on historical value, an 1865 dollar is equivalent to $16.26 in 2008. McCusker, "Historical Value of a Dollar," memorandum, Aug. 24, 2009. in possession of the author.

7. Secret Contract, Maximilian and Ángel Iturbide, Sept. 9, 1865; Emperor Maximilian to Josefa Iturbide, Sept. 16, 1865, Karton 16, Maximilian Papers, OS (also found in Agustín Iturbide collection, Georgetown University Library, Special Collections Division, Washington, D.C.); Bigelow, "Heir-Presumptive," 740.

8. Emperor Maximilian to Josefa Iturbide, Sept. 16, 1865, Karton 16, Maximilian Papers, OS; Paoli, *L'Impératrice Charlotte*, 121; Weckmann, *Carlota*, 204.

9. *Diario del Imperio,* Sept. 18, 1865; *Mexican Times*, Sept. 16, 1865.

10. Maximilian's other theme of the day was to honor the revolutionary José María Morelos. *Diario del Imperio*, Sept. 16, 18, 1865; Maximilian, Memorandum on uniforms, no date, Karton 16, Maximilian Papers, OS; Duncan, "Embracing a Suitable Past," 274; Hyde, *Mexican Empire*, 180 (quotation).

11. Alice Green Iturbide to Maximilian, Sept. 23, 1865 (quotation); Alice Green Iturbide in the words of Agustín Iturbide, undated, Karton 16, Maximilian Papers, OS.

12. Martín Castillo to Alice Green Iturbide, Sept. 28, 1865, Karton 16, Maximilian Papers, OS.

13. Alice Green Iturbide to Maximilian, Sept. 27, 1865, Karton 16, Maximilian Papers, OS (quotation); Bigelow, "Heir-Presumptive," 741.

14. *New Orleans Times*, July 9, 1866; Bigelow, "Heir-Presumptive," 741–742 (quotation).

15. Félix Eloin to Mariano Degollado, Sept. 29, 1865 (quotation), Martín Castillo to Intendant General, Sept. 29, 1865, Karton 16, Maximilian Papers, OS; *New York Times*, Jan. 9, 1866; Maximilian to Félix Eloin, Jan. 11, 1866, Charlotte and Maximilian Collection, WRC. Otilia Jordan de Degollado received an ivory crucifix, bearing the papal arms and royal crest, given to Maximilian and Carlota on their visit to Rome in 1864 on their way to Mexico. Tweedie, *Mexico as I Saw It*, 271–274.

16. Haslip, *Crown of Mexico*, 331.

17. Bigelow, "The Heir-Presumptive to the Imperial Crown of Mexico," 742 (quotation).

18. Bigelow, "Heir-Presumptive," 742; Corti, *Maximilian*, 726; Caroline de Grunne to Carlota, Jan. 25, 1866, in Weckmann, *Carlota de Bélgica*, 84–85.

19. Ridley, *Maximilian and Juárez*, 219; Edward L. Plumb to Benito Juárez, Sept. 8, 1865, Plumb Papers; Hanna and Hanna, *Napoleon III*, 197; Corti, *Maximilian*, 529; *Diario del Imperio* (Mexico City), June 11, 1866; *New York Times*. Matías Romero, June 20, 1867, Romero Collection, BLAC; in a low-key statement, telling the Mexican ministers that it was necessary.

20. Maximilian to Alfons de Pont, Sept. 19, 1865, as quoted in Corti, *Maximilian*, 530–531.

21. Martin, *Maximilian 10*, 189–190; Blasio, *Maximilian*, 114–115; Hyde, *Mexican Empire*, 119.

22. Maximilian to Pius IX, n.d., in Weckmann, *Carlota*, 303; Corti, *Maximilian*, 536, 621–624.

23. Romero in *Responsabilidades*, 11–12; Richard J. Gatling to Lew Wallace, Aug. 2, 1865; Lew Wallace to José María Jesús Carvajal, May 5, 1865; Lew Wallace to Ulysses S. Grant, April 18, 1865; Lew Wallace Papers, Microfilm roll F645, HIS. They prepared to buy Norwich Arms Company from John D. Mowry. Edward L. Plumb to Matías Romero, May 10, 1865, Plumb Papers; Miller, "Arms across the Border," 51 (quotation); Corti, *Maximilian*, 537.

24. Lecaillon, *Napoléon III et le Mexique*, 148–153; Ridley, *Maximilian and Juárez*, 212; Dabbs, *French Army*, 144, 224, 266–267.

25. Mignard, *Charles-Louis Du Pin*, 4 (quotation); Ridley, *Maximilian and Juárez*, 192, 194.

26. Puyo, "The French Military Confront Mexico's Geography," 142–143.

27. Dabbs, *French Army*, 146–147; Corti, *Maximilian*, 537–538; Hyde, *Mexican Empire*, 181–182.

28. Ratz, *Correspondencia Inédita*, 220; Maximilian to Napoléon III, Oct. 20, 1865,

Papiers et Correspondance de la Famille Impériale (Paris: Imprimerie Nationale, 1870), 97 (quotation); Dabbs, *French Army*, 145–146; Blasio, *Maximilian*, 61–62.

29. Dabbs, *French Army*, 146–147; Stevenson, *Maximilian*, 309–314; Ridley, *Maximilian and Juárez*, 228–229; Bigelow, "Heir-Presumptive," 743. Luis Blasio reported that the Black Decree was also signed by Maximilian's ministers: José Fernando Ramírez, Luis Robles Pezuela, José María Esteva, Juan de Dios Peza, Pedro Escudero Echánove, Manuel Siliceo, and Francisco de P. César (Blasio, *Maximilian*, 62).

30. Eugène Lefèvre, *Documents Officiels Recueillis dans la Secrétairerie Privée de Maximilien* (Paris: Armand Le Chevalier, 1870), 2: 254 (quotation); Thoumas, *Les Français au Mexique*, 310.

31. Corti, *Maximilian*, 539 (first and second quotation); Bigelow, "Heir-Presumptive," 743 (third quotation).

32. Thoumas, *Les Français au Mexique*, 311–312.

33. Friedrich Hotze to Obispo de Oaxaca, Dec. 1865, no day, Karton 30, Maximilian Papers, OS; Kératry, *La Contre-Guérrilla*, 204–205; Corti, *Maximilian*, 539–540; *La Orquesta*, Jan. 3, 1866.

34. Hyde, *Mexican Empire*, 180; *Mexican Times*, Feb. 24, 1866; Kératry, *Rise and Fall of the Emperor Maximilian*, 311.

35. Hyde, *Mexican Empire*, 180.

36. Hyde, *Mexican Empire*, 181.

Chapter 12. Like a Lost Soul

1. Edward L. Plumb to Benito Juárez, Oct. 9, 1865, Plumb Papers; Corti, 561; Hamnett, *Juárez*, 126, 139, 159, 201; Sheridan, *Memoirs*, 2: 223–224; Blumberg, "Diplomacy of the Mexican Empire," 84; Roeder, *Juárez*, 577, 578 (quotation); 613–614. Ortega reasserted his claims to the presidency in 1866. Roeder, *Juárez*, 660.

2. Roeder, *Juárez*, 613–616.

3. Napoléon III to Maximilian, Aug. 29, 1865, as reprinted in Corti, *Maximilian*, 541.

4. Maximilian to Napoléon III, Oct. 20, 1865, *Papiers et Correspondance de la Famille Impériale*, 96–97 (quotations); Haslip, *Crown of Mexico*, 339; Corti, *Maximilian*, 544; *El Pájaro Verde*, Oct. 13, 1866.

5. Edward L. Plumb to Charles Sumner, Oct. 26, 1865, Plumb Papers; Corti, *Maximilian*, 544.

6. Lubienski, *Der Maximilianeische Staat*, 99–100; Barker, *Distaff Diplomacy*, 100; Hyde, *Mexican Empire*, 157.

7. Announcement of prefect of Mérida, Nov. 30, 1864; José García Penales to Julia Campillo de Salazar, Dec. 10, 1866, Salazar Ilarregui Papers, Special Collections Library, University of Texas at Arlington; Maximilian to José Salazar Ilarregui, Dec. 14, 1864, Salazar Ilarregui Papers, HSA; Nelson A. Reed, *The Caste War of Yucatán*

(Palo Alto: Stanford University Press, 1964), 245. Boleslawski married Andrew Talcott's daughter. Lubienski, *Der Maximilianeische Staat*, 99–100; Corti, *Maximilian*, 443–445.

8. Napoléon envisioned an Anglo-Saxon rule over a large portion of the Americas. Corti, *Maximilian*, 445, 547 (quotation); Lubienski, *Der Maximilianeische Staat*, 100; Blasio, *Maximilian*, 63–64.

9. Haslip, *Crown of Mexico*, 339–340 (quotations); Blasio, *Maximilian*, 64.

10. Carlota to Maximilian, Nov. 8, 1865, in Ratz, *Correspondencia Inédita*, 224 (quotation); Blasio, *Maximilian*, 64.

11. Haslip, *Crown of Mexico*, 341 (quotation); Blasio, *Maximilian*, 64.

12. Haslip, *Crown of Mexico*, 342 (first quotation); Carlota to Maximilian, Nov. 16, 1865, in Ratz, *Correspondencia Inédita*, 233 (second quotation).

13. *L'Ere Nouvelle*, Nov. 19, 1865; *Revue Militaire de la Quinzaine*, Dec. 17, 1865, K25, OS; Carlota to Maximilian, Nov. 23, 1865, in Ratz, *Correspondencia Inédita*, 239 (quotation); José N. Iturriaga de la Fuente, *Escritos Mexicanos de Carlota de Bélgica* (Mexico: Banco de Mexico, 1992) 289 (quotation); Corti, *Maximilian*, 546–547; Maximilian to Mariano Degollado, Dec. 17, 1865, Joaquín and Mariano Degollado Papers, Benson Latin American Collection, University of Texas at Austin (hereafter cited Degollado Papers, BLAC).

14. Reed, *The Caste War of Yucatán*, 248–249; Carlota, "Viaje a Yucatán," in Weckmann, *Carlota*, 212–213 n.369; Haslip, *Crown of Mexico*, 340–341.

15. Haslip, *Crown of Mexico*, 342–343.

16. Carlota, "Relación del viaje," July 21, 1865, in Weckmann, 192–193, "Informe sobre el estado," 219–221.

17. Carlota to Maximilian, Dec. 8, 1865, in Ratz, *Correspondencia Inédita*, (quotations) 249; Reed, *The Caste War of Yucatán*, 248–249; Carlota, "Relación del viaje," July 21, 1865, in Weckmann, 193; Haslip, *Crown of Mexico*, 343–344.

18. Carlota to Countess of Grunne, April 9, 1866, in Reinach Foussemagne, *Charlotte*, 265 (quotation); Dominique Paoli, Memorandum on Carlota and her doctors, Oct. 8, 2009, notes in possession of the author. Some members of the Habsburg family with nervous disorders treated their ailments with morphine and opium and as a consequence became addicts. Catherine Radziwill, *The Austrian Court from Within* (London: Cassell, 1916), 127.

19. Reed, *The Caste War of Yucatán*, 248–249.

20. Blasio, *Maximilian*, 65.

21. Maximilian to Mariano Degollado, Nov. 12, 1865, Degollado papers, BLAC.

22. Communication no. 1, regarding celebration at Querétaro, July 13, 1865, *Corps Expéditionnaire: Correspondance Confidentielle*, 13/7 au 29/9/1965, G7, 99, *Expédition du Mexique*, 1862–1867, SHD; Haslip, *Crown of Mexico*, 341.

23. Maximilian to Bazaine, Dec. 3, 1865, Bazaine Collection, HC 378/388, HSA.

24. Achille Bazaine to his generals, June 3, 1864, Bazaine Papers, García Collec-

tion, BLAC; Maximilian to Achille Bazaine, Dec. 14, 1865, Bazaine Collection, HC 378/388, HSA (quotation).

25. Blasio, *Maximilian*, 66; Haslip, *Crown of Mexico*, 346 (quotation), 347; Military Return, December 1865, Karton 25, Maximilian Papers, OS. He made short excursions to the surrounding hillsides of Mexico City, like Tlalnepantla. *Diario del Imperio*, June 16, 1866.

26. Maximilian to Rudolf Günner, Jan. 10, 1866, Jan. 29, 1866; Karton 16, Maximilian Papers, OS; Haslip, *Crown of Mexico*, 347; Blasio, *Maximilian*, 66, 67 (quotation); *L'Ere Nouvelle*, Nov. 19, 1865. Construction and renovation continued as well at the National Palace and Chapultepec. Mrs. Kuhachevich to August Jilek, Jan. 27, 1866, Jilek Papers, Frederick R. Koch Collection, Beinecke Rare Book and Manuscript Library, Yale University (hereafter cited as Koch Coll., BL, YU); Ratz, *Tras las Huellas*, 128.

27. Blasio, *Maximilian*, 68, 69 (first quotation); Maximilian to Auguste Jilek, Feb. 4, 1866, Jilek Papers, Koch Coll., BL, YU (second quotation).

28. Haslip, *Crown of Mexico*, 347.

29. Blasio, *Maximilian*, 68.

30. Maximilian to Carlota, Dec. 25, 1865, in Ratz, *Correspondencia Inédita*, 256 (quotation); *Revue Militaire de la Quinzaine*, Jan. 2, 1866, Karton 25, Maximilian Papers, OS.

31. Carlota to Sophie, Feb. 1, 1866, in Weckmann, *Carlota*, 118; Blasio, *Maximilian*, 70.

32. Mrs. Kuhachevich to Auguste Jilek, Jan. 27, 1866, Jilek Papers, Frederick R. Koch Collection, Beinecke Rare Book and Manuscript Library, Yale University (hereafter cited as Koch Coll., BL, YU); Blasio, *Maximilian*, 67–68; Haslip, *Crown of Mexico*, 346 (quotation); Paoli, *Charlotte*, 133.

33. Leopold was cautioning Maximilian on uselessly paying for positive press. Lichtervelde, *Léopold First*, 320 (quotation); Haslip, *Crown of Mexico*, 344; Paoli, *Charlotte*, 133; Ratz, *Maximilian*, 1: 384.

34. Hyde, *Mexican Empire*, 184–185; Florencio Medina, Confirmation of Dr. Bilimek conservator of the Department of Natural History at the National Museum, Bilimek Records, May 2, 1866, GD 137, vol. 1, fs. 220, AGN; Carlota to Maximilian, Feb. 17, May 21, May 25, 1866, in Ratz, *Correspondencia Inédita*, 261–262, 287–290; Carlota to Philippe, March 2, 1866, Charlotte of Mexico Letters, 1856–1868, Archives of the Royal Palace, Brussels, Belgium (hereafter cited as ARP).

35. Blasio, *Maximilian*, 69–70.

36. Ratz, *Tras las Huellas*, 128; Maximilian to Auguste Jilek, Feb. 4, 1866, Jilek Papers, Koch Coll., BL, YU; Hyde, *Mexican Empire*, 186–187; Lorenza Fonda, interview, Miramar, June 9, 2009, notes in possession of the author; Maximilian to Carlota, March 17, 1866, in Ratz, *Correspondencia Inédita*, 270, and May 4, 1866, 280–281.

37. Blasio, *Maximilian*, 39.

38. Blasio, *Maximilian*, 74, 75 (quotation); Paoli, *Charlotte*, 144–145.

39. Blasio, *Maximilian*, 74; Paoli, *Charlotte*, 121, 123, 124 (quotation); Esta O. de Dávila, *Paradise in Mexico: Morelos and Its Capital, Cuernavaca* (Mexico City: Editorial Cultura, 1937), 64, 67. Dominique Paoli said the name of the woman could have also been María Ana Leguizano. She was born in Pachuca. Dominique Paoli, Memorandum on Concepción Sedano, Oct. 21, 2009, notes in possession of the author.

40. Ratz, *Correspondencia Inédita*, 8, 10, 40–42, 45, also Carlota to Maximilian, May 7, 1866, 284 (quotation); Mariano Ruiz, *Reminiscencias históricas de General Mariano Ruiz*, 62, Mariano Ruiz Papers, BLAC.

41. Blasio, *Maximilian*, 78.

42. Charles Blanchot quoted in Reinach Foussemagne, *Charlotte*, 263–264 (second quotation); Blasio, *Maximilian*, 78; Carlota to Maximilian, March 15, 21, 1866, Maximilian to Carlota, May 4, 1866, in Ratz, *Correspondencia Inédita*, 267–268 (first quotation), 274, 280. As mentioned elsewhere, some termed this road Paseo del Emperador.

Chapter 13. The French Repatriation

1. Barker, *Distaff Diplomacy*, 132, 133 (quotation), 134; Dabbs, *French Army*, 99, 238.

2. Reinach Foussemagne, *Charlotte*, 270–271; Dabbs, *French Army*, 164–166; Miller, "Arms across the Border," 59; Hyde, *Mexican Empire*, 164.

3. Belgian Josef Kowarz along with Mexican craftsmen made the saddle. When the Austrians logged it into the royal estate, they described the chaps and gun bag as being made of gorilla hair, being totally unfamiliar with the goats of Mexico. Mario Doeberl, Wagenberg, Schönbrunn, June 5, 2009, interview with M. M. McAllen and inspection of Mexican saddle to Franz Josef. Corti, *Maximilian*, 591–592.

4. Carlota to Philippe, March 7, 1866, Charlotte Letters, ARP; Blasio, *Maximilian*, 71; Aug. Scheler, "Chronique Belge de 1866," in *Annuaire Statistique & Historique Belge* (Bruxelles, Leipzig: C. Muquardt, 1867), 247–248; Félix Eloin, "Extraordinary Mission from Belgium," Letter Copy Book, Feb. 9, 1866, Charlotte and Maximilian Collection, WRC; Maximilian to Carlota, March 5, 1866, in Ratz, *Correspondencia Inédita*, 266 (quotation); Weckmann, *Carlota*, 97; C. M. Mayo, memorandum, July 30, 2012, in possession of author.

5. Dabbs, *French Army*, 175–177; Maximilian to Bazaine, Nov. 10, 1865, Bazaine Collection, HC 378/388, HSA (quotations); Lucius Avery to William H. Seward, Jan. 13, 1866, *Dispatches from U.S. Consuls at Matamoros, 1826–1906*, T18, Roll 4, NARA; Maximilian, "Tartine," Aug. 24, 1866, Karton 40, Maximilian Papers, OS.

6. Maximilian to Bazaine, Nov. 29, 1865, Bazaine Collection, HC 378/388, HSA (quotations).

7. Tomás Mejía to Godfrey Weitzel, Jan. 2, 1866, H. Exec. Doc. no. 73, 39th Congress, 1st Sess., 1866, 506; Godfrey Weitzel to C. H. Whittlesey, Dec. 24, 1865, Godfrey

Weitzel Manuscript Collection, MSS1498AV, Ohio Historical Society, Columbus, Ohio (hereafter cited as Weitzel Collection); Georges-Charles Cloué to Commander, Nov. 6, 1865, *Papers Relating to Foreign Relations*, 39th Congress, 2nd Sess., Part 3, 1867, 40 (quotation); Maximilian to Degollado, Nov. 12, 1865, Degollado Papers, BLAC.

8. Matías Romero to William H. Seward, Feb. 20, 1866; R. Clay Crawford to Godfrey Weitzel, Jan. 1, 1866, H. Exec. Doc. no. 73, 39th Congress, 1st Sess., 1866, 504–505.

9. Juan de Peza, Urgent News, Jan. 9, 1866, Karton 25, Maximilian Papers, OS; Hippolyte to Lucius Avery, Feb. 7, 1866, *Consular Dispatches from Matamoros*, Microfilm Reel 3, RG 281, NARA; Thompson, *Cortina*, 168; Mariano Escobedo to Godfrey Weitzel, Jan. 4, 1866, Godfrey Weitzel to C. H. Whittlesey, Jan. 7, 1866, Weitzel Collection.

10. Mariano Escobedo to Godfrey Weitzel, Jan. 7, 1866, Mariano Escobedo Papers, Bancroft Library, University of California at Berkeley, Berkeley, California (cited hereinafter as BL, UCB); Lucius Avery to William H. Seward, Oct. 20, 26, 1865, Jan. 13, 1866, *Dispatches from U.S. Consuls at Matamoros*, 1826–1906, Roll 4, NARA; *La Orquesta*, Jan. 27, 1866; Godfrey Weitzel to H. G. Wright, Dec. 29, 1865, Godfrey Weitzel to R. M. Hall, Jan. 6, 1866, H. G. Wright to Godfrey Weitzel, Jan. 14, 27, 1866, Weitzel Collection.

11. Maximilian to Bazaine, Jan. 11, 1866, Bazaine Collection, HC 378/388, HSA (first quotation); Félix Eloin to Charles Bombelles, Feb. 8, 1866, Charlotte and Maximilian Collection, WRC; Blasio, *Maximilian*, 71; Pitner, *Maximilian's Lieutenant*, 102 (second quotation), 103, 106; Ratz, *Tras las Huellas*, 116.

12. Hyde, *Mexican Empire*, 164 (quotations); Corti, *Maximilian*, 553–555, 557.

13. It was on this return that Dupin petitioned the court in Gallic to let him spell his name "Du Pin," to appear more aristocratic. Because he commanded a host of noblemen in the counterguerrillas, he could feel less outranked. Mignard, *Charles-Louis Du Pin*, 4 (quotation); Mignard, Memo, Feb. 18, 2009, notes in possession of author; *Pájaro Verde*, Jan. 22, 1866; *Mexican Times*, Feb. 3, 1866.

14. Corti, *Maximilian*, 567 (first quotation); Maximilian to Bazaine, May 16, 1866, Karton 40, Maximilian Papers, OS (second quotation).

15. Hyde, *Mexican Empire*, 183 (quotation); *Mexican Times*, Jan. 20, 1866.

16. M. A. Thiers, *Histoire du Consulat et de l'Empire, Faisant Suite à l'Histoire de la Révolution Française* (Paris: Paulin, 1849), 9: 542 (quotation); Corti, *Maximilian*, 574–578, 629–630.

17. Some suggested that the United States intervene militarily with the idea that it would receive Baja California and part of Sonora as compensation for forcing Maximilian and the French out of Mexico. Edward L. Plumb to Charles Sumner, Jan. 3, 1866, Plumb Papers; Corti, *Maximilian*, 578–579 (quotation), 585; Friedrich Anton Heller von Hellwald, *Maximilian I, Kaiser von Mexico* (Vienna: Wilhelm Braumüller, 1869), 469–473; Shaw, "McDougall of California," 129; William Seward to the Marquis de Montholon, Feb. 12, 1866, "Evacuation of Mexico by the French," H. Exec.

Doc. 93, 39th Congress, 1st Sess., 27–29; Almonte to Carlota, Apr. 17, 1866, in Weckmann, *Carlota*, 225.

18. Corti, *Maximilian*, 579.

19. Napoléon III to Maximilian, Jan. 15, 1866, Charlotte and Maximilian Collection, WRC (quotation); Paoli, *Charlotte*, 138.

20. Napoléon III to Maximilian, Jan. 15, 1866 (quotation); Maximilian to Félix Eloin, Feb. 28, 1866; Félix Eloin to Charles Bombelles, Feb. 8, 1866, Maximilian Collection, WRC; *New York Times*, March 20, April 20, 1866; John Bigelow to William Seward, April 6, 1866, "Evacuation of Mexico by the French," H. Exec. Doc. 93, 39th Congress, 1st Sess., 42.

21. Reinach Foussemagne, *Charlotte*, 275; Corti, *Maximilian*, 581–582.

22. Haslip, *Crown of Mexico*, 370; Reinach Foussemagne, *Charlotte*, 277.

23. Maximilian to Félix Eloin, Feb. 28, 1866 (second and third quotations) Charlotte and Maximilian Papers, WRC; Corti, *Maximilian*, 582 (first quotation); Reinach Foussemagne, *Charlotte*, 273; Roeder, *Juárez*, 622.

24. Maximilian to Carlota, February 22, 1866, March 17, 1866 (two letters), in Ratz, *Correspondencia Inédita*, 265, 270, 271 (quotations).

25. Maximilian to Félix Eloin, May 18, 1866, Charlotte and Maximilian Papers, WRC (quotation); Hanna and Hanna, *Napoleon III*, 275.

26. Hanna and Hanna, *Napoleon III*, 275; Maximilian to Auguste Jilek, Feb. 4, 1866, Koch Coll., BL, YU (quotation).

27. Maximilian to Auguste Jilek, April 26, 1866, Jilek Papers, Koch Coll., BL, YU (first quotation); Félix Eloin to José Manuel Hidalgo, Oct. 29, 1865, Maximilian to Félix Eloin, May 4, 1866 (second quotation), Charlotte and Maximilian Collection, WRC; Dabbs, *French Army*, 159, 161; Baron Karl Malortie, *Here, There and Everywhere* (London: Ward & Downey, 1895), 89; Corti, *Maximilian*, 595.

28. Charles Bombelles to Félix Eloin, Feb. 17, 1866; Félix Eloin to Stefan Herzfeld, March 24, 1866, Charlotte and Maximilian Collection, WRC; Corti, *Maximilian*, 582; Blasio, *Maximilian*, 71; Reinach Foussemagne, *Charlotte*, 269–270; Loysel appointed to military attaché to Legation of France, June 6, 1866, no. 267, État-Major général correspondance avec le Ministre, Nov. 18, 1865, to March 2, 1867, G7, 99, Expédition du Mexique, SHD.

29. Félix Eloin, notes in letter copybook, March 26, 1866, Charlotte and Maximilian Collection, WRC (quotations); Haslip, *Crown of Mexico*, 367; Reinach Foussemagne, *Charlotte*, 275.

30. Reinach Foussemagne, *Charlotte*, 275 (quotation); Félix Eloin, Letter copybook, March 26, 1866, Charlotte and Maximilian Collection, WRC; Caroline de Grunne to Carlota, June 26, 1966, in Weckmann, *Carlota de Bélgica*, 85.

31. France suffered a deficit of 50 million francs, calling for reduction in the military budget. French ministers Fould, Drouyn L'Huys, and Germiny repeated Napoléon's intentions to withdraw, and they did not have another "sou." Félix Eloin to Charles

Bombelles, Feb. 8, 1866, Félix Eloin to Stefan Herzfeld, March 24, 1866, Félix Eloin, notes, March 26, 1866, all found in Eloin's Letter Copybook, Charlotte and Maximilian Collection, WRC; Reinach Foussemagne, *Charlotte*, 277–278 (quotation).

32. Reinach Foussemagne, *Charlotte*, 278 (quotation).

33. Hyde, *Mexican Empire*, 200; Corti, *Maximilian*, 585–586.

34. John Bigelow to William Seward, March 22, 1866, "Evacuation of Mexico by the French," H. Exec. Doc. 93, 39th Congress, 1st Sess., 40–41; Blumberg, "Diplomacy of the Mexican Empire," 97–98.

35. Message of the President of the United States, March 20, 1866, 39th Cong, 1st Sess., House Exec. Doc. 73, 171–172; Blumberg, "Diplomacy of the Mexican Empire," 81.

36. Hellwald, *Maximilian I, Kaiser von Mexico*, 469–473; John Lothrop Motley, George W. Curtis, ed., *The Correspondence of John Lothrop Motley* (New York: Harper & Brothers, 1889), 2: 218, 245–247; Corti, *Maximilian*, 620; *New York Times*, May 24, 1866.

37. Blumberg, "Diplomacy of the Mexican Empire," 99–101; Maximilian to José Ignacio Durán, June 16, 1866, as quoted in Corti, *Maximilian*, 626 (quotation); Ratz, *Maximilian und Juárez*, 1: 384; Haslip, *Crown of Mexico*, 369 (quotation); Maximilian to Gregorio de Barandiarán, June 16, 1866, Karton 40, Maximilian Papers, OS.

38. Maximilian to Félix Eloin, May 18, 1866, Charlotte and Maximilian Papers, WRC; Corti, *Maximilian*, 587 (quotation).

39. Maximilian to Félix Eloin, May 18, 1866, Charlotte and Maximilian Collection, WRC (quotation); Jürgen Buchenau, *Mexico Otherwise: Modern Mexico in the Eyes of Foreign Observers* (Albuquerque: University of New Mexico Press, 2005), 71–75.

40. Félix Eloin to José Manuel Hidalgo, Oct. 29, 1865 (second quotation), Maximilian to Félix Eloin, Jan. 11, 1866, April 9, 1866 (first quotation), Félix Eloin to Charles Bombelles, Feb. 8, 1866, Charles Bombelles to Félix Eloin, Feb. 17, 1866, Charlotte and Maximilian Collection, WRC; Blumberg, "Diplomacy of the Mexican Empire," 91; Hyde, *Mexican Empire*, 200 (third quotation); Dabbs, *French Army*, 164; Reinach Foussemagne, *Charlotte*, 277.

41. Maximilian to Félix Eloin, Jan. 11, 1866, Charlotte and Maximilian Collection, WRC; Corti, *Maximilian*, 587–588 (quotations); Haslip, *Crown of Mexico*, 368.

42. Félix Eloin to José Manuel Hidalgo, Oct. 29, 1865, Charlotte and Maximilian Collection, WRC; Haslip, *Crown of Mexico*, 371; Corti, *Maximilian*, 589.

43. Hyde, *Mexican Empire*, 197 (first quotation), 198; Corti, *Maximilian*, 600 (second quotation), 601; Maximilian to J. M. Gutiérrez de Estrada, May 18, 1866, Karton 40, Maximilian Papers, OS; Maximilian to Carlota, July 18, 1866, in Ratz, *Correspondencia Inédita*, 300–302; also 273–274 (third quotation).

44. Maximilian to Félix Eloin, Feb. 28, April 9, 1866, Charlotte and Maximilian Collection, WRC; Paoli, *Charlotte*, 132; Bancroft, *History of Mexico*, 14: 217 n.10; Gustave Léon Niox, *Expédition du Mexique 1861–1867* (Paris: Librairie Militaire de

J. Dumaine, 1874), 562–563; Robert H. Duncan, "Maximilian's First Steps Toward the Global Marketplace (1864–1866)," in *Memorias del segundo congreso de historia económica, La historia económica hoy, entre la económica y la historia* (Asociación Mexicana de Historia Económica, Simposio 21, Mexico, 2004), 19.

45. Ulysses Simpson Grant, *Papers of Ulysses S. Grant, 1866*, ed. John Y. Simon (Carbondale: Southern Illinois University Press, 1988), 16: 192–193 (first and second quotations); Rister, "Carlota," 47 (third quotation); Paul D. Casdorph, *Prince John Magruder: His Life and Campaigns* (New York: John Wiley & Sons, 1996), 306; Anthony Arthur, *Gen. Jo Shelby's March* (New York: Random House, 2010), 169–170.

Chapter 14. The Empire Is Nothing Without the Emperor

1. *New York Times*, April 20, 1866; Bazaine to Napoléon III, Feb. 26, 1866, as reprinted in Corti, *Maximilian*, 590 (first quotation); Blasio, *Maximilian*, 78 (second quotation); *El Pájaro Verde*, Sept. 3, 1866.

2. Achille Bazaine to Jacques Randon, June 9, 28, Aug. 3, 1866, État-major général correspondance, SHD; Maximilian to Achille Bazaine, May 17, 20, 1866, Karton 40, Maximilian Papers, OS; Malortie, *Here, There and Everywhere*, 88; Report of Thun to José Salazar Ilarregui, April 14, 1866, Salazar Ilarregui Papers, HSA; Maximilian to Achille Bazaine, April 7, 1866, Bazaine Collection, HC 378/388, HSA.

3. Maximilian to Achille Bazaine, May 17, 1866, Karton 40, Maximilian Papers, OS; Roeder, *Juárez*, 623, 624; Maximilian to Félix Eloin, May 18, 1866, Charlotte and Maximilian Collection, WRC (third quotation); Corti, *Maximilian*, 614 (first, second, and fourth quotations); Carlota to Maximilian, March 19, 1866, 272, Maximilian to Carlota, May 1, 1866, 279–280, in Ratz, *Correspondencia Inédita*.

4. Roeder, *Juárez*, 623–624 (quotation); Maximilian to José María Lacunza, May 19, 1866, Karton 40, Maximilian Papers, OS; Dabbs, *French Army*, 282.

5. Reinach Foussemagne, *Charlotte*, 281 (first quotation); Corti, *Maximilian*, 615 (second quotation).

6. Roeder, *Juárez*, 624, 629–630; Léonce Détroyat, *La Intervención Francesa en Mexico: Acompañada de Documentos Inéditos*, trans. José Antonio Ruiz (Veracruz: Imprenta de El Progreso, 1868), 253–254; Maximilian to Achille Bazaine, June 3, 1866, Karton 25, Maximilian Papers, OS; Maximilian to Marshal Bazaine, July 5, 1866, Bazaine Collection, HC 378/388, HSA (quotation); Ratz, *Maximilian*, 1: 385.

7. Stevenson, *Maximilian*, 214–219; *El Cura de Tamajón*, 1–4; Ibsen, *Maximilian*, 24–29, 34–48.

8. Ratz, *Tras las Huellas*, 128–129.

9. Maximilian to Félix Eloin, June 9, 1866, Charlotte and Maximilian Papers, WRC; Duncan, "Political Legitimation," 41.

10. Haslip, *Crown of Mexico*, 374.

11. Maximilian to Achille Bazaine, June 3, 1866, Karton 25; Maximilian to Auguste Osmont, July 26, 1866, Aug. 5, 1866, Karton 40, Maximilian Papers, OS; Maximilian to Marshal Bazaine, July 5, 1866, Bazaine Collection, HC 378/388, HSA; Blumberg, "Diplomacy of the Mexican Empire," 104–105; Lubienski, *Der Maximilianeische Staat*, 62; Basch, *Memories of Mexico*, 5; Corti, *Maximilian*, 644–645; Magnus, *El Ocaso*, 83.

12. $3 million would have been nearly equivalent to $50 million in today's dollars. Thompson, *Cortina*, 178; Pitner, *Maximilian's Lieutenant*, 130; McCusker, "Historical Value of a Dollar," Aug. 24, 2009, memorandum in possession of the author.

13. Pitner, *Maximilian's Lieutenant*, 130–132, 133 (quotation); *Mexican Times* (Mexico City), July 7, 1866; Mariano Escobedo to Enrique A. Mejía, Feb. 1, 1866, May 16, 1866, Mariano Escobedo Papers, BL, UCB; Thompson, *Cortina*, 179.

14. Thompson, *Cortina*, 180; *New York Herald*, July 12, 1866 (quotation); Lucius Avery to William H. Seward, June 18, 29, 1866, *Dispatches from U.S. Consuls in Matamoros, 1826–1906*, RG281 Microfilm Roll 3, NARA; William Kelly to José San Román, June 21, 1866, José San Román Papers, CAH; "State of the Force and Situation of the Mexican Troops Commanded by Marshal Bazaine," Dec. 1865, Karton 25, Maximilian Papers, OS.

15. Joseph Cooper to José San Román, June 22, 25, 26, 1866, José San Román Papers, CAH; Tomás Mejía to Gen. de la Portilla, Aug. 6, 1866, Fondo 27, Tomás Mejía 1844–1866, Carpeta 1, Archivo Condumex; Franklin Chase to Matías Romero, Oct. 6, 1866, Romero Collection, BLAC; Miller, "Arms across the Border," 52; *Mexican Times* (Mexico City), July 7, 1866; *La Orquesta*, July 3, 1866; *El Pájaro Verde*, Oct. 13, 1866.

16. Maximilian to Antonio García, June 11, 1866, Karton 40, Maximilian to Achille Bazaine, June 24, 1866 (quotation), Karton 25, Maximilian Papers, OS; Félix Eloin to Maximilian, June or July 1864, no date, Charlotte and Maximilian Papers, WRC; Haslip, *Crown of Mexico*, 368, 378.

17. The *Tacony*, built for war, carried heavy batteries and large crews in shallow water. A side-wheeler steamer, she was armed with two sixty-pounder rifles and four eight-inch smooth-bores and four howitzers on the broadsides. The crew consisted of 144 men. She was important to the reoccupation by the Juaristas. Maximilian to Félix Eloin, June 9, 1866 (first quotation), Sept. 20, 1866 (second quotation), Charlotte and Maximilian Papers, WRC; Seaton Schroeder, *The Fall of Maximilian's Empire* (New York: G. P. Putnam's Sons, 1887), 12, 33–37; *New York Times*, Aug. 18, 1866; Corti, *Maximilian*, 627; *El Pájaro Verde*, Sept. 3, 1866; Lecaillon, *Napoléon III et le Mexique*, 188.

18. Roeder, *Juárez*, 620; *New York Times*, July 13, 31, 1866; Blumberg, "Diplomacy of the Mexican Empire," 83–85.

19. William H. Seward to Lewis Campbell, Oct. 25, 1866 (quotation), Records of the Headquarters of the Army, Entry 35, Box 1, RG 108, NARA; Miller, "Arms across the Border," 60.

20. Maximilian to Carlota, July 18, 1866, in Ratz, *Correspondencia Inédita*, 300–302; Fowler, *Santa Anna*, 327–329.

21. Robert W. Frazer, "The Ochoa Bond Negotiations of 1865–1867," *Pacific Historical Review* 11 (Dec. 1942), 397–398; Miller, "Arms across the Border," 34–41; Hanna and Hanna, *Napoleon III and Mexico,* 298. According to Miller, the Legion of Honor later greatly exaggerated their claims and petitioned Juárez for monetary compensation.

22. Sheridan, *Memoirs*, 2: 224–225; Lew Wallace to Sue Wallace, July 20, Aug. 7 (quotation), Oct. 22, 24, 1866, Lew Wallace Papers, IHS. Wallace persuaded Leonard Pierce, former American consul at Matamoros, to venture to Saltillo and Monterrey to sell arms. Lew Wallace to Sue Wallace, Aug. 27, Sept. 7, 1866, Lew Wallace Papers, IHS.

23. Maximilian to Joaquín Velázquez de León, May 18 (quotations), June 16, 1866, Maximilian to Mariano Degollado, May 1, 1866, Karton 40, Maximilian Papers, OS; Hyde, *Mexican Empire*, 199; Blumberg, "Diplomacy of the Mexican Empire," 104, 108; Maximilian, *Código Civil del Imperio Mexicano* (Mexico: Andrade y Escalante, 1866), 23–27; Magnus, *El Ocaso*, 109 n.

24. Blumberg, "Diplomacy of the Mexican Empire," 104; Détroyat, *La Intervención Francesa*, 227; Haslip, *Crown of Mexico*, 372–373; Roeder, *Juárez*, 640; Maximilian to Achille Fould, May 16, 1866, Karton 40, Maximilian Papers, OS; Magnus, *El Ocaso*, 77.

25. Détroyat, *La Intervención Francesa*, 229–231; Léonce Détroyat to Maximilian, July 6, 1866, as quoted in Corti, 634–635. Détroyat, born in Bayonne, came to Mexico as a ship's lieutenant under Admiral Jurien de la Gravière. Reinach Foussemagne, 280 n.4; Magnus, *El Ocaso*, 84.

26. Détroyat, *La Intervención Francesa*, 228–229.

27. Détroyat, *La Intervención Francesa*, 227.

28. Détroyat, *La Intervención Francesa*, 225–229; Reinach Foussemagne, *Charlotte*, 278–280.

29. Reinach Foussemagne, *Charlotte*, 266–267, 278; Haslip, *Crown of Mexico*, 370. Carlota inherited a fourth of the former queen's jewels valued at 70,305 francs, as well as a number of paintings, including Winterhalter's portrait of Carlota as a child. Weckmann, *Carlota*, 231.

30. "Broke the fleurs-de-lys in the sack," is a reference to France's July Revolution of 1830 in which the archbishop's palace was sacked and the fleurs-de-lys, the symbol of the monarchy, was removed from the public seal and buildings. Reinach Foussemagne, *Charlotte de Belgique*, 278.

31. Reinach Foussemagne, *Charlotte de Belgique*, 278.

32. Reinach Foussemagne, *Charlotte de Belgique*, 279.

33. Reinach Foussemagne, *Charlotte de Belgique*, 279–280.

34. Reinach Foussemagne, *Charlotte de Belgique*, 280.

Chapter 15. Beware of the French

1. Reinach Foussemagne, *Charlotte*, 292; Martin, *Maximilian*, 228–232; Corti, *Maximilian*, 642. They asked for payment in piasters, France's commercial currency used in French territories. One piaster equaled one peso or U.S. dollar. McCusker, "Historical Value of a Dollar," memorandum, Aug. 24, 2009. Memorandum in possession of the author.

2. Mrs. Kuhachevich to Col. Stabs-Arzt (no first name), Nov. 10, 1865 (quotations); Mrs. Kuhachevich to Auguste Jilek, Jan. 17, 1866, Jilek Papers, Frederick R. Koch Collection, Beinecke Rare Book and Manuscript Library, Yale University (hereafter cited as Koch Coll., BL, YU); Martin, *Maximilian*, 232; Kératry, *Rise and Fall of the Emperor Maximilian*, 150; Haslip, *Crown of Mexico*, 376–377, 426; Reinach Foussemagne, *Charlotte de Belgique*, 287.

3. Malortie, *Here, There and Everywhere*, 89–91; Martin, *Maximilian*, 232; Dabbs, *French Army*, 174 (quotation); Reinach Foussemagne, *Charlotte de Belgique*, 285–286.

4. Haslip, *Crown of Mexico*, 378–379.

5. Malortie, *Here, There and Everywhere*, 89.

6. Paoli, *L'Impératrice Charlotte*, 159; Concepción de Pacheco to Maximilian, Oct. 20, 1866, K40, Maximilian Papers, OS; Haslip, 378–379 (quotations); Malortie, *Here, There and Everywhere*, 93–95; Magnus, *El Ocaso*, 85.

7. Malortie, *Here, There and Everywhere*, 93–94 (quotation), 95; Haslip, *Crown of Mexico*, 380.

8. Malortie, *Here, There and Everywhere*, 96–97.

9. Malortie, *Here, There and Everywhere*, 97–99.

10. Haslip, *Crown of Mexico*, 381.

11. Martin, *Maximilian*, 236; Haslip, *Crown of Mexico*, 382.

12. Paoli, *L'Impératrice Charlotte*, 159; Carlota, "Informe sobre mi viaje," in Weckmann, *Carlota*, 200–201; Corti, *Maximilian*, 643–644; Martin, *Maximilian*, 237; Roeder, *Juárez*, 636.

13. Reinach Foussemagne, *Charlotte de Belgique*, 292; Haslip, *Crown of Mexico*, 377 (first quotation); Maximilian, "Tartine," July 15, 1866 (second quotation) Karton 40, Maximilian Papers, OS.

14. Maximilian, "Notations on the City of Mexico (Improvements) to the Fomento," July 21, 1866, Karton 40, Maximilian Papers, OS; *Diario del Imperio* (Mexico City), June 12, 13, 1866; Maximilian to Carlota in Ratz, *Correspondencia Inédita*, 313–314; *Mexican Times*, Nov. 25, 1865. However, work on the rail lines ceased when Maximilian could not pay $1.5 million. *New Orleans Times*, July 15, 1866.

15. Maximilian to Achille Bazaine, July 20, 1866, Karton 40, Maximilian Papers, OS; Lubienski, *Der Maximilianeische Staat*, 62; Loizillon, *Lettres*, 404–405; Corti, 644–645; Magnus, *El Ocaso*, 81.

16. Franz Thun to José Salazar Ilarregui, 1865, Salazar Ilarregui Papers, HSA;

Maximilian to Franz Thun, July 20, 1866, Maximilian, "Tartine," July 15, 1866, Karton 40, Maximilian Papers, OS; Martin, *Maximilian in Mexico*, 98; Loizillon, *Lettres*, 404–405; Hamann, *Con Maximiliano*, 175.

17. Loizillon, *Lettres*, 404–405.

18. Maximilian, "Tartine," Aug. 20, 1866, Karton 40, Maximilian Papers, OS; Maximilian to Carlota, July 18, 1866, in Ratz, *Correspondencia Inédita*, 300–301 (quotation); Emmanuel Masseras, *Un Essai d'Empire au Mexique* (Paris: G. Charpentier, 1879), 165; Blumberg, "Diplomacy of the Mexican Empire," 104; Martin, *Maximilian*, 190–191; Hanna and Hanna, *Napoleon III*, 277; Ratz, *Correspondencia Inédita*, 266–267; Ratz, *Maximilian*, 1: 384; *New York Times*, Aug. 18, 1866; Magnus, *El Ocaso*, 90, 97.

19. Maximilian, "Tartine," Aug. 20, 1866, Karton 40, Maximilian Papers, OS; Maximilian to Édouard Pierron, Aug. 4, 1866, as quoted in Corti, *Maximilian*, 651, 652 (quotation); Franklin Chase to Matías Romero, Sept. 24, 1866, Romero Papers, BLAC; *Diario del Imperio* (Mexico City), June 15, 1866; Martin, *Maximilian*, 218; *El Pájaro Verde*, Sept. 3, 1866.

20. Achille Bazaine to Maximilian, Aug. 12, 1866, as quoted in Corti, *Maximilian*, 653; *New York Times*, Aug. 18, 1866.

21. Nicolas Poliakowitz to Maximilian, July 26, 1866, Karton 16, Maximilian Papers, OS; Corti, *Maximilian*, 654 (quotation), 672; Roeder, *Juárez*, 636–637; *New York Times*, July 23, 1866; Norwich, *Absolute Monarchs*, 409; Magnus, *El Ocaso*, 77, 85.

22. Foussemagne, *Charlotte du Belgique*, 287–288; Paoli, *L'Impératrice Charlotte*, 159.

23. Reinach Foussemagne, *Charlotte de Belgique*, 288–289.

24. Reinach Foussemagne, *Charlotte de Belgique*, 289, 290 (quotation); Barker, *Distaff Diplomacy*, 158; Maximilian to Carlota, Aug. 7, 1866, in Ratz, *Correspondencia Inédita*, 312.

25. *El Pájaro Verde*, Sept. 14, 1866; Haslip, *Crown of Mexico*, 386, 387 (quotation); Malortie, *Here, There and Everywhere*, 109; Corti, *Maximilian*, 668.

26. Malortie, *Here, There and Everywhere*, 111.

27. Bigelow, "The Heir-Presumptive to the Imperial Crown of Mexico," 744; Haslip, *Crown of Mexico*, 386–387; Ángel Iturbide to Maximilian, June 14, July 13, 1866, Karton 16, Maximilian Papers, OS; Édouard to Agustín Cosme Iturbide, August 1866 (no day), Iturbide Papers, Georgetown University Library, Special Collections.

28. Bigelow, "Heir-Presumptive," 744.

29. Bigelow, "Heir-Presumptive," 744.

30. Ángel Iturbide to Maximilian, June 14, July 13, 1866, Karton 16, Maximilian Papers, OS; Édouard to Agustín Cosme Iturbide, August 1866 (no day), Iturbide Papers, Georgetown University Library, Special Collection.

31. Bigelow, "Heir-Presumptive," 744.

32. Bigelow, "Heir-Presumptive," 745.

33. Barker, *Distaff Diplomacy*, 196–197, 207 (quotation); Haslip, *Crown of Mexico*,

387–388. Some scholars have termed Eugénie "harebrained." Bock, *Prelude to Tragedy*, 480.

34. Barker, *Distaff Diplomacy*, 158; Haslip, *Crown of Mexico*, 388 (quotation).

35. The beautiful and celebrated Adrienne de Lannes, Countess of Montebello, also attended. Haslip, *Crown of Mexico*, 389.

36. Haslip, *Crown of Mexico*, 389–390.

37. Reinach Foussemagne, *Charlotte*, 290–291; Ridley, *Maximilian and Juárez*, 248; Haslip, *Crown of Mexico*, 390 (quotation).

38. Reinach Foussemagne, *Charlotte*, 291.

39. Carlota to Eugénie, August 13, 1866, in Corti, *Maximilian*, 943.

40. Malortie, *Here, There and Everywhere*, 112.

41. *New York Times*, Sept. 13, 1866; *El Pájaro Verde*, Sept. 15, 1866; Haslip, *Crown of Mexico*, 391; Malortie, *Here, There and Everywhere*, 112; Carlota to Philippe, Aug. 15, 1866, Charlotte Letters, ARP.

42. Haslip, *Crown of Mexico*, 391 (quotation); Corti, *Maximilian*, 673; Interview, Ámparo Gómez Tepexicuapan, Curator, Chapultepec, Oct. 16, 2009, notes in possession of the author.

43. Malortie, *Here, There and Everywhere*, 113 (quotation); *L'Estafette*, Sept. 16, 1866.

44. Carlota to Napoléon, Aug. 11, 1866, in Weckmann, *Carlota*, 174–177; Reinach Foussemagne, *Charlotte*, 292–293; Roeder, *Juárez*, 637; Corti, *Maximilian*, 669.

45. Haslip, *Crown of Mexico*, 392; Reinach Foussemagne, *Charlotte*, 293 (first quotation), 296 (second quotation).

46. Reinach Foussemagne, *Charlotte de Belgique*, 294–295; Dominique Paoli, memorandum on drugs and poisoning, October 4, 2009, notes in possession of the author; mentioned in Malortie, *Here, There and Everywhere*, 117.

47. Roeder, *Juárez*, 637–638; Reinach Foussemagne, *Charlotte*, 293 (quotation), 294–295.

48. Reinach Foussemagne, *Charlotte*, 290–291.

49. Carlota to the Conde del Valle, no day, 1866, Weckmann, *Carlota*, 145–146; Reinach Foussemagne, *Charlotte*, 297; *El Pájaro Verde*, Sept. 15, 1866; Hyde, *Mexican Empire*, 214.

50. Reinach Foussemagne, *Charlotte*, 297.

51. Roeder, *Juárez*, 638; Hyde, *Mexican Empire*, 214 (quotations).

52. Reinach Foussemagne, *Charlotte*, 297; Roeder, *Juárez*, 638, 639 (quotation); Haslip, *Crown of Mexico*, 395; Puyo, "The French Military," 141.

53. Roeder, *Juárez*, 639.

54. Roeder, *Juárez*, 639 (first and second quotations); Reinach Foussemagne, *Charlotte*, 300 (third and fourth quotation).

55. Reinach Foussemagne, *Charlotte*, 299.

56. Corti, *Maximilian*, 683 (quotation), 698; Michael Bordo to M. M. McAllen

Amberson, May 5, 2010, memorandum on the possible connotation of nonconvertible bonds with Mexico, in possession of the author; Bock, *Prelude to Tragedy*, 463.

57. Haslip, *Crown of Mexico*, 396.

58. The modern convenience of the telegraph from Europe to Mexico routed signals through the U.S. In this way, messages could be intercepted or stopped, which contributed to U.S. intelligence and its ability to intervene to oust the imperial government. Maximilian to Carlota, Aug. 28, 1866, in Ratz, *Correspondencia Inédita*, 324; Hyde, *Mexican Empire*, 238; Corti, *Maximilian*, 656, 943 (quotation), 944. Maximilian contracted with Richard L. Maury, Matthew F. Maury's son, to lay cable in the waters off Mexico to improve the system. *El Pájaro Verde*, Sept. 18, 1866.

59. Dabbs, *The French Army in Mexico*, 177.

60. Maximilian to Félix Eloin, Sept. 20, 1866, Charlotte and Maximilian Papers, WRC (quotations); Maximilian to Carlota, Sept. 20, 1866, in Ratz, *Correspondencia Inédita*, 329; Roeder, *Juárez*, 639; Corti, *Maximilian*, 656–658; Magnus, *El Ocaso*, 111–112.

61. Reinach Foussemagne, *Charlotte*, 299 (first quotation), 300; Hyde, *Mexican Empire*, 215 (second quotation); Basch, *Memories*, 15.

62. Reinach Foussemagne, *Charlotte*, 300.

63. Blumberg, "Diplomacy of the Mexican Empire," 106 (quotation); Hyde, *Mexican Empire*, 215.

64. *New York Herald*, Sept. 20, 1866; Haslip, *Crown of Mexico*, 398 (quotation).

65. Reinach Foussemagne, *Charlotte de Belgique*, 300–301 (quotations); along with Carlota to Maximilian, as quoted in Corti, *Maximilian*, 685.

66. Carlota capitalized "He" and "Him" in referencing Napoléon as the "Devil." Reinach Foussemagne, *Charlotte*, 300–301 (quotations).

Chapter 16. Someone Is Intent on Poisoning Me

1. Reinach Foussemagne, *Charlotte*, 306; Haslip, *Crown of Mexico*, 408–409.

2. Villa d'Este was owned by Archduke Rainer Joseph of Austria and then his heirs. Carlota to Maximilian, Aug. 26, 1866, Foussemagne, *Charlotte de Belgique*, 303–304 (quotation); Hyde, *Mexican Empire*, 79.

3. Reinach Foussemagne, *Charlotte de Belgique*, 304–305.

4. Reinach Foussemagne, *Charlotte de Belgique*, 304–305; Corti, *Maximilian*, 692–693; Lorenza Fonda, interview at Miramar, June 9, 2009, regarding Maximilian's correspondence with architects Karl Junker and Wilhelm Knechtel about the grounds of Miramar through Dec. 1866, notes in possession of the author.

5. Reinach Foussemagne, *Charlotte*, 305; Norwich, *Absolute Monarchs*, 402.

6. Reinach Foussemagne, *Charlotte*, 305.

7. Reinach Foussemagne, *Charlotte*, 305, 305 (first quotation); Interview with

Lorenza Fonda, Castello Miramare, June 9, 2009; Corti, *Maximilian*, 694 (second quotation); Maximilian to Auguste Jilek, April 26, 1866, Jilek Papers, Koch Coll., BL, YU.

8. Hyde, *Mexican Empire*, 220; Interview with Lorenza Fonda, Castello Miramare, June 9, 2009.

9. Hyde, *Mexican Empire*, 220; Corti, *Maximilian*, 694.

10. Tegetthoff had the ships sail in the formation used at the Battle of Lissa, July 20, 1866, in the Adriatic, a decisive victory over the Italian fleet. Foussemagne, *Charlotte de Belgique*, 305–306 (second and third quotations); Haslip, *Crown of Mexico*, 404 (first quotation); Maximilian to Wilhelm von Tegetthoff, Aug. 20, 1866, Karton 16, Maximilian Papers, OS.

11. Maximilian to Carlota, Sept. 20, 1866, in Ratz, *Correspondencia Inédita*, 329.

12. Magnus, *El Ocaso*, 89–90.

13. Maximilian to Carlota, Aug. 31, 1866, in Ratz, *Correspondencia Inédita*, 324.

14. Hyde, *Mexican Empire*, 220–221; Hamnett, "Mexican Conservatives, Clericals, and Soldiers," 204; Blumberg, "Diplomacy of the Mexican Empire," 104; Lubienski, *Der Maximilianeische Staat*, 65; Maximilian to Félix Eloin, Sept. 20, 1866, Charlotte and Maximilian Papers, WRC (quotation); *L'Estafette*, May 24, 1866; "Memorandum," 179, 181, and "Report, Martín del Castillo," 209, in Weckmann, *Carlota*; Magnus, *El Ocaso*, 102.

15. Loizillon, *Lettres*, 404.

16. Haslip, *Crown of Mexico*, 404–405; Hamann, *Con Maximiliano*, 91, 176–177; Lubienski, *Der Maximilianeische Staat*, 67. These hussars became known as the "Red Hussars" because their uniforms were entirely red, the only fabric color remaining in the French supplies at the time. Pitner, *Maximilian's Lieutenant*, 145.

17. Félix Eloin to Maximilian, Aug. 19, 1866, Charlotte and Maximilian Papers, WRC; Haslip, *Crown of Mexico*, 403–404; *New York Times*, Oct. 15, 1866 (quotation); Reinach Foussemagne, *Charlotte*, 307–308.

18. Reinach Foussemagne, *Charlotte*, 307–308.

19. Reinach Foussemagne, *Charlotte*, 309–310; Carlota to Philippe, Sept. 9, 1866, Charlotte Letters, ARP.

20. Blasio, *Maximilian*, 91, 93 (quotation); Reinach Foussemagne, *Charlotte*, 315.

21. Blasio, *Maximilian*, 91–92.

22. Blasio, *Maximilian*, 92.

23. José Luis Blasio to Maximilian, Sept. 26, 1866, Karton 25, Maximilian Papers, OS; Corti, *Maximilian*, 704–705; Blasio, *Maximilian*, 94–95; Reinach Foussemagne, *Charlotte*, 316.

24. Blasio, *Maximilian*, 95. Fr. Francisco Ramírez to Maximilian, Sept. 26, 1866, Karton 40, Maximilian Papers, OS; Blasio, *Maximilian*, 96–101.

25. Fr. Francisco Ramírez to Maximilian, Sept. 26, 1866, Karton 40, Maximilian Papers, OS; Reinach Foussemagne, *Charlotte*, 316. At Miramar, Carlota had the notion

that Pius had invited her to stay at the Quirinal, but that was contradicted by Velásquez de León. Weckmann, *Carlota*, 147 n.287.

26. Corti, *Maximilian*, 706; Blasio, *Maximilian*, 97–98 (quotation).

27. Blasio, *Maximilian*, 98; Reinach Foussemagne, *Charlotte de Belgique*, 316–317.

28. Blasio, *Maximilian*, 98; Corti, *Maximilian*, 707.

29. Norwich, *Absolute Monarchs*, 410; Corti, *Maximilian*, 707.

30. Blasio, *Maximilian*, 99; Reinach Foussemagne, *Charlotte*, 317.

31. Reinach Foussemagne, *Charlotte*, 317–318; Blasio, *Maximilian*, 100.

32. Blasio, *Maximilian*, 100–101 (quotation); Reinach Foussemagne, *Charlotte*, 317–318.

33. Haslip, *Crown of Mexico*, 420 (quotation); Hyde, *Mexican Empire*, 225.

34. Hyde, *Mexican Empire*, 225; Corti, *Maximilian*, 708.

35. Francisco Ramírez to Maximilian, October 9, 1866 (quotation), Karton 40, Maximilian Papers, OS; Blasio, *Maximilian*, 101; Haslip, *Crown of Mexico*, 420–421.

36. Haslip, *Crown of Mexico*, 421.

37. Blasio, *Maximilian*, 101; Reinach Foussemagne, *Charlotte*, 318; Haslip, *Crown of Mexico*, 422 (first quotation); Malortie, *Here, There and Everywhere*, 123 (second quotation).

38. Blasio, *Maximilian*, 102; Reinach Foussemagne, *Charlotte*, 318.

39. Reinach Foussemagne, *Charlotte*, 318; Blasio, *Maximilian*, 102; Haslip, *Crown of Mexico*, 423 (first quotation); Hyde, *Mexican Empire*, 226, 227 (second quotation); Conde de Couvray to Duke of Nemours, Oct. 11, 1866, in Weckmann, *Carlota*, 249.

40. Reinach Foussemagne, *Charlotte*, 318; Blasio, *Maximilian*, 103.

41. Blasio, *Maximilian*, 103.

42. Haslip, *Crown of Mexico*, 423; Hyde, *Mexican Empire*, 227–228.

43. Hyde, *Mexican Empire*, 227–228.

44. M. De Suárez to Maximilian, Oct. 6, 1866, Karton 16, Maximilian Papers, OS; Hyde, *Mexican Empire*, 228.

45. Hyde, *Mexican Empire*, 228–229; Reinach Foussemagne, *Charlotte*, 318; De Suárez to Maximilian, Oct. 6, 1866, Karton 16, Maximilian Papers, OS; Joseph I. Sirven, Joseph F. Drazkowski, and Katherine H. Noe, "Seizures among Public Figures: Lessons Learned from the Epilepsy of Pope Pius IX," *Mayo Clinic Proceedings* 82 (Dec. 2007), 1535; Haslip, *Crown of Mexico*, 424; Iturriaga, *Carlota de Bélgica*, 87–88.

46. Hyde, *Mexican Empire*, 230 (quotation); Haslip, *Crown of Mexico*, 424.

47. Reinach Foussemagne, *Charlotte*, 319; Carlota to Maximilian (quotation), Pope Pius IX, Frau von Kuhachevich, Leopold II, Oct. 1, 1866, Karton 16, Maximilian Papers, OS. These letters were later cosigned by Jilek, Bombelles, and Radonetz upon their arrival from Miramar.

48. Hyde, *Mexican Empire*, 231–232.

49. Haslip, *Crown of Mexico*, 426; De Suárez to Maximilian, Oct. 6, 1866 (quotation), Karton 16, Maximilian Papers, OS; Hyde, *Mexican Empire*, 232.

50. Blasio, *Maximilian*, 104; Hyde, *Mexican Empire*, 232–233; Reinach Fousse-magne, *Charlotte*, 320 (quotations).

51. Blasio, *Maximilian*, 104–105; Iturriaga, *Carlota de Bélgica*, 90.

52. Reinach Foussemagne, *Charlotte*, 321.

53. Blasio, *Maximilian*, 105.

54. Corti, *Maximilian*, 713.

55. Blasio, *Maximilian*, 107–108; Hyde, *Mexican Empire*, 233.

56. Blasio, *Maximilian*, 107.

57. Blasio, *Maximilian*, 106 (quotations); Martin, *Maximilian in Mexico*, 250; many of these attendants had been part of the Mexican delegation that invited Maximilian and Carlota to Mexico, July 26, 1863, Karton 9; Oct. 6, 1866, Karton 16, Maximilian Papers, OS.

58. Blasio, *Maximilian*, 106 (quotations); Letters from Carlota to Karl Bouslaveck, Jacob de Kuhachevich, Antonio Suárez de Peredo, Felipe Neri del Barrio, Manuelita del Barrio, Oct. 6, 1866, Karton 16, Maximilian Papers, OS; Reinach Foussemagne, *Charlotte*, 322.

59. Blasio, *Maximilian*, 107 (quotations). Many of the imperial staff remained in Europe indefinitely. Charles Bombelles to Félix Eloin, Nov. 9, 1866, Charlotte and Maximilian Papers, WRC.

60. Ramírez traveled to Europe as the almoner. Francisco Ramírez to Maximilian, Oct. 9, 1866, Karton 40, Maximilian Papers, OS; Blasio, *Maximilian*, 108; Corti, *Maximilian*, 714 (quotation); Reinach Foussemagne, *Charlotte*, 323.

61. Blasio, *Maximilian*, 108; Haslip, *Crown of Mexico*, 429 (quotation).

62. Blasio, *Maximilian*, 105.

63. Paoli, *L'Impératrice Charlotte*, 185; Dominique Paoli, memorandum, July 7, 2009, notes in possession of the author.

Chapter 17. Getting Out of the Toils of the French

1. Paoli, *L'Impératrice Charlotte*, 201.

2. Reinach Foussemagne, *Charlotte*, 325; Corti, *Maximilian*, 729 (quotation).

3. Loizillon, *Lettres*, 404–405; Maximilian to Joaquín Degollado, Oct. 9, 1866, Degollado Papers, BLAC.

4. Maximilian to Joaquín Degollado, Oct. 9, 1866, Degollado Papers, BLAC.

5. Dávila, *Paradise*, 64; Paoli, *L'Impératrice Charlotte*, 123–124 (quotations); Maximilian to Carlota, Aug. 31, 1866, in Ratz, *Correspondencia Inédita*, 324.

6. Maximilian to Carlota, Oct. 7, 1866, Karton 16, Maximilian Collection, OS; Haslip, *Crown of Mexico*, 436 (quotation).

7. Poliakowitz was a member of the civil list and facilitated many of the needs of the royal household from Veracruz. Maximilian to Domingo Bureau, October 8, 1866, Karton 40, Maximilian Papers, OS; Basch, *Recollections of Mexico*, 28 (quotation);

Ratz, *Maximilian und Juárez*, 1: 386–387; *El Pájaro Verde*, Oct. 10, 1866; Kératry, *Rise and Fall of the Emperor Maximilian*, 190.

8. Basch, *Memories of Mexico*, 23–24 (quotations); Haslip, *Crown of Mexico*, 431–432.

9. Josef von Riedel, statement, Oct. 11, 1866, Charlotte Letters, ARP; Iturriaga, *Carlota de Bélgica*, 92; "Josef Gottfried von Riedel," in *Österreichisches Biographisches Lexicon, 1815–1950* (Wien: Österreichisches Akademie der Wissenschaften, 1988), 137–138; Hyde, *Mexican Empire*, 240; Haslip, *Crown of Mexico*, 432 (quotation); Ratz, *Maximilian*, 1: 386.

10. Maximilian to Auguste Jilek, via Augustin Fischer, Nov. 27, 1866, Jilek Papers, Frederick R. Koch Collection, Beinecke Rare Book and Manuscript Library, Yale University (hereafter cited as Koch Coll., BL, YU); Basch, *Recollections of Mexico*, 28–29 (quotations); Magnus, *El Ocaso*, 100.

11. Medical notes on condition of Carlota, Auguste Jilek, Jan. 14–27, 1867, Jilek Papers, Koch Coll., BL, YU; Corti, *Maximilian*, 715, 716 (quotation); Paoli, *Charlotte*, 180.

12. Medical notes on condition of Carlota, Auguste Jilek, Jan. 10–27, 1867, Jilek Papers, Koch Coll., BL, YU.

13. Paoli, *Charlotte*, 184–85, 188; Reinach Foussemagne, *Charlotte*, 345.

14. Maximilian to Marshal Bazaine, July 5, 1866, Bazaine Collection, HC 378/388, HSA; Maximilian to Félix Eloin, May 28, 1866, Karton 40, Maximilian Papers, OS; Terrell, *From Texas to Mexico*, 72–73; Haslip, *Crown of Mexico*, 432; William Seward to Marquis de Montholon, Aug. 16, 1866, *Message of the President of the U.S. Relating to Mexico*, 39th Cong, 2nd Sess., House Exec. Doc. 76, 558–559.

15. Former Confederate John B. Magruder delivered this message. Schroeder, *The Fall of Maximilian's Empire*, 20, 39–41; Lewis D. Campbell to William H. Seward, November 21, 1866 (quotation), *Dispatches from U.S. Ministers to Mexico, 1823–1906*, M97, Reel no. 31, NARA. See also "A Cable from Napoléon," www.cia.gov/library/center-for-the-study-of-intelligence/kent-csi/vol2no3/htmlv02i3a12p_0001.htm, accessed March 1, 2010; *New York Times*, July 13, 1867; Dabbs, *The French Army in Mexico*, 167; Hanna and Hanna, *Napoleon III and Mexico*, 297.

16. The rifled needle gun was considered indispensible by the Prussians. Loizillon, *Lettres*, 405–406; Haslip, *Crown of Mexico*, 433 (quotation); Stevenson, *Maximilian*, 222.

17. Ministry of Treasury, report, October 1866; Édouard Pierron to Maximilian, Oct. 16, 1866, Karton 16, Maximilian Papers, OS.

18. Loizillon, *Lettres*, 403–404, 407.

19. Félix Eloin to Maximilian, Oct. 1, 1866, Charlotte and Maximilian Papers, WRC; Dabbs, *The French Army in Mexico*, 186–187; Stevenson, *Maximilian*, 232–233; Blumberg, "Diplomacy of the Mexican Empire," 106, 109–110; *El Pájaro Verde*, Oct. 19, 1866.

20. Haslip, *Crown of Mexico*, 440 (quotation), 441; Mignard, *Du Pin*, 18.

21. Haslip, *Crown of Mexico*, 433; Corti, *Maximilian*, 725 (quotation); Blumberg, "Diplomacy of the Mexican Empire," 100.

22. Hubert Howe Bancroft, *The Works of Hubert Howe Bancroft*, Vol. 14, *History of Mexico* (San Francisco: The History Company, 1888), 6: 262–263 n.85; Haslip, *Crown of Mexico*, 433–434.

23. Carlota suspected that Pierron was behind the recurring suggestions urging abdication coming from the French officers. Reinach Foussemagne, *Charlotte de Belgique*, 301; Corti, *Maximilian*, 719 (quotations); Loizillon, *Lettres*, 407.

24. Kératry, *Rise and Fall of the Emperor Maximilian*, 198 (quotation), 199; Dabbs, *The French Army in Mexico*, 178–179.

25. Loizillon, *Lettres*, 406–407; Hyde, *Mexican Empire*, 238–239; Dabbs, *The French Army in Mexico*, 178–179; *New York Herald*, Sept. 15, 1866.

26. Basch, *Memories*, 13–14; *El Pájaro Verde*, Sept. 14, 17, 1866; Ratz, *Maximilian und Juárez*, 1: 385 (quotation); *L'Estafette*, Sept. 18, 1866.

27. Basch, *Memories*, 35–36; Haslip, *Crown of Mexico*, 438; Dabbs, *The French Army in Mexico*, 187; Blumberg, "Diplomacy of the Mexican Empire," 106–107; Ratz, *Maximilian und Juárez*, 1: 385–368, 357; Magnus, *El Ocaso*, 121–122.

28. Maximilian to Carlota, Oct. 7, 1866, Karton 16, Maximilian Papers, OS; Haslip, *Crown of Mexico*, 436 (first quotation); *El Pájaro Verde*, Oct. 19, 1866; Kératry, *The Rise and Fall of the Emperor Maximilian*, 200 (second quotation).

29. Blumberg, "Diplomacy of the Mexican Empire," 108, 110, 112; James Creelman, *Díaz: Master of Mexico* (New York: D. Appleton, 1911), 248–250; Hyde, *Mexican Empire*, 241; Ratz, *Maximilian und Juárez*, 1: 387.

30. Bigelow, "The Heir-Presumptive to the Imperial Crown of Mexico," 748; Josefa Iturbide to Maximilian, Oct. 27, 1866, Karton 16, Maximilian Papers, OS (quotation).

31. Agustín Cosme Iturbide to Sabina Iturbide, Oct. 25, 1867, Iturbide Papers, Georgetown University Library Special Collections.

32. Maximilian to Alice G. Iturbide, Maximilian to Josefa Iturbide, Oct. 25, 1866, Karton 16, Maximilian Papers, OS. After fleeing Mexico, Josefa Iturbide moved to Paris, where her brother reported she spent lavishly, had a butler and servants, and wore her imperial diamonds on a regular basis. Bigelow, "The Heir-Presumptive to the Imperial Crown of Mexico," 748; Agustín Cosme Iturbide to Sabina Iturbide, Oct. 25, 1867, Iturbide Papers, Georgetown University Library Special Collections.

33. Basch, *Memories*, 31. Basch calls the house "El Olindo," but the name was thought to be "El Olvido."

34. Ramón de Obregón, Pelagio A. Labastida (first quotation), Carlos María Colina, Teodosio Lares (second quotation), Oct. 18, 1866; Luis de Arroyo, Teófilo Marin, Joaquin de Mier y Terán, Ramón Tabera, Juan N. de Prida, José Mariano Campos, Oct. 19, 1866; Melchor Uriarte, Joaquín Palacios, Ladies-in-Waiting Carlota

Escandón, Dolores G. de Elguero, Francisca E. de Landa, Oct. 20, 1866; Faustino Chimalpopoca, Francisco Villanueva, Mariano Degollado, Nov. 6, 1866, to Maximilian, Karton 16, Maximilian Papers, OS; Corti, *Maximilian*, 737; Basch, *Memories*, 28, 48.

35. Maximilian described Lacunza as a despot but capitulated to him anyway. Maximilian to Félix Eloin, April 9, 1866, Charlotte and Maximilian Collection, WRC; Basch, *Memories*, 15–16; Blumberg, "Diplomacy of the Mexican Empire," 108–109.

36. Basch, *Memories*, 25; Ratz, *Tras las Huellas*, 129.

37. Maximilian to Nicolas Poliakowitz, Oct. 27 (two letters; quotation), Oct. 31, 1866; Karl Schaffer to Poliakowitz, Nov. 3, 1866, Receipt of goods, Barque *Marie*, Dec. 8, 1866, Karton 40, Maximilian Papers, OS; Blasio, *Maximilian*, 117; Ratz, *Tras las Huellas*, 129; Ratz, *Maximilian und Juárez*, 1: 387.

38. Hyde, *Mexican Empire*, 241–242.

39. Corti, *Maximilian*, 744–745 (quotation); Basch, *Memories*, 53; Hyde, *Mexican Empire*, 242; Magnus, *El Ocaso*, 128.

40. Basch, *Memories*, 40, 41 (first and second quotations), 43 (third quotations); Corti, *Maximilian*, 741.

41. Stefan Herzfeld to Maximilian, Nov. 5, 1866, as quoted in Corti, *Maximilian*, 741–742; Roeder, *Juárez*, 643–644, 655–656; Hyde, *Mexican Empire*, 240.

42. Corti, *Maximilian*, 742–743, 745; Thompson, *Cortina*, 187–189; Basch, *Memories*, 46, 52; Roeder, *Juárez*, 655–666.

43. Domenech, *Juarez et Maximilien*, 3: 407 (first quotation); Blasio, *Maximilian*, 119 (second quotation).

44. Blumberg, "Diplomacy of the Mexican Empire," 109; Corti, *Maximilian*, 746–747 (quotations).

45. Blumberg, "Diplomacy of the Mexican Empire," 109 (quotation); Ratz, *Maximilian und Juárez*, 1: 388.

46. Blumberg, "Diplomacy of the Mexican Empire," 103, 110; Corti, *Maximilian*, 747–748; Ratz, *Maximilian und Juárez*, 1: 392; Magnus, *El Ocaso*, 133.

47. Augustin Fischer to Nicolas Poliakowitz, Nov. 10, 1866, Karton 16, Maximilian Papers, OS.

48. Basch, *Memories*, 29, 46–48; Corti, *Maximilian*, 738–739, 748–749; Blumberg, "Diplomacy of the Mexican Empire," 108–109; Hyde, *Mexican Empire*, 242–243.

49. Corti, *Maximilian*, 752.

50. Domenech, *Juarez et Maximilien*, 3: 406; Roeder, *Juárez*, 644; Ratz, *Maximilian und Juárez*, 1: 388 (quotation), 392.

51. Ratz, *Maximilian und Juárez*, 1: 402–404; Domenech, *Juarez et Maximilien*, 3: 409; Elton, *With the French in Mexico*, 177–178; Hanna and Hanna, *Napoleon III*, 290–291. Four million pesos in 1866 would be equivalent to over $60 million in twenty-first century terms. McCusker, "Conversion of 1865 Piasters to Contemporary American Dollars," Aug. 24, 2009, memo in possession of the author.

52. Maximilian to José Salazar Ilarregui, Feb. 1, 1867, Salazar Ilarregui papers, HSA; Basch, *Memories*, 49–50; 54–55.

53. "I will leave, the council is convened." Basch, *Memories*, 54 (first quotation); Domenech, *Juárez et Maximilien*, 3: 409–410 (second quotation); Blasio, *Maximilian*, 117; Hyde, *Mexican Empire*, 243; Ratz, *Maximilian und Juárez*, 1: 388–389.

54. Basch, *Memories*, 50–51, 55–56, 59 (second quotation), 77; Hyde, *Mexican Empire*, 243; Blumberg, "Diplomacy of the Mexican Empire," 111; Ratz, *Maximilian und Juárez*, 1: 389–391, 392 (first quotation).

55. Maximilian to Carlota, Nov. 27, 1866, in Ratz, *Correspondencia Inédita*, 337.

Chapter 18. Liberator I Will Be

1. Domenech, *Juárez et Maximilien*, 3: 409 (first and third quotations); Haslip, *Crown of Mexico*, 448 (second quotation); Lares implored Maximilian to go out and meet the people, but knowing Maximilian's health was again suffering, forbade it. Basch, *Memories*, 59.

2. Édouard Pierron to Maximilian, Dec. 31, 1866, as quoted in Corti, *Maximilian*, 762. "Suave, mari magno, turbantibus aquora ventis, E terra, magnum alterius spectare laborem; Non quia vexari quemquam est jucunda voluptas, Sed, quibus ipse malis careas, quia cernera suave est." Curiously, Lucretius counseled overcoming the fear of death. Basch, *Memories*, 57–58.

3. Maximilian to Félix Eloin, May 28, 1866, Karton 40, Maximilian Papers, OS; Hanna and Hanna, *Napoleon III*, 292; Dabbs, *The French Army in Mexico*, 199–200.

4. Achille Bazaine to François Castelnau, Jan. 25, March 1, 1867, *État-Major général correspondance avec le Ministre*, SHD; Domenech, *Juárez et Maximilien*, 3: 410; Hyde, *Mexican Empire*, 244; Corti, *Maximilian*, 758; Dabbs, *The French Army in Mexico*, 206.

5. Domenech, *Juárez et Maximilien*, 3: 412; Félix zu Salm-Salm, *My Diary in Mexico* (London: Richard Bentley, 1868), 269–270 (quotation); Corti, *Maximilian*, 758–759, 764.

6. U. S. Grant declined President Andrew Johnson's request that he go to Mexico, citing that he would be sent without a security detail into lands where Confederates had fled. Grant believed Johnson wanted to replace him with Gen. Sherman as secretary of war by sending him on an expedition. William T. Sherman, *Memoirs of William Tecumseh Sherman* (New York: D. Appleton, 1887), 2: 413; Sherman, *Memoirs of William Tecumseh Sherman* (New York: Library of America, 1990), 906; Franklin Chase to Matías Romero, Dec. 8, 1866, Romero Collection, BLAC; Stevenson, *Maximilian in Mexico*, 247–248; Seward, *Seward at Washington*, 362–363.

7. Casdorph, *Prince John Magruder*, 307–308; Sherman, *Memoirs of W. T. Sherman*, 906–908 (quotation); Franklin Chase to Matías Romero, Dec. 8, 1866, Romero Collection, BLAC.

8. Joseph Audenried to Mary Colket Audenried, Nov. 30 (quotation), Dec. 4, 7, 1866, Nau Collection; Stevenson, *Maximilian in Mexico*, 247–248; Sherman, *Memoirs*, 2: 418–420.

9. Lewis D. Campbell to William H. Seward, December 24, 1866, Dispatches from U.S. Ministers to Mexico, 1823–1906, Roll 31, NACP; Sherman, *Memoirs*, 2: 418 (quotation). Franklin Chase termed this sentiment Maximilian's "freak" inspiration, causing him to abandon his butterfly catching. Franklin Chase to Matías Romero, Dec. 8, 1866, Romero Collection, BLAC.

10. Joseph Audenried to Mary Colket Audenried, Nov. 30, Dec. 4, 7, 1866, Nau Collection; Stevenson, *Maximilian in Mexico*, 247–248; Sherman, *Memoirs of W. T. Sherman*, 906–908; Hanna and Hanna, *Napoleon III and Mexico*, 287.

11. Joseph Audenried to Mary Colket Audenried, Dec. 15, 1866, Nau Collection (first and second quotations); Sherman, *Memoirs*, 2: 418–420; W. T. Sherman to John Sherman, Nov. 7 [*sic*], 1866, in Sherman, *Sherman Letters*, 284 (third quotation); Casdorph, *Prince John Magruder*, 307–308.

12. Martin, *Maximilian in Mexico*, 7 (quotation); Rister, *Carlota*, 48.

13. Rolle, *The Lost Cause*, 111–112; O'Flaherty, *General Jo Shelby*, 302–307, 309–310; *Mexican Times*, (Mexico City), Nov. 19, 1866; Blumberg, "Diplomacy of the Mexican Empire," 112.

14. Galliffet ultimately led the 3rd Corps d'Afrique at the end of the Mexican expedition. He later achieved international fame in helping to suppress the Paris Commune in 1871, earning him the nickname "Red Marshal." Jules de Saint-Sauveur, *Les Derniers Jours de la Contre-Guérrilla au Mexique* (hereafter cited as *The Last Days of the Counterguerrilla*), Unpublished report, Maximilian, Emperor of Mexico Papers, UASC, 1–2 (quotation), Maximilian Papers, UASC; Mignard, *Du Pin*, 17; Ridley, *Maximilian and Juárez*, 128. The Belgians embarked on Jan. 20 and the Austrians on Jan. 21. Dabbs, *French Army*, 206, 215.

15. Saint-Sauveur, *The Last Days of the Counterguerrilla*, 3, Maximilian Papers, UASC.

16. Saint-Sauveur, *Last Days*, 3, Maximilian Papers, UASC.

17. Corti, *Maximilian*, 763.

18. Correspondencia de la Legación Mexicana en Washington durante la Intervención Extranjera, 1860–1868 (Mexico: Imprenta del Gobierno, 1885), 9: 614; Hanna and Hanna, *Napoleon III and Mexico*, 291–292, 292.

19. Hanna and Hanna, *Napoleon III and Mexico*, 292, 293 (quotation).

20. Dabbs, *French Army*, 195–197; Magnus, *El Ocaso*, 65.

21. Knechtel, *Las Memorias del Jardinero*, 188; Saint-Sauveur, *The Last Days of the Counterguerrilla*, 4, Maximilian Papers, UASC; Basch, *Memories*, 82–83; Hanna and Hanna, *Napoleon III and Mexico*, 293.

22. Saint-Sauveur, *The Last Days of the Counterguerrilla*, 4 (quotation), Maximilian Papers, UASC; Basch, *Memories*, 82; Dabbs, *The French Army*, 211.

23. Juan Nepomuceno Pereda to Maximilian (or Teodosio Lares), Dec. 22, 1866, Karton 16, Maximilian Papers, OS; Hanna and Hanna, *Napoleon III and Mexico,* 290.

24. Dabbs, *French Army,* 210–211; Blasio, *Maximilian,* 123, 127.

25. Blumberg, "Diplomacy of the Mexican Empire," 122; Hanna and Hanna, *Napoleon III and Mexico,* 285, 296; Bancroft, *Works of Hubert Howe Bancroft,* Vol. 14, *History of Mexico,* 269–270; Kératry, *Rise and Fall of the Emperor Maximilian,* 273 (quotation), 291; Haslip, *Crown of Mexico,* 457–458. Because the guards caught two men thought to be Liberal spies at the hacienda, for Maximilian's safety, they moved from La Teja back to the National Palace. Hyde, *Mexican Empire,* 248–249.

26. Juan N. de Pereda, undersecretary of the ministry, business report, Jan. 29, 1867, Karton 40, Maximilian Papers, OS; Basch, *Memories,* 84–85; Hyde, *Mexican Empire,* 248.

27. Ratz, *Maximilian und Juárez,* 1: 393–397.

28. Augustin Fischer, Inventory, Feb. 27, 1866–Feb. 1867, Fischer papers, HSA; Maximilian to José Salazar Ilarregui, Feb. 1, 1867, Salazar Ilarregui Papers, HSA; *New York Times,* Jan. 17, 1867; Ratz, *Maximilian und Juárez,* 1: 396.

29. Corti, *Maximilian,* 764; Hyde, *Mexican Empire,* 249–251; Kératry, *Rise and Fall of the Emperor Maximilian,* 294–295.

30. Blumberg, "Diplomacy of the Mexican Empire," 122 (quotation); Corti, *Maximilian,* 768–769; Haslip, *Crown of Mexico,* 458; Magnus, *El Ocaso,* 161.

31. Bazaine sold the coach that used to belong to Antonio López Santa Anna, which not even Juárez confiscated, Maximilian wrote in disgust to Stefan Herzfeld. Basch, *Memories,* 89–90, 143; Maximilian to José Salazar Ilarregui, Feb. 12, 1867, Salazar Ilarregui Papers, HSA; Masseras, *Un Essai d'Empire au Mexique,* 151–152; Salm-Salm, *Ten Years,* 170; Roeder, *Juárez,* 656.

32. Masseras, *Un Essai d'Empire au Mexique,* 157.

33. Maximilian to José Salazar Ilarregui, Feb. 12, 1867 (first and second quotations), Salazar Ilarregui Papers, HSA; Masseras, *Un Essai,* 155 (third quotation), 156 n.1.

34. Masseras, *Un Essai,* 151–152; Maximilian to José Salazar Ilarregui, Feb. 12, 1867 (quotations), Salazar Ilarregui Papers, HSA; Magnus, *El Ocaso,* 161.

35. Corti, *Maximilian,* 770 (first quotation); Maximilian to Carlota, Dec. 25, 1866, in Ratz, *Correspondencia Inédita,* 338 (second quotation).

36. Corti, *Maximilian,* 771–772.

37. Corti, *Maximilian,* 769; Hyde, *Mexican Empire,* 250; Bancroft, *Works of Hubert Howe Bancroft,* Vol. 14, *History of Mexico,* 263, 271–273; Elton, *With the French in Mexico,* 185.

38. Smart, *Viva Juárez,* 371; Roeder, *Juárez,* 663; Corti, *Maximilian,* 769; Hyde, *Mexican Empire,* 251. The customs house at Mazatlán took in nearly $100,000 annually. *El Pájaro Verde,* Sept. 18, 1867.

39. Masseras, *Un Essai,* 159; Smart, *Viva Juárez,* 371–372 (quotation); Benito

Juárez, *Documentos, Discursos y Correspondencia* (Mexico: Editorial Libros de México, 1972–1975), 11: 800.

40. Smart, *Viva Juárez*, 371–372 (quotations); Miller, "Arms across the Border," 39.

41. Smart, *Viva Juárez*, 372.

42. Masseras, *Un Essai*, 159; Corti, *Maximilian*, 770, 772–773; Haslip, *Crown of Mexico*, 459.

43. Salm-Salm, *My Diary in Mexico*, 36–37.

44. Masseras, *Un Essai*, 162 (quotations); Salm-Salm, *My Diary in Mexico*, 35; Haslip, *Crown of Mexico*, 493; Ratz, *Maximilian und Juárez*, 1: 399.

45. Masseras, *Un Essai*, 167 (quotation), 168–169; Ratz, *Maximilian und Juárez*, 1: 400.

46. On February 11 Maximilian, via his envoy M. E. Burnouf, approached Díaz about taking command of the imperial forces at Mexico City and Puebla. This would have removed Lares and Márquez from power, leaving the capitals in the hands of the Republicans. Masseras, *Un Essai*, 173–174 (first quotation); Kératry, *The Rise and Fall of the Emperor Maximilian*, 284; Hanna and Hanna, *Napoleon III and Mexico*, 295 (second quotation); Magnus, *El Ocaso*, 166, 169.

47. Masseras, *Un Essai*, 171, 173–174; Corti, *Maximilian*, 775; Blasio, *Maximilian*, 129; Basch, *Recollections of Mexico*, 104, Martin, *Maximilian*, 304; Ratz, *Maximilian und Juárez*, 1: 401.

48. Roeder, *Juárez*, 664; Ratz, *Maximilian und Juárez*, 1: 402–403.

49. Dano had stayed behind in Mexico to serve Maximilian and lamented that Maximilian would not go. "In a few days, this chance will be out of the question," he wrote Bazaine. Kératry, *Rise and Fall of the Emperor Maximilian*, 298. Jacques Randon to Achille Bazaine, Jan. 15, 1867, Bazaine Papers, García Collection, BLAC; Masseras, *Un Essai*, 153; Hyde, *Mexican Empire*, 251–252; Dabbs, *French Army*, 213–215.

50. Blumberg, "Diplomacy of the Mexican Empire," 123; Corti, *Maximilian*, 781.

Chapter 19. *War Is War*

1. Corti, *Maximilian*, 780.

2. Achille Bazaine to Intendant, Aug. 19, 1865, no. 9, Achille Bazaine to Engineering, Sept. 20, 1865, no. 12, *Corps Expéditionnaire: Correspondance Confidentielle*, 13/7 au 29/9/1865, SHD; Basch, *Memories*, 90–91; Hyde, *Mexican Empire*, 252; Smart, *Viva Juárez*, 376 (quotation); Basch, *Recollections of Mexico*, 103; Ratz, *Maximilian und Juárez*, 1: 400; Hanna and Hanna, *Napoleon III and Mexico*, 299.

3. Carlos Sánchez Navarro, *Tres Cartas Inéditas del Emperador Maximiliano* (Mexico City: Biblioteca Aportación Histórica, Vargas Rea, 1944), 19–24; Domenech, *Juarez et Maximilien*, 3: 412; Blasio, *Maximilian*, 109, 128 (quotation), 137; Dabbs, *The French Army*, 198.

4. Juárez, *Documentos*, 11: 799–800; Blasio, *Maximilian*, 130–131; Pitner, *Maxi-*

milian's Lieutenant, 178. A tertulia could be a dance or a party as well as an artistic presentation. Salm-Salm, *Ten Years*, 225.

5. Blasio, *Maximilian*, 130 (quotation), 131; Basch, *Recollections of Mexico*, 110.

6. Blasio, *Maximilian*, 131.

7. Salm-Salm, *My Diary in Mexico*, 25–26 (quotations); Haslip, *Crown of Mexico*, 465–466.

8. Agnes's father was William Leclerc Joy. David Coffey, *Soldier Princess: The Life and Legend of Agnes Salm-Salm in North America, 1861– 1867* (College Station: Texas A&M University Press, 2002); Haslip, *Crown of Mexico*, 465 (quotation), 466; Salm-Salm, *Ten Years*, 167.

9. Blasio, *Maximilian*, 132.

10. Blasio, *Maximilian*, 133 (quotation); Basch, *Memories*, 99–101.

11. Blasio, *Maximilian*, 134 (quotations); Basch, *Memories*, 101; Elton, *With the French in Mexico*, 185.

12. Magnus, *El Ocaso*, 258–259; Salm-Salm, *Ten Years*, 281 (quotation); Basch, *Memories*, 102. The town's aqueduct was known as Acueducto de Urrutia. Figueroa Domenech, *Guía general descriptiva de la República Mexicana* (Mexico: R. de s.n. Araluce, 1899), 524.

13. Maximilian to José Salazar Ilarregui, Feb. 12, 1867, Salazar Ilarregui papers, HSA; Salm-Salm, *Ten Years*, 281; Blasio, *Maximilian*, 135 (quotation); Salm-Salm, *My Diary in Mexico*, 33, 46; Basch, *Memories*, 102.

14. Blasio, *Maximilian*, 135; Salm-Salm, *My Diary in Mexico*, 34; Basch, *Memories*, 103; Maximilian to José Salazar Ilarregui, Feb. 12, 1867, Salazar Ilarregui Papers, HSA.

15. Maximilian to Félix Eloin, Feb. 23, 1867, Charlotte and Maximilian Papers, WRC; Blasio, *Maximilian*, 136; Salm-Salm, *My Diary in Mexico*, 41–42, 44; Basch, *Memories*, 104.

16. Hamnett, *Juárez*, 187.

17. Corti, *Maximilian*, 783–784.

18. Blasio, *Maximilian*, 137 (first quotation); Ratz, *Maximiliano und Juárez*, 2: 48–49 (second quotation).

19. Roeder, *Juárez*, 664; Blasio, *Maximilian*, 137–138. For more information on forced loans, see Amberson, *I Would Rather Sleep in Texas*, 192–193.

20. Hamnett, *Juárez*, 187–188; Haslip, *Crown of Mexico*, 468–469 (quotation); Ratz, *Maximilian und Juárez*, 2: 40.

21. Basch, *Memories*, 89 (quotations); Dabbs, *The French Army*, 212 n.132, 215–216; Charles Du Pin to Achille Bazaine, Feb. 19, 23, 1867, Jacques Randon to Achille Bazaine, Jan. 15, 1867, Bazaine Papers, García Collection, BLAC; Corti, *Maximilian*, 776; Joseph Audenried to Mary Colket Audenried, Dec. 4, 1866, Nau Collection; Magnus, *El Ocaso*, 171.

22. Kératry, *Rise and Fall of the Emperor Maximilian*, 300; Dabbs, *French Army*, 216, 274.

23. Juárez, *Documentos*, 11: 883–884; Corti, *Maximilian*, 786; Blasio, *Maximilian*, 140–141; Thompson, *Cortina*, 191; Basch, *Memories*, 118.

24. Blasio, *Maximilian*, 140–141.

25. Blasio, *Maximilian*, 142 (quotation); Magnus, *El Ocaso*, 260, 269.

26. Blasio, *Maximilian*, 142.

27. Salm-Salm, *My Diary in Mexico*, 127 (first quotation); Blasio, *Maximilian*, 144 (second quotation); Juárez, *Documentos*, 11: 885.

28. Salm-Salm, *My Diary in Mexico*, 53.

29. Salm-Salm, *My Diary in Mexico*, 54; Blasio, *Maximilian*, 143.

30. Blasio, *Maximilian*, 145.

31. Salm-Salm, *My Diary in Mexico*, 62 (quotation); Basch, *Memories*, 128, 130.

32. Basch, *Recollections*, 143–144.

33. Salm-Salm, *My Diary in Mexico*, 67–68; Basch, *Memories*, 130.

34. Mariano Escobedo to Benito Juárez, March 25, 26, 1867, in Juárez, *Documentos*, 11: 885–887; Corti, *Maximilian*, 787; Basch, *Memories*, 130.

35. Salm-Salm, *My Diary in Mexico*, 70.

36. Haslip, *Crown of Mexico*, 469; Salm-Salm, *My Diary in Mexico*, 71–72 (first and second quotations); Magnus, *El Ocaso*, 266–267 (third quotation).

37. Corti, *Maximilian*, 787–788.

38. Corti, *Maximilian*, 789–790; Blasio, *Maximilian*, 146–147; Blumberg, "Diplomacy of the Mexican Empire," 124.

39. Maximilian to Félix Eloin, March 21, 1867, Charlotte and Maximilian Papers, WRC; Basch, *Memories*, 135–136; Ratz, *Maximilian und Juárez*, 2: 87 (quotation).

40. Maximilian to Félix Eloin, March 21, 1867 (quotation), Charlotte and Maximilian Papers, WRC; Basch, *Memories*, 135–137; Blasio, *Maximilian*, 146–147; Blumberg, "Diplomacy of the Mexican Empire," 125; Bancroft, *History of Mexico*, 14: 334.

41. Corti, *Maximilian*, 790 (quotation), 791; Blasio, *Maximilian*, 147; Ratz, *Maximilian und Juárez*, 2: 89.

Chapter 20. The Enemy Is Here

1. Blumberg, "Diplomacy of the Mexican Empire," 125; Salm-Salm, *Ten Years*, 171–172 (quotation); Magnus, *El Ocaso*, 186.

2. Salm-Salm, *Ten Years*, 121; Corti, *Maximilian*, 791.

3. Blasio, *Maximilian*, 147–148.

4. Blasio, *Maximilian*, 149.

5. Ferdinand Wydenbruck to William Seward, April 6, 1867, *Letter of the Secretary of War*, Sen. Ex. Doc, no. 1, 40th Congress, 1st Sess., 57.

6. William Seward to Lewis D. Campbell, April 6, 1867, *Letter of the Secretary of War*, Sen. Ex. Doc, no. 1, 40th Congress, 1st Sess., 58; Seward, *Seward at Washington*, 364 (quotation).

7. Matías Romero to Sebastián Lerdo de Tejada, April 6, 1867, in Juárez, *Documentos*, 11: 929; Lewis D. Campbell to Sebastián Lerdo de Tejada, April 6, 1867, in Juárez, *Documentos*, 9: 931–932; Seward, *Seward at Washington*, 364–365; Haslip, *Crown of Mexico*, 479–480.

8. Seward, *Seward at Washington*, 364 (quotation); Magnus, *El Ocaso*, 213.

9. Roeder, *Juárez*, 656–657 (quotation); Corti, *Maximilian*, 776; Guedalla, *Two Marshals*, 127.

10. Hamnett, *Juarez*, 188–189 (first and third quotations); Smart, *Viva Juárez*, 382 (second quotation).

11. Magnus, *El Ocaso*, 267; Blasio, *Maximilian*, 148.

12. Blasio, *Maximilian*, 149.

13. Blasio, *Maximilian*, 149, 150 (quotation); Basch, *Memories*, 145.

14. Ratz, *Maximilian und Juárez*, 2: 86 (quotation); Corti, *Maximilian*, 794.

15. Hyde, *Mexican Empire*, 255; Ridley, *Maximilian and Juárez*, 260–261; Haslip, *Crown of Mexico*, 472–473.

16. Agustín C. Iturbide to Salina de Iturbide, Oct. 25, 1867, Iturbide Papers, Georgetown University Library, SC; Ridley, *Maximilian and Juárez*, 260 (quotation); Corti, *Maximilian*, 796.

17. Salm-Salm, *Ten Years*, 172–173; Ridley, *Maximilian and Juárez*, 260.

18. Porfirio Díaz to Matías Romero, May 3, 1867, in Juárez, *Documentos*, 11: 923; Salm-Salm; *Ten Years*, 172–173; Creelman, *Díaz*, 273–274 (quotation); Miller, "Arms across the Border," 40–41; *New York Herald*, May 24, 1867; Ámparo Gómez Tepexicuapan to M. M. McAllen, Interview at Chapultepec Palace, Oct. 17, 2009. Notes in possession of the author.

19. Salm-Salm, *My Diary in Mexico*, 146; Haslip, *Crown of Mexico*, 485; Smart, *Viva Juárez*, 382; Creelman, *Díaz*, 272–273; John C. C. Hill to James L. Hill, April 21, 1867, George A. Hill Jr. Collection, MC086, Herzstein Library, San Jacinto Museum, La Porte, Texas.

20. George W. Clark to Otilia Jordan de Degollado, April 16, May 6, 1867, personal collection of the author.

21. John C. C. Hill to James L. Hill, April 21, 1867, George A. Hill Jr. Collection, MC086.

22. Masseras, *Un Essai d'Empire*, 240; Salm-Salm, *My Diary in Mexico*, 119–120 (quotation); Basch, *Memories*, 146; Hyde, *Mexican Empire*, 255; Ridley, *Maximilian and Juárez*, 261; *New York Herald*, June 18, 1867; Magnus, *El Ocaso*, 173.

23. Salm-Salm, *My Diary in Mexico*, 121–122, 126–130; Blasio, *Maximilian*, 150; Pitner, *Maximilian's Lieutenant*, 175 (quotation). On April 10 Maximilian held a brief commemoration of his ascension to the Mexican throne by his signing of the Treaty of Miramar. Basch, *Memories*, 149–150.

24. *New York Herald*, June 18, 1867; Blasio, *Maximilian*, 150; Salm-Salm, *My Diary in Mexico*, 119, 122; Basch, *Memories*, 146.

25. Salm-Salm, *My Diary in Mexico*, 102–103.

26. Smart, *Viva Juárez*, 377; Hyde, *Mexican Empire*, 264–265.

27. Salm-Salm, *My Diary in Mexico*, 153–155.

28. Mariano Escobedo to Porfirio Díaz, April 28, 1867, Benito Juárez Papers, 1849–1872, BLAC; Blasio, *Maximilian*, 154; Masseras, *Un Essai d'Empire*, 239–240; Salm-Salm, *My Diary in Mexico*, 167–169, 170.

29. Blasio, *Maximilian*, 153–154; Masseras, *Un Essai d'Empire*, 240; Salm-Salm, *My Diary*, 171–175, 173 (quotation); Basch, *Memories*, 164, 164 n., 165; Corti, *Maximilian*, 798.

30. Salm-Salm, *My Diary in Mexico*, 174–175, 184; Corti, *Maximilian*, 798.

31. Salm-Salm, *My Diary in Mexico*, 178.

32. Salm-Salm, *My Diary in Mexico*, 174–175, 185–187; Haslip, *Crown of Mexico*, 4; Masseras, *Un Essai d'Empire*, 240–241, 244.

33. Salm-Salm, *My Diary in Mexico*, 190–191.

34. Blasio, *Maximilian*, 160–161 (quotations). López attempted to defend himself later and was not prosecuted. Jablonski is also spelled as Yablonski. Angel Pola, ed., *Los Traidores Pintados por si mismos: Libro Secreto de Maximiliano* (Mexico: Biblioteca Reformista, Imprenta de Eduardo Dublán, 1990), 193 n.1; Basch, *Memories*, 176–177.

35. Salm-Salm, *My Diary in Mexico*, 192–193.

36. Salm-Salm, *My Diary in Mexico*, 192, 193 (quotations); Hans, *Querétaro*, 289.

37. Salm-Salm, *My Diary in Mexico*, 192–193; Hans, *Querétaro*, 289.

38. Salm-Salm, *My Diary in Mexico*, 193–194.

39. Basch, *Memories*, 177.

40. Salm-Salm, *My Diary in Mexico*, 193–194; Blasio, *Maximilian*, 159–160; Ratz, *Tras las Huellas*, 172–173; Conrado Hernández López, "Querétaro en 1867 y la División en la Historia (sobre una carta enviada por Silverio Ramírez a Tomás Mejía el 10 de Abril de 1867)," *Historia Mexicano* 57 (Abril–Junio 2008), 1206–1207, 1211–1212.

41. Blasio, *Maximilian*, 159 (quotation), 160; Masseras, *Un Essai d'Empire*, 244–246.

42. Basch, *Memories*, 175–176, 181; Blasio, *Maximilian*, 161; Pitner, *Maximilian's Lieutenant*, 183.

43. Some accounts state that López went to deal with Escobedo with Maximilian's blessings. Juárez, *Documentos*, 11: 964–966; Pola, *Los Traidores Pintados por si mismos*, 185–188; Masseras, *Un Essai d'Empire*, 244–245; Corti, *Maximilian*, 801.

44. Hans, *Querétaro*, 287–288; Masseras, *Un Essai d'Empire*, 247.

45. Salm-Salm, *My Diary in Mexico*, 194 (quotation); Ratz, *Maximilian und Juárez*, 2: 51.

46. Salm-Salm, *My Diary in Mexico*, 195 (quotation); Blasio, *Maximilian*, 163; Pitner, *Maximilian's Lieutenant*, 178.

47. Salm-Salm, *My Diary in Mexico* (quotation), 195, 196; Haslip, *Crown of Mexico*, 476–477; Hans, *Querétaro*, 293; Pitner, *Maximilian's Lieutenant*, 178

48. Hans, *Querétaro*, 295–296 (first and second quotations); Haslip, *Crown of Mexico*, 476–477 (fourth quotation); Basch, *Memories*, 180 (third quotation).

49. Blasio, *Maximilian*, 164; Ernst Schmit Ritter von Tavera, *Geschichte der Regierung des Kaisers Maximilian I und die Französische Intervention in Mexiko, 1861–1867* (Wien und Leipzig: Wilhelm Braumüller, 1903), 372; Corti, *Maximilian*, 803–804 (quotation).

50. Schmit Ritter von Tavera, *Kaisers Maximilian*, 372 (quotation), 373; Ramón Corona to Benito Juárez, May 15, 1867, in Juárez, *Documentos*, 11: 991–992; Corti, *Maximilian*, 804.

51. Juan de Dios Arias to Pedro Santacilia, May 15, 1867, in Juárez, *Documentos*, 11: 962, 966, 1003–1004 (quotation); *New York Times*, June 11, 1867 (second quotation); Blasio, *Maximilian*, 164–165; Schmit Ritter von Tavera, *Kaisers Maximilian*, 372–373.

52. Benito Juárez to Felipe Berriozabal, May 15, 1867, *Letter of the Secretary of War*, Sen. Ex. Doc, no. 1, 40th Congress, 1st Sess., 61 (quotation); Schmit Ritter von Tavera, *Kaisers Maximilian*, 373.

Chapter 21. I Have Cared for You All

1. The legend holds that a friar named Margil planted his walking stick, which grew into a tree that produced branches in the shape of a crucifix. The Hapsburgs were obsessed by the thorns of the crown of Jesus and in their private collections held relics of what were believed to be remnants descended through the family. "Thorn from crown of Jesus," Hofburg Museum Catalog, Vienna, Austria. Also see www.las cronicasdelviejo.blogspot.com/2008/03, accessed Nov. 9, 2009. This plant, classified in the eighteenth century, is *Gleditsia triacanthos*, the honey locust, which is common to northern Mexico (Chihuahua and Coahuila). It is considered holy for the thorns that often form a spine-tipped cross. This specimen was likely transplanted from northern Mexico to Querétaro. Tom Wendt, Curator of Plant Resources, University of Texas at Austin, memorandum on cross-tipped thorn shrubs of Mexico specifically at Convento de la Cruz, Querétaro, 11 Jan. 2009, 10 May 2011, in possession of the author.

2. Basch, *Memories*, 181 (quotation); Blasio, *Maximilian*, 164–165; Schmit Ritter von Tavera, *Regierung des Kaisers Maximilian*, 372; Hans, *Querétaro*, 301–302.

3. Hans, *Querétaro*, 299, 301, 302 (quotation), 307.

4. Blasio, *Maximilian*, 164–165; Schmit Ritter von Tavera, *Kaisers Maximilian*, 372; Hans, *Querétaro*, 301–302.

5. During the final days of siege, the camp cook informed Maximilian that the men were rejecting horse meat. To set an example, Maximilian ate the meat, although rotten, and he developed food poisoning. Schmit Ritter von Tavera, *Kaisers Maximilian*, 374. Basch, *Memories*, 181 (quotation); Blasio, *Maximilian*, 165–164, 169.

6. Haslip, *Crown of Mexico*, 482.

7. Corti, *Maximilian*, 804–805.

8. Blasio, *Maximilian*, 167 (quotation), 169; Schmit Ritter von Tavera, *Kaisers Maximilian*, 375; Basch, *Memories*, 181; Mariano Escobedo to Benito Juárez, May 13, 1867, Juárez Papers, BLAC.

9. Basch, *Memories*, 180–181 (first quotation), 182; Blasio, *Maximilian*, 167 (second and third quotations); Schmit Ritter von Tavera, *Kaisers Maximilian*, 374.

10. Hamnett, *Juárez*, 188.

11. Blasio, *Maximilian*, 165; Hans, *Querétaro*, 309, 311–312, 313 (quotation); Pitner, *Maximilian's Lieutenant*, 179; Schmit Ritter von Tavera, *Kaisers Maximilian*, 376.

12. Basch, *Memories*, 181; Salm-Salm, *My Diary in Mexico*, 226 (quotation); S. Lerdo de Tejada to Mariano Escobedo, June 3, 1867, Romero Collection, BLAC.

13. Blasio, *Maximilian*, 168; Salm-Salm, *My Diary in Mexico*, 178–179; Schmit Ritter von Tavera, *Kaisers Maximilian*, 375.

14. Blasio, *Maximilian*, 168 (quotation); Salm-Salm, *Ten Years*, 190.

15. Agnes Salm-Salm, *Ten Years*, 185 (quotation); Magnus, *El Ocaso*, 209.

16. Haslip, *Crown of Mexico*, 481; Salm-Salm, *Ten Years,* 187 (quotation).

17. Haslip, *Crown of Mexico*, 481; Salm-Salm, *Ten Years*, 188–189 (quotations).

18. Hans, *Querétaro*, 315–316 (quotation); Blasio, *Maximilian*, 170; Schmit Ritter von Tavera, *Kaisers Maximilian*, 378.

19. Blasio, *Maximilian*, 170.

20. Salm-Salm, *Ten Years*, 190–191.

21. Mariano Escobedo to Benito Juárez, May 22, 1867, Juárez Papers, BLAC; Corti, *Maximilian*, 807; Salm-Salm, *Ten Years*, 191–192.

22. Salm-Salm, *Ten Years*, 191–192.

23. When Salm-Salm and an aide to Escobedo negotiated and wrote up these terms, Maximilian said, "Do it in an honorable manner; it is preferable to die than to humiliate oneself." Schmit Ritter von Tavera, *Kaisers Maximilian*, 379; Blasio, *Maximilian*, 172; Corti, *Maximilian*, 807.

24. Salm-Salm, *Ten Years*, 192–193.

25. William Seward to Ferdinand Wydenbruck, July 11, 1867, Romero Collection, BLAC; Seward, *Seward at Washington*, 364–365; Ferdinand Wydenbruck to William Seward, June 17, 1867, *Letter of the Secretary of War*, Sen. Ex. Doc, no. 1, 40th Congress, 1st Sess., 62; Haslip, *Crown of Mexico*, 478, 480.

26. Correspondencia de la Legación, 9: 612; Hamnett, *Juárez*, 188; Haslip, *Crown of Mexico*, 484; Seward, *Seward at Washington*, 365 (quotation).

27. Brian Hamnett, "La Ejecución del Emperador Maximiliano de Habsburgo," 237–238; Verónica Zárate Toscano, "Los Testamentos de los Presidentes del Siglo XIX," 261, both found in Luis Jáuregui and José Antonio Serrano Ortega, *Historia y Nación, II, Política y diplomacia en el siglo XIX mexicano* (Mexico City: El Colegio de México, 1998); Haslip, *Crown of Mexico*, 484; Mariano Riva Palacio to Rafael Martínez de la Torre, July 1867, in *Documentos Relativos*, 57.

28. Basch, *Memories*, 194; Blasio, *Maximilian*, 172; Salm-Salm, *Ten Years*, 193 (quotation); Pitner, *Maximilian's Lieutenant*, 181.

29. Blasio, *Maximilian*, 172; Salm-Salm, *Ten Years*, 193; Basch, *Memories*, 194 (quotations); Salm-Salm, *My Diary in Mexico*, 227; Schmit Ritter von Tavera, *Kaisers Maximilian*, 381. Revolutionary writer Cesare Cantù was a political ally and friend of Maximilian's in Italy and corresponded regularly with the sovereigns. Ratz, *Correspondencia Inédita*, 279.

30. Basch, *Memories of Mexico*, 194.

31. Salm-Salm, *My Diary in Mexico*, 227–228, 248 (first quotation); Blasio, *Maximilian*, 172–173 (second quotation); Pitner, *Maximilian's Lieutenant*, 181.

32. Basch, *Memories of Mexico*, 197.

33. Salm-Salm, *My Diary in Mexico*, 228 (first and second quotations); Basch, *Memories of Mexico*, 197 (third quotation); Coffey, *Soldier Princess*, 71.

34. Report by Baron Anton von Magnus, Aug. 19, 1867, in Corti, *Maximilian*, 808–809 (quotation); Juárez, *Documentos*, 11: 964; Ratz, *Tras las Huellas*, 177; Magnus, *El Ocaso*, 203.

35. Benito Juárez and S. Lerdo de Tejada, "Magnanimidad y Justicia," February 1867 (quotation), Romero Collection, BLAC; Hamnett, "La Ejecución del Emperador Maximiliano de Habsburgo," in Jáuregui and Serrano Ortega, *Historia y Nación*, 2: 236–237; Hall, *Mexico and Maximilian*, 213–215; Fowler, *Santa Anna of Mexico*, 3; Corti, *Maximilian*, 809; Basch, *Memories*, 190; Salm-Salm, *My Diary in Mexico*, 230.

36. Anton von Magnus to S. Lerdo de Tejada, June 2, 1867, Romero Collection, BLAC; Haslip, *Crown of Mexico*, 486; Lord Acton, *Historical Essays*, 168; *New York Herald*, June, 10, 1867. An alternate spelling of Hooricks is "Hoorikx" in Magnus, *El Ocaso*, 212.

37. Salm-Salm, *Ten Years*, 194–196 (quotations), 299; Basch, *Memories*, 195; Salm-Salm, *My Diary in Mexico*, 227, 231; *New York Times*, June 11, 1867.

38. Salm-Salm, *Ten Years*, 197.

39. Salm-Salm, *Ten Years*, 198.

40. Salm-Salm, *Ten Years*, 198–199 (quotation); Coffey, *Soldier Princess*, 70.

41. Corti, *Maximilian*, 808–809, 813; Haslip, *Crown of Mexico*, 486; Basch, *Memories of Mexico*, 193, Salm-Salm, *My Diary in Mexico*, 228; *New York Times*, July 16, 1867.

42. Salm-Salm, *My Diary in Mexico*, 231–232 (quotation), 233.

43. Salm-Salm, *My Diary in Mexico*, 238, 239 (quotation), 240, 244–245, 248–249; *New York Times*, June 11, 14, 1867.

44. Basch, *Memories of Mexico*, 196, 200–201, 203–204; Haslip, *Crown of Mexico*, 489–490 (first quotation); Salm-Salm, *Ten Years*, 204; Salm-Salm, *My Diary in Mexico*, 235; Magnus, *El Ocaso*, 203, 205 (second quotation), 211.

45. Magnus, *El Ocaso*, 206.

46. Haslip, *Crown of Mexico*, 490.

47. Hall, *Mexico and Maximilian*, 203.

48. Hall, *Mexico and Maximilian*, 203–204.

49. Hall, *Mexico and Maximilian*, (quotations) 204; Henry Wheaton, *History of the Law of Nations in Europe and America from the Earliest Times to the Treaty of Washington* (New York: Gould, Banks & Co.), iii–iv.

50. Hall, *Mexico and Maximilian*, 205–206.

51. Blasio, *Maximilian*, 173; Basch, *Memories*, 203; *La Sombra de Arteaga*, June 13, 1867; Hall, *Mexico and Maximilian*, 207 (quotation).

52. Salm-Salm, *My Diary in Mexico*, 253–255; Hall, *Mexico and Maximilian*, 208; Basch, *Memories*, 204 (quotation). According to Magnus, the Mexican Liberal army did not know the practice of changing the guard. Magnus, *El Ocaso*, 207.

53. Hall, *Mexico and Maximilian*, 217–223; Basch, *Memories of Mexico*, 196 (quotation); Haslip, *Crown of Mexico*, 489.

54. Hall, *Mexico and Maximilian*, 214–215.

55. Basch, *Memories of Mexico*, 207.

56. Haslip, *Crown of Mexico*, 491; Basch, *Memories of Mexico*, 208 (quotation).

57. Salm-Salm, *My Diary in Mexico*, 1 (facsimile of original note written by Maximilian); Haslip, *Crown of Mexico*, 491.

58. Salm-Salm, *Ten Years*, 214–215. In contemporary value, this would have been over $1.5 million. John J. McCusker, memorandum on historical currency evaluations, Aug. 24, 2009, notes in possession of the author.

59. Coffey, *Soldier Princess*, 75–76; Salm-Salm, *Ten Years*, 212.

60. Salm-Salm, *Ten Years*, 212; Coffey, *Soldier Princess*, 76.

61. Salm-Salm, *Ten Years*, 213.

62. Salm-Salm, *Ten Years*, 216 (quotations); Coffey, *Soldier Princess*, 77.

63. Salm-Salm, *Ten Years*, 217 (quotation); Coffey, *Soldier Princess*, 76.

64. Salm-Salm, "Diary of the Princess," in *My Diary*, 75; *La Sombra de Arteaga*, June 13, 1867; *New York Times*, July 16, 1867; Coffey, *Soldier Princess*, 77 (quotation).

65. *La Sombra de Arteaga*, June 13, 1867; *New York Times*, July 16, 1867; Ruiz, *Reminiscencias*, 63 (quotations), Mariano Ruiz Papers.

66. Riva Palacio and Martínez de la Torre, *Memorandum Sobre el Proceso del Archiduque Fernando Maximiliano de Austria* (Mexico City: Tomas F. Neve Impresor, 1867), 143–145; Juárez, *Documentos*, 12: 146; *La Sombra de Arteaga*, June 13, 1867; *New York Times*, July 16, 1867.

67. Basch, *Memories*, 237 (first quotation); *La Sombra de Arteaga*, June 13, 1867; *New York Times*, July 16, 1867 (second quotation).

68. *Le Figaro* (Paris), June 26, 1886; Haslip, *Crown of Mexico*, 493–494 (quotations).

69. Maximilian to Carlota in Corti, *Maximilian*, 817 n.46 (quotations); Creelman, *Díaz*, 291.

70. Salm-Salm, *My Diary*, 293 (first quotation); Corti, *Maximilian*, 817 (second quotation); Stevenson, *Maximilian*, 296–297.

71. Haslip, *Crown of Mexico*, 493; Magnus, *El Ocaso*, 241.

72. Salm-Salm, *My Diary*, 290 (quotation); Hyde, *Mexican Empire*, 284–285; Magnus, *El Ocaso*, 241.

73. Corti, *Maximilian*, 817.

74. Blasio, *Maximilian*, 169; Schmit Ritter von Tavera, *Kaisers Maximilian*, 484; Juárez, *Documentos*, 12: 154–155 (first quotation), 160; Basch, *Memories*, 215 (second quotation).

75. Salm-Salm, *My Diary*, 292; Basch, *Memories*, 216.

Chapter 22. ¡Viva Mexico! ¡Viva el Emperador!

1. William Seward to Benito Juárez, June 16, 1867, *Message from the President of the United States, Correspondence Relating to Recent Events in Mexico*, 40th Congress, 1st Sess., Sen. Exec. Doc. 20, 17; William H. Seward to Matías Romero, June 21, 1867, *Correspondencia de la Legación*, 9: 611; Corti, *Maximilian*, 819; Basch, *Memories*, 216.

2. Haslip, *Crown of Mexico*, 495; Salm-Salm, *Ten Years*, 222; Basch, *Memories*, 216 (quotation); Magnus, *El Ocaso*, 242.

3. Riva Palacio, *Memorandum*, 107–108; Ridley, *Maximilian and Juárez*, 270; Lord Acton, *Historical Essays*, 170.

4. Salm-Salm, *Ten Years*, 222.

5. Salm-Salm, *Ten Years*, 223; Coffey, *Soldier Princess*, 112 n.10.

6. William Seward to Ferdinand Wydenbruck, July 1, 1867, *Papers Relating to Foreign Affairs*, 40th Congress, 2nd Sess., Part 2, 56; Haslip, *Crown of Mexico*, 480; Corti, *Maximilian*, 825 (quotation).

7. Salm-Salm, *Ten Years*, 223.

8. Ridley, *Maximilian and Juárez*, 274–275 (quotation); Salm-Salm, *Ten Years*, 223–224.

9. Roeder, *Juárez*, 670–671.

10. Corti, *Maximilian*, 815–816; Hamnett, "La Ejecución," 236.

11. Corti, *Maximilian*, 819–820; Pitner, *Maximilian's Lieutenant*, 184; Maximilian to Pope Pius IX, June 18, 1867, in Juárez, *Documentos*, 12: 156 (quotation).

12. Hyde, *Mexican Empire*, 288 (quotation); Maximilian to Benito Juárez, June 19, 1867, in Juárez, *Documentos*, 12: 156.

13. Corti, *Maximilian*, 820 (quotation); Magnus, *El Ocaso*, 211.

14. Schmit Ritter von Tavera, *Kaisers Maximilian*, 484–485; Basch, *Memories*, 219–220; Corti, *Maximilian*, 820–821; Stevenson, *Maximilian*, 303. Notes from consultation regarding Maximilian's clothing at his execution, Katja Schmitz von Ledebur, July 8, 2009, Kunstkammer, Vienna, Austria, notes in possession of the author.

15. Schmit Ritter von Tavera, *Kaisers Maximilian*, 484, 485, 487 n.1 (quotations); Corti, *Maximilian*, 821; Basch, *Memories*, 220; *New York Daily Herald*, July 23, 1867.

16. Ratz, *Maximilian und Juárez*, 2: 50; Corti, *Maximilian*, 821; Hyde, *Mexican Empire*, 290–291; Ratz, *Tras las Huellas*, 198; Magnus, *El Ocaso*, 248.

17. Schmit Ritter von Tavera, *Kaisers Maximilian*, 485–486, 487 (second quotation); Haslip, *Crown of Mexico*, 497 (first and third quotations); *New York Daily Herald*, July 23, 1867.

18. *New York Daily Herald*, July 23, 1867 (first quotation); Schmit Ritter von Tavera, *Kaisers Maximilian*, 486 (second quotation); Corti, *Maximilian*, 822 (third quotation); Magnus, *El Ocaso*, 243–246.

19. Corti, *Maximilian*, 822; Hyde, *Mexican Empire*, 291 (quotation); *New York Daily Herald*, July 23, 1867; Magnus, *El Ocaso*, 247.

20. "Palabras del Emperador Maximiliano en su prisión en Querétaro, Mexico," note inscribed on reverse of *carte de visite* of Maximilian, ca. 1867 (quotation), in possession of the author; *New York Daily Herald*, July 23, 1867. See also Corti, *Maximilian*, 822 n.51; Riva Palacio, *Memorandum*, 115. There are slightly different versions, including one in Schmit Ritter von Tavera, *Kaisers Maximilian*, 487 n.2, that contains the words "I forgive everyone, I wish my blood to be spilled for the good of this country."

21. *New York Times*, July 10, 1867; Corti, *Maximilian*, 823; *New York Daily Herald*, July 23, 1867 (quotations); Magnus, *El Ocaso*, 249.

22. Schmit Ritter von Tavera, *Kaisers Maximilian*, 488 (quotation), 489 n.1; Basch, *Memories of Mexico*, 220–221; Hyde, *Mexican Empire*, 292; Corti, *Maximilian*, 823; *New York Times*, July 10, 1867; Magnus, *El Ocaso*, 247.

23. S. Lerdo de Tejada to Matías Romero, June 20, 1867, Romero Collection, BLAC; Ridley, *Maximilian and Juárez*, 277 (quotation); Salm-Salm, *My Diary in Mexico*, 313.

24. Ferdinand Wydenbruck to William Seward, June 20, 1867, *Message of the President of the United States*, Sen. Ex. Doc, no. 20, 40th Congress, 1st Sess., 62 (quotation); William H. Seward to Matías Romero, June 21, 1867, *Correspondencia de la Legación*, 9: 609; Seward, *Seward at Washington*, 365.

25. Juárez, *Documentos*, 12: 169–172; Roeder, *Juárez*, 670 (quotation).

26. Hanna and Hanna, *Napoleon III and Mexico*, 305 (first quotation); Lord Acton, *Historical Essays and Studies*, 173 (second and third quotations); Lecaillon, *Napoléon III et le Mexique*, 110; Haslip, *Crown of Mexico*, 500; *New York Times*, June 19 and 30, July 1 and 3, 1867.

27. Hanna and Hanna, *Napoleon III and Mexico*, 304.

28. Dabbs, *The French Army in Mexico*, 282; Domenech, *Juarez et Maximilien*, 3: 182, 194, 204, 210, 212, 221–222.

Epilogue

1. Ratz, *Tras las Huellas*, 208–209; Salm-Salm, *My Diary in Mexico*, 312 (quotation); Certificate, Vicente Licea, Oct. 7, 1867, DCCCVI, Carpeta 1, Archivo Condu-

484 Notes to Epilogue

mex; Basch, *Memories*, 221–222; Memorandum on Maximilian's clothing, Kunstkammer, July 8, 2009, Katja Schmitz von Ledebur; Magnus, *El Ocaso*, 248.

2. Magnus, *El Ocaso*, 248–252.

3. *Frank Leslie's Illustrated Newspaper* (New York), October 5, 1867; Blasio, *Maximilian*, 181; Hall, *Mexico and Maximilian*, 305; Ratz, *Tras las Huellas*, 209. Because Licea's inventory from the embalming did not list glass eyes, some surmised that they were obtained from a saint's statue. Konrad Ratz, memorandum on Maximilian's embalming, May 12, 2011, in possession of the author.

4. Ridley, *Maximilian and Juárez*, 281; Basch, *Memories of Mexico*, 221.

5. Roeder, *Juárez*, 670 (quotations); Seward, *Seward at Washington*, 365–366.

6. Hyde, *Mexican Empire*, 315.

7. *Frank Leslie's Illustrated Newspaper* (New York), October 5, 1867; Blasio, *Maximilian*, 181; Hall, *Mexico and Maximilian*, 305.

8. *Pájaro Verde*, May 31, 1873 (quotation); Tyler, *Santiago Vidaurri*, 155; Creelman, *Díaz*, 295.

9. Ridley, *Maximilian and Juárez*, 280; Hyde, *Mexican Empire*, 312 and 312 n.1; Creelman, *Díaz*, 281.

10. Benito Juárez to Matías Romero, Aug. 9, 1867, Romero Collection, BLAC; Ridley, *Maximilian and Juárez*, 281; *New York Daily Tribune*, July 23, 1867.

11. *Le Monde Illustré*, April 15, 20; May 18; June 1, 1867; *Harper's Weekly*, August 10, 1867; *Harper's New Monthly Magazine*, July 1867; Ross King, *The Judgment of Paris: The Revolutionary Decade That Gave the World Impressionism* (New York: Walker, 2006), 193, 206; *New York Times*, Apr. 14, June 19, 1867; David McCullough, *The Greater Journey: Americans in Paris* (New York: Simon and Schuster, 2011), 247, 251.

12. Carlota, "Para la exposición universal de Paris de 1867," in Weckmann, *Carlota*, 190.

13. McCullough, *Greater Journey*, 247; King, *Judgment of Paris*, 206.

14. King, *Judgment of Paris*, 206; Smart, *Viva Juárez*, 381; Corti, *Maximilian*, 825–826.

15. Corti, *Maximilian*, 826; Barker, *Distaff Diplomacy*, 162–163.

16. *La Orquesta*, July 24, 1867; Corti, *Maximilian*, 826 (quotation), 827; Plessis, *The Rise and Fall of the Second Empire*, 153; King, *Judgment of Paris*, 207.

17. King, *Judgment of Paris*, 207; Corti, *Maximilian*, 828 (first quotation); King, *Judgment of Paris*, 208 (second quotation), 209.

18. Corti, *Maximilian*, 826–827; Barker, *Distaff Diplomacy*, 162; Barker, excerpt of unpublished paper, Barker Papers, CAH.

19. Corti, *Maximilian*, 828–829.

20. *New York Times*, Oct. 23, 1867; Blasio, *Maximilian*, 181; Hall, *Mexico and Maximilian*, 312; Basch, *Memories*, 222; Juárez, *Documentos*, 12: 159, 160 (quotation).

21. Basch, *Memories*, 223; Hall, *Mexico and Maximilian*, 313.

22. *Frank Leslie's Illustrated Newspaper*, Oct. 26, 1867.

23. Blasio, *Maximilian*, 181; Corti, *Maximilian*, 830; *Frank Leslie's Illustrated Newspaper*, Oct. 26, 1867; Basch, *Memories of Mexico*, 223.

24. Blasio, *Maximilian*, 181; Corti, *Maximilian*, 830; *Harper's Weekly Journal of Civilization*, Feb. 29, 1868 (first, second, third quotations); Ratz, *Tras las Huellas*, 210; Ratz, *Tras las Huellas*, 210 (fourth quotation).

25. Blasio, *Maximilian*, 186–187; Basch, *Memories of Mexico*, 223. Salm-Salm and Eloin had been released by the Mexican government in November 1867 and sailed with Magnus to Europe in December. Magnus, *El Ocaso*, 290.

26. Jacob von Kuhachevich to Maximilian, June 28, 1867, Bazaine Papers, García Collection, BLAC; Paoli, *Charlotte*, 186, 190–191; Carlota to Philippe, July 6, 1867, Charlotte Letters, ARP.

27. Paoli, *Charlotte*, 186, 190–191, 196–197 (first and third quotations); Corti, *Maximilian*, 830 (second quotation).

28. Paoli, *Charlotte*, 184–185; Dominique Paoli to M. M. McAllen, March 25, July 9, 2009, regarding Carlota's mental diagnosis, notes in possession of the author; Iturriaga, *Carlota de Bélgica*, 100–101.

29. Paoli, *Charlotte*, 220–221, 225.

30. Paoli, *Charlotte*, 226–227.

31. Paoli, *Charlotte*, 234–236.

32. Marie Henriette wrote to Madame du Hulst, Jan. 14, 1868. Foussemagne, *Charlotte de Belgique*, 360; Paoli, *Charlotte*, 229–230 (quotations).

33. Blasio, *Maximilian*, 187–188.

34. Paoli, *Charlotte*, 225–226, 237 (first quotation), 238–239, 240 (second quotation), 241.

35. Ratz, *Tras las Huellas*, 65; Paoli, *Charlotte*, 242–243 (quotations); Haslip, *Crown of Mexico*, 504; Carlota put her foot on the rowboat on the first day of each month, a bizarre ritual. Iturriaga, *Carlota de Bélgica*, 96.

36. Coralie Vankerkhoven, *Charlotte de Belgique: Une Folie Impériale* (Brussels: Muette, 2012) 53–55, 180 (quotation).

37. Prince Michael of Greece, *The Empress of Farewells* (New York: Atlantic Monthly Press, 1998), 400–402; Dominique Paoli, memorandum regarding her boat rides, March 4, 2010, in possession of the author; Vankerkhoven, *Charlotte*, 63.

38. Prince Michael, *Empress of Farewells*, 408–411.

39. Baron von Eckhardt to Hélène de Reinach, January 23, 1927 (quotations), Charlotte and Maximilian Papers, WRC; *New York Times*, Jan. 20, 23, 1927. Weckmann disagrees with Reinach's telling of Carlota's final moments. He reports she said, "I expressed myself poorly in words, and I will suffer as a result." Weckmann, *Carlota*, 250.

40. Hyde, *Mexican Empire*, 315; Ridley, *Maximilian and Juárez*, 99–100; Harding, *Phantom Crown*, 97.

41. Roeder, *Juarez*, 724–727; Smart, *Viva Juárez*, 416; Hamnett, *Juarez*, 214–215, 225–227.

42. Baguley, *Napoléon III*, 367, 369–370; Barker, *Distaff Diplomacy*, 206; Lecaillon, *Napoléon III et le Mexique*, 187; Echard, *Napoléon III*, 302; James F. McMillan, *Napoléon III* (New York: Longman, 1991), 166–167; Williams, *Mortal Napoleon III*, 149–150.

43. Williams, *Mortal Napoleon III*, 107–108, 149–150, 164; Echard, *Napoléon III*, 241; Stevenson, *Maximilian*, 19 n.1.

44. Interviews: Ámparo Gómez Tepexicuapan, Chapultepec, Oct. 15, 2009; Dorotea and Mariliese Gudenus, Schloss Muelbach, June 5, 2009; Christiana von Habsburg-Lothringen, Vienna, June 5, 2009. Notes in possession of the author. See also Macías-González, "Presidential Ritual in Porfirian Mexico," in Samuel Brunk and Ben Fallaw, eds., *Heroes and Hero Cults in Latin America* (Austin: University of Texas Press, 2006), 91, 96–97.

45. Interviews with Gómez Tepexicuapan and Habsburg-Lothringen; Brunk and Fallaw, *Heroes and Hero Cults*.

46. Napoléon III to Maximilian, April 29, 1864, in Corti, *Maximilian*, 831 (quotation), 836; Carlota to Eugénie, June 18, 1864, in Corti, *Maximilian*, 836.

Selected Bibliography

Manuscripts and Archival Resources

Audenried, Joseph C. Letters, 1865–1866. The Nau Civil War Collection, Houston, Texas.

Barker, Nancy Nichols. Papers, Notes Relative to French in Mexico. Dolph Briscoe Center for American History, University of Texas, Austin, Texas.

Bazaine, Achille François. Papers, 1862–1873, Genaro García Collection. Benson Latin American Collection, University of Texas Libraries, Austin, Texas.

Carlota of Mexico. *The Llano de San Lázaro and the Camp of Cuajimalpa*. Mexico City: n.p., 1865. Maximilian von Habsburg Papers, Hispanic Society of America.

Charlotte and Maximilian Collection, 1846–1927. Woodson Research Center, Fondren Library, Rice University, Houston, Texas.

Charlotte of Mexico Letters 1856–1868, Archives of the Royal Palace, Brussels, Belgium.

Confederate Papers Relating to Citizens or Businesses. RG 109. National Archives and Records Administration, Washington, D.C.

De la Fère, María. "Recollections," 1907. Unpublished account. Maximilian, Emperor of Mexico Papers. Special Collections, University of Arizona, Tucson, Arizona.

Degollado, Joaquín and Mariano. Papers. Benson Library, University of Texas at Austin, Texas.

Degollado, Otilia Jordan de. Unpublished Letters. Private collection of the author.

Embalsamamiento de Maximiliano. Centro de Estudios de Historia de México, Condumex, Mexico City, Mexico.

Escobedo, Mariano. Papers. Bancroft Library, University of California at Berkeley, California.

Fischer, Augustin. Papers. Hispanic Society of America, New York, New York.

Hill, George A., Jr. English Document Collection. Albert and Ethel Herzstein Library, San Jacinto Museum of History, La Porte, Texas.

Jilek, Auguste. Papers. Frederick R. Koch Collection, Beinecke Rare Book and Manuscript Library, Yale University, New Haven, Connecticut.

Johnson, Andrew. Papers. Manuscript Division, Library of Congress, Washington, D.C.

Juárez, Benito. Papers, 1849–1872. Benson Latin American Collection, University of Texas at Austin, Texas.

Maximilian Collection. Special Collections, University of Arizona, Tucson, Arizona.

Maximilian's Clothing and Aztec Possessions of Mexiko. Kunstkammer, Kunsthistorisches Museum, Vienna, Austria.

Maximilian von Mexiko. Bildarchiv (Photographs), Vienna, Austria.

Maximilian von Mexiko. Information and reports on royal collars, scepters, medals. Schatzkammer and Hofburg Collections, Vienna, Austria.

Maximilian von Mexiko Papers. Haus-, Hof-, und Staatsarchiv. Manuscript Division, Library of Congress, Washington, D.C.

Maximilian von Mexiko Papers. Haus-, Hof-, und Staatsarchiv. Österreichisches Staatsarchiv, Vienna, Austria.

Mejía, Tomás. Papers. Archivo General de la Nación, Mexico City.

Miramar Castle. Art, Maps, and Manuscripts. Museo Storico, Ministero per i Beni e le Attività Culturali, Trieste, Italy.

Museo Nacional de Historia, Castillo de Chapultepec. Art, Artifacts, Maps, Manuscripts, and Illustrations. Instituto Nacional de Antropología e Historia, Mexico City.

Plumb, Edward. Papers. Manuscript Division, Library of Congress, Washington, D.C.

Relaciones Exteriores de México, Archivo General de la Nación, Mexico City, Mexico.

Romero, Matías. Collection, 1837–1899. Benson Latin American Collection, University of Texas at Austin, Texas.

Romero, Matías. "The Situation of Mexico, Speech Delivered by Señor Romero." Wm. C. Bryant & Co., 1864. Andrew Johnson Papers, Manuscript Division, Library of Congress, Washington, D.C.

Ruiz, Mariano. Reminiscencias históricas de General Mariano Ruiz. Benson Latin American Collection, University of Texas at Austin, Texas.

Russell, Lord John. Papers. The National Archives, United Kingdom, Surrey, England.

Saint-Sauveur, Jules de. "Les Derniers Jours de la Contre-Guérrilla au Mexique" (ca. 1867). Unpublished report. Maximilian, Emperor of Mexico Papers. Special Collections, University of Arizona, Tucson, Arizona.

Salazar Ilarregui, José. Papers. Hispanic Society of America, New York, New York.

Salazar Ilarregui, José. Papers. Special Collections Library, University of Texas at Arlington, Texas.

Wallace, Lew. Papers. Indiana Historical Society. Indianapolis, Indiana.

Weitzel, Maj. Gen. Godfrey. Manuscript Collection. MSS1498AV, Ohio Historical Society, Columbus, Ohio.

Government Publications

British Foreign Office. *British and Foreign State Papers, 1862–1863.* Vol. 53. London: William Ridgway, 1868.

Condition of Affairs in Mexico, Accompanying Message of the President of the United States, 39th Congress, 1st Sess., Exec. Doc. 73, 1865. Washington, D.C.: Government Printing Office, 1866.

Correspondance confidentielle, Nov. 18, 1865–March 2, 1867. Expédition du Mexique, Ministère de la Défense, G7, 99, Service Historique, Vincennes, France.

Correspondence Relative to the Present Condition of Mexico Communicated to the House of Representatives by the Department of State, 1862. Washington, D.C.: Government Printing Office, 1862.

Correspondencia de la Legación Mexicana en Washington Durante la Intervención Extranjera, 1860–1868. Vol. 9. Mexico: Imprenta del Gobierno, 1885.

Corta, Charles Eustache. *Mexique: Discours de M. Corta, Députe au Corps Législatif et de S. Exe. M. Rouher.* Paris: Typographie E. Pankoucke, 1865.

Dispatches from U.S. Ministers to Mexico, 1823–1906. National Archives and Records Administration, Washington, D.C.

Documentos Relativos a la Asamblea General de Notables que Dió por Resultado la Adopción del Sistema Monárquico en México y la Elección para Emperador de S. A. I. Y. R. El Archiduque Fernando Maximiliano de Austria. Mexico: Imprenta Literaria, 1864.

État-major général correspondance avec le Ministre, 1865–1867. Expédition du Mexique, Ministère de la Défense, G7, 99, Service Historique, Vincennes, France.

Maximilian of Mexico. *Código Civil del Imperio Mexicano.* Mexico: Andrade y Escalante, 1866.

Message of the President of the United States, 37th Congress, 2nd Sess., Exec. Doc. 100, 1862. Washington, D.C.: Government Printing Office, 1862.

Message of the President of the United States, Correspondence Relating to Recent Events in Mexico, 40th Congress, 1st. Sess., Sen. Exec. Doc. no. 20. Washington, D.C.: Government Printing Office, 1868.

Message of the President of the United States, "Evacuation of Mexico by the French,"

H. Exec. Doc. 93, 39th Congress, 1st Sess., 1866. Washington, D.C.: Government Printing Office, 1866.

Message of the President of the United States, Resolution Regarding Mexican Affairs, H. Exec. Doc. 20, 39th Congress, 1st Sess., 1866. Washington, D.C.: Government Printing Office, 1866.

Message of the President of the United States Relating to the Present Condition of Mexico, Jan. 29, 1867, 39th Congress, 2nd Session, House Executive Doc. 76. Washington, D.C.: Government Printing Office, 1867.

Orozco y Berra, Manuel. *Carta General del Imperio Mexicano*, 1864.

Papers Relating to Foreign Affairs, 40th Congress, 2nd Sess., Part 2. Washington, D.C.: Government Printing Office, 1867.

Papers Relating to Foreign Relations Accompanying the Annual Message of the President, 39th Congress, 2nd. Sess., Part 3. Washington, D.C.: Government Printing Office, 1867.

Papiers et Correspondance de la Famille Impériale. Paris: Imprimerie Nationale, 1870.

Records of Headquarters of the Army, RG108, National Archives and Records Administration, Washington, D.C.

Responsabilidades Contraidas por el Gobierno Nacional de México en los Estados Unidos, en Virtud de los Contratos Celebrados por sus Agentes. Mexico: Imprenta del Gobierno, 1867.

Books

Aburto, J. Bernardo. *De Miramar a México: Viaje del Emperador Maximiliano y de la Emperatriz Carlota, desde su Palacio de Miramar cerca de Trieste hasta la Capital del Imperio Mexicano*. Orizaba, Mexico: Imprenta de J. Bernardo Aburto, 1864.

Acevedo, Esther, Fausto Ramírez, and Jamie Soler Frost, eds. *La Fabricación del Estado, 1864–1910*. Los Pinceles de la Historia series. Mexico City: Patronato del Museo Nacional de Arte, Instituto Nacional de Bellas Artes, 2003.

Acton, Lord John Emerich Edward Dalberg, and John Neville Figgis, eds. *Historical Essays and Studies*. London: Macmillan, 1907.

Amberson, Mary Margaret McAllen. *I Would Rather Sleep in Texas*. Austin: Texas State Historical Association, 2003.

Arthur, Anthony. *General Jo Shelby's March*. New York: Random House, 2010.

Baguley, David. *Napoleon III and His Regime: An Extravaganza*. Baton Rouge: Louisiana State University Press, 2000.

Bancroft, Hubert Howe. *History of the Pacific States of North America*. Vol. 9. San Francisco: History Company, 1888.

———. *The Works of Hubert Howe Bancroft, Vol. XIV, History of Mexico*. Vol. 6. San Francisco: History Company, 1888.

Barker, Nancy Nichols. *Distaff Diplomacy: The Empress Eugénie and the Foreign Policy of the Second Empire*. Austin: University of Texas Press, 1967.

Basch, Samuel. *Memories of Mexico: A History of the Last Ten Months of the Empire*. Trans. Hugh McAden Oechler. San Antonio, Texas: Trinity University Press, 1973.

Basch, Samuel. *Recollections of Mexico: The Last Ten Months of Maximilian's Empire*. Ed. and trans. Frank Ullman. Wilmington: Scholarly Resources, 2006.

Bazaine, Achille. *La Intervención Francesa en México según el Archivo de Mariscal Bazaine*. 2nd ed. Vol. 2. Mexico City: Editorial Porrúa, 1973.

Betts, Benjamin. *Mexican Imperial Coinage*. n.p.: Organization of International Numismatists, 1899.

Bigelow, John. *Retrospections of an Active Life*. Vol. 3. New York: Baker and Taylor, 1909.

Black, Shirley. *Napoleon III and Mexican Silver*. Silverton, Colorado: Ferrell Publications, 2000.

Blasio, Luis. *Maximilian Emperor of Mexico: Memoirs of His Private Secretary*. Ed. Robert H. Murray. New Haven: Yale University Press, 1934.

Bock, Carl H. *Prelude to Tragedy: The Negotiation and Breakdown of the Tripartite Convention of London, October 31, 1861*. Philadelphia: University of Pennsylvania Press, 1966.

Brunk, Samuel, and Ben Fallaw. *Heroes and Hero Cults in Latin America*. Austin: University of Texas Press, 2006.

Buchenau, Jürgen. *Mexico Otherwise: Modern Mexico in the Eyes of Foreign Observers*. Albuquerque: University of New Mexico Press, 2005.

Campos, Ruben M. *Chapultepec, Su Leyenda y Su Historia*. Mexico: Talleres Gráficos de la Nación, 1922.

Carmona, Michel. *Haussmann: His Life and Times, and the Making of Modern Paris*. Trans. Patrick Camiller. Chicago: Ivan R. Dee, 2002.

Casdorph, Paul D. *Prince John Magruder: His Life and Campaigns*. New York: John Wiley & Sons, 1996.

Castelot, André. *Maximilien et Charlotte du Mexique: La Tragédie de l'Ambition*. Paris: Librairie Académique Perrin, 1977.

Chávez, Octavio. *Charrería, arte y tradición*. Mexico City: Fomento Banamex, 2008.

Chynoweth, W. Harris. *The Fall of Maximilian*. London: Self-published, 1872.

Coffey, David. *Soldier Princess: The Life and Legend of Agnes Salm-Salm in North America, 1861–1867*. College Station, Texas: Texas A&M University Press, 2002.

Corti, Egon. *Maximilian and Charlotte of Mexico*. Trans. Catherine A. Phillips. 2 vols. New York: Alfred A. Knopf, 1929.

Creelman, James. *Díaz, Master of Mexico*. New York and London: D. Appleton, 1911.

Cunningham, Michele. *Mexico and the Foreign Policy of Napoleon III*. Hampshire, England: Palgrave, 2001.

Dabbs, Jack A. *The French Army in Mexico, 1861–1867.* The Hague: Mouton, 1963.

Dávila, Esta O. de. *Paradise in Mexico: Morelos and Its Capital, Cuernavaca.* Mexico City: Editorial Cultura, 1937.

Davis, William C. *An Honorable Defeat: The Last Days of the Confederate Government.* New York: Harcourt, 2001.

De Havilland, John. *Le Mexique sous la Maison de Habsbourg.* Vienna: C. Gerold, 1863.

De las Torres, Martín. *El Archiduque Maximiliano de Austria en Méjico.* Madrid: Librería de D. A. San Martín, 1867.

Détroyat, Léonce. *La Intervención Francesa en Mexico: Acompañada de Documentos Inéditos.* Trans. José Antonio Ruiz. Veracruz: Imprenta de El Progreso, 1868.

Domenech, Emmanuel. *Juarez et Maximilien.* Vol. 3 of *Histoire du Mexique.* Paris: Librairie Internationale, 1868.

Dunbar, Edward E. *The Mexican Papers, the Mexican Question, the Great American Question.* New York: J. A. H. Hasbrouck, 1860.

Echard, William E. *Napoleon III and the Concert of Europe.* Baton Rouge: Louisiana State University Press, 1983.

Elton, James F. *With the French in Mexico.* London: Chapman and Hall, 1867.

Fabiani, Rossella. *Il Museo Storico del Castillo de Miramare.* Vincenza: Terra Firma, 2005.

Fowler, Will. *Santa Anna of Mexico.* Lincoln: University of Nebraska Press, 2007.

Galeana de Valadés, Patricia. *Las relaciones Iglesia-Estado durante El Segundo Imperio.* Mexico: Universidad Nacional Autónoma de Mexico, 1991.

Grant, Ulysses Simpson. *The Papers of Ulysses S. Grant, 1866.* Ed. John Y. Simon. Vol. 16. Carbondale: Southern Illinois University Press, 1988.

Guedalla, Philip. *The Second Empire: Bonapartism, the Prince, the President, the Emperor.* New York: G. P. Putnam's Sons, 1922.

———. *The Two Marshals, Bazaine–Pétain.* New York: Reynal & Hitchcock, 1943.

Gurza Lavalle, Gerardo. *Una Vecindad Efímera: Los Estados Confederados de América y su Política Exterior Hacia Mexico, 1861–1865.* Mexico City: Instituto Mora, 2001.

Gutiérrez de Estrada, J. M. *Cartas Dirigidas al Excimo Sr. Presidente de la República.* Mexico City: Impresa por I. Cumplido, 1840.

Habsburg, Ferdinand Maximilian von. *Recollections of My Life.* Vols. 1–2. London: Richard Bentley, 1868.

———. *Reglamento para el Servicio y Ceremonial de Mi Corte.* Mexico City: n.p., April 10, 1865.

Hall, Frederic. *Mexico and Maximilian.* New York: Hurst, 1880.

Hamann, Brigitte. *Con Maximiliano en México: El Diario del Príncipe Carl Khevenhüller 1864–1867.* Mexico: Fondo de Cultura Económica, 1994.

Hamnett, Brian. *Juárez.* London: Longman Group, 1994.

Hanna, Alfred Jackson, and Kathryn Abbey Hanna. *Napoleon III and Mexico: American Triumph over Monarchy.* Chapel Hill: University of North Carolina Press, 1971.

Hans, Albert. *Querétaro: Souvenirs d'un Officier de l'Empereur Maximilien.* Paris: E. Dentu, Libraire, 1869.

Harding, Bertita. *Phantom Crown.* Mexico City: Ediciones Tolteca, 1960.

Haslip, Joan. *The Crown of Mexico: Maximilian and His Empress Carlota.* New York: Holt, Rinehart, and Winston, 1971.

Hellwald, Friedrich Anton Heller von. *Maximilian I, Kaiser von Mexico.* Vienna: Wilhelm Braumüller, 1869.

Hyde, H. Montgomery. *Mexican Empire: The History of Maximilian and Carlota of Mexico.* London: Macmillan, 1946.

Ibsen, Kristine. *Maximilian, Mexico, and the Invention of Empire.* Nashville: Vanderbilt University Press, 2010.

Iturriaga, José N. *Escritos Mexicanos de Carlota de Bélgica.* Mexico: Banco de Mexico, 1992.

Jáuregui, Luis, and José Antonio Serrano Ortega. *Historia y Nación, II, Política y Diplomacia en el Siglo XIX Mexicano.* Mexico City: El Colegio de México, 1998.

Joseph, Gilbert Michael, and Timothy J. Henderson. *The Mexico Reader: History, Culture, Politics.* Durham, N.C.: Duke University Press, 2002.

Juárez, Benito. *Apuntes para Mis Hijos.* Mexico City: Universidad Nacional Autónoma de México, 2003.

Juárez, Benito. *Documentos, Discursos y Correspondencia.* Ed. Jorge L. Tamayo. Vols. 11–12. Mexico: Editorial Libros de México, 1972–1975.

Kératry, Emile de. *La Contre-Guérrilla Française au Mexique, Souvenirs des Terres Chaudes.* Paris: Librairie Internationale, 1868.

———. *The Rise and Fall of the Emperor Maximilian.* Trans. G. H. Venables. London: Sampson Low, Son and Marston, 1868.

King, Ross. *The Judgment of Paris: The Revolutionary Decade That Gave the World Impressionism.* New York: Walker, 2006.

Knechtel, Wilhelm. *Las Memorias del Jardinero de Maximiliano.* Ed. Ámparo Gómez Tepexicuapan. n.p.: Jean-Gérard Sidaner, 2011.

Kollonitz, Paula. *The Court of Mexico.* Trans. J. E. Ollivant. London: Saunders, Otley, and Co., 1867.

Laurent, Paul Louis Marie. *La Guerre du Mexique de 1862 à 1866, Journal de Marche du 3e Chasseurs d'Afrique.* Paris: E. de Soye Imprimeur, 1867.

Lecaillon, Jean-François. *Napoléon III et le Mexique.* Paris: Éditions L'Harmattan, 1994.

Leonardini, Nanda. *Santiago Rebull.* Mexico City: Círculo de Arte, 1999.

Lichtervelde, Louis de. *Léopold First: The Founder of Modern Belgium.* Trans. Thomas H. Reed. New York: Century, 1930.

Loizillon, Pierre Henri. *Lettres sur l'Expédition du Mexique, Publiées par sa Sœur, 1862–1867.* Paris: Librairie Militaire de L. Baudoin et Cie, 1890.

Lubienski, Johann. *Der Maximilianeische Staat, Mexiko 1861–1867, Verfassung, Verwaltung und Ideengeschichte.* Wien: Böhlau Verlag, 1988.

Magnus, Anton von. *El Ocaso del Imperio de Maximiliano visto por un Diplomático Prusiano: Los Informes de Anton von Magnus a Otto von Bismarck, 1866–1867.* Ed. Konrad Ratz. Mexico, D. F.: Siglo Veintiuno Editores, 2011.

Mallon, Florencia. *Peasant and Nation.* Berkeley: University of California Press, 1995.

Malortie, Karl. *Here, There and Everywhere.* London: Ward & Downey, 1895.

Martin, Percy F. *Maximilian in Mexico.* New York: Charles Scribner's Sons, 1914.

Masseras, Emmanuel. *Un Essai d'Empire au Mexique.* Paris: G. Charpentier, 1879.

McCullough, David. *The Greater Journey: Americans in Paris.* New York: Simon and Schuster, 2011.

McMillan, James F. *Napoleon III.* New York: Longman, 1991.

Mignard, Gérard. *Charles-Louis Dupin, Un intellectuel baroudeur né à Lasgraïsses.* Self-published, 1997.

Motley, John Lothrop. *The Correspondence of John Lothrop Motley.* Ed. George W. Curtis. Vol. 2. New York: Harper & Brothers, 1889.

Napoléon III. *Histoire de Jules César.* New York: D. Appleton, 1865.

Niox, Gustave-Léon. *Expédition du Mexique, 1861–1867.* Paris: Librairie Militaire de J. Dumaine, 1874.

Norwich, John Julius. *Absolute Monarchs: A History of the Papacy.* New York: Random House, 2011.

O'Flaherty, Daniel. *General Jo Shelby.* Chapel Hill: University of North Carolina Press, 2000.

Palmer, Alan. *Twilight of the Habsburgs.* New York: Atlantic Monthly Press, 1994.

Paoli, Dominique. *L'Impératrice Charlotte: Le Soleil Noir de la Mélancholie.* Paris: Éditions Perrin, 2008.

Pilcher, Jeffrey. *¡Que Vivan los Tamales! Food and the Making of Mexican Identity.* Albuquerque: University of New Mexico Press, 1998.

Pitner, Ernst. *Maximilian's Lieutenant: A Personal History of the Mexican Campaign, 1864–1867.* Trans. Gordon Etherington-Smith. Albuquerque: University of New Mexico Press, 1993.

Plessis, Alain. *The Rise and Fall of the Second Empire, 1852–1871.* Cambridge: Cambridge University Press, 1989.

Pola, Angel, ed. *Los Traidores Pintados por si Mismos: Libro Secreto de Maximiliano.* Mexico: Biblioteca Reformista; Imprenta de Eduardo Dublán, 1900.

Radziwill, Catherine. *The Austrian Court from Within.* London, New York, Toronto: Cassell, 1916.

Randon, Jacques Louis César Alexandre. *Mémoires du Maréchal Randon.* Vol. 2. Paris: Typographie Lahure, 1877.

Ratz, Konrad. *Correspondencia inédita entre Maximiliano y Carlota*. Mexico City: Fondo de Cultura Económica, 2003.

———. *Maximiliano und Juárez*, vol. 2, *"Querétaro-Chronik."* Graz, Austria: Akademische Druck- u., 1998.

———. *Tras las Huellas de un Desconocido: Nuevos Datos y Aspectos de Maximiliano de Habsburgo*. Patricia Galeana de Valadés, prologue. Mexico City: Conaculta, INAH, 2008.

Reinach Foussemagne, Hélène de. *Charlotte de Belgique, Impératrice du Mexique*. Paris: Pon-Nourrit, 1925.

Ridley, Jasper. *Maximilian and Juárez*. New York: Ticknor and Fields, 1992.

———. *Napoleon III and Eugenie*. New York: Viking Press, 1979.

Rister, Carl Coke. *Border Command: General Phil Sheridan in the West*. Norman: University of Oklahoma Press, 1944.

Riva Palacio, Mariano, and Rafael Martínez de la Torre. *Memorandum Sobre el Proceso del Archiduque Fernando Maximiliano de Austria*. Mexico City: Tomás F. Neve Impresor, 1867.

Rodríguez Prampolini, Ida. *La Crítica de Arte en México en el Siglo XIX, Estudios y Documentos*. Mexico City: Universidad Nacional Autónoma de México, 1997.

Roeder, Ralph. *Juárez and His Mexico*. 2 vols. New York: Viking Press, 1947.

Rolle, Andrew F. *The Lost Cause: The Confederate Exodus to Mexico*. Norman: University of Oklahoma Press, 1965.

Salm-Salm, Agnes. *Ten Years of My Life*. New York: R. Worthingon, 1877.

Salm-Salm, Félix. *My Diary in Mexico*. London: Richard Bentley, 1868.

Salvucci, Richard J. *Politics, Markets, and Mexico's "London Debt," 1823–1887*. Cambridge: Cambridge University Press, 2009.

Sánchez Navarro, Carlos. *Tres Cartas Inéditas del Emperador Maximiliano*. Mexico City: Biblioteca Aportación Histórica, Vargas Rea, 1944.

Scheler, Aug. *Annuaire Statistique & Historique Belge*. Bruxelles, Leipzig: C. Muquardt, 1867.

Schmit Ritter von Tavera, Ernst. *Geschichte der Regierung des Kaisers Maximilian I und die Französische Intervention in Mexiko, 1861–1867*. Wien und Leipzig: Wilhelm Braumüller, 1903.

Schofield, John M. *Secret Mission to Paris Regarding the French Empire in Mexico, 1865–1866*. Reprint of *Century Quarterly*, 1897. Laurel, Maryland: Preservation Reprint #8210, Wordmax Books, n.d.

Schoonover, Thomas D. *Mexican Lobby: Matías Romero in Washington, 1861–1867*. Lexington: University of Kentucky Press, 1986.

Schroeder, Seaton. *The Fall of Maximilian's Empire*. New York: G. P. Putnam's Sons, 1887.

Schwaller, John F. *The History of the Catholic Church in Latin America: From Conquest to Revolution and Beyond*. New York: New York University Press, 2011.

Seward, Frederick W. *Seward at Washington as Senator and Secretary of State, a Memoir.* New York: Derby and Miller, 1891.

Sheridan, Philip. *Personal Memoirs of P. H. Sheridan.* Vol. 2. New York: Charles L. Webster, 1888.

Sherman, William T. *Memoirs of William Tecumseh Sherman.* Vol. 2. New York: D. Appleton, 1887.

———. *Memoirs of William Tecumseh Sherman.* New York: Library of America, 1990.

Sherman, William T., and John Sherman. *The Sherman Letters: Correspondence between General and Senator Sherman from 1837 to 1891.* Ed. Rachel Sherman Thorndike. New York: Da Capo Press, 1969.

Smart, Charles Allen. *Viva Juárez: The Founder of Modern Mexico.* Philadelphia: J. B. Lippincott, 1963.

Smith, Susan Deans. *Bureaucrats, Planters and Workers.* Austin: University of Texas Press, 1992.

Steinberg, Jonathan. *Bismarck: A Life.* New York: Oxford University Press, 2011.

Stevenson, Sara Yorke. *Maximilian in Mexico.* New York: Century, 1899.

Suárez Argüello, Ana Rosa. *Un Duque Norteamericano para Sonora.* Mexico City: Consejo Nacional para la Cultura y las Artes, Dirección General de Publicaciones, 1990.

Terrell, Andrew Watkins. *From Texas to Mexico and the Court of Maximilian, 1865.* Dallas: Book Club of Texas, 1933.

Thomas, Hugh. *The Golden Empire: Spain, Charles V, and the Creation of America.* New York: Random House, 2011.

Thompson, Jerry D. *Cortina: Defending the Mexican Name in Texas.* College Station: Texas A&M University Press, 2007.

Thoumas, Charles. *Les Français au Mexique, Récits de Guerre (1862–1867).* Paris: Bloud et Barral, 1891.

Tweedie, Mrs. Alec. *Mexico as I Saw It.* London: Hurst and Blackett, 1901.

Tyler, Ron, Douglas E. Barnett, Roy R. Barkely, Penelope C. Anderson, and Mark F. Odintz, eds. *The New Handbook of Texas.* 6 vols. Austin: Texas State Historical Association, 1996.

Tyler, Ronnie C. *Santiago Vidaurri and the Southern Confederacy.* Austin: Texas State Historical Association, 1973.

Vankerkhoven, Coralie. *Charlotte de Belgique: Une Folie Impériale.* Brussels: Muette, 2012.

Victoria, Queen. *The Letters of Queen Victoria: A Selection from Her Majesty's Correspondence and Journal between the Years 1862–1878.* Ed. George Earle Buckle. Vol. 1. New York: Longmans, Green & Co., 1926.

Weckmann, Luis. *Carlota de Bélgica: Correspondencia y Escritos Sobre México en los Archivos Europeos (1861–1868).* Mexico City: Editorial Porrúa, 1989.

Wheaton, Henry. *History of the Law of Nations in Europe and America from the Earliest Times to the Treaty of Washington.* New York: Gould, Banks & Co., 1845.

Williams, Frances Leigh. *Matthew Fontaine Maury, Scientist of the Sea.* New Brunswick, N.J.: Rutgers University Press, 1963.

Williams, Roger L. *The Mortal Napoleon III.* Princeton: Princeton University Press, 1971.

Articles/Papers

Barker, Nancy Nichols. "France, Austria, and the Mexican Venture, 1861–1864." *French Historical Studies* 3, no. 2 (Fall 1963), 224–245.

Bigelow, John. "The Heir-Presumptive to the Imperial Crown of Mexico." *Harper's New Monthly Magazine,* April 1883, 735–749.

Blumberg, Arnold. "The Diplomacy of the Mexican Empire, 1863–1867." *Transactions of the American Philosophical Society* 61, part 8 (Nov. 1971), 5–47.

Duncan, Robert H. "Political Legitimation and Maximilian's Second Empire in Mexico, 1864–1867." *Mexican Studies* 12, no. 1 (Winter 1996), 27–66.

———. "Embracing a Suitable Past: Independence Celebrations under Mexico's Second Empire, 1864–1866." *Journal of Latin American Studies* 30, no. 2 (May 1998), 249–277.

———. "Maximilian's First Steps toward the Global Marketplace (1864–1866)." In *Memorias del segundo congreso de historia económica, La historia económica hoy, entre la economía y la historia* (Asociación Mexicana de Historia Económica, Simposio 21, Mexico, 2004), 19.

Edison, Paul. "Conquest Unrequited: French Expeditionary Science in Mexico, 1864–1867." *French Historical Studies* 26, no. 3 (2003), 459–495.

Ellis, L. Tuffly. "Maritime Commerce on the Far Western Gulf, 1861–1865." *Southwestern Historical Quarterly* 77, no. 2 (Oct. 1973), 210–211.

Frazer, Robert W. "The Ochoa Bond Negotiations of 1865–1867." *Pacific Historical Review* 11, no. 4 (Dec. 1942), 397–398.

Gómez Tepexicuapan, Ámparo. "El Paseo de la Reforma, 1864–1910." In *Historia del Paseo de la Reforma.* Ed. Wendy Coss y León (Mexico City: Instituto Nacional de Bellas Artes, 1994), 27–53.

Hamnett, Brian. "Mexican Conservatives, Clericals, and Soldiers: The 'Traitor' Tomás Mejía through Reform and Empire, 1855–1867." *Bulletin of Latin American Research* 20, no. 2, (2001), 187–209.

Hernández López, Conrado. "Querétaro en 1867 y la División en la Historia (sobre una carta enviada por Silverio Ramírez a Tomás Mejía el 10 de Abril de 1867)." *Historia Mexicano* 57, no. 4 (Abril–Junio 2008), 1206–1212.

Miller, Robert Ryal. "Arms across the Border: United States Aid to Juárez during the

French Intervention in Mexico." *Transactions of the American Philosophical Society* 63, part 6 (December 1973), 5–60.

Nuñez y Domínguez, José de J. "Los Cumpleaños de la Emperatriz." *Divulgación Histórica* 2, no. 8 (June 15, 1941), 394–396.

O'Connell, Marvin R. "Ultramontanism and Dupanloup: The Compromise of 1865." *Church History: Studies in Christianity and Culture* 53, no. 2, (1984), 200–217.

Pani, Erika. "Dreaming of a Mexican Empire: The Political Projects of the 'Imperialistas.'" *Hispanic American Historical Review* 82, no. 1, (Feb. 2002), 1–31.

Puyo, Jean-Yves. "The French Military Confront Mexico's Geography." *Journal of Latin American Geography* 9, no. 2 (2010), 138–157.

Rister, Carl Coke. "Carlota, a Confederate Colony in Mexico." *Journal of Southern History* 11, no. 1 (Feb. 1945), 33–50.

Shaw, William L. "McDougall of California." *California Historical Society Quarterly* 43, no. 2 (June 1964), 123–129.

Sirven, Joseph I., Joseph F. Drazkowski, and Katherine H. Noe. "Seizures among Public Figures: Lessons Learned from the Epilepsy of Pope Pius IX." *Mayo Clinic Proceedings* 82, no. 12 (Dec. 2007), 1535–1540.

Newspapers

El Cura de Tamajón, Monterrey, N.L., Mexico
Diario del Imperio, Mexico City
L'Ere Nouvelle, Mexico City
L'Estafette, Mexico City
The Extraordinary, Mexico City
Le Figaro, Paris
Harper's New Monthly Magazine
Harper's Weekly
The *Illustrated London News*
London News
The *Mexican Times*, Mexico City
Le Monde Illustré, Paris
Monterrey Monitor, Monterrey, Mexico
New Orleans Times
New York Daily Tribune
New York Herald
New York Semi-Weekly Times
New York Times
La Orquesta, Mexico City
El Pájaro Verde, Mexico City (Ultra-Clerical Party publication)

Revue Militaire de la Quinzaine, Mexico City
La Sociedad, Mexico City
La Sombra de Arteaga, Querétaro
Tri-Weekly Telegraph, Houston, Texas

Reports, Interviews, and Correspondence

Bordo, Michael. Memorandum on nineteenth-century economics and non-convertible bonds in Europe. Rutgers University, New Brunswick, N.J., May 7, 2010.

Doeberl, Mario. Memoranda on wagons, carriages, and saddles. Wagonberg, Schönbrunn, Vienna, Austria, June 5, 18; Oct. 8, 21, 2009.

Fabiani, Rosella. Interview and correspondence on Miramar and Maximilian's designs for the building and art collection, Castello Miramare, Trieste, Italy, June 9, 2009. Lorenza Fonda, contributor, June 9, Oct. 15, 2009; Feb. 8, 10, April 2, 2010.

Gómez Tepexicuapan, Ámparo. Information on the artifacts and life of Maximilian and Carlota, Castillo de Chapultepec, the capital of Mexico City, and Maximilian's contributions to its infrastructure. Castillo de Chapultepec, Mexico City, Oct. 15, Nov. 5, 6, 18, Dec. 2, 2009.

Guerra, Enrique. Collection of documents, ephemera, and artifacts on Maximilian von Habsburg. Linn, Texas. December 2009–December 2010.

Hamnett, Brian. Memoranda regarding Benito Juárez. Essex, England, Jan. 2009–Feb. 2010.

Kuster, Thomas. The contents of the Schatzkammer and royal accoutrement of Maximilian. Kunsthistorisches Museum, Vienna, Austria. May–June 2009.

Lusher, Ted. Collection of artifacts and historical documents from Mexico's Second Empire and Maximilian von Habsburg. Austin, Texas.

McCusker, John J. Memorandum and report on historical valuations of piaster, thaler, franc, dollar, and peso in relation to one another, San Antonio, Texas, August 24, 2009.

Mignard, Gerard. Memoranda regarding Charles Du Pin and other matters of the Second Empire. Paris, France. January–December 2009.

Paoli, Dominique. Memoranda regarding Carlota and her health. Paris, France. August 2008–November 2009.

Ratz, Konrad. Memoranda regarding Maximilian and Carlota. Vienna, Austria. April 2009–May 2011.

Rueda, Salvador. Interview on Maximilian's attempts to assemble artifacts for the Imperial Museum of Mexico, Castillo de Chapultepec, INAH, Mexico City, Mexico, Oct. 15, 2009. Subsequent memoranda, November 2009–March 2010.

Van Bussel, Gerard. Curator of Nord und Mittelamerika, Museum für Völkerkunde, Vienna, Austria, Information on Aztec artifacts from Mexico. October 6, 7, 2009.

Wendt, Tom. Curator of Plant Resources, University of Texas at Austin, memorandum on cross-tipped thorn shrubs of Mexico specifically at Convento de la Cruz, Querétaro, and taxonomic history of cypress trees in Mexico. Memoranda, Jan. 11, 2009, March 4, 2010, May 10, 2011.

Acknowledgments

Family and friends from my childhood helped to inspire this book, especially my uncle, Pedro A. Chapa Quiroga, who served under Venustiano Carranza during the Mexican Revolution. Chapa trained as one of Mexico's first pilots, constructing airplanes from kits shipped into Mexico by rail, in order to bomb Doroteo Arango (Pancho Villa) and other revolutionaries fomenting violence in northern Mexico. After working to assimilate a new plan for Mexico with his compatriots, in 1917 he donned a disguise to enter Querétaro in order to sign the controversial constitution he knew would define Mexico through the twenty-first century. After embarking in the air travel industry in the new and progressive Mexico, Chapa rose to become minister of aviation and brought Pan American Airlines to Mexico. Chapa remained a diplomat and staunch representative of the country, expanded travel in Mexico, and sought to transform the country into a thoroughly modern competitor in the world market.

Chapa and his wife, my aunt Mildred McAllen de Chapa, spoke a great deal about Mexico's history, and especially as citizens of Cuernavaca, memories of the Second Empire of Mexico, that of Emperor Ferdinand Maximilian von Habsburg and his wife, Empress Carlota, surrounded them. Chapa, like many Mexicans, was very interested in their realm, the international glamour, the courtly excess, and Mexico's sovereignty as a European issue, as well as the struggle to return to a republic, which left an indelible impression on the psyche of the Mexican people, still wrestling to find a new postrevolutionary identity in the twentieth century.

Since those days of long stays with my uncle and aunt in Cuernavaca in the 1970s through the 1990s, my interest in Mexico and its associations with the United States and Europe never waned. I return as often as I can, despite the political climate. The investigations for this book began in 1997 as I researched my first book on the history of U.S.–Mexico relations. Over the years, I have been intrigued by the fantastic yet frequently unclear or inaccurate stories of Maximilian and Carlota. This version is told from an American point of view, without major detours to examine lineage or peerage of European royalty or extensively explaining their political theater's shifting boundaries.

In this narrative history, while relying on well-known English-language accounts, I also utilized sources published in Mexico, Germany, Austria, and France. My own transcriptions from private archives, and those of interpreters, employed known and little-known documents that enhanced the panorama of Mexico during the Second Empire. This includes the lives of the sovereigns and their court, their philosophies and feelings, the motives of the military officers attempting to conquer Mexico, the defensive strategies of Benito Juárez and his Republican generals, and the U.S. intervention. My aim is to tell this history in a succinct manner, in a way that may be appreciated by all readers.

A number of people helped complete this book and are owed much gratitude. A profound thank-you goes to my children, Margaret, Alicia, and Argyle, who supported and traveled with me to far-flung places during the research. In the United States, many thanks go to the gracious Don Lamm with his encyclopedic and creative mind and to his colleagues Christy Fletcher and Melissa Chinchillo who agented this book. I am grateful to Trinity University Press and director Barbara Ras. In Texas, a heartfelt thank you is extended to Caroline Alexander Forgason, Juan Ruiz Healy and his wife, Patricia, Belinda B. Nixon, Elizabeth McAllen Roberts; Father Bob Wright of the Oblate Fathers; and John J. McCusker, Ben Vaughan, and Richard Salvucci at Trinity University in San Antonio; Ted Lusher of Austin; Gerald J. Ford of Dallas; Enrique E. Guerra, Melissa and Enrique E. Guerra Jr. of Linn; Jerry Thompson of Texas A&M International University at Laredo; John Wheat at the Dolph Briscoe Center for American History and Michael Hieronymous and the staff of the Nettie Lee Benson Library, University of Texas at Austin. Also, thank you to Jeffrey Pilcher at the University of Michigan, Linda Arnold at Virginia Tech, Michael Bordo at Rutgers University, as well as staff members at the Library of Congress, Washington, D.C.; Hispanic Society of America in New York; the Getty Research Institute in California; the United

States Army Military History Institute, Carlisle Barracks, Pennsylvania; and Arizona State University. This book could not have been written without the superb translations of Joan Wallace and Ralf Weber von Froisberg. Thanks are also extended to research assistant Jamie Boldrick and transcriber Robyn Straus.

In Mexico City, much gratitude goes to the considerate and generous Salvador Rueda Smithers and Ámparo Gómez Tepexicuapan at Castillo Chapultepec; the staff of the Condumex archives; Rodrigo Rivera Lake and Marisa Fernandez; and in Monterrey, to Patricio Milmo. In Austria, gracious thanks for the enormous assistance and guidance provided by Countess Cynthia M. Kinsky and her husband, Count Rudolf Kinsky, who opened many doors during my investigations and research in Vienna. Additional gratitude is conveyed to Archduke Dr. Michael Salvator von Habsburg-Lothringen; Archduchess Christiana von Habsburg-Lothringen; Countess Martin Gudenus at Schloss Muelbach; Frau Dr. Susanna Brandis at Schloss Glaswein. Also, thanks to Vernon J. Rosen, Nikola Donig, Gerhart Tötschinger, Christl Naderer, and the staff of the Österreichisches Staatsarchiv. At the Habsburg palace of Schönbrunn, thanks to Mario Doeberl at the Wagonberg as well as Thomas Kuster and Franz Kirchweger at the Schatzkammer and Kunsthistorisches Museum; Gerard van Bussel, curator of Nord und Mittelamerika, Museum für Völkerkunde; Peter Prokop at the Bildarchiv; Konrad Ratz for his direction and assistance and to his son, Wolfgang Ratz, for his translations. At Miramar Castle at Trieste, Italy, I thank Rossella Fabiani along with Lorenza Fonda and the staff. In Paris, grateful appreciation goes to Gérard Mignard, Chevalier de Palmes Académiques; and at La Sorbonne, Dominique Paoli. In Essex, England, many thanks to Brian Hamnett, an outstanding expert on Benito Juárez who helped greatly, along with Will Fowler at St. Andrews, Scotland. In Germany, H.S.H. Ambassador Prince Stefan of Liechtenstein. Lastly, thank you to Gustaaf Janssens at the Archives of the Royal Palace, the staff of the Musée Royal de l'Armée et d'Histoire Militaire in Brussels, Belgium, and the Ministère de la Défense, Service Historique, in Vincennes, France.

Illustration Credits

MIM insignia on half-title and title page: Courtesy of the Lusher Collection, Austin, Texas

Frontispiece: Bildarchiv, Österreichische Nationalbibliothek, Vienna, Austria

page

4   Abel Briquet Collection, Library of Congress, Washington, D.C.

6   Collection of M. M. McAllen. (M. M. M. Collection)

6   François Aubert Collection, Musée royal de l'armée et d'histoire militaire, Brussels, Belgium

9   Courtesy of the Hispanic Society of America, New York

16   *Frank Leslie's Illustrated Newspaper*, Sept. 3, 1864, Courtesy of Sheridan Libraries, Johns Hopkins University, Baltimore, Maryland

26   M. M. M. Collection

28   Cesare Dell'Acqua, ca. 1866, Castello di Miramare, Trieste, Italy

32   M. M. M. Collection

35   M. M. M. Collection

41   M. M. M. Collection

48   M. M. M. Collection

57   Courtesy of Library of Congress, Washington, D.C., LC-USZ62-22169

61   *New York Herald*, July 30, 1863

63   Paul Emilie Miot, *Voyage of the Magellan*, Courtesy of Research Library, Getty Research Institute, Los Angeles (2004.R.8.)

70   Courtesy of Library of Congress, LC-USZ62-73934

74   M. M. M. Collection

76   F. Galvez, ca. 1865, Courtesy of Enrique E. Guerra Collection, Linn, Texas

82   Courtesy of Library of Congress, Washington, D.C.

86   François Aubert, ca. 1864, Courtesy of Getty Research Institute, Los Angeles (96.R.122)

88   Courtesy of the Hispanic Society of America, New York

89   Courtesy of McAllen Ranch Archives, Linn, Texas

91   Courtesy of McAllen Ranch Archives, Linn, Texas

99   Cesare Dell'Acqua, 1867, Courtesy of Castelleto di Miramare, Trieste, Italy

105   Abel Briquet Collection, ca. 1875, Library of Congress, Washington, D.C.

125   Cesare Dell'Acqua, 1867, Courtesy of Castelleto di Miramare, Trieste, Italy

131   Abel Briquet, Library of Congress, Washington, D.C., LC-USZ62-138426

133   William Henry Jackson, Library of Congress, LC-D4-3922

133   Jean-Adolphe Beauce, ca. 1865, Courtesy of Castelleto di Miramare, Trieste, Italy

135   Bildarchiv, Österreichische Nationalbibliothek, Vienna, Austria

149   Jean-Adolphe Beauce, ca. 1865, Courtesy of Castello di Miramare, Trieste, Italy

161   *Le Monde Illustré*, March 4, 1865, Paris, France

168   *Députation des tribus sauvages, dans le jardin du quartier général à Mexico, le chef portant en sautoir une médaille du roi Louis XV*, Courtesy of Hispanic Society of America, New York

169   Jean-Adolph Beauce, ca. 1865, Museum of Franz Ferdinand, Artstetten, Austria.

171   *London Illustrated News*, May 20, 1863

189   *Le Monde Illustré*, Aug. 12, 1865

200   Courtesy of Museo Nacional de Historia, CONACULTA-INAH-MEX

217   François Aubert, ca. 1864, Courtesy of Getty Research Institute, Los Angeles (96.R.122)

223   Private collection, San Antonio, Texas

226   Courtesy of Kunsthistorisches Museum, Wagonberg, Schönbrunn, Vienna

227   *Harper's Weekly*, Feb. 9, 1867

247   Courtesy of McAllen Ranch Archives, Linn, Texas

318   François Aubert, ca. 1864, Courtesy of Getty Research Institute, Los Angeles (96.R.122)

333   *Cartotgrafía de Querétaro*, Gobierno de Estado, 1978

330   Courtesy of the Lusher Collection, Austin, Texas

371   François Aubert, 1867, Musée royal de l'armée et d'histoire militaire, Brussels, Belgium

386   Courtesy of Museo Nacional de Historia, CONACULTA-INAH-MEX

387   François Aubert, 1867, Musée royal de l'armée et d'histoire militaire, Brussels, Belgium

389   M. M. M. Collection

391   Courtesy of Museo Nacional de Historia, CONACULTA-INAH-MEX

394   François Aubert, 1867, M. M. M. Collection

395   *Frank Leslie's Illustrated Newspaper*, October 5, 1867

397   *Le Monde Illustré*, June 22, 1867

399   *La Orquesta*, Mexico, July 24, 1867

400   *Frank Leslie's Illustrated Newspaper*, Oct. 26, 1867

401   *Harper's Weekly*, Feb. 29, 1868

402   Bildarchiv, Österreichische Nationalbibliothek, Vienna, Austria

403   Bildarchiv, Österreichische Nationalbibliothek, Vienna, Austria

In Gallery

1   [The Imperial Habsburgs] Bildarchiv, Österreichische Nationalbibliothek, Vienna, Austria

2   [Édouard Drouyn de L'Huys] Courtesy of Museo Nacional de Historia, CONACULTA-INAH-MEX

    [Achille Fould] M. M. M. Collection

3   [Gen. Miguel Miramón] Courtesy of Library of Congress, Washington, D.C., LC-USZ62-40078

    [Gen. Leonardo Márquez] Courtesy of Museo Nacional de Historia, CONACULTA-INAH-MEX

    [Imperialista Gen. Tomás Mejía] Courtesy of the Enrique E. Guerra, Linn, Texas

    [Imperialista Gen. Ramón Méndez] Courtesy of the Lusher Collection, Austin, Texas

4   [Jean Pierre Isidore Alphonse Dubois de Saligny] Courtesy of Museo Nacional de Historia, CONACULTA-INAH-MEX

    [Charles Lennox Wyke] Courtesy of Library of Congress, Washington, D.C., LC–USZ62-49325

    [Juan Prim] Courtesy of Museo Nacional de Historia, CONACULTA-INAH-MEX

5   [José Manuel Hidalgo y Esnaurrizar] Courtesy of Museo Nacional de Historia, CONACULTA-INAH-MEX

[Admiral Jean-Pierre Jurien de la Gravière] Courtesy of Museo Nacional de Historia, CONACULTA-INAH-MEX

5   [Félix Eloin] Courtesy of Museo Nacional de Historia, CONACULTA-INAH-MEX

6   [Santiago Vidaurri] Courtesy of Library of Congress, Washington, D.C., LC-USZ62-22170

[José Salazar Ilarregui] Courtesy of Museo Nacional de Historia, CONACULTA-INAH-MEX

[Matías Romero] Courtesy of Library of Congress, Washington, D.C., LC-USZ62-9838

7   [Count and Gen. Franz von Thun] Courtesy of Museo Nacional de Historia, CONACULTA-INAH-MEX

[Charles Bombelles] Courtesy of Museo Nacional de Historia, CONACULTA-INAH-MEX

8   [Dolores Quesada de Almonte] Courtesy of Museo Nacional de Historia, CONACULTA-INAH-MEX

[Manuela del Barrio] Courtesy of Museo Nacional de Historia, CONACULTA-INAH-MEX

9   [Pelagio Antonio de Labastida y Dávalos] M. M. M. Collection

[Pietro F. Meglia] Courtesy of Museo Nacional de Historia, CONACULTA-INAH-MEX

[Luis Blasio] Courtesy of Library of Congress, Washington, D.C., LC-USZ62-131409

10 [Maximilian with Feliciano Rodríguez] Courtesy of Roberto Yslas Carmona, Mexico City, Mexico

[*cochero*] Courtesy of Museo Nacional de Historia, CONACULTA-INAH-MEX

[French officer] M. M. M. Collection

11 [Father Augustin Fischer] Courtesy of Augustin Fischer Papers, Hispanic Society of America, New York, New York

[Mariano and Otilia Jordan de Degollado] Courtesy of Enrique E. Guerra Collection, Linn, Texas

12 [Josefina de Iturbide] Courtesy of Museo Nacional de Historia, CONACULTA-INAH-MEX

13 [William H. Seward] M. M. M. Collection

[Matthew Fontaine Maury] M. M. M. Collection

14 [Prince Félix Salm-Salm and Princess Agnes] Roger D. Hunt Collection at the United States Army Military History Institute, Carlisle, Pennsylvania

15 [French Gen. Félix Charles Douay] Courtesy of Library of Congress, Washington, D.C., Lot 3112, No. 53 (LC-USZ62-131340)

15 [Gen. François Castelnau] Courtesy of Library of Congress, Washington, D.C., LC-DIG-ggbain-20719

[Mariano Riva Palacio] Courtesy of Museo Nacional de Historia, CONACULTA-INAH-MEX

[Frederic Hall] Courtesy of Library of Congress, Washington, D.C., LC-USZ62-131349

16 [Imperialistas held prisoner at Querétaro] M. M. M. Collection

Index

Acapantzingo, Cuernavaca, Morelos, Mexico: 221.

Acapulco, Guerrero, Mexico: 218.

Albert Edward, Prince of Wales: 398.

Albert of Saxe-Coburg Gotha: 28, 31, 69.

Algeria: 16, 49, 51, 78, 110, 157, 160, 171, 172, 205, 254.

Almonte, Dolores Quesada de: 5–7, 136, 262, 267.

Almonte, Juan Nepomuceno: 5–6, 57, 58, 62, 64–65, 67–68, 75, 78, 85–86, 90, 93, 95, 101–102, 104–105, 112, 115, 128, 141, 143, 193, 239, 250–251, 262, 271, 281.

Antonelli, Giacomo: 126, 282–284, 286–288.

Arab troops: 63, 81, 112, 159–161, 171, 205.

Arms, ammunition: 123, 127.

   French and Imperialist troops: 13, 67, 73–74, 78, 83, 85–87, 93, 112, 139, 160, 174, 185, 246–247, 312, 315, 320, 335–336, 349.

   Liberals: 85, 88, 107–108, 112, 187, 160, 185, 187, 205, 249–250, 321, 347, 360.

Arteaga Magallanes, José María: 208.

Austria: 20–23, 25, 27, 30–34, 36–37, 57–58, 66–67, 100, 114, 120–121, 127, 163–164, 167, 225–227, 234, 237–239, 250, 261, 264, 276, 278, 298, 308, 343, 387–388, 400–401, 405, 410.

Austrian troops in Mexico, Army and Navy: 4–5, 7, 21–25, 32–34, 67, 100, 114, 120, 122, 126, 157, 159, 161, 170, 175–176, 196, 207, 212, 230, 234, 237–240, 242–243, 246, 247, 259, 279, 299, 302, 304–305, 307–309, 311–313, 315–317, 319, 321, 326, 329–330, 346–347, 364, 369, 390, 401, 403, 406.

Audenried, Joseph: 313–314.

Azcárate, Miguel María: 18, 146.

Aziz, Abdul, Sultan of Turkey: 398.

Bagdad, Tamaulipas, Mexico: 159, 229–230, 247.

Bahnsen, Johannes H.: 368.

Baja California, Mexico: 44, 163, 183, 230, 258–259.

Basch, Samuel: 296, 302, 304, 306, 329, 336, 338, 352–354, 359–361, 365–366, 373–374, 378–379, 384, 393, 400, 402–403.

Bazaine, François Achille: 5, 16–19, 78–79, 81, 82, 85–88, 92, 95, 101–108, 110–112, 115, 117–118, 144, 148–150, 153–154, 156–158, 160–162, 164–166, 171–172, 174–178, 180, 182–184, 187, 195–197, 201–202, 206–207, 216, 217, 218–219, 230–231, 239, 244, 246, 254–255, 264, 267, 270, 278, 295, 302, 307, 318.

Bazaine, François Achille *(continued)*
Marriage: 187–188, 189.
Return to France: 344.
Sonora: 193
Troop withdrawal: 196, 218, 228, 233, 242–243, 248, 250–251, 259–261, 271–272, 279, 298–301, 303–304, 306, 310, 312–313, 315, 322, 326–328, 335–336.
Bazaine, Josefa (Pepita) de la Peña y Azcárate: 188, 189, 302, 317, 318, 321, 344.
Belgian army: 68, 123, 157, 170, 175–176, 196, 205, 213, 227, 236, 242–244, 256, 259, 279, 300, 304–305, 309, 312, 316, 321, 330, 390, 407.
Benjamin, Judah P.: 163.
Bigelow, John: 180, 186.
Bilimek, Dominik: 132, 221, 234, 302, 305, 310, 366, 379.
Bismarck, Otto von: 149, 261, 398–399.
Black Decree: 206–208, 210, 212, 231–232, 272, 303, 310, 373, 377.
Blanchot, Charles: 78–79, 223.
Blasio, José Luis: 133–134, 136, 165, 168, 180–181, 195, 198–199, 216, 218–219, 221–223, 242, 280–282, 290–291, 304, 329, 331–332, 334, 336–338, 342, 345–346, 350, 352–355, 359, 361, 366, 403, 406.
Blondeel, Édouard: 213, 215.
Boleslawski, Gustav von: 212, 319.
Bombelles, Charles Albert: 7, 139, 167, 177–178, 219, 226, 255–256, 285, 290, 296, 298, 379, 403.
Bombelles, Heinrich: 21, 139.
Borromeo, Edoardo: 287.
Botany: 22, 35, 132, 166, 168, 221, 245, 300, 358.
Bouchout Castle, Meise, Belgium: 1, 407–408.
Bouslaveck, Karl: 255, 281, 284, 286, 289, 291, 293, 296.
Bringas, Bernabé: 306, 310.
Brownsville, Texas: 187, 250, 314.
Budin, Nicolas: 106, 236.
Buenavista, Mexico City: 189, 321.

Bureau, Domingo: 5–6.
Burnouf, Karl: 195, 319.

California: 163, 184, 192–193, 204, 249, 370.
Campbell, Lewis D.: 249, 313–314, 323, 343–344.
Campbell-Scarlett, Peter: 152, 307–308.
Cañada, La, Puebla, Mexico: 12
Canales, Servando: 111, 187.
Carlota of Belgium (Marie Charlotte Amélie Augustine Victoire Clémentine Léopoldine): 1, 3–5, 6, 7–19, 25, 28, 35–37, 40, 59, 66–70, 73, 90, 100, 114, 116–117, 119–120, 122–124, 125, 126–127, 130, 132, 134–140, 148, 149, 156–157, 160, 162–168, 170–179, 188–192, 197, 220–224, 226–228, 231, 233–234, 236–237, 240, 242, 245, 249, 251–253, 272, 295, 317, 329, 348, 377–378, 383, 390, 397, 410.
Appeal to Napoleon III: 265–271.
Childhood: 28–29.
Childless: 198–201, 203.
Clergy: 150–155, 170, 181.
Death: 408.
In Italy: 31–34.
Marriage: 29–31, 32.
Mental illness: 268, 281–293, 295–297, 299, 302–304, 307, 310, 319, 321, 323, 404–409.
Mission to Europe: 254–258, 261–271, 273–294, 298.
Regent: 140, 144–147, 181–182, 194.
Returns to Belgium: 405–407.
Yucatán: 212–215, 218–219.
Carvajal, José María Jesús: 109, 111–112, 205, 247, 330, 332.
Castagny, Armand: 158, 178.
Castelnau, François de: 299–300, 303, 311–312, 316–317, 319–320.
Castillo, Severo del: 337, 355, 357.
Castillo y Cos, Martin del: 202, 222, 254, 266, 269, 286, 291–292, 295.
Catholic Church: 12, 14, 18, 22, 29, 39–40, 43, 46, 48–49, 51, 53, 69, 77, 94–95, 99, 103–104, 105, 142–143, 150–156, 170, 216, 238–240, 250, 260, 280, 289, 389, 407.

Religious toleration: 31, 40, 43, 100, 103, 150, 152, 155, 250, 283.

Cavalry of the Empress: 170, 256.

Cazadores: 242, 244, 297–298, 301, 312, 337–339, 348, 350.

Cerro de las Campanas, Querétaro, Querétaro, Mexico: 332, 336–337, 341, 355–356, 378–379, 384–385, 386.

Cervantes de Morán, Guadalupe: 136.

Chapultepec: 130, 133, 134, 136–137, 139–140, 161, 164–165, 168–169, 190–191, 200, 202, 222, 239, 245, 272, 278, 302, 305, 317, 347.

Chase, Franklin: 159–160, 313.

Chihuahua, Mexico: 108–109, 112, 158, 163–164, 183–185, 210, 249, 259, 313–314, 323.

Cholula, Puebla, Mexico: 14, 89, 177.

Civil War, United States: 45, 50–51, 67, 70, 82, 118, 159, 162–163, 168, 178–179, 185–187, 190, 201, 208, 228–229, 248, 291, 330.

Clerical Party (Church party): xii, 15, 43, 53, 62, 73, 95, 102, 104, 106, 126, 150, 154–156, 181, 240, 260, 272, 304.

Cloué, Georges-Charles: 228–229, 258, 313, 336.

Colonies: 118, 156, 176, 179, 186, 191–194, 208, 240–241, 272, 314–315, 408.

Comonfort, Ignacio: 40, 42–43, 87, 107.

Confederate States of America

Colonization: 156, 178–180, 185, 190–194, 240–241, 248, 314–315.

Migrations to Mexico: 60, 66, 68, 83, 106–108, 118, 162–163.

Conservative Party (Monarchists): xii, 11–12, 39–40, 42–46, 53, 64, 67, 73, 86, 89, 95, 99–102, 104, 115, 150–151, 165, 178, 260, 272, 280, 304, 306, 309–310, 312, 316–320, 326–328, 335, 379, 389.

Convent of the Capuchines, Querétaro: 365–368, 383, 393, 396.

Convent of La Cruz: 332, 338–339, 345, 351–352, 355–362.

Convent of the Teresitas, Querétaro: 361, 363–365, 373.

Convention of La Soledad: 64–65.

Convention of London: 60, 62.

Córdoba, Veracruz, Mexico: 5–6, 9–10, 65, 72, 98, 110, 128, 192, 257.

Corio, Giuseppe: 7, 167.

Corona, Ramón: 324, 335, 356.

Corps Législatif, Paris, France: 55, 77, 161, 172–173, 225, 233, 235, 273.

Corta, Charles Eustache: 172–173.

Cortina, Juan Nepomuceno: 109, 111, 158–159, 187.

Corwin, Thomas: 60, 162.

Counterguerrillas: 85, 91, 92–93, 107, 110–112, 158–159, 176, 185, 206, 208, 246–247, 279, 300, 315.

Crawford, Richard Clay: 229–230.

Crimea: 25, 49–50, 75–76, 78.

Cuernavaca, Morelos, Mexico: 218–223, 233–234, 241, 245, 255, 278, 295, 304–305, 319, 329.

Custer, George Armstrong: 186.

Dandolo: 214, 305, 308, 310, 313.

Dano, Alphonse: 179–180, 231, 312, 316, 327, 389.

Davis, Bette: xii.

Degollado, Mariano: 136, 179, 202, 204.

Degollado, Otilia Jordan: 136, 220, 348.

De la Portilla, Nicolás: 341.

Del Barrio, Felipe Neri: 254.

Del Barrio, Manuela: 22, 266–267, 282, 285–287, 289–292.

Détroyat, Léonce: 251, 253, 255.

D'Huart, Frédéric Victor: 227, 237.

Díaz, Porfirio: 74, 89–90, 109, 160–161, 172, 184, 307, 324, 326, 340, 344, 346–350, 362, 396, 409.

Dios Peza, Juan de: 175.

Doblinger, Mathilde: 289–290.

Domenech, Henri Dieudonné: 238.

Douay, Félix: 78, 85, 101, 107, 156, 158, 171, 178, 187, 196–197, 242, 260, 344, 407.

Drouyn de L'Huys, Edouard: 179–180, 195, 203, 269.

Du Barail, Charles François: 81, 84, 89, 103, 128–129.

Dunlop, Hugh: 60, 62–63.

Du Pin, Charles Louis (also Dupin): 84–85, 90, 91, 92, 110–112, 158–159, 205–206, 231, 236, 247, 300, 315, 335.

Egypt: 24, 33, 84, 93, 110, 170, 180, 205, 208, 218, 398.

Elisabeth (Sisi) of Bavaria: 25, 119–120, 124. *Elizabeth:* 305, 401.

Eloin, Félix: 7, 127, 152, 177, 191, 194–195, 202, 213, 234–239, 279–280, 307, 341, 383, 403.

El Paso del Norte, Chihuahua, Mexico: 158, 183–184.

England: 6, 27–29, 31, 39, 47, 50, 55–56, 58–59, 61, 65, 68–70, 72, 97, 100–101, 115–116, 119, 127, 190, 197, 202, 236, 238, 241, 245, 250, 380–381, 409.

Escobedo, Mariano: 89, 90, 109, 184, 187, 210, 228–230, 246–247, 260, 300, 314, 324–325, 335, 338–339, 342, 344, 349–350, 354, 356–358, 360–365, 368, 373–376, 378, 380, 383–384, 393–394, 399.

Escudero y Echánove, Pedro: 213.

Eugénie, María de Guzmán de Palafox y Kirkpatrick, Condesa de Teba, empress of France: 14, 16, 25–26, 47, 48, 49–50, 52, 60, 65, 72–73, 93, 97, 106, 117, 124, 135, 150, 152, 154, 170–171, 195, 197, 211, 225, 236, 238–239, 254, 299, 344, 384.
  Carlota's mission to France: 263–271.
  Maximilian as emperor of Mexico: 55–56, 66, 68, 99, 119, 121.
  Maximilian's execution: 398–399.

Europe, geopolitical change: 27, 30, 32–33, 49, 149, 152, 157, 225, 232, 237–239, 255, 261, 264, 275–276, 298–299, 372.

Favre, Jules: 77, 83, 171.

Ferdinand I: 24.

Finances: 40, 45, 50, 54, 62, 65, 83, 100, 108, 111, 117, 119, 121, 156, 158–160, 162, 172–174, 184, 196–197, 205, 211, 228, 234–236, 240, 243–244, 250–252, 254, 267–270, 274, 279–280, 298, 309–310, 312, 319, 325, 335, 340, 342, 354, 398, 410.

Fischer, Augustin: 204–205, 250, 272, 278,

296, 302, 304–306, 308, 310, 319–320, 325, 340–342, 347–348.

Food: 12, 80, 134–135, 137–138, 148, 180–181, 215, 220, 230, 284–285, 288–289, 332, 337, 340, 345, 347, 349, 351, 354, 358, 360–362, 366, 404.

Foreign Legion: 60, 78, 87, 110, 117, 137, 148, 233, 241, 243, 247, 250, 300–301, 311, 319.

Forey, Louis Elie Fréderic: 76–79, 83–88, 90, 93–95, 101–102, 161.

Fould, Achille Marcus: 77, 115, 117, 157, 172, 195, 234, 266, 269–270.

Foury, Ferdinand-Louis: 227.

French army evacuation: 65, 101, 115, 118, 157–158, 170, 179–180, 211, 232, 233, 235, 237–238, 240, 242, 245, 247–249, 253, 259–260, 262, 271, 273, 279–280, 294, 297–298, 301–302, 308, 313–314, 316, 319–323, 348.

French Foreign Ministry: 46, 75.

Friant, Jean Nicolas: 246, 260, 295, 297–298, 301.

Galliffet, Gaston Alexandre de: 315.

García de Aguirre, Manuel: 327.

Garibaldi, Giuseppe: 276, 388.

German unification: 261, 398–399.

Gibraltar: 24, 126.

González Ortega, Jesús: 44–45, 54, 83, 88–89, 184–185, 210, 260, 370.

Goytía, Manuel E.: 324.

Grant, Ulysses S.: 162, 186–187, 190, 228–230, 240, 313.

Grill, Antonio: 198, 222, 329, 352, 366.

Guadalupe, Nuestra Señora, Shrine: 15–16.

Guaymas, Sonora, Mexico: 83, 259.

Günner, Rudolf: 218, 341.

Gutiérrez de Estrada, José María: 46–47, 57–58, 66–68, 98–99, 106, 115, 118, 123, 126, 151, 204, 239–240, 249, 260, 262, 309, 379.

Gwin, William M.: 118, 193–194.

Habsburg dynasty: 21–24, 37, 66, 100, 120–122, 141, 152, 233, 237, 278, 302, 306, 308, 389, 410.

Habsburg, Ferdinand von: 21–22.

Habsburg, Franz Josef von: 20–22, 25, 27, 30–33, 35, 36–37, 58, 66–67, 100, 114, 116, 152, 167, 244, 275–276, 323, 343, 364, 399–401, 404–405, 410.
  Family Pact: 120–124, 127, 226–227, 237–238, 261–262, 308, 387–388.
Habsburg, Franz Karl von: 20–22.
Habsburg, Karl Ludwig von: 20, 35, 122, 188, 238, 323, 414.
Habsburg, Ludwig Victor von: 20, 35, 122, 402.
Habsburg, Maria Anna Karolina von: 20.
Hacienda de la Teja: 145, 317–320.
Hacienda Socyapán: 302.
Hall, Frederic: 370, 372–373.
Hammerstein, Freiherr von: 319, 326.
Hans, Albert: 356, 359, 361.
Haussmann, Georges-Eugène: 27.
Herzfeld, Stefan: 296, 304–305.
Hidalgo y Costilla, Miguel: 39, 143–146.
Hidalgo y Esnaurrizar, José Manuel: 46–48, 50–52, 55–58, 84, 98–99, 106, 123, 204, 211, 235, 238–239.
Hill, John C. C.: 348.
Hofburg Palace, Vienna: 119, 131, 188, 297, 403.
Hofmann, Julius: 131.
Hooricks, Frederic: 367, 370.
Hot lands (terres chaudes): 84–85, 92, 176, 218, 315.
Huasteca, La: 84, 90, 97, 111–112, 158, 279, 315.
Hugo, Victor: 83, 388.
Hülsemann, Johann Georg Ritter von: 71.
Hussars: 218, 230, 279, 295, 315, 319, 330, 334, 346–347, 351–353, 355–356

Iglesias, José María: 324.
Imperialists (Monarchists): xii, 6, 14, 63, 80–81, 84, 88, 95, 99, 107–109, 112, 156–160, 165, 175, 178, 182–183, 185, 190, 193, 195, 207–208, 210, 228–229, 240, 242, 245–247, 249, 260–261, 267, 272, 300, 302, 306–309, 320–321, 324–330, 335–337, 339–341, 343, 346–351, 353–356, 358–363, 367, 370, 373, 383, 390, 396.
Independence from Spain, Mexican: 38–40, 143–146, 166, 201, 301.

Indigenous groups: 11, 142–143, 169–170, 176, 181.
Iribarren, José María: 341.
Isthmus of Tehuantepec: 44, 185, 259, 272.
Italy: 21, 23, 30, 33–34, 46, 66, 75, 166, 275–277, 366, 388.
Iturbide, Agustín I: 39, 46–47, 199.
Iturbide, Alice Green: 199–203, 263–264, 303.
Iturbide, Ángel: 199–200, 202.
Iturbide, Josefa: 199–201, 220, 303.
Iturbide, Salvador: 199, 262.
Iturbide y Green, Agustín de: 199, 200, 202-203, 303.
Iztaccihuatl (Volcano): 12, 14–15, 219, 278.

Jablonski, Antonio: 352.
Jäger: 242.
Jeanningros, Pierre: 180, 279.
Jilek, Auguste: 170, 277, 285, 290, 293, 296–297, 404.
Johnson, Andrew: 179, 186–187, 193, 232, 248, 298, 313, 364, 381.
Juárez, Pablo Benito: xi–xii, 4, 10–12, 14, 18, 37, 41, 52, 54–55, 57–62, 64–65, 68, 70–71, 78, 81, 83–84, 93, 107–109, 116–117, 128, 140, 144, 152, 161–162, 172, 178–179, 193–194, 203, 205, 209, 222, 228–229, 248–250, 253, 280, 306, 309, 312–314, 319–320, 323–328, 335, 338, 343–344, 346, 348, 357.
  Chihuahua: 109–110, 158, 163, 183–187, 206–208, 210.
  Death: 409.
  Family: 41–42, 109, 210.
  Reform: 42–46, 51, 53, 57, 94, 103–104, 126, 140, 150, 153–155.
  Restoration to power: 237, 357–358, 360, 362–373, 377–383, 387–388, 390, 394–396, 398–399, 401, 408, 410.
Juaristas. *See* Liberals

Kayser, Carl Gangolf: 131, 219.
Khevenhüller, Karl: 177, 222, 279, 319, 326, 403.
Kickapoos: 168, 169, 170.
Kirby Smith, Edmund: 185, 190.
Kodolitsch, Alfons von: 176, 230, 279, 311, 347.

Kollonitz, Paula: 8,10, 13, 126.
Kuhachevich, Jacob von: 7, 133, 255, 281, 284, 288–289, 291, 404.

Labastida y Davalos, Pelagio Antonio: 15, 18, 43, 46, 53, 57, 69, 94–95, 101–106, 150, 153, 155–156, 173, 188, 201, 260, 304, 322.
Lacunza, José María: 260, 305, 329, 334, 357.
Ladies of the Court: 11, 67, 132–133, 136–137, 182, 213, 220, 254–257, 261, 265–267, 283, 304.
Laeken, Palace of, Belgium: 27–29, 31–32, 405–408.
Lago, Alfred de: 308, 312, 320, 366–367, 374, 378, 394, 400.
Langlais, Jacques: 210–211, 234–236, 240.
Language: 7, 11, 13, 36, 38, 80, 84, 140, 142, 155, 177, 299.
Lares, Teodosio: 95, 141, 155, 260, 278, 304–306, 309, 312, 318–320, 325–326, 329, 334, 341.
Legion of Honor (American): 249, 324, 347.
Leguizano. *See* Sedano, Concepción
Leopold I of Belgium: 22, 28, 29–31, 37, 59, 68–69, 115–116, 134, 151, 156, 177, 195, 220, 236, 252, 323.
Leopold II of Belgium: 29, 220, 227–228, 236–237, 262, 286, 380, 405–408.
Lerdo de Tejada, Miguel: 40, 43.
Lerdo de Tejada, Sebastián: 41, 313–314, 324, 343, 363, 381, 387, 394.
Leva (forced conscription): 94, 312, 319, 342.
Liberals (Juaristas, Republicans): xii, 4, 13, 39–40, 43–45, 54, 58–59, 65, 68, 74–75, 77, 80, 83–85, 90–91, 93, 107–108, 111–112, 117, 138, 141, 144, 148, 158–160, 163, 171, 175, 178, 184–185, 187–188, 206–208, 210, 218, 224, 228–229, 231, 242, 247–249, 260–261, 267, 271, 280, 300–301, 305–307, 314–315, 318, 321, 323, 325–326, 328, 330–332, 335–336, 338, 340–341, 343–344, 347–350, 352–356, 359–361, 363, 369–370, 379, 383, 388, 396, 502.
Licea, Vicente: 393, 395.
Lincoln, Abraham: 51, 58, 60, 71, 82, 159, 162, 179, 183.

L'Hérillier, Edmond Aimable: 139, 172, 225.
Loizillon, Pierre Henri: 80–81, 90, 95, 101–102, 259, 279, 299.
Lombardy, Italy: 21, 30, 32–34, 36, 275–276, 399.
López, Miguel: 10, 16, 256, 300, 327, 329, 334, 351, 352, 353–355, 358–361, 367.
Louis Napoléon Bonaparte. *See* Napoléon III
Louis Philippe of France: 25, 28–29, 51, 252.
Loysel, Charles: 175, 190, 196, 235–236, 238, 407.

Magnus, Anton von: 149, 278, 330, 367, 370–372, 379–381, 384–385, 387, 394, 400.
Malaria: 115, 150, 294.
Malortie, Karl: 256–257.
Maria Amalia of Brazil: 24.
Marie-Amélie of France: 5, 25, 28, 119, 252, 265.
Marie Charlotte Amélie Augustine Victoire Clémentine Léopoldine de Saxe-Coburg Gotha. *See* Carlota of Belgium
Márquez, Leonardo: 44, 64, 73, 75, 81, 89, 101–102, 107, 152, 308–309, 316–317, 319–323, 326–328, 330–331, 334–335, 339–340, 346–348, 350, 363, 396.
Martínez de la Torre, Rafael: 370.
Mastai-Ferretti, Giovanni Maria. *See* Pius IX, Pope
Matamoros, Tamaulipas, Mexico: 83, 109, 158–160, 187, 197, 228–230, 243, 246–248, 259, 314.
Maury, Matthew Fontaine: 190–192, 208, 240–241.
Maximilian von Habsburg, Ferdinand: xii, 6, 32–33, 35, 46, 125–127, 143, 149, 159, 162–163, 188, 239, 400.
    Abdication: 251–253, 270, 280, 294, 299, 301–313, 315, 317, 320, 327, 357.
    Arrival in Mexico: 3–16, 17, 18–19, 128–129.
    Arts and Anthropology: 166–167, 215, 245–246, 398.
    Botany: 22, 35, 132, 168, 221, 300, 358.
    Capture: 351–357, 365–367, 369–371, 377–381.

Catholic church: 69–70, 104, 126, 142, 150–156, 170, 204–205, 240, 250, 272, 275, 278, 304.

Carlota: 28–31, 32, 33–36, 119, 122, 124, 140, 144–145, 164, 182, 197–198, 211–213, 216, 220–221, 223, 234, 245, 251–257, 271, 274–275, 285–286, 288, 291–297, 302, 310, 378, 404.

Chapultepec: 130–132, 137–139, 143, 161, 164–166, 168–169, 191, 200, 202, 222, 239, 245, 272, 278, 302, 305, 317, 347.

Childhood and Education: 20–24.

Civil list: 132, 143, 166, 216, 235, 261, 291, 298, 319.

Colonists: 178–180, 185–187, 190–192, 240–241, 315.

Commander in chief of Austrian navy: 23–25, 126, 244, 276–278.

Court: 69, 127, 132, 136, 345.

Cuernavaca: 218–223, 245, 255, 278, 295, 304–305, 319, 329.

Embalming: 393–395, 401, 409.

Escape plan: 350–351, 353–354, 356, 369, 371, 373–376.

Execution: 379, 381–389.

Family Pact: 66–67, 100, 114, 120–123, 127, 226–227, 238, 261, 308, 388.

Finance: 156, 160, 165, 170, 172–175, 197, 216–217, 235, 240, 248, 250–251, 258, 265, 270, 298–299, 310, 312, 319–320, 335, 354.

Franz Josef: 120–123, 226–227, 244.

Funeral: 402–403.

Government, staff: 128, 133–134, 139, 141–143, 149–150, 165–166, 176–178, 189–190, 258, 260, 278, 300, 302, 310–312, 318, 322, 360–361, 364–366, 370, 384.

Horses/Riding: 21, 134, 135, 139, 143–145, 164, 181, 327, 332, 338, 355, 359.

Interment: 402–404.

Invitation to become emperor of Mexico: 36–37, 40, 52, 56–58, 65–68, 96–98, 99, 100–101, 106–108, 112, 115–117, 119–120, 123–124.

Iturbide, Agustín: 198–204, 263–264, 303–304.

Juárez, Benito: 68, 115–116, 183, 206–210, 253, 280, 309, 312, 324–329, 338, 343–344, 346, 357–360, 362–373, 378–383, 387–388, 394–396, 398.

Leopold I: 27–28, 37, 68–69, 220, 323.

Military/Cazadores: 152, 157, 161–162, 165, 175–176, 195–197, 206–208, 211–212, 217–218, 225, 228–232, 237, 242–244, 246–247, 259–261, 279–280, 294–295, 300–302, 307, 331, 334, 336–340, 348–349, 353, 357.

Miramar: 33–34, 125, 188, 275–277.

Napoléon III: 25–27, 66, 68, 71, 97, 100, 106, 114–115, 117–119, 121, 156–158, 163, 173, 194–195, 225–226, 230–232, 236, 249–250, 267–269, 272–273, 294, 298, 307, 309, 311, 316–317, 320, 388, 390, 398–400, 409.

Public relations: 145–146, 147–148, 170, 195, 204, 206, 227, 234, 238, 245.

Sonora, Mexico: 118, 193–194, 377.

Trial: 371, 373–378.

Mazza, Antonio: 42.

Mazza y Juárez, Margarita: 42, 109.

McLane, Robert M.: 44–45, 64.

Meglia, Pietro Francesco: 151–156, 170, 250.

Mejía, Tomás: 14–15, 44, 64, 102, 107–108, 111, 142, 158–160, 185, 187, 228–230, 247–248, 278, 300, 319, 323, 325, 328, 331–332, 334, 337, 343, 348, 351, 354–357, 363, 373–374, 376, 378–379, 381–383.

Execution: 384–388, 393.

Méndez: Ramón: 176, 208, 323, 325, 328, 334, 338, 348, 350, 360, 363.

Mensdorff, Alexander von: 237.

Metternich, Richard Klemens von: 21, 36, 52, 58, 67, 114, 121, 269, 388, 399, 410.

Mexico City: 5, 8, 14–17, 40, 43–45, 55, 62, 64–65, 78, 80, 83, 87, 105, 115–116, 130–131, 137, 140, 143–144, 146–148, 150, 156, 165, 167, 172, 174–175, 178, 189–190, 192–193, 196, 202, 210, 213, 216, 218, 220–221, 223–224, 227, 234, 237, 239, 243, 245–246, 248, 250, 254, 256, 258, 263, 272, 279, 300–301, 303–304, 306–308, 312–313, 315–319, 324–331, 335, 340–342, 346–349, 357, 362–364, 367, 370, 389, 395–396, 401.

French evacuate: 321–323.

Mexico City *(continued)*
  French occupation: 93–94, 96–98.
  Lakes: 1, 130, 145, 254, 258, 347.
Miramar Castle: 13, 33–34, 36, 66, 69,
  97–98, 116, 118, 120–124, 125, 131–132,
  156, 168, 204, 234–235, 251, 273–277,
  280–281, 285, 287, 292, 296–298,
  305, 307, 312–313, 316, 366, 372, 383,
  403–405.
  Convention of Miramar: 170, 230, 235,
    250–251, 277, 301.
Miramón, Concepción: 370, 373, 382, 390.
Miramón, Joaquín: 324–325.
Miramón, Miguel: 44–45, 54, 62, 102, 107,
  152, 158, 308–309, 319, 324–325, 327–
  328, 331–332, 334–337, 340–341, 343,
  345–346, 348–350, 354–357, 370–371,
  373–374, 376–379, 381–383.
  Execution: 384–388, 393.
Monarchists. *See* Imperialists; Conservative
  Party
Money, means of exchange: 51, 54, 159, 165,
  172, 192, 205, 211, 421 n. 3, 424 n. 43, 460
  n. 1, 469 n. 51.
Monroe Doctrine: 51, 71, 98, 162, 186, 280.
Monterrey, Nuevo León, Mexico: 108–109,
  116, 158, 180, 192, 228, 243, 246, 248,
  279, 314.
Montholon, Charles F.: 16, 176, 180, 297.
Morelia, Michoacan, Mexico: 98, 107, 112,
  147.
Morny, Charles Auguste de: 45, 55, 270.
Motley, John Lothrop: 237.
Murphy, Tomás: 320, 329, 341.
Music: 18, 85, 89, 92, 96, 123, 137, 188, 214,
  221, 257, 329.

Napoléon Bonaparte: 25, 49, 78, 199.
Napoléon III (Louis Napoléon): xi–xii, 5,
  15–16, 25, 26, 27, 29, 33, 38–39, 45–46,
  49–52, 55, 59–63, 65, 70–72, 74–78,
  83–85, 93–97, 101–102, 104, 108, 110, 113,
  124, 131, 141, 143, 155–157, 160, 162–163,
  171–175, 178–180, 184, 186, 188, 193–197,
  203, 206, 210–211, 226–228, 230–231,
  237, 244–245, 261, 272, 278–279,
  294–295, 306–307, 309, 317, 410.
  Carlota: 157, 170–171, 224, 239, 252–255,

  262–275, 281, 283, 285, 289, 292, 294,
  296.
  Châlons, Camp: 265–266, 271.
  Death: 409.
  Eugénie: 172–173, 195, 225, 239, 398–399.
  Maximilian as emperor: 36–37, 56, 58,
    66–69, 97, 99–100, 106, 114–115,
    117–119, 121–122, 124.
  Maximilian's abdication: 320.
  Maximilian's execution: 388, 390,
    396–400.
  Troop withdrawal: 218, 225–226, 232–236,
    238, 240, 242–243, 248–251, 272, 294,
    298–299, 301, 311, 314, 316, 320, 335, 344.
National identity: 38, 40, 365.
Nationalities: 40, 63, 110, 171, 205, 230, 337.
National Palace, Mexico: 18–19, 93, 95, 130,
  131, 134, 136–137, 145, 147, 165–167,
  188–189, 202, 208, 216, 222, 265,
  295–296, 305, 320, 322, 410.
Nevado, El, volcano: 148.
New York, New York: 82–83, 109, 163, 184,
  203, 205, 210, 237, 247, 249–250, 272,
  280, 306–307.
Noriega, Manuel: 340, 346–347.
Novara: 3, 5–7, 23, 34, 114, 122–124,
  126–128, 278, 400, 401, 402.

Oaxaca, Oaxaca, Mexico: 40–42, 58, 74,
  109, 157, 160, 161, 162–163, 172, 184, 302,
  307, 324, 340, 408.
Ocampo, Melchor: 41, 44–45, 54, 64.
O'Horán y Escudero, Tomás: 326, 348
Order of the Golden Fleece: 16, 31, 98.
Order of Guadalupe: 16, 132, 146, 291.
Order of Malta: 123.
Order of the Mexican Eagle: 132, 339.
Order of San Carlos: 132–133, 201.
Orizaba, Veracruz, Mexico: 3, 11–12, 63–65,
  72–73, 75, 77–80, 84, 115, 161, 180, 291,
  295, 297, 302–311, 313, 315, 327.
Ortega, Eulalio: 370, 372, 377.
Osmont, Auguste Adolphe: 246, 260, 278,
  295, 297–298, 301.
Otomí: 14, 44, 142, 383.
Otterbourg, Marcus: 316.

Pacheco, Concepción de: 256.

Palacios, Miguel: 366, 375, 380.

Paris, France: 25–27, 46–47, 52, 57, 72, 75, 77–78, 84, 91–92, 96–98, 103, 106, 110, 112, 115, 117–121, 123–124, 136–137, 143, 146, 151–152, 156, 161, 166–167, 170–173, 180, 188, 193–194, 196, 199, 201, 203, 206, 225, 231, 233–236, 238–239, 245, 250, 254–255, 258, 262–265, 270–273, 275, 279, 281, 292, 294, 311, 314, 327, 344, 396–399, 409.

Paso del Macho, Veracruz, Mexico: 9–10, 72, 213, 257.

Pesos (Mexican): 11, 13, 40, 45, 65, 83, 108, 125, 136, 138, 160, 162, 172–174, 199, 211, 214, 235, 240, 244, 250, 254, 263, 269, 309, 319, 323, 335, 342, 354, 367, 369, 374–375, 410.

Philippe, Count of Flanders: 29, 227, 286, 292.

Pierron, Édouard: 232, 255, 298–301, 306, 308, 311.

Pitner, Ernst: 230, 246, 348, 373, 403.

Pius IX, Pope (Giovanni Maria Mastai-Ferretti,): 30, 69, 70, 103, 120, 126, 151–152, 272, 275, 280, 283, 285–288, 290, 383, 389.

Platón Sanchez, Rafael: 374.

Poliakowitz, Nicolas: 133, 295, 305, 308.

Popocatépetl (volcano): 12, 14–15, 131, 219, 256, 278.

Preston, William: 118, 163.

Prussia: 27, 31, 33, 66, 149, 152, 157, 225, 230, 232, 237–239, 255, 261, 264, 275–276, 298–299, 330, 367–368, 372, 398, 409.

Public relations of the empire: 94, 100, 170, 204, 208, 238.

Puebla de Los Angeles, Puebla, Mexico: 12–14, 40, 42–43, 64–65, 71–75, 76, 77–79, 81, 83–85, 86, 87, 88, 89–91, 93, 97, 101–102, 109, 115, 147, 150, 160–161, 175–176, 184, 188, 190, 198, 201–202, 255, 257, 259, 299, 303–304, 315–317, 326, 328, 340, 346–347, 349, 409.

Pyramids: 14, 167, 170, 177, 180, 215.

Quadrille: 13, 19, 137, 139, 214.

Querétaro, Querétaro, Mexico: 44, 98, 112, 144, 187, 323, 325–332, 333, 334–348, 354–355, 357–360, 362–364, 367–368, 370–371, 374–376, 379–381, 383–385, 387, 395–396, 398, 401.

Radetzky, Joseph: 22, 33.

Radonetz, Edouard: 287, 292, 383.

Rains, Claude: xii.

Ramírez, Francisco: 204.

Ramírez, José Fernando: 141, 163, 176, 199, 211, 213, 278.

Randon, Jacques Louis César: 195, 266, 269–270, 311, 409.

Rebull, Santiago: 131, 166.

Rechberg-Rothenlöwen, Johann Bernhard: 36, 114.

Reforma, La: 39–44, 47, 50–51, 54, 57, 62, 73, 94, 103–104, 117, 126, 410.

Régnier, Alexandre Philippe: 56, 244–245.

Regules, Nicolas: 324, 334.

Republicans. *See* Liberals

Rességuier, Olivier: 212, 319.

Riedel, Josef Gottfried von: 296–297.

Río Chiquihuite, Veracruz, Mexico: 9, 72.

Río Frío, Mexico, Mexico: 15, 72, 227, 256, 316.

Rio Grande: 158–159, 169, 184–187, 228–229, 230, 246–247, 313–314.

Rivadeneira, Ignacio: 361, 393.

Riva Palacio, Mariano: 370, 377.

Riva Palacio, Vicente: 208, 306, 321, 324, 358–359, 363, 370.

Robles Pezuela, Luis: 141.

Rome: 27, 34, 46–47, 49, 53, 57–58, 71, 81–82, 109, 123, 126, 150–151, 162, 170, 183, 185–186, 194, 204–205, 237, 239–240, 250, 272, 281–283, 285, 287, 290–292, 295, 304, 325, 329, 343, 388.

Romero, Matías: 58, 71, 81–82, 109, 162, 183, 185–186, 194, 205, 237, 343, 388.

Rueda Auza, Juan: 374.

Saddle: 12, 90, 111–112, 135–136, 148, 164, 226, 227, 257, 282, 331, 350–351, 359, 397.

Sadowa, Battle of: 261–262, 298.

Saillard, Édouard: 233.

Saint Cloud, Château: 25, 99, 262, 264, 266–267, 269.

Saint Sauveur, Jules de: 315–316.

Salas, Mariano: 6, 95, 104.
Salazar Ilarregui, José: 212, 214, 260, 322.
Salazar Ruíz, Carlos: 208.
Saligny, Alphonse Dubois de: 46, 54–55, 61–62, 64–65, 73, 75–76, 78, 84–85, 89, 93, 95, 101–102.
Salm-Salm, Agnes: 330–331, 342, 362–364, 367–369, 374–375, 381–382.
    Jimmy: 330, 362, 369, 374, 376.
Salm-Salm, Félix: 330–332, 334, 337–339, 345, 348–353, 355–356, 360–361, 365–366, 369–370, 373, 383, 393.
San Blas, Nayarit, Mexico: 83, 259.
San Francisco, California: 83, 249.
San Juan de Ulúa, Veracruz, Mexico: 3, 8, 93.
San Luis Potosí, San Luis Potosí, Mexico: 44, 84, 93, 104, 107–108, 158, 160, 180, 187, 196, 247, 301, 321, 323, 325, 331, 335, 360, 362–363, 368–369, 371, 376, 380–382, 394.
San Martín Zoquiapan, Puebla, Mexico: 14.
Sánchez Navarro, Carlos: 329, 341.
Santa Anna, Antonio López de: 39, 42, 45, 57–58, 67–68, 115, 144, 249.
Santa Gertudis, Battle of: 246–247.
Schaffer, Karl: 340–341.
Scherzenlechner, Sebastian: 7, 127, 152, 177–178.
Schofield, John M., 186.
Schönbrunn Palace: 20, 100, 130.
Sedano, Concepción: 222, 223, 295.
Semelder, Friedrich: 195, 255, 404.
Seward, William H.: 58, 60, 78, 81–82, 109, 162–163, 179–180, 183, 186–187, 203, 232, 237, 248–249, 297–298, 314, 343–344, 364–365, 380–381, 383, 387–388, 395.
Sheridan, Philip Henry: 186–187, 228–230, 240, 250, 314.
Sherman, William Tecumseh: 38, 186, 240, 313–314, 323.
Sierra Gorda, Mexico: 44, 351, 369, 370, 383.
Sisal: 214.
Soledad, La, Veracruz, Mexico: 9, 64–65, 72, 93, 111, 213.
Sonora, Mexico: 44, 51, 118, 141, 156, 163–164, 183, 193–194, 258, 377.

Sophie Friederike Dorothea von Wittelsbach of Bavaria, Archduchess of Austria: 20–22, 25, 119, 122, 124, 262, 309, 323, 400, 403.
Soria y Breña, Manuel de: 379, 384–385.
Spahis: 160, 171.
Spain: 6, 23–24, 38–39, 45, 47–48, 50–51, 54–55, 58–62, 65, 68, 71–72, 99, 115, 127, 143, 380.
Stanton, Edwin: 82, 240.
Suárez Peredo, Juan Antonio: 254, 284, 289, 291.
Sudan: 84, 110, 218.
Supremos Poderes: 352–353.
Susquehanna: 313–314.

Talcott, Andrew: 193.
Tavera, Ramón: 301, 327.
Tegetthoff, Wilhelm von: 24, 276–277, 400–402.
Temple, Henry John, Lord Palmerston: 50, 58–59, 97.
Tertulia: 245, 329.
Thiers, Adolphe: 77.
Thun-Hohenstein, Franz Graf: 175–176, 178, 204, 218, 255–256, 259.
Thun-Hohenstien, Guido: 152.
Toluca, Mexico, Mexico: 98, 148–149, 315, 323, 325.
Treaty of London: 59–60.
Treaty of Miramar: 118, 121, 156, 234, 316, 372.
Trieste, Italy: 24, 33, 66, 123, 125, 126, 221, 237, 276–277, 280, 285, 383, 400, 401, 402–403, 406.
Tüdös, José: 329, 366, 384–385.
Tuileries: 87, 97, 117, 121, 188, 194, 314, 396.

Union Army (U. S.): 68, 77, 160, 162–163, 178, 185–186, 229, 248, 288.
United States: 3, 38–39, 44–47, 48–52, 55–56, 58–60, 63–67, 70–71, 77, 81–82, 97–100, 109, 111, 117–118, 158–160, 162–164, 167, 169, 178–180, 183–187, 191–194, 198, 202–205, 208–212, 228–232, 235, 237–238, 243, 246–250, 258, 262, 265, 272–273, 280, 297–299, 300, 303, 310, 313–316, 319–320, 338,

343–344, 364–365, 370–372, 377, 381–382, 388–390, 395, 397, 400.

Aid for Mexican Liberals: 163, 187, 190, 192, 194, 203, 205, 211, 229–230, 232, 240, 248–250, 313–315, 364, 388.

United States Congress: 81, 98, 162, 186, 192, 202–203, 211, 232, 237, 248, 250, 298, 388.

Universal Exposition of 1867, Paris: 396–399.

Uraga, José López: 107, 213, 278–279, 304.

Uriarte, Juan E. de: 13.

Uxmal, Yucatán, Mexico: 215.

Van der Smissen, Alfred: 175–176, 222, 300, 316, 330, 404.

Vásquez, Jesús M.: 370, 372, 377.

Vatican, Rome: 30, 43, 47, 53, 103, 126, 150–153, 155, 204, 250, 272, 278, 281–283, 285, 287–290, 295, 297, 310, 389.

Velázquez, de León, Joaquín: 127, 141, 204, 250, 284, 286–287, 292.

Venice, Italy: 31–33, 276.

Veracruz, Veracruz, Mexico: 3, 4, 5–6, 8–11, 19, 41, 45, 53, 59–60, 62–65, 72–73, 77–80, 84–85, 87, 89–93, 111, 115, 126, 128, 137, 144, 171–172, 174, 192–194, 197, 203, 207, 213–214, 216, 218–219, 227, 230, 239–240, 247–248, 255, 257, 259, 279, 295, 299–300, 305–306, 308, 312–313, 315–316, 321, 327–328, 335–336, 340, 364, 394, 396, 400–402.

Victor Emmanuel, King of Italy: 276.

Victoria, Queen of England: 28, 31, 59, 63, 68–69, 97, 100, 119, 126, 152, 380.

Vidaurri, Santiago: 107–108, 160, 245, 278, 329–331, 341, 396.

Vieil, Antonin: 295.

Vienna, Austria: 9, 20–22, 31–32, 36, 46, 57, 119, 122, 124, 130–131, 167, 170, 237–239, 244, 258, 261–262, 281, 296–297, 308, 323, 365, 374, 394, 400, 402–403, 406.

Wallace, Lew: 185, 190, 205, 249–250.

Weitzel, Godfrey: 228–230.

Wickenburg, Edmund Graf: 319.

Wine: 50–51, 125, 132, 134, 137–138, 148, 181, 215, 222, 230, 245–246, 297, 310, 314, 325, 337–338, 341, 351, 359, 366, 369.

Woll, Adrian: 78, 178.

Wydenbruck, Ferdinand von: 162, 237, 343, 364, 381, 387.

Yellow fever: 3, 5, 63, 75, 78, 84, 90, 115, 258, 335.

Yucatán, Mexico: 46, 108, 144, 211–216, 218–219, 231, 245, 255, 260.

Zacatecas, Zacatecas, Mexico: 83, 107, 225, 321, 323–325, 327, 332, 343.

Zapotec: 41, 142.

Zichy, Félix von: 7.

Zouaves: 16, 60, 68, 74, 76, 87, 94, 104, 106, 148, 149, 157–158, 189, 245, 315.

Zuloaga, Félix: 43–44, 64.

About the Author

M. M. McAllen was raised on a storied south Texas ranch and writes about the history of the Southwest and Mexico. Her first book, the award-winning and best-selling *I Would Rather Sleep in Texas* (2003), depicts families from the area and the blending of cultures against the backdrop of the Mexican-American War, the Civil War, and upheavals along the border. Her second book, *A Brave Boy and a Good Soldier: John C. C. Hill and the Texas Expedition to Mier* (2006), tells the 1842 biography of thirteen-year-old Texan John C. C. Hill, who was captured in battle and later adopted by Antonio López de Santa Anna, president of Mexico. This saga of one boy's survival and success won numerous awards and has become a curriculum standard in a number of Texas schools. She has written book introductions and contributed to anthologies.

McAllen has appeared on the PBS series *History Detectives*—in an episode about the origins of the Chisholm Trail—and has contributed to *Faces of America*, Henry Louis Gates's series on the origins of famous citizens. She continues to research and write articles on transborder topics and has contributed to various books and anthologies. She lives in San Antonio.